THE HISTORY OF **THE TIMES**

VOLUME I
'THE THUNDERER' IN THE MAKING
1785–1841

VOLUME II
THE TRADITION ESTABLISHED
1841–1884

VOLUME III
THE TWENTIETH CENTURY TEST
1884–1912

VOLUME IV
150th ANNIVERSARY AND BEYOND
Part I 1912–1921
Part II 1921–1948

VOLUME V
STRUGGLES IN WAR AND PEACE
1939–1966

VOLUME VI
THE THOMSON YEARS
1966–1981

WILLIAM REES-MOGG
EDITOR OF *THE TIMES*
1967–1981

THE HISTORY OF

THE TIMES

VOLUME VI

THE THOMSON YEARS 1966–1981

by

John Grigg

TIMES BOOKS
LONDON
1993

British Library Cataloguing in Publication Data

History of the Times.
Vol. 6: Thomson Years, 1966–81
I. Grigg, John
072.1

ISBN 0-7230-0610-5

Published by Times Books,
A Division of HarperCollins*Publishers*
Typeset by Rowland Phototypesetting Limited
Printed in Great Britain
by Butler and Tanner, Frome and London

CONTENTS

LIST OF ILLUSTRATIONS

Acknowledgements
Most of the photographs in this book have been supplied by *The Times* Picture Library. The publishers would also like to thank the following for permission to reproduce photographs: Margaret Allen, Jessica Douglas-Home, the National Union of Journalists, Paul Routledge.

Some abbreviations

C.D.H	Denis Hamilton
C.D.-H.	Charles Douglas-Home
FT	Financial Times
HTT	The History of the Times
IoJ	Institute of Journalists
ITO	International Thomson Organisation
M.J.H.	Marmaduke Hussey
NATSOPA	National Society of Operative Printers, Assistants and Media Personnel
NGA	National Graphical Association
NPA	Newspaper Publishers' Association
NUJ	National Union of Journalists
Op. ed.	The page opposite the leader page
R.H.T.	Roy Thomson
SLADE	Society of Lithographic Artists, Designers, Engravers and Process Workers
SOGAT	Society of Graphical and Allied Trades
TBH	Thomson British Holdings
TBN	Times Business News
TEB	Times Executive Board
TEMC	Times Executive Management Committee
TNHL	Times Newspapers Holdings Limited
TNL	Times Newspapers Limited
TT	The Times
TTO	The Thomson Organisation
TUC	Trades Union Congress
W.R.-M.	William Rees-Mogg

Unless otherwise stated, all documents mentioned in footnote source references are in *The Times* archive at Wapping.

INTRODUCTION

THE FIRST VOLUME of *The History of The Times* was published in 1935, the year of the paper's 150th anniversary. It covers the period from the birth of the paper, as the *Daily Universal Register*, in 1785, to the death of its great (perhaps greatest) editor, Thomas Barnes, in 1841. The second volume, appearing four years later, on the eve of the Second World War, takes the story on to 1884 and deals largely with the powerful editorship of Thomas Thadeus Delane (1841–1877). The third volume, published two years after the war, describes the period 1884–1912. This was a time of troubles for the paper, including the episode of the Pigott forgeries in the late 1880s, which aggravated financial difficulties that were relieved only when control of the paper passed to Alfred Harmsworth, Lord Northcliffe, in 1908. The fourth volume, covering the years 1912–1948, came out in two parts in 1952, the second part, obviously, extending to a time very close to the date of publication. The authorship of these first four volumes was anonymous, following the rule traditional on the paper and still in force while they were being written. But it has long been an open secret that they were directed and substantially written by Stanley Morison.

Volume V differs from its predecessors in being the work of a named author, Iverach McDonald, writing after the anonymity rule had ceased to apply. (It was ended, as will be seen, early in the period of the present volume.) Another distinctive feature is that it reaches back over some of the ground already covered, beginning in 1939 rather than 1948, and in fact giving, as well, a further backward glance at the Munich crisis in 1938. The reasons for this overlapping are cogently stated by the author, though the necessity for it was unfortunate. Since Volume V was brought out in 1984, in time for the paper's 200th anniversary, it was also, more questionably, thought appropriate to add a ten-page epilogue covering the period with which the present volume will be concerned. Principally, however, Volume V describes the editorship of Sir William Haley (1952–1966), and the circumstances leading to the transfer of ownership from the Astor family, who had followed Northcliffe, to the Canadian-born Lord (Roy) Thomson, already proprietor of the *Sunday Times*.

Volume VI will be the first in the series to have the unity of dealing not only with a single family ownership (Roy and Kenneth Thomson), but also a single editorship, that of William Rees-Mogg. It will also be the first to have been written by an outsider. Whereas Stanley Morison and his collaborators were members of the staff of the paper during the last part of the time they cover, and Iverach McDonald was a member of it throughout his period (for most of it a senior member), my own connection with the paper began some years after the Thomson period, during which I had nothing whatever to do with it except as a reader. This relative detachment means, no doubt, that my treatment lacks the intimate understanding that the earlier authors were able to bring to theirs. On the other hand there may possibly be some compensating gain in objectivity and perspective.

The volume begins with the Thomson ownership and ends with the paper in the hands of Rupert Murdoch. The intervening years saw many dramatic events in the world, and in the United Kingdom a state of turbulence and discord unmatched since the early years of the century. In Northern Ireland the communal conflict which had been in abeyance for fifty years was violently revived, with the result that Great Britain became, once again, directly involved in the affairs of Ireland. At the same time the country as a whole was afflicted by a mounting industrial crisis, which threatened not only the basic health of the economy but the authority of the state itself. In this crisis the newspaper industry was a particularly hard case, and Times Newspapers Limited the hardest of all, since the company eventually engaged in a trial of strength with the print unions which caused *The Times* (with the *Sunday Times* and the Supplements) to be out of circulation for nearly a year.

My aim has been to follow, in principle, the rubric laid down at the beginning of the series, that the History should be 'what its title professes, no more and no less'. In other words, I have tried above all to tell the story of *The Times* during the Thomson period, and not to make it an excuse for writing a general history of the times. It would have been impossible, however, to do this comprehensibly, let alone readably, without providing the context of events and issues in which the paper existed – which were, indeed, its *raison d'être*. If I have therefore been generous in the provision of context, I have no regrets, because I am sure it is better to give too much than too little. Only readers with a specialist interest in newspapers, and little interest in anything else, could be content with an account of *The Times* narrowly focused upon its internal affairs, and quoting its reports and comments without adequate explanation of the subject-matter. The present volume should give a suitably strong impression of the paper's internal life, including its painful vicissitudes on the business side. Nevertheless, without being general history in disguise, the book is meant to appeal, like the paper itself, to the general intelligent reader.

Most attention is given to those aspects which chiefly characterise *The Times*, and which represent its greatest strength. Above all, it is a political newspaper, reporting and reacting to public affairs at home and abroad. Its leading articles have always been a most important feature, and Rees-Mogg was, pre-eminently, a writing editor with emphatic (if changeable) opinions and an arresting style. Though not, like Haley, a 'hands-on' administrator, he defined the character of the paper in his time no less clearly. Essential, too, was the work of heads of department and specialists, and of the correspondents who kept the paper supplied with news and commentary from their various vantage-points. The book does justice, I hope, to their personalities and to their contributions.

In addition, *The Times* has been a forum for debate, in which views not necessarily shared by the paper have found an outlet. Under Rees-Mogg this function was, on the whole, faithfully discharged on the op. ed. page. But above all the free expression of opinion and whimsy flourished in 'Letters to the Editor', and I have throughout drawn extensively on this marvellous feature, as well as devoting to it a section of one chapter. No part of the paper is more justly loved and admired. Special notice has also been taken of other features for which *The Times* is universally known, such as its obituaries, its law reports, its court page and, not least, its crossword. (Strangely, the crossword has not hitherto been mentioned in the History, though it has been one of the paper's favourite features since it was started in the 1920s.)

The book has been written according to a pattern which is broadly chronological and episodic, rather than thematic. Each chapter consists of a miscellany of sections in which editorial and business matters alternate, instead of being segregated into solid, indigestible chunks. This pattern is also intended to convey the often bewildering variety of events, in the office and in the outside world, with which those running the paper had to deal. The sections are marked by noticeably wider spaces in the text and their subject matter is indicated not only by the summary at the beginning of each chapter but by the headings above every right-hand page.

Inevitably there has been some arbitrariness in the choice of incidents recorded in detail, and of features appraised; also, of the degree of attention given to individuals. A work of this kind, however substantial and comprehensive, has to be partly impressionistic or it would go on for ever. Nevertheless, I trust I have not neglected anybody or anything of major significance.

The book does not deal at all with the Supplements, which are separate publications. Before the Thomson period the editor of *The Times* exercised a godfatherly supervision over both of them (Haley, in particular, taking a close interest in the *TLS*), but in the new dispensation they were hived off under the general aegis of Denis Hamilton as editor-in-chief of Times Newspapers. Rees-Mogg had no more editorial responsibility for them than he had for the *Sunday Times*, and their story, interesting though it is, has no place in an account of the Thomson *Times*. It should, however, be noted that to the two existing Supplement titles *The Times Higher Education Supplement* was added in 1971.

When Sir Edward Pickering asked me to write this volume, he had in mind a book of 100,000 words; but when I started to write it, it soon became apparent that it would run to more than twice that length. Consequently, it has taken more than twice the originally contemplated time to write (and further delay was caused by illness during one year). Throughout, Sir Edward has shown a constancy of kindness and patience for which I can never thank him enough. He has also given me much practical help, drawing on his incomparable experience of the newspaper world, on both the editorial and the managerial sides.

Mr Rupert Murdoch, the present proprietor of *The Times*, is of course ultimately responsible for the great facilities, and the complete freedom, with which I have been able to carry out my task. He also talked to me very openly about his take-over of the paper. On both counts I greatly appreciate his help and support.

Apart from Sir Edward Pickering – and, I would particularly add, my wife – two people have read the full text and given me the benefit of their comments. The first to do so was Lord Gilmour of Craigmillar, who read it with the utmost promptitude, despite being under heavy pressure of work himself, and who made many detailed suggestions of the greatest value. Thanks to him, some mistakes have been corrected and numerous improvements made. I am deeply grateful to him for his generous labour.

Later, on Sir Edward's initiative, but with my full agreement, it was read by Mr Simon Jenkins, who also reacted to it most warmly and helpfully. I am very grateful to him, too, and have done my best to take his constructive remarks into account.

Among the very many key witnesses whose recollections I sought, only one declined to see me, the present Lord Thomson of Fleet, but he was good enough to give clear answers to certain questions that I put to him in writing. Those to whom I have spoken are too numerous to be listed here in full, though many of their names appear in footnote source references throughout the book. But I must mention specifically (in alphabetical order) a few who have given me an exceptional amount of their time, or who have helped me with documents, or both. They are: Miss Margaret Allen, Sir Gordon Brunton, Mr George Clark, Mr Michael Cudlipp, Mr Robert Fisk, Mr John Grant, the late Sir Denis Hamilton, Mr Louis Heren, Mr E. C. Hodgkin, Mr M. J. Hussey, Miss Enid Knowles, Professor Innis Macbeath, Mr Michael Mander, Mr Michael Leapman, Lord Rees-Mogg and Professor Hugh Stephenson. My debt to them, and to all the others who have spoken to me, is immense.

When I started work the archive of *The Times*, then still at Gray's Inn Road, was run by Mrs Anne Dickson, who gave me unstinted help. But before long she handed over to Miss Melanie Aspey, whose knowledge and dedication to her job are matched only by her cheerful good nature. These qualities were tested, but not found wanting, by the removal of the archive to Wapping. To her, and to her colleagues, Mr Eamon Dyas and Miss Caroline O'Sullivan, my warmest thanks are due.

In addition, I am much obliged to Mr Michael Roffey, *The Times*'s picture library manager, for helping me to find illustrations for the book; to Mr Douglas Matthews for compiling the index with his usual skill and a conscientiousness beyond the line of duty; and to Mr Barry Winkleman and Mr Thomas Cussans for their zealous cooperation in seeing the volume through the press.

The book was typed by Miss Jean Walton, to whom as always I record my special gratitude.

J.G.

I

The new proprietor • The good soldier Hamilton • Character of an editor • Rees-Mogg takes over

ROY HERBERT THOMSON was seventy-two when he took control of *The Times* in 1966. He had started life with few advantages. His father, whose great-grandparents emigrated to Canada from Dumfriesshire in the late eighteenth century, was a rather feckless barber. His mother, born in Somerset, worked as a hotel chambermaid before her marriage. Growing up in Toronto on the edge of poverty the young Thomson dreamt of making his fortune. After several false starts, and when he was middle-aged, the dream began to become true.

It happened in a way he had never planned. In the 1930s, as a struggling salesman of radio sets in the bleak north of Ontario, he borrowed money to buy, in succession, three radio stations, mainly to provide entertainment for his customers and so make the task of selling less difficult. One of the stations, in the small town of Timmins, operated from the same building as the local newspaper, which in due course he acquired, above all as a medium for advertising. This was the first step in a process that led to the accumulation of a newspaper empire comprising well over a hundred titles, of which *The Times* became the 138th.

He had no natural interest in journalism or desire to exercise political influence through the press. As he gradually expanded from the obscure beginning at Timmins, he continued to favour the acquisition of papers which had a monopoly of the readership within their communities, so offering the maximum scope for selling space. The much-quoted, though perhaps apocryphal, remark that editorial content is 'the stuff you separate the ads with' is a pretty fair summary of his attitude.

Up to a point this was conducive to editorial freedom. Since his interest in newspapers was essentially commercial, he saw no reason to interfere with editors so long as their work resulted in healthy balance-sheets. His papers were not used as instruments for the propagation of any line dictated by him. But they were used as instruments for making as much money as possible, and there was a tacit assumption that editors would avoid threatening the prosperity of their papers by giving gratuitous offence to the readership. In practice their independence was thus significantly circumscribed, and it is hardly surprising that his papers tended to reflect the prevailing opinions and prejudices of the communities they served.

By the early 1950s he was a major North American press tycoon, owning newspapers in the United States and the Caribbean, as well as an ever growing number in Canada. But he was no longer content with life in his native land and the focus of his ambition was changing. Though still ardent in the pursuit of wealth, he was also hankering after other marks of worldly achievement. Concurrently, or consequently, his thoughts were turning towards Britain.

Three events in his life helped to change its direction. His business partner, Jack Kent Cooke, who was also his closest boon companion, deserted him; his wife, Edna, died; and an attempt to enter Canadian federal politics ended in defeat. In 1953, nearing the age of sixty, he opened a new phase of his career by acquiring the *Scotsman* and a residence in Edinburgh. At the same time he transferred nominal control of his North American and Caribbean businesses to his son, Kenneth.

Thomson was determined to show Canada, and more especially Kent Cooke, that he could succeed on his own in Britain. But he recruited, if not another partner, certainly a most able lieutenant, in the Scot James Coltart, who came to him from the Beaverbrook organisation. With Coltart's help he secured, in 1956, the franchise for Scottish Television. Despite the refusal of many Scottish bigwigs to join him in the venture, this turned out to be – in his own famous phrase – 'a licence to print money'. Three years later he assumed a central position in the British newspaper industry when he gained control of the Kemsley group, including the *Sunday Times*.

Yet it was not only for the purpose of winning fresh business laurels that he had moved to Britain. Though in one part of his nature a typical self-made North American, contemptuous of Old World snobbery, in another he was by no means immune to the charm of those traditional values that he affected to despise. Having become very rich in Canada, he wanted to become respectable in the land of his ancestors. In particular he had set his heart on a title, preferably of the hereditary sort; and, since he was disqualified from receiving one as a Canadian citizen, he decided in 1963 to take out British nationality, making sure that the prime minister, Harold Macmillan, was aware of the fact. His message to Macmillan was 'duly noted', and the following year he was raised to the hereditary peerage as Lord Thomson of Fleet.

This brought him a profound sense of fulfilment, but did not transform him into a glorified fuddy-duddy. He remained the dynamic capitalist he had always been, still at pains to cultivate his reputation for folksiness, simplicity of life, and readiness to turn or save a buck. Much as he enjoyed being a British nobleman and public figure, he did not give himself airs. Far from buying a large country estate he lived in a modest villa in Buckinghamshire, travelling to and fro by commuter train. With his shabby ill-fitting clothes and thick pebble glasses he seemed the quintessence of ordinariness, which in many ways he was.

The mixture of motives that had prompted his move to Britain was most evident in his purchase of *The Times*. The mere fact of becoming chief proprietor of a newspaper universally, if somewhat naïvely, regarded as the organ of the British establishment caused him very great satisfaction, for the sake of which he was prepared to give almost unlimited financial pledges. Yet he was confident that the need to act on them would be strictly limited in practice, because he had every intention of making the paper a big commercial success. While appreciating to the full the kudos of owning it, he was looking for substantial profit from it as well.

How he succeeded in becoming *The Times*'s chief proprietor is described in detail in Volume V of this History, so need only be summarised here. Since 1964 the paper had been committed to a programme of modernisation, development and expansion, but without the financial or managerial resources to back it. Lord Astor of Hever who, as Major J. J. Astor, had acquired control of the paper after Northcliffe's death in 1922, had been driven to live abroad in 1962 by the Selwyn Lloyd budget of that year, which made the American sources of his wealth vulnerable to British death duties. Earlier, he had transferred most of his shares in the paper to his eldest son, Gavin, who in 1959 became chairman as well.

Gavin Astor's position was from the first almost impossible. Though not a conspicuously clever man, he was worthy, sensible, and more up-to-date in outlook than his father. Yet Lord Astor, even after moving to the South of France, retained the title of co-chief proprietor and continued to be treated as effective boss by senior figures on the paper, including the editor, Sir William Haley. Moreover, he was legally debarred from making over the trust income that he received from America, which could otherwise have been used to finance *The Times's* development. As chairman, therefore, Gavin Astor had responsibility without power, while as principal owner he came to view *The Times* as a property which he could not afford to develop on his own, and in which too much of his fortune was locked up.

The programme of expansion belatedly launched in 1964 brought matters to a head. For *The Times*'s sake he had long thought this necessary and desirable, but once it began his sense of isolation increased and the need to find somebody at least to share the burden became acute. The most natural solution, from many points of view, would have been a deal with the *Observer*, which was housed in a wing of *The Times*'s building, printed on its presses, and edited by Gavin Astor's first cousin, David Astor. But unfortunately the *Observer* was itself very short of cash and so incapable of helping to boost *The Times*. Another solution discussed was merger with the *Guardian*; but this proposal, whose journalistic merits were anyway extremely doubtful, ran into stiff opposition on the *Guardian*'s side, led by the paper's editor, Alastair Hetherington, and in due course had to be abandoned. Merger with the *Financial Times* seemed a much better prospect, and would probably have gone through if the Pearson family, which controlled the *FT*, had been anything like as keen on the idea as its managing director, Lord Drogheda. But the Pearsons had serious misgivings and in the end made Gavin Astor an offer that he was more or less bound to refuse.

When the *FT* scheme collapsed some arrangement with Thomson became almost inevitable, if only as a last resort. Though his interest in *The Times* had been known since 1963, it had met with a consistently negative response. To both the Astor family and senior members of the staff he seemed, at first, a thoroughly unsuitable person to control the paper. Despite his recently acquired badges of British rank, he was still far from measuring up to *The Times*'s cherished concept of the gentleman-proprietor. His brashness, his philistinism and his unashamedly commercial attitude to newspapers all grated, and there was also a legitimate fear that *The Times*'s identity would be submerged in an organisation such as his.

Thomson went to great lengths to allay this fear, and to demonstrate his sense of *The Times*'s uniqueness. He proposed the formation of a new company, Times Newspapers Limited, whose board would consist of four members appointed by himself, four Astor-appointed members, and four national directors expressly charged with using their blocking third position to uphold *The Times*'s dignity and independence. The *Sunday Times* would be put into the company along with *The Times*, and there would be an editor-in-chief to coordinate the two papers' activities, to allocate budgets and to plan for the future.

But each paper was to have its own editor, whose essential freedom would in no way be threatened or diminished by the role of the editor-in-chief. In particular it was stressed that whoever was editor of *The Times* would enjoy, as of right, the unfettered political autonomy that tradition and (allegedly) the national interest required.

During the negotiations Thomson had to agree that he would not be chairman of the new company, or even a member of the board; also that the chairman for three years should be Haley. Financially, he did both well and badly. In obtaining 85 per cent of the new company's stock, to the Astors' 15 per cent, at a maximum cost to himself of £3,300,000, he undoubtedly had a good bargain so far as it went, since the assets to be transferred included the buildings at Printing House Square, whose estimated value was £4,500,000. But this tight deal with the Astors was more than offset by the laxness of his attitude towards the paper itself, which he undertook, more or less without qualification, to maintain for ever in the style to which it was accustomed.

The agreement was initialled on September 30 1966, and the following day the paper carried a statement by him in which he said: 'I am a great admirer of *The Times*, and its special position throughout the world will now be safeguarded *for all time* [author's italics]'. It is true that he added the words 'as well as its commercial prosperity', but in context these must have been read almost as an afterthought: certainly not as a *sine qua non* for the durability of the pledge he was giving. His deal with the Astors was referred to the Monopolies Commission, and in his appearance before it he reaffirmed his commitment to the paper. As he wrote later:

> Not once but many times I told them that I was only taking on *The Times* because I reckoned its rescue and restoration to health would be a worthy object and perhaps a fitting object for a man who had made a fortune out of newspapers. I knew, I said, that I was going to lose a lot of money before *The Times* became viable again, and if it ever did become a profitable concern it would very likely never repay the big sums, the millions, we would have to invest in it. We knew that, my son and I, yet we were prepared to devote a large amount of our private fortune to that end'.[1]

---

1 Roy Thomson, *After I was Sixty*, p.173. It was arranged that *The Times*'s losses should be covered in the last resort by Thomson Scottish Associates, in which Roy and Kenneth Thomson were the sole beneficiaries. Outside shareholders in the wider Thomson Organisation were thus protected.

Despite his admission that the paper might never make money, and his apparent willingness to subsidise it indefinitely, it is clear that his practical intentions were very different. For he also told the Commission that he expected to lose a million in the first year, and that he might have to provide five million before he could make *The Times* viable. Between his open-ended pledges and his more measured plans there was a potentially dangerous incompatibility.

On December 21 Douglas Jay, President of the Board of Trade, told the House of Commons that the Monopolies Commission had decided the proposed transfer of *The Times* would not be against the public interest. He also announced that he accepted this conclusion and therefore consented to the transfer. The period of Thomson ownership had now definitely begun.

The following day it was announced that Sir William Haley would be relinquishing the editorship at the end of the year, to become chairman of the new board, and that until his successor was appointed early in the New Year the managing editor, Iverach McDonald, would be in charge of the paper. Meanwhile there was no mystery about who was to be editor-in-chief of the two papers involved in the deal. It had been known since October that this post would be held by Denis Hamilton, who had been editor of the *Sunday Times* since 1961.

Charles Denis Hamilton's career resembled Thomson's in one respect, if in no other: it owed almost everything to his own qualities and nothing to inherited privilege. Born in Middlesbrough in 1918, the son of a maintenance engineer working for Dorman Long, he won a scholarship to the local high school where, however, he did not shine academically. He was a much keener boy scout than student, and scouting took him to other parts of Britain as well as to some places abroad. An avid reader of newspapers, he contributed scouting notes and occasional features to the *North-Eastern Daily Gazette* while still a schoolboy; and when he left school at the age of seventeen he decided, instead of trying for a university place, to join the *Gazette* as a junior reporter. Within ten years he was right-hand man to the paper's proprietor, Lord Kemsley, though nobody at the time could have predicted such a spectacular rise.

His prospects were transformed by the Second World War. When it broke out he was already a Territorial officer in the Durham Light Infantry, but by the time it ended he was a lieutenant-colonel with a leadership record that few men of his age could rival. He had commanded battalions, even at times brigades, in action, and had been awarded an immediate DSO for repelling a German attack between Nijmegen and Arnhem in December 1944. On demobilisation he returned to an £8-a-week job on the *Newcastle Chronicle*, another Kemsley paper in his home area, to which he had moved shortly before the war. But in next to no time he was summoned to London to be personal assistant to Kemsley himself. The provincial reporter turned war hero thus became, overnight, a powerful figure in national journalism.

Soon afterwards his wife, Olive, and their young family joined him in London. In due course they also acquired a home in Sussex. But Hamilton never forgot his origins in the North, where as a child he had witnessed the terrible effects of the Depression. Though his politics were Conservative, he believed wholeheartedly in the necessity for a Welfare State and was, in many ways, an archetype of the postwar consensus (later so much abused). His Conservatism was very close to that of Harold Macmillan, who between the wars had represented Stockton, just up the Tees from Middlesbrough. Like Macmillan, he was also much influenced in his political attitudes by what he had observed and experienced in the army. Class warfare was deeply repugnant to him, and he could never easily regard any compatriot as an enemy. To him the problems of editorship or newspaper management were akin to those of military command, and he worked instinctively on the principle that there were no bad men, only bad officers.

After four years as personal assistant he became editorial director of all the Kemsley newspapers, among which the *Sunday Times* was pre-eminent. Though he did not actually edit this paper under Kemsley, he gave its fortunes a decisive boost by the practice that he initiated of buying books for advance serialisation. His purchases included such outstanding best-sellers as Nicholas Monsarrat's *The Cruel Sea*, Arthur Bryant's presentation of Alanbrooke's war diary, Alan Moorehead's account of the Russian revolution, and Charlie Chaplin's autobiography. But his greatest coup was the serialisation of Montgomery's memoirs, which brought the paper a permanent addition of 100,000 readers. (He had, of course, served under Monty in 21 Army Group, and he became one of the field-marshal's few close friends in retirement. Later, Monty's official biography was written by one of his sons, Nigel.)

When, in 1959, Kemsley without warning sold all his newspapers to Thomson, Hamilton was shocked and disillusioned. He had served his employer loyally and might have expected to be treated with more consideration. But in the event the change turned out well for him.

Thomson took him on and proved a more congenial father-figure than Kemsley.

Though Hamilton was grateful to Kemsley for giving him his big chance, and for many incidental favours, he found Thomson a more impressive chief, who was prepared to give him at least as much scope, and who had none of Kemsley's pomposity. Both proprietors hankered after titles, but whereas Gomer Berry from Merthyr Tydfil, as well as becoming Lord Kemsley, equipped himself with grand houses in London and the country, where he entertained lavishly, seeming in every way anxious to conceal his obscure beginnings, Roy Thomson from Toronto had no such pretensions or *mauvaise honte*.

He and Hamilton formed an effective partnership, the slim, trim figure of the younger man contrasting piquantly with that of his roly-poly boss. In 1961 Hamilton was appointed editor of the *Sunday Times*, and his comparatively short time in the job was, apart from his war service, the most fulfilling in his life. The paper was already doing very well, but under his direct control it did even better. By the end of 1964 its circulation had risen from about 850,000 (when Thomson acquired it) to nearly 1,300,000, and Hamilton was named Journalist of the Year. When his editorship ended two years later the circulation was 1,500,000.

His prodigious success was achieved partly by a continuation of the practice of buying books for pre-serialisation, which had already paid off so handsomely in increased sales. But there was more to it than that. He was a remarkable picker of journalists, and excellent at getting the best out of those he picked. Though he wrote very little himself, he maintained a high standard of writing in the paper, while also making sure that the contents were lively and varied. He appointed William Rees-Mogg his leading writer on politics and economics; later his deputy. He created the Insight feature, with Clive Irving as head of the team producing it. He implemented Thomson's 'brainwave' of a colour magazine, choosing Mark Boxer as its first editor, and Boxer's friend Tony Snowdon as one of its photographers.[1] He launched a separate pull-out Business News, with Tony Vice in charge. Finally, in 1966, he brought the dynamic editor of the *Northern Echo*, Harold Evans, to Gray's Inn Road as his chief assistant.

Clearly Hamilton satisfied the prime requirement of a Thomson

---

1 Hiring Lord Snowdon was, of course, a public relations coup, quite apart from his artistic value to the paper. But it seemed excessive that Thomson and Hamilton were waiting at the front door of Thomson House to receive him when he reported for his first day's work.

editor: he produced a paper which had buoyant sales and a powerful appeal to advertisers. Was it also a great newspaper, and was he a great editor? These are terms of art, for which there can never be agreed definitions. But if one test of greatness in a newspaper and its editor is the capacity to challenge readers' prejudices on a major issue, and to face unpopularity on such a scale as to incur heavy loss of sales and advertising, it has to be said that Hamilton and his *Sunday Times* do not pass that test. Perhaps only two post-war British editors do: David Astor of the *Observer* and Alastair Hetherington of the [still *Manchester] Guardian*, who both took a line during the 1956 Suez crisis which, though substantially vindicated by history, went against the overwhelming weight of popular and commercial opinion at the time.

The *Sunday Times* supported the Eden government over Suez, and so gained a lot of readers at the *Observer*'s expense. Indeed it was that episode, combined with the first effects of Hamilton's pre-serialisation purchases, that restored the *Sunday Times*'s briefly lost lead over its rival. In 1956 Hamilton was not yet editing the paper, but he was editorial director of the group and to that extent bears responsibility for its profitably erroneous stance in the Suez crisis. As editor under Thomson he certainly did make the *Sunday Times* less stuffily conformist than it had been in Kemsley's day, when (as he put it) the paper showed a '*Pravda* like fidelity' to the Conservative Party.[1] For instance, he ran some articles critical of Macmillan at the very time when Thomson was anxiously awaiting his peerage (which, in the event, was awarded on Sir Alec Douglas-Home's recommendation, though to honour a pledge given by Macmillan). He also had considerable admiration for Harold Wilson during the early phase of his leadership of the Labour Party, when he was talking about the white heat of technological revolution – a concept whose meaning might be somewhat obscure, but which seemed altogether preferable to red revolution.

Under Hamilton the paper, though still essentially Conservative, was undoubtedly less partisan than it had been. Above all it was less political. Believing as he did that 'the public wanted something different on a Sunday', he set out to provide a good all-round weekend read, with wide coverage of interests and activities other than politics.[2] He catered for people whose working lives were, he judged, mainly in business or the professions, and whose thoughts at weekends increasingly turned to sport, travel, science, the arts, gardening and

1 C.D.H., *Editor-in-Chief*, p.58.
2 Op. cit. p.104.

other recreations. He was careful not to give them a surfeit of politics, and did not as a rule subject them to a didactic editorial line, though he firmly advocated British membership of the European Community, reflecting in this Thomson's view as well as his own.[1] The *Sunday Times* under him was, therefore, more entertaining than challenging, but he broadened the field of Sunday journalism and within that field was the greatest of impresarios.

When Thomson acquired *The Times* Hamilton was only forty-seven, and his appointment as editor-in-chief of the daily and Sunday joined together as Times Newspapers seemed to promise even more fruitful and rewarding years ahead. But in fact he had reached the pinnacle of his career, and the future was to prove a reverse slope. There would still be important achievements in his life, but the story would be far more of disillusion, travail and frustration. The post of editor-in-chief conferred glory rather than substance, more especially in regard to *The Times*, the independence of whose editor had been guaranteed to the Monopolies Commission. As for the additional post of chief executive, this was one for which he was miscast, all the more so in view of the worsening state of the economy and of labour relations in the newspaper industry. Over the next fourteen years he was to be made painfully aware that there could be bad men as well as bad officers.

If he had wanted to be editor of *The Times*, the job could probably have been his for the asking. He had played a key part in the negotiations leading to the deal with the Astors, thereby enhancing Thomson's already high regard for him and sense of obligation to him. Above all he was an editor after Thomson's heart, and the new proprietor told the Monopolies Commission that he was satisfied Hamilton would be the best editor for *The Times*. Among others sharing this view were three members of the Commission – Noel Annan, Francis Williams and Donald Tyerman – who personally urged him to take the job.[2] He was tempted, but resisted the temptation. Why?

Perhaps the imaginary prospect of guiding the fortunes of two famous papers tempted him more. At the time he may have been scarcely less dazzled than others were by the title editor-in-chief. But

---

1 Thomson's belief in European unification was based on his intense admiration of the United States. He assumed that the American experience was strictly relevant to Europe. Hamilton's attitude resulted more from his sense of the need to transcend national rivalries which had caused two devastating wars.

2 C.D.H., op. cit., p.139. Tyerman had himself been a candidate for the editorship of *The Times* in 1955 (when Haley was appointed), having been assistant editor since 1944. He was editor of the *Economist* from 1956 to 1965.

he certainly also felt that he owed it to Thomson to shoulder what appeared to be the larger responsibility. A further, and perhaps the clinching, cause of his decision was that he doubted his ability to edit *The Times*. It was one thing to edit a Sunday paper whose political content was deliberately kept within bounds; quite another to edit a daily with a legendary reputation for political news and views.

There was no need for him to be deterred by the fact that he was not a writing editor, because the same had been true of Delane. But Delane's detailed knowledge of politics and politicians far exceeded his. Moreover, he may not have been quite sure that his stamina would be equal to the task. From childhood he had been 'tortured by migraine', suffering attacks of it three or four times a week, except (curiously) in battle.[1] As editor of the *Sunday Times* he had been a systematic delegator, but even with the maximum delegation editing a daily was bound to make much heavier demands.

Whatever the reason, or combination of reasons, he decided that another man should edit *The Times*. But at the turn of the year the world was still unaware who that editor would be. Meanwhile Hamilton embodied the new regime to which many members of *The Times* staff reacted with hostility, assuming it to be a *Sunday Times* take-over. Their resentment was further aroused when, the day after the deal was officially sanctioned, they read in a gossip column a report of Hamilton's views on the future of the paper, in which however he was also quoted as saying that he would be visiting them after Christmas and had already formed, from afar, a good opinion of them. ('They've had a long wait to see the sort of chap I am . . . They must have a damn good staff there. They are doing very well'.)[2] When he came to Printing House Square on December 28 to meet senior editorial writers some of the damage was immediately repaired. 'I got the impression,' one of them noted in his diary, 'of a nice chap who is perhaps still a bit unsure of himself.'[3]

The following day, at 4.30 p.m., Haley took his last conference. He thanked his colleagues for their 'help, support and friendliness through fourteen and a quarter years'. Iverach McDonald replied with a tribute in which he said that he 'never knew a man who so completely let his yea be yea and his nay be nay – a great gift for an administrator'. He had provided 'excitement, a youthful zest for the chase, a sense of romance, a never-fading enthusiasm in the daily business of

---

1 C.D.H., op. cit., p.6.
2 *Evening Standard*, 'Londoner's Diary', December 22 1966.
3 Diary of E. C. Hodgkin, entry for December 28 1966.

producing a paper and getting it away'. He was, McDonald concluded, 'the most independent-minded editor of *The Times* since Barnes'.[1]

Haley's departure from the editorial chair left a vacuum that McDonald was to fill in an acting capacity. But his reign lasted little more than a fortnight. On January 12 1967 speculation about the editorship was at last brought to an end. After the board meeting of Times Newspapers Limited (TNL) held that day at Printing House Square, it was announced that Harold Evans would edit the *Sunday Times* and that the new editor of *The Times* would be William Rees-Mogg.[2]

Rees-Mogg himself had known for several months that he was destined for the post, having been told by Hamilton when he returned from his summer holiday the previous year. At about the same time there was a leak in the *Daily Mirror*, to which he had to give the lie when congratulated by Quintin Hogg at the Conservative party conference. He had accompanied Thomson and Hamilton when they visited the prime minister, Harold Wilson, at Chequers in September, and this may have been the source of the leak.

In retrospect his appointment seems almost inevitable, granted Hamilton's decision to be editor-in-chief. But it did not seem inevitable at the time and the *Mirror* story was generally discounted. One who discounted it was McDonald, the strongest inside candidate for the job, who had the impression, when he visited Hamilton in the country shortly before Christmas, that the matter was still open. And if seniority, competence and loyalty had been the only qualifications required he might well have been chosen. He had been with *The Times* for over thirty years. Of Caithness extraction, but educated at Leeds Grammar School, he had come to the paper in 1935 from the *Yorkshire Post*. After starting as a sub-editor he had soon established himself as a foreign specialist, within three years paying visits to the Soviet Union, serving briefly as correspondent in Berlin, and then becoming diplomatic correspondent. With first-hand knowledge of Continental Europe, and excellent natural judgement, he formed views on foreign

---

1 *Times Newspapers House Journal*, issue for January–March 1967.

2 This was the third meeting of the new board. The first, on December 30 1966, was little more than a formality. At the second on January 4 1967, Hamilton's appointment as editor-in-chief was confirmed, as was Gavin Astor's as life president and Haley's as chairman for a period to expire, at latest, by the company's third annual general meeting. It was agreed that when he stood down he would be succeeded by Kenneth Thomson, who was meanwhile appointed deputy chairman.

policy much at variance with those of *The Times* during the 1930s and 1940s, when it advocated, successively, appeasement of Hitler's Germany and Stalin's Russia.

McDonald did not, however, resign in protest against the aberrations of the Dawson and Barrington-Ward years. As a good lieutenant he carried out his duties, offered advice, but did not break ranks. This might suggest that his temperament was not entirely that of a leader. Certainly it could be argued against him as a potential editor that he had very little experience of dealing with home affairs. Much the same could be said of the only other serious candidate from the inside, Oliver Woods, most of whose distinguished service to the paper had been as colonial correspondent or colonial editor. Among outsiders the most impressive contender was Charles Wintour, whose work as editor of the *Evening Standard* was widely admired. But he could not help being associated with the militant anti-Europeanism of his former employer, Lord Beaverbrook (d. 1964), which conflicted with Thomson's pro-EEC stance. Another person mentioned, though also as an outsider, was Geoffrey Cox, editor of Independent Television News and formerly chiefly known for his work on the *News Chronicle*. But in fact none of these candidates had any real chance of being appointed, because none of them had ever worked with Hamilton.

Rees-Mogg on the other hand had been Hamilton's deputy on the *Sunday Times* for the past two years, and before that City editor and then political and economic editor. Aged only thirty-eight, he had the advantage of relative youth without the disadvantage of inadequate credentials. Before being recruited by Hamilton in 1960 he had been chief leader writer and assistant editor on the *Financial Times*, having been picked in 1952 straight from Oxford by that paper's formidable editor, Gordon Newton. The managing director, Lord Drogheda, had noticed a profile of Rees-Mogg in the Oxford students' magazine *Isis*, in which he was said to begin each day reading the *FT* in bed. This prompted Drogheda to make enquiries about him at Oxford and then to bring his name to Newton's attention, with swiftly positive results.[1]

His background was very different from Thomson's or Hamilton's, or for that matter Haley's, in that he was a child of privilege. His paternal ancestry consisted of a long line of Somerset squires, the Moggs, joined by marriage in the early nineteenth century to a Welsh

1 Drogheda, *Double Harness* (memoirs), p.136. The *Isis* profile was written by a group of undergraduates from the (then) ladies' college, Somerville, but the key sentence is attributed to Shirley Williams, future Cabinet minister and co-founder of the SDP.

family from Wick in Glamorgan, the Reeses. Though he became a big earner, and was always interested in improving his fortune, his career was from the first assisted by very substantial independent means. In London he lived near the heart of things, in Smith Square, Westminster, and he had in Somerset a home of the stately kind, Ston Easton Park, which, however, he sold during his editorship of *The Times*, moving to a smaller house in the same area.

Yet he was far from being a 'pure' specimen of English county stock. His mother was Irish-American, Roman Catholic, and an actress. She had appeared in New York with Sarah Bernhardt, at a time when the veteran French *tragédienne* was being hissed off the Paris stage for taking parts (such as Rostand's *L'Aiglon*) no longer suited to her age and physique. Rees-Mogg also had American blood, though of a different kind, on his father's side, since his paternal grandmother was descended from John Winthrop, the first governor of Massachusetts.

Despite being brought up in his mother's faith, Rees-Mogg was sent not to a Roman Catholic school but to Charterhouse, where he came under the inspiring influence of Robert Birley, then headmaster. Like Birley he won a Brackenbury scholarship to Balliol, but unlike Birley did not get a first in history at the end of his time at Oxford. Much later he expressed gratitude to a friend for advising him to persist in trying for the presidency of the Union (students' debating society) rather than concentrate on his schools (final examinations). This, he said, had changed his life for the better.[1] Whether or not it would have been impossible for him to achieve both distinctions, as several people have done within living memory, it is a fact that he was elected president of the Union but had to be content with a second class in history.

Already, a superficially rather shy manner concealed almost boundless self-confidence and ambition, of which contemporaries sometimes caught a glimpse. George Steiner remembered him, 'straw-hatted, on a spring afternoon in Balliol', saying that two jobs would greatly tempt him, the Exchequer or *The Times*.[2] When he and Nigel Lawson were young journalists together on the *FT*, their editor considered that, of the two, Rees-Mogg was more likely to go to the top in politics, Lawson in journalism.[3] Certainly Rees-Mogg was very political in the early phase of his career. He stood as a Conservative for the hopeless

---

1 W.R.-M. to Hugh Shetton, March 14 1977.
2 George Steiner to W.R.-M., January 14 1967.
3 Sir Gordon Newton talking to author.

seat of Chester-le-Street in County Durham, at a by-election in 1956 and at the 1959 general election. Afterwards on several occasions he came near to being selected for a safe seat. During the brief premiership of Anthony Eden he published a very respectful biography of the leader (which he later refrained from mentioning in his *Who's Who* entry). Until 1964 he served on a number of Conservative policy committees. But in that year a long period of Conservative dominance came to an end, and perhaps partly for that reason he seems to have decided, *faute de mieux*, that his destiny lay in journalism rather than politics.

Abandoning his hope of a career in the House of Commons did not, however, diminish his interest in political ideas or the political process, which was, indeed, one of his outstanding qualifications for editing *The Times*. But even before he severed formal links with the Conservative party on his appointment as editor, he was showing a markedly more detached attitude and broadening his political sympathies to include, at any rate, the Liberal party of Jo Grimond and many individuals on the right of the Labour party. Soon he was describing himself not as a Tory but as a Whig. 'I am . . . particularly glad to see you refer to yourself as a Whig', he wrote in 1972 to a peer with a resonant historical name, who had served in Macmillan's Conservative government. 'The two self-avowed Whigs in this office are myself and Bernard Levin so I feel we are a very select party'.[1]

This Whiggishness may seem eccentric, even perverse, in a country squire of the old faith. But it has to be understood that there was nothing remotely ultramontane about Rees-Mogg's Roman Catholicism. The Pope with whom he felt the closest spiritual affinity was not the living Pope in Rome, but rather a Pope who had lived two centuries before in eighteenth-century England: the poet Alexander Pope, who had no truck with the Jacobites, accepted the rationalism of his friend Bolingbroke, and regarded himself as a disciple of Locke. Rees-Mogg certainly believed in institutions, morality and social discipline; but he had a no less rooted belief in personal liberty. Indeed, he valued order largely because it was, in his view, the necessary precondition of freedom.

His marriage, in 1962, to Gillian Morris, brought him great happiness and helped to shape his character and habits as he approached the most important phase of his career. In the little book expounding his religious faith, which he published while he was editor of *The Times*, he writes:

---

1 W.R.-M. to Lord Lansdowne, April 20 1972.

> Religion enters into all the details of life, not as a conscious element of sacrifice, but as a background of love and gratitude. The moment when the husband comes home in the evening, an occasion for tea in England and often for a cocktail in the United States, is one of the cherished moments in most happy marriages. Somewhere there is an unexpressed sense of gratitude to God for the security of that moment.

It has to be said that 'the security of that moment' is unfamiliar to most editors and their families, who on most days of the week do not expect to be together in the early evening. But Rees-Mogg would not allow his home life to be sacrificed to the exigencies of his profession; though not as a rule home in time for tea, he usually managed to be there by cocktail-time (a term which was, however, figurative in his case, because he virtually gave up alcohol after an attack of jaundice when he was young).

The sanctity of the home was, to him, vital to the preservation of decent standards in every department of life: the very basis of civilisation itself.

> The obvious social and sexual problems, delinquency, drug-taking, alcoholism, suicide, promiscuity, inability to keep a job, gambling, violence, all seem to be closely related to loss of stability of the home. It is the common experience that they occur in stable and unstable homes, but in a much larger number of cases where the marriages have failed. It is evident that such social problems are on the increase, and the increase has followed the rise in the divorce rate . . .[1]

In the press, as in politics, domesticity has never been easy to maintain. But Rees-Mogg was determined to maintain it, and he did so, at whatever cost to his job.

Shortly before he moved to *The Times*, and when he already knew that he would be appointed, he published in the *Sunday Times* a remarkable letter to his newborn son Thomas. To some this appeared rather self-indulgent and embarrassing, but anyone seeking to understand Rees-Mogg should be grateful for it, because it is a most revealing document. In it he says (only a few passages can be quoted, to give the flavour of the whole):

---

1 The passages quoted are from W.R.-M., *An Humbler Heaven*, pp.64–6.

> I hope that you will have a long and happy life and that you will never be Prime Minister, a much overrated job. It would already be antiquated to wish that you should grow up to be an English gentleman, and the suggestion of social snobbery would be unacceptable to you, but I do hope you will grow up an independent and kindly man of your word, and that is much the same ideal . . . There is, of course, the possibility that you will live to see the end of the world, as indeed may I. That possibility you should not worry about too much. If the progress of science and the lack of progress of man does produce the end of the world, one might just as well be there to see it . . . The problem is rather that we seem to be in a stage when the new technology is destroying the old civilisation, but is not building a new one in its place. Europe is apparently going the way of America, America is going the way of California and California is going to the devil and Mr. Reagan . . . Fashion has become a dominant influence in the lives of the unfortunate people who are most afflicted by this cultural decadence . . . This cuts off swinging people from the rest of society, with whom they have almost wholly ceased to communicate, and makes the King's Road and Carnaby Street an ambulatory hospital for the temporarily deranged . . . The truth is that the important things do not change. What matters to man is birth, an experience you have recently had, marriage and death. God matters . . . and so do all kinds of creative work. Love matters, both romantic love and friendship, and even more married and family love . . . Honesty and courage are the backbone of life. Beauty matters. Good nature matters a lot, and so does good humour. And most men need, for their sins, to have some success in life, if they are to be happy . . . Humility matters, and is the most difficult of the virtues. Some physical objects matter . . . It matters that one should love one's neighbour, and it is far from easy to do so . . . Shakespeare matters to most civilised people and Alexander Pope matters to some of us.[1]

In this article Rees-Mogg summarised his philosophy and showed that in many ways he was opposed to the spirit of the age. His ideals, those of the English gentleman-scholar combined with those of the sophisticated East Coast American WASP (white Anglo-Saxon Protestant, though the 'P' obviously did not apply in his case) had come under heavy challenge, on both sides of the Atlantic, in the 'Swinging

1 'Letter to my newborn son', *Sunday Times*, October 30 1966.

Sixties'. He deplored the new mass culture which in Britain he associated with the King's Road and Carnaby Street, in America with California and Ronald Reagan (then about to serve his first term as governor of the state). Fearing the effects of fashionable ignorance and licence, Rees-Mogg was a self-conscious elitist and champion of traditional morality.

It was easy to caricature him as a relic from the past, absurdly out of touch with the modern world. Quite apart from his views, he could neither type nor drive a car, and even by the standards of most contemporary rich people his way of life was extraordinarily sheltered. Yet it is always dangerous to judge from externals. Rees-Mogg was not all that he seemed; or rather, what appeared on the surface was not the whole man. Though in some ways antiquated, in others he was markedly less conservative than many of his critics. Above all, he had unusual ability, flair, and a character that quietly but effectively imposed itself.

His mind was lucid and he had a talent, unsurpassed in his time, for stating a case with cogency, style and speed. His leading articles, which were usually models of clarity – whatever the merits of the argument – and often enlivened with memorable phrases, were either written straight off or, sometimes, dictated. The fact that he did not compose them on a typewriter is hardly significant. More serious was his total lack of experience as a reporting journalist, which meant that as an editor he was like a general appointed to command an army in the field having previously only served on the staff. But, despite practical limitations from which most of his colleagues and subordinates were free, he soon won their respect for the quality of his intellect, as well as for some more personal qualities.

The ideal of gentlemanliness that he expounded for the benefit of his son was the ideal that he followed himself, and with a fair measure of success. People found that they could trust him; he was a man of his word, and he gave support to his staff when it was needed. Without conveying a particularly strong impression of warmth, he was amiable, equable and courteous, even under provocation. His very distinctive voice – with a sort of impediment that was part click, part lisp – had considerable charm and did not have to be raised to carry authority. A tall man, with a bit of a stoop, and wearing as a rule a rather loose double-breasted suit, he might have been a family solicitor with donnish proclivities; and an air of pawkily humorous wisdom enhanced the effect.

Congratulating him on his 'succession to the greatest editorial chair in the world', his former colleague Nigel Lawson (then editing the

Spectator and not yet an MP) wrote, with perhaps a hint of comradely sarcasm: 'Of all my generation I have always felt that you were the only one who was absolutely cut out to be Editor of *The Times*, for you were the only one with the real *Times* gravitas'.[1] This was true up to a point, but also slightly misleading. To the extent that he had always been serious beyond his years, that he looked the part of an editor of *The Times*, and that he could turn a leader in a way that did credit to the paper, the term gravitas certainly applied to Rees-Mogg. But in the sense implying consistency of judgement and contempt for the more popular aspects of journalism it did not wholly apply. His judgement was, in fact, more volatile than either his appearance or his editorial style suggested. Though on some issues, such as Europe, his opinion held firm throughout his editorship, on several others it proved changeable. As for his approach to the job, it was different from that of all previous editors in that, whereas they had shunned publicity for themselves, he almost courted it, giving numerous press or radio interviews and appearing quite often on television. We have seen that at Oxford he preferred debating – one of the performing arts – to scholarship, and it may be of some relevance that his mother had a stage career. He was a fascinating mixture of responsibility and recklessness. Those who knew him best became aware that his dignified demeanour concealed a streak of exhibitionism and a certain taste for journalistic sensation, of which he seemed at times to be conscious himself, and half-ashamed.

'You'll put in William, I suppose, and then just run him', Thomson had said to Hamilton when discussing future arrangements on *The Times*. 'No, Roy, I'll give him 95 per cent freedom', was Hamilton's reply, as he recalled it nearly twenty years later.[2] But Hamilton did not, in the event, have even 5 per cent control over Rees-Mogg. The new editor was determined to have all the freedom enjoyed by editors under the Astor regime, and the guarantees of editorial independence given to the Monopolies Commission ensured that he would get his way. Asked by Hamilton to set out his views on a command structure before the deal went through, Rees-Mogg argued that there should be

1 Nigel Lawson to W.R.-M., January 13 1967.
Another friend, Keith Kyle, writing to congratulate him, said that the announcement recalled the first occasion on which his name appeared in the journal he was now to edit, an occasion which led *The Times* to apologise, in the smallest print Kyle had ever known it to use, 'for having in error described the new President of the Oxford Union as Rees-Hogg'. Kyle added that this recollection 'should deserve a footnote in the next volume of the History' (a comment now fulfilled). Kyle to W.R.-M., January 16 1967.

2 Talking to author.

a clear division of labour between editor-in-chief, editor and managing editor:

> The Editor-in-Chief is responsible for how the paper develops; the Editor is responsible for what the paper says, both in its opinion and in its news columns; the Managing Editor is responsible for how the paper works. When the division is made between an Editor and a Deputy Editor [the relationship between him and Hamilton on the *Sunday Times*] the last word on political policy must remain with the Editor. When the division is made between an Editor and an Editor-in-Chief then the last word on political policy must still remain with the Editor. Here there may be a naval comparison – the Captain does not cease to be responsible for his ship even if he has a senior officer on board who is responsible for the whole fleet.[1]

Rees-Mogg, in fact, did not merely have 'the last word on political policy', but the complete word from first to last. He felt no obligation even to inform Hamilton of a line he was proposing to take, and there were to be occasions when the editor-in-chief only knew of an important policy departure by *The Times* when he saw it in the paper. It suited Rees-Mogg that Hamilton, in addition to handling the business affairs of the group, including labour relations, should normally conduct on behalf of *The Times* negotiations for serial rights, which had been such a speciality of his on the *Sunday Times*. He was also quite often consulted by the editor on staff appointments. But in general his impact upon the character of the paper during the Thomson years was, compared with the editor's, almost negligible.[2] Whatever its editorial successes and failures during the period, whatever its merits and defects, Rees-Mogg was overwhelmingly responsible.

Immediately after the board meeting on January 12, McDonald was summoned to be told what had been decided. It is strange indeed that he was not told earlier. Nobody who had worked with him could have doubted that he was a man to be trusted with a secret. Haley had advance knowledge of the decision and ought, surely, to have shared it with McDonald, who had been his candidate to succeed him. But

1 W.R.-M. to C.D.H., undated document in Hamilton papers; also referred to in C.D.H., op. cit., pp.139–40.

2 He was to have far more influence with the new editor of the *Sunday Times*, Harold Evans.

McDonald reflected afterwards that it was characteristic of him not to do so, for the reason, or on the pretext, that the decision had not yet been formalised.

At 6 p.m. on the same day, when the news had been broken to McDonald, Hamilton broke it to about a dozen senior members of the editorial staff. He paid a warm tribute to McDonald (in whose room the meeting was held) for the way he had held the fort, but said that the board had decided a younger man was needed for the editorship. McDonald would, however, be associate editor. He commended Rees-Mogg as 'a person of high intellect, great understanding, but capable also of great firmness'. He asked them not to spread the news for a quarter of an hour, to give him time to reach Thomson House in Gray's Inn Road and make a similar statement there.

In the view of one of those present, that should have been the end of the meeting, but:

> McD[onald] jumped up and said in a rather strained voice (he had been sitting gloomily by the corner of his own desk) that he would like fully to endorse all that D[enis] H[amilton] had said. He thought that had he been ten or even five years younger a different decision might have been taken. As it was, he would in similar circumstances have made the same appointment. He would continue to go on . . . Here his voice broke, and he repeated, almost with a sob, 'to go on . . .'

His colleagues 'left embarrassed'.[1]

The following day Rees-Mogg made his debut at Printing House Square, attending the midday conference in the editor's room. According to the same witness, he:

> shook hands rather limply with each of us. He sat in the Editor's chair, and O[liver] W[oods] on his right 'took' the conference . . . everyone talking rather louder and with more emphasis for the benefit of the newcomer.

After some discussion of the day's news, he addressed the company, saying that he envisaged 'a period of 2 or 3 months when there would be considerable changes, then a year or two of consolidation, and then

1 E. C. Hodgkin's diary, entry for January 12 1967. Earlier that afternoon McDonald had been telephoned by the PA and the *Evening News* to ask if they could take pictures of him. So he had assumed they knew more than he did, with the result that his disappointment, when it came, was all the more acute.

a further expansion'. He gave a few detailed instances of what he had in mind, then:

> said he had always been a very professional journalist (nobody knew what to make of that), and that he regarded it as a privilege to be associated . . . etc.

He 'made a good impression in a rather donnish way'.

After lunch he wrote his first leader, talked to E. C. Hodgkin about proposed staff changes, and took the 4.30 p.m. conference. In a gesture that certainly did not anticipate his future routine, he returned for a couple of hours or so after dinner, when among other things he was introduced to some of the night staff. In the car going home, accompanied by Hodgkin, he talked mostly about Balliol.[1]

So ended his first day in charge of *The Times*. It happened to be Friday the 13th.

1 Hodgkin diary, entry for January 13 1967. Hodgkin also was a Balliol man, but had been at the college some time before Rees-Mogg, who was fifteen years his junior. He had succeeded McDonald as foreign editor in 1965.

II

Unchanged strategy • New look for the paper • No purge of editorial staff • Lone voice in the boardroom • Premature launch of TBN *• An old man and the sea*

THE FIRST ISSUE of the new house journal for both Times newspapers had a yellow cover on which the grinning face of Roy Thomson appeared through a jagged black hole with the inscription 'Whaam'. The issue contained a message from William Haley stating that, while the two journals involved in the merger would remain 'independent entities, each with its own character', the company itself was 'one whole' with the purpose of creating 'a corporate sense and a common interest'. Denis Hamilton, in his message, declared that 'one of the most important means of moving forward [lay] in pooling resources'. He also announced that the year's major project for *The Times* would be a separately folded business section, and he set as the paper's first target a normal size of 32 pages and a sale of 400,000. The next two or three years would, he said, be 'immensely difficult', but he was quite confident of the outcome.[1]

Apart from the idea of pooling resources, the strategy adopted by the new regime was not in itself new. Essentially it was a continuation of the strategy for survival to which the management of *The Times* had become committed during the last phase of the Astor regime. The inspiration for this was a report by the firm of City accountants Cooper Brothers and Company, commissioned in the autumn of 1957 and delivered early the following year. As well as recommending drastic changes in the system of management, the Cooper report made sweeping suggestions for improving *The Times*'s editorial appeal. These included making the style of the paper less ponderous; having more news (with shorter items) and placing news on the front page; reducing the space allotted to leaders; increasing the number of special features; giving more space to trade and industry; relaxing the anonymity rule;

1 *Times Newspapers House Journal*, January–March 1967. With the next quarterly issue this publication changed its name to *Times News*. From July it began to appear every other month, or occasionally for a single month.

and brightening the paper's appearance by changes in typography and layout. The proposed circulation target was to be 400,000 within five years and 600,000 within ten (from an existing 250,000 plus).

The Cooper inquiry was prompted by *The Times*'s increasing sense of weakness in relation to its competitors. On the score of readership it had been left far behind by the *Daily Telegraph*, whose circulation had risen from about 100,000 in the 1920s to well over a million in the 1950s, while that of *The Times* had oscillated, but at a much lower level.[1] To the bulk of the educated middle class the *Daily Telegraph* had become the prime source of jobs as well as news; it had established a decisive lead in the very important field of classified advertising. Despite maintaining a far more numerous staff of correspondents and reporters, at home and abroad, it was a highly profitable newspaper, whereas *The Times* in 1957 made a loss.

A more recent competitor in the fight for readers was the *Manchester Guardian*, which put news on its front page in 1952 (the *Telegraph* having done so in 1939). Seven years later it dropped the 'Manchester' from its title, and in 1961 started printing in London. Its circulation, which had risen from about 80,000 at the end of the war to 180,000 at the end of the 1950s, in 1962 passed that of *The Times*. The *Guardian* was now the national quality newspaper of the centre-left, and it also made a strong appeal to younger readers.

Yet the most serious challenge, perhaps, came from the *Financial Times*, which was achieving in the sphere of business and finance the sort of primacy that *The Times* had long been assumed to possess in all the leading departments of national life. Just when 'Top People Take *The Times*' was being launched as a promotional slogan, top people in the City were beginning to find the *FT* a more than adequate substitute. This development coincided with a shift in the balance of power from politicians to financiers, businessmen and technocrats, and with a shift within the City itself from the old *Times*-orientated establishment to new forces less respectful of tradition. It was during the 1950s that the change became apparent. At the beginning of the decade the City editor of *The Times* was automatically given precedence, at City lunches and similar functions, over the editor of the *FT*; by the end of the decade their positions were reversed.[2]

With a circulation that rose in the 1950s from 57,000 to 122,000, and with a growing market of a kind particularly attractive to many

1 1923, 163,000; 1938, 203,000; 1950, 255,000; 1952, 232,000; 1956 (Jan.), 218,000; 1957, 235,000; 1961, 253,000. (Round figures).
2 Sir Gordon Newton talking to author.

advertisers, the *FT* was hitting *The Times* in readership, revenue and prestige. Moreover, it was continually broadening the range of interests for which it catered, providing excellent coverage of the arts, science and technology, social problems and leisure pursuits, as well as the best specialist information within its own sphere. Like *The Times* it was acquiring a unique reputation, but unlike *The Times* it did not have to live on reputation alone.

The Cooper report called, in effect, for simultaneous action on every front: to chase the *Daily Telegraph*'s big circulation, to emulate the *Guardian*'s liveliness, and to recapture ground lost to the *FT*. Some felt that the philosophy of the report was fundamentally misconceived. Stanley Morison, for instance, rejected as heresy the whole idea of aiming at a much wider readership, arguing that *The Times* had to be the organ of 'a strong, educated, efficient, informed governing class', by which he meant the political and administrative class.[1] Haley, though unhappy about some aspects of the report, could not agree to such a restriction of *The Times*'s appeal. He was a thoroughgoing elitist, but his idea of the British elite embraced almost anyone capable of reading *The Times*.

At any rate, after a lot of discussion and several years' delay, he began to act on lines indicated by the report. On May 3 1966 *The Times* appeared with news on its front page, with more lower-case headlines, and with a redesigned masthead from which the royal coat of arms had been dropped.[2] The paper also acquired a diary, a political cartoon and a regular woman's page. These and other changes boosted the circulation to over 300,000 by the end of the year. But they also made the need for a change of ownership more acute, since the rapid rise in circulation increased costs long before there could be any compensating benefit in higher advertisement revenue. For a paper which derived three-quarters of its revenue from advertisements, and only a quarter from sales, this was clearly a disastrous development. The old regime had started to put a new strategy into effect without the necessary financial resources. The new regime now provided the cash without questioning or reassessing the strategy.

---

1 Memorandum to the chief proprietors, April 1958; quoted in Oliver Woods and James Bishop, *The Story of The Times*, p.344. Morison (1889–1967), eminent typographer and principal author of the first four volumes of the present History, was associated with *The Times* for nearly thirty years.

2 It was restored by Harold Evans on July 29 1981, the day Charles Prince of Wales was married to Lady Diana Spencer.

Rees-Mogg shared Haley's view rather than Morison's of the readership at which *The Times* should aim. In the first of many interviews that he gave as editor he said:

> I believe *The Times* ought to be the natural main newspaper of a very large proportion of what I call the seriously occupied people of the country – business people, those in universities, doctors, politicians, civil servants – and a much wider band than that as well. We certainly want it to be a newspaper with a broader area of circulation.

At the same time he promised that traditional standards would be maintained. Obtaining a wider audience for the paper would 'not mean popularizing, distorting, sensationalizing or trivializing the news'.[1]

Four days after his appointment he announced his first major change:

> From Monday January 23 personal by-lines will be used in *The Times* where appropriate, and subject to the following guiding rules:
>
> 1. Turnovers by staff men or women should normally carry a personal by-line, together with the office of the writer – e.g.: 'By Louis Heren, Our Washington Correspondent'.
> 2. The Drama, Music and other critics on the Arts Page should have personal by-lines for their normal full-length notices. (Brief notes should not normally carry names.)
> 3. Sports writers should also use their names for full-length reports of matches or events . . .
> 4. The Political, Diplomatic, Labour and other specialist writers may in exceptional circumstances be given a personal by-line when they write a major revelatory or explanatory piece, but not when they are reporting a White Paper or other routine news. They should always be given a by-line on weekly or feature columns . . .
> 5. Outstanding dispatches from correspondents and reporters at home and abroad can be given personal by-lines, but this should be exceptional. The principle of the reporting of current news without personal by-lines will be maintained.
>
> W.R.-M.
>
> January 17 1967

1 Reported in *The Times*, January 13 1967.

The rule of anonymity was part of *The Times*'s special cachet, and the ending of it, though recommended by the Cooper team, had been firmly resisted by Haley, who feared that signed writing would invite exhibitionism, impair objectivity, and detract from *The Times*'s corporate authority. Rees-Mogg had no such fears. Replying to one of the few readers who wrote to complain of the change, he counter-attacked hard: 'I do not accept that an anonymous writer must always be regarded as writing with more authority and less bias than if he writes under his own name; indeed the opposite is often the case'.[1] And to another critic he suggested that many writers might be inhibited by feeling 'a striking phrase . . . inappropriate in an anonymous article, let alone a striking judgement'.[2] Among the paper's editorial staff there was almost universal acquiescence in the change. Only one resigned in protest: Windsor Davis, the Parliamentary correspondent, who said at his farewell party that before he came to *The Times* (from the *Daily Telegraph*) 'I knew Windsor Davis, and didn't think much of him, but to be called Parliamentary correspondent of *The Times* – that was really something'.[3] On the other hand, many undoubtedly welcomed the introduction of by-lines; for instance, Heren in Washington, who found that it enhanced his reputation not only among readers, but among the people he reported.[4] Since Rees-Mogg had no intention of being a self-effacing editor, it would have been hard for him to deny his colleagues the opportunity to shine as individuals, even if he had thought it right to do so.

On January 18 there was a leader by him entitled 'The Idea of *The Times*', in which he asserted the paper's qualitative superiority in one vital respect:

> There is no paper in the country which does not rightly claim independence – yet there does still remain perhaps a certain shade of difference. Other papers have a duty of independence. *The Times* has a vocation to it.

---

1 W.R.-M. to Rowland Bowen, February 6 1967.
2 W.R.-M. to Sir Bernard Darwin, April 27 1967. Darwin objected only to ending the anonymity rule, and to the 'thumbnail photographs' of regular contributors which began to appear at the same time, and which reminded him of the BBC's 'tedious and unimaginative habit' of using signature tunes. Other changes in the paper he warmly approved. (Darwin to W.R.-M., April 24 1967.)
3 Hodgkin diary, entry for February 16 1967. Oliver Woods made a presentation to Davis, who returned to the *Telegraph*.
4 Louis Heren, *Memories of Times Past*, p.223.

He added that this vocation had only once been 'really in peril – in the influence exerted by the leading Ministers on the appeasement policy of *The Times*'. Thus, almost casually, the new editor of the paper disowned the record of a fairly recent predecessor.

This leader had a significant side-effect on the layout of the centre pages. Since it occupied three columns, it created such pressure on the rest of the leader page that something had to give; and one of the features put there in the changes of the previous May – the diary – was switched to the opposite page, where it remained. As a result, it became possible at any time to expand the space for leaders without cramping unduly the space available for letters and the turnover.

Early in February further big changes were announced, in a circular to staff.[1] The Personal column, which had been moved to page 2 when news was placed on the front page, was to be transferred to the back page, which it would share with Births, Marriages and Deaths, and the crossword. Pictures, for long an established feature of the back page, would be moved to the inside. Pages 2 and 3 would be devoted to home news, 4 and 5 to foreign news, 6 and 7 to sport as well as general news pictures, 8 and 9 to the arts and women's topics. The Parliamentary and Law reports would be interspersed within pages 6–9. Page 10, to the left of the leader page, would remain a special news page also containing (since January 18) the diary. Page 12 would accommodate Court and social news, and obituaries. Extended business coverage would start at page 13 and would be followed by appointments and classified advertising. There would also be regular columns by three staff men – David Wood on Whitehall, Louis Heren from Washington and Kyril Tidmarsh from Moscow – as well as one by Ian Trethowan, BBC political commentator and future director-general, on current politics.

These changes came into effect from February 13 and, since they had meanwhile been announced and explained to readers,[2] the letters column that day contained some reactions. The chief ground of complaint was the removal of pictures from the back page, but Mr. W. Sing of Saffron Walden, still evidently sore about losing the old front page, wrote 'One will now be forced to read *The Times* from back to front'. Mr. C. Gascoyne wrote from Morecambe, in the stateliest French, requesting 'de temps en temps (chaque semaine par exemple) une pièce en français provenant de Paris'. Mr. D. L. Miles of Andover, ignoring the contents, merely asked 'Could you not print on a paper

1 February 7 1967.
2 In a leader written by Rees-Mogg, 'The plan of a newspaper' February 9 1967.

which lights a fire?' In general, however, it is safe to assume that readers welcomed the new arrangement of contents, which provided, as was claimed, a more logical run-through for news, features and advertising. The *Daily Telegraph* and *Guardian* soon paid their rival the sincerest compliment, by following suit.

Rees-Mogg was at pains to demonstrate to his new colleagues that he was not the spearhead of a *Sunday Times* invasion of Printing House Square. The editorial staff of the main paper, as distinct from the Business section, remained much as it had been before the merger. Leader writers, heads of department and foreign correspondents were mostly either confirmed in their positions or promoted. A. P. Ryan, a former assistant editor and recently literary editor, did retire; but at sixty-seven he was of an age to do so. Oliver Woods lost his exclusive connection with the paper when he was appointed deputy to the editor-in-chief. But most senior figures from the previous regime were at least equivalently employed on the Thomson *Times*, and the same pattern was followed at other levels. As the paper's activities expanded new people were brought in, but to reinforce rather than to displace the old guard, which by and large held its own in the early Thomson years.

Indeed, throughout the whole Thomson period the personnel side was controlled by an old *Times* man, John Grant, who may therefore be seen as a rather striking symbol of continuity. Grant was a Lancastrian from Burnley, who was sent to school just across the Yorkshire border, at Giggleswick. Geoffrey Dawson's country estate was in the neighbourhood, and he was a governor of the school, in which capacity it fell to him to present young Grant with a prize: an early and prophetic link with *The Times*. The next stage of Grant's education was at Balliol, where before the war he read classical Mods. During the war he served in the army, mainly as an adjutant in India, returning to Oxford afterwards to read not Greats, but English. Having completed his interrupted university career he decided to be a journalist, and went first as a graduate trainee to the *Liverpool Post & Echo*. From there he was recruited by the *Manchester Guardian* (as it then still was) as a general reporter and, for two years, part-time military correspondent. In 1955 he succeeded his friend Bobby Jessel (who had died of leukaemia) as defence correspondent of *The Times*. Five years later Haley, whom he greatly admired, appointed him home news editor. Not long after the change of ownership he became managing editor. Genial but sharp-minded, he served the new regime loyally and efficiently, drawing on his wartime experience of administration and man-management, though many regretted, and with reason, that he was no longer free to exercise his notable talent as a writing journalist.

Though the old *Times* establishment could hardly complain that it was under-represented in the new, there was one recruit from the *Sunday Times* who, from the first, challenged traditional methods and attitudes, and so created a feeling of unease which was to grow, over time, into serious resentment. This was Michael Cudlipp, whose title when he joined the paper was assistant editor (night), but whose impact was soon out of all proportion to his rank and seniority.

Michael Cudlipp was, indeed, still a young man – four years younger than Rees-Mogg – when he moved to *The Times*. Son of Percy Cudlipp, nephew of Reginald and Hugh, he was born in the Fleet Street purple. Eager as a boy to pursue the family trade, he disregarded his father's wish that he should go to Cambridge after his schooling at Tonbridge, preferring instead to go straight into journalism. Hamilton, who for the same reason had spurned the opportunity of a university education, took him on for Kemsley newspapers and arranged for him to start on the *South Wales Echo* in Cardiff. From there he went as a sub-editor to the *Manchester Evening Chronicle*, and in 1958, when he was only twenty-four, Hamilton brought him to London as news editor of the *Sunday Times*, in which capacity he achieved great success.

His arrival at *The Times* was greeted without enthusiasm. The night news staff regarded him as a potential menace, and Hodgkin, at their first meeting, thought he seemed 'a confident rather lowering old schoolboy'.[1] But Rees-Mogg had formed a very good opinion of him at the *Sunday Times*, and in their new relationship came to depend upon him increasingly. Their qualities were complementary: Rees-Mogg with a trained and sophisticated mind, more interested in policy than news, and deliberately rationing his time on the job for the sake of family life; Cudlipp very intelligent but under-educated, quintessentially a news man, and prepared to sacrifice almost everything to his work. As time went on, he became in most respects the paper's effective editor during the long weekday evening and night hours; also on Sundays, when Rees-Mogg was away from the office and not always in touch even by telephone.

Cudlipp's routine at *The Times* initially involved starting work there at 11 a.m., a quarter of an hour before the morning conference,

1 Hodgkin diary, entry for February 9 1967.

and leaving at about 9.15 p.m. But before long he changed it to arriving in the early afternoon and staying until 1–2 a.m. He lost no time in introducing a television set into the news room, because he felt it necessary to know what the television news was carrying. This, as he put it, was 'contrary to the hallowed doctrine that nothing was news until it had appeared in *The Times*'.[1] The innovation was surely overdue, though some colleagues said that he became rather obsessed by the television news, to the extent of going to often absurd lengths to give *The Times* a lead story that had not appeared on television. In any case he was prone to make drastic changes in later editions, with the result that stories would go out unread and were likely, therefore, to contain mistakes as well as misprints. Another consequence was that trains were quite often missed because the production side could not cope with the demands that he made upon it.

Whatever his faults, however, they were mainly due to excess of zeal, and were more than offset by the vitality and urgency that he brought to his task. Most of those who worked with him eventually acknowledged the value of his contribution, though many continued to deplore some of his methods. When he left the paper in 1973 Rees-Mogg said that he deserved to be 'a major figure in Volume VI of *The History of The Times*'. The comment was just and will prove to have been correct.

The news-gathering resources of the paper were swiftly developed after the merger, and all concerned had the heady sensation that anything worth doing could be done. Haley had cared passionately about news, but lacked the wherewithal to build up an adequate service. He was always, as he said, having to count candle-ends. Now at last there was money to match long-felt needs. Soon the number of home news reporters had risen by more than a third, and the paper's representation abroad was enhanced by regular appointments in South Africa, Japan and South America, while subscription to Agence France Press gave access to the only Western staff correspondent in China.

One early innovation was a news service run in partnership with the scientific journal *Nature*. Rees-Mogg felt that *The Times*'s coverage of science had been patchy, and his idea was to offer a service analogous to the law reports, enabling laymen to know what was happening in the world of science generally, and scientists themselves to be informed of developments outside their own special fields. The link was arranged between Rees-Mogg and Maurice Macmillan – Macmillans' being the publishers of *Nature* – and the *Times/Nature* news

---

1 Talking to author.

service soon proved its worth. It was retained despite the appointment, in due course, of a regular science correspondent, and was still going strong long after Rees-Mogg had ceased to be editor.

In February a News Team was set up for the rapid intensive coverage of special situations and emergencies. At the outset the team was five strong and led by a *Times* man, Peter Evans. Its first notable success was the following month when the tanker *Torrey Canyon* was wrecked off Cornwall and discharged an oil slick threatening beaches, birds and fish over a wide area. As soon as the news came through a light aircraft was chartered to fly Evans and two other members of the team, and a photographer, to an RAF station in Cornwall, where Evans at once arranged for himself and the photographer to be flown over the wreck. At the same time the two other journalists were being driven to Newlyn, where they talked to survivors and rescuers. In particular, one of the journalists, who happened to be a Dutch-speaker,[1] was able to talk to members of the Dutch salvage crew whose captain had been killed while trying to get aboard the tanker. As a result of these concerted efforts the team's account, which made all but the first edition, was the fullest and most dramatic to appear in next morning's papers. Other successes followed; also some failures. Later the separate News Team was found to be a luxury the paper could no longer afford, and its functions were largely subsumed in the ordinary foreign and home news departments. But in the early Thomson days its creation was symptomatic of the confident spirit then prevailing.

While the editorial department was in a state of quickened activity, the board room was certainly not idle. The headquarters of Times Newspapers Limited was established at Printing House Square as a gesture to *The Times*, and the main board met there ten times in 1967, with Haley as chairman.[2] In the middle of the following year an executive board was set up, under Hamilton's chairmanship, to 'assist in arriving at policy decisions and where appropriate make recommen-

---

1 Dan van der Vat.

2 Apart from Haley, the TNL board consisted at first of Kenneth Thomson (deputy chairman); Lord Shawcross and Sir Donald Anderson ('national' directors appointed by Gavin Astor); Lord Robens and Sir Eric Roll ('national' directors appointed by the Thomson Organisation); James Coltart and Gordon Brunton (representing the Thomson Organisation); Kenneth Keith (representing Gavin Astor, though in fact he had also advised Thomson); Denis Hamilton; Geoffrey Rowett (general manager and former managing director of the *Sunday Times*); and George Pope (deputy general manager, and still general manager of *The Times*).

dations to TNL main board'.[1] The executive board met at least monthly (except in August), and often several times a month, with the result that the main board took to meeting rather less frequently. In addition, Hamilton created management committees for the two papers, over which he presided and which normally also met in the board room. *The Times*'s management committee held its first meeting on January 23 1967, and in all met twenty-one times during that year.[2]

Whether the time spent in these conclaves was wholly justified is open to question. For the most part they did not serve for taking decisions or discussing problems in depth, but rather for the formal exchange of information between people who were anyway exchanging it all the time in the ordinary course of business. Indeed, at the end of 1969, meetings of the management committees were discontinued in favour of 'information and discussion meetings to be held quarterly by the chief executive on an informal basis'.[3] There was, moreover, a fundamental unreality about the boards and committees, in that Thomson himself did not sit on any of them. As we have seen, he had undertaken not to be chairman or even a member of the TNL board, and he naturally did not choose to serve on any subordinate body, which would in any case have ceased to be subordinate through the mere fact of his presence on it. Yet as chief proprietor and moving spirit of all the Thomson enterprises he could not have been ignored by his lieutenants, even if they had wished to ignore him. In fact, they had no wish to do so, and he had no intention of detaching himself from the business of managing and developing *The Times*. Behind the scenes he was in constant touch and ceaselessly active. In Hamilton's words, 'Roy was never off the telephone to me from the minute I'd taken over'.[4]

Ostensibly he was willing to provide all the money that might be needed to make *The Times* profitable in the long run. But in his own mind there was a more limited commitment and a more strictly defined

---

1 Regular members of the executive board, apart from Hamilton, were the two editors, the general manager, the personnel director, the publishing director, the marketing director, the technical director, and the director for senior management development. To these were added a financial director and an overall advertisement director. Others were invited to attend from time to time.

2 The original members of this committee were Hamilton, Rees-Mogg, Oliver Woods, Geoffrey Rowett, G. R. Pope, Barry On, Harry Henry and Thomas Cauter. Others often attended by invitation. At the same time three sub-committees were formed: for advertising, circulation and production.

3 Minutes of TNL executive board, November 17 1969. The *Times* management committee had a total of forty meetings during its existence of just under three years.

4 C.D.H., op. cit., p.145.

aim. Though he did not set his thoughts down in black and white, and never properly examined their implications, there can be little doubt that he felt committed to spending £5 million over five years, but not necessarily anything more, since he expected the paper to be paying its way by the end of that period. Despite statements from time to time suggesting that there was no limit to what he would spend, in reality he had £5 million over five years in mind, and was not seriously entertaining the idea of an indefinite subsidy.

He was confident that *The Times* could quite swiftly raise its circulation to a level where it would compete with the *Daily Telegraph*, while leaving the *Guardian* far behind. Part of the strategy for achieving this was to make the paper more attractive to readers without charging them any more for it. While the product was being enlarged and improved at great cost, and to the accompaniment of lavish publicity, the price was to be held at 6d until further notice. Price had, indeed, often been an effective weapon in circulation wars, not least in *The Times*'s own history. In March 1914, when Northcliffe cut the price of *The Times* from 2d to 1d, sales immediately leapt from under 50,000 to 150,000, bringing them more or less into line with those of the *Daily Telegraph* and the *Morning Post*, both already selling at 1d. By 1930 newspaper prices had risen again, but in that year William Berry, the first Lord Camrose, cut the *Telegraph*'s price from 2d to 1d and doubled its circulation overnight. In 1937 it absorbed the *Morning Post* and by 1939 the circulation of the joint paper exceeded 750,000. Meanwhile *The Times*, selling still at 2d (until 1938, when the price was raised to 3d) stayed with a circulation around 200,000. Geoffrey Dawson would say, during this period, that the *Telegraph* was 'the hell of a pennorth'. So indeed it was, but with extraordinary insouciance *The Times*'s management took no retaliatory action and allowed the *Telegraph* to establish its enormous lead.

Holding *The Times*'s price at 6d in 1967 could not, unfortunately, be expected to have the same effect as what Northcliffe had done in 1914 or Camrose in 1930. On the first occasion the price of *The Times* had been brought down to the same level as that of its competitors, so that it could fight them on equal terms; on the second, the *Telegraph*'s price had been reduced to half that of *The Times* (and *Morning Post*), so that it had a decisive advantage in the market. But in 1967 the price of the *Guardian* was 5d and that of the *Telegraph* 4d. Both papers, therefore, were undercutting *The Times* by a significant margin. In these circumstances, to believe that *The Times* could rapidly overtake the *Telegraph*, or even beat the *Guardian* out of sight, was surely to believe in miracles – all the more so, when it was assumed that £5 million would be enough to do the trick. Even if it had been possible to achieve such an increase so quickly, *The Times* lacked as yet the productive capacity to handle it, as events were to prove. Moreover the time-lag between additional sales and the advertising revenue to sustain them, already apparent in the latter part of 1966, was bound to be a growing problem.

So far as the *Financial Times* was concerned there was a price advantage, since it was selling at 8d in 1967. But in other respects the *FT* was more favourably placed, having a select readership which guaranteed extremely strong support from certain categories of advertiser, and being under no compulsion to accelerate its sales' growth beyond what seemed to be the natural rate. Yet the Cooper-Thomson strategy (as we may term it) required a simultaneous attack on all *The Times*'s competitors, including the *FT*. While aiming for a much bigger circulation within a few years, the paper had also to aim for the sort of people who bought the *FT* and the sort of advertisers who took space in it.

Among senior staff only one man dissented from the basic strategy and tried to prevent its adoption. This was Harry Henry, marketing director of the Thomson group. The minutes of the first meeting of *The Times*'s management committee contain the bald record that 'On circulation targets H. Henry said that medium- and long-term targets for circulation increase would take time'.[1] But Hamilton tells us that Henry submitted a paper to himself and Thomson in which he argued that:

> the decision to go for 500,000 copies would only bring disaster; that the *Telegraph*, the *Financial Times* and the *Guardian* had gone so far ahead that there weren't enough AB readers (readers in the professions and higher income groups) left to be picked up. To succeed in achieving a sale of half a million copies, the extra readers would have to be won from existing readers of the other newspapers; and he very much doubted whether it would be worth the vast expenditure of money and effort.

Henry's paper was, Hamilton says, discussed by the board, which we should perhaps understand to mean the management committee, because there is no evidence that the TNL board discussed it. At all

1 January 23 1967.

events, 'the consensus was against him'; he was 'the odd man out'.[1] The strategy went ahead.

For competing with the *Financial Times* the principal instrument was to be the *Times Business News (TBN)*, whose scope and character were under consideration before the end of 1966. In early December Rees-Mogg sent Hamilton a 'strictly confidential' memorandum on the subject. After listing what he saw as the reasons for the success of the *Sunday Times*'s business section, he argued that most of them existed, or could be made to exist, for *The Times*. It would be necessary to recruit a minimum of forty-five journalists to launch *TBN*, of whom about thirty could be drawn from *The Times's* existing staff. The eventual number might be about sixty. The launch should be 'as early as possible in order to forestall possible competition'. Granted the capacity to produce a satisfactory section, they 'should not be ashamed to develop and improve it in public'. The earliest feasible launching date was, in his view, February 1 1967, though 'the fallback date' could be April 1. The only significant competition would come from the *Financial Times* and the *Daily Telegraph*. It would be wrong to copy the *FT*: *TBN* would be 'only about 40 per cent City and 50 per cent industrial', so the *FT* could 'retain its monopoly as the financial daily'. The *Telegraph* was another matter, because it could produce a business section with a much larger circulation. In that event it might be necessary to reduce the price of *The Times*, 'a course one could otherwise hope to avoid'.[2]

By the end of the following month Rees-Mogg may have become slightly more cautious about the time for launching. He said then that 'examination of the problems and opportunities of a separate 8 pp. (minimum) section on Business News' would begin on February 13, leaving only six or seven weeks to the latest launching date he had proposed. Hamilton, himself under relentless pressure from Thomson, says that at this point he 'did rather press William to pull his weight' to ensure an early launch.[3] It is unlikely that he had to press very hard. The editor was as keen as anyone to get *TBN* started, and it was he who had suggested an early date to guard against the danger of pre-emptive action by a rival. Whatever subsequent doubts he may

---

1 C.D.H., op. cit., pp.144–5.
2 W.R.-M. to C.D.H., December 6 1966. This seems to be the only reference in writing to even the possibility of cutting *The Times*'s price.
3 Op. cit., p.145.

have had were clearly soon resolved, because in mid-February it was agreed that the launch should be on Budget day, April 11.[1]

The business section was to be edited by Anthony (Tony) Vice, who had been performing the same task on the *Sunday Times*. Like Rees-Mogg he had gone from Oxford – where he read PPE – straight to the *Financial Times*. After his apprenticeship there he worked briefly on *The Times*, as a leader-writer on finance and economics under Haley. But most of his experience, before moving to the *Sunday Times*, was on the *Daily Telegraph*, whose professionalism he much admired. A lively, enthusiastic man, he was also nervy and rather vulnerable. When the *TBN* ran into serious difficulties his temperament became an addition to them, though it has to be said that most of the difficulties were not of his making.

By early April a supposedly adequate minimum staff had been signed on, including recruits of high quality such as Joe Roeber from the *Economist* and Frances Cairncross for whom, at twenty-two, it was to be the first job in a distinguished career. But the star recruit was a thirty-year-old principal from the Treasury, with a first in PPE from Oxford, where he had also been president of the Union. Peter Jay was a son of Douglas Jay, the President of the Board of Trade who had given the Government's consent to Thomson's acquisition of *The Times*, and who had himself worked on the paper for four years between the two wars. Moreover Peter Jay's father-in-law, James Callaghan, was chancellor of the exchequer at the time, and so head of the department of state in which he was employed. When he asked his mentor, Sir William Armstrong, if his career in the service would be prejudiced by these family connections, Armstrong hinted that it might be. He was anyway feeling rather restless, and when a journalist friend, John Morgan, suggested to him at a party that he should join *The Times*, he gave a 'vaguely positive' reply.[2] On the strength of it Morgan approached Rees-Mogg, who had never met Jay but, realising at once that he would be a considerable catch, telephoned him and asked him to talk to Vice. As a result, he became economics correspondent of *TBN*, and soon his influence extended to the paper as a whole

---

1 Minutes of Times Management Committee, February 6 and 20 1967. Rees-Mogg was emphatic in retrospect that he did not contest the choice of date. (Talking to author.)

2 Jay talking to author. Sir William Armstrong, later Lord Armstrong of Sanderstead (d.1980), was at the time joint permanent secretary to the treasury. His advice rested on more than hunch, since in 1964 he had been obliged to sack Jay as his private secretary to allay the suspicions of George Brown, then secretary of state for economic affairs while Callaghan was chancellor.

as economics editor. Though there were important issues, particularly Europe, on which he and Rees-Mogg did not agree, he became one of the editor's closest colleagues over the next ten years and, at one point, a decisive influence on his thinking. At editorial conferences his interventions were often dazzling, and his intellectual agility could be used in odd ways, as when he once wrote an article in which the first letter of each paragraph serially spelt out the name of a girl with whom he had been having lunch. His contribution to the first issue of TBN was a signed 'preview' of his father-in-law's budget.

In his leader on the day of launching Rees-Mogg said that *TBN* would have the advantage of 'a really able young team'. It would have 'a valuable educational role, not merely inside industry, but about industry', since there was a disastrous barrier 'between the profit-earning businessman or profit-directed business executive and the fee or salary-earning professional man or civil servant', which he hoped *TBN* would help to break down.[1]

That evening the launch was celebrated at a dinner for two hundred at the Savoy, at which Thomson was present though Hamilton acted as host. There was no high table, but a number of small tables with a member of TNL presiding at each. A large screen was erected in the dining room and, during the first part of dinner, cameras at Printing House Square showed preparations for getting the paper to press. Later Rees-Mogg addressed the gathering from his office. Among the guests there were, of course, many leading City men, industrialists and advertising agents, but also a variety of well-known people from other fields, including four previous chancellors of the exchequer: R. A. Butler, Harold Macmillan, Peter Thorneycroft and Selwyn Lloyd. The Chancellor of the day, Callaghan, arrived after his budget appearance on television, and made an impromptu speech. Macmillan, too, was prevailed upon to speak, and gave a light-hearted review of bygone budget days.

There was a hard sell from Hamilton when he claimed that *The Times* was now read by the entire meritocracy: not only 'the upper echelons of government, the law, the civil service and the professions', but also 'the whole of the business world . . . technologists and engineers'. *TBN* was only the first of many projects that *The Times* would undertake. Thomson spoke in his best Monopolies Commission vein. Though the paper must 'for its own self-respect be profitable one day', nevertheless he was certain that, if there was ever 'conflict between a chance to make money and an opportunity to fulfil its

1 'The New Business News', April 11 1967.

editorial mission then it would always choose the latter'.[1] To this sort of stuff many of the guests must have preferred the contribution of Warren Mitchell, then a household name for his role as Alf Garnett in the television series *Till Death Us do Part*, who did 'a hilarious sequence about *The Times* going into business'.[2]

The launch was preceded by an extensive publicity campaign. Two thirty-second peak hour spots were reserved on national television. Space was taken in many national and local newspapers. Poster sites were booked on tube and commuter stations. Five hundred thousand leaflets promoting *TBN*'s coverage of the Budget were distributed to the homes of prospective readers. Just about all that advertising could do was done. It is, however, notorious that advertising is a waste of money unless and until the product is right; and unfortunately much was wrong with *TBN*. The launch was soon acknowledged to have been premature, and the whole idea of a separate, 'backset' business news was before long being called in question. *TBN* in its original form was to have a troubled life, for reasons that will appear. But meanwhile, for a brief space, its creators were full of optimism about its future, and about what it could do for the fortunes of the paper.

Its introduction occasioned, or coincided with, a number of other changes. The sports pages replaced the old business section opposite the Court page. Television and radio were placed on the last left-hand page before the end. The title of the diary was changed from 'As It Happens' to 'The Times Diary', with the promise that it would, in future, be 'more of a news and personalities column than its predecessor'.[3] Above all, the make-up throughout the paper was changed from seven broadish (13½-em) columns to eight rather narrower (11½-em) columns per page. This change, which some readers naturally regretted, brought *The Times* into line with other quality newspapers. It was dictated by the need to make, within reason, the most economical use of available space.[4]

The one element in forward planning for *The Times* which was, of course, entirely new and in no way foreshadowed by the Cooper report

1 *Times News* (new name for house journal) issue for April–June 1967. Some lady members of the staff were indignant that the Savoy party was an all-male occasion.
2 C.D.H., op. cit., p.146.
3 Leader on April 11 1967, quoted above.
4 It was decided on March 20 1967 that the minimum size ever for the whole paper should be 20 pp.; the normal size when parliament was sitting, 24 pp.; for July–August, 22 pp.; minimum for launch week, 28 pp. (16 main, 12 *TBN*).

was the proposed pooling of resources with the *Sunday Times*. Hamilton had stressed the importance of this and Geoffrey Rowett, general manager of the combined enterprise, acted in the right spirit by spending his mornings at Thomson House in Gray's Inn Road and his afternoons at Printing House Square. Because of the merger, he said, the two newspapers could have 'the benefit of both worlds'.[1] In fact it did not turn out thus. Amalgamation of bureaux abroad proved unworkable, and cooperation at home was limited. To the extent that the staffs of the two papers mixed at all, they did not mix well. But on one story, already current at the time of the merger, successful joint action was achieved. This was the story of Sir Francis Chichester's solo voyage of circumnavigation in his yacht *Gipsy Moth IV*.

For the outward part of the voyage, from Plymouth to Sydney N.S.W., exclusive newspaper rights were shared by the *Sunday Times* with the *Guardian*; but for the return journey *The Times* took the *Guardian's* place. The arrangement was that, for a fee of £1,500, Chichester would provide an interview piece before leaving Sydney, a weekly message of up to 500 words during his journey home, and a concluding signed article after his arrival in England. The *Sunday Times* paid £2,000 for similar, but complementary, reports; and the two papers made joint arrangements for syndication throughout the world.

As a result *The Times* obtained two outstanding scoops. The first was when *Gipsy Moth* ran into a terrific storm in the Tasman Sea within twenty-four hours of leaving Sydney. During the night of January 30 the yacht was struck by a huge wave and for a few moments capsized, though fortunately it righted itself after part of the cockpit had been torn away and most of the contents of Chichester's cabin thrown into a jumble. On February 1 *The Times* was able to run a story on the front page under the three-column headline CHICHESTER SAFE AFTER CAPSIZE IN STORM, with details of the incident and the fact that he had refused help. The story was quoted on late television bulletins the night before, from the paper's early editions, and the following day late editions of other papers gave the news, mainly with due acknowledgment to *The Times*. The Canberra correspondent, Stewart Harris, who had helped to produce Chichester's copy before

1 *Times News*, April–June 1967. Rowett, forty-one in 1967, had been on convoys to Russia while serving in the Royal Navy during the war. Then, after qualifying as a chartered accountant, he worked for a time as a director of companies in Africa, based in Rhodesia. He joined the *Sunday Times* in 1965.

he left Australia, was warmly thanked by his superiors for efficiency in transmitting the message.[1]

The greater scoop, which was also truly an example of pooled resources, occurred when Chichester was rounding Cape Horn. On March 20 he radioed his position to Murray Sayle of the *Sunday Times* who, together with about thirty journalists from other papers, was waiting at Punta Arenas on the Magellan Strait. Under the noses of his rivals, and despite atrocious weather, Sayle took off in a yellow Piper Apache piloted by a Chilean, Captain Rodolfo Fuenzalida. *Gipsy Moth* was sighted south of the Horn, and Sayle managed to take a picture. Regaining Punta Arenas, within twenty minutes he caught a plane to Santiago, where just after midnight he had the picture processed and wired. It arrived in time to appear, somewhat blurred but unique, in later editions on March 21, forming with Sayle's accompanying account the lead story under a five-column headline THE FIRST PICTURE OFF CAPE HORN.

The following day Chichester was still the front-page lead story, with the veteran sailor's own report under a three-column headline CHICHESTER TELLS HOW HE DID IT:

> Conditions have been bad . . . I survived last night, but it's a test of nerves sailing into a black night which you know is stuffed with rocky islands . . . The ogre of the Horn did not approve. As I rounded the Horn I was running before a sea which was building up fast. My cockpit was filled five times. . . .

There was also that day a first leader on the subject, entitled 'Round the Horn'.[2]

A knighthood had been conferred on Chichester while he was in Sydney, and on July 7, at his triumphant homecoming, Elizabeth II gave him the accolade in person at Greenwich, using the sword with which Elizabeth I had knighted Francis Drake after his voyage of circumnavigation in the *Golden Hind*. It was a popular gesture, and Chichester perhaps deserved it for sailing round the world alone at the age of sixty-six after recovering from lung cancer, and towards the end of a career which had begun with pioneer flying. Yet there was,

1 James Bishop, features editor, to Stewart Harris, February 1 1967. Harris had 'some pretty fair fights' with Chichester and his wife, Sheila, who was with him during the interlude in Australia. But 'what I liked about them both was that however abrupt and bad-tempered the end of one encounter might be, it never made the slightest difference to the beginning of the next'. (Harris to Bishop, February 8 1967.)
2 *The Times*, March 22 1967.

in fact, little analogy between him and the earlier Sir Francis; as little as between the two queens Elizabeth and their respective ages. The ceremony at Greenwich was a last flicker of the 'new Elizabethan' cult that had become so obtrusive in the 1950s.

The true equivalents of Elizabethan seafarers were not sailors – even lone sailors – travelling with radio equipment and abundant tinned stores, but rather the astronauts who were beginning the exploration of Space. The Chichester story appealed to the imagination, certainly, but to a backward-looking imagination. It also appealed to all who, in recent years, had taken to sailing as a recreation, and as a means of escape from the modern world. As such it was good for British self-esteem – and good copy for *The Times*.

III

Making leaders count • Harold Wilson's hour • Rees-Mogg's antipathy to Wilson • Musings of a European • The Six-Day War • Editor and proprietor • Defending Mick Jagger

CONCERNED though Rees-Mogg was to improve *The Times's* news coverage and to rationalise the arrangement of its contents, unquestionably it was the paper's opinion-forming role that interested him most. For a politician *manqué* this was natural enough, but the priority that he gave to leader-writing and the systematic evolution of policy was no mere self-indulgence, since it also reflected his understanding of the paper's historic character and peculiar strength. In this he differed markedly from his predecessor. Whereas Haley had devoted himself to supervising every aspect of the paper from day to day – to the extent of becoming, as some were inclined to say, a glorified sub – Rees-Mogg concentrated upon policy and for the rest delegated drastically. Haley's desk was always littered with galleys, but they were not very often seen on Rees-Mogg's, and Haley was regularly hard at work at Printing House Square long past the hour when Rees-Mogg equally regularly left for home.

Haley was by no means indifferent to politics. He had certain broad political attitudes, mainly derived from nineteenth century Liberalism, and he wrote a fair number of political leaders, some of which deserve to be remembered. Yet somehow they are not remembered – apart from one, at the time of the Profumo scandal, in which he took a heavily moralistic line.[1] On far more important policy issues he failed to carry much weight, and in any case it was not a rule with him to give policy-making his sustained and detailed attention. During the Suez crisis, for instance, he was absent in the United States for seven

1 In June 1963 The Conservative war secretary, John Profumo, had to resign after misleading the House of Commons about an extramarital relationship. HTT, Vol.V, p.359.

'testing weeks'.[1] Though there were frequent meetings of leader-writers while he was editor, they were seldom attended by him. Rees-Mogg, on the other hand, instituted meetings at 11 a.m. on Tuesday mornings at which he would preside over the discussion of specific policy issues, sitting (as soon became habitual) in a rocking chair. At the first of these meetings, on February 17 1967, swing-wing aircraft, decimal currency and cigarette advertising were among the topics discussed. The new editor at once impressed his colleagues with his ability to see all round a subject, and his determination to influence the course of events.

On average Rees-Mogg's output of leaders was not much larger than Haley's, and it was only under the stimulus of a general election that he wrote significantly more.[2] But what he wrote tended to have more impact. Moreover he kept a closer eye on the work of his colleagues, often arguing with them privately while supporting publicly whatever they had written. Under him the paper's editorial line thus became more forceful and authoritative.

The leader-writing team was large, an inner core of frequent contributors being supplemented by numerous specialists who contributed occasionally. There were also continual changes: new people joining while others dropped out. But the principal members remained throughout Rees-Mogg's editorship or, at the very least, for a number of years; and nearly all of them were inherited from the previous regime. McDonald wrote quite often, chiefly on Russia and Eastern Europe. Hodgkin's parish was the Middle East, though he could turn his hand to almost any subject. Charles Douglas-Home, defence correspondent since 1965, wrote on the Middle East and other matters as well as on defence. Richard Harris, the paper's China hand, wrote on the Far East; also on the Indian subcontinent. Roy Lewis remained the chief leader-writer on colonial affairs, though with growing help from a new man, Michael Wolfers, on the ground in Africa. Another young man, Patrick Brogan, wrote many leaders on France.

For home policy Rees-Mogg's chief lieutenant was Owen Hickey, who had been with the paper since 1954. A classical scholar and a Roman Catholic, with a farm in Co. Tipperary, he wrote most of *The Times*'s leaders on Ireland as another Ulster crisis began to escalate. He in turn had a versatile and prolific lieutenant in Geoffrey Smith,

---

1 HTT, Vol.V, p.265.

2 In 1966 Haley wrote forty-two leaders. Rees-Mogg's annual scores during his first four years were: 1967, forty-five; 1968, forty-eight; 1969, thirty; 1970, sixty-four. In the last-mentioned year eighteen of the leaders were written during the election month of June.

an Edinburgh University graduate still in his thirties, who had joined the paper in 1961 and started writing leaders in 1965. Another home affairs specialist who wrote a considerable number of leaders until his election to Parliament in 1970 was Norman Fowler, who had come to *The Times* from Cambridge in the same year as Smith.

On economics and finance Peter Jay contributed quite often to the main leader column, as well as to that of *TBN*. Among others who did the same were the *TBN* editor, Tony Vice, Maurice Corina (recruited from the *Financial Times*), Joe Roeber (from the *Economist*) and Hugh Stephenson (from the Diplomatic Service).

The transfer of power at *The Times* occurred at a moment when events at home and abroad were more than usually challenging to editorialists. In Britain Harold Wilson's decisive victory in the general election of 1966 had given Labour – for what turned out to be a brief period – the air of being the natural party of government. In 1964 a long spell of Tory rule was brought to an end when Wilson's Labour Party narrowly defeated the Conservative Party under Sir Alec Douglas-Home (uncle of *The Times*'s defence correspondent), who a year previously had succeeded Harold Macmillan as party leader and prime minister.

Under another leader the Tories might well have won their fourth election in a row, but the circumstances in which Douglas-Home was chosen caused a split in the party's higher ranks, which must have damaged it in the eyes of the public. In particular, the rather formidable Iain Macleod refused to serve under Douglas-Home and later published an article in the *Spectator* suggesting that Home's selection as leader had been engineered by a cabal of Old Etonians.[1] This highly misleading account was just what the Labour party needed and, in the atmosphere of the time, may have been enough to sway the relatively small number of votes that determined the result of the election.

Had Labour lost again in 1964 it is likely that a realignment would have occurred on the left, involving the Liberal party under its attractive leader, Jo Grimond. In all probability Labour's socialist doctrines would have been re-examined and gradually modified, while Wilson, who in any case had been a Liberal in his youth, might well have looked for ways of cooperating with Grimond, in the process shedding

---

1 January 17 1964. The piece was technically a review of Randolph Churchill's account of the Tory leadership crisis. Macleod was editor of the *Spectator* at the time.

or marginalising the left-wing ideologues in his own party. As it was, such fundamental change was postponed to a later date.

Meanwhile the Labour leader applied to his divided party the superficially unifying balm of office and patronage. No man could have been better suited to this role. An essentially middle-of-the-road, not to say conservative, politician, Wilson had risen in the party by sheer cleverness and hard work, combined with a judicious pretence of being on the left. When Hugh Gaitskell unexpectedly died in 1963, Wilson was elected leader in his place, despite serious misgivings on the part of many of his colleagues. The Gaitskellite candidate, George Brown, inspired far more affection, but his tendency to get drunk, aggravating or reflecting an erratic temperament, made him seem too risky a choice.

Having won the party leadership by, in some measure, pandering to the left, Wilson achieved national leadership by managing – just – to convince the electorate that he was a modern-minded pragmatist. Instead of socialism, with its implied threat of confiscation and increasingly egalitarian taxes, he offered the British people the vaguer, but less menacing, nostrum of technological revolution, which to many – including, as has been said, Denis Hamilton – was not without appeal. For party reasons he had also to campaign with a pledge to get rid of Britain's independent nuclear deterrent (which he called Britain's 'so-called independent so-called deterrent'), and this no doubt came near to costing him the election. But once he was in power the pledge was unceremoniously dropped.

For eighteen months he had to govern with a Parliamentary majority of fewer than five.[1] But in March 1966 he went to the country again and was returned with an overall majority of ninety-six. There had been time for his moderation, but not for his weaknesses, to become apparent.

The Conservatives meanwhile had acquired a new leader, Edward Heath. In 1965 Douglas-Home had changed the method whereby Tory leaders were chosen, from the shadowy backstage processes which had done duty for so long, and which had aroused so much controversy in his own case, to direct election by Conservative MPs. Since his own suitability for the leadership had been called in question – not least by Rees-Mogg in a wounding article in the *Sunday Times*[2] – he decided not to stand under the new procedure. If he had stood he would almost

1 At first the majority was four, but it dropped to two after Labour lost a by-election in January 1965.
2 July 1965.

certainly have been elected and would thus have given his position as leader the democratic legitimacy, as it were, which it had so far been thought to lack. But he had lost the will to lead, and in the ensuing contest Conservative MPs chose Heath in preference to the less dynamic Reginald Maudling.

Their choice also gave them a leader strikingly, and intentionally, different from Douglas-Home: a grammar-school boy from a modest home who had gone to Oxford before the war on a scholarship, and who, as a Conservative student there, had signalled his independence of mind and political courage by opposing the Munich agreement (at a time when Douglas-Home was Neville Chamberlain's PPS). In the House of Commons he had shown the same qualities, above all by early championing the cause of European unity with full British participation.

Heath's ideas were, however, more remarkable than his manner of expressing them; there was no magic in his speeches, and his public personality was altogether rather wooden. All the same it was hoped that his tough debating style and excellent head for facts and figures would make him a match for Wilson. In the short term they did not. Wilson at first had no difficulty in maintaining his ascendancy in Parliament, and in the 1966 election he had the advantage of fighting as an incumbent prime minister against a new leader of the opposition who had never held the premiership.

On becoming editor of *The Times* Rees-Mogg severed all formal links with the Conservative party. Yet he was still of course the same man, with the same fundamental sympathies and antipathies. Despite his best efforts to be impartial, it was only natural that he should retain some prejudice in favour of his old party and against Labour. And these prejudices were strongly reinforced by personal feelings.

Heath he had every reason to admire, as a Conservative who knew the time of day and as a dedicated European. Moreover the Conservative leader was another Balliol man, who had also been president of the Oxford Union. Rees-Mogg could feel an almost proprietary interest in his leadership, having as a commentator on the *Sunday Times* helped to bring it about, in however small a way. Regard at the time was mutual; Heath told Rees-Mogg that his appointment as editor was regrettable only because it removed him for ever from 'the sphere of active politics', to which many would have welcomed his return.[1]

1 Edward Heath to W.R.-M., January 23 1967.

Rees-Mogg's feelings for Wilson were even less warm than for Labour as a party. He honoured the memory of Gaitskell, partly no doubt because it *was* a memory – to a person with any degree of political commitment the best leader of an opposing party is always likely to be a dead one – but also because he genuinely respected Gaitskell's stand against neutralism, and his attempt to rid his party of the Clause Four incubus. Rees-Mogg's favourite Labour politicians tended to be Gaitskellites such as Roy Jenkins, whose reasons for being resentful and suspicious of Wilson he could well understand.

In addition, he had reasons of his own. When, in the autumn of 1966, he visited Chequers with Thomson and Hamilton, the prime minister made the worst possible impression on him, and deepened his mistrust. As recorded in the last volume of this History, Wilson then told Thomson that the first thing he should do, if the Monopolies Commission were to approve his acquisition of *The Times*, 'ought to be to get rid of David Wood', the paper's political correspondent.[1] Wilson's vendetta against Wood was an early symptom of the virtual paranoia about the press from which he increasingly suffered. He felt that Wood, instead of being used by him (his normal way with the Lobby), was being used against him, and the biggest provocation may have been Wood's success in identifying ministerial sources without actually putting names to them.[2]

Thomson left Chequers after dinner, but Rees-Mogg and Hamilton stayed the night. Rees-Mogg was not yet editor, though Wilson probably realised that he would be given the job. At any rate Rees-Mogg did not feel called upon to comment on the prime minister's request, one way or the other. Yet he was shocked by its impropriety, all the more so as the change of ownership was still in the balance, with the government the ultimate arbiter. His already low opinion of Wilson was decisively confirmed.[3]

In his very first *Times* leader, written within hours of arriving at Printing House Square, he argued 'The Case for George Brown', using as his peg a recently published *New York Times* article on Brown by Anthony Lewis, which the *Observer* was about to reproduce. Brown, who had been foreign secretary since the previous August, had also been the Gaitskellite candidate against Wilson for the Labour leadership. To defend him was in some degree to reflect upon Wilson.

---

1 HTT, Vol.V, p.365.
2 David Wood talking to author.
3 W.R.-M. talking. He spent the night in a four-poster bed formerly occupied by Harold Macmillan, and the final unpleasantness of the visit was that his hot-water bottle leaked.

According to the leader, Brown's manners were 'indeed rough' by the standards of polite society, but they were 'the manners of an original'. People should not leap from the correct judgement that he was 'an odd character' to the incorrect one that he was disqualified thereby from 'holding high office successfully'. High politics was 'not a suitable occupation for ordinary men':

> The greatest statesmen of Britain have not been ordinary men. To move the affairs of nations requires either remarkable skill or remarkable force of personality. The greatest statesmen of Britain have not been ordinary men, nor have they been polite men . . . SIR WINSTON CHURCHILL and WILLIAM PITT were both sociable drinkers; LLOYD GEORGE and PALMERSTON could not be trusted with women; CHATHAM, perhaps the greatest of them all, was actually mad while Prime Minister.

As for Brown, 'one would not invite him to cucumber sandwiches with one's maiden aunt – but he is a remarkable man with some of the qualities and all the courage of a great statesman'.[1]

In retrospect the argument of this leader seems rather absurd, since whatever Brown's merits he was really not comparable as a statesman with the historic figures mentioned. Yet in Rees-Mogg's eyes he had the advantage of not being Wilson, and of being courageous where Wilson was devious, in particular on the Common Market issue. The leader was anyway notable for its colourful and arresting style, which was to command attention for Rees-Mogg's opinions, right or wrong, over the next fourteen years.

He showed a few weeks later that he could be critical of Heath, in a leader entitled 'The Organization of an Opposition'. Prompted by a resignation from the Shadow Cabinet which Heath had accepted in a 'rather abrupt' manner, he suggested that Heath had yet to learn 'the proper value of political humbug'. But the editor's intention was clearly to be helpful and constructive:

> MR. HEATH is at present the victim of a good deal of unreasonable and some merely disappointed criticism . . . There is no evidence that any other leader would have done better or indeed as well . . . Yet the fact that he is the Conservatives' natural as

1 January 14 1967. Two days later a letter was published from Miss Meriel E. D. Biggs of Weybridge, in which she said: 'As a maiden aunt of some years' standing . . . I should be brazenly delighted to have Mr. George Brown's company if he would accept my cucumber sandwiches'.

> well as actual leader for the coming years makes it all the more important that [he] should himself consider the drawbacks of the present system, which are to some extent the drawbacks of his own methods of work.

It was wrong that the Conservative Research Department and the Conservative Political Centre were under direct Central Office control, and that even decisions to publish pamphlets had to be taken 'at the highest level'. It was equally wrong that Heath's front-bench colleagues were not given enough independence. Quintin Hogg, for instance, should be freer to speak to the right of the party, and Edward Boyle to the left. The result of existing arrangements was that 'big men [were] being treated as though they were little men'.[1]

At the beginning of the year Grimond had retired as Liberal leader, any immediate hope of realignment on the left having been dashed by the 1966 election result. While remaining in the House of Commons he was succeeded as leader by Jeremy Thorpe, another former president of the Oxford Union. Rees-Mogg wished Thorpe well, and up to a point was quite well disposed to the Liberal party, to whose residual Whiggishness his own Whiggish side could respond. Another merit of the Liberals, in his view, was that they had an excellent record on Europe.

It might be thought, incidentally, that Rees-Mogg's early changes to the paper's appearance and style would have included dropping the traditional practice of setting personal names in capital letters, as in the leaders already quoted in this chapter. But he showed a rather surprising reluctance to make the change, and resisted it for about eighteen months. The last use of capital letters for personal names in a *Times* leader was on Saturday 27 July 1968. The following week the change was made to lower case, though quietly, without announcement.

Despite its numerically strong majority in Parliament, the Wilson government's position in 1967 was always vulnerable. Economically, its chief source of trouble was trying to maintain an unrealistic exchange rate for the pound. Soon after the 1966 election it had to impose a credit and pay freeze, which had the effect of holding back industrial expansion, hitting the balance of payments, and

1 February 8 1967. The shadow cabinet member who had resigned was Ernest Marples.

undermining foreign confidence in sterling. It also caused a swift drop in the government's popularity at home, with the result that it began to lose seats at by-elections. On that account alone Labour MPs would have become restive; but in fact it was by no means the only cause of disaffection. Many of them deplored Wilson's failure to dissociate Britain from America's war in Vietnam, and when in early 1967 he showed that he was about to perform a volte-face on the Common Market – visiting, with Brown, all the capitals of the Six between January and March – many deplored that as well (though the two groups were not, of course, identical).

Wilson's problem was that he was simultaneously disappointing left-wingers and Labour traditionalists whose support had been useful to him in his rise to the top, and the wider public which had taken seriously his self-projected image as a moderniser and economic wizard. His alienation from a large number of Labour MPs became apparent at the end of February when sixty-two of them abstained in a defence vote. This provoked him into saying, at the ensuing party meeting, that every dog was allowed one bite but if biting became a habit the dog's licence might not be renewed. At the same time he was involved in a silly row over D-notices (the voluntary system of press censorship in matters of national security) whose details are too trivial to be gone over here but which, in the event, permanently damaged his relations with the press. In a leader commenting on both incidents, Rees-Mogg said of the D-notice affair that it reflected 'the PRIME MINISTER's fascination with security and party conspiracy problems', and of the other, which was 'much more serious', that Wilson should 'not underrate the power of Parliament'. Dog metaphors were 'usually a mistake in democratic politics'.[1]

In general the editor was unable, at this stage, to mount a full-blooded assault on the prime minister, because on issues of policy the scope for criticism was limited by his own views (on the economy and Vietnam) or by Wilson's change of tack (on the Common Market). While believing that devaluation was likely to occur, sooner or later, under a Labour government, Rees-Mogg did not necessarily wish it to occur and in any case would have felt debarred from advocating it, on patriotic grounds. His attitude to the Vietnam war was essentially the same as the government's, and of course he could only be pleased at the signs of Wilson's conversion to a pro-EEC policy, whatever his doubts about the motives.

In early April he wrote a characteristic leader of the think-piece

1 'The mistakes of a fortnight', March 4 1967.

variety, in which he mused on the current psychological state of France, Germany and Britain. After two paragraphs on Jung's theory of the loss of energy in individuals, he applied it at the collective level and related it to the countries in question:

> Great nations, that is those with a long history and a strong sense of national identity, need to operate at full stretch, just as able men or fast horses need to do. When they are not working at full stretch, when their energy is diverted from external objects, then they suffer from all sorts of depressions, delusions, and social difficulties.

In the case of France, de Gaulle had succeeded in providing 'an outlet for national pride and for the psychic energy of his country'. This was 'a very great achievement and the source of his power'. Germany had 'followed a different course' and was suffering from a repression of energy, a fear of energy, and 'a strong association between national energy and national guilt'. Britain had shown 'some persistent elements of fantasy, of the belief that past honours can be brought back not through the present but by turning away from the present'. Yet the work open to all three was that of 'remaking' the European community of nations.[1]

It was significant that he wrote of it as something to be remade rather than as a completely new departure. His view of Europe's future was thus closer to de Gaulle's than to that of the federal enthusiasts whose ideals were embodied in the Treaty of Rome. At the beginning of May the paper carried a single leader by him, occupying two columns to the full depth of the page, in which he gave detailed consideration to de Gaulle's 'insights' on Europe. These had to be looked at, 'not because he is wholly right, but because he is the one living European statesman of genius'.

The first, that Europe must be independent of both the United States and the Soviet Union, had been 'interpreted in French policy in a way that [had] sometimes been too rigorous and sometimes premature'. Yet the basic principle of independence was just, and Europe was 'only Europe in the hands of Europeans'. The second, that France was the 'natural heartland of Western Europe', was true, though should not be taken to mean 'perpetual French political dominance' or to justify 'the exaggeration of France's power on her own'. The third, that 'Europe must be united as a consequence of the history of

1 'The energy of nations', April 8 1967.

the European nations and not against the grain of history', was in some ways inadequate, yet 'historically intelligible'. Europe ought, indeed, 'to welcome and preserve identities of the European nations'. He ended with a statement of the obvious, that the immediate future of Europe was again in de Gaulle's hands, and that it was a humiliating reflection on Britain that it should be so.[1]

In another think-piece, at the end of May, he considered the reasons for Britain's relative lack of authority in the Sixties. Neither major party was united. Labour divisions were obvious, and on the Conservative side Maudling and Boyle were 'interventionists', while Enoch Powell and Keith Joseph were 'virtually laisser-faire economists'. Britain was therefore in a situation where 'the main economic problems facing the country [had] in succession defeated the ability of both parties, and neither party [had] developed a consistent new body of doctrine for dealing with them'. At present the country was

> very far from a coalition situation, and indeed a new coalition to impose old ideas would be the worst solution of all. Yet in these circumstances a realignment of men and ideas cannot be ruled out, though if it happens it will be events which will produce it.

Policies of national regeneration would have to include 'much better incentives to management, higher investment, freedom from restrictive practices, import policies and more effective encouragement to technological advance'.[2]

Suddenly, at the beginning of June, the attention of politicians and journalists was diverted to the Middle East, as war erupted there between Israel and its neighbours Egypt, Jordan and Syria. The ulterior causes of conflict are all too well known, but the principal immediate cause was the removal, at President Nasser's request, of the United Nations' presence on the Egyptian-Israeli border. Towards the end of May Egyptian forces consequently occupied Sharm El Sheikh, the peninsula dominating the entrance to the Israeli Red Sea port of Eilat, whose use was thus altogether denied to Israeli shipping by closure of the Gulf of Aqaba.

Tension had meanwhile been growing between Israel and Syria, with which Egypt was once again cooperating despite the break-up,

---

1 'Post-Imperial but pre-European', May 1 1967.
2 'The maze of the 1960s', May 20 1967.

three years previously, of their brief political union. Jordan almost inevitably became involved in the Arab coalition, while Iraq and Saudi Arabia made limited gestures of solidarity from a safe distance. There were reasons for fearing an early attempt to destroy the Jewish state by concerted action, though it is unlikely, in fact, that Nasser intended to start a war.

In any case, the Israelis did not wait to be attacked but started the war themselves on June 5 with a pre-emptive strike which virtually destroyed the Egyptian air force. Over the next couple of days they carried out further devastating strikes against air bases in Syria and Jordan. On June 7 Israeli troops captured Gaza and realised the most cherished goal of Zionism by occupying the whole of Jerusalem. Next day President Nasser and King Hussein of Jordan asked for a cease-fire, and the day after that the Syrians had to follow suit when the Israelis broke through their defences on the Golan heights and advanced towards Damascus. The so-called Six-Day War ended with the Arab armies comprehensively beaten, and with Sinai and the formerly Jordanian West Bank in Israeli hands.

The Times's coverage of the war was as thorough as Israel's military victory. Charles Douglas-Home, the defence correspondent, flew out to report from Israel, while Norman Fowler (who spoke French) was sent to Syria, Peter Hopkirk reported from Cairo and Nicholas Herbert, the Middle East correspondent, from Beirut. On the leader page, Rees-Mogg's first reaction was pro-Israeli. Whereas the Arabs apparently wanted to destroy Israel as a nation – which could not be allowed by the United States or Britain – the Israelis' objective was limited, 'to destroy for the time being the aggressive capacity of at least one of her enemies' (Nasser). But in a turnover article on the same page Hugh Thomas made the point that the Israelis were this time on their own, without the benefit of collusive military action by the British and French.[1]

When it was clear that the Israelis had nonetheless won, Douglas-Home wrote sagaciously from Tel Aviv:

> . . . one important product of Israel's air strikes . . . is that the next time it may be the Arabs who carry out a pre-emptive strike . . . Israel's dominance is real, but it will only last politically as long as it will take Egypt to buy or borrow a new air force . . . Egypt has already lost no time in turning a military defeat into a

1 'This time Israel bears the brunt in isolation', June 6 1967. Rees-Mogg's leader the same day was entitled 'The aims of war'.

> propaganda victory over the West . . . In spite of the plaudits, the victory flags going up, the spontaneous clapping at press conferences, one can see no finality in Israel's victory here.[1]

On June 10 Rees-Mogg's leader, 'The Light that Failed', praised Nasser's 'good idea of a modern Arab nation working in unity' and his 'good administration'. Moreover, while deploring his vendetta against Israel, which had been 'an utter failure', it admitted that 'to be moderate against Israel would have denied him the essential element of enthusiasm in the Arab world'. On the same day, and the same page, there was a turnover by the anti-Zionist Hodgkin stating the case for internationalising Jerusalem:

> 'For centuries', said Renan, 'the world will dispute the possession of Jerusalem. An invisible attraction will draw thither people of various races'. That is so, and it would be better for all races, including the Israelis, if they all had a share in the city's government.

In the correspondence column the lead letter was from Sir John Glubb, reminding readers of Jordan's record as a loyal ally of Britain.

Rees-Mogg was very pleased with *The Times*'s performance in the war, above all with that of Douglas-Home to whom he wrote:

> Apart from thanking you in person, I wanted to do a special letter, if only for the archives of the paper, to thank you for your work in Israel. I thought it was of quite exceptional quality and gave us much the best coverage of the war from the Israel side. It has been very widely commented on and much admired.[2]

Among those impressed by *The Times*'s coverage, and not least by Rees-Mogg's final editorial, was an American politician soon to stage what would be described as the most remarkable comeback since Lazarus. In a letter to Thomson, Richard M. Nixon wrote:

> During a brief visit to London at the height of the Mid-East crisis, I had the rare privilege of reading the coverage as well as the lead editorial on the crisis which appeared in the TIMES.
>
> I just wanted you to know that from the standpoint of fair

1 Douglas-Home's report, filed from Tel Aviv on June 8, appeared as a turnover the following day under the heading 'Problems of Israel's quick victory'.
2 June 14 1967.

> and objective reporting as well as perceptive editorial comment, I don't think I have ever seen a better all-round job. I thought for example your editorial, 'The Light that Failed', was really a superb sample of eloquent editorial comment on a very difficult subject.[1]

Thomson sent this letter to Rees-Mogg, with a covering note:

> Dear Bill,
>
> Attached, for your information. I have acknowledged it to Mr. Nixon.
>
> Yours sincerely
> Thomson of Fleet.[2]

Something should be said here of Rees-Mogg's relations with the proprietor. Evidently Thomson's understanding of the younger man was still limited, or he would not have addressed him as 'Dear Bill'. Rees-Mogg was the most unBillish person imaginable, and no one was encouraged to abbreviate his Christian name in any version.[3] Thomson had also shown serious misjudgement in suggesting that he would be 'run' by Hamilton.

All the same the two were more than slightly acquainted before becoming, respectively, proprietor and editor of *The Times*. Rees-Mogg had been a Thomson employee since 1960, and had been made to feel that the boss had rather a soft spot for him. When he married (in 1962) he and his wife were lent Thomson's villa at Cap d'Ail for part of their honeymoon.[4] It was Rees-Mogg's impression that Thomson, having missed out on higher education, was prone to admire those who, like himself, could be regarded as intellectuals. At the same time he seemed to have a fatherly and protective attitude towards one who, though financially literate, needed to be sustained by his mastery of business.[5]

---

1 Written from New York, June 27 1967.
2 July 6 1967.
3 Very few people ever did so, though Reginald Maudling once wrote to him as 'Dear Willie' and Duncan Sandys as 'Dear Bill'. In neither case was the mistake repeated.
4 The French Riviera was not at all Thomson's scene, but since Beaverbrook had a villa at Cap d'Ail the next Canadian-born press lord may have felt obliged to have one there too. The decor included rather too much tartan, but the food was excellent.
5 W.R.-M. talking to author.

A few weeks after the Six-Day War Thomson stayed with the Rees-Moggs at Ston Easton.[1] This must have reflected a closer relationship, and made it closer still. The following year Rees-Mogg sent Thomson tentative evidence concerning a local ancestor on his mother's side:

> When you were down in Somerset we took you on the old road to Bath which passes next to the village of Camerton . . . In March 1825 John Skinner, the rector of Camerton, wrote a longish note in his diary about the Coombes family. I should be very surprised if this family were not related to your mother as they came from the very area in which her father must have worked.
>
> The most interesting character is the Reverend William Coombes, 1744–1822, who became a Catholic priest and played a large part in founding Downside Abbey where he is buried. I was discussing this with our local priest who said that the Abbey had just recently been given Dr. Coombes' books and they thought, as a family memento, that you might like to have one. I enclose the book together with a copy of the relevant pages of John Skinner's diary.

Thomson wrote a warm letter of thanks, beginning 'Dear William'.[2] He had learnt the form.

Such personal amenities would have counted for little if Thomson had doubted Rees-Mogg's fitness to be editor of *The Times*. But there is no evidence that he had any doubts on this score, even though Rees-Mogg was unable to satisfy one of the requirements normally mandatory for a Thomson editor, that of producing a paper that made money. Thomson started, as we have seen, with a quite different attitude towards *The Times*, and to the extent that his old instincts reasserted themselves after just a few years of heavy loss-making, Hamilton rather than Rees-Mogg was the casualty. Though the editor had the effective power, the editor-in-chief was held responsible for what went wrong.

From Rees-Mogg's point of view Thomson was the ideal proprietor, in no way threatening his editorial freedom but, on the

---

1 The weekend of July 21 1967.

2 W.R.-M. to R.H.T., June 11 1968; R.H.T. to W.R.-M., June 26 1968. Thomson's mother's surname was Coombs, but the 'e' could easily have disappeared on the way to Canada, or after arrival there. Its absence does not necessarily disprove the suggested connection with the Revd William Coombes. Thomson had already shown intense interest in his Scottish ancestral roots.

contrary, defending it against threats from outside. On one occasion a leading industrialist complained of a photograph in *TBN* in which he appeared between two monkeys, mentioning ominously that he was a friend of the proprietor. When Thomson was shown the complaint his immediate reply was 'Never pay any attention to anyone who says he's a friend of mine'.[1] With such an assurance of moral support Rees-Mogg could safely ignore pressure from business interests. But Thomson, on his side, knew that Rees-Mogg would never outrage any large section of *The Times*'s readers or advertisers. He would never attack religion or seriously criticise royal personages – two potential exercises of editorial freedom to which the proprietor's tolerance would not have extended. No political, economic or social issue would be handled in such a way as to give massive offence to *The Times*'s readership. Under Rees-Mogg the paper would be intelligent, stimulating and never wholly predictable, but would keep within certain bounds. The good relations between editor and proprietor rested, therefore, on a sense of security that was mutual.

The Sixties witnessed a profound change in the tastes and behaviour of the young. Even before the age of majority was lowered to eighteen (in 1969) parental control over teenagers of both sexes was breaking down. The main reason was money. At a time of very high employment most school-leavers were entering jobs and receiving rates of pay unimaginable to an earlier generation. Affluence had never been more widespread, and parents enjoying a measure of it for the first time tended to be reluctant to lecture their children on the need for frugality and self-denial. Yet in the absence of admonition there was little else they could do, because young people in work were no longer dependent upon their elders for the means to finance their leisure pursuits.

Among these, the most conspicuous was sex. Easy contraception, permissive legislation and a further decline in the influence of Christian values together produced a climate in which early sexual experience became normal; indeed – granted the tyranny of fashion – almost obligatory. Many parents, moreover, were themselves affected by the climate and to that extent deprived of such moral authority as they might have had – since the offspring of adulterers or divorcees were unlikely to be inspired by them to observe a strict code of sexual conduct. The phenomenon of teenage sex was not, of course, entirely

1 W.R.-M. talking to author. Though he referred the matter to Thomson, Rees-Mogg was satisfied in retrospect that he would have rejected the complaint anyway.

new (Romeo and Juliet alone being evidence to the contrary), but it was, surely, unprecedented in scale, and also closely associated with another modern movement, that of female emancipation.

Anger and protest were, at any rate superficially, characteristic of youth during the period. But it was often less obvious what they had to be angry about, or how much serious thought and effort they were prepared to devote to the ostensible subjects of protest. Social and racial, as well as sexual, equality were popular causes, as was unilateral nuclear disarmament (to a generation born since the end of the Second World War, and largely ignorant of history). But, apart from participating in the occasional march or signing the odd petition, most of the youthful enthusiasts contributed little to any public cause, being too busy savouring the unfamiliar freedom of their private lives. Much of the protest was, indeed, related to their own origins rather than to anything external to themselves. Young people from the new ethnic minorities had grievances that were unquestionably genuine. But denunciations of 'the system' or 'the establishment' by white working-class or middle-class youth were altogether less convincing. Often the former were merely working off their resentment of unprivileged home backgrounds (looking back in anger), while also insulting the privileged world that they were in the process of joining. At the same time children of the bourgeoisie were rejecting its values as a way of needling their parents, and to demonstrate their 'classlessness'.

Another distinctive feature of youth at the time was a growing keenness to experiment with narcotic drugs, which naturally led to a mounting problem of addiction. The smoking of cannabis derived, in part, from the Caribbean community, in which it was traditional. But a wider cause of the narcotics' phenomenon was precisely that it was distinctive as between young and old, so providing another way for the young to assert their independence. And again parents were at a disadvantage, if they were smokers and/or drinkers, since the question could plausibly be asked: if nicotine and alcohol are acceptable, why not cannabis? The argument that pot was in some respects more dangerous, above all because it could introduce smokers to more powerful and deadly members of the narcotics' family, may have been valid but was not self-evidently so.

The spirit of the young found its artistic expression in pop music, by which in turn it was greatly stimulated. Most of the themes of the contemporary youth culture were present in the music and lyrics of leading pop singers and groups. Youth culture and pop culture were, indeed, essentially one. The craze began in America, but caught on in Britain; and early in the Sixties the native product achieved world-wide dominance with the triumph of the Beatles, whose regional, proletarian, erotic and vaguely idealistic image was perfectly suited to their age and generation.

To many older people the pop scene was utterly abhorrent and a symptom of cultural disintegration. Others, however, recalled that the waltz had once aroused similar fears, and argued that the music of pop had considerable interest, even though the words might be crude and banal compared with the sophisticated lyrics of, say, Cole Porter. In any case, all who wanted to keep in touch with the young had to come to terms with pop, and Harold Wilson was seen to be making a symbolic gesture (as well as one convenient to himself, in view of his political connection with Liverpool) when he recommended the Beatles for MBEs.

Under Haley *The Times* had observed social and moral developments in the Sixties with distaste. When, at the beginning of the decade, a jury in the High Court decided that *Lady Chatterley's Lover* was not obscene, he wrote a leader strongly regretting the decision. Three years later, at the time of the Profumo scandal, his most famous leader proclaimed that it *was* a moral issue. Though the Beatles' music was discussed by the paper's music critic, and reference made to the 'chains of pandiatonic clusters' discernible in it, Beatlemania and all that it represented was beneath Haley's notice.[1]

His successor's inner feelings about pop culture were much the same as his; but there the resemblance ended. In Rees-Mogg's view *The Times* could not afford to appear too stuffy, or to be manifestly out of sympathy with the young, if it were to achieve the great expansion of readership that it was thought to need. He may also have judged that the dangers inherent in pop culture could best be counteracted by winning the confidence of the young, and by showing careful discrimination in his treatment of their idols and fantasies. In keeping with this approach he was quick to condemn sensationalism in the reporting of drugs cases, remarking that 'for some news editors the word "drugs" now activates the same conditioned reflex as "mods and rockers" or "security scandals" have at other times'.[2]

Before long a case arose which enabled him to demonstrate his attitude with dramatic effect. On the last day of June, at West Sussex quarter sessions at Chichester, two members of the Rolling Stones pop group were sentenced for drug offences: Keith Richard to one year's imprisonment and a £500 fine for smoking cannabis, and the

---

1 HTT, Vol.V, pp.359–61 and p.226.
2 'A dangerous press campaign', February 28 1967.

group's leader, Mick Jagger, to three months' imprisonment and a fine of £100 for being in possession of four amphetamine tablets. At the same time a man with whom they had been staying (at West Wittering) received a heavier sentence for possessing heroin.

The Rolling Stones were then nearing the peak of their fame. Whereas the Beatles had become almost respectable after visiting Buckingham Palace to collect their medals (though John Lennon would later return his), the Stones had a violent and anarchic style which sent their fans into ecstasies but filled many sober citizens with disgust, even dread. The group embodied all the characteristics for which pop was loved or hated, seeming as it did either a challenge to traditional taboos or a threat to civilisation, according to taste. And what was true of the group was more especially so of Jagger himself. With his thick-lipped mouthings and corybantic contortions he powerfully expressed the group's message, such as it was; and since he was known to have a middle-class background, and to have been a promising student at the London School of Economics, his credentials as a rebel seemed all the more valid.

The day following the sentences, July 1, *The Times*'s first leader was devoted to the subject. Written by the editor and entitled 'Who Breaks a Butterfly on a Wheel?' it concentrated on the case of Jagger. Though he and his colleague were appealing, and the case was therefore still *sub judice*, the circumstances were held to be 'sufficiently unusual to warrant . . . discussion in the public interest'. Jagger had been convicted 'purely on the ground that he possessed four Italian pep pills, quite legally bought but not legally imported without a prescription'. If the Archbishop of Canterbury (Michael Ramsey), after his recent visit to the Pope (Paul VI), 'had bought proprietary airsickness pills on Rome airport, and imported the unused tablets into Britain on his return, he would have risked committing exactly the same offence'. This was 'about as mild a drug case as [could] ever have been brought before the Courts', and the normal penalty for it would have been probation.

Yet there were many who took 'a primitive view' of the matter and felt that Jagger had 'got what was coming to him'. Such people resented 'the anarchic quality of the Rolling Stones' performances', disliked their influence on teenagers, and regarded them as a symptom of decadence. As a sociological concern this might be reasonable, and at an emotional level it was 'very understandable', but it had nothing at all to do with the legal case. 'There must remain a suspicion that Mr. JAGGER received a more severe sentence than would have been thought proper for any purely anonymous young man'.

This leader provoked a great deal of comment, not least in the form of letters to the editor. On July 3 Anthony Kenny from Chancery Lane disputed its main conclusion. Why should the court disregard the fact that Jagger was 'an idol and an influence on young people'? In return for wealth, fame and influence, did he not have some special responsibilities relevant to his sentence? On July 4 letters on the subject occupied the entire correspondence column, with pride of place given to one from John Osborne – still, in the public mind, a radical figure – who commended the leader as 'a reassuring and welcome contrast to the odd silence from most of Fleet Street about such a newsworthy subject'. Two days later Dr. R. A. Sayce from Worcester College, Oxford, praised the editor's 'brave defiance of the *sub judice* rule', which was undesirable when 'used as a screen for injustice'. On the same day, however, Quintin Hogg asked: 'Would it not perhaps be better to leave the sentences . . . to the Court of Appeal (Criminal Division), who, after all, will have the benefit of a full transcript of the evidence, and the arguments of counsel on both sides?'

It had been understood that the Court of Appeal would not be able to hear the appeals during the current term, and that they would have to be held over until the autumn. But in the event they were heard on the last day of the month, when the sentences on Jagger and Richard were quashed by a court presided over by the Lord Chief Justice (Parker). Meanwhile the two defendants had been out on bail. Jagger later recalled that on July 1 he was alone in a cell at Brixton when a warder brought him a copy of that day's *Times* with the comment 'Well, it seems you'll be out soon'; and he was, indeed, released within hours.[1] At the appeal hearing on July 31 the decision to quash the sentences was greeted with 'a chorus of screams, claps and gasps' from the public gallery.[2]

After his discharge, which was made conditional on good behaviour, Jagger attended a press conference staged by Granada Television and gave an exclusive interview to *The Times*. Later in the day Granada spirited him by helicopter to a garden in Essex (that of the county's lord lieutenant), where he was interviewed by a quartet of notables: Lord Stow Hill, a former Labour home secretary, Father Thomas Corbishley, a leading English Jesuit, Dr. John Robinson,

---

1 Mick Jagger talking to author. Some newspaper reports suggest that he was released the previous afternoon, but the recollection of his counsel, Michael (later Lord) Havers, was that bail was applied for at once but not granted until the following day, July 1. (Conversation with author.) Jagger was driven from Chichester to Brixton after the trial.

2 News report in *The Times*, August 1 1967.

suffragan bishop of Woolwich – and William Rees-Mogg.[1] This *World in Action* programme, transmitted the same evening, was a brilliant media stunt but not otherwise of much value. Such questions as whether society was corrupt and how far freedom should go were discussed in a necessarily inconclusive manner, and the questioners, with the creditable exception of Rees-Mogg, tended to do too much of the talking themselves. Jagger, for his part, made some vaguely aggressive remarks, but his lack of revolutionary purpose must have been obvious to anyone of normal intelligence. Reviewing the programme next day, Julian Critchley commented shrewdly that 'the butterfly who had escaped the wheel' was 'perhaps more of a Cabbage White than a Red Admiral'.[2]

Nevertheless his exclusive interview appeared in next morning's *Times* on the page opposite the leader, and under the headline 'Mr. Mick Jagger speaks his mind'. 'I really do feel a responsibility to my fans', he was quoted as saying. 'We don't want power over people', but 'if people continually push this generation by pushing the people who are its leaders, they will really alienate them'. He did not work for the money, but liked life. His purpose was not to build a socialist state, but to reach a state at which he was at one with himself and the world.

In a passage that might, surely, have landed him and the paper in trouble – if the authorities had been looking for trouble – he said:

> I think pot's more respectable than ten years ago; much more chichi. I don't see what's wrong with going on trips. I don't see what's wrong with not going on trips either. It's up to me to pick the things I want to do and I will. What I do with my consciousness is my business.

But he showed insight into the cause and nature of his own cult when he referred to the people of earlier generations whose minds had been 'twisted by strikes, depressions and wars', and added: 'They've been on a bigger trip than any of us – they've had the opportunity for danger and excitement'.[3]

---

1 Stow Hill, better known as Sir Frank Soskice, was home secretary for the brief period 1964–5. Corbishley was a popular theologian and pioneer of ecumenism in his church. Robinson acquired a misleadingly *outré* reputation with his book *Honest to God* and by appearing as a witness for *Lady Chatterley's Lover*.

2 August 1 1967

3 Same date. The interview was conducted by Stephen Jessel, who said of Jagger: 'He is quieter and has much more grace of manner than one would have expected . . . But the quality that impresses one most . . . is his overwhelming self-possession'.

The Jagger controversy did much to establish Rees-Mogg's style of editorship, since it enabled *The Times* to change its image in the eyes of a certain sort of avant-garde, and more especially of the younger generation, while remaining suitably Olympian. The 'butterfly' leader undoubtedly influenced opinion and was probably decisive in obtaining an earlier hearing of the Rolling Stones' appeal than had, at first, seemed likely. Other newspapers followed *The Times*'s lead, and such arguments appearing in the serious press provided a most helpful reinforcement to the efforts of defence counsel. Yet Rees-Mogg's words could not fairly be interpreted as glorifying the Rolling Stones or the culture that they represented; still less as condoning the use of narcotics by the young. Indeed, in a long leader in mid-July he came to the firm conclusion: 'For the young and inexperienced the psychedelic drugs are a type of conjuring with superior power which must be dangerous and wrong, and the more powerful their effect the more dangerous they must be'.[1]

Some traditional-minded viewers may have been rather shocked at the spectacle of an editor of *The Times* hobnobbing with a pop star in a country garden, and not a few readers must have felt uneasy about the prominence given to Jagger's views in the paper. But Rees-Mogg had no regrets. Some time later he could still claim to have enjoyed his televised encounter, while asserting his belief that it did 'no harm to take part in a happening from time to time'.[2] There was, as has already been noted, a streak of exhibitionism in him, which his apparent shyness and aloofness belied. In a sense, he and Jagger were both showmen. Yet personal showmanship was not his prime motive for handling the issue as he did. He had good reason to feel that he had won new support for *The Times* without betraying the paper's essential standards, or his own.

---

1 'Blessing in shades of green', July 15 1967. This leader's title was taken from the eighteenth-century mystical poet, Christopher Smart, who was 'clinically insane'. Various methods of inducing ecstasy were mentioned, including religious contemplation, sexual 'and particularly romantic' love, music, and 'the vision of nature of the romantic poets', and finally mental illness. The state of mind resulting from the use of hallucinogenic drugs had, it was argued, less in common with Christian or Eastern mysticism, or with the natural mysticism of Wordsworth, than with the mysticism of the psychoses.
2 W.R.-M. to John Sheppard, January 22 1969. It was Sheppard, apparently, who persuaded the lord lieutenant of Essex to allow his garden to be used for the 'happening'.

IV

Devaluation and a new chancellor • A brush with Downing Street • Stern line on honours • Shift of view on Vietnam • Two assassinations • Firm stand on race

WHEN HE BECAME prime minister Harold Wilson vowed that he would keep sterling flying high, and for three years the exchange rate was defended. During the sterling crisis of July 1966 some members of the cabinet, led by George Brown, strongly argued for devaluation, but Wilson carried the day against them, at the same time bringing in a programme of austerity which included a year-long freeze of wages and prices. This curtailed economic growth, with the result that a year later the figure of unemployment was, at nearly half a million, the highest July figure since 1940. Moreover the trade gap, though negligible in the first quarter of 1967, was widening again even before the Six-Day War and temporary closure of the Suez Canal added heavily to the adverse balance by boosting oil and shipping costs.

In early August Rees-Mogg was saying privately that 'Wilson would clearly not stay the course – the whole situation was crumbling around him'.[1] This was a premature judgement. As yet there was little sign of another sterling crisis and in some ways the prime minister seemed more dominant than ever. At the end of the month he reshuffled his cabinet, dropping the anti-Marketeer Douglas Jay and assuming direct control of economic affairs with his protégé, Peter Shore, to assist him.[2] Despite considerable disaffection in the trade unions and a general loss of popularity, shown in by-election losses, the government did surprisingly well at Labour's party conference, held at Scarborough.

---

1 *The Cecil King Diary, 1965–1970*, entry for August 3 1967 (p.137). Rees-Mogg had been dining the night before with King's son, Michael.
2 Shore was appointed secretary of state for economic affairs, taking the place but not the authority of Michael Stewart, Brown's successor in the office. Stewart became first secretary of state.

In particular a resolution of support for the government's economic policies, which might well have been lost, was carried.

For this narrow but important victory the chancellor, James Callaghan, received much credit. His speech at the end of the debate was by common consent exceptionally powerful, and may well have swayed enough votes to determine the result. In the anonymity of a *Times* leader his son-in-law praised his courage but questioned his policy. Was the only way to break out of the stop-go cycle 'at the bottom'? Could the country be made efficient and prosperous only by first enduring a regime of austerity?

> The answer must essentially depend on whether full employment, capacity production, buoyant profits, and high investment are more or less favourable than a prolonged economic winter to the necessary structural changes in the economy. Formal economics gives no final answer to this fundamental problem. But the weight of technical argument tends to reinforce the commonsense view that rapid economic change is, like flowers, likely to thrive best in the sun. People are more willing to surrender what they have if they can see a good chance of something better. Fear and insecurity breed resistance to change and restrictive defensive attitudes to innovation. We are still harvesting in rigid and wasteful industrial practices the consequences of the inter-war years of privation and failure.[1]

A few days after the party conference attention was diverted from Labour's present to its past by the death of Lord Attlee on October 8. *The Times* next day marked the occasion not only with an obituary occupying four full columns, but also with a leader written by Hickey. Attlee used to be underrated, it said, but now his 'dry and matter of fact manner', and his 'inability to dramatize his leadership', were generally preferred to Churchill's flamboyance and 'the studied television personalities of his successors'. His Indian policy and fidelity to the Anglo-American alliance were to be admired, but his failure to lead Britain into the European Coal and Steel Community was a historic mistake. At home his most lasting achievement, the large extension of the welfare state, had proved so popular that all later governments had been 'frightened to do any more than a few running repairs', even though the original structure was 'audibly creaking in

1 'Brave but probably mistaken', October 4 1967. Peter Jay's first leader for the main paper had been written at the end of August, though he had already written a fair number for *TBN*.

social conditions quite different from those for which it was designed'. His measures of nationalization had 'stood one test of time, that of survival', though 'in the political dogfight that went on around them, for which the Opposition was as much to blame, serious thought about the management and development of the industries became a casualty'.

In the same judicious vein the leader ended:

> Lord Attlee was reared in the British school of twentieth century class politics. He was a most estimable product of it, deeply conscious of the social deprivations of large sections of the people, and seized of the moral purposes of politics. His earnestness and quiet demeanour deepened a little the joylessness of postwar socialism, which contributed something to its downfall. It was a school for politicians which had marked limitations. The categories in which it arranged political experience had only partial relevance to the postwar world. Yet ATTLEE's particular qualities of tenacity, common sense and moderation – with the occasional strong flash, such as his India policy – were of service to Britain at the time, and they will be remembered.[1]

Attlee was spared – if only by a matter of weeks – the spectacle of another Labour government forced, as his had been, into devaluing the pound. Just as a seamen's strike had helped to cause the 1966 sterling crisis, so in the autumn of 1967 strikes in the Liverpool and London docks, and a threatened strike on the railways, did much to undermine confidence. All the same the final crisis, in mid-November, took most commentators by surprise. Until the last week financial journalists were not sounding any note of alarm, but by Thursday November 16 the situation was out of control. On that day Callaghan, perhaps over-mindful of the way Cripps had been savaged for denying devaluation shortly before it occurred, failed to make such a denial under questioning in the House of Commons. It was then assumed that the decision had been taken, as in fact it had been, and newspapers felt free to comment accordingly. In a leader on the chancellor's equivocal reply, *The Times* more or less opted for devaluation: 'Nothing . . . could be less useful than further borrowing in support of a policy which could not be shown to be realistic'.[2] The following day it was more explicit; as between a very tough loan and a devaluation

1 'Clement Attlee', October 9 1967.
2 'Mr. Callaghan's reply', November 17 1967.

of, say, 12½ to 15 per cent, the second seemed to be the better of the two alternatives available'.[1] Yet it was not until 9.30 p.m. on Saturday November 18 that the Treasury announced a devaluation of 14.3 per cent, from $2.80 to $2.40. The excessively long delay cost the country about $200 million.

In Monday's paper the front-page lead headline covering the full width of the page was 'Prime Minister defends devaluation'. This referred to Wilson's broadcast the night before, in which he used the unfortunate phrase that the 'pound in your pocket' would not be worth less. Though he could justly claim that the phrase was torn from its context and unscrupulously exploited by his opponents, it never ceased to plague him; and he later admitted that he had made a mistake in toning down the extent of the defeat his government had suffered, whatever the causes.[2] *The Times*, in a single big leader, described the devaluation as a confession of failure, while stressing the need to take full advantage of it.[3] And in his column the same day Ian Trethowan raised the question of the chancellor's future: 'However much Labour people may respect Mr. Callaghan as a person, they will not lightly forgive the man who, more than anyone, has been responsible for rounding off the most disastrous political treble of modern times: 1931, 1949, 1967'.[4]

Callaghan was not slow to hint that he was going, but of course his responsibility was shared by Wilson, all the more so since at the end of August the prime minister had taken direct control of economic policy. In any case Callaghan was too important a man to lose from the government; he had to be persuaded to stay. On November 29 it was announced that he would be moving from the Treasury to the Home Office, and that the home secretary, Roy Jenkins, would be taking his place as chancellor.

No appointment could have been more congenial to the editor of *The Times*. Jenkins was a politician after Rees-Mogg's heart: another Balliol man, yes, and also another former officer of the Oxford Union (though as secretary and librarian, not president). He was a devoted Gaitskellite, but with the merit of being, unlike Gaitskell, a fervent European. Moreover, among Gaitskell's younger disciples he had shown the most conspicuous aptitude for government, having been

---

1 'Right rate for Europe', November 18 1967. Both leaders were written by the editor.
2 H. Wilson, *The Labour Government 1964–1970: A Personal Record*, pp.465–6. He had made it quite clear in his broadcast that prices would rise as a result of devaluation. The offending phrase was, as it happens, suggested to him by a Treasury brief.
3 'Harsh opportunity', November 20 1967, written by the editor.
4 'Mr. Callaghan's personal dilemma', November 20 1967.

raised at once, in 1964, to senior office, and having made a success of both the posts he had held, as minister of aviation and home secretary. He was also a thoroughly civilised man, by Rees-Mogg's standards, with interests and tastes by no means confined to politics. He had a strong historical sense, and wrote history. He was amusing and sociable, and there was no partisanship in his choice of friends. Above all, he did not allow his political and official life, seriously as he took it, to monopolise his existence. Though extremely effective when he was on the job – quick to master subjects and take decisions – he believed that his working day should, as a rule, end in good time for dinner, subject only to the requirement of returning to Westminster for important votes.

In a leader on December 1 Rees-Mogg welcomed the new chancellor and expressed high hopes of what he might achieve. His 'combination of economic understanding, parliamentary skill and political judgment' made him probably 'the most promising appointment to the Exchequer since HUGH GAITSKELL in 1950, though that was a mixed blessing'. The first phase of his task, which would last about eighteen months, would be 'to ensure that real incomes fall to take account of the devaluation'. But in his 1969 budget Jenkins should be able 'to start the more cheerful process of creating a favourable climate for economic expansion in Britain'. Many might think that the end of the Labour government was near, but there was no reason to accept this view. 'If MR. JENKINS'S economic policy is successful, then there will be a considerable probability that the Labour Party will win the next election by a comfortable majority. If the policy fails then indeed everything else fails'. A week later the editor wrote: 'The question is whether the Government will have the courage to push [Jenkins's] policy through. Will the Opposition have the magnanimity to support them?'[1]

The advent of Jenkins as the Wilson government's new star may have improved *The Times*'s attitude towards the government itself; but it did nothing at all to improve relations with the prime minister. On the contrary, ill-will was considerably aggravated by Peter Jay's signed column in *TBN* on November 23, entitled 'Devaluation – who was to blame?' The question was answered unequivocally: the two villains of the piece were Macmillan and Wilson, the first for 'presiding over

---

1 'Mr. Jenkins's duty', December 1 1967; 'Courage and magnanimity', December 8 1967.

the period in which the economic seed corn stemming from the 1949 devaluation was frittered away', the second for 'refusing to admit the basic facts of the economic situation and then pursuing policies which made devaluation inevitable'.

The story of Wilson's role was, according to Jay, 'beyond belief'. Ever since he took office in 1964 he had been the 'prime mover' behind maintaining the old exchange parity. Two days after the election that brought him to power he held a meeting with Brown and Callaghan at 10 Downing Street, at which no officials were present. A 'firm, irrevocable' decision was then taken 'on political grounds' that devaluation was out of the question; and there was no doubt that, among the three, Wilson was the leading protagonist of orthodoxy. Again, in July 1966, it was the prime minister who decided that any price had to be paid to defend sterling; and that was why, departing from precedent, he himself rather than the chancellor announced the crisis package to the House of Commons. On two occasions before the 1966 crisis economic aides had submitted categorical advice that devaluation was a necessary pre-condition of any coherent future economic or foreign policy. In mid-1965 a memorandum to this effect was ignored and denied further circulation on the prime minister's personal instructions, and early in 1966 he ordered that a draft report on the same lines be destroyed – though in fact one copy of the draft survived.

More incredibly still, having taken such an adamant stand against devaluation, he showed complete disregard for official advice on the ways and means to maintain it. 'He surely knew that if he announced Britain's application to join the Common Market last spring without any other steps, then devaluation would inevitably follow'. And at the end of August he 'must have known that the H.P. relaxations which were announced to celebrate his assumption of economic overlordship were bound to lead to devaluation within a matter of months'.

But what of the chancellor's role? His son-in-law ended by posing the question, and replying in somewhat enigmatic terms:

> No one will perhaps ever know what in his heart Mr. Callaghan's real attitude was, if indeed he had one. Like King Henry VIII's Cardinal Wolsey he judged that the only viable policy was the King's policy, whatever its strengths and weaknesses. And like Cardinal Wolsey his aptest epitaph as Chancellor . . . will surely be: – 'Had I but served my God with half the zeal/I served my King, he would not in mine age/Have left me naked to mine enemies'.

The historical analogy was not at all flattering to Wilson; but it was not particularly flattering to Callaghan, either.

Jay's article created quite a sensation, as was only to be expected in view of his close connection with both the chancellor and a cabinet minister recently sacked by Wilson, not to mention the fact that he had been a civil servant in the treasury before joining *The Times*. The evening after its appearance Wilson was questioned about it when he faced a panel of financial journalists on the ITV programme *This Week*. Jay was to have been one of the interrogators, but the invitation to him was withdrawn at 11 a.m. In his absence Nigel Lawson asked about the article, and Wilson replied that it was not for him to comment on 'a very slanted article by a former civil servant', because to put the record straight would involve giving 'a great deal of information which should not be made public'. He went on to imply that Jay was out of touch with ordinary people, but – significantly – did not deny what had been alleged about his rejection of advice, for which in any case there is positive corroboration in Barbara Castle's diary.[1]

Immediately afterwards, on another television programme, Jay insisted that his information was 'wholly accurate', and claimed to have come by it 'in the normal course of [his] journalistic activities', not when he was a civil servant. Moreover, he had not discussed the piece with his father-in-law either before or after it was written. Indeed he had not spoken to Callaghan for two or three weeks.[2] (But, viewers must have wondered, had there been a similar lack of contact between his wife, Margaret, and her father? And had nothing been repeated?)

Next day the two interviews were reported on the front page of *The Times*, with a picture of Jay: the sort of personal exposure that would formerly have been unthinkable for a *Times* man. And until Parliament rose for Christmas the opposition tried to make some use of the affair, with Jock Bruce-Gardyne in particular repeatedly asking the prime minister about the circumstances in which the invitation to Jay to be one of his questioners on *This Week* was withdrawn. Wilson's reply was that 'a journalist with experience of prices and incomes, and industrial matters', would be preferable. He was also able to say that

1 Thomas (later Lord) Balogh, who was Wilson's principal economic adviser, said that 'there *had* been two memos to Harold advocating devaluation, and that he . . . had signed both – one in the spring of 1965 and the other in March 1966. But he insisted that Harold had been quite right to suppress them, otherwise there would certainly have been leaks'. (*The Castle Diaries 1964–70*, entry for November 27 1967, p.330.)

2 Jay was appearing on *The Frost Programme*. Both programmes went out during the evening of November 23 1967.

the company had apologised for announcing the list of interviewers before it had been cleared with Downing Street.[1]

Meanwhile Sir Laurence Helsby, joint permanent secretary of the treasury and head of the civil service, had written to Rees-Mogg expressing himself 'much troubled about some aspects of Peter Jay's article' and asking for an 'informal talk'. After a delay of three days the editor replied:

> . . . I think this is a rather difficult matter. I have Peter Jay's assurance that none of the matters to which he referred in his article or in his broadcast were derived from his experience as a civil servant, but that he was told them afterwards quite separately. [By whom?] As you know, he was appointed to work away from the central control of the economy shortly after the Labour Government was returned in 1964 . . .
>
> Naturally, in the ordinary course of events, I should be delighted to discuss the matter with you on an informal basis. However the Prime Minister has already attacked Peter Jay on television, and Downing Street have made a number of statements about the circumstances in which Peter Jay was taken off the Prime Minister's television programme which are, so far as I can establish, unreliable. The Prime Minister's own statement on television was open to an interpretation that could have been misleading. In these circumstances I don't think that I can come and see you without at any rate further clarification of the matters which we should discuss.[2]

In the nature of things it was scarcely credible that Jay had no relevant knowledge deriving from his official experience, and in fact the government could have proved that he had by producing a document that he had initialled. Moreover, in mid-1966 he had written a memorandum in favour of devaluation, and had nearly resigned on the issue. He was now indignant with Wilson for putting it around that he had always wanted to devalue, but had been advised against doing so by the Treasury, when he (Jay) knew that the opposite was the truth. Another cause for resentment was that his father had recently been dropped from the cabinet. On the government's side, it

---

1 Wilson answered Parliamentary questions on the subject on November 28, December 5 and December 19. The words quoted are from the second exchange. During the third, Maudling intervened from the opposition front bench; but it was never possible to make much of the Jay affair as a censorship issue.

2 Helsby to W.R.-M., November 24 1967; W.R.-M. to Helsby, November 27 1967.

was obviously inexpedient to pursue a vendetta against Callaghan's son-in-law, and prudence overcame any urge to enforce the rules. At a party given by the publisher Robert Maxwell, at Headington Hall, Jay was informed by the attorney-general himself (Sir Elwyn Jones) that the decision had just been taken not to prosecute him.[1]

Devaluation was a severe blow to Wilson's prestige, and Jay's article made it all the more so by emphasising his responsibility for maintaining the old parity at all costs. It also provided de Gaulle with an additional pretext for again vetoing British entry to the Common Market, at one of his superbly theatrical press conferences on November 27.[2] But in December the prime minister to some extent restored his authority by masterly handling of a crisis within the Cabinet on the issue of selling or not selling arms to South Africa. Though a strong group of ministers, including Brown and Callaghan, favoured arms sales, Wilson managed to worst them completely without driving any of them to resignation.

On New Year's Day 1968 the editor reasserted *The Times*'s traditional self-denying ordinance in the matter of honours. Noting that in the list just published there were awards explicitly for journalism, as well as for broadcasting, he described this as a 'disturbing precedent'. The principle of a government bestowing honours on journalists was 'highly objectionable' because, 'Human nature being what it is, people are influenced by honours and even more by the expectation of honours'. It was thus that the Conservative whips managed the House of Commons during the 1950s and early 1960s, 'and a backbencher of that period who did not in thirteen years become a knight was something of a rarity'. If it were to be regarded as normal for journalists to accept honours in a prime minister's gift, this would 'inevitably lead to attempts to manage newspapers by offering the prospect of ribbons and titles to their staff'.[3]

For more than a century and a half *The Times* could take pride in the fact that its proprietors and editors rigorously eschewed honours, and that only the very occasional *Times* journalist accepted one. The Walters kept their virtue while more and more newspaper owners were

---

1 Jay talking to author.
2 The text of his press conference was printed in full in *The Times* the following day, while a leader commented:- 'It is . . . marvellous to behold a man of 77 capable of such feats of memory and wit . . . producing an illusion to cover what are, in fact, a number of deeply rooted prejudices all of them impervious to reason'.
3 'Honours for journalists', January 1 1968.

becoming press lords. Not until John Astor became Lord Astor of Hever in 1956 did a chief proprietor of *The Times* succumb, and he did so only after consulting the editor, Haley, who found casuistical arguments to justify his acceptance of a peerage.[1] But the same Haley, though already knighted for his work as director-general of the BBC, would never have accepted an honour as editor of *The Times*, and indeed laid down the rule that no *Times* journalist should accept one either during or after his or her service on the paper.[2]

Rees-Mogg, even before his New Year leader, had shown that Haley's rule would also be his. When, in the 1967 Birthday list, *The Times*'s labour correspondent was awarded an honour, the editor circulated a tough memo:

> We have all been pleased by the well-deserved award of the CBE to Mr. Wigham . . . However, this cuts across the informal but long-standing tradition that members of the editorial staff of *The Times* do not accept Honours either from foreign Governments or from the British Government. Mr. Wigham tells me he was not aware of this tradition. I feel therefore it is necessary to establish it on paper.
>
> In future no member of the editorial staff . . . will be allowed to accept any Honour. I shall be taking steps to make it clear to the appropriate authorities that this is the case.

But there was to be one significant exception:

> This prohibition does not apply to life peerages, should they be offered, because they are functional appointments rather than awards.[3]

With Rees-Mogg's attitude in mind, Hamilton had some misgivings about accepting a knighthood in 1976, and was at pains to point out to his colleague that the citation was for services to the arts – in particular for the exhibitions he had organised – rather than for his journalistic work. He might have felt at less of a moral disadvantage

1 'It was agreed that as he had no influence on the policy of the paper, for him to become Lord Astor of Hever would raise no question about its independence. His other activities alone justified the honour'. (Haley on Astor in the *DNB* 1971–1980 volume.)

2 Note from Haley, February 25 1954, and letter to Sir Edward Bridges, July 25 1954. One victim of Haley's austerity was McDonald, who was forbidden to accept the Legion of Honour.

3 June 13 1967.

had he been able to foresee that Rees-Mogg himself would accept a knighthood within months of relinquishing the editorship in 1981.

American involvement in Vietnam, which had increased throughout Kennedy's presidency, developed under his successor into full-scale war not only against the guerillas inside South Vietnam (the Vietcong) but against North Vietnam as well. By the beginning of 1968 there were more than half a million American troops in South Vietnam, while vain attempts were being continued to bomb the North into submission. The Communist leader there, Ho Chi-minh, though no puppet of China or Russia, could count on the support of both against the United States; and the Russians' rivalry with China ensured that they would be particularly assiduous in supplying him with material aid, including anti-aircraft weapons. Within South Vietnam the Vietcong were proving equally undefeatable, partly because the South Vietnamese regime, propped up by the Americans, was a thoroughly unpleasant dictatorship, and partly because the rebels were not of a different race, as the Communists had been in Malaya, but were fellow-Vietnamese. President Lyndon Johnson had been lured by the military establishment into a disastrous escalation which could not lead to victory, as even his hitherto hawkish secretary of defense, Robert McNamara, was beginning to see. It was Johnson's cruel dilemma that he wanted to end the war while his enemies were unwilling to end it on any terms that he could accept, since they felt that time was on their side.

Until *The Times*'s change of ownership coverage of Vietnam had been limited, consisting mainly of agency reports. But under the new dispensation it was at once given a much higher profile. A promising reporter, Fred Emery, was switched from Tokyo to become South-East Asia correspondent and, so far as Vietnam was concerned, he was to be assisted on the spot by another *Times* man, David Bonavia.[1] In due course the services of a *Sunday Times* special correspondent, David Leitch, were also made available to the paper.

Early in 1968, at the time of the Tet festival marking the Buddhist new year, the Vietcong launched an offensive throughout the country, in which all the main American bases were simultaneously attacked. Saigon itself was temporarily threatened, while the old imperial

1 Emery, having a wife and children, chose to be based in Singapore. Bonavia, unmarried, was based in Saigon – though he got married in December 1967. In any case Emery was often in Vietnam.

capital, Hué, was captured and held by the rebels for twenty-six days. When the Tet offensive began Emery was away covering some riots in Mauritius, but he immediately returned to the scene of more serious action, being flown to Singapore in an RAF aircraft, and from there to South Vietnam in an aircraft of the Royal Australian Air Force.[1] On February 20 the paper led with a big front-page story from him, dateline Hué:

> The American Marine battalion engaged in reducing the fanatical communist resistance in [the] citadel had by this evening lost about half its combat strength in what has become a hellish battle. Indeed, after spending two days witnessing heavy casualties in ferocious house-to-house fighting . . . I would venture to say that the situation is precarious for the Americans unless reinforcements are sent in.

But it would, he said, be difficult to reinforce even by air; the helicopter in which he arrived had been hit by sniper fire.

Hué was, in fact, recaptured. But the Tet offensive convinced Emery, and many others, that the Americans had an impossible task in Vietnam. Louis Heren in Washington had his doubts about the war, despite his sympathy for, and good standing with, the president. In a turnover on February 23 he gave an obviously first-hand account of Johnson's dissatisfaction with Britain's attitude to the war. Harold Wilson's suggestion that only a narrow gap had to be bridged to bring peace to Vietnam reduced him 'to the homely expletives of the Texas hill country'. He was also concerned about Britain's 'accelerated withdrawal' from East of Suez. Australia, 'which he seems to regard as a second Texas', was a good ally; but there were too few Australians.[2] This was hardly fair to Wilson, who had backed American policy in Vietnam to an extent that most members of his party found deplorable.

The Times's editorial line at the beginning of 1968 was that there could never be 'a purely military solution in Vietnam'.[3] This could be taken to assume the need for military victory as a prelude to political negotiation, and such was, indeed, still the prevailing assumption. To anyone as pro-American and anti-communist as Rees-Mogg the idea

---

1 These privileged and (from the service point of view) irregular trips were, to Emery's embarrassment, reported prominently in the paper on February 16 1968. He had mentioned them in a message to Cudlipp, but had not wished them to be published.
2 Heren had recently received the John F. Kennedy award of $10,000 for his book, *The New American Commonwealth*.
3 'The equation of battle', January 31 1968.

of effective defeat for the Americans in Vietnam was, as yet, inadmissible. But before long, in response to events both in Vietnam and in the United States, a shift of view became apparent. Early in March, when it was reported that the American commander in Vietnam, General William Westmoreland, was asking for 206,000 more troops to be sent there, and when the first presidential primary, in New Hampshire, was imminent, a leader entitled 'The Pentagon's War' ended:

> General Westmoreland's request may . . . have the effect of forcing a fresh assessment of the war by the Administration. Already there are signs that American opinion is in a more critical mood than the pollsters reported soon after the Vietcong [Tet] offensive. In the New Hampshire primary SENATOR MCCARTHY is expected to attract a vote on a scale greater than that of purely intellectual protest, while MR. NIXON's emphasis on 'winning the peace' after ending the war has significance. If it becomes clear that the public is not behind what it assumes are the Pentagon's plans for the next stage of the war the politicians may begin to think in terms of extrication.[1]

Political thinking was certainly transformed when Senator Eugene McCarthy, the peace candidate, went far beyond attracting votes 'on a scale greater than that of purely intellectual protest', to emerge nearly top of the Democratic poll in New Hampshire. Next day *The Times* carried a front-page story that Senator Robert Kennedy, stimulated by McCarthy's success, was preparing to enter the campaign against Johnson for the Democratic nomination.[2] Soon afterwards it was reported that General Westmoreland had been relieved of his command, and about a week later Johnson announced on television that he would not be a candidate for re-election. At the same time he announced that the bombing of North Vietnam would cease.[3]

Commenting on the fall of Johnson, the *Times* leader (written by Hodgkin) was generous:

> A reaction could come quickly. Taking stock of MR. JOHNSON's presidency, as the world now must, and comparing him with his immediate predecessors in office and – still more – with his

1 March 11 1968.

2 March 14 1968. The story, a scoop for Heren, was illustrated by a large picture of Kennedy, and a small one of McCarthy.

3 General Westmoreland's dismissal reported March 23 1968; Johnson's announcement, April 1 1968.

> possible successors, he regains much of the stature he had when his reputation was at its highest. Now is the time to remember MR. JOHNSON's claim to be one of the great reforming Presidents.[1]

America's war in Vietnam was being fought by a conscript army, and the draft operated in such a way that the well-off could easily avoid it. The human price of the war was, therefore, being paid disproportionately by the poor, among whom a disproportionate number were black. Johnson's outstanding achievements in the promotion of civil rights were tragically offset by his commitment to a war which, among its many ill-effects, could only be damaging to that cause. Unrest at home was, moreover, accompanied by an alarming growth of violence; between 1960 and 1968 crimes of violence in the United States increased by 57 per cent.

The Republic's general state of travail was brought into sharp focus by the assassination of two famous citizens, one black, one white. *The Times*'s coverage of these events was curiously uneven. At the beginning of April the black civil rights leader, Dr. Martin Luther King, was shot dead in Atlanta, Georgia. His obituary in later editions of the paper on April 5 ran to only two columns, not of full depth and without a picture, though a small picture appeared with the lead news story on the front page. The opening words of the obituary were hardly felicitous – 'Dr. Martin Luther King, vitriolic champion of Negro civil rights in the South' – though the piece did go on to stress that his campaign had been non-violent. On April 6 he was the subject of an appreciative first leader (by Richard Davy), while the obituary was repeated for the benefit of those who had not seen it the day before.

Vastly more space was given to the assassination, two months later, of Senator Kennedy, who was shot in Los Angeles at the moment of victory in the Californian primary. On June 6, before his death was confirmed, most of the front page was devoted to the story of his shooting. The following day his obituary occupied six whole columns, with a large picture, while the same page also carried tributes from the Pope, the Archbishop of Canterbury, and others. On the same day the whole of the op. ed. page, apart from the diary, consisted of material on Kennedy, including a report from Heren in Washington, one from Innis Macbeath in New York, and a poem by the Russian

1 'Mr. Johnson withdraws', April 2 1968.

dissident poet, Yevtushenko. There was also a leader under the heading 'He stood for justice' (by Hodgkin), and, as a three-column turnover, extracts from an essay and a book by Kennedy (both probably ghost-written).

Why such a very marked contrast in the scale of treatment accorded to these two victims? Kennedy was, indeed, a US Senator, and had been US attorney-general under his brother and under Johnson, whereas King had never held any official position. Even so, the two were of more nearly equivalent importance than the space allotted to them would suggest. Racial prejudice can be discounted, for a reason that will soon appear. The explanation must lie in the Kennedy cult, of which Bobby Kennedy was the chief beneficiary after his brother's murder, and which his own then served to enhance. The Kennedy mystique was potent throughout most of the world in the Sixties, conveying, however spuriously, a sense of up-to-date intelligence and youthful idealism. Few at the time were impervious to this mystique, and they did not include Rees-Mogg, who, moreover, can hardly have failed to be a little influenced by the fact that the family in question was Irish-American Roman Catholic, like his mother's.

Between the Luther King and Bobby Kennedy assassinations Britain experienced its most impassioned political controversy of the decade. This was started by Enoch Powell, Conservative MP for Wolverhampton South-West, in a speech delivered on April 20 at the annual meeting of the West Midlands Conservative Political Centre at the Midland Hotel, Birmingham. Powell was a former minister of health, and currently spokesman on defence in Heath's shadow cabinet. The subject of the speech was coloured immigration, which came within the shadow sphere of a senior colleague, Quintin Hogg. No prior notice of the speech's contents was given to Hogg or to Heath, though the text was widely circulated in advance to newspapers, and the occasion was covered on television.

The issue itself was by no means new. In the late 1950s the effects of unrestricted immigration from the Caribbean and the Indian subcontinent were already acutely felt in some areas of the country, including the West Midlands, and the demand for action to curb the flow was then voiced, above all, by a Conservative backbench MP, Sir Cyril Osborne. In 1962 the Macmillan government carried through the first Commonwealth Immigrants Act, which the Labour Party opposed, but which some on the right regarded as insufficiently stringent. When the Conservative party went into opposition the most persistent advocate of tighter control was, for a time, a former cabinet minister, Duncan Sandys. Powell, however, though a representative of one of the areas affected, was as yet very quiet and restrained on the issue.

Meanwhile Labour, in power, enacted the first measure to penalise racial discrimination in Britain, the Race Relations Act of 1965. Two years later the issue of race was intensified by fear that about 200,000 Asians from Kenya might claim their right to move to Britain as citizens. There was also pressure from the left to strengthen the law against discrimination. As opinion in the country became increasingly polarised, Heath had to deal with conflicting currents in his own party. His task was difficult enough without gratuitous aggravation from a colleague.

Powell's decision to provide it was relatively sudden, though his conversion to a hard line on race was apparent by the beginning of 1968, several months before his Birmingham speech. A visit to the United States in the autumn of 1967 confronted him with the reality of racial conflict in big cities, and made him more alive to the danger of it in Britain. Knowing the force of feeling among many of his white constituents, and observing the generally strong response to Sandys's interventions, he may have decided to lead a movement that he could no longer oppose or ignore. He was unlikely to be inhibited by any special tenderness towards the leadership of his party, since he had been a rival contender for the succession to Douglas-Home and regarded Heath with a mixture of resentment and intellectual superiority. In February 1968 he fired his first shot with a speech at Walsall, in which he emphasised the threat of mass Asian immigration from Kenya. Within a month the government had rushed through a measure – opposed by some prominent Conservatives, though not by Heath or the opposition as a whole – limiting the entry of Kenya Asians to 1,500 annually. Powell can hardly have failed to have a sense of being the master of events.

His Birmingham speech two months later was a more wide-ranging attack, as well as more elaborately stage-managed. Parts of Britain, he said, were undergoing a 'total transformation to which there is no parallel in a thousand years of English history'. The remedies he proposed were that coloured immigration should be cut 'to negligible proportions', and that repatriation or 're-emigration' should be very actively encouraged. While acknowledging the principle of equal rights for all citizens, he used it to argue that no citizen 'should be denied his right to discriminate in the management of his own affairs between one fellow-citizen and another'.

The substance of the speech was, therefore, tough; but it was the tone and phraseology that made it explosive. His argument was dramatised by the use of anecdotal evidence, including the story of an old woman in his constituency (brought to his notice in a letter from Northumberland) who had 'lost her husband and both her sons in the war', and whose life was now being made a misery by the blacks dominating her street. This had become 'a place of noise and confusion'; her windows were broken and she found 'excreta pushed through her letterbox'. But the most lurid passage in the speech involved a quotation from Virgil which Powell the populist orator owed to Powell the classical scholar. 'Like the old Roman', he said, he foresaw 'the river Tiber foaming with much blood'.[1] He was all too clearly suggesting that the few isolated race riots that had already occurred in Britain were only the prelude to racial conflict on a much larger scale.

In Heath's view, the speech could only have the effect of increasing tension. He also saw it as a direct challenge to himself. His immediate response, therefore, was to drop Powell from the shadow cabinet. Had he not done this he would have been faced with the resignation of Hogg; yet it is unlikely that he needed any additional spur.

April 20 being a Saturday, the speech was first reported in the Sunday papers, and the dailies had twenty-four hours to consider their reactions. In any case, the issue did not take Rees-Mogg by surprise. *The Times*'s Midland correspondent, Brian Priestley, who was based in Birmingham, had warned him of worsening racial problems in the area.[2] Throughout the week 11–16 March the paper's op. ed. page had carried a News Team inquiry on the theme 'The Black Man in Search of Power'. The last three articles in the series dealt with the problem at home, and the final one, on the Saturday, stressed the danger of racial polarisation in Britain. Entitled 'The eleventh hour', it ended: 'If the Government of Britain, one of the world's upper-class nations, cannot help the coloured poor inside and outside her gates, then, like the working class after the Russian Revolution, they will look for other friends . . . For black men are not simply in search of power. They are also in search of justice'.

To Powell *The Times*'s attitude on the racial issue seemed soft, and his Birmingham speech included an unmistakable attack on the paper: 'There could be no grosser misconception of the realities than

1 '. . . bella, horrida bella, / et Thybrim multo spumantem sanguine cano'. (*Aeneid*, book 6, lines 86, 87).
2 Priestley to W.R.-M., March 6 1968.

is entertained by those who vociferously demand legislation as they call it "against discrimination", whether they be leader-writers of the same kidney, and sometimes on the same newspaper, which year after year in the 1930s tried to blind this country to the rising peril which confronted it, or archbishops . . .' In commenting on the speech on Monday April 22 Rees-Mogg was, therefore, in a sense reacting to personal criticism; but the disgust that he expressed was none the less genuine.

His leader, 'The evil speech', began by commending Heath's decision to dismiss Powell, which 'required courage'. The speech was 'disgraceful', not because it advocated still tighter control of immigration, or even – though the idea might be 'quite impractical' – because it suggested larger grants to encourage re-emigration. It was disgraceful, above all, because it was 'calculated to inflame hatred between the races, not only of white against black, but also of black against black'.

> The more closely one reads the text of MR. POWELL's speech, the more shameful it seems. The language, the innuendoes, the constant appeals to self-pity, the anecdotes, all combine to make a deliberate appeal to racial prejudice. This is the first time that a serious British politician has appealed to racial hatred, in this direct way, in our postwar history. It occurred within a couple of weeks of the murder of MARTIN LUTHER KING and the burning in many American cities. It is almost unbelievable that any man should be so irresponsible as to promote hatred in the face of these examples of the results that can follow.

Under home news the same day the speech itself was substantially reproduced, with comments from various Conservatives; Nicholas Scott strongly opposing it, Duncan Sandys and Teddy Taylor on the whole backing it, and Michael Heseltine sounding a more ambiguous note.[1] The following day's lead story reported that the shadow cabinet was behind Heath. There were front-page pictures of Powell opening fan-mail and of Heath drinking black-and-white ale at a brewing exhibition, while on the op. ed. page Norman Fowler discussed the state of public opinion on race, concluding that it had been insufficiently prepared for the government's new race relations bill.

Correspondence on the issue flourished as the controversy grew.

---

1 The speech, he said, had 'split the Conservative Party down the middle', and he called on Heath to 'spell out Conservative policy in detail'.

In two columns of letters on April 23, one from David le Vay of Harley Street stated simply: 'Mr. Powell's crime is to have said what every Englishman thinks'. But two days later the Revd Kenneth Clark of Westbury-on-Trym replied that this calculation erred, in his view, 'by a good many million Englishmen'. A number of Powell's constituents, including two with Asian names, wrote a joint letter protesting against the 'ostrich-headed ideas of politicians, archbishops and woolly minded liberals all of whom live well away from the ghettoes of Wolverhampton'. But this was soon followed by another letter from constituents condemning the speech.[1]

The authenticity of Powell's beleaguered old woman was questioned by Ann Dummett of Oxford, who wrote that an almost exactly similar story had been told to her recently about an old woman living in London. 'It would be interesting indeed to know just how many old ladies in how many parts of the country have had the experience related by Mr. Powell or, alternatively, from what source such scurrilities emanate'. A London solicitor, however, disputed the suggestion that stories of people having their doors fouled with excreta were apocryphal. He could testify to having sworn evidence of such practices.[2]

Some letters were prompted by the march to Westminster on April 23 of thousands of London dockers demonstrating in favour of Powell. The high commissioner for Kenya, J. N. Karanjia, wrote: 'When I drove to Parliament yesterday . . . I was shocked and surprised to be shouted at and booed by the assembled throng of dockers. My driver, who is a Kenyan, was also shouted at and told to go back to Jamaica!' A TGWU official, Brian Nicholson, wrote that the march had 'done enormous damage to the dockers' cause'; and J. P. Anderson of Taunton, commenting on the picture of a dignified Sikh walking past a jeering crowd of dockers, wrote: 'If we had to choose between the London dockers and the Sikh I know my answer. Export the dockers and import the Sikhs.'[3]

A letter from Canon F. W. Cocks, rector of St. Peter's, Wolverhampton, where Powell and his wife had taken communion the morning after his speech, insisted that a report of his being congratulated by a member of the congregation should not be misunderstood. There was no general approval of the speech on the part of local Christians,

1 Letters appearing April 23 and 25 1968.
2 M. A. Spry of Hanger Lane replying, April 27 1968, to Ann Dummett, April 24 1968.
3 Karanjia, April 25 1968; Nicholson and Anderson April 27 1968.

who were, on the contrary, 'doing their best to remove prejudice and create harmony'.[1] This letter was reprinted in the *Wolverhampton Express & Star*, whose editor, thanking Rees-Mogg for permission, said that his paper had already received 5,000 letters on the issue, very few of them up to *The Times*'s standard.[2]

Rees-Mogg was certainly open to the charge of living 'well away from the ghettoes of Wolverhampton'. The problems of large-scale coloured immigration were not very obtrusive in Smith Square, Westminster, or in rural Somerset. All the same, the stand he took is not invalidated by his lack of first-hand knowledge, which in any case he soon sought to remedy by a visit to the West Midlands. This was organised for him by the regional correspondent, Priestley, who wrote afterwards that it had been 'a great tonic to us all up here', and had done 'a great deal to improve our local contacts'.[3] Meanwhile the race controversy had given way to one on the ethics of transplants, following the first British heart transplant operation in early May. But there was a subliminal reminder in the picture of the National Heart Hospital's team of three, appearing on the front page on May 4, since one of them, S. Khoja, was dark-skinned.

1 April 26 1968.
2 Clement Jones to W.R.-M., April 27 1968.
3 Priestley to W.R.M., June 21 1968.

V

Haley's farewell • Cecil King and coalition • 'Student power' and the Paris événements • *Prague's blighted spring • Death in Hove*

AT THE END of 1967 Sir William Haley retired early from the chairmanship of Times Newspapers Limited, to move to Chicago as editor-in-chief of the *Encyclopaedia Britannica* (a post which did not suit him at all, and in which he did not last long). His place as chairman was taken by Kenneth Thomson.

On leaving *The Times* Haley opted for a lump sum of £15,750, with a pension consequently reduced from £6,000 to £4,500 a year. His departure was marked by various ceremonies and presentations. From the senior staff he received a Georgian silver box, presented to him by Iverach McDonald at a small gathering on December 19 1967, when both men made speeches that 'evoked a touch of emotion', and when Lady Haley was not forgotten, receiving a bouquet and a handbag.[1] Two days later there was a larger meeting, attended by Roy Thomson, members of the staff at all levels, pensioners, and others who had left the paper's service. Haley came to the meeting within hours of a motor accident on the Embankment which had left him with a gash on his forehead. After Denis Hamilton had paid a tribute to him, and given him a book containing 1,400 signatures, he replied with a speech in which he summed up his achievements as editor and praised some of his colleagues by name. But the speech's most notable feature was a ringing reassertion of his philosophy. Recalling that on a similar occasion at the end of his time as director-general of the BBC he had warned that 'the morons [were] on the march', he declared:

> What I am going to say now I have said before but I believe it so deeply that I will go on saying it until I die. The truth is that there *is* a difference between right and wrong, and there *are* things we should not be ready to compromise. There is no half-way house between honesty and dishonesty. There are things which are bad and false and ugly, and no amount of argument or

1 *Times News*, January–February, 1968.

> specious casuistry will make them good or true or beautiful. It is time that these things were said and time for the press to say them.

Such was the swansong of a man of absolute values in an increasingly relativist age.

On March 19 1968 Roy Jenkins introduced what Harold Wilson later described as 'the most punishing Budget in Britain's peacetime history',[1] proposing tax increases of £923 million in a full year. This received a somewhat bleak welcome from *The Times*. In his leader on the budget Rees-Mogg wrote:

> [Jenkins's] strategy involves him in great risks and it has involved him in individual decisions which seem exaggerated or mistaken. Yet there is underlying the Budget a coherent policy for strengthening the economy. It is a policy which has some chance, though perhaps not a very good one, of being brought successfully to fruition.[2]

The word 'exaggerated', as used, could only mean that in some respects the budget was tougher than it need have been. In the event it turned out to be not tough enough. (By contrast Jenkins's 1969 budget, though criticised by *The Times* from the opposite standpoint, proved in the event to be excessively severe.)

Despite such criticism Rees-Mogg remained extremely well-disposed towards Jenkins, though a less favourable view of him was represented in the paper by Jay. At the same time hostility to Wilson was unflagging. In the May borough elections Labour suffered sweeping losses, and the following day (May 10) the Labour-supporting *Daily Mirror* came out with a demand for Wilson's resignation under the headline ENOUGH IS ENOUGH. The piece was written and signed by Cecil Harmsworth King, a nephew of Northcliffe and chairman of the International Publishing Corporation (IPC) which owned the *Mirror*. His attack, claiming that Britain faced 'the greatest financial crisis' in its history, was particularly damaging since he had been, until writing it, a director of the Bank of England. *The Times*, while dissenting from his adverse view of the government's post-devaluation

1 H. Wilson, *The Labour Government 1964–1970*, p.513.
2 'Nasty but necessary', March 20 1968.

strategy, gave substantial backing to his onslaught on the prime minister:

> He has lost the confidence of senior Cabinet colleagues. In financial and business circles he is judged to postpone difficult decisions until it is almost, or quite, too late, and even then to shy away from their full consequences. By the public he is sensed to have become a weak Prime Minister, and one who is more adept at political presentation than fashioning policies. He stands in the way of any revival of confidence in a Labour administration. It cannot be assumed that a peaceful change of leader would in itself restore confidence and authority. It can be assumed that without a change those lost necessities will be a great deal more difficult to recover.[1]

Three weeks later King lost the the chairmanship of IPC in a palace revolution. His fellow-directors suddenly asked him to resign and, when he refused to do so, dismissed him. The reasons for this coup had more to do with his conduct of IPC than with the political line he had been taking, though both reflected an arrogance that many had come to regard as intolerable. Nevertheless his opinions were, for a time, much in demand, not least by Rees-Mogg, who in any case was somewhat attracted by his way of thinking. Both men were frustrated politicians, with conflicting mandarin and maverick impulses. Soon King was writing articles for *The Times*, and by the end of the year he had a five-year contract, including the use of a Rover 3.5 saloon with chauffeur. Like two of the paper's national directors, Lords Shawcross and Robens, Rees-Mogg shared at this time King's interest in promoting a coalition government, as the only alternative he could see to the Labour government under Wilson. In early December he went public with the idea in a three-column leader. After describing, in lurid terms, all that was wrong with the country, he wrote:

> The classic answer is well known. In circumstances of this kind the first thing that has to be done is to restore confidence in the ability of the Government to govern. The best way to do that is to have a coalition or national government to overcome the emergency. Such a government can assert its authority; it can check rising anarchy which shows itself equally in the universities,

1 'Can they still govern?' May 11 1968 (a Saturday). This leader was the joint work of Hickey and Jay, Rees-Mogg being doubtless in the country.

> on the football trains and on the factory floor. The hooliganism and wrecking tactics of a small minority can only threaten the nation if the nation passively submits to the threat . . .
>
> It is not difficult to conceive of a policy which would work, or of a government which could enforce it. It is much more difficult to see how to establish such a government, and almost impossible to see it being done before things get worse. Too many Conservatives still think that in two years' time they will inherit power at a general election like a plump chicken to put in the pot. It will not be like that. The nation has limited confidence in the Opposition on its own and two years is too long to wait.
>
> The obstacles in the Labour Party are even greater. The Prime Minister is a difficulty. No one can expect the Conservatives to serve under him; he is as much the architect of our misfortunes in 1968 as Neville Chamberlain . . . in 1939. No need to condemn him; scarcely now any need to discuss him; his astonishing complacency at every stage of his disastrous administration condemns itself.[1]

There was no indication of how the desired national government could, in practice, come about, nor any name proposed of a suitable person to lead it. For several days the correspondence columns were full of letters for and against the coalition idea, but it was significant that no major politician, indeed no major figure of any kind, gave it overt countenance. Whether or not it was a good idea, it clearly rested on a false premise, since the Conservatives were, in fact, to 'inherit power' in eighteen months' time. Moreover the not-worth-discussing Wilson would still be leading the Labour Party – would indeed be returning to the premiership – at the next election but one. Rees-Mogg's leader does not score heavily for prescience.

It was, however, a striking manifestation of his editorial independence, since he wrote it without even informing the editor-in-chief. Hamilton later recalled his 'intense anger' when, leaving for Switzerland with Roy Thomson on an early plane from Heathrow, he bought a copy of the paper and read the leader. In his view he ought to have been consulted about such a shift in policy, even though the editor was bound to have the last word.[2] And he must have been even more incensed to find, in Switzerland, that the article was 'widely attributed' to King.[3]

---

1 'The danger to Britain', December 9 1968.
2 C.D.H., op. cit., p.144.
3 C.D.H. talking to King on December 10 1968, as reported in the latter's diary entry for the following day. (King, op. cit., p.221.)

No doubt on his return he mentioned this to Rees-Mogg, who must have been scarcely less annoyed to hear that he was regarded abroad as King's mouthpiece. Within days he received a letter from King, whose contents and tone can only have added to his uneasiness:

> Dear Rees-Mogg,
>
> I have on recent occasions had lunch alone with the French, German and American Ambassadors, with the last of whom I am on very good terms. I have also had lunch with Sir John Stevens who is now a member of the Committee of Treasury at the Bank of England. I am giving Marsh lunch today and having lunch with Heath on Sunday. I have other less eminent but equally valuable contacts. I wrote a piece about the financial situation for the *Financial Times* 2–3 weeks ago, which they praised but did not print. Perhaps it was too realistic. Anyway I am going to Kuwait on January 7th but before that I am having lunch with Sir Maurice Parsons, Deputy Governor of the Bank, on December 31st. I should then know what is going on as well as anyone who does not see the secret figures. I am proposing to submit a piece that day for your approval. It is bound to be gloomy as the insiders all predict the collapse of the £ and the franc early in the coming year – by early I mean not later than April. Optimism is limited to academic economists and ministers.
>
> With all good wishes,
> Yours sincerely
> Cecil H. King[1]

Rees-Mogg's reply was guarded, with just a hint of coolness:

> Dear Mr. King,
>
> Thank you very much for your letter . . . I find these conspiracy allegations very tedious.

---

1 King to W.R.-M., December 16 1968. The American ambassador at the time was David Bruce. Richard (later Lord) Marsh was minister of transport in the Wilson government. King found him, at their lunch, 'not very informative'. 'He didn't see how a coalition could be established – under whom?' The meeting with Heath was less intimate than King's letter suggested. King and his wife (Dame Ruth Railton, founder of the National Youth Orchestra) were in fact invited, along with a number of others, to Heath's annual carol service at Broadstairs. 'There was no political talk. Ted always puzzles me. He is a nice man and an honest one . . . He has no understanding of politics or public opinion but then that is true of most politicians these days.' It was, perhaps, truer of King himself. (King, op. cit., entries for December 16 and 23 1968, pp.223 and 225–6.)

I should prefer to put off the article until February. I entirely agree with your view of the situation which conforms with what I have been able to learn, but I think it is important that we should not let these conspiracy mongers believe that *The Times* is running a campaign. If you wanted to write and place an article elsewhere early in January I should of course entirely understand and would be very happy to run it myself when we have given another six weeks or so for time to pass.

With many thanks and all good wishes for Christmas,

Yours sincerely

William Rees-Mogg[1]

King dethroned was becoming more maverick than mandarin, while for Rees-Mogg, secure on his editorial throne, it was the other way round. He did not wish to be involved in any conspiracy to destabilise the government by talking sterling down; still less when it would be thought that he was only a subordinate conspirator, working under King's dictation. King continued for some time to write for the paper, but his influence was already on the wane. In June 1969 Rees-Mogg returned an article of his on 'Insecurity', saying that it might 'lower the quality of the series', and in February 1970 another was returned, on 'Love'. In 1973 King's contract was terminated.[2]

One of the dangerous symptoms referred to in Rees-Mogg's coalition leader was rising anarchy in the universities. Student unrest was, indeed, a widespread phenomenon in the late Sixties, and it contributed to a feeling that 1968 might, like 1848, be a year of revolutions. In the West a general cause of it was the weakening of adult authority, already discussed in another context. But each country had additional causes of its own; in the United States, for instance, it was the Vietnam war that chiefly inflamed the campuses.

During the week May 27–31 the paper ran a series of articles on 'Students in Revolt', produced by Richard Davy with the help of

---

1 W.R.-M. to King, December 17 1968.

2 King's arrangement with *The Times* entitled him to £1,500 a year for five years, plus £500 a year for 'consultancy' and payments for individual articles. Under the last two headings payments to him had been made regularly, but under the first he had not been paid since January 1969. In January 1973, therefore, he was paid £6,000 to cover the four annual instalments still due to him, £500 for his last year's consultancy fee, and £1,000 to compensate him for the loss of car and chauffeur: a total of £7,500. (Enid Knowles, personal assistant to the editor-in-chief, to Cecil King, January 22 and February 13 1973.)

foreign correspondents throughout the world, and of Victoria Brittain as chief researcher in London. The first article had as its theme 'The lesson of campus violence – it gets results', and began by stating that the student population of the world had more than doubled during the past ten years. The second was on 'Guevara: symbol of eternal political youth'. The third described a number of contemporary student radicals, with pictures of Tariq Ali, David Adelstein, Daniel Cohn-Bendit and Karl-Dietrich Wolff. The fourth argued that there was no international conspiracy behind the revolt. The fifth and last discussed what the general public thought of students.

While these articles were appearing the news columns were filled with reports from Paris, where a student uprising seemed to be causing a crisis of the Gaullist regime. These *événements* gave acute topicality to the students series. In France the number of university entrants had quadrupled since the war, with most of the expansion occurring during the ten years since de Gaulle returned to power in 1958. But there had been no corresponding improvement in facilities, and the system of higher education remained overcentralised and, in many ways, old-fashioned.

The crisis could probably have been avoided if the authorities had acted with firmness at the outset. A demonstration by Sorbonne students, reinforced by ideological militants from the new suburban campus at Nanterre, was allowed to get out of hand. There was no intervention while barricades were set up in the Latin Quarter, and it then cost the police a night of violence to pull them down. Students occupied the university buildings, where they began to debate the transformation of society in continuous session; and the trouble spread to provincial universities. Meanwhile there was concurrent action by industrial workers, though the country's largest and Communist-led trade union, the CGT, did not sympathise with the students and was keen at first to settle with the government. At one point ten million people had stopped work, but the strike was never general and in particular food supplies to the capital were maintained.

In the early stages of the crisis first the prime minister, Georges Pompidou, and then President de Gaulle himself, were out of the country. Even when they were at home their manifest uncertainty how to handle the situation made it worse. There had already been signs that the president, now in his seventy-eighth year, was losing some of his legendary judgement and flair for action; and such signs became more apparent as the crisis developed. In a televised broadcast on May 24 he managed to convey an impression of weakness, and during the next few days he underwent a personal crisis, in which he was near to resigning and going into voluntary exile. But the evidence of a vacuum of power tempted the Communists into abandoning the caution they had hitherto shown. The CGT called for mass demonstrations demanding a Popular Front government, and this emergence of a serious Communist threat turned the tide of public opinion. De Gaulle returned to Paris, after a mysterious absence, and on the evening of May 30 gave a highly successful radio broadcast, in which he announced that parliament would be dissolved for fresh elections. The same evening there was a huge demonstration of his supporters in Paris, and when the elections were held they resulted in a Gaullist landslide.

The Times's coverage of these events was extensive, though inevitably somewhat confused. The News Team moved in and produced a lot of copy, while the correspondent in Paris, Charles Hargrove, also sent substantial reports. On May 30, the very day the government was about to reassert its authority, Patrick Brogan wrote an op. ed. piece on the achievements of the Fifth Republic, which to most readers must have seemed the equivalent of an obituary. The following day the lead story was 'French army reported to be surrounding Paris', and low down on the front page was a News Team report of the big Gaullist demonstration in Paris following the president's broadcast. On page 8 a piece by Charles Douglas-Home, on the detached attitude of the French army, contained a remark that was even more important than he may have realised: 'It is being said in Paris that the President . . . met two French corps commanders, General Massu from the French force in Germany, and General Hublet commanding all the divisions in north-east France'. The meeting, it was suggested, had taken place at Mulhouse.

De Gaulle had indeed met Massu, but at Baden-Baden, having flown there secretly by helicopter. (His daughter Elisabeth was at Mulhouse; hence, possibly, the mention of that place.) The meeting with Massu was decisive, partly because it reassured the president of the army's loyalty, but above all because it restored his personal morale. On arrival he had greeted the general with the memorable words '*C'est foutu, Massu*', but after two hours' talk he was back to his normal confident form. The full story and true significance of this fascinating encounter were not known for some time; meanwhile the rumour quoted by Douglas-Home was at least a near-miss.

The 1968 *événements* in Paris were, towards the end of May at any rate, seen as revolutionary by most British observers, including *The Times*. Some welcomed them as such; Paul Johnson, for instance, then editor of the *New Statesman*, echoed Wordsworth's rapture at the time of the original French Revolution (though he, like Wordsworth, later changed his position drastically). A more typical reaction, which was also that of *The Times*, combined a certain smugness at the discomfiture of one who was felt to have shown hubris, more especially at Britain's expense, with apprehension at the possible consequences for French democracy and the Western alliance.

In fact, the situation in France was never anything like as revolutionary as it seemed. Most of the students were more interested in establishing their right to cohabit (to 'make love not war') than in changing the basis of society, and most of the industrial workers who went on strike did so to improve their pay and conditions rather than to destroy the capitalist system. In 1789 Paris was a genuinely revolutionary place, from which revolution spread to the rest of the country. Hence Disraeli's comment that France was 'a kingdom with a republic for its capital'. By 1968 the revolutionary spirit, even in Paris, was more apparent than real.

What was true of France was even truer of other Western countries where social and political unrest occurred in 1968. The various movements were never desperate or comprehensive enough to threaten the established order. In one country of the Communist bloc, however, deep popular feeling seemed likely for a time to bring about real revolution. That country was Czechoslovakia.

In January 1968 Alexander Dubcek became first secretary of the Czechoslovak Communist Party, having previously been the Communist leader in Slovakia. His advent to power marked the Russians' abandonment of Antonin Novotny, who had ruled the country with an iron hand since 1953. He was detested not only as a particularly rigid and ruthless Stalinist, but also (in Slovakia) because of his contemptuous attitude to Slovaks. The Russians thought they could trust Dubcek, who had been educated in the Soviet Union and went out of his way to proclaim his loyalty to Communism and the Warsaw Pact. In welcoming his appointment they believed they would merely have to deal with an equally dependable, if more humane and generally acceptable, *apparatchik*. But they soon found that they had misjudged the man and, above all, the state of affairs in his country.

Even before Novotny fell there had been some economic decentralisation and a limited relaxation of censorship. But these changes only made people more avid for freedom. Whatever Dubcek's intentions at the outset, he soon responded to the mood of the masses. At the beginning of February he made a speech extolling democracy, and at the same time removed a number of hard-liners, including the security chief, from the party hierarchy. Two months later he published 'The Czechoslovak Road to Socialism', a programme for creating freedom and diversity, political as well as economic, within a still ostensibly socialist state. This earned him the support of Tito and the Italian communists, and of course much admiration in the democratic West. But it was denounced by Brezhnev and other leaders of the Soviet bloc, and also caused some division between reformers and anti-reformers in his own party ranks.

In June Warsaw Pact manoeuvres were held in Czechoslovakia, after which Russian tanks lingered on in the country. But the reformers did not take the hint. They put Dubcek under increased pressure with their 'Two Thousand Words' demanding continuous movement towards democracy. A period of parleying ensued, with the Russians apparently uncertain what to do; and at the beginning of August their tanks were withdrawn. But on August 20 they returned, together with units from East Germany, Poland, Hungary and Bulgaria. Dubcek was taken to Moscow where he was subjected to rough treatment. At the end of the month he effectively capitulated to Russian demands, though he remained formally in office until the spring of 1969 – a very different spring from the previous year's.

At the time of Dubcek's appointment as party leader, in January, *The Times* shared the generally sceptical view of him.[1] But when, the following month, Richard Davy was in Prague, he quickly sensed that big changes were on the way. Since the Thomson take-over Davy had been roving correspondent in Eastern Europe, with a car and ample expenses.[2] Though he went down with 'flu soon after his arrival in Prague, and so was afraid he would be scooped by other British journalists, in fact what he gathered from his sources gave the paper a notable scoop, which took the form of an op. ed. piece, dateline Prague February 23, entitled 'Breath of freedom in Czechoslovakia'. In this he said that the Dubcek regime was attempting 'nothing less than a fundamental reconstruction of the political system designed to separate the functions of party and state and introduce elements of real democracy'. The impact on Prague's intellectual life was 'dramatic'; once again the pre-communist past was becoming 'a legitimate source of inspiration', with, for instance, *Literarny Listy*, magazine of

1 'Nothing startling should be expected of the new leader, MR. ALEXANDER DUBCEK' (leader, 'Promotions in Prague', January 1968).
2 He had been on the paper's editorial staff since 1955, and a special writer on foreign affairs since 1961.

the Writers' Union, running 'a witty article on the toleration edict of the Emperor Josef II'. It was obvious to Davy that 'the original heart of central Europe' was 'beginning to beat again in place of the Russian transplant'.

In March Davy visited Poland, but there was no spring in the air there and he was soon thrown out. Rees-Mogg wrote to commiserate with him, and to thank him for the 'really brilliant work' he was doing.[1] Though he was called home to edit the 'Students in Revolt' series, he returned to Czechoslovakia and was there on and off until shortly before the the Russians invaded. Another of the paper's foreign correspondents who reported at the time quite often from Prague was Dessa Trevisan, a Yugoslav married to an Italian. Towards the end of May Charles Douglas-Home visited the country and formed the interesting view that there might be some danger for the West if the Dubcek experiment were to succeed. A genuinely democratic socialism might, he argued, lead 'to a western Communist Party assuming a new respectability which the Communists have not yet had in sufficient measure to carry them over the threshold of government.[2]

Douglas-Home was in the country again two months later, when Russian forces were still there after the Warsaw Pact manoeuvres, though supposedly in limited and decreasing numbers. At Zilina, on the Slovak-Polish border, he was detained at gun-point and held for eighteen hours before being ordered out of the country. Back in England, he gave a full account of the incident in an op. ed. piece, stating that the size of the units he had seen made a mockery of Russian claims to be withdrawing.[3] At about the same time Hodgkin spent a week in Prague, meeting many people in Davy's company, but finding it hard to distinguish truth from rumour.

He also found that most of the leading writers and politicians were on holiday, since July and August were 'as sacred on the Continent as the weekend in England'.[4] So far as the key politicians were concerned, this was an illusion. In late July they became involved in talks with the Russians and other Warsaw Pact 'partners', held at places near the Soviet border and at Bratislava. Davy kept in touch with these talks through a member of the Central Committee, who was hearing all the time from his colleagues and who passed on what he heard in the relative safety of pseudo-casual walks in the streets of

1 W.R.-M. to Richard Davy, March 27 1968.
2 Op. ed. piece appearing on May 24 1968.
3 July 27 1968.
4 Hodgkin diary: recollections of Prague visit written up later, on September 1 1968.

Prague. Yet what Davy heard was, through no fault of his informant, misleading. The mere fact that the Russians were talking, combined perhaps with the seasonal atmosphere noted by Hodgkin, created a false sense of security. As a result the invasion on August 20 took everybody by surprise, and when the tanks rolled into Prague neither Davy nor any other representative of *The Times* was there.

For on-the-spot reporting the paper had to rely, at first, on Tad Szuk of the *New York Times*. But every day for a week there were op. ed. pieces by Davy, whose remarkable informativeness was due to a stroke of luck. On the morning of the invasion a Czech journalist on the staff of *Literarny Listy*, who happened to be on holiday in London, walked into Davy's office at Printing House Square. His name was Igor Hajek, and he was equipped with a receiving set of exceptional power. Davy at once arranged for him and his radio to occupy a corner of the office, where, over the ensuing days, he was able to monitor broadcasts by dissident groups throughout Czechoslovakia. *The Times* thus had a monitoring service that was even better than the BBC's, because the Czechs at Bush House were *emigrés* who lacked Hajek's intimate knowledge of contemporary conditions and personalities in their homeland. The paper also showed to advantage as a journal of record by printing the full text of Dubcek's tragic address to his nation at the end of August.[1]

The Times's handling of the Czech crisis earned the paper a lot of admiration, and one of those who wrote to congratulate Rees-Mogg was his old teacher, Robert Birley:

> *Never*, I should think, in the long history of Pedagogy has any schoolmaster received quite the honour I have been granted during the last fortnight. For the Russian authorities have selected two English newspapers to attack – first, by Mr. Malik in the Security Council debate – the Editor of the *Observer*, and second [by] Izvestia – the Editor of *The Times* – and both were my pupils. I congratulate you most warmly – and incidentally I think the reporting and treatment of the Czech crisis in *The Times* has been absolutely first-rate.[2]

---

1 August 28 1968. Two days later the paper printed an extensive report of a recorded broadcast by Josef Smrkovsky, president of the National Assembly, in which he said that the country had been 'suddenly occupied by an enormous military power which it was absolutely hopeless and impossible to resist in like manner'. Smrkovsky had given Davy an interview in April. Though one of the earliest advocates of reform, he had also shown that he was aware of the need for caution.

2 Sir Robert Birley to W.R.-M., September 3 1968. Birley wrote to Rees-Mogg frequently, at length, and in his own hand. Rees-Mogg's replies tended to be relatively brief, and typewritten.

It is hard to guess which would have given the greater pleasure, Birley's approval or *Izvestia's* disapproval. Both were worth having.

A very old man, who had protested in vain against *The Times*'s less creditable handling of an earlier Czech crisis, died in a flat at Hove on August 11. He was John Walter IV,[1] great-great-grandson of his namesake who founded the paper in 1785. His death, which occurred three days after his ninety-fifth birthday, was inevitably described as 'the end of an era';[2] and he was, indeed, the last member of his family to play an important part in the paper's life, though he never exercised control.

As a young man he was active on the editorial side. In 1899 he covered both the disarmament conference at The Hague and the retrial of Dreyfus at Rennes. He also paid frequent visits to the paper's correspondents in foreign capitals, before becoming himself its correspondent in Madrid. From the time of his father's death in 1910 until the Thomson take-over in 1966 he had to be content with the role of junior partner, first to Northcliffe and then to Major (later Colonel) J. J. Astor, whose emergence as chief proprietor after Northcliffe's death he did much to promote.

With his knowledge of Europe he saw the danger of appeasing Hitler, and when, in the spring of 1938, *The Times* published a leader arguing that Czechoslovakia should cede the Sudetenland to Germany, he remonstrated strongly with the editor, Geoffrey Dawson. But he had neither the power nor – since he fully supported the principle of editorial independence – any desire to impose his view, and Dawson unfortunately did not defer to his superior wisdom.

The paper's obituary of him on August 12 was substantial and warm in tone, but made no reference to his behind-the-scenes stand against appeasement. Nor was there any leader to salute the last of the Walter proprietors. In the course of his long life he had seen the family lose control of the paper, after nearly a century and a quarter. He had seen Northcliffe come and go, and then the Astors. Finally, he had seen the Thomsons come, but even he could not live quite long enough to witness their departure.

---

1 The number attached to him in this History, though he preferred to be known as John Walter V out of regard for the memory of his paternal uncle John, who was drowned in 1870 before he could succeed John Walter III (his father) as chief proprietor.
2 *Times News*, July–September 1968.

VI

Uneasiness in the board room • Men on the moon • Overboard for Biafra • Northern Ireland: troops in • Lady in waiting

BY THE AUTUMN of 1968 it was becoming clear that the paper's economic strategy, essentially inherited from the previous regime, was not fulfilling the best hopes of the new management. The daily net sale was in the region of 425,000, but in order to achieve this more than 500,000 copies had to be printed, which imposed almost intolerable strain on all departments. Existing capacity did not, in fact, allow for printing more than about 460,000 copies per issue without detriment to the general standard of the product, more especially to editorial and distribution schedules.

The capacity in question was not simply mechanical, but a combination of mechanical and human. On the human side, it was traditional that *The Times*'s presses could be run only at the rate of 28,000 copies per hour unless special payments were made to increase the rate to 35,000–40,000 copies per hour. Management was, therefore, faced with the prospect either of not being able to expand the circulation much beyond the level it had reached, or of having to incur costs that would make nonsense of budgetary targets.

Advertisement revenue could not be looked to as the potential saviour. Though this had improved overall by 20 per cent since the autumn of 1967, the competition of the *Daily Telegraph* with its big circulation, and of the *Financial Times* with its unique advantages, severely limited the scope for improvement. The advertising people took the view that until the paper's circulation reached 500,000 little could be done to increase its share of the available business.[1]

In these circumstances the demands of the proprietor began to seem incompatible with the extent of his readiness to commit resources. On September 12 Hamilton informed his colleagues on the executive board that Thomson had so far waived his dividends in order to finance the paper, but that he wished to see a sales figure of 500,000

1 Management committee, November 18 1968.

swiftly attained. A month later Hamilton had to say that development expenditure on *The Times* would continue until the ABC figure reached a six-monthly average of 500,000, *or until December 31 1969, whichever was the sooner.*[1] In other words, Thomson was no longer willing to provide an open-ended and indefinite subsidy for the paper, if indeed that had ever been his true intention. He was effectively setting a deadline for the paper to be in the position of paying its way, and that deadline was little more than a year ahead.

The aim was totally unrealistic and should have been opposed as such at the outset. It never had been sensible to imagine that the circulation could be raised to a level remotely competitive with that of the *Daily Telegraph* at a cost of only £5 million in development expenditure, when there was so much else to which money was being committed, notably the attempt to produce a business section that might compete with the *Financial Times*. Moreover, the substantial increase in circulation that was achieved during the first two years of the Thomson regime owed much to the policy of holding down the price, which in turn distorted the economics of the paper and inevitably added to the need for subsidy. For *The Times* to have any chance of growing on the scale, and at the speed, that Thomson demanded, it was necessary for a very much larger sum than £5 million to be invested in its development. If this was not apparent at the end of 1966, it should have been abundantly so by the end of 1968.

Even at an artificially competitive price the paper was not quite achieving its circulation targets, and the overprinting involved in trying to maximise sales normally resulted in a high figure of unsold copies, which adversely affected budget performance. Yet in mid-1969 Hamilton was still saying that 'the rule must be availability'.[2] He was also planning a sales drive in the autumn, to be carried through to the following Whitsun, even though he admitted that the price might meanwhile have to be put up, because it would be impossible to do this during the period August 1970 to February 1971, when the country would be switching to decimalisation. In the circumstances it is hard to understand how he or any of his colleagues can have seen any hope of a breakthrough within the time-limit set by Thomson.

No doubt he was uneasy about the strategy, but he was so committed to it, and under such pressure from the proprietor, that he could only keep slogging ahead like the British army on the Somme. Most of his colleagues by now also had their reservations, which can

1 TEB, October 17 1968. (Author's italics.)
2 TEB, June 26 1969.

sometimes be inferred from their recorded comments. Yet nearly all were in some degree the victims of wishful thinking, which Thomson himself did much to encourage by the uncertain signals that he gave. In the very month that his supply of development money for the paper was due to expire, he was still capable of writing: 'I am confident that *The Times* will be commercially viable in the early Seventies. *Until then I will see that it is not stinted for anything it needs*.'[1]

Rees-Mogg, for his part, was among the more extravagant optimists, looking forward to a circulation of up to a million 'by the second half of the 1970s'.[2] In any age other than the present such an aspiration could have been described as reaching for the moon. But the phrase was out of date, because American astronauts were now achieving in reality what the Thomson *Times* was failing to achieve metaphorically.

In accordance with Rees-Mogg's policy of greater coverage for science, special efforts were made to ensure that the first moon landings were well reported. During the preparatory period *The Times* printed, on January 6 1969, colour pictures of the earth taken from sixty miles above the moon: the first time news pictures in colour had ever appeared in the paper. That morning, on the BBC's Radio 4 *Today* programme, Cudlipp was interviewed about what was clearly regarded as a significant event. One of the interviewers described the pictures as 'really excellent' and added that it was 'quite a surprise' to see them in *The Times*. But another, less obligingly, said that he had seen them the previous week in the *Reading Evening Post*. Cudlipp explained that local papers had a different printing process, which was 'all right for small-circulation papers' and could take colour. Hamilton was delighted with the pictures, soon afterwards telling the management committee that they 'opened the concept of using colour aggressively in advertising'.[3]

Meanwhile confidential notes were circulating in anticipation of the landings projected for the summer. On New Year's Day Colin Webb wrote to John Grant, with a copy to the editor, drawing attention to the fact that the Americans were planning to send two men to the moon in July. As a result the features editor, James Bishop, made detailed dispositions which he outlined in a memorandum on

---

1 Article in *CPU*, quarterly journal of the Commonwealth Press Union, December 1969 issue. (Author's italics.)
2 TEB, November 12 1968.
3 January 20 1969.

January 23. Pearce Wright, the paper's science reporter, was to be sent to Houston for some months in advance of the target date. His work was to be backed up by the staffs of the Washington and New York offices, and nearer the time by a member of the News Team. There was to be colour, again, in connection with the landings, and features on as many aspects of the space programmes, Soviet as well as American, as could be included. Bishop stressed the importance of secrecy: 'Please do not leave this paper where others might see it'.[1]

On the whole the planned coverage worked out well. On June 3 there was an 'edge of the moon' colour inset, which was the occasion for bringing the production figure to the all-time record of 574,000, with an estimated sale of over 490,000 for that particular issue. As the time for the landings approached, the activities of NASA were regularly and expertly reported from Houston; and on July 21 man's first steps on the moon were duly celebrated by blockbuster reporting on the front page, and by a Rees-Mogg leader in extra-large type entitled 'Wonder of the World', in which he compared the astronauts' achievement with 'the conquest of Everest or the great voyages of discovery'. (The second was a correct analogy, but the first, surely, not correct at all. With the oxygen and other facilities available to the Hunt expedition the conquest of Everest, though quite a distinguished feat, was in no way comparable with what such pioneers as Columbus and Vasco da Gama had achieved, or with the latest human triumph achieved by Armstrong and Aldrin.)

The leader went on to say that the conquest of the moon was also 'a reproach', since 'the nation which personifies this and other advances is unable to solve social problems which should perhaps be simpler but are more difficult'. In a rather striking passage Rees-Mogg considered what might follow from the event:

> It may be little more than a brilliantly lit blind alley, a successful act of scientific curiosity, but also an intrusion into an atmosphere so alien that it will remain of as little use to man as the much more convenient explorations of the polar regions . . . or it may lead to a whole series of further explorations, to a new way of life for man . . .

The idea that the human race might resign itself to being earthbound in perpetuity, or until it came to share the extinction of the dinosaurs,

1 Bishop had been features editor since 1965, having joined the paper in 1955 and served as its correspondent in New York 1960–4.

shows the editor's mind at its most conservative; though typically it remained open to a more adventurous hypothesis.

When the second pair of astronauts (Conrad and Bean) travelled to the moon in November, the paper recorded the event less lavishly but with thoughtful accompanying comment. Shortly after the launch, while the men were still on their way to the moon, there was a leader written by Wright in which he described a profound difference of opinion within NASA on the desirability of further manned space flights in the immediate future:

> The scientists can make a good case for advancing science in planetary exploration and space astronomy with unmanned craft which would cost a fraction of the more showy manned flights. They can claim with some justification to have proved their case by the Mariner experiments in August, when unmanned satellites discovered so much about the nature of the surface and atmosphere of Mars.[1]

NASA soon decided, indeed, to abandon the over-ambitious plan to send manned craft to Mars in just over ten years.

All the same the successful second landing on the moon was greeted by the paper in more unequivocally positive terms than the first. In a leader, also by Wright, it was stated: 'No matter what the future of manned space flight, the adventure in space has left an indelible mark on man. He is no longer bound by the earth and its atmosphere'.[2]

In the late 1960s Western opinion was stirred to the depths by a foreign struggle scarcely less emotive than the Vietnam war. This was the civil war in Nigeria, which followed a declaration in May 1967 by Colonel E. O. Ojukwu, leader of the Ibo tribe, that the eastern region of the country would become independent under the name of Biafra. As always in such matters the rights and wrongs of the dispute were complex, but the case for maintaining Nigeria's unity as a federation was strong, and the Nigerian government continued to be recognised by most of the world's states, including Britain. Biafra was recognised by only four states, all African: the anglophone Zambia and Tanzania, and the francophone Ivory Coast and Gabon.

Yet support for Biafra was far greater than the extent of formal

---

1 'Science overshadowed', November 15 1969.
2 'The costly moon', November 25 1969.

recognition suggests. France provided arms through its African associates, thereby prolonging a war which might otherwise have ended in 1968. Moreover the French government gave its moral blessing to Biafra, while hinting that formalisation of the process was only a matter of time. In addition two formidable lobbies, affecting political and public opinion in many countries, were largely mobilised on behalf of Biafra. Since Ojukwu and many other Ibos were Roman Catholic, Roman Catholics worldwide tended to be Biafra-sympathisers; and since Egypt was actively helping the Nigerian government, Israelis and Zionists everywhere had a similar tendency.

The contrasting images of the two principals were very important, too. The Nigerian leader, General Y. D. Gowon, with trim moustache, was a Protestant Christian from the predominantly Muslim north of the country. He was decent and courageous, and later to prove magnanimous in victory, but meanwhile no match at all for the bearded Ojukwu in the art of public relations. Gowon's origins were humble, and his finishing schools had been Sandhurst and Camberley (though in later years, after his fall from power, he was to study at Warwick university and earn a Ph.D.). Ojukwu was the son of a millionaire holding a British knighthood, and his education had involved reading history at Oxford as well as military training at Eaton Hall. Of the two, Gowon 'looked and sounded far less assured, certainly honest and well-meaning but naïve and lacking in confidence', whereas Ojukwu was 'a born talker' with 'a politician's sense of theatre', creating 'a marvellously reassuring atmosphere of sanity, patience and moderation'.[1]

The British government not only recognised federal Nigeria, but was a vital supplier of arms to it, as was the Soviet Union (a fact which did nothing to advance the Nigerian cause in the United States, quite apart from other pro-Biafran influences at work there). Support for Nigeria against the attempted secession also came from the Conservative opposition in Britain. But by 1969 the British press and other media were giving a lot of coverage to the horrors of the war, from which Biafra generally came across as the victim. Of no paper was this more true than *The Times*, which in February went overboard for Biafra, editorially as well as in the news columns.

This development coincided with Rees-Mogg's decision to send Winston S. Churchill junior to Nigeria. His recruitment for the paper was announced with some ceremony on January 4 1969:

---

1 John de St. Jorre, *The Nigerian Civil War*, p.94 and p.131.

> Mr. Winston Churchill will be taking on special and exclusive assignments for *The Times* during 1969. He will be working particularly in the foreign field, covering international crises and emergencies wherever they may occur. His reports will supplement those contributed by the regular team of *Times* correspondents throughout the world.

Soon afterwards *Times News* recorded that, although Churchill's illustrious grandfather and namesake had never written for *The Times*, his *World Crisis* had been serialised by the paper in 1923, and early in his career he had 'nearly' become a war correspondent for it. At the battle of Omdurman in 1898, when two of its correspondents were wounded, Churchill senior 'filled the gap with a long descriptive telegram, but it wasn't sent because Kitchener refused to allow a serving officer to act as a war correspondent'. On the other hand young Winston's father, Randolph, 'did get into print in *The Times* on frequent occasions'.[1]

The new recruit was twenty-eight. His previous experience of journalism had been covering the Six-Day War, and the recent Democratic Convention in the United States, for the *Evening News*. Another man might have felt crushed by the name he bore, but unfortunately he seems not to have found it crushing enough. He had no special qualifications for writing about a civil war in West Africa, and lacked the genius which, in rare cases, can atone for ignorance. Nevertheless his reports from Nigeria were, from the first, exceptionally self-confident and opinionated.

Swiftly making up his mind that the Nigerian government was a ruthless bully under sinister foreign influence, he moved to Biafra and from there started filing highly tendentious stories. On February 21 the paper's front page carried one, dateline Umuahia the previous day, under the headline 'Winston S. Churchill reports from Biafra. Civilians die in bombing raid on clinic':

> At 10.08 local time today the town of Umuahia was bombed by a Nigerian Air Force jet. The Russian-made, twin-engine bomber made its run-in from the north . . . releasing its bombs at an altitude of 1,000 ft. over the most densely populated area of this town of 40,000 inhabitants which has been swollen to more than 200,000 by the influx of refugees . . . A clinic for nursing and pregnant mothers was in session . . . The bombs landed on the

1 *Times News*, January-February, 1969.

> clinic, demolishing it . . . Eight people were killed and more than 20 wounded, all of them civilians . . . I saw the naked and mutilated bodies of a young woman and her infant child lifted on to a sheet of corrugated iron . . . A Roman Catholic priest, making the sign of the cross in blessing, leant over the corpse of an old man whose body had been lacerated by flying fragments.

A few days later Churchill was reporting again from Umuahia, to which he seemed intent on giving the emotive power in the outside world that Guernica had acquired during another civil war: 'It is clear that the Egyptian pilots hired by Nigeria regard Biafra as a free bomb zone'.[1] He might have added that his grandfather and the British air staff had taken the same view of German cities during the Second World War, with consequences far more cruel and devastating than anything seen in Biafra.

Commenting on Churchill's reports of Nigerian air raids, Rees-Mogg wrote:

> The British and Russian Governments, as the most important powers supplying arms to the Federal Government . . . share a special responsibility for these events . . . For a British Government to supply arms to forces committing these deliberate acts of terror and slaughter must damage and has damaged the moral standing of Britain in the world. The Government should take immediate action to inform itself about these matters and should take every step in its power to bring these atrocities to an end.[2]

Yet if Britain's 'moral standing in the world' had survived its own 'deliberate acts of terror and slaughter' against Cologne, Hamburg, Berlin, Dresden and other major cities in Germany, there was surely little to fear in that respect from the supply of arms to Nigeria.

In the same leader it was stated that Churchill was returning home after his brief foray, and that 'special reports' by him, summing up his impressions, would be published during the coming week. These appeared as four op. ed. pieces at the beginning of March.[3] In the last his conclusion was that the Nigerian federation could not be sustained, and that a military solution was out of the question. This view was endorsed by the editor in further leaders.[4] In the correspondence

1 February 26 1969.
2 'The Biafra bombings', February 28 1969.
3 March 3, 4, 5 and 6 1969.
4 'Not a war to be won', March 13 1969; 'To stop the war', March 14 1969.

columns there were plenty of letters supporting Churchill, though also some criticising his one-sidedness, including a dignified protest from the Nigerian high commissioner.[1]

Within a year his judgement of the future course of events was dramatically falsified when Biafra collapsed and the Nigerian federal forces achieved a comprehensive military victory. Roy Lewis, the paper's acknowledged expert on Africa, had always predicted that this would be the eventual outcome, but he was not sent to cover the war and his opinion was politely disregarded.[2] Why did Rees-Mogg lose his balance on the Biafran issue? Since he knew virtually nothing of black Africa, his views could only be second-hand. Were they also prejudiced? At the time he was attacked, by John Junor in the *Sunday Express*, for being part of a Roman Catholic conspiracy in support of Biafra; but he indignantly rejected the charge that his line on the subject reflected religious bias.[3]

Some years later a Nigerian, who had written his doctoral thesis at London university on the international aspects of his country's civil war, wrote to Rees-Mogg to ask why *The Times* was converted to the Biafran cause in 1969. Rees-Mogg replied:

> The reason . . . was quite simple and had nothing to do with religion. We sent more than one correspondent to cover the war and we found in each case that our correspondents came back and advised us to support the Biafran side. The crucial instance of this was the reporting of Mr. Winston Churchill. He is of course not a Roman Catholic and went to Nigeria with an open mind but basically with Federal sympathies. He became a convinced supporter of Biafra as a result of his work there and as I had sent him to Nigeria in order to help form the paper's view I was naturally very much influenced by that.[4]

This explanation, though doubtless sincere, is somehow not very convincing. It fails to explain why Lewis, the obvious man to have sent to Nigeria, was not sent, or why the judgement of a very young

1 March 5 1969.
2 Lewis, who had joined the paper from the *Economist* in 1961, was not strictly a member of the staff between 1967 and 1971. But during this interlude he continued to work for the paper much as before, though as an outside contractor. When the Nigerian civil war ended Rees-Mogg did send him, belatedly, to report on the country.
3 W.R.-M. to John Gordon, editor-in-chief of the *Sunday Express* April 16 1969, and Gordon's reply, April 18 1969.
4 Dr. Fred Ogunbadeho to W.R.-M., March 14 1975, and W.R.-M.'s reply, March 25 1975.

man with negligible background knowledge was treated as oracular after only a few weeks in the country. One is tempted to suspect that the editor was more influenced than he realised himself by a lobby that swayed the feelings of so many of his co-religionists, and that Churchill's reports were persuasive because they reinforced a definite, if unconscious, prejudice.[1]

Within the United Kingdom as well there were growing signs, in 1969, of a civil conflict involving tribal and religious passions, also with a potent international dimension. This was a revival of the age-old Irish Question, which had bedevilled British politics in the nineteenth and early twentieth centuries, but which had been quiescent since the 1921 Irish Treaty and the subsequent defeat of those who rebelled against it in the South.

The immediate causes of what happened in Northern Ireland in the 1960s are fairly easy to explain. After partition, the Protestant and Unionist ascendancy there was maintained for four decades with stubborn immobilism, more especially during the twenty-year rule of the first Lord Brookeborough, described in his *Dictionary of National Biography* entry as 'a lazy man of limited ability and considerable charm'. At the same time the Free State in the South was turned, mainly by Eamon de Valera, into an inward-looking and somewhat priest-ridden republic, whose neutrality during the Second World War was thought by many in the United Kingdom to have cost thousands of British sailors' lives and made the Battle of the Atlantic a far closer-run thing than it need have been.

In 1963 Brookeborough was succeeded as prime minister of Northern Ireland by a man of a different generation and outlook, Terence O'Neill (later Lord O'Neill of the Maine). O'Neill took the initiative in holding meetings with the Irish Taoiseach, Sean Lemass, who was a veteran of the 1916 Easter Rising but nevertheless also keen to put

---

1 But Rees-Mogg was not alone in admiring Churchill's Nigerian reports. James Bishop, the features editor, wrote on March 6 1969 to thank him for 'making such a splendid start' to his association with *The Times*, and to say that his reports would 'prove to be a turning point in British policy'. Churchill's association with the paper did not, in fact, last all that long. After numerous further assignments in 1969, in Iran, Israel, Egypt and South Africa, as well as reporting on the homeless in Britain, and after a trip to Australia in February 1970, his appearances in the paper became infrequent and there were arguments about the terms of his contract. In October he left, with a letter of thanks from Rees-Mogg assuring him that his coverage of Biafra would be 'part of the history of *The Times* in recent years' (October 2 1970). So indeed it is.

relations between the two parts of Ireland on a better footing. For a time O'Neill's policy transformed the atmosphere, though his aloof and rather condescending manner made it hard for him to win affection, as distinct from respect, in any quarter. Moreover his failure to consult his colleagues before inviting Lemass to Belfast made him vulnerable to rivals on his own side, who could exploit the feeling of hard-liners that he was a traitor to the Protestant and Unionist cause.

Even so his experiment might have succeeded but for a combination of bad luck and bad judgement. The bad luck was that 1966 marked the fiftieth anniversary of the Easter Rising, and in an island where historical, or quasi-historical, memory is a perennial bane this was bound to be an occasion for demonstrations by Nationalists. To have banned them would have been inconsistent with his more liberal approach, yet by allowing them to take place he aroused traditional Unionist fears and resentments. There was still much support for him, however, among ordinary people in both communities, and when in late 1968 he broadcast an appeal for reconciliation the response was overwhelming. Had he then immediately held an election in the province, for which there was just enough time before Christmas, he would probably have been returned with a decisive mandate. But unfortunately he delayed until the New Year, and the delay was fatal, because meanwhile the spirit of goodwill resulting from his broadcast was largely dissipated.

In January a Nationalist march from Belfast to Londonderry led to clashes with hard-line Unionists, and the election, when it was held, gave him only a technical victory, not the landslide that would have given him the authority for further bold measures. Delaying the election was his crucial error of judgement.[1] Soon afterwards he was replaced as prime minister by a less adventurous Unionist, James Chichester-Clark (later Lord Moyola).

At this period *The Times's* coverage of Northern Ireland was intermittent and patchy. There was no regular correspondent there, nor would one be appointed for several years yet. The affairs of the province were normally covered by the paper's North of England correspondent, John Chartres, as an additional chore. Only when there were riots or other obviously newsworthy occurrences were people sent from London to report them *ad hoc*. Rees-Mogg himself took

1 Even Bernadette Devlin had tried to persuade her radical Nationalist colleagues not to go ahead with the march, because she felt that in the ecumenical climate created by O'Neill's broadcast it would not command enough support from ordinary members of their community.

a curiously detached view of Northern Ireland, despite its growing importance. Perhaps the emotions deriving from his Irish-American ancestry conflicted with those of a patriotic and, on the whole, conventional English gentleman, leaving him confused on the Irish Question and reluctant to become seriously involved in it.

In general *The Times*'s attitude was typical of *bien pensant* opinion in Great Britain, in treating the civil rights movement in Northern Ireland more or less uncritically, while dismissing Unionist opposition to it as utterly prejudiced and benighted. For instance, when five members of the News Team were sent to observe a civil rights demonstration in Londonderry as 'independent eye-witnesses', their reports showed 'Loyalists' (the word pointedly used in inverted commas) invariably in a bad light, but contained no perceptible criticism of the demonstrators.[1] The truth was more complex. There was, indeed, considerable justice in the demand for improved civil rights for the Nationalist minority, but also a good deal of exaggeration and some falsification. Anyone in Britain might have been forgiven for believing that, until 1966, the minority was denied all political rights, whereas in fact it was only in local elections that the principle of 'one man one vote' did not apply. For elections to the Westminster Parliament and the provincial assembly at Stormont Nationalists had always been fully enfranchised. Moreover, if the minority in Northern Ireland had been truly oppressed, as was so often suggested, it is hardly likely that its numerical strength would have grown, as it did, substantially in the period following the Second World War, while the population of the Republic was declining.[2]

Unionists were not wholly wrong to regard the civil rights movement as a stalking horse for republicanism, whose real aim was not to secure fair play for the minority in Northern Ireland, but rather to impose that minority's will upon the majority. Yet extreme Unionists did their cause enormous harm by opposing all demands, whether reasonable or unreasonable, and by expressing themselves in the language of religious bigotry. Even moderate Unionists were no match for their opponents in the competition to influence outside opinion, since the Gaelic-Irish are far superior to the Scotch-Irish as communicators.

---

1 Op. ed. report, November 18 1968.

2 It is no answer to say that Nationalists/Roman Catholics stayed in Northern Ireland because they could not afford to lose its Welfare State benefits. Had they moved to Great Britain, as they were perfectly free to do, and as so many of their Southern co-religionists did, they would have had the same benefits with none of the oppression to which, it was claimed, they were subject in Northern Ireland.

In August 1968 the Ulster crisis entered a new phase with the despatch of British forces to assist in maintaining law and order, and more especially to protect the minority. The decision to send troops was precipitated by violence in Belfast and Londonderry on a scale that the Stormont government could not, by itself, control. On August 15 almost the whole of *The Times*'s front page was devoted to these events, with a headline across eight columns 'Five are killed in new Ulster riots'. The main story was that the Stormont government had called for troops to support the Royal Ulster Constabulary in Derry, and it was said that by the evening of the previous day 'the general situation had appeared calmer because of the arrival of 400 British troops'. The reporter in Derry was John Chartres, while Stephen Jessel and Julian Mounter were reporting from Belfast.

The paper's first leader the same day, written by Hickey, concluded that troops would be required in Northern Ireland 'in strength and for a longish period of time'. This in turn would necessitate 'some redistribution of political responsibility'.[1] It was clear, however, that the author was thinking only of redistribution as between the British and Northern Ireland governments. He was not anticipating the direct rule from London to which, before very long, what was happening would inevitably lead.

Next day there was another banner headline, 'Belfast rioters use machine guns', and an op. ed. piece by Douglas-Home, who had joined Jessel and Mounter in Belfast. In a leader Brogan hinted at the intractableness of the problem that the British were trying to tackle:

> The real moment of difficulty will arrive when the British Government starts looking beyond the barricades towards the next political stage. As the civil rights movement in the United States has shown, the removal of legal discrimination and the establishment of the principle of 'one man one vote' is not enough to eradicate the hatreds of generations. Even if the Stormont Government were to push through a complete civil rights programme, granting the Catholics' every last demand, relations between majority and minority in Northern Ireland would be saturated with suspicions. Both sides will be building legends out of the violence that has already taken place.[2]

---

1 'What the troops mean', August 15 1969.
2 'Arms over Ulster', August 16 1969.

Meanwhile the home secretary, Callaghan, who was the minister chiefly responsible for dealing with Northern Ireland and its devolved government, had been giving McDonald an off-the-record briefing. There was no doubt, he said, that the troops' intervention had 'radically changed the situation'. He stressed that they were under the control of Her Majesty's Government, not under that of 'Chichester-Clark and his men', who were therefore 'no longer in full control of Ulster'. He (Callaghan) was seeking to influence Stormont through the appointment of advisers, including senior policemen and a political officer to be attached to the GOC Northern Ireland. If the Ulster government were to prove incapable of governing, then HMG would 'have to consider setting aside the constitution'; but 'that point was by no means reached yet, and probably would not be'.[1]

At the end of the month Callaghan visited the province, and Fowler was sent to cover his visit. On August 29 there was a front-page picture of him receiving a 'warm welcome' from a woman in the Bogside. The years ahead would give his uniformed compatriots in Northern Ireland plenty of experience of warm welcomes of a different sort.

In November the paper's education correspondent, Brian MacArthur, had a long interview with the new shadow education secretary, Margaret Thatcher. Though at pains to indicate that her position would not be all that different from Sir Edward Boyle's, she gave MacArthur to understand that it was her distinctive intention to preserve 'a top tier of grammar schools within a national system of mostly comprehensive education'. Her other principal concerns would be 'how to obtain sufficient resources for education; manpower and the recruitment of science teachers and graduates; and defining how best central government should carry out its duty to promote education'.

Within a decade her doings and sayings would be occupying columns of the paper almost daily. But on November 7 1969 she may well have been content with a friendly interview appearing on page 10.

1 Memorandum from McDonald to the editor, August 15 1969.

VII

War of Hodgkin's article • Busting a police racket • Moment of truth • New talent • Treatment of the arts • Book pages • Lightning Waugh

AFTER A VISIT to the West Bank of the Jordan in the autumn of 1969 the foreign editor, E. C. Hodgkin, recorded his impressions in a turnover which provoked an exceptionally lively war of words. This territory (and the Gaza Strip) had been occupied by the Israelis since the Six-Day War, and Hodgkin found the mood of the Arabs there 'perhaps similar to that in occupied France at the beginning of 1942'. He described the severity of the occupation regime in some detail, showing how curfews and the destruction of houses were used as collective punishment, stating that suspects were often held for months without trial, and giving instances of disproportionately harsh prison sentences for young offenders. He also, more vaguely, alleged torture. 'A common belief in the occupied areas . . . is that anyone suspected of belonging to a guerrilla organization or of helping one in any way is tortured as a matter of routine, and there is a great body of evidence to support this belief.' (Perhaps for reasons of space the evidence was not adduced.)

To the Israelis' argument that tough measures were forced upon them he replied:

> Naturally, the Israelis say that everything is the fault of the guerrillas – the fedayin. If they would only stop their raiding and bomb throwing there would be no need for repression. Perhaps not. But it seems ingenuous to expect the Palestinian Arabs not to react to an alien military occupation as other people everywhere else react. Indeed, they have a stronger reason not to lie still because they fear that occupation is only the preliminary to annexation.

In Hodgkin's view, their fears were justified:

> Israelis see the Jordan River as historically and strategically a natural frontier. So the new settlements go up on the West Bank,

> the new buildings rise like mushrooms in and around Jerusalem, the new military roads and communications are constructed. These are evidence of a people determined to stay where they are.

Another reason for guerrilla activity was that the Palestinians could expect no support from the West, where double standards prevailed:

> If there are demonstrations in Prague against the Russian occupiers, they say, you applaud; if there are reports of torture in Greece you insist on investigations; if bombs go off in Athens you say this is only to be expected, and cheer; if South Africa keeps 'suspected terrorists' in gaol for months without trial you protest. But similar things can happen all the time in occupied Palestine, and the world remains indifferent.

Hodgkin concluded that the only hope of avoiding 'a long drawn-out war' lay in handing over the occupied territories to the United Nations 'for a transitional period'.[1]

In the large correspondence that followed this article most writers were merely rationalising their prejudices. The tendency was either to savage Hodgkin as an Arab propagandist or to hail him as a Daniel come to judgement. There was, however, particularly weighty support for him from John Reddaway, who had served as a UN relief commissioner on the West Bank and in Gaza during the Six-Day War and for a year afterwards. While acknowledging the 'humanity and objectivity' of the Israeli officer who had usually accompanied him as he went about his work, he nevertheless described Hodgkin's report as 'sober and accurate'. On the other hand Louis Velleman, an experienced Dutch correspondent who had recently covered the same ground as Hodgkin, and whose approach was, he claimed, 'too critical for some Israeli authorities', felt obliged to say that his conclusion on the general merits of the case was 'about the opposite of Mr. Hodgkin's'.

An ingeniously pro-Israeli letter from the maverick Labour MP Reginald Paget began by agreeing with Hodgkin that military occupation had continued too long, but went on to argue that it should give way to annexation, which was 'the only available alternative' granted that Israel's neighbours would not make peace or even acknowledge her right to exist. The Arab inhabitants of the occupied territories

1 'Grim reports of repression in Israel-occupied lands', October 28 1969. There was corroboration for what Hodgkin said about the punitive destruction of Arab houses in a report by Brogan from the West Bank that appeared the previous day, and in a Reuter's report from Gaza published on October 31.

should be invited to take an oath of loyalty, or be expelled with compensation for their property. There was plenty of room for them 'in the Arab lands which support scarcely half the population they carried in Biblical times'. Palestinian refugees should be absorbed by other Arab countries and given the chance to establish their personal independence, instead of being 'kept as propaganda exhibits'. Population movements were, after all, 'the normal consequence of unsuccessful war'.

A Conservative MP with Zionist sympathies, Philip Goodhart, pointed out that Hodgkin was allowed to go where he liked and talk to whom he liked during his visit, 'a freedom generally absent in Nazi-occupied France or Soviet-occupied Czechoslovakia'. The Middle East was 'a hard, tough part of the world', and Goodhart suggested it did 'not need much imagination to envisage the sort of occupation policy that the Arabs would have adopted in Israel if the outcome of the Six-Day War had been different'.

Some Zionist reactions were intemperate to the point of hysteria. In Parliament Julian Snow attacked *The Times*, implying an anti-Semitic motive for Hodgkin's article:

> Is it surprising to find that sort of article in *The Times* newspaper? Those of us who were politically conscious in the years 1938 to 1940 will remember the pretty friendly attitude of *The Times* to the Nazi Government. I am personally not surprised that that newspaper, which was friendly to the Nazi Government and its sinister and terrible anti-Semitism, should now see fit to publish an article like that.

In the same debate the Labour veteran Emanuel Shinwell accused the Tory MP Dennis Walters of anti-Semitism, a charge that Walters challenged him to repeat outside the protection of Parliamentary privilege.

After a few days Rees-Mogg entered the controversy with a leader in which he powerfully defended the paper's honour and the integrity of his foreign editor. He began by reaffirming the paper's basic support for Israel, and its opposition to El Fatah and 'the general intransigence of the Arab powers'. He found it 'interesting' that Hodgkin's article, and *The Times* generally, 'should be attacked with such passion by so many of the supporters of Israel'. After pointing to Hodgkin's record 'as a student of Middle Eastern affairs and as a conciliator rather than a propagandist' he turned to what had been said in the House of Commons by Snow and Shinwell:

> There are a number of things to be said about this response. In the first place it is obviously hysterical. If a calmly argued report of the conditions of the Arab people in the occupied territories is equated with the anti-Semitism of the Nazis, then nobody except an avowed Israeli propagandist can be allowed to discuss the state of Israel at all . . . *The Times*, like members of the House of Commons, is in the business of discussing public policy. We expect to be banged about from time to time and, on the whole, enjoy it rather than otherwise. We do not like being called anti-Semitic because that is a whole world away from our position. It is, however, clearly damaging to the interests of the state of Israel. It does Israel harm by pretending that she is a special kind of state which either can do no wrong or, when she does wrong, must not be criticized because of the memory of the wrongs that have been done to the Jews by other nations. In fact Israel's survival depends in the end upon her being accepted as an ordinary state, accountable for her actions, deserving of continuous scrutiny . . . Only an ordinary state will ever have ordinary neighbours.

He ended:

> There is no subject which needs closer scrutiny than the conduct of a military power in alien, hostile and conquered territory. Of course no British newspaper will ever lose the consciousness of the wrongs that the Jewish people have suffered in this century and are suffering or could suffer again in the eastern European countries. The wrongs of the Jews cry out to heaven, but they do not cry out so loud that the wrongs of the Arabs need not be heard.[1]

Anyone amenable to reason on the Arab-Israeli issue might have found this leader persuasive, but it did little to mollify Zionists, while anti-Zionists noted the explicit confirmation of a bias in favour of Israel. The leader was entitled 'To be fair to both', but the issue unfortunately was one on which fairness to both sides was impossible, since their interests were irreconcilable. Rees-Mogg, a moderate pro-Israeli who wanted a square deal for the Palestinians, was doomed to seem either too fair or not fair enough, according to the point of view. Yet he went to some lengths to avoid being pressurised, or of giving the slightest appearance of being open to improper influence.

---

1 November 1 1969.

When, in 1971, some ladies demonstrated outside *The Times*, and later gave him a bottle of Bristol Cream sherry as a Christmas present because he had treated them kindly, he solved the moral dilemma by keeping and drinking the sherry while sending a cheque for its value to the Chief Rabbi, to be applied to a charity of his choice.[1]

In the summer of 1969 two Scotland Yard detectives set out to blackmail a young South London criminal, Michael Perry. After handing him a piece of gelignite, ostensibly for his inspection, they took it back and warned him that his fingerprints on it would land him in gaol for several years unless he would either name a receiver of stolen goods whom they were seeking or make a payment to them of £200.

Perry felt that their conduct was violating the 'honour among thieves' principle. Though he had a record, he was a small-time operator whose activities were not normally such as would earn him a substantial prison sentence. To him and his mates it seemed that the detectives' trick was in breach of the rules of a game which they sometimes played with Scotland Yard. He mentioned his predicament to a friend who had earlier answered an advertisement from journalists on *The Times* investigating an antiques' burglary racket, and the friend advised him to approach *The Times* for help.

The task of interviewing Perry was entrusted to Gareth Lloyd of the News Team, who immediately asked another member of it, Julian Mounter, to join him. Both had learnt their trade on local newspapers, where they had much experience of reporting court proceedings and so had been made aware of the degree of thoroughness needed to establish a case that would stand up in court. After talking at length to Perry, and to others connected with him, Lloyd and Mounter were convinced that he was telling the truth. But they knew there was no way of proving his story to be true short of listening to conversations between him and the officers he said he was paying, Detective Inspector Bernard Robson and Detective Sergeant Gordon Harris, both of Scotland Yard's C9 division.

Perry's story suggested that the incident which had caused him to approach *The Times* might be only the tip of an iceberg of corruption. He and his friends alleged that in most units at Scotland Yard and in the London area there was someone who could be bought. This wider allegation was so serious that Rees-Mogg felt justified in giving the investigation his full backing.

The journalists first asked for permission to listen to a telephone

1 Exchange of letters, January 1972.

call from Perry to Robson and Harris, and permission was granted. Then a call was tapped which involved a third officer, Sergeant John Symonds of Camberwell police station. Symonds and Robson proposed meetings at which Perry would hand over money, and the journalists were authorised to record these meetings. In the event recordings of such encounters were carried out over a period of weeks, with the surveillance techniques becoming ever more elaborate.

Towards the end of the investigation meetings held in Perry's car were recorded on four tape-recorders. He had one tiny instrument strapped to his arm, and a microphone hidden under his jacket which transmitted to a vanity case held by a sound assistant standing at a nearby bus-stop or other convenient location, as well as to a third recorder in the car's boot. A fourth, also in the boot, was connected with a microphone under the dashboard. By these methods perfect recordings were obtained, which proved everything that Perry and his friends had alleged. In addition a photographer was used to provide a pictorial record.

Before each meeting Perry was searched, and Mounter would take the serial numbers of the bank-notes he was carrying. After each meeting he was stripped and searched again, when it would be found that the money was missing. He was also required to make a full statement on each occasion, as were the sound engineer and his assistant. Each night, moreover, Mounter and Lloyd made their own signed statements. At Printing House Square a large part of the home newsroom was turned over to the investigation. Banks of typists with headphones transcribed tapes of the detectives receiving bribes. Scores of documents were stored in heavy steel filing cabinets to which only the two journalists had keys. Somehow secrecy was preserved.

When the dossier was complete, Rees-Mogg decided that it should not merely be handed to Scotland Yard, where in the absence of additional pressure there might well be a cover-up, but that there should be simultaneous publication in the paper. So on the night of November 28, when next day's first edition was already out, Mounter and the news editor, Colin Webb, took a copy of it to Scotland Yard, together with reels of tape and a pile of documents. They were received 'politely but with an air of contempt'.[1]

In November 29's paper a compressed version of the story appeared on the front page under three-column headlines: 'Tapes reveal planted evidence. London policemen in bribe allegation'. The front page also reported a statement from Scotland Yard to the effect that notice had

1 Memorandum from Mounter to author.

been taken of the matter and that an inquiry was in hand. Inside, on the op. ed. page, there was a fuller account of the investigation, from which Rees-Mogg quoted key passages in his relatively short but pungent leader the same day:

> On November 5, in the course of a meeting outside the Grove public house, Detective Inspector Bernard Robson of Scotland Yard said: 'When I stuck that in your hand that's there for keeps . . . I told you in the car that with that jelly I would stand there, and believe you me you could say what you liked, and it would make no — difference. So don't think you've wasted your money. You've got off well because you haven't put up a buyer which I really wanted'.
>
> This . . . admits to planting evidence on a man who might be charged with a crime, admits to a willingness to commit perjury in order to obtain a false conviction, admits to making money in return for not prosecuting, and urges the young man to whom he was talking to act as an *agent provocateur* in order to allow the Inspector to arrest another man on a charge of receiving stolen goods . . .

The implication of remarks made by Detective Sergeant Symonds was 'particularly disquieting':

> [He] devoted some time to offering advice to the young man on how best to pursue a criminal career. In the course of that advice he implied that he would not be able to help the young man if he got into trouble outside the London area because 'country coppers are swedes' – that is, presumably, that they are too thickheaded to be corrupt – and elsewhere warnings are given against the uniformed branch in London. There is however a claim that this officer was in a position to look after his criminal clients in the Metropolitan area . . . 'I'm in a little firm in a firm . . . anywhere in London I can get on the phone to someone that I know I can trust, that talks the same as me . . .'
>
> This may have been exaggerated in order to impress but . . . It is important in justice to the Metropolitan police, and in particular to the plain-clothes branch, that the most stringent inquiry should now be made.[1]

November 29 was a Saturday, but the story was much discussed

1 The leader was tellingly entitled 'A little firm in a firm'.

over the weekend, with many questioning *The Times*'s methods. On Monday December 1 Maurice Edelman, a Labour MP who was also an author and journalist, was quoted as saying it was quite wrong to have 'denounced these police officers in a way which, had court proceedings already begun, would have constituted contempt of court'. The following day there was a report that the shadow cabinet felt 'deep disquiet' about what appeared to be trial by newspaper. A significantly different view, however, was expressed by Ted (Lord) Willis, creator of the TV series *Dixon of Dock Green* (which showed the police in a very favourable light). According to Willis: 'Every now and then a newspaper must come across a tremendous scandal where it is necessary to name names. Otherwise there is a danger, as one has known in the past, of an elaborate cover-up'. Explaining that under the Police Act 1964 alleged misdemeanours within the police were to be investigated by the police themselves, he commented: 'There are many of us who feel that this is wrong. We ought to have independent inquiries'.[1] Soon afterwards the home secretary announced that 'in view of the wide public interest someone independent should be associated with the investigation of allegations recently published in *The Times*'.[2]

The man appointed was Frank Williamson, HM Inspector of Constabulary. Though a policeman, he was formerly from the Manchester CID and in no way connected with the Met. It was the first time any outside officer had been brought in to help investigate an allegation against Scotland Yard, and as such was deeply resented in many quarters there. Among the other officers involved in the investigation there were some whose eagerness to arrive at the truth was, to put it mildly, open to question. One in particular, Chief Superintendent Bill Moody, was already suspected of corruption and later sent to prison for it. Lloyd and Mounter were made to feel that they were on trial themselves, and had good reason to fear that dirty tricks were being used against them. It would have been more suitable if the home secretary had excluded Met officers altogether from the inquiry. Yet Williamson, despite being only an individual from outside 'associated' with the work, was a man of such integrity and zeal that he managed to ensure that justice was done. Without him the investigation would probably not have resulted, as it eventually did, in the corrupt detectives' being charged, convicted and gaoled.[3]

---

1 December 1 1969. Surprisingly, no letters about the affair appeared in the correspondence columns during the week following disclosure.
2 December 9 1969.
3 Robson and Harris were tried in March 1972. Symonds skipped the country and was for some years a fugitive abroad, before returning to face trial in 1981, when he too was sent to prison.

In rejecting an appeal by Robson and Harris, Lord Justice Edmund-Davies went out of his way to praise the two journalists whose evidence had broken the racket:

> It would be churlish were we to fail to make mention of the great public service rendered by these two reporters. It was, it would appear, mainly their intrepidity and skill which laid bare the hideous cancer which, if unchecked, could have done even greater and incalculable damage to law enforcement.[1]

It was Rees-Mogg, however, who had to take the big decisions: first, to permit the use of tape-recorders and other forms of secret surveillance, and then to publish the story instead of merely handing over the evidence and hoping for the best. Of course he was excited at the thought of achieving a major scoop, but would not have acted as he did without believing that disclosure was in the public interest. There were many critics of his decision, including some within the office; but he had staunch support from people who mattered, notably Hamilton and the legal adviser to Times Newspapers, James Evans.

Callaghan, who was home secretary at the time, later conceded that events were to show Rees-Mogg had been 'only too correct' in assuming he had to publish the report without giving Scotland Yard prior warning.[2] Above all, the decision was approved by a man who knew too well the extent of corruption in the Met, but whose efforts to tackle it from within had so far been frustrated. Robert Mark, who was deputy commissioner at the time, writes in his memoirs:

> The method of revelation bordered on the sensational . . . It read more like the *People* or the *News of the World* than *The Times*. . . There are disadvantages arising from public disclosure on television or in newspapers of matters likely to be subject to criminal investigation and trial. A very important one is that a fair trial may not thereafter be possible. Another is that even if the allegations are true, the wrongdoer is forewarned and is given the opportunity to take evasive or other action. As a generalization it can fairly be said that such disclosures are rarely in the public interest . . . Why, then, did a newspaper with a worldwide reputation to sustain behave in this uncharacteristic manner? The answer is quite simple. The editor and his legal advisers did not

1 June 26 1973 (report next day in *The Times*).
2 James Callaghan, *Time and Chance*, p.254.

> believe that if the allegations against the detectives were disclosed privately to the Metropolitan Police they would be properly investigated. He decided, therefore, to bring the matter into the open even at the risk of prejudicing a fair trial for the accused. *At the time and in hindsight I thought his decision was absolutely right.*[1]

It can hardly have been a coincidence that Mark was appointed commissioner in 1972, with the top priority, as was generally understood, of cleaning up the Yard. By 1975 nearly 300 officers had been removed, by means of legal action or enforced resignation. Such were the benefits of *The Times*'s controversial disclosure. Though police corruption was far from being eliminated, a strong blow against it had, undoubtedly, been struck.

Rees-Mogg received an IPC Investigative Journalism award for his part in the business, and the last to grudge it to him were the journalists whose work on the ground he had sanctioned and loyally supported. Years later, when he came under attack for his role as vice-chairman of the BBC, Mounter, by now director-general of Television New Zealand, wrote from the other side of the world to defend him:

> While we waited for the trials of the police officers . . . my colleagues and I knew the true loneliness of journalists who have published only to be damned. [But] throughout this period, Sir William resolutely backed his staff and bravely repudiated criticism of . . . tough, adventurous, inquiring journalism. More than one executive at *The Times* wobbled under the pressure. Sir William did not . . . I have always been grateful for his solidarity in that situation and admired his stand on other occasions.[2]

No press award could have been more worth having than such a tribute, paid spontaneously and long after the event.

In September 1969 the publishing director, Derek Jewell, told his colleagues that, although *The Times's* circulation was continuing to grow in excess of estimates, 'we did not have the impetus we had two years ago and the curve was now beginning to flatten'. The print order for July and August had been forced down, to reduce the level of unsolds. This policy of avoiding too high a print order 'should ensure

---

1 Sir Robert Mark, *In the Office of Constable*, p.107. (Author's italics.)
2 Letter to the *Listener*, April 7 1988.

that by December the figure [would] reflect a true sales situation'.[1]

Other developments were to make the end of the year even more emphatically a moment of truth. On October 20 the paper's cover price was at last raised, from 6d to 8d,[2] with the result that the curve of sales, already flattening, turned down sharply. The December figure of 401,000 was 18,000 fewer than the previous December's. The Thomson regime's immediate goal of half a million was to remain a mirage, to say nothing of Rees-Mogg's even more ambitious projections. The average daily sale of 431,721 for the year 1969 was to prove the highest achieved in any year of the Thomson ownership. Even 400,000 was never again reached; the figure for 1970 was 388,406, and well before the end of the decade average sales would have fallen below 300,000.

On December 12 a letter was sent by the chief executive to every member of *The Times*'s staff, at his or her private address. The message conveyed in this letter could be summarised as 'the party's over'. The general assumption that Thomson would indefinitely subsidise the paper and finance its expansion was understandable enough in view of his various statements. But Hamilton himself had been brought up against the reality of a strictly limited commitment on Thomson's part, and it was now his unpleasant duty to explain the true position to the staff.

His letter began with upbeat paragraphs about the growth of the paper over the past three years. But before reaching the end of the first page readers were introduced to the bad news:

> However, there is another and alarming side to the picture. As fast as we take in more money we pay out more still in our costs of production. Our total revenue is now running at a rate 77 per cent better than 1966. The figure for our costs has jumped by 100 per cent.

Even after cutting back on promotion, and despite the price rise and an anticipated increase of £1.2 million in advertisement revenue, the following year's losses could be of the order of £1 million.

> Plainly this will not do. *After three years no-one is going to*

1 Minutes of Times Management Committee, September 22 1969. Jewell was viewed by traditionalists as a particularly disturbing representative of the Thomson management.

2 The board of TNL had given Hamilton discretion to choose the date for raising the price at its meeting on September 29 1969. The concessionary rate of 3d less than the cover price was retained for students, for whom the new rate was, therefore, 5d.

> *continue to pour in money at this rate* . . . The paper must break even in 1971. [Author's italics.]

Every department had to contribute to the campaign to increase revenue and trim costs. But the biggest contribution had to come in the area of wages and salaries, which was consuming over 51 per cent of the paper's revenue.

> The wages and salaries bill has increased by over 88 per cent in three years. It was £2,423,000 in 1966. It is £4,563,000 today, and will spiral still faster if we do not take action . . . Most of what we need can be achieved by voluntary departures and early retirement, on fair terms, to produce a smaller working staff.

He then touched on an issue which was to become all-important in the coming decade and beyond, but which had long been shirked by British newspaper managements:

> In addition, we should examine all restrictive working practices, some of which date back to a profitable and smaller paper but have no relevance whatsoever when *The Times* is struggling for its life. The larger the size of *The Times* the better our chances of breaking even – at present we hurt ourselves by quite disproportionate charges for big issues.

He said he was 'personally starting talks with executives and representatives of the chapels'.

Before long Printing House Square would be too small for producing *The Times*, so a site had been acquired in Gray's Inn Road, next to the existing *Sunday Times* site, where a new building for the paper would be erected. There would then be 'excellent working conditions and the most modern equipment' for both newspapers and the *Times* supplements in juxtaposition. The idea seemed logical, neat and cost-effective, but events were to show how dangerous it is to plan without due regard for tradition and the human factor.

The letter ended on a note of optimism which must have seemed a bit forced even at the time:

> We have a unique opportunity to develop ourselves into a really efficient organisation so that when we move we shall be soundly based for a great future. I personally face the future entirely confident there is sufficient goodwill and sense of responsibility.

> *The Times* will be 200 years old in 1985. Many who work on *The Times* today will thus be taking part in the celebrations of the first double century of a paper published daily in Britain throughout that time. You can judge the strength of my confidence when I say we are already planning histories and other activities for this great anniversary.[1]

In retrospect, the words have a sad irony. The double-century would indeed be celebrated, but in 1985 the paper would have a different owner and a different editor, and Hamilton's association with it would have ceased.

The impact of his letter was considerable, as it was meant to be. McDonald wrote to his son, Ian, in Washington in an attempt to soften the blow:

> It is to be taken seriously, of course, but not tragically; there is no crisis . . . There may be fewer foreign trips for one thing, and fewer men sent on a job. Some of the departments – I am not speaking of the editorial ones so much – have got swollen with staff and there may be a period when many vacancies are not filled . . . Nobody who is doing good work need have any fears.[2]

Inevitably, though, there was much uneasiness among the paper's journalists, and above all a sense of disillusionment. For three years it had seemed that nothing would stand in the way of improving and expanding the paper; more especially that editorial activity of all kinds would be conducted without serious financial constraint. Now it was felt that the paper was returning, if not to Haley's predicament of counting candle-ends, at least to a state of relative austerity. The new regime's confident morning was at an end, and the spirit of it would never be recaptured.

Nevertheless, in a 'strictly confidential' memorandum at the beginning of 1970, Rees-Mogg took a doggedly optimistic line. The document reads as an intended vindication of his own stewardship at a time when

---

1 The need for an explanation to staff was raised at the TEB meeting on October 23 1969. The precise wording of Hamilton's letter was agreed, with amendments, at the board's meeting on December 9 1969, and before being sent it was also vetted by Gordon Brunton, managing director of the Thomson Organisation.

2 December 14 1969. Ian McDonald was appointed assistant Washington correspondent in 1967. In 1973 he took a job with the IMF, leaving *The Times* with the editor's thanks and an option to return.

circumstances might possibly be calling it into question. After defending the performance of *TBN* at somewhat excessive length, and with a degree of special pleading, he drew attention to all that had been achieved in other editorial departments, including the one which was most strictly his own. 'In 1966 it was widely believed that the leading article as a journalistic influence was dying. In fact *Times* leaders have played a very important part in the attraction of interest to the paper.'

He particularly stressed what had been done in the way of editorial recruitment. 'There is no doubt that the quality of the younger staff of *The Times* is exceptionally high, both intellectually and in professional ability.' Among 'the more obviously glittering Presidents of the Union or Fellows of All Souls' he singled out for mention David Bonavia, who after his service in Vietnam had become the paper's Moscow correspondent, and who spoke 'two Chinese dialects fluently, as well as Russian'. It was on journalists of his sort that the future depended, since he was still in his mid-twenties, and the fact that many of the paper's best correspondents were, like him, young helped to attract its audience, 'the youngest proportionately of any paper'.[1]

People were indeed keen to work for the Thomson *Times*, and in the early years Rees-Mogg had to give gentle rebuffs to quite a number of distinguished journalists working for other newspapers, or in broadcasting, who had approached him with requests for jobs. For instance, when a new Washington correspondent was due to be appointed in early 1970, Andrew Knight of the *Economist* wrote to offer himself for the job, and Rees-Mogg replied in very flattering terms, saying that he had always hoped Knight would work for the paper 'one day', but that on this occasion the Washington post had to go to an existing member of the staff or there would be ill-feeling and loss of morale.[2]

If not all who wished to write for the paper had their desire fulfilled, Rees-Mogg had little difficulty in obtaining the services of almost anyone he wished to recruit. There were quite frequent changes among the columnists whose pieces appeared, day by day, on the op. ed. page.

---

1 The Editorial Development of The Times (a review after three years), January 1970. It is interesting that Rees-Mogg seems to have regarded the presidency of the Union and a fellowship of All Souls as roughly equivalent. We can understand why he set so much store by the former, since he described the latter as offering 'the same sort of permanent distinction as being made a Cardinal'. (Letter to Robert Jackson congratulating him on his election to an All Souls fellowship, November 1968.) Another fellow of All Souls on the staff was Edward Mortimer.

2 Andrew Knight to W.R.-M., February 12 1970, and W.R.-M.'s reply. In 1974 Knight became editor of the *Economist*. (In 1990, twenty years after his initial approach, he did become associated with *The Times*, in an exalted though non-editorial capacity.)

When Trethowan left to concentrate on work at the BBC, his political column was taken over by the philosophic Tory, Ronald Butt, who was to prove a durable figure on *The Times*, and who for the time being continued to write for the *Sunday Times* as well. Trethowan welcomed his successor, saying that he was 'particularly glad to think there [would] be no respite for the little man in Downing Street'.[1] Another regular columnist at the end of the 1960s was the Canadian Leonard Beaton, who had made his name as defence correspondent of the *Guardian*. Yet another was the academic and Labour MP, John P. Mackintosh, whose inclusion had the ostensible purpose of giving the columns some semblance of political equity. 'I think it would be a very good thing', the features editor wrote, 'if we could add to their coverage by publishing the occasional piece that is more clearly Labour orientated'.[2] Mackintosh, however, was hardly representative of the Labour party at the time. Though admirable and gifted, he was well to the right of the party, and his view of its leader was much the same as Trethowan's, Butt's or Rees-Mogg's. What he wrote in *The Times* may well have ensured his regrettable exclusion from the Wilson government.[3]

In the autumn of 1969 Mark Boxer, who had been the first editor of the *Sunday Times* colour magazine, and was now assistant editor of the whole paper, started to produce pocket cartoons for *The Times*. These appeared two or three times a week in the diary section, and soon became a popular feature. The central figures in the cartoons were a couple called Simon and Joanna Stringalong, representing the trendy left-wingery then prevalent among middle-class 'communicators'. They thought a lot about 'the middle-class dilemma', and their son Tristram was nicknamed *Le Rouge* when he led the first infants' revolt at his local primary school. Boxer signed his cartoons 'Marc'. A good early specimen showed Simon Stringalong reading the headline 'Murdoch attacked for muck-raking', and Joanna saying to him: 'The middle-class dilemma is never resolved, Simon. We all felt guilty about not taking the *Sun*; now I suppose we'll feel guilty if we do'.[4] Soon

---

1 Trethowan to James Bishop, March 6 1969. Trethowan became the BBC's managing director of Radio in 1969, and in 1977 director-general of the BBC, after a brief interlude as head of BBC Television. Had 'the little man in Downing Street' been able to read the letter quoted, his worst suspicions about prejudice against him at the BBC would have been confirmed.

2 Bishop to Mackintosh, January 3 1968.

3 'Bob Mellish told me I "might have been in the Government by now but for your articles in *The Times*". So at least some of those in the Government read them!' (Mackintosh to Bishop, November 12 1969.)

4 October 2 1969. The *Sun* had recently been acquired by Rupert Murdoch, having failed as a new incarnation of the old trade union and Labour party *Daily Herald*.

after the Marc cartoons began to appear Antonia Fraser wrote about them in a guest column:

> Like characters in an Anthony Powell novel, one soon begins to compare the people one knows to Marc's characters, rather than the other way round, because his brilliant hieroglyphic creations clearly have stronger and more demoniac personalities than any possible prototypes . . . Whereas Osbert Lancaster's Maudie Littlehampton and even her drop-out/debutante daughter Jennifer are eternal English types, Marc is limning away at a new class.[1]

In 1969 a new arts editor was appointed, to succeed the veteran John Lawrence, who had held the post for twenty years and had been with the paper since 1919. The new man, to start work in 1970, was John Higgins, whom Rees-Mogg had persuaded to leave the *Financial Times*, so provoking the wrath of the *FT*'s managing director, Lord Drogheda:

> Gordon [Newton] . . . told me . . . that you were taking John Higgins from us. This is a real blow, and to me personally because I have had a lot to do with the *FT* taking an interest in the Arts. I had understood from Gordon that you had a sort of gentleman's agreement with him on the subject of 'poaching'. I hope that it is not supposed to be a purely one-way agreement.

Rees-Mogg was emollient, but unrepentant:

> My greatest worry in offering John Higgins the job was that I feared it would distress you personally . . . On the other hand I had to fill a post . . . to cover both the Arts and the Saturday Review and I felt that it would not be fair to John Higgins to exclude him from consideration. Yet if one considered him, he was obviously the outstanding person.

He contested what Drogheda said about poaching:

> I don't have a non-poaching agreement with Gordon and there have been a number of cross-appointments on both sides. We do naturally try to avoid causing difficulties for the other paper and we have recruited something like fifty financial journalists for the

1 'A trendy world': op. ed. column, October 25 1969.

> Business News in the last couple of years of which only two or three have come from the *FT*.[1]

At all events Higgins joined *The Times*, at a starting salary of £6,500, soon to rise to £6,750. But it was not apparently the money that tempted him. At the *FT* he would have a larger and more attentive readership. He came on the understanding that he would be a contributing editor, with opera as his special sphere of interest.[2]

Higgins inherited two major specialists, William Mann (music) and Irving Wardle (drama). Mann had been the paper's music critic since 1960, and before that assistant music critic since 1948. He was an eminent authority, who had written books, or parts of books, about Bach, Wagner, Richard Strauss, Britten and Tippett. Despite a tendency to drink too much his work seldom suffered (though there was an occasion when he stopped between the Bath Festival and Cardiff at a market town where the pubs stayed open all day, with the result that a performance of *Der Freischütz* went unreviewed). His attempt to treat the Beatles as educated musicians (in the 'pandiatonic clusters' piece already mentioned) was an uncharacteristic lapse. Normally he stood for the highest standards, regardless of fashion.

To new music he was kindly disposed, though not to excess, as in this summing-up of a violin concerto by David Blake, receiving its first performance at a prom:

> The models are good, and shown to be viable, the loans generously repaid with personal interest. The sags of tension and the moments of orchestral traffic jam militate against the piece. It succeeds in charm and evocation, and in displaying the stellar qualities of Miss [Iona] Brown's violin playing, a treat for the ear if not always for the accompanist: Sir Charles Groves and the BBC Symphony Orchestra were kept on their toes, sometimes caught with heels close to the ground. There is enough originality and imagination in the new concerto to please audiences all over the country, maybe elsewhere.[3]

Readers were unlikely to feel that they could hardly wait to hear the piece; yet the composer must have been reasonably encouraged.

Wardle was, perhaps, the best dramatic critic of the 1970s, a decade

---

1 Drogheda to W.R.-M., May 31 1969, and the latter's reply, June 2 1969.

2 Higgins talking to author. Newton, he felt, was much less exercised than Drogheda about his departure from the *FT*.

3 Review of promenade concert, Albert Hall, August 20 1976.

when, in Higgins's view, daily reviewing came back into its own, after having been somewhat eclipsed in the 1960s by the Sunday reviewing of Kenneth Tynan and Harold Hobson. His judgement of plays could be relied on by ordinary playgoers as well as by *cognoscenti*. When Tom Stoppard's *Rosencrantz and Guildenstern are Dead* came to London as a National Theatre production, having first appeared as a fringe event at the previous year's Edinburgh Festival, he hailed it as 'an amazing piece of work', for which he knew of 'no theatrical precedent'. But he assessed it carefully:

> There are times when the author, like his characters, seems to be casting about for what to say next. But for most of the time he walks his chosen tight-rope with absolute security.
>
> In its origin this is a highly literary play with frank debts to Pirandello and Beckett; but in Derek Goldby's production these sources prove a route towards technical brilliance and powerful feeling.[1]

Wardle's appraisal of actors was often chastening, for their own benefit. For instance:

> After his brilliant recent work in *Too True to be Good*, Romeo marks a return to Ian McKellen's worst mannerisms; the alternation of slack-jawed uncoordination and spasms of headlong energy (most of his exits are taken at the run), and imposed contortions of slurred and staccato speech intended to convey extreme emotions.[2]

Wardle was a master of the overnight review, an art-form threatened by new technology, with its earlier deadlines.

Also inherited from the previous regime were John Percival, who continued to write well about ballet throughout the period, and John Russell Taylor, who was writing film reviews when Higgins took over. Soon he left to teach film in America, and David Robinson replaced him. But after a time Taylor was persuaded to return as visual arts correspondent, since Guy Brett, who had been doing that job for some years, seemed to Higgins to take too little interest in figurative art.

As arts editor Higgins saw little of Rees-Mogg except, with others, at conferences, when the discussion seldom turned to artistic themes.

---

1 Review 1967.
2 Review of performance at Stratford, April 2 1976.

He was left almost entirely free to run his pages, though with a degree of self-censorship, since he was careful not to provoke the editor by, for instance, reviewing films containing a lot of sex and violence. Rees-Mogg only once rang him to complain about a piece in the arts pages. The offending author was Kingsley Amis.[1]

The Saturday Review which provided an outlet for arts material as well as other features, was inserted between the op. ed. and leader pages. The flavour of it may be gathered from a sample issue towards the end of 1969. The lead feature, on page i, was a piece by Dr. Henry Durant, 'Was Nelson a Suicide?', suggesting that the hero might have planned his own death in the hope (evidently vain) of making Emma Hamilton and their daughter Horatia financially secure. Page ii was devoted to entertainments and weekend broadcasting; page iii to reviews of art, theatre, TV, radio and music; pages iv–v to book reviews (including pieces on Elizabeth Longford's *Wellington: The Years of the Sword* and Thomas Jones's *Whitehall Diary*); page vi to gardening, chess and bridge; page vii to 'Eating In' and 'Eating Out', features on cookery, restaurants and City pubs; page viii to travel, with an article on Ibiza, 'this septic isle'[2]

In his report on editorial developments, already quoted, Rees-Mogg described the Saturday Review as 'a popular innovation, particularly with women, but in a rather minor key. He hoped that in future it would 'develop minority interests in the worlds of leisure and antiques as well as providing an attractive weekend coverage of books and the arts'.

The Saturday Review was inspired by the success of the *Financial Times*'s cultural pages on Saturday, and it was therefore natural that Higgins should be given overall control of it, in addition to his duties on other days of the week.

For a time the Saturday Review included book reviews, as we have seen. The first person to be put in charge of them, succeeding A. P. Ryan, was Michael Ratcliffe, an import from the *Sunday Times*, where he had been J. W. Lambert's deputy as literary and arts editor. A Lancastrian, educated at Cheadle Hulme grammar school and (as a scholar) at Christ's College, Cambridge – where he was a pupil of John Plumb, and got a first in the second part of the history tripos – Ratcliffe had come to the *Sunday Times* by way of the *Sheffield Telegraph*. Before Higgins arrived, the books page was under the features

---

1 Higgins talking to author.
2 November 8 1969.

editor, and it was a comparatively recent feature, having been started by Haley in 1955. Previously the existence of a Literary Supplement also published by *The Times* had been thought to absolve the parent paper of any obligation to review books, despite the obvious difference and disparity of the two publications.

As well as book reviews, Ratcliffe ran a literary gossip column in the Saturday Review, written by Alex Hamilton under the name of 'Pooter'. But this was discontinued before the end of his literary editorship, as was the experiment of using the Saturday Review as the vehicle for book reviews, mainly because it failed to attract the expected advertising support from publishers. Instead, books went back to being regularly reviewed in the main paper on Thursdays, with also a single book reviewed on Mondays. In 1972 Ratcliffe ceased to be literary editor, while remaining (without a drop in salary) as the paper's lead reviewer under his two successors. For the rest of the Thomson period he contributed a 1,200-word book review every week, while also writing a weekly 400-word piece on television.

This arrangement was presented as a *fait accompli* to the next literary editor, Ion Trewin, but fortunately the two men were already friends and never ceased to get on well. Trewin, son of the well-known dramatic critic, J. C. Trewin, had not been to university and so had lost no time in pursuing his ambition to be a journalist. After working for the *Western Independent* in Plymouth (the paper on which, incidentally, his parents had met), he moved to the *Sunday Telegraph*, and from there came as a very young recruit to the Thomson *Times*, to work on the diary. He stayed as literary editor until 1979 when he decided to forsake journalism for publishing.

Though book reviews as a whole remained outside the Saturday Review, Trewin arranged for paperbacks to be reviewed there once a month. This was a pioneering move, followed in due course by other papers. It enabled various popular genres of literature, such as the Western, to be noticed. (When a piece on that subject appeared, there was a telephone call from the fashionable bookshop, Hatchards, on behalf of a customer who had heard that Westerns had been written about in *The Times* and could not believe it was true.) Trewin was always looking for ways of extending the coverage of books beyond the books page, and found he could often manage to infiltrate suitable pieces into other sections of the paper. For instance, *TBN* could take reviews of books on business or finance, and Margaret Allen, as features editor, was particularly cooperative.

Rees-Mogg took an interest in the books page, though his involvement in it was less passionate and active than Haley's had been. There was no Rees-Mogg equivalent of the Oliver Edwards column. Haley continued to contribute; notably, Trewin persuaded him to review the Everyman series, which had been his prime literary resource as a young man. Rees-Mogg liked to drop in to look at books, or to discuss them, but he seldom jogged the literary editor's arm or questioned his choice. He did, however, object to Ratcliffe's use of Brigid Brophy as a reviewer, and he said that he would like to be consulted before Enoch Powell was ever asked to contribute to the page.

When Trewin resigned in July 1979, with effect from November, he wrote to Rees-Mogg to apologise for having to do so at a bad moment in the paper's fortunes, and to thank him for all his support.[1] Trewin's successor was Philip Howard, who had been on the paper since 1964 as the most stylish and gifted of home news reporters. A classical scholar, with a background of Eton (as a colleger) and Trinity College, Oxford, he was above all a *Times* man of the choicest vintage. Altogether, the books page during the Thomson period was at least as good as that of any other daily, apart perhaps from the *Financial Times*, though it never quite achieved the authority and compelling quality of the *Observer*'s or the *Sunday Times*'s literary pages, with their outstanding regular reviewers.

A new and, as it turned out, short-lived contributor in 1970 was Auberon Waugh, who was retained as a weekly columnist for an initial period of six months, his pieces to appear on Saturdays.[2] Though he had published a few novels, and had worked for the *Daily Telegraph*, the *Catholic Herald*, the Mirror Group and the *Spectator*, he was as yet relatively little known. But his style and outlook appealed to Rees-Mogg, and it is easy to see why. They had three important affinities: membership of the old church, a squirearchical base in Somerset and a taste for journalistic excitement. Waugh lost no time in showing just how exciting he could be.

His first piece, entitled 'Assessing Sir Alec', discussed the former prime minister and actual foreign secretary with withering contempt. What could account for such a man's success? He was admired by the British as an amateur, and because he 'enshrine[d] every saloon-bar Napoleon's hope of being Prime Minister'. But the real explanation,

1 Trewin to W.R.-M., July 25 1979. Trewin had been Higgins's deputy as arts editor, as well as literary editor.

2 James Bishop to Waugh's agent, Pat Kavanagh, February 27 1970. He was to be paid £50 per column.

which 'no political commentator ha[d] yet ventured to suggest', was 'that the Douglas-Home Phenomenon started as a cruel practical joke', played on his colleagues by Harold Macmillan.

> Mr. Macmillan's Douglas-Home joke was primarily against Lord Butler, of course. In its secondary effect, it was against those Tory politicians – Mr. Macleod and Mr. Powell – who took politics seriously. Finally, I suspect, it was against the entire Conservative Party, which fell into its allotted role like an enormous elephant into a submerged pit.

At the foot of the piece there was the announcement 'Mr. Waugh will be writing regularly for *The Times*'.[1] In fact he was to write only irregularly, and not for long.

His second piece was more far-reachingly provocative, though reactions to it must have surprised even the author. It was illustrated by a poster, put out by the Health Education Council, of a pregnant male with a sad expression, bearing the caption 'Would you be more careful if it was you that got pregnant?' Waugh's piece began:

> Sir James Frazer, author of *The Golden Bough*, would surely have had a ready explanation of the Health Education Council's poster advertising contraception, which depicts a pregnant male. He would have pointed out that many primitive religions included accounts of male births in their mythology and portrayals of it in their art, and that even today there is widespread belief throughout Islam that Allah will be born to a man. For that reason (or so I have always been told) many Muslims wear trousers of a particular design, irreverently known as Allah-catchers. Our newest religion . . . has merely taken a leaf from the Koran. Was it for this that we fought the Crusades?[2]

Outrage at this insulting reference to Islam was manifested only after some delay, but then in no uncertain fashion. The source of indignation was not Iran, where the Khomeini revolution had yet to occur, but Pakistan. A fortnight after the piece appeared there was a report on page 5 of the paper: 'Pakistan riot over *Times* article'. This gave the news that students demonstrating against the article had forced their way into the British Council library in Rawalpindi, 'burning books and breaking

1 March 7 1970.
2 'A leaf from the Koran', March 14 1970. The 'newest religion' was advertising and the culture associated with it.

windows'. Earlier in the week the British high commissioner had been summoned to the foreign ministry to be told that 'the article had hurt the feelings of the people of Pakistan'.[1] The demonstration doubtless resulted from the attitude of the Pakistani government, rather than vice versa. The official statement on the alleged effect of the article on popular sentiment in the country recalls F. E. Smith's notorious comment on the second reading of the Welsh Church bill in 1912, that the bill had 'shocked the conscience of every Christian community in Europe'. The high commissioner might have echoed the 'chuck it' theme of G. K. Chesterton's brilliant satirical riposte on that occasion.[2]

Taking their cue from the Rawalpindi students, the day after the *Times* report from Pakistan 250 British Muslims staged a march on Printing House Square. Fortunately they did not break in or commit any large-scale arson, but contented themselves with burning a copy of the *Sunday Times*. (It was a Sunday, and no copy of *The Times* was available.) A six-man deputation handed a letter to the foreign news editor, J. C. (Jerry) Caminada:

> We, the Muslims in Britain:
> 1. Condemn *The Times* and Mr. Auberon Waugh for the baseless article.
> 2. Demand that *The Times* should make a public apology . . .
> 3. Demand that the apology be published in a prominent place . . .
> 4. Demand that *The Times* give an undertaking not to publish any articles that are calculated to distort and misrepresent Islam and might injure the feelings of Muslims throughout the world.[3]

The Times would not, of course, bow to these demands, least of all to the fourth, and the incident was soon closed. It was, however, a modest foretaste of what would happen nearly two decades later, when Salman Rushdie's *The Satanic Verses* was published. In 1970 there was no Islamic fundamentalist 'pope' to pronounce sentence of death against Waugh, and he was not obliged to go into hiding under

---

1 News report, March 28 1970.

2 Chesterton's poem ended:

> Talk about the pews and steeples
>   And the cash that goes therewith!
> But the souls of Christian peoples. . .?
>   Chuck it, Smith!

3 News report, March 30 1970.

police protection. If his days as a *Times* columnist were already numbered, it was not because he had given offence to Muslims throughout the world, but rather because he had made a dangerous enemy within the office.

This was Douglas-Home, who was appointed features editor while Waugh was writing for the paper and thus became the departmental head with whom he had to deal. Douglas-Home may have had mixed feelings about Waugh's sensational second article, but there was nothing mixed about his reaction to the first. His family loyalty was aroused by the contemptuous treatment of Sir Alec, and he did not forgive. Waugh was the sort of contributor who needs a protector, and in the ordinary way Douglas-Home would have backed him against all critics, since the new features editor was normally a strong supporter of those who wrote for him. But as criticism of Waugh mounted – even subs finding some of the things he wrote offensive – Douglas-Home used it to ensure that his contract would not be renewed after the probationary six months. Indeed, Waugh stopped writing even before the contract ended, his last column appearing on July 18.

Rees-Mogg was in many ways sorry to lose him, but faced with having to choose, as he saw it, between Waugh and Douglas-Home, he had no hesitation in sacrificing the columnist. Waugh did not bear him any ill-will, as a letter written shortly before the break shows:

> My anxieties only began when Charlie told me – informally, and in quite a friendly way – that so far as he had any influence in the matter, my agreement . . . would not be renewed when it ran out, and he would oppose any suggestion that I should write a regular Comedy Corner. Almost certainly his attitude is dictated by nothing more than a dislike for my writing . . . I should not like you to suppose that my sadness would make the memory of these past months any less warm, or my gratitude towards you any less intense.[1]

Douglas-Home's clannishness may, in this instance, have warped his judgement and caused him to do the paper a disservice. Though Waugh's writing could occasionally go over the top, it was always readable and often brilliant. Other papers were to benefit from the talent that *The Times* lost.

1 Waugh to W.R.-M., 'personal and confidential', July 19 1970. In retrospect Waugh had no doubt that Douglas-Home's dislike was due to the attack on his uncle. (Written note to author, and A. Waugh, *Will This Do?*, pp.201–2.)

VIII

Wilson out, Heath in • The White Swan affair • Editorial changes • Enter Bernard Levin • New joy for cruciverbalists

ELECTIONEERING was in the air from the very beginning of 1970. Despite the Government's humiliating defeat at the hands of the trade unions the year before, when Barbara Castle's industrial relations bill had to be withdrawn in the face of union resistance – aided by some important Labour politicians, notably Callaghan – a genuine improvement in the state of the economy heralded a revival of Labour's fortunes. On New Year's Day Jenkins lifted restrictions on currency for foreign travel. On February 3 the gold and dollar reserves reached their highest level for two years, even after substantial repayments of debt. The monthly trade figures were on the whole good and sterling was all the time gaining strength.

The political climate seemed to be responding to these favourable economic trends, as the Conservatives' massive opinion poll lead of the past three years began to slip away. In real voting, the GLC elections on April 9 showed a modest movement to Labour, which was enough to win them control of the ILEA. In the borough elections held in the first week of May the swing to Labour seemed to be accelerating; in England and Wales Labour had a net gain of 443 seats, the Tories a net loss of 327. On May 13 Gallup in the *Daily Telegraph* gave Labour a lead of 7.5 per cent. Two days later Wilson asked the Queen for a dissolution and announced that the general election would be held on June 18.

Most people thought it likely that Labour would win, and Rees-Mogg was no exception. Though his disapproval of Wilson remained as strong as ever, he made considerable efforts to ingratiate himself with the prime minister during the months preceding the election, no doubt for the paper's sake. In October 1969 he wrote to Wilson direct asking for an early meeting and expressing the hope that good relations between them could be restored. But Wilson, replying through his press secretary, offered no more than the possibility of 'a word' if Rees-Mogg were to attend a forthcoming reception at Downing Street for the American astronauts.[1] Again, in early May, Rees-Mogg was told that the prime minister's diary was too full for him to contemplate a meeting 'in the very near future'.[2] Nevertheless, soon after the election was called, Rees-Mogg swallowed his pride and his sincerity to the extent of writing to the press secretary: 'Please give the Prime Minister my personal best wishes for his campaign. I hope I shall have a chance to see him later in the summer'.[3] If, technically, the second sentence could be regarded as ambiguous, the first could hardly be read otherwise than as a wish for Wilson's, and his government's, victory at the polls.

In fact, of course, Rees-Mogg desired a different outcome, though he had to prepare for the result he did not desire since the evidence suggested it was the more probable. He saw some hope, however, that Labour's chances might be damaged by Jenkins's last budget, introduced on April 14. In this the chancellor, despite having a revenue surplus of nearly £2,500 million, conceded only £175 million in tax cuts, and left all the major indirect taxes on consumers unchanged. Commenting on this budget in a leader the following day, Rees-Mogg wrote:

> Mr. Jenkins has the reputation of being both a responsible and a clever Chancellor. Yesterday's Budget will do more to enhance his reputation for responsibility than for cleverness . . . as he sat down at the end of his speech, [he] must . . . have been aware that his colleagues with marginal seats could not feel that he had made their election any easier.

In the same leader the editor referred to the government's defeat by the trade unions, and stressed the importance of trade union reform:

> One might have guessed . . . that the Prime Minister and the Chancellor had decided on a short Budget and an early election, so that the great battle to put the unions in their place could be fought after the election was over. Whichever party wins will have to fight this battle. For the Labour Party, the Prime Minister's defeat over last year's Industrial Relations Bill will prove merely to have been unfinished business if he is returned to power.[4]

---

1 W.R.-M. to Wilson, October 6 1969. J.T.W. Haines to W.R.-M., October 9 1969.
2 Haines to W.R.-M., May 4 1970.
3 W.R.-M. to Haines, May 21 1970.
4 'Chancellor's motto "never again"', April 15 1970.

When the campaign proper began Rees-Mogg put the paper, and himself, into top gear. Coverage of the election, described as 'unparalleled', was to include opinion polls by Marplan, psephological commentary by Professor Richard Rose, 'analysis in depth' given every Saturday by the News Team, an election diary by Leonard Beaton, daily impressions of constituency contests from Land's End to John o'Groats by Patrick Brogan, examination of the parties' broadcasting techniques by Chris Dunkley, and a series of articles, entitled Minority View, in which 'well-known people outside politics' were to say how they saw the issues. Rees-Mogg, for his part, wrote no fewer than eighteen leaders during the campaign. Deprived of the opportunity to fight as a candidate, he made the most of his position to influence the nation's choice.

There was no question of keeping an open mind until the end of the campaign. His first leader on May 19, which ran to three columns with cross-heads, had a clear message summed up in the last paragraph:

> To the Labour Party's credit there is an unprecedentedly good current balance of payments situation which is nevertheless a little past its best . . . [This] is threatened by wage inflation and was the result of devaluation rather than any underlying improvement in the relative efficiency of our economy. The experience of Labour rule in terms of rising prices, rising taxation, rising unemployment, and low industrial growth, has been decisively inferior to the most recent experience of Conservative rule. Judged by the economic criteria which the Labour Party used to gain office in 1964 and to retain it in 1966, the present Government has a wholly inadequate claim on the electorate in 1970.[1]

The one good thing he had to say about Labour's record was, as can be seen, heavily qualified. Yet it was only two days later that he sent his private message of unqualified goodwill to the prime minister.

In the same issue Marplan was giving Labour a 2.7 per cent lead, 'equal to a 60 overall majority', while on the op. ed. page Rose was explaining that the Tories needed a minimum swing of 4 per cent to win. Throughout the first week the paper carried turnover articles by Adam Fergusson setting out the Labour case.

When Heath launched his party's manifesto Rees-Mogg broadly welcomed it, and in particular praised the leader's foreword, finding

1 'The record is the issue', May 19 1970.

it 'considerably more personal than the stylized rhetoric which is customary'.[1] On June 9, in what he thought might be his last shot in the campaign, because a newspaper strike was imminent, he gave unequivocal endorsement to the Conservatives precisely because Heath was their leader:

> Victory for Labour will certainly make it more complacent and even arrogant, but defeat would equally be bad for the Conservatives. It would not project Mr. Powell into power, but it would endanger the serious attempt to make the Conservatives a Party of practical reform. At a difficult moment Mr. Heath does us the honour of not pandering to our national complacency. We should support the party which tells the truth in critical times.[2]

Powell and his views on race were featuring prominently in the campaign. Though still excluded from the shadow cabinet, he was an accredited Conservative candidate, and he commanded far more public and media attention than most of the party's leaders. On June 3 his importance in the campaign was gratuitously boosted when a cabinet minister attacked him in terms recalling Churchill's fatal 'Gestapo' speech in the 1945 election. The minister in question was Anthony Wedgwood Benn, or Tony Benn as he chose to be called. Speaking at the Central Hall, Westminster, Benn said: 'The flag of racialism which has been hoisted in Wolverhampton [Powell's constituency] is beginning to look like the one which fluttered twenty-five years ago over Dachau and Belsen'. This remark, which was headline news throughout the next day's press, was a godsend to the Conservatives and deeply embarrassing to Labour, many of whose natural supporters were equally natural supporters of Powell on the racial issue. Heath, who in January had described Powell's latest outburst on race as 'an example of man's inhumanity to man which is absolutely intolerable in a Christian civilized society', was able for a change to defend him, challenging Wilson to disown Benn, which the prime minister virtually did.

Benn's immoderate words were no less of a gift to Rees-Mogg, who wrote:

> No one will suppose, least of all Mr. Powell, that *The Times* has been too kind to Mr. Powell in the past. Nevertheless Mr. Benn's

1 'The right questions', May 27 1970.
2 'One last word', June 9 1970.

> statement . . . is irresponsible and untrue. Mr. Benn is, of course, an exceptionally silly man, though able and pleasant enough. That is, however, no excuse. Anyone could see that this sort of attack would strengthen Powellism because it is so obviously false. Mr. Benn's language is that of an hysterical ninny; he has made race an issue in the election, which Mr. Powell's election address had failed to do.[1]

Partly, no doubt, to mitigate the impression of relentless partisanship, Rees-Mogg singled out the odd non-Tory for honourable mention. Michael Foot was extolled as a good MP with 'a sense of history, a sense of humour, a sense of wit and a sense of the moods of Parliament . . . above all, courage'.[2] Laura Grimond, Asquith's granddaughter and wife of the former Liberal leader, was warmly recommended to the electors of West Aberdeenshire.[3] But the editor's most extravagant praise was reserved for another woman, Shirley Williams: 'If one had to pick a single Labour MP in whose social conscience one would trust it would be Mrs. Shirley Williams . . . She is one of the very rare women who could become Prime Minister (and perhaps should) without losing a scrap of her good nature and charm, and without thinking any better of herself for it'.[4] There was also a lament for the departure from politics of the liberal Tory Sir Edward Boyle, which suggested that 'modern British politics [were] not sufficiently attractive to men of powerful mind'.[5]

For a whole week of the campaign, June 9–12 inclusive, the

---

1 'Mr. Benn makes an Issue of Race', June 5 1970. Congratulating Rees-Mogg afterwards on *The Times's* election coverage, the experienced political journalist Hugh Massingham wrote: 'Your leader on W. Benn was masterly – a real scorcher' (Massingham to W.R.-M., July 6 1970). The previous autumn, after sitting between Kenneth Thomson and Rees-Mogg at a *Times* lunch, Benn had committed to his diary his own view of Rees-Mogg: '[He] is a completely Edwardian figure . . . he has absolutely no sense of modernity about him at all and yet somehow you're not afraid of those sort of people any more because you don't feel that they command much power'. (Tony Benn, *Office Without Power*, entry for November 24 1969, p.213). The unconscious irony of this comment is that in many ways Benn was distinctly the more old-fashioned of the two.

2 'Men not puppets', June 2 1970.

3 'The Asquith ideal', June 8 1970. But she was not elected, having the misfortune to be confronted by a Conservative candidate who, at the time, was something of a popular hero: Colonel Colin Mitchell ('Mad Mitch').

4 'Does Labour care?', June 4 1970. Another of her merits was that, as an Oxford contemporary of Rees-Mogg, she had written the article in *Isis* which, by a curious chance, brought him his first job. (See p. 13 chapter 1.)

5 'Intellect in politics', June 3 1970. Boyle was leaving politics to become vice-chancellor of Leeds University. He received a life peerage in the dissolution honours, and was thereafter known as Lord Boyle of Handsworth.

national dailies were closed by a printers' strike. But they were back in circulation to report and comment on the last few days, when it still seemed almost certain that Labour would win. On the eve of the poll Rees-Mogg sadly acknowledged that, despite wide variations in the opinion polls, the consensus of them suggested that 'a Labour victory [was] a near certainty and a landslide victory a considerable possibility'. This did 'not conform to the pattern of the argument'; the electorate, he implied, was about to act perversely and illogically.[1] On polling day the front-page lead story had the headline 'Three polls show Labour ahead'. Yet the story itself contained two pointers to the actual result. The first reported an Opinion Research Centre poll mentioned on television the previous night, and due to be published (in the London *Evening Standard*) during the day. This gave the Tories a 1 per cent lead – the first poll to show them ahead since the campaign began. The other significant item in the story was that surveys in selected Midlands constituencies indicated that 'the Conservatives could still turn the tide'. In the same issue the psephologist Rose ended his final piece: 'In so far as Mr. Powell has managed to make immigration important, there is . . . the prospect of at least a few swings reflecting divisions on race, not class'.

Beaton's last campaign notebook was gloomily entitled 'The Tory hierarchy: not a team, not an opposition', with pictures of Maudling, (Sir Keith) Joseph, Macleod, Hogg, Powell and Heath. The last Minority View article, by the Warden of All Souls, John Sparrow, was disparaging of Wilson; and the editor's last leader, after a lengthy denunciation of British indifference to the outside world, concluded inevitably with an attack on the prime minister:

> We are not at all interested in the world . . . What we do not think our business would stock a library, and what we do think our business would not fill a paperback. If this really is the nation we have become then this will be a dangerous election to win; if Mr. Wilson does win, it will be by exploiting this odious mood.[2]

---

1 'Against the tide', June 17 1970.

2 'Dead to the world', June 18 1970. Some readers, however, may have been tempted to regard the overwhelming amount of its space that *The Times* devoted to the election as a prime example of British parochialism. Incidentally, the Minority View feature did not quite live up to its billing. Most of those who contributed to it were 'outside politics' only in the limited sense of not being MPs. Men such as Lords Radcliffe, Harlech and Redcliffe-Maud, not to mention Sparrow, would have been on anybody's list of establishment figures. One of the few exceptions was the playwright Arnold Wesker.

When the results started to come in it was soon apparent that he had not won. Having chosen the anniversary of Waterloo for polling, he found that the day was his rather than Heath's Waterloo. 'Conservative victory looks assured' was *The Times* headline next day, across the full width of its front page. In the event the Conservatives were returned with 330 seats to Labour's 287, and an overall Commons majority of thirty.

The causes of this unexpected Tory triumph have been much discussed, but can never be exactly determined. Jenkins's failure to bribe the electorate in his April budget was probably not as important a factor as Rees-Mogg hoped it might be, or as some Labour ill-wishers were pleased to make out subsequently. After all, it had not prevented Labour from doing conspicuously well in the borough elections, which occurred a fortnight after the budget. On the other hand it was undoubtedly bad for Labour that the trade figures announced on June 15 showed a deficit of £31 million. This seemed to call in question Jenkins's (valid) claim to have turned the economy round, which was the government's principal asset. Rising unemployment – though the rise was modest indeed by later standards – was another awkward issue for Labour, brilliantly exploited by Macleod in a TV election broadcast late in the campaign. The newspaper strike in the last full week, against the background of Labour's capitulation to the unions over the reform of industrial relations, and the Conservatives' pledge to introduce such reform, must also have influenced voters. The racial issue must have influenced them, too, to judge from the differentially high swings to Powell himself and other Tories in his area; and the issue of race overlapped with that of law and order, since many were indignant about the threatened disruption of a South African cricket tour, which had led to its cancellation at the government's request. Above all Labour's campaign was dangerously bland and complacent, as many remarked at the time. Despite warning his colleagues at the outset not to take the result for granted, Wilson adopted a presidential style which involved largely forgoing his normal cheeky combativeness. Democracy likes to be wooed with some ardour, but in the 1970 election Wilson seemed to be treating the British people as a husband of some years' standing, secure in his rights.

Scarcely had Rees-Mogg completed his election marathon than he was faced with a wholly unexpected challenge within the office. This took the form of a letter from a powerful group of colleagues complaining about changes, actual and apprehended, to the character of the paper. Dated July 7, the letter read:

> In view of the changes in the editorial character of the paper which are under consideration, it is appropriate that we should express our concern about certain earlier changes that have been made in the past few years.
>
> We recognise the need for innovation and evolution of style, and we agree that many of the things that have been changed needed to be changed. But the general effect of what has been done, and of the manner in which it has been done, has been to diminish the authority, independence, accuracy, discrimination and seriousness of *The Times*. These are chief among its essential values. To the degree that they are lost *The Times* departs from its true tradition, and forfeits the principal editorial factor in its commercial success.
>
> It is because we are sure you are determined to uphold the tradition of *The Times* as a paper of the highest quality that we now address you. We believe we can make a constructive contribution to the proposals under consideration, provided we are given an opportunity to discuss them with you and others directly involved, and provided the discussions take place at a formative stage. We accordingly ask for the opportunity.

This letter was signed by twenty-nine members of the editorial staff, and since they did so roughly in alphabetical order the top signatory was Michael Baily, the transport correspondent. He was also the prime mover in the affair, though his importance was eclipsed by that of others persuaded to sign, most notably Hodgkin, Hickey, Douglas-Home, Richard Harris, John Hennessy (sports editor), Roy Lewis, Brian MacArthur (education correspondent), Innis Macbeath (labour correspondent), Geoffrey Woolley (letters editor) and David Wood.[1] Conspicuously absent from the list were McDonald, Grant, Bishop and Cudlipp, the last-named being, indeed, the principal, though unspecified, target of the protest.

How did it come about? Baily, 'a quiet man but one with strong feelings', had approached a number of colleagues about forming a

1 The other signatories were Patrick Brogan, Jerome (Jerry) Caminada, James Greenwood, John Greig, George Clark, Clifford (Cliff) Longley, Robert (Bob) Jones, Kenneth Mackenzie, Hugh Noyes, Moira Keenan (the only woman), A. M. Rendel, Geoffrey Smith, David Spanier, Hugh Stephenson, Colin Watson, Stuart Weir, Michael Wolfers and Alan Wood. Hickey, Greig and Wolfers signed *in absentia*.

society to preserve *The Times*'s standards, and had called a meeting to be held at 7 p.m. in an upper room of the White Swan tavern in Farringdon Street. Those invited arrived 'singly or in groups . . . with a nod to the man behind the bar, like nineteenth-century anarchists or the IRA coming silently to their rendezvous'. During the discussion, which lasted two hours, Harris 'sensibly suggested' that Rees-Mogg should be treated as someone whose heart was in the right place, but whose head needed to be strengthened 'in the fight for a common objective'. At the end of the meeting 'it was agreed that the situation was too urgent for the formation of committees etc., and that a letter should be drafted immediately for submission to [Rees-Mogg]'. The job of drafting it was referred to Hickey, Harris and Bob Jones, a reporter from *Business News*.[1] For a few days the resulting draft lay in a drawer in Harris's office, which occupied a strategic position at the angle of two passages. There people dropped in to sign.[2]

As usual in such cases the sources of discontent were various, and the text of the letter alone suggests some confusion of thought and motive. Yet it is safe to assume that the remonstrance would never have been made if the paper had still been expanding freely and confidently. People who have grievances tend to keep quiet about them when things are going well, because it is hard to quarrel with success. But at the first sign of trouble disaffection sets in. Hamilton's letter to staff in December had served notice that the euphoria of the early Thomson phase was at an end, and it was only natural that people with doubts and resentments, hitherto hidden, should be tempted to bring them out into the open.

Most of those who signed the letter were representatives of the pre-Thomson *Times*, and it was perhaps inevitable that they should try to pin the blame for what had gone wrong on newcomers from the *Sunday Times*. Of these the most important were Hamilton, Vice, Cudlipp and Rees-Mogg himself, all of whom had their critics. But of the four, Cudlipp was by far the most unpopular. His brash and thrusting methods had caused a lot of offence, and were felt by many to have lowered the paper's tone. Hodgkin was recording a widely held view when he described him at the time as 'a jumped up enthusiast of no intellect who intrigues and bullies and has no conception of what a responsible newspaper should be'.[3] The judgement was unfair, and Hodgkin later formed a much better opinion of Cudlipp.[4] But in 1970

1 Hodgkin diary, entry for July 3 1970.
2 Harris talking to author.
3 Ibid.
4 'I think increasingly well of him, though I know that a year ago . . . I thought he had neither taste nor judgment'. (Hodgkin diary, entry for June 29 1971.)

traditionalists regarded him as the most disastrous recruit from the *Sunday Times*, whose power and influence had to be checked if the paper's reputation was to be saved.

Much of what they objected to in his conduct was due to an excess of the enthusiasm noted by Hodgkin, itself one of his most valuable qualities. In following up a story he was apt to telephone people late at night, sometimes even breaking into their sleep. In exceptional circumstances this might be justified, but as a general rule it was clearly undesirable, as were some other manifestations of his enthusiasm. Yet it was probably more for his virtues than his faults that he was disliked and resented by some old *Times* hands. His kind of zeal would have been appreciated by those who created the paper's unique reputation, but was less congenial to those currently living on it. *The Times* made its name in the nineteenth century through a matchless combination of news, independence and progressive technology. As it then gradually became what was known (in a later idiom) as the establishment newspaper, some of the qualities that originally made it great tended to atrophy, and to be replaced by a smug self-sufficiency which exasperated Northcliffe when he gained control of the paper early in the present century. 'After the sale the Old Guard in the editorial departments – the "Black Friars" or "Brethren" as Northcliffe called them – continued doggedly to resist innovations. In them they saw nothing but the thin ends of countless unwelcome wedges.'[1]

The 1970 equivalents of Northcliffe's Black Friars took a similar view of changes introduced by the Thomson regime. There was much talk of the paper going down-market. But what exactly was meant by this? In an academic work published three years later a whole chapter was devoted to 'The Vulgarization of *The Times*,' in which many of the examples cited relate to the period 1966–70. One, typically, is concerned with the undue attention paid to pop stars:

> Would *The Times* ever before . . . 1966, even in the silly season of August, have run as its second story on the home-news page the information, illustrated by two photographs, that the then Mrs. John Lennon had missed a train and wept? But the new *Times* explained unblushingly in its obituary of Brian Epstein . . . that the Beatles are the best-known people in the world – and therefore, it followed for the new paper, the best worth reporting

---

1 Woods and Bishop, op. cit., p.204.

on all occasions. Pop stars' pictures at about the same time began alternating with royalty on the court page.[1]

Admitting that *The Times* 'needed to abandon the ruling classes in favour of the educated' while maintaining continuity, the author saw no merit in the changes that had actually occurred:

> What in fact happened was that in 1966 *The Times* became panicky about its Victorian tradition and in 1970 found that a modern alternative was not easy to come by. Instead of bringing *The Times*'s real identity into a changed world *The Times* was changed to suit the trends, and the result was . . . a style, it would seem, for a nation with little that could be called public opinion, with no capacity for generating a language in which the political world can be discussed and where all political decisions . . . must therefore be left to people who cannot be responsible to a public . . . The paper's language had to change, but the difference between change and decay was not understood.[2]

In the course of a long and almost entirely denigratory chapter some valid points were made, but the indictment as a whole seems flawed as well as ponderous. Was it not, after all, perfectly true that the Beatles were just about the best-known people in the world in the late 1960s, and would it, in that case, have been right for *The Times* to continue to treat them as no more than a musical phenomenon, as it had done in Haley's day? Rees-Mogg's policy towards the pop scene, as shown most impressively in his handling of the Jagger drugs case, was to recognise its enormous social significance while maintaining the paper's intellectual and moral standards. To the accusation that he failed to understand the difference between change and decay he could reasonably reply that traditionalist critics, including perhaps most of the signatories of the White Swan letter, failed to understand the difference between taking a paper down-market and bringing it up to date.

By no means all of those who signed the letter were, however, temperamentally opposed to change. As well as the old guard element there was a group of 'Young Turks', led by Douglas-Home, of which

---

1 Ian Robinson, *The Survival of English: essays in criticism of language*, chap. 4, pp.102–3.

2 Ibid., p.144. The Robinson critique was reviewed in the Sept.–Nov. 1973 issue of *Times News*, the review (by Eric MacHardy) ending: 'If it is a consolation to Mr. Robinson he may be assured that *The Times* will continue to be a great newspaper long after he and his pompous essays are forgotten'.

other members were Macbeath, Stephenson, Geoffrey Smith and Longley. The position of Douglas-Home as a leading figure in the cabal is of special interest, partly for the obvious reason that he was to be the paper's next editor but one, but also because he was already one of the liveliest and most influential members of the senior editorial staff, though still in his early thirties. (He was born in 1937.) Douglas-Home was ambivalent in a way not infrequently found among talented aristocrats, more especially those belonging to a cadet branch. He wanted to be accepted as a thoroughgoing professional, which indeed he was; yet he also had a not always well concealed sense of superiority to some of his professional colleagues from less privileged backgrounds. His character was further complicated by a distinctly 'chippy' attitude towards people with academic credentials, deriving from the fact that, although a scholar at Eton, he had not attended a university. A natural leader, he almost identified with a man whose biography he wrote, Field Marshal Erwin Rommel, and was much given to speaking in military metaphors. Brave and dashing, he was also capable of ruthlessness, and of disguising his true opinions and intentions. Sharing Rees-Mogg's patrician outlook, and Cudlipp's activist approach, he nevertheless saw much to criticise in both men and felt that he could run the paper better than they did. His signature on the White Swan letter had less to do with outraged conservatism than with self-assertiveness and driving ambition.

Rees-Mogg, for his part, had no doubt that the letter was a challenge to his authority, despite the soft soap inserted for his benefit. He knew that Cudlipp was far more unpopular than he was, but rightly regarded his unpopularity as due, in large measure, to power conferred by himself and exercised on his behalf while he was enjoying the pleasures of home life. The veiled attack on Cudlipp had to be treated, therefore, as an attack on himself at one remove.

Deciding that the best form of defence was counter-attack, he summoned the signatories of the letter to his office at 10 a.m. the day after it reached him – the time being deliberately chosen for its inconvenience to some who would normally have come in later. When they were assembled in his room, he did not for a moment condescend to discuss the letter's contents but subjected them to a dressing-down of calculated severity. Feeling that his confidence in them had been abused, and that they were unjustly accusing him of inaccessibility, he showed an anger that was certainly genuine, though his Thespian genes may have helped him to appear even angrier than he was. Beyond question the tactics worked. Argument at the time would have been fatal, since it would have suggested weakness and self-doubt. By confining himself to an effective show of righteous indignation he reimposed his authority and regained the initiative.

Another advantage that may, at least partly, have been due to the shock tactics he employed was that the incident was kept at the time, and for some years afterwards, a total secret from the outside world. He would have wished it to be so in any case, but one of the White Swan confederates might possibly have leaked the story if it could have been presented as a triumph for them. There was, however, no way it could be so presented.

Rees-Mogg's indignation was strongest against Hodgkin, by whom he felt seriously hurt and let down. Hodgkin was not only foreign editor but deputy editor (though due to relinquish both posts in the near future). He was also a Balliol man. Rees-Mogg had felt he could count on him, and in return had backed him to the hilt over his controversial West Bank article. It had seemed unthinkable that Hodgkin would fail to bring any complaint he might have about the running of the paper direct to himself, to be discussed privately between them. Towards Hodgkin alone, therefore, he had an *Et tu Brute* feeling, and their relations never truly recovered from the wound, partly because Hodgkin may have been too proud or too reserved ever to express quite adequately the regret that he undoubtedly came to feel. Yet there was no complete estrangement, and they continued to work together more or less satisfactorily, with Hodgkin in the more limited role already agreed before the incident, until he retired from the paper two years later.

Hickey, though a colleague of comparable seniority, was rather less resented, because Rees-Mogg had never felt quite as close to him as to Hodgkin. He was also in Ireland when matters came to a head, and his absence from the final scene in the editor's room may have made him appear rather less closely involved in the business than in fact he had been. Towards other signatories of the letter, and notably towards the Douglas-Home group, Rees-Mogg showed an extraordinary indulgence. Far from being punished for their cheek, they received during the rest of his editorship every mark of favour. Douglas-Home himself, already about to move from defence to features, was later appointed to other major posts, and was Rees-Mogg's preferred candidate to succeed him when he resigned as editor in 1981. In his discriminatory goodwill towards the Douglas-Home group Rees-Mogg was not merely making allowances for youthful indiscretion; he was also showing a shrewd awareness that they were potentially dangerous enemies – or useful allies.

The White Swan letter called for more consultation, with special reference to impending changes. But some of the most important changes had already been decided on, and for the future Rees-Mogg's freedom of action remained essentially unimpaired. At the same time it suited both sides to establish a formal system of consultation. On July 28 *The Times*'s NUJ Chapel appointed a panel of journalists to discuss with the editor and management 'all matters affecting the conduct of the paper except leader policy', and the first such meeting took place the following day. Thereafter meetings were held at monthly or longer intervals, with little to show for them in practice. The existence of the panel was of some cosmetic value, but its influence on editorial and management decisions was marginal.

On June 22 Douglas-Home's transfer from defence to features was announced, to take effect from July 27. (The outgoing features editor, Bishop, was to move to another sector of the Thomson empire, where he would soon become editor of the *Illustrated London News*.) On July 7 – the day before the conspiratorial gathering at the White Swan – it was announced that McDonald and Hodgkin would, from the beginning of August, be joint associate editors, thus forming with the editor and Hickey the team of senior leader-writers, but having no administrative duties. McDonald was to relinquish the additional title of deputy editor, and Hodgkin the foreign editorship. He had for some time been asking for more leisure, and was fully in agreement with the change. He had also himself suggested the person appointed to succeed him, Louis Heren.

Heren was the paper's star foreign correspondent, whose story was, moreover, a *Times* romance. Brought up in a London East End slum, he had been recruited as a messenger when he left school because his father (who died when he was four) was a printer on the paper. For Heren *The Times* provided a more than adequate substitute for secondary and university education. An assistant editor, C. W. Brodribb, one day spotted him reading *Nostromo* in an alcove and mentioned the fact to others. Soon Stanley Morison began to take an interest in him and helped him to become a reporter. As such he would often, before the Second World War, volunteer for the chore of weekend duty in the old building at Printing House Square. He loved having the house more or less to himself, sleeping in a bed with 'crisp linen sheets' after a shower in the 'well-appointed bathroom', being called on Sunday morning with a cup of tea, and then having a breakfast of eggs and bacon in the next room while reading the Sunday papers and marking stories worth following up.[1]

1 Louis Heren, *Memories of* Times *Past*, pp.201–2.

War service in the army gave him a taste for foreign travel, and when he returned to the paper after the war it was not long before he asked to be sent abroad. For the next twenty-three years, in a succession of postings, he made his name as one of the best foreign correspondents in the paper's history. After reporting brilliantly, and often dangerously, from India, the Middle East, Korea, Malaya and Germany, in 1960 he was appointed head of the Washington bureau. His decade in this job was in reality the pinnacle of his career. In 1970 he was ready to come home, mainly because his wife was ill (in fact dying), and if he was to return it had to be to a post worthy of him. Nothing less than the foreign editorship would, it seemed, have been adequate.

Yet he was to find life in London in many ways anti-climactic and frustrating. His new post was not simply that of foreign editor, but of deputy editor (foreign), while Cudlipp was appointed deputy editor (home) with responsibility for the day and night production of the paper. This Heren-Cudlipp dyarchy was to prove unsatisfactory, since the two men did not work well together and their respective spheres were imperfectly defined. In any case Heren disliked the new Printing House Square building that had replaced, in the early 1960s, the old one he remembered so fondly from his youth. His impressions as he took up his duties were clearly unfavourable:

> I found that at least one thing had not changed . . . The endearing but occasionally infuriating habit of not being told what was expected of one had survived. Rees-Mogg gave me a distracted smile, but nothing more. Cudlipp . . . was no more communicative as he bustled about with a clipboard. My new secretary led me to my office, a large glass box with views of the square and the river to the right of my desk and of the editorial floor to the front. She said that it was very functional, but I sighed for the book-lined rooms of the old building.[1]

Before long he moved down from the higher editorial floor to the news room, where he had a little glass cubicle looking out on the subs. This made for more friction with Cudlipp.

To the post of assistant editor (night), briefly held by Davy, a *Sunday Times* man, Michael Hamlyn, was appointed,[2] while that of night editor was given to R.M.W. Hardy (whose predecessor,

---

1 Heren, op. cit., p.229.
2 He had been news editor on the *Sunday Times*.

E. MacHardy, was moved to a new job developing the foreign news services of Times Newspapers). Fowler having been elected to Parliament in June, his home affairs post was given to Peter Evans, the race relations correspondent, and the two functions were merged to save one specialist. Further economies were effected by not replacing two home reporters and two subs, while the Business News staff was cut by three.

Abroad, there was a cut of one reporter in Paris, and in Washington the financial correspondent was transferred to the *Sunday Times* payroll. Heren's post there went to Emery, who was not replaced as Far East correspondent based in Singapore. The Singapore office was closed, and the Far East was in future to be covered by the correspondent in Japan (Michael Hornsby), the correspondent in Australia (Stewart Harris), and a China specialist working from Hong Kong on a retainer. Early in 1971 the post of correspondent in Canada was temporarily abolished.[1] After all these changes the total saving on editorial staff was to be over £14,000 in what remained of 1970, or nearly £33,000 in a full year.

Another consequence of the economy drive was the further restyling of the paper that occurred in September 1971. For this, as in 1967, the principal consultant was Clive Irving.[2] The changes of layout were intended to give the paper 'a tighter and more classical style', eliminating the wastefulness of 'big headings, large white spaces and blown-up pictures'. It would thus be 'easier to give the news in full, to give important dispatches at length and to provide both comprehensive and interesting coverage'. There was to be more space for home and foreign news, for the arts, for women's features and for leaders and letters.[3]

The last result was achieved by what was, perhaps, the most noticeable of the changes: the disappearance of the turnover article. It may

---

1 Not surprisingly, the closing of the separate office in Canada was an emotive issue, though Thomson himself seems to have made no attempt to avert the decision. Over the next two years there were protests from the British High Commissioner in Canada. (Peter Hayman to W.R.-M., February 26 1971 and May 18 1973), and a British Conservative politician wrote to the editor: 'I thought you ought to know that quite a few people in Canada are hurt that *The Times* . . . rather tends to treat Canada as an offshoot of America'. (Geoffrey Finsberg MP to W.R.-M., March 21 1973.) In 1974 John Best was appointed Ottawa correspondent.

2 He was appointed 'executive consultant' for the second half of 1970, and was to be paid £3,000 on the understanding he would give the paper not less than 50 per cent of his time. He was also engaged to write a fortnightly column on communications during the last quarter of the year, at £75 per column.

3 'Look as you wish to be', September 21 1970: Rees-Mogg's leader explaining the changes.

have been feared that many readers would be upset by this change. Certainly there was no explicit announcement of it; it was just allowed to occur. To judge from published letters, however, there was little adverse reaction to it, or to any of the other changes. One reader of sixty years' standing wrote to say that, when he first saw them, he had nearly given the paper up, but that he had since changed his mind and found it 'better than ever'.[1] The last turnover was a curious piece by F. Rubin on Russian experiments in hypnopaedia or sleep teaching, in which it was claimed that the technique had been successful for bona fide educational purposes, but that there was no evidence it could be used 'for forced or subliminal mass indoctrination'.[2] Nevertheless, a clergyman was encouraged: 'Your article . . . is understandably a tonic to us preachers. Clearly we achieve more than our own wildest dreams'.[3] With the turnover gone, there was room for three columns of leaders and four of readers' letters, which became the normal pattern.

Rees-Mogg was always open to suggestions for improving the paper's appearance and style, provided they were not put to him in the form of an organised demonstration. He was also well aware that one item at least, in the White Swan remonstrance was valid: the complaint that there were too many inaccuracies in the paper. There was nothing new in this complaint. He had answered numerous letters from readers on the subject, explaining carefully that the main cause of the trouble was that the paper was operating beyond its real printing capacity, with the result that there was too little time for proof-reading and too little scope for correcting mistakes in later editions. Now, with the circulation much reduced after the price rise, conditions were less stressful and soon, consequently, there was less talk of inaccuracy in the main paper – though such talk persisted about the Business News.

On one editorial feature Rees-Mogg's standards were set; he had no doubt at all that his policy on leaders was right. In his view they were of paramount importance, and he was also confident that his own way of writing them was the proper way and good for the paper. Most people, fortunately, seemed to agree with him, though there were some carpers. For instance, during the election campaign Thomson received a letter from John North, author and former director of the London Press Exchange, in which he offered some criticisms of *The Times* under Rees-Mogg's editorship, including a particularly scathing reference to his leader of June 9. This he described as

1 Letter to the editor from D. J. Simpson, September 25 1970.
2 'Sleep learning is no longer just a dream', September 19 1970.
3 Letter to the editor from the Revd R. Kissack, September 22 1970.

a shocker. Three columns under the caption ONE LAST WORD. Fit only for retired gentlemen in Bournemouth with time on their hands – and, I don't doubt, *The Times* in them.

Thomson thanked North for giving 'the benefit of [his] advice', and sent the letter on to Hamilton without comment.[1] Whether or not any word of it reached Rees-Mogg, he never showed the slightest inclination to modify his style of leader-writing.

Like the captain of a ship the editor of a paper can feel very lonely, and Rees-Mogg's sense of solitude was intensified by the White Swan affair. Soon, however, he acquired a uniquely close and like-minded colleague. Early in the New Year it was announced that a new columnist would be writing for the paper twice-weekly, on Tuesdays and Thursdays; and there was nothing low-key about the announcement. Among the epithets used to describe him by 'admirers and detractors' alike were, it was said, 'savage, clever, cunning, cruel, witty and brilliant'. The paragon in question was Bernard Levin.[2]

On the face of it, he and Rees-Mogg were markedly different, and few would have predicted that they would become soul-mates. Though Levin's background was by no means deprived, and he was, like Rees-Mogg, a public-school product (in his case, Christ's Hospital), he was far from being a squirearchical figure. Moreover, his higher education had been at the London School of Economics and his early political sympathies were quite strongly left-wing. While Rees-Mogg was making his name in journalism as a weighty political commentator, Levin was making his as a cheeky debunker of politicians, writing parliamentary sketches for Ian Gilmour's *Spectator* under the pen-name 'Taper'. And whereas Rees-Mogg long aspired to be a Conservative politician, Levin never aspired to be in politics at all, much less to be a candidate for the Conservative party. There was also a big contrast in prose styles, Rees-Mogg's being classical with a touch of neo-gothic, Levin's extravagantly baroque.

Yet these differences concealed fundamental affinities, and Rees-Mogg himself soon identified one of the most significant when he told Lord Lansdowne that he and Levin were 'the two self-avowed Whigs'

---

1 North to R.H.T., June 10 1970; R.H.T. to North June 15 1970.

2 Announcement on the front page, January 15 1971. Levin had been working for the *Daily Mail*. Rees-Mogg had approached him several years earlier, but he was not then prepared to make the move. *The Times* was to pay him £75 per column, with four weeks' paid holiday during the year: a total annual payment of £7,800.

on *The Times*'.[1] Levin indeed shared Rees-Mogg's passion for civil and religious liberty, and his attitude to his own Jewish community was rather similar to Rees-Mogg's to the Roman Catholic church. Both men hated obscurantism and exclusiveness, and both prided themselves on being rational while having, in fact, a pronounced tendency to be swayed by emotion. There were other resemblances. Both were curiously unmodern in their habits. Neither drove a car, and though Levin did type, unlike Rees-Mogg, it was not until 1989 – and then most reluctantly – that he exchanged his typewriter for a word-processor. Both loved the theatre and had a strong theatrical streak. Finally, Rees-Mogg secretly shared a characteristic of which Levin made no secret at all: the desire to stir people up and cause sensations.

During the rest of his time as editor Rees-Mogg found Levin not only a star contributor to the paper, but an indispensable source of encouragement, advice and amusement to himself. He was Father Joseph and Touchstone in one, and his place of work at Printing House Square both symbolised and assisted his role. When he arrived, there was no office available for him so he was 'temporarily' assigned a desk in Rees-Mogg's outer office. There he and his secretary became fixtures, and when the paper moved to Gray's Inn Road they occupied a similar position. Most mornings Levin would drop in on the editor for a chat; Rees-Mogg liked to try out ideas on him. Their relationship involved serious discussion mixed with light-hearted banter. One day when Rees-Mogg was dictating a leader to Levin's secretary, in the absence of his own, Levin came into the room just as he was saying 'Full stop'. Seeing Levin, he added: 'I'm sure you hear that more often from me than from Bernard'. On another occasion, when discussing a leader, he said to Levin: 'I'll provide the nouns – you provide the adjectives'.[2]

As well as all the talk, there was a constant flow of memoranda from Levin and, when he was abroad, of postcards. One typical Levin memo reads:

> A letter to the Editor this morning begins 'Sir, Do you ever wonder whether Mr. Levin is a fit contributor to your columns?' I have drafted a reply which begins 'The Editor frequently wonders whether Mr. Levin is a fit contributor to his columns, and *always* concludes that he is'.[3]

---

1 See p. 15 Chapter 1.
2 Levin talking to author.
3 Levin to W.R.-M., November 20 1972.

His postcards from abroad would often refer to what many regarded as an obsession with Wagner. For instance: 'On a strictly non-attributable basis, I am prepared to admit that Schubert is better than Wagner. If made public, however, I shall deny it and sue you'.[1]

Levin's first column for the paper coincided with a national postmen's strike, which prompted a long opening flight in his best parenthetical manner:

> For my part, I rather welcome the present dispute, in the agreeable knowledge that while it lasts the wicked (with whom I couple the name of the Inland Revenue) will cease from troubling me, and the weary (under which heading I include those correspondents who write to tell me to go back where I came from, heedless of the fact that I came from Camden Town and have no intention of going back there if I can help it) be at rest. Like, I suppose, most sensible men I have already made my own arrangements for meeting the emergency; I have laid in an ample store of cleft sticks, and my faithful bearer, Abdul the Fleet-footed, is putting dubbin on his sandals even as I write these words.

In view of his later hard line on trade union militancy, it is intriguing to record that in this dispute he sympathised wholeheartedly with the strikers.[2]

In 1970 one of the paper's most cherished features acquired new dimensions when the crossword editor, Edmund Akenhead, brought in two innovations: a *Times* crossword championship, and occasional jumbo puzzles. The former, held in conjunction with Cutty Sark whisky, was so popular that the first round, involving the correct solution of any one of five puzzles appearing in May, produced more than 20,000 qualifiers. Further eliminating rounds were needed to reduce the field to manageable proportions. The jumbo puzzle, with a twenty-seven letter square, was introduced as an additional attraction for bank holidays.

Akenhead had been editor of the feature since 1965, and he held the post throughout the Thomson period, retiring eventually in 1983 (to be succeeded by John Grant). He was a solicitor, educated at Rugby, who after attaining the rank of lieutenant-colonel in the Glider

1 Levin to W.R.-M. from Dornbirn, Austria, June 1978.
2 'Strikers in search of an incomes policy', January 19 1971.

Pilot Regiment during the war, entered the Colonial Service on the legal side and was sent to Tanganyika. There, in his plentiful leisure from government conveyancing, he diverted himself and others by exercising his skill as a conjurer, by acting and producing with the Dar es Salaam Players, and by compiling crosswords (his first appearing in the *Tanganyika Standard*).

The end of empire liberated his talents for fruitful employment at home, and when Jane Carton gave up the job of *Times* crossword editor – in which her husband, Ronald, had served a pioneering stint of thirty years – Akenhead was appointed to succeed her. He led a team of ten compilers, including two women, one of whom, Joyce Cansfield, had been Scrabble champion of Britain. A particularly brilliant member of the team was Brian Greer, mathematician and lecturer in psychology at Queen's University, Belfast. Akenhead himself compiled one puzzle a week, and all the jumbos. His mind was constantly attuned to anagrams and other cruciverbal devices. When his son introduced a girl friend called Celia, he is reputed to have exclaimed, with eyes agleam, 'Ah yes, mad Alice'.

The supremacy of the *Times* crossword within the genre is almost universally acknowledged, and owes much to the wit, as well as the ingenuity, of the clues. These were qualities on which Akenhead insisted, and which he was at endless pains to develop.

IX

The new government • Garden House sentences • Nasser and de Gaulle • Hamilton replaced as chief executive • End of the backset TBN • *Decimalisation and Rolls-Royce*

THE GENERAL ELECTION'S unexpected result posed a problem for the editor. In place of a government to which he was instinctively opposed he found himself dealing with one that he instinctively favoured. And what was true of the governments was even more true of their respective leaders, since he approved of Heath as much as he disapproved of Wilson. At the same time he had to maintain *The Times*'s independence, and this now involved suppressing, or at any rate masking, a favourable prejudice rather than a hostile one.

He achieved the necessary detachment partly by not seeing too much of the new prime minister: a self-denial made easier by Heath's complementary desire not to be too close to any journalist and not to seem as obsessed with the media as his predecessor had been. During his premiership Rees-Mogg's meetings with him were just about as infrequent as, during the previous three or four years, with Wilson. In addition there were issues on which the paper could disagree with the government, among which the most substantial was that of arms for South Africa.

Heath was under pressure from his right wing to lift the sanctions directed against the illegal Ian Smith regime in Rhodesia, but – with *The Times*'s full support – was unwilling to do so unless Smith accepted certain conditions which would, in effect, nullify the purpose of his rebellion. In the circumstances it suited the prime minister to make a limited concession to the right on South Africa, by selling arms ostensibly for use in defending the sea-lanes, but not for internal use. This involved him in some acrimony with other Commonwealth countries, but he stood firmly on Britain's right to act as its government thought fit. *The Times* took the view that any commercial advantage to Britain was more than offset by resulting trade boycotts, and that the defence and Cold War arguments used to justify the policy were defective in their own terms. 'To sell arms to South Africa is the simplest and most direct way to increase the risk of war and of communist penetration. If the Government wants to destroy its own policy this is the right way to do it'.[1]

The new government's chief concerns were, however, domestic and European. Its economic policy had much in common with what later came to be known as Thatcherism, and the man expected to be foremost in giving effect to it was Iain Macleod, whom Heath appointed chancellor of the exchequer. Unfortunately, within a month of taking office, Macleod suddenly died on July 20 after an operation for appendicitis. *The Times*'s obituary of him was excessively reverent and not very perceptive, failing to bring out the element of inspired adventurer that was the key to his character.[2]

Who was to succeed him? Maudling had been chancellor before, but was now home secretary and anyway somewhat lukewarm in his attitude to the EEC. Keith Joseph, a former housing minister and now at the DHSS, was a man of superior intellect and known to be interested in economics. But Heath's choice was Anthony Barber, less obviously gifted than Joseph, and with slightly shorter cabinet experience, yet a former treasury minister and, above all, a committed European, already charged with the task of negotiating British entry. No doubt Heath regarded him as a thoroughly like-minded and reliable executant for the most important business facing the administration. *The Times* described his appointment as not the only possible one but 'the most logical'.[3]

On the day this leader comment appeared, an op. ed. piece by Philip Howard, most stylish of the paper's younger writers, turned a study of the red grouse into a reflection on contemporary Britain:

> In the autumn grouse persecutes grouse: there is annual gladiatorial contest, as aggressive cock grouse seize territories and drive away gentle grouse into packs, which drop out, with nothing to eat, and nowhere to go, except over the butts. The researchers have observed old cock grouse, who have been evicted from their territories by abrasive, aggressive young birds, pine away from what they describe as 'social stress', even though there is still plenty of food around for surplus birds. Life and death on the

---

1 Leader, 'No arms for South Africa', October 15 1970.
2 July 22 1970.
3 Leader, 'Mr. Barber's role', July 27 1970.

grouse moor, in fact, turns out to be shockingly like the rat race in the big city.[1]

Any readers who may have been disturbed by recent changes of style and tone in the paper can only have been reassured by this piece.

Barber's first budget, introduced in the autumn, cut income tax by 6d in the pound (from the following April) and corporation tax by 2½d (from January). The cost of school meals was to be increased, though poorer families' entitlement to free meals was extended. Free school milk was stopped for children over seven – earning the nickname 'milk-snatcher' for the new minister of education, Margaret Thatcher – and cheap welfare milk for the population generally was discontinued, though retained for expectant and nursing mothers, and for children under five. NHS prescription charges were put up, as were charges for spectacles and dental treatment.

The Times devoted two leaders to this budget. In the first the chancellor's strategy was commended, if only as a step in the right direction. The second argued that the cuts were not to be seen as damaging to the welfare state, but rather as necessary for maintaining it on a viable basis.[2] In neither leader was there any reference to a proposal which was to exercise *Times* readers far more than cuts in milk or school meals: the proposal to charge for entry to national art galleries and museums. In the House of Commons this was greeted with cries of 'Shame' from some Labour MPs, though not mentioned by Roy Jenkins in his immediate response to the chancellor's statement. In *The Times* it provoked a lively correspondence which continued for weeks.

The first letter was from the president of the Museums Association, who did not oppose charges for all museums – only for those whose natural attractiveness was not such as to make the handicap of a charge bearable – but who was convinced it would be the unanimous view of his colleagues that the proceeds of charges should go towards improving museums' services.[3] There was support for the chancellor, some of it light-hearted: 'What a pity Mr. Barber did not come sooner! If his predecessor of 1850 had thought of imposing a charge for admission to museums the penurious Karl Marx would have been kept out of the reading room of the British Museum, and *Das Kapital* would not have been written'.[4] And a past president of the Royal Academy

---

1 'Greater dangers than "the glorious twelfth"', July 27 1970.
2 'Creating room to move' and 'No Attack on Welfare', October 28 1970.
3 From Hugh Scrutton, October 30 1970.
4 From W. J. Rasbridge, Epsom, November 3 1970.

wrote: 'We pay when we go to concerts to hear music; why then should we not pay when we go to galleries to see pictures? Is there not some relation between the cost of things to us and our appreciation of them? In spite of the popular song, the best things in life are *not* free'.[1]

The weight of opinion, however, was against the proposal. A leading and public-spirited art dealer wrote: 'I am saddened . . . as I feel the principle is wrong even if the proceeds are to be used to benefit the galleries concerned. [But] if the sums raised are to be annexed to the Treasury, thus becoming merely a further form of taxation, I feel I would want to reconsider carefully my own loans to the national collections. Other owners who have lent their works of art so that they may be freely enjoyed by the public . . . may share this view'.[2] Various heads of fine art schools or departments wrote to protest,[3] as did two of Britain's most famous painters.[4] The *Annual Register* for 1970 recorded that 'the letter pages of *The Times* were full of distinguished names adding their support to the opponents of museum admission charges'.

It was not until mid-December that *The Times* committed itself editorially on the issue, and then it took the government's side, using the familiar argument that art, in the visual sense, should not be uniquely privileged when other forms of artistic expression were subject to charges. More money should be made available to museums and galleries from public funds, though not by allowing each institution to earmark for its own use the money raised by charging for entry.[5] The government's case, thus supported by *The Times*, was logically unassailable; but in politics, and more especially English politics, even supposedly educated opinion is more likely to be swayed by irrational feeling than by logic. The museum charges proposal caused far more trouble than it was worth, and its implementation was repeatedly postponed. Meanwhile it damaged the government's reputation among people who should have been its most ardent well-wishers. Heath was unusual among prime ministers in being a genuine aesthete. Moreover, he gave his arts minister, Lord Eccles, a seat in the cabinet, and his desire to control public expenditure did not preclude a generous attitude towards funding the arts. Yet through the maladroit attempt to charge for admission to museums his government came to be described (by John Betjeman) as philistine.

---

1 Sir Charles Wheeler, PPRA, November 5 1970
2 Hugh Leggatt, November 7 1970.
3 Sir William Coldstream and others, November 9 1970.
4 Ben Nicholson and Graham Sutherland, December 16 1970.
5 'Paying for Admission to the Museums', second leader, December 15 1970.

On the major issues of the Heath administration – Europe and trade union reform – Rees-Mogg could support the government with enthusiasm and total commitment. On most others, apart from arms for South Africa, his instinct was to give Heath the benefit of any doubt. For example when, in October, super-ministries of industry and the environment were set up, and the overseas development administration was absorbed into the foreign office, *The Times* commented: 'Most of the changes should be welcomed, though it remains to be seen how they work out in practice'.[1] The tone was essentially positive, and the qualifying clause merely platitudinous.

The readiness of the Rees-Mogg *Times* to defend the younger generation against excessive judicial severity, already shown in the Jagger case, was evident again when six Cambridge students were sentenced by Mr. Justice Melford Stevenson for their part in a violent demonstration at the Garden House Hotel in Cambridge, protesting against a dinner organised by sympathisers of the colonels' regime in Greece. The six were arrested, in what many regarded as an arbitrary manner, from a crowd of several hundred demonstrators, and they received sentences of between nine and eighteen months, while the two of them who were not British (a South African and a Brazilian) were recommended for deportation.

In a leader which attracted considerable notice *The Times* described these sentences as 'of a severity that raise[d] important questions of public policy'. How far did it matter that the citizens concerned were students? The judge, in passing sentence, had said: 'These offences are not less serious because many of you are living wholly or in part on public money'. 'Not less serious', the leader commented, 'but no more serious either. Whether any student is receiving a public grant for his education must be irrelevant in a court of law'. As for exemplary sentences, they could on occasion be justified, but it was 'a good rule that an exemplary sentence should be no more severe than [was] necessary to set an example'. For most of the students 'the mere fact of imprisonment would have been enough':

> A prison sentence of six months or less for a first offence does not have to be suspended when it is for an assault, or a threat of violence, or for having or possessing a firearm or an offensive weapon. So Mr. Justice Melford Stevenson was not forced to

1 'A better machine for policy', October 16 1970.

> impose longer sentences in order to ensure that the offenders were sent to prison at all, and it must seem that while he was right to take a serious view of a deplorable affair he has been very severe.[1]

In the big correspondence that followed, the chairman of the Cambridge University Conservative Association was one who disagreed with *The Times*. 'Had this particular violence been committed by anyone else in the community, for example a gang of skinheads, a sentence of 18 months, whether in Borstal or in prison, would be considered far from harsh, perhaps even too lenient'. Double standards in the law should be avoided.[2] Most of the letters, however, supported the line taken in the leader.

One aspect of the judgement to which the leader did not refer, but which came up in the correspondence, was the judge's remark in his summing-up that some senior members of the university, who had appeared as witnesses in the trial, might have exerted 'evil influence' over their students and so helped to provoke the crime. Six dons wrote emphatically denying this charge, against which, they said, there could be no redress.[3] And their letter was swiftly followed by one from the heads of their faculties defending them on character grounds.[4]

The latter part of 1970 witnessed the sudden deaths of two men who, in their different ways, had been outstanding national leaders, and who had also successfully twisted the British lion's tail. On September 28 President Gamal Abdel Nasser of Egypt died of a heart attack in Cairo, and the following day *The Times* carried an obituary of him occupying four columns running to slightly more than half the depth of the page. There was also a leader, written by the editor, in which Nasser was described as 'the greatest leader of an Arab country in his generation', who nevertheless 'bore responsibility for several great disasters for his country and region'. He was 'in modern history, perhaps in all her history since Roman times, the first great Egyptian leader of Egypt'. The appraisal concluded:

> The Middle East might have been an easier place in which to make peace if he had never lived; it is certainly a harder place in

1 'Student sentences' (Smith), July 4 1970.
2 Jim Powell, July 6 1970.
3 Dr. Elias Bredsdorff and others, July 6 1970.
4 Lord Kahn and others, July 7 1970.

> which to maintain any kind of security or order because he has died now. Yesterday there were three certainties in the Middle East: Israel, Russian power and Nasser. Now there are only the two certainties left: Israel and Russia. No man can tell what will happen to the rest.[1]

The price of oil and then resurgent Islamic fanaticism would provide answers that Rees-Mogg did not foresee.

On the op. ed. page Hodgkin discussed the future of the region after Nasser, starting with the proposition that he was probably the only man who could have sold a settlement with Israel to the Arabs. Since he was head and shoulders above all his associates, it was impossible to guess who would succeed him as leader.[2]

Unlike Nasser, Charles de Gaulle was no longer in office when he died at Colombey-les-deux-Eglises on November 9, having resigned the presidency two years before. He was also nearly thirty years older, and manifestly his talents and achievements were far more impressive than Nasser's. Suitably, therefore, the paper gave him an obituary covering two whole pages, with four illustrations. There were also two op. ed. pieces relating to him, interviews on page 5 with Lords Avon and Montgomery and Sir Louis Spears, and a leader by Hodgkin which began with a quotation from the English translation of de Gaulle's *Le Fil de l'Épée* and ended with the magnificent closing words of his war memoirs given in French (from 'Vieille France, accablée' to 'la lueur de l'espérance').

The leader suggested that the history of the Second World War, and the subsequent founding of the Fourth Republic in France, might not have been very different 'if de Gaulle had been arrested by the Pétainists in Bordeaux'. But what could not be questioned was that in 1958 he had 'saved France from a military dictatorship which would have led inevitably to civil war and which would, among its many consequences, have let the Common Market die at birth'. At the age of sixty-seven he had 'saved the state and the republic and led France safely and legally out of the morass of the Algerian war'. He governed 'the least easily governed European state' for ten years, and left a greater mark on the country than any man since Napoleon.

There was, indeed, a contrast between the 'solemn wisdom' of his speech in Westminster Hall and the 'growing obsession with a bogy to which he gave the collective label Anglo-Saxon'. Yet 'no rebuffs

---

1 'The death of Nasser', September 29 1970.
2 'After Nasser, what kind of future for Middle East?' (same date).

could kill in Britain the realization that a century, once rashly dedicated to the Common Man, was uncommonly lucky to have fostered the genius of a de Gaulle and a Churchill'.[1]

In his letter to the staff at the end of 1969 Denis Hamilton had said that the paper 'must break even in 1971'; but it was soon obvious that this intention would not be fulfilled. For the period to the end of March the cumulative loss on Times Newspapers exceeded forecast by nearly £250,000,[2] and at the end of May the finance director, W. M. Brown, was predicting for the year a trading shortfall against budget of £721,000.[3] In the autumn Hamilton was told by the Thomson Organisation, at a meeting with its managing director, Gordon Brunton, that his preliminary budget for 1971 was 'inadequate' and would have to be revised. Brunton called for 'a fundamental review' of Times Newspapers' 'entire operation with a view to reducing the non-variable costs in 1971 by £1 million'.[4]

The trouble was due, of course, overwhelmingly to *The Times*, and more especially to its poor performance in advertising. By the middle of the year its net advertisement revenue was down £475,000 against budget. Everything that was being done to save money, or increase revenue, in other departments was more than counteracted by the decline in advertising volume. Compared with 1969 *The Times* had lost, to April, 1 per cent overall in market share, while the *Guardian* had gained the same percentage; and bookings for the coming half-year were down more than 15 per cent.[5] Since the price rise in October 1969 circulation had moved sharply into reverse, but even while it was growing the readers gained were largely (though from educated backgrounds) in the C1 category, and therefore of extremely limited interest to advertisers.[6] Rates were considered high in relation to the number and quality of readers, and in these circumstances the temptation to offer cut-price sales of space, or 'contra' arrangements whereby advertisers paid in kind rather than cash, was not always resisted. Such practices, or the mere suspicion of them, inevitably further undermined confidence in the paper as an advertising medium.

Insufficient revenue from advertisements was the worst problem,

1 'Charles de Gaulle', November 11 1970.
2 TEB, April 23 1970.
3 TEB, May 28 1970.
4 TEB, October 28 1970.
5 TEB, May 28 1970.
6 TEB, March 19 1970.

but by no means the only one. The drop in circulation after the 1969 price rise, though of course anticipated in principle, turned out to be rather steeper than expected. For the six months to June the average sale was about 25,000 below the budgeted figure.[1] The educated C1 readers who had represented so large an element in the growth of circulation while the price was held down, deserted in droves when the price went up. It was raised again, to 9d., in mid-June, and at first there were indications that this might not affect sales significantly. But a wholesalers' dispute which lasted for a fortnight at the end of September, and unhappily coincided with a campaign to promote the re-designed paper, served to accelerate the downward trend.[2] In November the price was raised yet again, to 1s., which meant that the price of *The Times* had doubled in little more than a year.

Hamilton had expressed the hope, in his letter to staff, that all engaged in producing the paper would suggest to him ways of saving money. But by the middle of the year it had to be reported that the unions had given little or no support to what was euphemistically called the Profit Improvement Programme; so it seemed necessary for management to take the initiative.[3] At a meeting attended by forty-two fathers of chapels from all the unions and their sub-units Hamilton stood on a chair, Monty-style, and announced that two folders (printing presses) would have to be closed, with the loss of about 120 man-weeks' work in the machine room. After some initial shock the decision was accepted, on the basis of thirteen weeks' notice or pay in lieu for the men made redundant. At the same time a joint management-unions consultative committee was set up which, it was hoped, would facilitate the implementation of further changes. In fact it did not make much progress. By September the general manager, Rowett, was reporting 'a slow start' and 'lack of urgency or interest'.[4]

With such a record of failure on the business side, and such a dubious outlook, the need for personal as well as policy changes was inescapable. Before the end of the year the advertisement marketing director, J. P. Macfarlane, who had only quite recently joined the executive board, left with a handshake of £5,000.[5] But a more important scapegoat was needed, and the obvious candidate was Hamilton himself. At the beginning of 1971 it was announced that he would be succeeding Kenneth Thomson as chairman of Times Newspapers

1 TEB, July 23 1970.
2 TEB, October 22 1970.
3 TEB, May 28 1970.
4 TEB, September 3 1970.
5 TNL board meeting, November 30 1970.

Limited, while the latter was to become co-president (with Gavin Astor) of TNL and joint chairman of the Thomson Organisation. The job Hamilton was assuming, however, was of far less consequence than the one he was giving up, for he was to relinquish the position of chief executive. His successor in it was to be M. J. Hussey, from Associated Newspapers.

Until the Thomson take-over of *The Times* Hamilton's career had never faltered. After his brilliant war service he had become first Kemsley's, then Thomson's, indispensable lieutenant. He had shown mastery in the negotiation of large-scale deals and in editing a quality Sunday newspaper. With his appointment as editor-in-chief of the two Times newspapers, and chief executive of the company that was to run them (and the supplements), he seemed to have reached an apotheosis of power and opportunity.

Yet the first of these posts sounded more powerful than it really was, while the second required experience that he largely lacked. Basically and by original choice a journalist, he had excelled at mobilising the talents of a team of journalists, and at judging the tastes and interests of an increasingly prosperous weekend readership. He had also proved a most accomplished courtier and diplomat in the service of two formidable businessmen. But he was not, in the true sense, a businessman himself. He had never been responsible for coordinating the manifold activities and often competing elements of a big commercial enterprise, in such a way as to make it profitable. At the *Sunday Times* he had made a notable contribution to the paper's fortunes, but as the leader, as it were, of one department of the orchestra, rather than as the conductor.

In 1967 he was thrust into a role for which, by temperament and training, he was ill-equipped. His relationship with Thomson, and with the Thomson Organisation, was full of ambiguity. The proprietor's attitude to *The Times*, and his numerous other commitments, led him to adopt a position of managerial detachment which did not come naturally to him and which was, therefore, essentially a sham. Hamilton did not have a free hand. Thomson was nagging at him all the time and, worse still, giving inconsistent guidance. At the outset Thomson seemed to be offering unlimited support for the policy of dashing for growth; but when the results were not what he expected he abruptly reverted to type and decided that *The Times* would have to live within its means. Had he been prepared to continue subsidising it to even half the extent of the losses his family were to incur from it before the end of the 1970s, the policy of expansion might conceivably have succeeded. As an alternative, he might have discarded the philosophy of the Cooper report and concentrated upon exploiting the paper's unique prestige, without trying to compete with the *Daily Telegraph*'s circulation or the *Financial Times*'s special appeal. What he actually did made the worst of both worlds.

Hamilton cannot escape a substantial share of blame. Like Thomson himself and all other senior Thomson men, with the sole exception of Harry Henry, he was seduced by a mistaken policy, which he personally compounded by mistakes of his own attributable to unfamiliarity with the sort of work he was doing. He erred, moreover, in imagining that Thomson would allow any newspaper of his, even *The Times*, to run indefinitely at a heavy loss, whatever he might say. But Hamilton should not carry more than his fair share of blame, nor should others, including more especially Thomson, be exempted from blame. Hamilton was Thomson's chief executant, rather than an independent chief executive. As chairman of the company he was now to have even less control of its affairs, and he turned increasingly to the promotion of cultural events, such as exhibitions.

His successor was very different from him superficially, and up to a point genuinely. Whereas Hamilton was a grammar-school boy who never went to university, and who served in line regiments, Marmaduke James Hussey was educated at Rugby and Trinity College, Oxford, and his war service was in the Grenadier Guards. Though his background was not exactly grand, it was certainly privileged; and he entered the grand world with his marriage to Lady Susan Waldegrave, a friend and lady-in-waiting of the Queen. Another difference was that Hussey, unlike Hamilton, had spent his entire working life on the business side of newspapers. He had never been a journalist but had joined the Rothermere press (Associated Newspapers) as a management trainee in 1949, becoming a director in 1964 and managing director of Harmsworth Publications (*Daily Mail* and *Evening News*) in 1967. He had ample experience of running newspapers; also of closing them down. He knew at least as much about newsagents, paper manufacturers, print unions and advertisers as he did about journalists.

There was also a very apparent contrast of temperament. Hamilton was reserved and noted for his pregnant silences; Hussey was ebullient to the point of heartiness, with a big laugh. Nobody would ever have accused Hamilton of being bonhomous, though he was almost invariably courteous. Hussey's bonhomie was so robust and indiscriminate that anyone not naturally responsive to it might have wrongly suspected it of being false. Perhaps this difference, as well as the circumstances in which they were thrown together, made it inevitable that the two men would never get on. Yet the difference itself may have been partly a symptom of something very profound that they shared. Hamilton's extreme reserve and Hussey's extreme ebullience may, in a sense, have been different ways of dealing with a problem that they had in common: that of living with chronic pain.

Hamilton, as we have seen, suffered from bouts of agonising migraine, to which he had been subject since childhood but which may have been aggravated when an ammunition dump was blown up as he was accepting the surrender of a German division at the end of the war. After this he was in hospital for months. Hussey had an even longer hospital experience, resulting from terrible war wounds. Hardly had he joined his battalion at Anzio in January 1944 than he was hit at point-blank range by sub-machine-gun bullets. Left for dead he was nevertheless taken prisoner and nursed at first by Italian nuns, under whose care he had a leg amputated. Transferred to a camp in south Germany, he underwent surgery for his shattered spine. At the end of 1944 he was repatriated, and as he was carried out of the prisoner-of-war camp, on what happened to be his twenty-first birthday, the German commandant and a guard-of-honour were on parade, with a band. For several years afterwards he was in and out of hospital, but a combination of surgeons' skill and his strength of character enabled him to walk, though always with a stick and always painfully. A natural athlete and Oxford 'blue' (for cricket, though he could have had one for rugby as well) he was turned by the war into a permanent cripple.

Both Hamilton and Hussey were prime examples of soldierly virtue and this was not the only underlying resemblance between them. Despite the tough capitalist image that he cultivated, Hussey was far from being a right-wing ideologue. His patriotism, like Hamilton's, was laced with social idealism; he had plenty of sympathy for life's victims. Moreover, his approach to industrial relations was in one vital respect not so very different from Hamilton's. Though he reckoned he understood trade unionists, and certainly had far more practice than Hamilton in dealing with them, fundamentally his approach was that of the officer and gentleman; and he was to pay a heavy penalty for it. He was also, like Hamilton, to suffer eventually for carrying out a policy that he believed to be that of his proprietor.

Meanwhile he made no attempt to soften the impact of Hamilton's fall, or propulsion upstairs. In place of Hamilton's executive board he swiftly set up an executive management committee, of which he was chairman and from which Hamilton was excluded. If, however, those who appointed Hussey were hoping that he would be equally detached and ruthless in his attitude to Rees-Mogg, it was soon clear that they had miscalculated. In fact a close alliance developed between the editor of *The Times* and the new chief executive. Both were Oxford men, and both were history scholars. Hussey's bluff manner camouflaged not only his physical suffering, but also the intellectual streak in him. An even closer bond, perhaps, was Somerset. The Waldegraves were Somerset grandees, and the Husseys had a house in Waldegrave territory. Rees-Mogg was a representative of the Somerset landed gentry, with a home in the county. Like-mindedness on the job was thus reinforced by neighbourly contact at weekends.

Since its highly publicised launch in April 1967 the separate *Times Business News* 'backset' (in the technical term), had considerable achievements to its credit. It provided good economic analysis, particularly by Peter Jay, Hugh Stephenson, Frances Cairncross and the editor, Tony Vice. It was notably strong in the sustained day-by-day coverage of financial news stories. In September 1969 it introduced the computerised setting of Stock Exchange prices, a pioneering exercise in Britain. Nevertheless it was plagued by inaccuracy, and in its challenge to the *Financial Times* – the purpose for which, above all, it existed – it never showed any sign of succeeding.

Much of the trouble was due to its having been launched prematurely, under relentless pressure from Thomson. Many of the journalists recruited for it were young and inexperienced. The subs and readers were too few in number, underpaid, and for the most part unfamiliar with the type of material they were handling. The production base, anyway inadequate for a paper that was expanding so rapidly, was most acutely inadequate for *TBN*, an operation of great complexity in which the need for precision of detail was absolute. Even strengths could be turned into weaknesses by flaws in the production process; computerised price-setting seemed to Vice 'like putting a 10 hp car on to a motorway'.[1] In April 1970 the *TBN* price list had a first edition error rate of 50 per 1,000 shares, compared with the *FT*'s rate of 15 per 1,000 shares.[2]

Apart from share prices, TBN early acquired a reputation for gross factual errors, and such reputations, once acquired, are hard to live down. In 1967, for instance, the British Motor Corporation was angered by a report that BMC was producing 17,000 cars a month, when the correct figure was 17,000 a week; and the Finnish ambassador was incensed to read a report in which Finland was described as an Iron

---

1 Talking to author.
2 Memo from A. Vice to J. Webb, copy to W.R.-M. (among others), April 21 1970.

Curtain country.[1] Such mistakes persisted, and there were also endless complaints about the proliferation of literals. By mid-1970 it was recognised that *TBN* had a bad name for inaccuracy, while the *FT* remained the accepted paper of record for financiers and businessmen, and that consequently *The Times* rarely got long company reports.[2]

Rees-Mogg had hoped that *TBN* would break down the barrier 'between the profit-earning business man or profit-directed business executive and the fee or salary-earning professional man or civil servant'.[3] Yet the prejudice against business, as distinct from finance, was not so easily removed. From within the office Joe Roeber was protesting, at the end of 1968, about *TBN*'s relative neglect of industry. Most so-called business journalists were, he argued, in reality City journalists by training and interest. 'We live in the City; more for social reasons than anything else, the peak of the business community is occupied by the City; many of our friends . . . work in the City. It is, in short, an inescapable part of the London climate. But we should fight against it'.[4] Though Roeber himself soon left for the United States, his criticism seems to have had some effect, because in 1969 it was decided to strengthen the production of industrial news, which would in future 'occupy the greater part of expanding editorial space'.[5] Unfortunately the expansionary phase was about to end.

Long before economy became the order of the day *TBN* was having difficulty holding its staff. Within two years of its launch twenty members of the editorial staff, or one-third of the total, had resigned. One reason was the attraction of salary prospects elsewhere – not least because the *FT* was fighting back hard – but another was that the open-plan accommodation for *TBN* at Printing House Square was so crowded that many were working close to the minimum space of 45 sq. ft. per person laid down by the GLC.[6] In the new climate created by Thomson's decision to stop subsidising *The Times*'s growth there could be no question of increasing the staff of *TBN*. On the contrary Vice was asked for cuts, and in November 1970 he proposed to reduce the editorial establishment over 13 per cent, from seventy-four to sixty-four.[7]

Meanwhile the future of the section as a separate entity was being ardently debated. Vice himself had no doubt that *TBN* should remain

1 Confidential memo from McDonald to W.R.-M., August 25 1967.
2 Memo on *TBN* from unspecified source, June 30 1970.
3 Vice to W.R.-M. and others, May 27 1969.
4 Roeber to W.R.-M., copies to Vice and Jay, December 11 1968.
5 Vice to W.R.-M. and others, May 27 1969.
6 Vice to W.R.-M., copy to C.D.H., November 13 1968.
7 Vice to W.R.-M., copy to J. Grout, November 23 1970.

backset. When the idea of incorporating the section in the main paper was first mooted, he argued that the differential cost of backsetting was about £250,000 a year (£150,000 for extra paging and £100,000 for extra editorial overheads), and that this had to be considered in relation to business advertising revenue of over £2 million a year.[1] He did not, perhaps, convincingly demonstrate that the scale of business advertising was directly due to backsetting as such, and certainly he failed to convince a management which was concerned, above all, to reduce costs, and which had been bombarded for some time with anecdotal evidence about the thousands of *TBNs* left daily as detritus on commuter trains. At the end of 1970 it was announced that *The Times* would be appearing as a single integrated paper during the holiday period, though it was also stated that *TBN* might reappear as a separate section after the holiday.[2]

In fact, it did not reappear. Hussey lost no time, after his assumption of power in the New Year, in seeking the views of those responsible for selling space in the paper. These were conveyed to him in a 'strictly private and confidential' memorandum from Macfarlane's successor, R. L. Willsmer. Donald Antcliffe, though 'ambivalent as usual', said he was prepared to accept there would be no loss of revenue from financial advertising if *TBN* were included in the main paper. Michael Weston reported that media directors 'with very rare exceptions' disliked the backset *TBN*, and that news that the section would continue within the paper 'would lead to a resurgence of confidence among media buyers'. David Teague, on behalf of Classified, was 'totally in favour of a one-section paper', while Bryan Todd for Marketing thought that 'the differential readership between the two sections should encourage advertisers'. Willsmer added that his own views accorded 'very closely with those of the media directors'. He had always regarded *TBN* 'as a bit of a joke', and was sure that 'a good, tightly controlled, business section within the main paper would do a tremendous amount to restore confidence in the future of *The Times*'.[3] Hussey agreed, and the temporary integration became permanent for the rest of the Thomson period.[4]

1 Vice to C.D.H., October 31 1968.
2 *TT*, December 21 1970.
3 R. L. Willsmer to M.J.H., copy to C.D.H., January 12 1971.
4 But there was no formal announcement of the change, and readers who wrote to ask about *TBN* were told: 'While the present economic trends continue, it is probable that Business News will be paged into the main paper. However, occasions will arise when we will reappear as a separate section'. (Specimen letter sent to W.R.-M. for inspection by Dennis Topping, February 15 1971.)

The end of backsetting appropriately coincided with the departure of its chief defender, Vice. In the New Year he left not only the paper, but journalism, for a senior position at Rothschilds' bank. Though his temperament may not have been ideal for the role of editor, he lacked neither energy nor ideas, and the tribulations of *TBN* during its early phase were largely due to circumstances beyond his control.

His successor, Hugh Stephenson, though not the first choice for the job, was to hold it with marked competence for ten years.[1] A Winchester scholar, he had gone on to New College, Oxford, and he was yet another who had been president of the Oxford Union. He had also been Peter Jay's best man, and it was Jay who persuaded him to leave the diplomatic service and join *The Times*. His promotion to a key post on the paper, while only in his early thirties, was a striking example of Rees-Mogg's indulgent attitude to younger signatories of the White Swan letter.

On February 15 1971 Britain went over to a decimal currency, and on that day *The Times* announced its price simply as 5p, having for some days previously given it as 'one shilling (5p)' to get readers used to the change. In a leader the paper commented sadly on the event and its precipitating cause:

> By February 15, 1971, the poor penny has shrunk so far in value, and therefore in importance in everyday exchanges, that its translation into something else is no longer of great significance. It is to inflation as much as to their own perseverance that the improvers owe the realisation of their hopes today.[2]

The lead story that day, however, was not the decimalisation of the currency but the nationalisation of Rolls-Royce. In 1968 the Rolls-Royce Company had signed a fixed-price contract with Lockheed for supplying several hundred RB-211 engines for its TriStar aircraft, still on the drawing-board. Government finance was pledged as backing for the project, but over the next two years its costs soared – partly another consequence of inflation – and in November 1970 the Heath government, while agreeing to add £42 million to the £47 million already provided from public funds, said that the company was

1 The post was offered first to an outsider, the editor-in-chief of the *Director*, who turned it down. (Stephenson talking to author.)
2 'Reckoning the change', February 15 1971. The new penny has since become as 'poor' as the old one was then.

changing its top management. Even so confidence was not restored and Rolls-Royce shares continued to fall.

On February 8 the House of Commons was informed that the company was going into liquidation, since its losses on the project were likely to exceed net assets and the government was unwilling to provide any more help. This was indeed startling news. Rolls-Royce was one of Britain's most prestigious companies and celebrated throughout the world. In the words of the *Annual Register*, 'If the Bank of England itself had collapsed the shock could scarcely have been greater'. But for Tories there was a further shock, since the government went on to say that it would be acquiring the aero-engine and certain other divisions of the company. This act of nationalisation by a Conservative government was condemned by Enoch Powell, and caused uneasiness among many members of the party.

The Times on the other hand, in a leader on decimalisation day, supported the government's decision, stressing the argument that the parts of Rolls-Royce that were being nationalised were vital for national defence:

> It can fairly be described as a tough tactic, but in the circumstances a necessary one. Once Rolls-Royce was bankrupted by the RB-211 contract, the Government had to find a way to preserve what was capable of being preserved, and of protecting the national interest.

The failure of Rolls-Royce was due to 'a simple and massive commercial misjudgement'.[1] Yet *The Times* would not apply the pure capitalist thesis that such misjudgements should be left to do their worst, with no attempt on the part of government to mitigate their ill effects.

---

1 'Broken rules that led to the downfall of Rolls-Royce', February 15 1971.

X

Page seven girl • Priceless unpaid contributors • EEC entry: France the key • Editorialising on the grand scale • Vote won, treaty signed • Weekend in the country • Evolution of features

'**WHAT'S A NICE** girl like you doing in a firm like this?' was the caption of an advertisement for Fisons which occupied the whole of page 7 of *The Times* on March 17 1971. The 'nice' girl in question was certainly nice-looking. She was also stark naked, and brushing her hair. The pretext for using such an illustration to advertise a firm manufacturing farm and garden chemicals and pharmaceutical products was exceptionally far-fetched. Ostensibly the advertisement was for Bisks, a line of slimming biscuits that Fisons was producing. Everyone who bought a packet of Bisks was entitled to join the Bisks Slimmers' Club, and it was alleged that 100,000 had joined, 'including the nice girl up there who modelled for one of the advertisements'.

The immediate question in the minds of many traditional readers of the paper when they saw the advertisement must have been: 'What's a nude girl like you doing in a newspaper like this?'. Such an attitude was, indeed, well reflected in the correspondence that ensued, but it also showed many taking a more light-hearted view of the matter. One who disapproved strongly was Trevor Abbott from Martyr's Green in Surrey:

> Sir, Well, well, even *The Times* has succumbed at last. Let me say I was more than mildly surprised to discover a full page nude photograph in your paper; particularly since it bore absolutely no relation to the product advertised. It has long been apparent that advertisers have lost all sense of scruple and for a quality paper such as yours to support this is very saddening.

But James Marchant from Bletchley was humorously relaxed:

> Before the crescendo of protest becomes deafening, may I voice

my appreciation of the consummate good taste displayed by your advertiser on page seven . . . ? I hope this delightful picture has the same effect on *The Times*'s circulation as it does on mine.

T. J. Owen wrote from Leeds to express his displeasure:

I do not wish to take up space . . . except to state that *The Times* should not use such matter which degrades womanhood and uses the female body as an eye-catcher. Too much emphasis on nudity seems to me to obscure the main issue which is that sex is merely a part of the more important matter of love and respect.

But such solemnity was not for C. Pratsides of Greenford, Middlesex:

It's disgusting! Disgraceful. Quite plainly it's too much. How can I, a regular subscriber to this paper, be expected to listen (along with the world) with humble awe when *The Times* speaks . . . when, in all innocence, whilst expecting to come across the Law Report, or the Science Report, or something, I turn to page seven and am suddenly confronted with a full page spread of a naked . . . that is, of a young . . . er, of a rather attractive . . .

Well, anyway, Sir, I was shocked. The very foundations of our society have been rocked. Dare I suggest that this is but an omen of things yet to come? The mind boggles at what Chairman Mao is going to do with this.

And it wasn't even in colour. Tut, tut.

Andrew Symonds of Cuckfield, Sussex, shared T. J. Bowen's view, asking:

Are you trying to drive away your readers by subscribing to the present advertising belief that it is only sex and nakedness that sells? If you want to maintain the position claimed by your own advertisements, surely you had better eschew the nudes and pay more respect to womanhood.

But S. F. Shore from the Minories, London EC3, conveyed a hint of criticism with a lighter touch:

Presumably as a result of your today's edition, there will be a mass change of subscriptions from *Playboy* magazine to *The Times*.

And the best letter of all, which was also the shortest, came from F. S. Macdonald, Masters' Common Room, St. John's School, Leatherhead. It read simply:

> 'Topless People Take *The Times*'?[1]

Of all *The Times*'s regular features none was more admired than 'Letters to the Editor', which gave it the benefit of first-class material for which it did not have to pay, provided an incomparable channel of communication with its readers, and often generated news stories which other papers had to copy. In March 1971 Robert H. Yoakum of Lakeville, Connecticut, wrote a piece about the feature in *Newsday*, and one of the Senators from Connecticut, Abraham Ribicoff, was so impressed by it (or possibly so anxious to do a good turn to his constituent) that he had the article reprinted in the *Congressional Record* for May 4 1971.

Under the heading 'In London town, there is only one "God" and his name is "Letters to the Editor"', Yoakum wrote:

> If it is true that Hell hath no greater fury than a woman scorned . . . the letter writer who has been rejected by *The Times* of London must come in a close second.
>
> To understand the bitterness with which unprinted writers assail *The Times* one must remember that the publication of a letter in that paper is, for some Britishers, the one clear way to earthly immortality.
>
> Think of the frustration that builds up: 90,000 people wrote to *The Times*. . . last year; approximately 85,500 didn't get in. Even so most rejected writers keep trying, hoping that the portals of heaven will someday open.

He gave examples of some who had succeeded, over time. Hockley Clarke had done particularly well with more than forty letters published, on such subjects as birds, animals, tomato plants, bats, caterpillars, hotels, the Christmas post, chemical sprays, railway closures and wintering in England. H. F. Martin had been less fortunate. During a long life he had written seven letters to the editor, of which three had been published: on roast duckling, bloaters and farming finance.

---

1 Letters to the Editor, March 19 1971, running down the whole of the right-hand column of the leader page. None of the letters printed was from a woman.

Another correspondent, Philip G. Sharp, annoyed at the non-appearance of what he thought a good letter, had complained to a friend that it seemed one had to be a member of the Athenaeum to get a letter accepted. So how, he asked, did one become a member of the Athenaeum? The friend's reply was that 'he thought the first step towards membership was to get a letter published in *The Times*'.

One who had never had a letter published was nevertheless content to have received an acknowledgement, which was, he felt (according to Yoakum), 'to have moved in the foothills of immortality'. Only grosser spirits would seek public proof of the editor's regard.[1]

Since 1953 the person who embodied and mediated the editor's godlike power over correspondence had been Geoffrey Woolley, and he was to continue as letters' editor until 1980, when he was succeeded by Leon Pilpel. A vintage *Times* man, Clifton and Cambridge educated, Woolley had joined the paper as a sub just before the war and returned to it in 1945 after service in the army. His happiest time was working under Haley, because Haley took a special interest in the correspondence columns. Nearly every day after lunch he spent three-quarters of an hour with Woolley going through the day's letters and making a selection for the following day's paper. Rees-Mogg had no such routine. His sessions with Woolley were intermittent, though when he did give his attention to letters he often became fascinated. He tended, however, to be unmethodical about them and there were cases of letters being buried in his tray, leading to complaints that they had not been acknowledged.

Woolley was punctilious about acknowledging letters, replying personally to at least forty a day, often at considerable length. The idea of saving trouble by having a few stock answers would never have occurred to him. He treated all his correspondence about letters to the editor as strictly confidential, not to be preserved in the archive. (He destroyed it after three to four months.) Though the volume of letters that he had to handle was exaggerated by Yoakum – the correct figure for 1970 being not 90,000, but just under 63,000 – it was nevertheless very large. In 1968, the year of Enoch Powell's Birmingham speech, it rose by 13,000, and Rees-Mogg then appointed a deputy letters' editor, Norman Grenyer, to help Woolley cope with the increased flow. The figure oscillated from year to year, with general elections as well as specific controversies tending to give it a boost. But after 1967 there were never fewer than 1,000 letters (on average)

1 Yoakum knew *The Times* well, because he acted as a stringer for it, as well as writing for *Newsday* and other American journals.

a week, and often many more. This was more than double the volume when Woolley took over as letters' editor.

He also witnessed a considerable expansion in the variety of people writing to the paper. Politicians, the City and Oxbridge were no longer so easily predominant as they used to be, but were joined by trade unionists and the students and staff of new universities. Clergymen and barristers were rather less in evidence than in the past. These changes did not displease him, though some manifestations of the Thomson *Times* did. He was a party to the White Swan remonstrance.[1]

In 1976 an anthology of letters to the editor since 1900 was published jointly by Times Books and Allen & Unwin. It was entitled *The First Cuckoo*, and there was a foreword by Bernard Levin, who recalled two early, unsuccessful, attempts to get letters published in *The Times*, but who could 'nowadays claim to be not so much a correspondent himself as the cause of correspondence in others'. Yet he did not wish to seem too superior:

> Is there any difference between the impulse that drives a man to write letters to the newspapers and that which impels his neighbour to write for a living? I rather think not; we are all, gentlemen and players alike, engaged in the business (a very curious business, when you come to think of it) of expressing our views to thousands, or even millions, of people who have not invited us to do so.

In any case there was no doubt, he said, that if a man was going to write for nothing 'he would rather do so in *The Times* than anywhere else'.[2]

---

1 When Woolley retired in 1980, he was succeeded as letters editor by Leon Pilpel, formerly chief sub-editor of the paper.

2 *The First Cuckoo* was clearly a success, because it was followed by *The Second Cuckoo* (1983), *The Third Cuckoo* (1985) and *The Last Cuckoo* (1987). For all four the choice of letters was made by Kenneth Gregory. Woolley knew nothing of the original publication until one day, as he was going in to see Rees-Mogg, Levin called from his outer office: 'I've just written a foreword for your book'. Awkward explanations followed and Woolley was then asked to contribute a short 'preface', which appeared together with Levin's foreword and an 'introduction' by Gregory.

The 'first cuckoo' letter that inspired the title was from R. Lydekker, FRS, who reported hearing a cuckoo in his Hertfordshire garden on February 4 1913, but who had to confess a few days later that he had been deceived by a bricklayer's labourer imitating the bird's call. Both letters are reprinted in *The First Cuckoo*, with the interesting editorial note that Delius's *On Hearing the First Cuckoo in Spring* was first performed (in Leipzig) on October 2 1913.

A few of the letters quoted by Yoakum in the piece that found its way into the *Congressional Record* are also reprinted in *The First Cuckoo*.

The most important business of the Heath government was negotiating British admission to the European Communities, and in this, of course, *The Times* and its editor were most enthusiastic supporters. It could well be argued that the Wilson government had failed in its attempt because it made the mistake of trying to isolate the French, and more especially of trying to play the Germans off against them: a procedure that reached its nadir in the so-called *affaire Soames* in February 1969.[1] Heath was determined not to make the same mistake, as was early explained to *Times* readers by Leonard Beaton in an op. ed. piece under the headline 'Switching to France'. The big difference between the Wilson and Heath governments was, Beaton suggested, that the former felt its 'primary aim' should be 'a close working relationship with the West Germans', whereas the latter felt that 'the success of British policy in Europe depend[ed] on a special relationship with France'.[2]

At the same time EEC members in general were said to be moving away from ideological federalism and towards a pragmatism more congenial to British taste. In a leader-page article from Brussels, David Spanier wrote that political union was not for the moment the primary interest. The whole attitude in Brussels was 'down to earth and down-beat', and he quoted President Pompidou's recent speech at Strasbourg in which he called, Gaullistically, for a Europe of nation-states. The basic fact, according to Spanier, was that 'all Six' wanted Britain to join, and that France seemed to be becoming 'more friendly day by day'.[3]

Pompidou had been elected President of France almost exactly a year before the election of the Heath government in Britain. Though created politically by de Gaulle – who had appointed him straight to the premiership in 1962, when his experience was little more than that of an academic and banker – Pompidou had distanced himself somewhat from the General after the 1968 disturbances, which had led to his replacement as prime minister by Couve de Murville. Yet

1 De Gaulle had invited the British ambassador, Christopher Soames, to an intimate lunch at the Elysée, at which only their wives were present, and had spoken very freely of the possibility of modifying the Treaty of Rome to make British participation easier; also of how France and Britain could work together in the longer-term European future. Under strong pressure from the foreign office Wilson soon afterwards conveyed the gist of this conversation to the German chancellor, while the foreign office briefed ambassadors to other EEC countries. It was not long before the story leaked to the press, causing justifiable fury in France.

2 July 1 1970.

3 'Europe today: more market, less community', July 2 1970. Britain was soon to find that the 'down to earth attitude' took the form of extremely tough bargaining.

when de Gaulle suddenly stood down after failing to get his way in a referendum on regional government and reform of the Senate, Pompidou was, *faute de mieux*, the Gaullist candidate for the presidency. De Gaulle did not take part in the campaign, and said nothing against him in public, with the result that he had the double benefit of being formally Gaullist while seeming to be his own man.

He was, in fact, very different from de Gaulle, being essentially a man of compromise. Yet there was nothing of the anglophile sentimentalist about him and his initial attitude to Britain's third attempt to join the Continentals' club was coolly sceptical. While the British negotiator, Geoffrey Rippon, was having a hard time with the Council of Ministers, Pompidou gave a press conference in Paris in which he said: 'It is readily recognisable that the British have three qualities – humour, tenacity and realism. I am inclined to think we are still rather at the humour stage'. Though he went on to say that he had no doubt tenacity would follow, and that he hoped realism would triumph 'in the end', it was clear that he had no intention of letting Britain in on easy terms.[1]

Indeed it was feared in London that he might achieve the effect of a third veto, without imposing it directly, by insisting on terms that would be unacceptable. De Gaulle was not only out of office but, since November, no longer in the world. Yet it seemed that his spirit of hostility to British entry might still be very much alive.

Heath's commitment to a European future for Britain was, however, free from the ambivalence that had marred Macmillan's and Wilson's approaches. Even before he and Pompidou got to grips with each other, the latter was becoming aware that this British prime minister would probably be prepared to make the necessary sacrifices. In early April *The Times* carried a front-page story 'France wants Britain in EEC in spite of suspicions'. It had Rees-Mogg's byline, and followed an unattributable interview with Pompidou at which *The Times*'s Paris correspondent, Hargrove, acted as interpreter.

The story began on an encouraging note:

> President Pompidou sincerely wants the negotiations for British entry to the EEC to succeed. He is not raising difficulties for their own sake or laying traps for us. This was the clear impression with which I was left after a visit to Paris over the past few days.

Failure in the negotiations would, in the French view, 'poison

1 January 21 1971.

Anglo-French relations for years to come'. Yet there were essential matters which France had to pursue. The position of sterling was a tricky, but vital, issue. France considered that 'the EEC should not be at a disadvantage as a result of the sterling system, either in terms of access to the European market, or the commitments that might be involved in a future sterling crisis, arising from the existence of sterling balances'. It was certainly expected by 'French government opinion' that the questions of Caribbean sugar and New Zealand butter could be settled by compromise. But these 'secondary matters' were 'not points upon which the success of the negotiation really turn[ed]'. The report ended positively, while emphasising the need to satisfy French interests:

> No one in Paris doubts that the man who will take the final decision is President Pompidou himself, or that he is politically entirely free to take what decisions he thinks right. In France there is a problem of government, not of public opinion. Neither President Pompidou's ultimate good will towards Britain, nor his determination to protect the interests, as he sees them, of France and the European Community, can be doubted.[1]

This interview was not only a journalistic scoop, but also something of a diplomatic coup. It was read by Heath in Bonn the morning after his arrival there for talks with the German chancellor, Willy Brandt, and it gave him a reassuring signal. Though he must already have had a good idea of Pompidou's state of mind from diplomatic sources, it was a further encouragement that such on the whole helpful views were expressed, even if unattributably, to the editor of *The Times*.

The following month Heath was in Paris himself for a summit meeting with Pompidou that was to prove decisive. If the two leaders had failed to get on at their first serious encounter, the chances of success in the negotiation might still have been blasted; but in fact they did get on very well indeed. After the first day of talks there was a picture of them together in the garden of the Elysée Palace, with a front-page story from Hargrove and Patrick Brogan: 'No one could have wished for a more encouraging sign than the atmosphere of

---

1 April 5 1971. The reference to Caribbean sugar and New Zealand butter as secondary matters, which should not be allowed to decide whether or not Britain's application failed, was Pompidou's parting remark to Rees-Mogg as the interview ended. (Incidentally, the President's assistant *chef de cabinet* at the time, who later became his *chef de cabinet*, was a family friend of the Rees-Moggs.)

tonight's state banquet'.[1] Next day's lead story, with another picture of the two leaders, was: 'Mr. Heath and M. Pompidou agree the way is now open for Britain'. And a short leader, entitled 'Reconciliation in Paris', commented that the immediate purpose of the Paris talks had been achieved.[2]

At the joint press conference with which the conference ended Pompidou said: 'Many people believed that Great Britain was not European and did not wish to become European, and Britain wanted to enter the Community only to destroy it. Many people also thought that France was ready to use all kinds of means and pretexts to impose a new veto on British entry'. Then, turning to Heath, he added: 'You see before you tonight two men who are convinced to the contrary'. The change from his press conference in January could hardly have been more marked, and the way was indeed open for the agreement of terms between Britain and the Six.

Shortly before the Paris summit Rees-Mogg treated the paper's readers to one of his grandest exercises in editorial leadership. In a series of five leaders under the general heading 'The Prospect of Britain' he reviewed the current state of the nation and indicated right courses for the future. Each article was three columns wide and ran to almost the full depth of the page. The series stimulated a large correspondence, and Anthony Howard wrote in the *Observer* that nothing to rival it had been seen in the British press 'since the days when J. L. Garvin himself used to deliver the milk of the word in great churns . . . every Sunday'.[3] The articles were soon made available in booklet form.

The first was entitled 'Fathers and sons: the critique of the young'. The second asked the question, 'What is the British disease?'. The third discussed 'Mr. Heath's historic gamble'. The fourth was concerned with 'The politics of reconciliation'. The fifth considered the choice facing Britain: 'Dead failure or new start'.[4] All were written in the distinctive style which enabled Rees-Mogg to be Olympian without being boring.

---

1 May 21 1971. The same day Rees-Mogg wrote to Heath: 'I have never been much given to congratulating Prime Ministers. Perhaps I may be allowed to do so in this case. You will know the overriding importance that we attach to this issue'.
2 May 22 1971.
3 May 9 1971.
4 April 28, 29 and 30, and May 3 and 4, 1971. The booklet containing the articles was on sale from May 20, price 15p plus 5p postage.

In the second article, which took stock of Britain's apparent loss of the capacity, or the will, to create wealth, he stressed that there could be no purely materialist remedy for this material disease. National revival could not be inspired by economic motives alone. 'Some nations make civilisation a by-product of the creation of wealth; Britain is more likely to make wealth a by-product of the creation of a worth-while civilisation'. In the fourth article he warned against equating reconciliation with relaxation. 'One of the most unfortunate attitudes in British politics has been to regard the centre as weak and extremists as strong. A policy of reconciliation will incur just as many enemies, and probably nastier ones, than any other. It will require a willingness to exercise authority'.

Not surprisingly, the series ended with a strong statement of his European faith:

> The final and perhaps the most important requirement is cultural, the civilisation of Europe. Britain is a confluence of European influences, of Anglo-Saxons and Danes, of Normans, of the lasting influences of the Christian religion. One of our royal mottoes is in French, another in German; we have a European Royal Family. The reason that Europe can hope to work together is that our civilisation is one, though our nations are several. A Europe of Dante, Voltaire and Goethe which is not also the Europe of Shakespeare would be only half made.[1]

Thus he claimed the highest spiritual, moral and aesthetic grounds for his advocacy of British entry,

In early July the government published its White Paper on the terms for accession, which were debated by the Commons at the end of the month without a vote, and then discussed throughout the country during the summer recess. The Conservative party was seriously divided on the issue, though much less seriously than Labour. Wilson, the Labour leader, was soon denouncing the terms with ferocity and seeming to cast doubt on joining at all, while George Brown and Michael Stewart, each of whom had served as foreign secretary under

---

1 De Gaulle's trio of representative European writers was Dante, Goethe and *Chateaubriand*. The last-named was a natural choice for the General, whose own thought and style were much influenced by the Romantic anti-Bonapartist with his roots in the *ancien régime*. It is interesting that the liberal English Catholic Rees-Mogg should have regarded Voltaire as the representative French writer.

him, both said they would have accepted the terms obtained by the government, as did George Thomson, who had been Labour's negotiator with the EEC. Above all Jenkins, the deputy leader, dissociated himself from the Wilson line. The majority of the public, to judge from opinion polls, was opposed to British entry, but Heath had no intention of holding a referendum. Despite an earlier promise, much quoted against him, that he would take Britain into the EEC only with the 'full-hearted' assent of the British people, prudence and constitutional propriety alike required that Parliament should decide.

On 21 October the House of Commons began a six-day debate on a motion to approve in principle the government's decision 'to join the European Communities on the basis of the arrangements . . . negotiated'. The following day two letters appeared side by side in *The Times*. One read: 'The undersigned, being full-time teachers of economics in British universities, believe that the economic effects of joining the Common Market, taking both short and long-term effects into account, are more likely to be unfavourable than favourable to Britain'. The other was identical, except that the words 'favourable' and 'unfavourable' were transposed. Each had several dozen signatories, though the list of 'antis' was slightly longer than the list of 'pros'. Heath referred to the letters in his speech winding up the debate on the sixth day:

> Economists have lined themselves up in the columns of *The Times*. One [list] was a quarter of an inch shorter than the other, but on what basis can one make a judgment on a quarter of an inch in *The Times*? (Laughter).

The Commons' vote certainly did not reflect the prevailing opinion of the economists. 'Parliament gives a resounding Yes to Europe with MPs' majority of 112' was the main headline on October 29. The day before the paper had predicted that sixty-six Labour MPs would vote with the government, in defiance of the whip. In the event sixty-nine in all, led by Jenkins, broke ranks and voted for the motion, while twenty more abstained. On the Conservative side there were thirty-nine anti-Market rebels (and two abstentions), but they were not defying the whip, because the party managers had decided it would be safer, as well as embarrassing for Labour, to let Tory MPs have a free vote. A full list showing how all MPs voted was printed with the parliamentary report.

In his leader on the historic vote Rees-Mogg showed that, for him, the arguments of the economists, one way or the other, were essentially irrelevant:

> The most important point about the European development is not indeed the economic benefits which may flow – though they could well help to reduce unemployment – not the business opportunities, nor even the direct political opportunities, but the development of understanding. It is the creation of a European consciousness.[1]

This was his insistent theme.

Early in the New Year the treaty of accession was signed by Heath on Britain's behalf. (At the same time Denmark and the Republic of Ireland also joined.) Wilson declined to attend the ceremony in Brussels, but George Brown accepted. Since it took place on a Saturday, January 22, the story was no longer news for Monday's papers. The picture on the front page of Monday's *Times* was not of Heath signing the treaty, but of Heath celebrating at a lunch that he gave next day for diplomats and officials who had been involved in the negotiation. Sitting on his right was Mrs. Palliser, wife of the British ambassador to the Communities and daughter of the Belgian Euro-pioneer, Paul-Henri Spaak; on her right was the British ambassador to France, Christopher Soames.

The whole of page 4 was devoted to texts of the accession documents, edited by Spanier. On the op. ed. page there was a piece by Robert Jackson on 'Europe's search for new symbols of authority', and one from Hargrove in Paris on 'How President Pompidou has put his trust in Mr. Heath'; while David Wood wrote about the impending task of getting the necessary legislation through Parliament. Wood also had a piece on the leader-page, a character-sketch of the prime minister:

> My own contribution to the understanding of Mr. Heath would be a reminder that he was a most formidable and tough Chief Whip, the first Chief Whip to lead the modern Conservative Party. That training made him the surest exponent of governmental power of his generation.[2]

All of Heath's toughness and skill were needed to force the

---

1 'Citizens of Europe', October 29 1971.
2 January 24 1972.

European Communities Bill through the House of Commons. The Labour pro-Europeans felt that they had done their bit by ensuring a big vote for the principle of entry; but having willed the end they showed no sign of willing the means. At the same time the prime minister had to contend with a small but implacable minority of Conservatives led by Enoch Powell. As a result the second reading was carried, in February, by only eight votes; but for support from the Liberals the measure would have been lost. Later, a guillotine motion imposing a timetable was carried by eleven votes. Only through the fullest use of 'governmental power' in Parliament did the bill eventually become law.

In July 1971 Rees-Mogg invited his senior editorial colleagues for a working weekend at his home in Somerset. Their wives were asked, too, for pleasure rather than business, and most accepted. A number of the guests were met by Gillian Rees-Mogg at Bath station on the Friday evening (July 9) and driven to Ston Easton in three cars. After a dinner of paté, sole and profiterolles they all watched Harold Wilson on television before retiring for the night.

Next morning the group was joined by Douglas-Home (who was staying with his father-in-law in Gloucestershire). The subject of the first session was Europe's future development. Stephenson spoke, according to Hodgkin, 'with particular clarity and command', and in the ensuing discussion most of the questions were asked by Douglas-Home. Half-way through the morning attention switched to the 'enlarged role' that *The Times* might play, on which Rees-Mogg expounded his views, mentioning both the new features that he had in mind and the need to make the paper's normal coverage more Europe-orientated. Some fear was expressed that ordinary home news and the rest of foreign news might, as a result, suffer.

The whole party then met for drinks in the sunshine in front of the house, followed by lunch consisting of melon, chicken in white sauce and ice-cream with red currants. During the afternoon session Hodgkin, for one, had some difficulty in keeping awake. In the evening the group dispersed.[1]

A report on the weekend's deliberations was afterwards prepared by Spanier. The amount of space available for West European

1 Hodgkin, op. cit., entries for July 9 and 10 1971. At that date it was still worthy of note that Wilson was watched 'on *colour* TV'. His performance was judged 'most insincere'.

coverage might not, it was felt, be maintained at quite the one page per day thought necessary during the negotiations, which in any case was normally proving to be about three columns in excess of requirements. As well as the news reports there should also be more correspondence from Europe, since readers on the Continent were to be encouraged to write letters for publication. The paper was thought to be well served by its representatives in Rome, Paris, Brussels and Bonn, though a second correspondent would be appointed to Brussels after British entry, and *Business News* stringers in Paris and Milan. At the same time home specialists were to be urged 'to take as lively an interest in their subjects within the Community as they could'.

There was much talk of a Saturday Review of Europe, which might have the additional virtue of eliminating, or at least reducing, the loss incurred by the paper on Saturdays, currently about £8,000 a week. This could include articles that would inform or entertain 'in a way that daily despatches did not always allow', European law reports, pieces by outside columnists, and material from various Continental newspapers. The intention would be 'to establish *The Times* as a paper of breadth as well as depth in its European coverage', while giving 'British readers a strong feel of life in the Community'. Conversely, 'European readers, who might increase by 10 per cent a year (present circulation 18,000 in the Community) should get a strong feel of British life'.

Looking ahead ten years, Rees-Mogg saw *The Times* as 'the English language European newspaper of record, just as it was in Britain', with 'a particularly strong economic coverage' (leaving to the *FT* the specialist role in that field) and with 'a much harder news sense than *Le Monde*'. The sense of the meeting was that the process should 'start cautiously', but that the paper should be 'ready to go further and faster'.[1]

Many of the ideas canvassed at Ston Easton underwent considerable modification before they were realised, and some were never realised at all. Yet the gathering was generally agreed to be worthwhile, and not least for its effect on the participants' morale. As Hodgkin commented: 'It was good having a specific problem to talk about, and a limited number of people, who all know each other well, talking about it. It gave those present a feeling of being the cabinet of the paper'.[2]

1 Report from Ston Easton, signed D.S., July 23 1971.
2 Hodgkin, op. cit., July 10 1971.

A large part of the paper came under the heading 'features'. The features editor was responsible for the turnover article (while it lasted), the op. ed. page, including columns and the diary, the women's page, all special features (such as the Chichester story), serialisation and the travel section of the Saturday Review; in all, a very extensive empire. The Thomson period was one during which, throughout the British press, features were gaining ground relative to hard news, and this trend was reflected in *The Times*.

At the time of the transfer the features editor was James (Jim) Bishop, who had been on the paper since 1955, in a variety of capacities at home and overseas. He stayed in the post under the new regime until 1971, when he left to be the successful editor of another Thomson publication, the *Illustrated London News*. Though a devoted admirer of Haley, Bishop was not on that account prejudiced against the wave of innovation associated with Cudlipp. On the contrary, he got on with Cudlipp very well, and it was probably for that reason that he was not asked to sign the White Swan letter.[1] He had the good fortune to be features editor during the time of expansion, when money was freely available. He had a budget of his own, a previously unheard-of luxury, and one of his first acts was to offer attractive fees to contributors, instead of the beggarly payment which – on the principle that the honour of writing for *The Times* was its own reward – had long been traditional.

Bishop's team consisted principally of his deputy, D. N. Herbert, the women's page editor, the fashion editor, the home page editor, the art editor (not to be confused with the arts editor), the literary editor (later transferred to arts), and the travel correspondent. When Douglas-Home succeeded Bishop in 1971 there was also a change of deputy, and the new deputy features editor was Margaret Allen, the outstanding woman journalist on the paper during the Thomson period.

Allen came from Droylsden in Lancashire, the daughter of a Roman Catholic father and a Protestant mother, and the only intellectual member of a working-class family. Her father was a tool-maker and Labour party stalwart. From being taught by nuns at a local church grammar school she won a scholarship to the London School of Economics, and after graduating from there got a job on the *Investors' Chronicle*. In her mid-twenties she was deputy City editor of the *Evening Standard*. She joined *The Times* in 1963, and two years later

1 He was sure, in retrospect, that if he had been asked he would have tried to persuade the protesters that they were mistaken. (Bishop talking to author.)

Haley made her assistant City editor. Early in the Thomson period she was rather unhappily employed on *TBN* features, but then she had three enjoyable years on special reports before being appointed deputy features editor. In 1971 she was a divorcée of ten years' standing (from William Davis, financial journalist and one-time editor of *Punch*), and she had two young daughters whom she often brought into the office.

Despite a powerful femininity to which several of her male colleagues were far from immune, she wished to compete with them on entirely equal terms and felt that the women's page catered too little for professional working women like herself.[1] This page was run, for three years after the transfer, by its original editor, Susanne Puddefoot. She was a footballer's daughter from Blackpool, with a degree in modern and medieval languages from Cambridge (Girton). Towards the end of 1969 she was showing signs of strain and Bishop decided that she had to be replaced, while praising the 'talents and skill' that had enabled her to establish the page.[2] Her successor was Moira Keenan, who had been working for some time with Ernestine Carter on the *Sunday Times*. Keenan brought many qualities to the task, but was fighting a losing battle against cancer. When at length she died, in the latter part of 1972, no new appointment was made to the post of women's page editor. Increasingly the attempt was made to desegregate women's features in the paper, a process that Allen did her best to advance, since she felt there was no more point in having special pages for women than special pages for men. Her idea was that all features should, in principle, have a general appeal.

One women's page feature that did not long survive Keenan, with whom it had been closely associated, was known as 'growing point', and was concerned with female and family matters. Others proved more durable, such as Prudence Glynn on fashion, Sheila Black on shopping, and Dr. Hugh Jolly on paediatrics. A representative bill of fare for the 'second features page' (no longer women's page) in the mid-1970s consisted of a profile on Monday, fashion on Tuesday, a column by Helen Hayman and a piece by Dr. Jolly on Wednesday, 'shopping around' by Sheila Black on Thursday, and a piece by two reporters on homelessness on Friday. In the same week the op. ed. page carried the usual three columns by Levin, on Tuesday, Wednesday and Thursday, as well as other material ranging from a piece on the Tory leadership by Maudling to one on the Mafia by Gaia

---

1 Memo from Allen to the editor, Cudlipp and C.D.-H., October 12 1972.
2 Bishop to Puddefoot, October 2 1969.

Servadio.[1] By this time Douglas-Home was home editor and Allen, since 1973, was features editor in his place, as she was to remain for the rest of the Thomson period.

A key figure in the development of the paper's appearance was Jeanette Collins, who was art editor from 1966 to 1970, and design editor (a title less easily confused with that of Higgins, the arts editor) until her retirement in 1979. Her influence was felt throughout the whole paper, and Rees-Mogg told her that her work was comparable with that of Stanley Morison in the 1930s.[2] Her chief contribution was a new, 'modular' layout, which required copy to be fitted into spaces of varying size and shape, rather than run on from column to column, as previously. There was, of course, a considerable price to be paid for this change, since much good material, in reports or features, was lost as it was arbitrarily cut to fit the Procrustean beds provided by the new design. But, on the credit side, this appearance of the paper undoubtedly became less dull and predictable. Visually, the modular layout was a major improvement.

1 February 1975. Under Douglas-Home an analysis was done (in January and February 1971) showing that out of 178 features 93 were written by members of the staff and that they divided (excluding Levin) 91 on home subjects and 71 on foreign. 122 were 'immediately topical, either reacting to news or anticipating news stories'. At home the most neglected subject was education; abroad, Latin America.
2 W.R.-M. to Jeanette Collins, March 12 1979.

XI

Barber cuts taxes • Papist and Presbyterian • A contentious bill • Embattled Levin • Law reporting • Dermatitis strike • Benevolent feudalist

GETTING INTO EUROPE was the government's principal policy, but scarcely less important, and complementary, was its attempt to recreate at home the conditions for a free market economy. This desirable state was to be achieved partly by fiscal measures and partly by the reform of industrial relations.

In his first proper budget, introduced on March 30 1971, Barber cut taxation by nearly £550 million. Selective employment tax (SET) was halved, as a first step towards its abolition. Together with purchase tax it was anyway due to be replaced by value added tax (VAT) if and when Britain became a member of the EEC. Corporation tax was reduced by 2½ per cent, and there was relief for people with high incomes, the top rate of tax being brought down from 88 per cent to 75 per cent. At the same time old-age pensions were increased by £1 a week for single people and £1.60 a week for couples.

On *The Times*'s front page next morning, under the lead story reporting the budget's main provisions, David Wood described the package as cautiously reflationary, while Hugh Noyes, lobby correspondent, wrote of the delight of Conservative MPs ('Mr. Barber comes out from the shadows and backbenchers find a Chancellor'). There was also a report that even the general secretary of the TUC was, up to a point, favourably impressed ('Nudge in the right direction, Mr. Feather says'). On inside pages, as well as two-and-a-half pages devoted to Parliament, with the budget statement in full, there was also, on page 2, a summary of the Green Paper on VAT.

In his leader on the budget Rees-Mogg applauded the chancellor's 'coherent political strategy', saying that he had taken advantage of 'a period of opportunity' in a way which might provide a 'starting point for a revival of confidence in British industry'. But it would be easier to judge the budget's effect in a few weeks' time. Some people, when the chancellor sat down, found his proposed measures 'strongly inflationary', but 'a closer look at the budget arithmetic' suggested that it might not prove reflationary enough, in view of 'the urgent need to halt the present rise in unemployment'.[1]

The figure of unemployed for March, published soon afterwards, showed that at nearly 830,000 it had risen by about 200,000 since the end of the previous year. This was a large percentage rise for a single quarter, though the total was still modest indeed compared with the levels of unemployment that had been experienced forty years earlier, and would be experienced again a decade later. Since the Second World War full employment had been the commonly accepted basis of policy, whichever party was in power, as free trade had been a century earlier; and to nearly all politicians and political commentators, left, right and centre, any idea of a return to mass unemployment was taboo. The amount of overmanning, or concealed unemployment, in the British economy was not as yet generally recognised. Rees-Mogg for his part would remain for some time broadly representative of the postwar consensus on economic policy. What came to be regarded as genuinely 'radical right' thinking still had little appeal for him, and as late as the end of 1973 the liveliest source of such thinking, the Institute of Economic Affairs, was complaining of *The Times*'s neglect of its publications.[2]

The government's approach to the reform of industrial relations had three main objectives: to bring the trade unions effectively within the law and so (it was hoped) diminish their power; to increase the authority of national trade union leaders within their unions; and to enhance the freedom of individual workers. All three objectives were, in themselves, entirely rational, even laudable. Legal immunities which had served to redress the balance in favour of employees at a time when employers were overwhelmingly powerful – because there was no policy of full employment, and social security was still very limited – had become anomalous in the drastically altered circumstances of post-1945 Britain. Trade union power within the community had grown out of proportion, while within the unions power had shifted from national officials to shop stewards or (in many cases) unofficial leaders on the shop floor. Moreover this power was seldom obtained or exercised in a genuinely democratic fashion. Trade union ballots were more often open than secret, and there was much

1 'A radical Tory budget', March 31 1971.
2 Arthur Seldon to W.R.-M., December 3 1973.

intimidation of potential dissidents. During the immediate postwar period the flawed state of British trade unionism was not too apparent in practice, because leaders and rank-and-file alike were, on the whole, moderate. But since the end of the 1950s the trend towards militancy had been growing, and by the late 1960s it had become sufficiently menacing, particularly in the form of unofficial strikes, to stir even a Labour government into an attempt to reform industrial relations.

Whatever was wrong with British trade unions in general was to be found in an aggravated form in the newspaper industry. It had long been a matter of sardonic comment that the press, so much given to lecturing others on the need for better industrial relations, had signally failed to set an example in its own sphere. Trade unions on the print and production side were a byword for conservatism, restrictive practices and problems of demarcation, while on the journalists' side the big union, the NUJ, was often seduced by false notions of working-class solidarity, and the more moderate Institute of Journalists (IoJ) was too small, relatively, to be effective. Managements, for their part, were forever sacrificing the long-term interests of the industry to the needs or opportunities of the moment. Faced with the threatened loss of an edition or a whole day's issue, not to mention more prolonged loss of sales, they were all too prone to give way; and if by chance some management ever decided to stand firm there would nearly always be at least one rival ready to exploit the situation for its own immediate gain. Finally, however inadequate labour relations may have been, here and there, in the provincial press, they were at their worst on national newspapers, in London.

The vicissitudes of Labour's *In Place of Strife*, and the Tories' commitment to industrial relations' reform, gave Rees-Mogg the idea that he ought to upgrade the treatment of labour affairs in the paper. Accordingly, in 1969, he appointed a labour editor where previously there had only been a labour correspondent; and his choice for the new post was a representative of the Haley *Times*, Innis Macbeath.

Macbeath was a Presbyterian Scot born and educated in Belfast, where his father was a professor. At Queen's University, Belfast, he read history with a strong emphasis on economics. After working for a few years on the *Glasgow Herald* he joined *The Times* in 1957 as a general reporter covering home and foreign affairs. (He spoke four foreign languages.) In 1964 he was sent to report from the Americas, North and South, and in 1967 became chief of bureau in New York. Two years later he was the only foreign journalist to receive a Dumont Award for Journalism, and soon afterwards was brought home to be labour editor. As such he was to have a correspondent and two assistants under him, and was to be responsible for features on labour matters. He was also meant to take a leading part in the formation of policy.

Unfortunately the arrangement did not work out well, mainly because the necessary confidence and harmony were never established between him and the editor. Macbeath did not start as an expert on labour relations, but knew a lot more about the subject than Rees-Mogg. During his time as a general reporter he had covered a number of industrial disputes and had acquired a considerable knowledge of some trade unions. Moreover, while in America he had observed the workings of the Taft-Hartley legislation, which many British Conservatives regarded as a hopeful and instructive model. He once sent a piece explaining that the 'cooling-off period' provided in that legislation had become a virtual dead-letter, but since it arrived on a day when there was to be a leader arguing that cooling-off periods were vital the piece was spiked. This was a bad omen for Macbeath's future role.

Rees-Mogg wanted him to analyse trade unions as commercial businesses were analysed, but Macbeath felt there was little analogy. Without expecting his labour editor to give uncritical endorsement to the Tories' industrial reform legislation, Rees-Mogg no doubt assumed that he would be broadly sympathetic to the measure, whereas in fact he was unmistakably hostile to it. Rees-Mogg considered that he 'went native' and became, willy-nilly, a defender of trade union privileges: an impression naturally strengthened by his activities as chairman of the federated NUJ and IoJ chapel on *The Times*, to which post he was elected in early 1970. He, on his side, regarded the editor's approach to industrial relations as ignorant and capricious. Both men genuinely believed themselves to be free from political partisanship. Rees-Mogg had severed all formal links with the Conservative party on becoming editor, and Macbeath later took pride in having been asked, at one time or another, to stand as a parliamentary candidate by four parties, without having ever given up his independence. Yet fundamentally Rees-Mogg was, of course, a Conservative, while of all parties the Conservative was the one Macbeath seemed least likely to support.

Beneath their differences on policy lay a profound difference of temperament. Cardinal Manning may have said that there was only a thin plank between a Papist and a Presbyterian, but he could not have said it of these representatives of the two religious traditions. Macbeath disapproved of Rees-Mogg's 'highness', if not consciously of his churchmanship, then certainly of the aura of high table and high society that surrounded him. One incident, as described by Macbeath, vividly illustrates a puritan professional's resentment of what seemed to him lazy and lordly amateurism:

> The nightly ceremony of the editor seeing the paper away in the composing-room . . . was valued, and Sir William Haley was proud of his familiarity with production methods. Rees-Mogg, caring little for such things, ended the ceremony, but put nothing in its place.
>
> Years later, composing-room workers remember the night when he turned up with some friends to show them the paper in production. Rees-Mogg and his guests were in evening dress. One guest asked: 'Who is that man? What does he do?' Rees-Mogg said he didn't know and asked a supervisor.
>
> Two electricians were passing, and one said, indicating the editor: 'Who is that man? What does he do?' The other electrician said: 'He doesn't know'.[1]

There was truth on both sides. Macbeath did become over-involved in the minutiae of trade unionism, both in the country and inside the office, to the extent of being unable, often, to see the wood for the trees. Rees-Mogg did tend to be rather too Olympian, and his remoteness from some departments of the paper, including those physically producing it, was a defect in his style of leadership. Yet there were great merits in both men, which each became increasingly incapable of appreciating in the other.

Early evidence of Macbeath's attitude was that he signed the White Swan letter. Further and frequent clashes ensued. He would have liked to be transferred to some other specialisation, but Rees-Mogg felt disinclined to make a change while the Industrial Relations Bill was going through, and during the initial stages of its operation. There may have been some advantage to the paper in the tension between editor and labour editor; without it, coverage of the legislation might have been more uniform, and in particular fewer dissident views might have found their way on to the op. ed. page. On the whole, however, the incompatibility of two such important figures was clearly unfortunate. In October 1972 Macbeath went to the length of telling Tony Benn that the *Times* NUJ chapel had protested to the editor about

1 'How they put the paper to bed': article by Macbeath in the *New Statesman*, December 19 1980.

the way he (Benn) was being treated in the paper.[1] Eventually, in April 1973, his health temporarily undermined, Macbeath left to become Plowden Professor of Industrial Relations at the London Business School.[2]

In its leader on the 1970 Queen's Speech *The Times* referred to the forthcoming trade union reform in terms which reflect Macbeath's authorship:

> The trade union movement must eventually accept some legal standing less anomalous than it has now. What happened in 1969 has made the prospect much more unpalatable. The Government is so deeply committed that it cannot retreat. But that is all the more reason for the most anxious care that the months which a major Bill must in any event require for gestation are used to ensure that it is not born overweight.[3]

The government's proposals were published in October in the form of a 'consultative document'. The headline on the main front-page story was 'Line by line Commons fight likely on Tory proposals to fine industrial offenders', while pages 5, 12 and 13 were given over entirely to the document's text. On the op. ed. page there were two interesting pieces on the government's scheme. Andrew Shonfield saw it as an advance on its Labour predecessor, but nevertheless made some criticisms. The responsible minister, Robert Carr, and his colleagues were trying 'to restrict the scope for industrial action much too severely', seeming not to understand that trade unions were 'in the last resort fighting organisations'. K.W. Wedderburn, professor of law at London University, attacked the proposals on a broad front, accusing the government of ignoring 'the research work in recent years by experts of many different viewpoints'. His article ended:

> The sensible proposals . . . are submerged beneath a plan for a legally regulated system which will reduce the power of unions and workers . . . The Government – above all its legal officers –

1 Tony Benn, *Office without Power: Diaries 1968–72*, entry for October 3 1972 (p.453), Macbeath's first name is misspelt 'Innes' and he is described as 'Industrial Correspondent' of *The Times*.
2 He had lost a lot of weight and had thrombosis in a vein, causing eye trouble. (This account of the relations between Macbeath and Rees-Mogg is largely based on talking to both.)
3 July 3 1970.

> should beseech themselves in Cromwellian fashion to reconsider at least the timetable for this revolutionary measure and come to the table for genuine consultation on substance not just detail.

On the same day the leader, 'Fair and moderate reform', contained hardly any criticism at all.[1]

The 'revolutionary' or 'fair and moderate' measure went ahead, unchanged in substance. Because of its size and complexity (it had 170 sections) it occupied the attention of Parliament for sixty days before receiving the Royal Assent on 5 August 1971. Its effect was to repeal previous labour laws and substitute a new framework for industrial relations. Such legal immunities as were left to trade unions were to be enjoyed only by those that registered under the act. There was a new concept of 'unfair industrial practice', and there were to be new rights for individual trade unionists, such as protection from unfair dismissal and improved terms of notice. Instead of the closed shop as it had previously existed, there was provision for 'agency shop' agreements which would have much the same effect, though individuals could be exempted on grounds of conscience. A National Industrial Relations Court was set up to adjudicate in all matters falling within the ambit of the act, with power to impose heavy fines on recalcitrant unions. The secretary of state for employment could ask the court to order ballots and cooling-off periods in what he might judge to be situations of emergency.

Predictably, the Industrial Relations Act was anathematised by the entire labour movement. The TUC, at its meeting in September, instructed all affiliated unions not to register under the act, and later suspended or expelled the thirty-odd that did. Syndicalism was a powerfully reviving force within the unions and even constitutional-minded leaders tended, therefore, to be swept into all-out defiance of the measure, which involved rejecting the will not only of Parliament but of the electorate as well. Having scotched the recent attempt of a Labour government to reform them, the unions were unlikely to show any mercy to a Conservative government, even though, unlike its Labour predecessor, it had a mandate for reform. Left-wingers relished the opportunity for mass demonstrations and other organised action against the 'class enemy'. As for the parliamentary Labour party, it also included many class warriors, who joined cheerfully with their ideological soul-mates in the unions. All the same a majority of its

---

1 October 6 1970. Seven years later Wedderburn became a life peer, as Lord Wedderburn of Charlton, on Callaghan's recommendation.

members probably felt embarrassed at having to fight indiscriminately against a measure with some, at least, of whose provisions they were known to agree. In spite of themselves moderate Labour MPs, like moderate union leaders, felt obliged to act on the principle of *pas d'ennemis à gauche*.

It could be argued that the measure was, indeed, 'born overweight', and that its authors underrated the difficulties of enforcement in the climate of the time. As a means of bolstering the authority of responsible union leaders against unofficial trouble-makers, and of weakening the strike weapon, it had little success. Equally futile was the 'cooling-off period' device, whose uselessness Macbeath had observed in America. Nevertheless, if everything else had gone well for the government, the act as a whole might gradually have won acceptance, while its imperfections could have been amended away. But everything else did not go well, and within less than three years the act was engulfed in a larger cataclysm.

During its passage through Parliament Macbeath made occasional written comments, as well as doing what he could to mobilise a variety of comment on the op. ed. page. Usually he wrote himself, as it were, from the wings, in the business section. For instance:

> Dismissals cases under the Bill will determine in the end 'in accordance with equity and the substantial merits of the case', which is the yardstick for contract cases already. The byways and crannies of the Bill are full of interesting speculative matter for barrack-room lawyers. We shall have, as the judge said when Sir Alan Herbert's Mr Haddock arrived in court again, 'some jolly litigation'.[1]

While the bill was in the Lords there was an interesting Saturday review column by Baroness (Dora) Gaitskell. The Tories' 'silent built-in majority' would make victory for the government in the Lords 'meaningless' (she must have meant morally). The bill stirred 'deep political loyalties and alignments', and Gaitskell's widow hinted at a conflict within herself when she said: 'Some of us may have reservations about the strategy and tactics in the war against the bill, but no one should underestimate the clash of philosophies between the two parties'.

She turned with obvious relief to criticism by lawyers of a bill which so many of her supposed colleagues were preparing to fight illegally:

1 'Prospects of jolly litigation', *TBN*, May 14 1971.

> On May 17 we came to what I thought was the most crucial part of the Bill, the clauses dealing with the enforceability of collective bargaining agreements. I was anxious to hear what the lawyers had to say, as they would have to administer the law. I was not disappointed. One after another they proceeded to demolish the legal edifice that the Government had built up . . . First the eminent solicitor Lord Tangley – who had been a member of the Donovan Commission . . . The eminent judge, Lord Wilberforce, Lord of Appeal, followed . . . In a brilliant and constructive analysis of this measure he pointed out that collective agreements 'are not simple – that they are of a diverse and often sophisticated kind and not really suitable to be brought into the ordinary legal process'. Like others who have studied collective agreements he suggested . . . 'some more sensitive and sophisticated procedure which would bring collective agreements under the law, but not under lawyers' law – the law of contract and the law of judges'.

And so on. She ended by quoting Burke: 'To innovate is not to reform'.[1]

The name of Wilberforce would soon be like a knell to the Conservative Party. Meanwhile the bill became law: or at any rate what Lady Gaitskell and her learned ally speciously called 'lawyers' law'. *The Times* produced a guide to the act, largely written by Macbeath.

In March 1971 the Rothermere press (Harmsworth Publications) decided to merge their ailing tabloid, the *Daily Sketch* with its prosperous sister-paper, the *Daily Mail*. The decision was implemented swiftly and secretively, and there were, of course, redundancies. There was also a dispute about terms. Bernard Levin, still trailing clouds of the left-wing, anti-boss sentiment that had inspired his youthful thinking, wrote with bitter irony in his column: 'I will say this much for the Rothermeres: they remain in character, even at times of crisis. The staffs of the *Daily Mail* and *Daily Sketch* discovered that the papers were to be merged when the *Mail*'s Geneva correspondent telephoned to sympathise'.

The piece proceeded from one vituperative paragraph to another. One passage conveyed a double-edged poisoned dart:

> There were a few touches of grotesque humour. One such was

1 June 12 1971.

> the resignation (as chairman of Harmsworth Publications) of Lord Rothermere, who then left the country, together with the announcement that he was being succeeded in the position by his son, Vere (known throughout the organization as 'mere') Harmsworth. It was thus left to Harmsworth to announce the closure and the sackings . . .[1]

Levin's attack would have had awkward implications in any case. The Rothermere press was not only his, but Hussey's, previous employer, which both had only recently left. Malicious motives were bound to be suspected, however unjustly. The piece also created further friction between Rees-Mogg and Macbeath, who had written – before Levin – a piece about the *Mail-Sketch* affair, explaining the issues, only to be told that it could not be published because, as father of the chapel, he was ex officio a member of the NUJ's Central London branch committee, which was involved in the dispute. But above all the piece caused trouble to the paper for a reason that can be gathered from a headline on the following day's front page: 'Lord Rothermere to sue *The Times*'.

In those days the public was thought to be more sympathetic than the judicial bench to the cause of free comment by newspapers, and there were special reasons for thinking this where Levin was concerned. On *The Times*'s side it was felt, therefore, that a jury trial would be advantageous. The Rothermere side, clearly making the same calculation, applied for the case to be heard by a judge. In the court of first instance the decision went in favour of the Rothermeres. *The Times* appealed, and after some months the Court of Appeal reversed the decision. The Rothermeres then took the case to the House of Lords which, after further delay, upheld the decision of the lower court and ordered that the case be tried by a judge. Faced with this prospect *The Times* was advised to settle out of court, and did so.

Levin had often been very rude about lawyers in print, and his pen had not spared some of the highest legal officers in the land. This background must surely have influenced the attempt to secure a jury trial and, when the attempt failed, the decision to settle. If judges in general were believed to have a rather low opinion of journalists, Levin was a journalist to whom the average judge was likely to be particularly hostile. Moreover, while the Harmsworth libel action was *sub judice*, Levin tempted Providence with what was regarded, by many lawyers, as one of his most scandalous and outrageous attacks.

1 'Profit and dishonour in Fleet Street', March 19 1971.

The former lord chief justice, Lord Goddard, died on May 29 at the age of ninety-four. Little more than a week later Levin's column, headlined 'Judgment on Lord Goddard', was the equivalent of a death sentence on the dead man's reputation. Goddard's bias against both defendants in the Craig-Bentley case in 1953 was, Levin said, 'as undisguised as it was unjudicial'. And he said much else in the same vein.

Anticipating the point on which the fury of his critics would chiefly focus, he replied in advance:

> . . . I am aware, many a pen must be twitching, especially in the Temple, to write to *The Times* denouncing this column as, in the traditional phrase, 'a cowardly attack on a dead man'. Let the writers know this: that I wrote and published such sentiments, and stronger ones too, while Goddard was alive, and not merely while he was alive but while he was still Lord Chief Justice.[1]

Many did, indeed, write to *The Times*. And it was no coincidence that soon afterwards Levin was blackballed by the Garrick Club, in whose membership lawyers form a substantial element.

Throughout the controversy Rees-Mogg gave him solid support. Whatever his precise opinion of Levin's views on any particular matter, he regarded him as a contributor of unique value, as well as a friend. When the Harmsworth case was eventually settled, in April 1973, Levin wrote to him:

> Now that it is all over, I am sure we are well shot of it . . . We might have done better, but the chances were at least even that we might have done worse, certainly from a financial point of view. I am sorry it ever happened, and I am sure you are right when you say that if we had been working together longer at the time it would have come out differently. And thank you very much for your calmness and support throughout . . .

Rees-Mogg replied:

> . . . I am sure we were right to settle and equally sure that one cannot conduct a newspaper on the footing that one will never run the risk of a libel action, and in particular that your sort of

1 June 8 1971.

> column could not be written on that basis . . . I was very grateful to you for the calm way in which you treated the whole thing and enjoyed seeing it through together.[1]

Would it have come out any differently if they had been working together longer? One has to wonder.

Levin's provocation could not alter the fact that *The Times* was more or less obligatory reading for lawyers, because its law reports were in a class apart. Through its traditional link with the Incorporated Council of Law Reporting it was able to provide a better coverage of the courts than any other paper. None of its rivals had access to this source of reporting by professional lawyers, which was and remained a unique privilege. During the Thomson period the editor of the law reports, who handled the material that came from the reporters of the Incorporated Council, was Jack Evans.

In 1970, however, it was decided that the paper should have a legal correspondent, as the *Daily Telegraph* already had, to write about the law in a way that would interest ordinary readers of the paper. While the law reports would remain indispensable reading for lawyers, it was felt that they should be supplemented by less technical and more wide-ranging treatment of the subject. The first legal correspondent to be appointed, Simon Courtauld, lasted only about a year. He was succeeded, in June 1971, by a thirty-year-old Franco-South African, Marcel Berlins.

Berlins' parents had migrated to France from the Baltic states. His father, of Latvian Jewish origin, was running a small hotel in Marseilles when France fell in 1940. Soon he was active in the Resistance, and to avoid capture by the Gestapo he moved with his family to a remote village in the Lubéron region, where Marcel, the only child, spent his earliest years. After the war, in 1951, his parents moved to South Africa, where he completed his schooling and read law at the university of Witwatersrand. His experience of South Africa left him with a fervent dedication to justice in the broadest sense. In 1964 he returned to France to read for a law doctorate at the Sorbonne, but there were problems about his national service, and about his desire to switch subjects, with the result that, three years later, he moved to London. There he got a job under Evans on the *Times* law reports, which he combined with reading, mainly in the evenings, for a LL M degree at

1 Levin to W.R.-M., April 9 1973; W.R.-M. to Levin, same date.

the London School of Economics. In 1969 he became a civil servant in the lord chancellor's department, and it was while he was working there that he was asked, much to his surprise, to be *The Times*'s legal correspondent.

The approach to him was made by Grant, after various other candidates had been considered but turned down for one reason or another. Grant remembered him as a recent junior working on law reports, but had little else to go on and took him largely on trust. He did, however, make a point of asking Berlins one question – was he 'a shit'? – explaining that there was no place for such a person on *The Times*. His reply must have been satisfactory, and it was not long before Grant's choice was seen to be as inspired as it was bold. By 1974 Berlins was a valued member of the editorial team, not only producing admirable, lively reports and analyses of issues within his own field, but also writing leaders on various other topics, including cricket and pop music. (He contributed the obituary leader on Elvis Presley.) His special mentor was Hickey, but he also liked and respected Rees-Mogg. In 1978 he was able to cover the Steve Biko trial in South Africa, when he happened to be there for his father's funeral.

The paper did not appear at all on Wednesday July 28 1971, and the following day's paper had this announcement on the front page:

> We regret that *The Times* was not published yesterday, owing to an industrial dispute in the machine room. The present issue carries news covering the day that was missed as well as the normal coverage of yesterday's news.

Thursday's paper consisted, in fact, of thirty-four pages, compared with twenty-six on Tuesday and twenty-eight on Friday.

In one respect, not mentioned in the announcement, the one-day strike on the 28th was an unfortunate landmark in the paper's history. Though *The Times* had been involved, along with others, in national newspaper strikes, never before had it been stopped on its own. Ostensibly the strike was caused by the decision to make permanent the integration of business news into the main paper, and to end back-setting. At first this change was said to be only temporary, with Rees-Mogg for one hoping that *TBN* might once again become separate and self-contained. Meanwhile the machine-room men continued to receive a backsetting bonus – until the decision in July, which prompted the chapel to ask for thirteen weeks' notice or pay in lieu. The management refused on the grounds that the men had been receiving the bonus for months, in effect for doing nothing.

The dispute over the bonus was the occasion for the strike, but not its true precipitating cause, which was something quite different and rather more human. The weather was very hot, and several of the machine-room men developed dermatitis. Under the previous regime a nurse, or even a doctor, would have been sent to attend to the men from the Middlesex Hospital, of which John Astor was chairman. But the Thomson management told them to go to their own doctors and get a prescription. This grievance, trivial in itself, tipped the balance in favour of a strike.[1]

The Times's printers were, traditionally, the aristocrats of Fleet Street, and labour relations on the paper had long been regarded as the best in the industry. Louis Heren, whose father was a *Times* printer, describes the harmonious, if feudal, spirit that prevailed during the Astor period:

> Britain was of course a deferential society in those days, but everybody who worked for *The Times* was supposed to be a member of one big happy family known as the Companionship. We were not employees or hands, but Companions joined in a mystical union dedicated to producing *The Times*. Astor was the Chief Companion. It was taken very seriously, and those who thought it a joke – and there must have been some – kept quiet if only because of the advantages. They were considerable. For instance, the Companionship ran the staff restaurant – not the usual canteen but a real restaurant with linen tablecloths, fresh flowers, uniformed waitresses and a licence to sell beer, wines and spirits most hours of the day and night. It also ran the sports ground in Ravensbourne, Kent, and a number of clubs ranging from cricket and golf to music and amateur dramatics.[2]

The change after Thomson took over was gradual, and only after the move from Printing House Square to Gray's Inn Road were its consequences disastrous. But already in 1971 there was a clear premonition of trouble to come. Many of the material advantages remained under Thomson, though not all, as the dermatitis affair

1 Innis Macbeath, unpublished memoir of life at *The Times*.
2 Heren, *Memories of Times Past*, pp.4–5.

showed. Above all, the sense of solidarity uniting all departments, editorial, management and production, was weakening.

Only a week or so before the dermatitis strike Lord Astor of Hever died at Cannes, and his death was an apt reminder of the old regime and its values. His obituary, which ran to 3½ columns, was throughout almost reverent in tone, as for instance in this passage on his 'constant care for the harmony and well-being of the staff':

> In addition to ensuring that the company provided for their health and comfort in working hours and for their pensions on retirement, John Astor did all in his power to encourage their games and pastimes. For many summers before the last war he and his wife entertained the staff, their wives and their friends at immense gatherings at Hever Castle, running sometimes to over 3,000 guests. John and Violet Astor were happy and friendly hosts. As each year was added to the last there grew a link of affection between John Astor and his staff that was intensely personal. It showed itself from time to time in gifts that were made to him by the staff on significant occasions. These he cherished.[1]

The following day there was a first leader on Astor, a gesture that had been denied to his co-proprietor, John Walter. The leader recalled the firm guarantee of editorial independence given by the regime that succeeded that of Northcliffe:

> He [Astor] and John Walter . . . saw that the future editor must have his position defined more clearly than before. The two proprietors could appoint an editor and, if need be, dismiss him: they could advise and warn, and would expect to be informed by him on matters of great concern. Yet the editor would be editor . . .

John Astor kept faithfully to his side of the bargain despite, allegedly, occasional uneasiness about the line the paper was taking:

> He kept to it even though there were times – during the years of appeasement, during the term of the first Labour government after the war, or in the years of the Stalinist menace – when he

1 July 20 1971. Astor had died the previous day.

> would privately disagree with the policy of the paper. He would express his opinion, often by way of a question or two: he would not insist.[1]

The leader was written by McDonald, who makes a similar claim for Astor in Volume V of this History. But one has to ask how strong his anti-appeasement views were in the 1930s if no reference to them occurs in any diaries or memoirs of the period, to say nothing of the columns of *Hansard*. Was he so scrupulous in giving no public indication of differing from his editor that he censored himself as an MP? If so, his sense of priorities was surely wrong, since his duty to the country was presumably even greater than his duty to *The Times*. It seems more likely, however, that his views were so vaguely articulated as to be hardly worth the name. As Haley says in his *DNB* entry, he was not 'politically inclined', but went into Parliament because he felt it was expected of him.[2] At any rate, despite any opposition to appeasement that he may have expressed, with the more knowledgeable support of Walter, the policy of the paper was unaffected.

This prompts a brief digression on the relationship between newspaper owners and editors, and its bearing on the freedom and quality of the press. Few would deny that quality newspapers have to be free newspapers, and that one of the freedoms most necessary for them is, in principle, that of their editors from proprietorial interference. But should the principle be absolute, and is it, in any case, enough to ensure quality? So far as the freedom of its editors was concerned, *The Times* lived through a golden age under Astor. Unlike Northcliffe, he did not interfere at all, and his non-interference has earned him general praise. But did the paper in his day enhance its reputation for honest and full reporting, wise judgement and fearless campaigning? Certainly it did not. The Astor period was, on the contrary, one of exceptional, perhaps unique, degradation, in the sense that it was the period when *The Times* stood (if that is the right word) for the appeasement, successively, of Hitler and Stalin, the two most dreadful and devastating tyrants known to history.

The two editors responsible for this shameful double, Geoffrey Dawson and R.M. Barrington-Ward, were both men of high ability

---

1 'John Astor of *The Times*', July 21 1971. In the same issue there was a follow-up obituary tribute from Thomson, full of mind-numbing platitudes – 'greatest admiration and affection', 'integrity and independence', 'always put his sense of duty first', 'a very fine newspaper owner and a very fine man'.

2 Astor was Conservative MP for Dover from 1922 to 1945. Haley says nothing of his private dissent on policy issues.

and personal virtue. Nevertheless they were capable of leading the paper hideously astray. Dawson was twice editor: first under Northcliffe, whose style as a proprietor was made genuinely intolerable towards the end by dementia, and caused Dawson to resign in 1919; then again under Astor, who left him entirely to his own devices. If an editor only needed freedom from proprietorial interference to produce admirable results, Dawson's second editorship should have been far better than his first. Yet in fact the reverse is surely true. There can be little doubt that his first was the better, or that both he and the paper benefited immensely from the active involvement of Northcliffe who (so long as he was sane) was not only an inspired journalist but also a patriot with a knowledge of certain subjects, including Germany and the phenomenon of manned flight, that few of his contemporaries could match. As for Dawson's second editorship, one has to say that he did not extend to his editorial staff the perfect freedom that he himself enjoyed, but allowed his obsessive commitment to appeasing Hitler to influence his handling of news stories and his attitude to colleagues' comments.

The truth seems to be that freedom of the press and the quality of journalism depend upon conditions that cannot be too strictly defined. As in most, if not all, spheres of human activity, personal qualities and their interplay are all-important. A proper balance did not, of course, exist at *The Times* towards the end of the Northcliffe regime. In another sense it was even more disastrously absent during the Astor period.

Yet, whatever his intellectual and political limitations, and however questionable his non-interventionist stance, John Astor was a truly decent and benevolent man, fulfilling in his life the dream of his father, William Waldorf, who left America because it was 'not a fit place for a gentleman to live', and who, in England, provided himself and his family with the appurtenances of aristocracy. John, educated at Eton and New College, Oxford, completed the process of assimilation. During the First World War, in which he lost a leg, he married a war-widow from a noble Scottish family: Violet, daughter of the 4th Earl of Minto. Together they made Hever a suitably splendid country extension of the neo-feudal regime at Printing House Square. For all his diffidence of manner and genuine humility of spirit, Astor had natural authority, deriving even more from his character than from his wealth; and he served many good causes, including *The Times*, devotedly according to his lights.

XII

Direct Rule in Ulster • Resident reporter • A joke misfires • Union militancy blows the government off course • Unemployment and inflation – which the principal enemy? • A curious rumour • Ill-defined diary

THE ARRIVAL OF British troops in Northern Ireland in August 1969, though at first welcomed by members of the minority community for whose protection they had chiefly been sent, was soon exploited by republican extremists for their own purposes. The troops were represented as an alien army of occupation, whose function was to uphold the Unionist/Protestant ascendancy and to hold the Nationalist/Roman Catholic population down. There were, moreover, inevitably faults and blunders on the army's side, which could be used further to prejudice minority opinion; as, for instance, when a five-year-old girl died after being accidentally knocked down by an army vehicle during a day of rioting in Belfast, in February 1971. Communal violence was all the time increasing, more troops had to be sent, and there was also a struggle within the IRA, between the Official and Provisional wings, from which the Provisionals were emerging as the dominant force.

In March Chichester-Clark was succeeded as prime minister of the province by Brian Faulkner, an adept but widely distrusted politician, who had made life difficult for O'Neill. Faulkner's reputation as a hard-liner was, however, spurious. The motive for his hostility to O'Neill had been more personal than political, and his true colours were those of a somewhat Wilsonian pragmatist.[1] In any case hard-line Unionism was now championed by more ostentatiously unyielding figures; above all by the Revd Ian Paisley and his Democratic Unionist Party. In the Republic the Fianna Fail government was led by the mild but quietly determined Jack Lynch, who had succeeded Lemass as a

1 There are, indeed, analogies between his relationship with O'Neill and Wilson's with Gaitskell.

compromise candidate when there was deadlock between two more favoured rivals. One of these was Lemass's son-in-law, Charles Haughey, who became minister of finance under Lynch. But in May 1971 he was sacked from the government, and three weeks later was charged with conspiring to import arms illegally. During the trial it was revealed that large sums from a fund administered by him, supposedly for the relief of distress in Northern Ireland, had found their way to the two wings of the IRA. Though a Dublin jury acquitted him, Lynch did not bring him back into the government until forced to do so, four years later, by his popularity with the party rank-and-file.

At the time of the gun-running scandal Lynch gave an off-the-record interview to Hickey, in which he would not say much about the scandal itself, because the trial was still pending, but did make his attitude to the North and its troubles reasonably clear. He had told Nationalist deputations from the province that 'they must look for protection from the British Army (a thing he found it hard to do)', because he had no intention of supporting them physically. 'He would allow his government to fall rather than become arms supporters in an Irish civil war'.[1]

The other prime minister concerned, Heath, had little knowledge of Ireland, North or South, and disliked what he knew. English and Anglican to the core, he regarded Irish politics as sheer introversion and most Irish religion as pure bigotry. His home secretary, Reginald Maudling, was if possible even less sensitive to the Irish and their predicament, scarcely bothering to conceal his distaste for Northern Ireland and speaking of 'an acceptable level of violence' as the best that could be hoped for there. Even this callously limited objective was not achieved by the methods that the Heath government chose to employ. In August 1971, after a visit by Faulkner to London, detention without trial of terrorist suspects was introduced, while the British military presence in Northern Ireland was further reinforced. Immediately about 300 people were rounded up, but since most of them were Catholics, and some of them innocent, the result was an intensification of minority feeling against the army, and a victory, in effect, for the IRA. Violence escalated in the province, and there was also a war of words between London and Dublin. Despite attempts to reduce the temperature during the following month, and a meeting of the three prime ministers at Chequers at the end of September – the first such meeting since Ireland was partitioned – it was clear that there would

1 Report of interview from Hickey to W.R.-M., May 27 1970.

be no significant progress so long as detention remained. There were allegations of ill-treatment of detainees, and of brutal methods of interrogation, which the government set up a committee to investigate.[1] This showed a certain lack of confidence, without removing the basic grievance.

On January 30 1972 the army was involved in a major incident, which led to a fateful political decision. Civil rights activists in Derry went ahead with an illegal march, despite the obvious danger that more extreme elements would use it to provoke conflict with the security forces. Conflict duly occurred. After the 10,000 marchers had dispersed, gangs of youths began to throw stones at the troops. The first battalion of the Parachute Regiment was ordered to pursue the stone-throwers, and afterwards claimed to have come under heavy fire from IRA snipers. Certainly the paras opened fire themselves, killing thirteen unarmed men. The day soon passed into republican folklore as 'Bloody Sunday', though of course equally innocent blood, and far more of it, had already been shed by the IRA in the course of its murderous campaign.

Next morning's main news story in *The Times* was headlined '13 civilians are killed as soldiers storm the Bogside', and the story itself, from Brian Cashinella and John Chartres, described what had happened as 'by far the worst day of violence seen in this largely Roman Catholic city since the present crisis began in 1969'. A senior officer of the Official IRA in Derry was quoted as saying, in a tape-recorded interview 'with journalists from the Republic', that all members of his organisation had been given freedom to shoot as many British soldiers as possible in retaliation. Bernadette Devlin, the fiery republican MP for Mid-Ulster, was quoted as describing the incident as 'mass murder by the Army', who had 'shot up a peaceful march'.

In its leader the paper commented that the 'dreadful day's work in Londonderry [would] carry Northern Ireland another stage towards a finally ungovernable condition'. Since there was 'the usual flat contradiction' between the official account and what some eye-witnesses were saying, it was 'imperative that the truth of the matter be established to the reasonable satisfaction of the British people – and of the Irish people too if such a thing were possible'. The responsibility of those who had insisted on holding the march was stressed:

1 The committee reported in November, criticising some of the methods used for interrogating suspects. The government then appointed another committee, of privy councillors, to review existing techniques of interrogation.

> The decision announced by Mr. Faulkner a fortnight ago that the general ban on processions and parades would be extended for a year was publicly resented by the Orange organisations. By the organisers of the Roman Catholic minority it was received as a challenge immediately to be taken up.
>
> The men who purport to speak for that community now in effect deny the legitimacy of the Stormont Government . . . The prohibition was met with defiance. It must be presumed that those who are inciting the Catholics to take to the streets know very well the consequences of what they are doing. Londonderry had a taste of those consequences last night.

The army was in a position where it could not win. As for the ruling Unionist Party, if it were to split the time and place must be right. 'Now is neither. The Unionist Party is one of the elements out of which the immediate political construction of the province will have to be built. Its disintegration would compound the chaos'.[1]

The following day most of the front page was occupied by further news of the incident and its repercussions. The main headline was 'Sweeping Dublin demands to London as envoy is recalled', and it was reported that a judicial inquiry was being set up. In the left-hand column the parliamentary correspondent, Hugh Noyes, described a dramatic scene in the House of Commons:

> Miss Bernadette Devlin, arms flailing and fists flying, launched herself across the House of Commons today in an attack on the Home Secretary, Mr. Maudling, as that normally unflappable minister was answering questions on the events in Northern Ireland . . .
>
> Mr. Maudling's glasses were sent flying as the diminutive, mini-skirted MP for Mid-Ulster threw herself at the government front bench. The Home Secretary had already been called a liar several times by Miss Devlin, but words, for once, appeared to fail her . . . 'That murderous hypocrite' was all that could be heard above the uproar as she took off from her seat on the opposition back benches.
>
> No one could remember a similar incident in the Commons in recent years . . .
>
> What astonished the House today was that Miss Devlin appeared to have escaped with not even a warning, let alone a

1 'The new tragedy in Ulster', January 31 1972.

suspension. An attempt to raise the incident as a contempt of the House was not allowed by Mr. Selwyn Lloyd, the Speaker.

On pages 4 and 5 there was extensive further coverage of the shooting, with conflicting eye-witness statements, including Cashinella's which, like one also quoted from Simon Winchester of the *Guardian*, suggested that the army had over-reacted. According to Cashinella: 'Before the paras went in, and the troops at the bottom of William Street were being stoned, the situation did not seem much worse to me than that faced by the police at the Grosvenor Square anti-Vietnam demonstration'.

In its leader the paper again took a firm and realistic line. Accepting that not only republican opinion in Ireland, but public confidence in Britain and foreign opinion ('not to be ignored'), had been affected by the tragic occurrence in Derry, it agreed that the proposed inquiry was necessary. All the same:

> . . . neither its appointment nor its findings, whatever they are, will alter the fact that Londonderry, January 30, 1972, is now a potent part of Irish political mythology. It was the day the British paras went blazing into the Bogside and gunned down the innocent. As a statement of fact that is probably a travesty. As a belief impervious to contrary evidence it is a fact in its own right. Political calculation must reckon on it.

The leader warned against premature attempts to find a political solution. 'Until the Catholic representatives [were] ready for negotiation and free to enter into it, further initiatives towards a new political settlement [would be] so many wasted words'.[1]

By an unpremeditated irony the paper carried the same day, sandwiched between the op. ed. and leader pages, a special report entitled 'Ireland: the island for all seasons', in which the manifold charms of the country, or anyway part of it, were colourfully set forth. Which was the missing part? There was no mention at all of Northern Ireland, or any of its numerous attractive features. 'The island' should have

1 'The Deaths in Derry', February 1 1972. The inquiry into the affair, which was conducted by the lord chief justice, Lord Widgery, on his own, resulted in a report, published in April, which was a balancing act, though tilted distinctly in the army's favour. The army's tactics were criticised, but the charge that there had been a deliberate decision to use lethal force was rejected. Naturally, as *The Times* foresaw, the report made no impression on Irish republican opinion.

read 'the Republic'. Across the bottom of the two middle pages there was an advertisement from the Irish Tourist Board.[1]

After 'Bloody Sunday' there were almost daily reports of atrocities in Northern Ireland. On March 10, in an article on the op. ed. page, Philip Howard reviewed fifty years of the Northern Ireland parliament, Stormont (actually opened in June, 1921). To judge from its contents, Howard's piece might have been an inspired trailer for Stormont's impending demise. He argued that Stormont had not fulfilled Burke's specification of what was needed for a parliamentary machine to work properly, that it should be 'a deliberate assembly of ONE nation, with one interest, that of the whole'.[2]

A fortnight later Stormont was suspended and direct rule from London imposed. At the same time it was announced that detention without trial would be phased out, and that regular plebiscites would be held on whether or not the Border should remain. Heath had come to the conclusion that he must take drastic action to counter the harm that the Ulster disturbances were doing to Britain's reputation abroad: in the United States and, from his point of view more especially, among Roman Catholics in the European Community. At meetings in London Faulkner had been asked to surrender all responsibility for security in Northern Ireland to the British government. If he had acceded to this demand, the Stormont regime would have been reduced to a cipher. Not surprisingly he resigned rather than accede to it, and his government disappeared with him. Instead of the devolved administration a Northern Ireland Office was set up on the analogy of the Scottish Office, as part of the United Kingdom government. To the post of secretary of state for Northern Ireland Heath appointed a senior and most trusted colleague, William Whitelaw, at the time lord president of the council and leader of the House of Commons.

---

1 Same date. The paper's special reports, edited by John Greig, were important as receptacles for advertising; but for that very reason it was never easy to ensure that the contents were manifestly and incontestably up to the standards of objectivity which many expected of *The Times*. In May 1967 some eyebrows were raised when, at the time of a state visit to Britain by King Faisal of Saudi Arabia, the paper carried a twelve-page special report on that country, with a front-page introduction headlined 'Welcome guest from a changing land'. The report contained no advertisements, but vigilant readers could find at the foot of p.II the following announcement: 'Publication of this number has been made possible by the payment of a charge by the Government of Saudi Arabia equivalent in amount to the cost of the advertising that a special number of this size would normally carry'. In other words, the whole report was an advertisement, which might be considered doubtfully in accordance with the Code of Advertising Practice's rule that advertisements 'in the style of news or editorial' should be readily identifiable as advertisements.

2 'Stormont: to pity the plumage of a dying bird', March 10 1972.

The destruction of Stormont was, of course, a prime objective of the IRA, so there needed to be the assurance of enormous compensating benefits to justify giving such a prize, and such encouragement, to the enemy. Yet how could there be any such assurance? *The Times* recognised that the step was a gamble, but felt that it might pay off if the opportunities that it presented were swiftly exploited.

> The move to direct rule could provide a short space, a few weeks or a few months, of opportunities for political movement. If it is made the basis of action in that time, the advantages would be gained, and perhaps the worst of the risks avoided. That would mean a rapid attempt to negotiate a construction of consent between the communities. If so, direct rule would prove justified, but the chance will not last long.[1]

Time would show what use would be made of the chance, and what would become of the resulting 'construction'. Meanwhile one stark fact was established, though many in Britain failed at first to appreciate its baleful significance. The British government and parliament had resumed direct responsibility for at least a part of Ireland, a burden from which they had been free since the early 1920s. The buffer of a devolved regime – the only example in practice, as has been wryly observed, of Gladstonian Home Rule – was removed, so that the full onus and odium of trying to govern Irishmen were, once again, on Britain.

'Bloody Sunday', which caused Heath to undertake the fundamental change of policy just described, also prompted Rees-Mogg to reconsider his policy of having no resident *Times* correspondent in Northern Ireland. Despite the multiplication of incidents and the general political deterioration since British troops were sent in, and even more since detention without trial was introduced, reporting from the province was still on an *ad hoc* basis up to, and during, the traumatic events in Derry early in 1972. Chartres remained the regional correspondent physically closest to Ulster, who was therefore normally expected to be first on the scene when anything important occurred, or seemed likely to occur. He was in Derry to cover the civil rights march that led

---

1 Leader, 'The responsibility comes home', March 25 1972. The author, as of other leaders quoted in this section, was Hickey.

to the shooting, though Cashinella was also there and others quickly followed.

Between 'Bloody Sunday' and the imposition of direct rule, however, a resident correspondent was installed in Northern Ireland. He was Robert Fisk, who represented a new generation of *Times* men, having been born in 1946 and recruited for the paper since the Thomson take-over. From his home at Maidstone he was sent as a boarder to Sutton Vallance, only twelve miles away, because his father wanted to make a man of him. He hated the place, but perhaps did acquire there, or at any rate develop, some of the qualities that were to mark him as a journalist, more especially courage and independence. One day he was beaten by a prefect for reading a book (on Jan Masaryk's defenestration) instead of cheering the school side at a football match. This made him so angry that he broke the cane and jabbed the boy's face with one of the bits, nearly putting out an eye and leaving a permanent scar. (The boy in question turned up as an officer in Northern Ireland while Fisk was there, and they became quite good friends.)

After Sutton Vallance Fisk took a job for six months on the *Newcastle Evening Chronicle* (Hamilton's old paper) before going to Lancaster university, where he read English and Classics. He then worked for three years on the *Sunday Express* ('Town Talk') before joining *The Times*. He had no Irish blood, but had visited Northern Ireland from Lancaster and found the place so interesting that, when he was interviewed by Cudlipp and Grant, he said he would like to cover it for the paper. Before long his wish was fulfilled.

His byline appeared for the first time on a report from the province on February 11 1972, and thereafter with increasing frequency. As he settled in he lost no time in establishing contacts with nearly all parties and groups, including the IRA, and in obtaining good sources in the army and the RUC. He also did a crash course of reading on Irish history, and among the many books he read the two that influenced him most were *The Ulster Crisis* by A.T.Q. Stewart and the third volume of Tom Jones's *Whitehall Diary*. His approach to the job was that of an impassioned truth-seeker and communicator of news, to whom the highest moral imperative was that he should inform the public. In any conflict between his vocation as a journalist and his duty as a patriot, he had no hesitation in allowing the former to prevail. With such a philosophy he could hardly fail to run into trouble with the authorities, while in the process making his name as a great reporter.

Perhaps appropriately, direct rule in Northern Ireland came into force on April 1, after the necessary legislation had been rushed through.

On the same day *The Times* carried an item which was to cause the paper some embarrassment and to cost the travel correspondent his job. In connection with a Saturday Review feature on Thomas Cook, the travel agency, about to celebrate the centenary of its first round-the-world tour, there was an announcement that the company was offering a thousand such tours during the coming summer at 1872 prices, or £220.50 per tour. The itinerary was to take in Cape Kennedy, the Great Barrier Reef, Fujiyama, the Taj Mahal, the Valley of the Kings and a dozen world capitals. Applicants were told not to send money 'at this stage', but merely to write indicating interest. Their letters were to be addressed to 'Miss Avril Foley, Cook's Special Holiday', and either handed in at local offices of the company or posted to its headquarters in London.

The announcement was, of course, an April fool, though its author claimed that he wrote it only as a private joke and never meant it to appear in print. On March 24 John Carter, the travel correspondent, knowing that there was to be a Thomas Cook feature, wrote the spoof item in an idle moment and put it on the desk of Margaret Allen, then assistant features editor, with whom he shared an office. According to him, he attached to it a note 'Not for the news pages', with exclamation marks. Margaret Allen was out of the room at the time, but when she came back he remarked casually that she might be amused by the piece. She made no reply, and he realised afterwards that she must have failed to register what he said. Anyway he then left for Jamaica and on his return went home for the weekend of April 1, which was also Easter weekend.

Meanwhile the spoof copy became detached from the warning note and absorbed into the production process. Before it appeared in print it was read, marked and revised in the usual way. Obviously many subs and others were taken in by it, and their gullibility was matched by that of a large number of the paper's readers who equally failed to spot the significance of 'Avril Foley'. Several hundred people rang to speak to 'her', and nearly 3,000 wrote letters. Someone at the Press Association, however, saw through the hoax, which was reported next day with some *Schadenfreude* by two Sunday newspapers.

Cudlipp was in charge on Sunday, and he immediately put out a statement, which he read to Carter over the telephone – Carter having been shocked to see the spoof announcement in Saturday's paper on his return from Jamaica – to the effect that the piece was intended as a joke 'by an individual member of *The Times* staff', and that the paper apologised for the inconvenience caused. Cudlipp also rang Rees-Mogg in Somerset, where he happened to be having tea with Hussey, and they agreed that Carter would have to go – a harsh decision. After some huffing and puffing by the NUJ chapel, which did nothing to improve Rees-Mogg's relations with Macbeath, Carter was dismissed as travel correspondent though retained as a regular contributor. Cook's did not demand his head, but on the contrary pleaded for him; and they were reimbursed (by him) for the trouble they had experienced. But Rees-Mogg nevertheless felt that substantial damage had been done to the paper's reputation, and that Carter had acted so irresponsibly he could not be kept on as travel correspondent[1]. Margaret Allen was so upset about the incident that she offered to resign, but her offer was turned down.

For a time the Heath government's hard line with the unions, and its resistance to what it regarded as inflationary wage demands in the public sector, seemed to be working. But by the end of 1971 things had gone badly wrong. In Scotland the consortium of Upper Clyde Shipbuilders, put together by Tony Benn when he was minister of technology under Wilson, was proving unviable, as British shipbuilding became less and less competitive in the world market. In June 1971 the government announced a plan to close the Clydebank and Scotstoun yards and to concentrate at Govan-Linthouse. The workforce was to be cut by more than two-thirds, and a liquidator was appointed for UCS. But the workers at Clydebank, led by two Communist shop stewards, James Reid and James Airlie (both of course Jimmies), occupied the yard and started a 'work-in'. Their action was supported by Benn, though he knew it to be illegal. Wilson, characteristically, refused either to condemn or condone it.[2]

There were also mass demonstrations in support of the 'work-in', one in Glasgow being reputedly the largest seen in Scotland since the war. The government, convinced by the chief constable of the city that there was a grave threat to public order, began to recede from its firm stand. The following year all four yards were taken over by an American corporation, Marathon, after the government, instead

1 Carter had been with the *Sunday Times* before joining *The Times*, and his long service to the Thomson Organisation should have counted in his favour. Soon afterwards the incident was leaked in the form of a mock-Elizabethan satirical piece in the *Spectator*, 'Master Mogg and the Merrie Peregrine' by 'Volcanus Tempestivus'.
2 Benn, op. cit., diary entries for June 14 and July 29 1971, p.349 and p.363.

of pulling out, had committed further enormous sums of public money. The 'work-in' did not end formally until October 1972, and then only on terms that guaranteed the minimum number of redundancies.

Grave as was the setback inflicted by the Clyde workers, that inflicted by the miners was even worse. In 1971 the ten-year reign of Lord Robens as chairman of the National Coal Board came to an end. Originally appointed by Macmillan, he had been an outstanding success in the job, closing uneconomic pits and halving the labour force in the mines while preserving peace in the industry. His advantage was that he combined managerial skill with political experience, since he had been a Labour MP for many years, representing a mining constituency, and had briefly served as minister of labour at the tail-end of the Attlee administration. The new chairman, Derek Ezra, was a technocrat who had made his career in the NCB and had no political experience at all. Yet the chairmanship of a nationalised industry is, at the best of times, as much a political as an industrial job, and never more political than when the government of the day is at loggerheads with labour.

On January 9, 1972 the National Union of Mineworkers began a strike in support of a pay claim that far exceeded the NCB's offer. At first the strike had little effect, because there were large coal stocks and the winter was mild. But at the beginning of February a picket was accidentally killed by a lorry at Scunthorpe, and the Labour side in Parliament reacted almost hysterically, one ex-miner MP shouting that unless the government acted to end the strike he would advocate 'violence, violence, violence'. At the same time a new form of industrial action, for which both the NCB and the government were unprepared, started to make itself felt. This was the blocking of supplies to power stations through mass picketing at depots, and the refusal of railway workers to move coal or coke. On February 9 the government declared a state of emergency, enabling it to restrict the use of electricity by, among other things, cutting the working week in factories from five to three days. The following day a crowd of 6,000, including pickets from Yorkshire organised by a rising NUM activist, Arthur Scargill, successfully defied the police at Saltley coke depot, Birmingham, and the same day the employment secretary, Robert Carr, announced the immediate appointment of a committee to inquire into the dispute. This committee, under the chairmanship of a law lord, Wilberforce – whose criticisms of the industrial relations bill were, as we have seen, quoted with approval by Dora Gaitskell – reported with amazing speed on February 16, acknowledging that the miners had 'a just case for special treatment' and recommending a pay increase for them of three times the NCB's original offer (which, too late, it had improved on since). Utterly at odds though Wilberforce's recommendation was with the government's proclaimed policy, the cabinet at once accepted it.

The miners, however, seeing that the government was on the run, judged that still more could be obtained and rejected the Wilberforce award. Heath then felt obliged to abandon another of his principles by calling both sides of the industry to 10 Downing Street for direct talks, which involved the further humiliation of having to postpone a visit to Chequers by President Pompidou. After hours of negotiation the dispute was eventually settled, with the miners receiving £5 million a year more than the £85 million already recommended by Wilberforce and accepted by the cabinet. It was an overwhelming victory for them, and of course an equivalent defeat for the government.

Industrial conflict in Britain had to vie for attention in *The Times*, as in Whitehall, with the concurrent disturbances in Northern Ireland, the completion of British entry into the European Community, and much else. All the same the Clydeside and miners' disputes received extensive coverage and ample, if at times somewhat ambiguous, comment. Macbeath's attitude to both disputes was so even-handed that it was often hard for him to give clear guidance. But on the whole his sympathies were with Labour, and he seems to have underrated trade union power. Thus in October 1971 a leader written by him suggested to the organisers of the Clyde 'work-in' that the time might have come to end it:

> In London tonight the Upper Clyde Shipbuilders controversy will reach a determining point . . . If there is agreement the 'work-in' will have an honourable place in the unique history of labour on the Clyde. If the demonstration is pressed too far, the long-term effects will be damaging . . . In the short run, Clydeside cannot afford to press indignation too far. No one can compel industrialists to put their money there; merely attract them . . . both workers and prospective employers must have some assurance for the future.[1]

The point, surely, was that in politically sensitive areas the government could be forced, by trade unions and employers alike, to put public money into uneconomic industries.

1 'The crisis on Clydeside', October 12, 1971. The negotiations in London referred to in the leader were far from being the end of the matter, and the 'work-in' lasted another year.

Similarly, Macbeath tended to sympathise with the miners while apparently underrating their strength. As the strike began he wrote:

> Miners are not well paid. During the past ten years, while their numbers have halved, their members have slipped from near the top to well down the industrial scale . . . Miners do not blame the NCB . . . for the need to close the pits and the difficulty of finding jobs outside mining. They do resent the collective social attitude which creates this difficulty. A meagre offer as a result of government policy is therefore doubly vexatious.[1]

When the state of emergency was declared he wrote that the government had to act 'to conserve the nation's fuel supplies and, no less, to forestall if it [could] greater injury and distress outside the pits and the power stations'. Yet the tone of this leader was one of warning to the miners not to overplay their hand.[2] On the front of the same issue the pickets at Saltley were reported as saying 'Saltley's coke mountain has blood on it', and the chief constable of Birmingham as telling how 500 miners had travelled 'from distant parts' to join in action that was 'illegal and tantamount to intimidation'.[3]

In *TBN*, also on February 9, there was a leader by Hugh Stephenson, the section's editor, on the choice facing the government in the Upper Clyde affair. Stephenson, like Macbeath, was a man of intellect and conscience who tried hard to be objective, but whose natural affinities were with the moderate left. He wrote:

> After Rolls-Royce, the Upper Clyde must be the industrial experience that has most upset the Government's pre-election vision . . . Put simply, if the Government decide to do nothing, shipbuilding in Scotland will go to the wall. If the Government decide, on industrial or social grounds, that there should continue to be a shipbuilding industry in Scotland (or anywhere else for that matter) they will have to agree to subsidise it.

Since the amount of capital required was beyond the capacity (or, he might perhaps more accurately have said, the willingness) of private credit institutions to provide, the government had 'little option but to put up the necessary money for the Upper Clyde'. At the same time it should support attempts 'to regulate internationally direct and indirect

1 'Stubbornness on both sides', another Macbeath leader, January 10, 1972.
2 'The state of emergency', February 9 1972.
3 The report was from Arthur Osman, Birmingham (same date).

subsidies given by all governments to their respective shipbuilding industries'.[1]

At the height of the mining dispute, after the appointment of Wilberforce and before his report, Rees-Mogg wrote a leader in which he, too, tried to be fair to both sides, though with an equally natural tendency to look at the dispute from a moderate-right angle. There was bound, he said, to be bitterness as millions of people were thrown out of work and further millions exposed to cold and darkness in their homes. But conciliation was 'often assisted by analysis and seldom by condemnation'. He admitted that the miners were 'only moderately paid', but on the other hand inflation was 'a vital threat to the welfare of this country'. It was not a simple question of right and wrong. The NCB 'must regret that their current offer . . . was not made before the strike started when it would have had a better chance of acceptance'. Yet the miners also were open to criticism; some of their picketing had 'gone far beyond the peaceful picketing that [was] allowed by law'. He ended that it was not 'a time to indulge in bitterness', but 'a time for reason'.[2] Unfortunately reason did not really come into it; the dispute was essentially a trial of strength which the miners won.

A few days later, on the eve of the Wilberforce report, Rees-Mogg wrote a big leader in which he sought to identify 'the defects of government which [had] contributed to the present situation'. The department of employment, he decided, was not to blame. The government's economic policy, which 'depended upon a willingness to face confrontation', had at first been 'remarkably successful'; and even though it could not be assumed that the miners would get a lot more than Heath would regard as reasonable, they would have done so after 'a long and major strike', which would be 'not exactly an incentive to other unions to think that they [could] imitate the miners'. This was to prove over-optimistic; the railwaymen soon imitated them all too effectively.

The sphere of government which, in his view, had shown itself to be seriously defective was the department of trade and industry, which had failed to anticipate the damaging potential of the strike, more especially the new form of picketing. (He might have added that the press, including *The Times*, had been just as weak in its industrial intelligence). Finally, he made the good point that the home secretary, Maudling, should not have been expected to act as chairman of the

1 'Upper Clyde: the choice', *TBN* leader, same date. Stephenson was, at the time, a Labour councillor in Wandsworth. In 1982 he became editor of the *New Statesman*.
2 'A time for reason', February 12 1972. His point about the effects of power cuts was aptly illustrated, on the front page, by a picture of John Davies, the industry secretary, 'in his candlelit home'.

emergency committee while he was also 'the minister responsible for Northern Ireland at the most difficult stage to date of that crisis'. It was clear that Northern Ireland should be treated as 'a full-time Cabinet job', and that the home secretary should no longer be asked to 'combine it with his other responsibilities'. The leader's conclusion was an endorsement of firmness, but on one vital condition. 'The tougher a government's line, the less it can afford mistakes'.[1]

In January 1972 the figure of unemployed broke the one million barrier, a moment of acute psychological significance to politicians and commentators inured to the post-war norm of full employment. Anything that might suggest a possible return to pre-war levels of unemployment was generally regarded as socially unacceptable and, for the party in power, electoral poison. On the day the figure was announced Heath was subjected, in the House of Commons, to a show of abuse from the Labour benches so prolonged that the sitting had to be suspended. But Heath needed no Labour attacks to make him thoroughly unhappy about unemployment at over a million. He was a child of the 1920s and 1930s, sharing with most people of his generation a dread of mass unemployment.

At the same time pay demands from the miners and other workers were threatening to push inflation to levels that would endanger the health of the economy. The dilemma facing the government was, therefore, which to regard as the greater evil, unemployment or inflation, when a choice of policies had to be made. The same dilemma confronted those who offered economic advice to the government in the columns of newspapers.

The Times argued that to reconcile the two needs, of maintaining employment and controlling inflation, the best device was a voluntary incomes policy. There was, indeed, a surprisingly large consensus at the time in support of some kind of incomes policy, as Jay pointed out in a *TBN* leader. He made much of an apparent shift away from pure free market orthodoxy by Professor F.A. Hayek, in a new note to some of his work republished by the Institute of Economic Affairs. Jay drew special attention to Hayek's statement that 'the only hope of escape from the vicious circle would seem to be to persuade the trade unions in general to agree to an alternative method of wage determination which, while offering the workers as a whole a better chance of material advance, at the same time [would restore] the flexibility of the relative wages of

1 'The good reasons and the bad', February 15 1972.

particular groups'. While Hayek seemed to favour some form of profit-sharing, which united him strangely 'with Lord Brown and with the socialist ideas of Robert Owen', Jay concluded that 'others of less visionary disposition [would] prefer to plug away at the more palpable task of developing an incomes policy based on consent'.[1]

The government, for its part, continued to hope for an agreed incomes policy, but meanwhile showed quite clearly that reducing unemployment had become its overriding priority. In the budget introduced on March 21 (three days, incidentally, before the decision to impose direct rule in Northern Ireland), Barber cut taxes by £1,200 million. Two and three quarter million people at the bottom end of the scale were exempted altogether from tax, and the top rate of purchase tax was brought down to 25 per cent, while pensions and other state benefits were increased by 12½ per cent. An Industrial Development Executive was to be set up, and this seemed no different in principle from the Industrial Development Corporation which the government had been quick to abolish when it came to power. The purpose of the new body was to inject about £315 million into the economy in 1973–5, and more than twice that amount in 1975–6.

Reporting from Parliament, David Wood wrote: 'It was the budget to surpass all budgets, *if inflation is disregarded.* Everybody drew a lucky number'. In reality, inflation was more or less disregarded by the government. So it was by *The Times*, which made no reference at all to the subject in its leader on the budget. The chancellor had done a lot, the leader said. 'Yet even so it is by no means certain whether he has done all that was required of him on either economic or social grounds. *From now until the end of their term of office, the Government will be judged above all on their ability to reduce the level of unemployment*'. It was doubtful that the measures announced in the budget would be enough.[2]

Shortly beforehand, when the government had been forced to surrender to the miners, Rees-Mogg in effect advocated appeasement of the unions. The public had reached the stage of being disillusioned with the government, but could be won back if the lessons of recent events were properly learnt. This would not be achieved if Heath decided that he had been insufficiently tough, but rather if he reached the opposite conclusion. 'He should take no notice of critics who

1 'Wanted – an incomes policy', February 15 1972. Lord Brown was an industrialist and recently trade minister in the Wilson government.
2 Wood's front-page report on reactions to the budget in the House of Commons, and leader 'Neither bad, nor very good', March 22 1972. (Author's italics.)

despise conciliation. "George, be a King" is bad advice to a Prime Minister – after all it cost Britain America'.[1]

On February 27 1972 the following report appeared in the *Observer*:

> *Editor of Times for Cabinet?*
> Could it be that the Prime Minister is considering making William Rees-Mogg, editor of *The Times*, a member of a reconstructed Cabinet this summer?
>
> Mr. Rees-Mogg, 43, who once contested and has since been rejected by selection committees in four safe Tory seats, would have to be given a peerage.
>
> It is being suggested that he might be called on to serve in a post connected with presenting Government policy to the outside world. It was widely felt during the miners' strike that the Government's case was going by default, and that, with each Minister involved in his own department and the Prime Minister more interested in devising than in selling his policies, it might be useful to have a senior Minister specialising in this field – rather as Mr. William Deedes performed as Minister without Portfolio for Mr. Macmillan.
>
> Mr. Rees-Mogg said yesterday that he had heard nothing about this idea and that certainly no approach of any kind had been made, though there has been a persistent rumour along these lines in the City. He added that his ambitions were at present wholly satisfied with *The Times's* links with Europe.
>
> He has been on friendly terms for many years with Mr. Heath, who has visited the Rees-Moggs socially at their house in Smith Square . . .
>
> There is a precedent for such a leap directly from *The Times* to a Ministerial appointment and a seat in the Lords. In 1964 Mr. Wilson appointed Alun Gwynne-Jones, *The Times* Defence Correspondent, now Lord Chalfont, as Minister of State at the Foreign and Commonwealth Office. And Heath himself brought John Davies into the Cabinet – which might have taught him a lesson.[2]

1 Leader, 'A turning-point for Mr. Heath', March 8 1972.

2 John Davies had been appointed straight to the Cabinet, first as minister of technology, then as trade and industry secretary in 1970. Though he had been elected to the House of Commons that year, his previous experience had been exclusively as a businessman (apart from wartime service in the army). He was, from the first, ill at ease in politics, and of course he was thrown in at the deep end. Later in 1972 he was moved to the sinecure post of chancellor of the Duchy of Lancaster.

Was there any truth in the rumour? Heath later said that there was none whatever, so far as he was concerned. He had neither offered, nor contemplated offering, a ministerial post to Rees-Mogg.[1] This is easy enough to believe, because Rees-Mogg was surely of far more use to him as a particularly sympathetic editor of *The Times* than he could possibly have been as minister in charge of the government's public relations. To have lured him away from the editorship would have been to run the risk of an editor who could hardly have been more friendly and might well have been less so.

But could Rees-Mogg have been lured? Is there any reason to suspect that he inspired the rumour, consciously or unconsciously? Might people who knew him well, in the City or elsewhere, have gathered from the way he was talking that he would be amenable to such an offer? His reaction to the idea, as quoted in the *Observer*, was hardly an unequivocal denial. He said that no approach had been made to him, and that his ambitions were 'at present' satisfied by his work at *The Times*. But he was careful not to say that he would refuse any invitation to join the government, since editing *The Times* was the summit of his ambition.

There is further evidence of his state of mind in an exchange of letters with Donald Trelford, who was the *Observer*'s deputy editor at the time. Rees-Mogg had evidently rung Trelford as soon as he saw, or heard of, the *Observer*'s first edition on the Saturday night, because Trelford at once wrote:

> Dear Mr. Rees-Mogg,
>
> You may have noticed that after the first edition we moved our story about you to Pendennis, which seemed to me to be the proper place for political speculation of that sort. I'm very glad you rang, because the authority with which the story was first presented seemed to carry an implicit editorial endorsement which wasn't merited. On the other hand, it may turn out to be true – *and if that is what you would like, I hope it is*. In any event, I hope we haven't caused you undue embarrassment.
>
> Yours sincerely
> Donald Trelford

Rees-Mogg dictated his reply, presumably from Somerset, on Monday morning:

---

1 Talking to author.

Dear Mr. Trelford,

Thank you very much. I am grateful to you for moving it into the diary. *I should think it is very unlikely to prove true.* I was sorry to bother you last Saturday.

Yours sincerely

pp. William Rees-Mogg

(Dictated by the Editor but signed in his absence to avoid delay).[1]

Later, Rees-Mogg was quite sure he had never wanted to exchange his editorial chair for a seat in the government. As he recalled, the story had been 'put about by Jeremy Thorpe', who probably told the *Observer* and certainly told him. The 'suggested author of the scheme was Lord Carrington'. He would 'not have dreamed of accepting the offer if it had been made'.[2] At the time, however, he seems to have given Trelford the opposite impression when they spoke on the telephone: an impression that his letter after the weekend can have done nothing to remove. We should remember, too, that he had excluded from his general anathema against honours for *Times* staff the acceptance of life peerages, describing them as 'functional appointments rather than awards'.[3] It is hard to share his subsequent conviction that he would have refused the offer; memory plays us all tricks. But the question is academic because the offer was not made, and for good or ill he had to remain a politician *manqué*.

Trelford had told Rees-Mogg that the rumour about his future belonged properly to the *Observer*'s gossip column, 'Pendennis'. What of *The Times*'s own gossip column, or diary, 'PHS'? The feature was one of the innovations brought in at a late stage of the Haley regime, when it was entrusted to Harman Grisewood.[4] Rees-Mogg's first choice as diary editor was Roger Berthoud, well qualified by previous service on the *Evening Standard*'s 'Londoner's Diary', one of the most successful gossip columns in the British press. He joined the paper and started work in April 1967.

Berthoud, son of an industrialist turned diplomat, went to Rugby and read modern languages at Cambridge before entering a City firm

1 Donald Trelford to W.R.-M., February 26 1972; W.R.-M's reply, February 28 1972. (Author's italics.)

2 W.R.-M. to author, March 28 1988. Carrington was defence secretary, and soon to be chairman of the Conservative Party.

3 Memo dated 13 June 1967 (quoted on p. 74 above).

4 See HTT, vol.V, p.407.

as a trainee. But he did not stay there long, because his talent for journalism was spotted by Edward Pickering, then editor of the *Daily Express*. After working for a time in the *Express*'s Manchester office, he was switched within the same group, in 1960, to the 'Londoner's Diary' team, becoming editor of the feature in 1965. At *The Times* he had four people working under him. One of the original quartet, Tony Aldous, soon established himself as a pioneer specialist on town planing and the environment. Berthoud himself was particularly strong on diplomatic gossip (not surprisingly, in view of his connections); also on the world of literature and the arts. In this he had many useful contacts, including Henry Moore, whose life he later wrote. When he took the job he told Rees-Mogg he did not want to do it for more than two years, and in 1969 he left to become correspondent in Bonn.

His successor was a member of his 'PHS' team, Ion Trewin, who had come to *The Times* from the *Sunday Telegraph* in 1967. Like Berthoud, he believed that the feature's main purpose was to be newsy, and he prided himself on a number of scoops. One concerned the appointment of George Gale as editor of the *Spectator* in 1970. After hearing from a friend, at third hand, that this was imminent, Trewin put through a call late in the evening to the *Spectator*'s printers at High Wycombe, where the journal was about to go to press, and asked if he could just check the wording of the announcement, implying that its contents were well known. The printers told him that they had not yet received the copy, but had been told to leave a space for it. With nothing firmer than this to go on he decided to run the story, and the gamble paid off. He was often given good political stories by Wood, and Douglas-Home was another fertile source. But perhaps the best source of all was Peter Fleming, who would ring every other day and refused to be paid for his stories, being entirely satisfied to see them in the paper. (Thus Fleming rounded off a record of varied service to *The Times* which began in 1932, when he undertook an equally unpaid assignment in the hinterland of Brazil.)

The diary was now placed across the bottom of the op. ed. page, having at first, for a short time, occupied a vertical column there. But although it had a settled position it failed to acquire a settled character. Under Berthoud and Trewin it concentrated on news, and during the early years of the Thomson period it had the necessary resources. But after 1970 it suffered, like every other part of the paper, from the new emphasis on economy. In 1972 Trewin asked for a change of job and was, as we have seen, appointed to succeed Ratcliffe as literary editor. His replacement on the diary was Michael Leapman, who had been doing well as the paper's correspondent in New York. He had come to journalism from a minor public school via national service, but no university; his first published work appeared in the *Spectator* while he was serving in the navy. After working for papers in Cyprus and Iran, on the *Scotsman*, and on the pre-Murdoch *Sun* as a foreign affairs specialist, he joined *The Times* in 1969, on Cudlipp's initiative.

Leapman was less interested than his predecessors in political or any other kind of gossip. He felt that 'PHS' could to some extent meet the need for feature material, in which, in his view, the paper as a whole was rather weak. He therefore gave the diary a lively personal character, and to judge from letters at least a section of the readership responded to his style of editing it. His most distinctive contribution was the long-running saga of his allotment, which started when he wrote about the difficulty of obtaining allotments from various public bodies and the Water Board was moved to offer him one in Brixton. The progress of this patch through the seasons, and the culinary use that Leapman made of its produce, occupied many column-inches of diary and evoked much sympathetic advice and anecdotage from readers. Yet he did not wholly disdain the more normal subject-matter of a diary, and during the 1974 election caused some annoyance to Alastair Burnet of ITN by drawing attention to his involvement in Conservative policy-making. (His own political inclinations, such as they were, were towards the left.) During his time as diary editor he normally worked with only two assistants.

When, in 1977, he returned to New York, he continued to write Monday's diary from there, and the feature soon became little more than a succession of self-contained pieces, contributed by individual members of the staff at home or abroad. Thus in the first week of November 1978 Wednesday's diary (on the first of the month) was written from Brussels by Michael Hornsby, Thursday's was an arts diary by Martin Huckerby, Friday's was from Douglas-Home in Helsinki, Saturday's was a sports diary by 'A.N. Other', Monday's came from Leapman in New York, and Tuesday's was a London diary by Howard. After the stoppage the same pattern was resumed, but there were many on the paper who disapproved of it, and soon a number of them got together to write to the editor:

> We should like to ask you if you would be willing to consider re-instating the original form of PHS diary, in place of the present series of individual pieces on different days.
>
> As reporters we find all too frequently that there are items of news and ephemera which are not suitable for the relatively serious news columns of *The Times*, yet would both interest and

> amuse our readers. The present system effectively prevents publication of such pieces.
>
> It has been borne in upon us by friends, relatives and members of the public that there is a very strong demand for the restoration of the old style of diary. In discussions with readers about the paper, no subject is mentioned so often as the need for a return to a diary column with continuity of approach and authorship. We are convinced there would be no lack of stories for such a PHS diary revived under the right auspices.

Rees-Mogg replied emolliently, saying that he would reconsider the form of the feature, but questioning one of the arguments put to him:

> In fact, when we had a diary of the kind you suggest, it only intermittently attracted a sufficient flow of the sort of ephemeral stories to which you refer and it was a frequent complaint of diary editors to me that they were not getting the tips and paragraphs from other members of the staff which they had hoped for.[1]

At all events, no important change resulted, though the three middle days of the week were soon devoted to London diaries, so making the feature slightly less of a Cook's tour.

The Thomson/Rees-Mogg regime undoubtedly failed to make the *Times* diary a serious competitor to, for instance, the *Daily Telegraph*'s 'Peterborough'. Though shortage of resources after 1970 is some excuse, the main trouble was that it never acquired the necessary consistency, continuity and character, with a settled format, and so never became the irresistible and vital feature of the paper that a good diary should be.

---

1 Annabel Ferriman & others to W.R.-M. (undated), and his reply, January 30 (or 31, the figure is illegible) 1980. Berthoud was among the thirty-odd signatories of the letter. The diary's last editor during the period was Peter Davalle.

XIII

Royal matters • Exclusive notice-board • Signs of schism on the left • Dealings with Mr. Wilson • Ugandan Asians, and the relentlessness of Enoch Powell • Religion as news

WHILE THE MINERS' strike in support of their pay demand was imminent, Parliament had to consider a more august case where increases of remuneration were required. The civil list payments to the Queen and other members of the royal family had been unchanged for ten years, and it was clearly necessary to adjust them to take account of inflation. But the question was not entirely straightforward. In addition to the money voted by Parliament, the Queen and the Prince of Wales had the benefit of immunity from tax on their income from, respectively, the Duchy of Lancaster and the Duchy of Cornwall. Sovereigns were also exempt from death duties on their personal estate, which must therefore have accumulated greatly since Queen Victoria's time. The Prince of Wales, following a precedent set by his uncle, the future Edward VIII and Duke of Windsor, had voluntarily been paying half of his Duchy of Cornwall income to the treasury; but the remaining half undoubtedly represented a very large untaxed income. The Queen, for her part, agreed during the civil list discussions in 1971 that she would in future forgo payments from the civil list into her privy purse, receiving money from Parliament solely for the discharge of her public duties. Labour members of the select committee appointed to advise Parliament on increases in the civil list – who, apart from the lone republican, William Hamilton, were unimpeachably monarchist and moderate – nevertheless felt that the Queen's resources resulting from tax immunities ought to be divulged, if only to the committee, so that they could be taken into the reckoning when civil list increases were calculated. The Queen, however, instructed her servants to make no disclosure, and the government, which had a majority on the committee, acquiesced in her refusal.

The Times at first took a view very similar to that of the opposition.

In a well-argued leader, written by Hickey, it pointed out that at no period in history had 'the monarch's income, possessions or occupations been neatly divisible into the two categories private and public'. The Queen's tax exemptions should be taken into account by the committee, because they derived from her unique public status:

> In so far as the Queen's income and estate has certain tax exemptions not available to her subjects, they may be said to be possessed 'in right of the Crown', and it has for long been established that revenues enjoyed 'in right of the Crown' are taken into account when consideration is given to the Civil List.

There was no call for 'an inquisition into the Queen's notional wealth'. Art treasures and other such hereditaments were held in trust for the future; they generated no income, and the sovereign would never dispose of them. Moreover, the matter of disclosures should be approached 'with discretion, avoiding tendentious comparisons, in the knowledge that the royalism of the people . . . favours an impressive and generous style of monarchy'.[1] This eminently reasonable argument failed to influence either the Queen or the government, and at the end of the year increases were duly voted without any 'means test' having been applied.

Meanwhile nothing was left to chance by Buckingham Palace lobbyists. Sir John Colville, who had been the Queen's private secretary when she was Princess Elizabeth, wrote a letter for publication in which he declared that it was 'an impertinence to demand that the Queen should reveal her private affairs'. In a covering letter to Rees-Mogg he wrote:

> The fact that I was once H.M.'s Private Secretary is doubtless forgotten so that nobody is very likely to conclude that the attached letter, if you see fit to print it, is a put-up job. Nor is it, except that I have reason to think it makes a point which H.M. would like to make and which cannot easily be made by anyone immediately connected with the Household or indeed the Government.[2]

---

1 'Inspection of the royal finances', May 29 1971.

2 Sir John Colville to W.R.-M., June 4 1971. If Colville had read Hickey's leader of a few days previously, he chose to ignore the argument that the public and private aspects of the monarchy were not 'neatly divisible'. He was a clever man, but a quintessential courtier (in turn to Neville Chamberlain and Churchill, and later to the Queen before her accession). His letter for publication appeared as the lead letter on June 9 1971.

The 'point' was that estimates of the Queen's private wealth that were being bandied about were purely speculative, without any evidence to support them. But that, surely, was precisely why opposition members of the committee were asking for evidence; they wanted to deal with fact rather than speculation. Moreover, it could fairly be asked why, if the Queen's wealth was so much less than some were suggesting, she did not avail herself of the opportunity to give the lie to exaggerated reports of it by making the truth known, at least to the committee.

Rees-Mogg allowed himself to be persuaded by Colville, or perhaps needed no persuading. In reply to Colville he said: 'I think it is a very good thing to remove some of these very exaggerated rumours. It is a pity that the Select Committee has at least one committed republican on it'.[1] By December the paper's line had shifted away from that of Hickey's leader and had become indistinguishable from the government's.[2]

There was a rather bizarre sequel, when the 'one committed republican' provided the paper with some excellent free copy. In a speech on the civil list Hamilton had described the Prince of Wales as 'a twerp', but at the end of February *The Times* carried a letter from Hamilton, to which it drew attention on the front page. The letter read:

> Sir, The Oxford Dictionary defines a 'twerp' or 'twirp' as 'an insignificant or contemptible fellow'.
>
> Chambers' 20th Century Dictionary says it could mean a 'cad'.
>
> And the Penguin English Dictionary says it means a 'silly fool; an unimportant person'.
>
> I have never personally met Prince Charles. But I do not think any of the above descriptions fit. I therefore take this opportunity of publicly and unreservedly apologising for so describing the Prince in the House of Commons.
>
> I believe him to be a sensible, contented, pleasant young man. Who wouldn't be contented and pleasant with a guaranteed untaxed annual income of £105,000 a year, which is likely to be doubled or even quadrupled, automatically, within the next five years.
>
> Yours sincerely
> W. W. Hamilton

---

1 W.R.-M. to Colville, June 8 1971.

2 Leader, 'Money for the monarchy', December 3 1971. This was written by Geoffrey Smith and followed publication of the select committee's report the previous day.

The front-page story mentioned the public and unreserved apology, but not the sting in the tail.[1] The sting, however, was not particularly venomous, and readers must have reflected that if that was the worst Britain's one overtly republican MP could produce there was little to be feared from British republicanism. They must also have been amused to observe such a vaunted enemy of the 'establishment' showing that for him, too, the appropriate, even inevitable, place to explain a controversial remark was the correspondence columns of *The Times*.

At the end of May the paper spread itself with coverage of the death of the Duke of Windsor in Paris. There were reports from there (Hargrove) and from New York (Peter Strafford), together with a selection of pictures of incidents in the Duke's career, on the page opposite the obituary. This occupied a full page and was illustrated by a suitably informal picture of the Duke smoking a pipe. The obituary gave proper emphasis to his activities as Prince of Wales – obviously the most important and fruitful phase of his life – and also praised his good work as governor of the Bahamas. It was a generous, and on the whole balanced, piece. The op. ed. page reproduced material from the paper's coverage of the abdication, including the leader, 'King Edward's choice', that appeared on December 11 1936.

The paper's valedictory leader on the Duke was Rees-Mogg at his best:

> The demand made on Edward VIII was that, for reasons of her unsuitability, he should renounce his intention to marry the woman of his heart. He chose instead to renounce the throne. The demand seems harsh. It was harsh, but it was not wrong at the time it was made, the only time in relation to which it makes sense to call it either right or wrong. As for the choice between renunciations that he made, nothing that happened later either to the monarchy or to himself dictates the conclusion that he was wrong.
>
> It says much for the British monarchy that the shock and sorrow of those events did not impair its strength. For that, part of the credit belongs to the Duke of Windsor, who was determined to minimise the disturbance of his abdication. He would countenance neither intrigue nor recrimination. He may have felt unable to sustain in loneliness the burden of his responsibilities, but he was never more mindful of them than in the manner

1 Front-page story and letter to the editor, February 24 1972.

of his going, and in the patience with which he accepted an unnecessarily absolute disbarment from the kind of service to his people to which he had been born and bred.[1]

Three months later there was another, and sadly premature, royal death when Prince William of Gloucester was killed in an air accident. It turned out to be the occasion for the last leader written by Hodgkin, who was paying his final visit to the office before retiring. He had been trying to think of a suitable subject when the news came in. After consulting McDonald on the telephone he wrote 350 words on the prince – 'a curious theme to go out on'[2]

The royal family's doings were, of course, recorded day by day on the court, or social, page, one of the paper's best-loved features. The Court Circular, initiated by George III in 1803 to counter misstatements in the press, retained its own perennial style, archaic and stately. For example: 'By command of the Queen, the Lord Wallace of Coslany (Lord in Waiting) was present at Heathrow Airport, London, this afternoon upon the departure of Mr. France René (President of the Republic of Seychelles) and bade farewell on behalf of Her Majesty'. Heathrow was a very new sort of place, and the Republic of Seychelles even newer. But such disturbing novelties were made at least tolerable when touched by the magic of the Court Circular.

Just as the human race has a special terminology to distinguish it from the rest of creation ('exhumed' for 'dug up', and so on), the Court Circular had a special terminology for the royal family to distinguish it from the rest of the human race. When a royal personage had a birthday it could not be a mere birthday, but had to be the *anniversary* of that person's birthday. Apart from royalty, even the most illustrious had to be content with mere birthdays, as recorded in the 'birthdays today' section which had appeared on the social page since 1963.

---

1 Reports, features, and leader 'The Duke of Windsor', May 29 1972. The Duke was buried at Frogmore after lying in state for two days in St. George's Chapel, Windsor. 'Over 57,000 people filed past his coffin . . . and many people saw a certain irony in that only in death was he accorded the dignity of a former monarch and his widow invited for the first time to stay as the guest of the Queen in Buckingham Palace'. (*Annual Register*).

2 Hodgkin, diary entry for August 28 1972. Rees-Mogg and Hodgkin parted on friendly terms, despite the permanent shadow cast by the White Swan affair. Shortly before Hodgkin left, the editor said he would miss him but hoped he would go on writing for the paper, because he had a style which was 'clear, but contemporary', unlike his own and Hickey's which were 'rather old-fashioned', (diary, July 31 1972). In October Rees-Mogg gave a small dinner for Hodgkin at the Garrick.

During Rees-Mogg's time the range of people qualifying for inclusion in this section was considerably widened. The names of media and showbiz personalities began to appear, which some no doubt regarded as a betrayal of standards but which could be fairly said to reflect the changing values of British society. For the same reason he decided to include more names from the world of commerce, writing to the editor of *TBN*:

> As you know many people feel very flattered when they see their birthday mentioned in *The Times*. I think we are somewhat over-represented among the official classes and under-represented with businessmen. I would be grateful if you would send the Social Page Editor a list of businessmen . . . Perhaps they should include the Chairmen and Managing Directors of the 100 largest of *The Times* 500.[1]

The editor of the social page, appointed in 1967, was Margaret Alexander, who did the job throughout the Thomson period, having been with *The Times* since 1950. She was responsible for the whole of the page except the obituaries, which had their own editor (and will be discussed later). Room was found on the page for miscellaneous items which did not conflict with its tone, such as pieces on religion, science or archaeology. But essentially the page served as a notice-board for 'top people'. Many of the items were, in effect, advertisements paid for by the individuals concerned. These included most announcements of forthcoming marriages, wedding and christening reports, funerals and memorial services, private and commercial entertaining, and the details of schools (independent of course) reassembling for a new term. Some such items were of sufficient news value to be put in free of charge: for instance, the marriages and funerals of major public figures, the wills of known people, and announcements for the half-dozen or so leading public schools. But most were paid insertions.

Traditionally the social page carried early each year a list of the season's private dances. But at the beginning of the Thomson regime there was a dreadful rumour that this practice might be discontinued.

1 W.R.-M. to Vice, undated. Rees-Mogg also maintained the rule that the birthdays of members of *Times* editorial staff should not be published, though directors of TNL could appear in the list. (W.R.-M. to Margaret Alexander, December 12 1967.) He showed good sense as well as compassion in reinstating in the list the name of a former Conservative MP and junior minister who had been dropped when his career was ruined by a homosexual scandal. (Ian Harvey to W.R.-M., August 25 1973; W.R.-M. to Harvey, August 29 1973.)

The resident governor of the Tower of London was moved to write to Thomson himself:

> Dear Lord Thompson [*sic*],
>
> I have been asked by my wife to write to you as she keeps meeting anxious mothers who wonder when the usual list of this season's dances is to appear in *The Times*. We understand from your Social Editor that the decision lies with you as to when the list is to be published – if indeed it is going to be published at all.
>
> Alarm is spreading amongst the 'deb' mothers, my wife included, who it seems are finding difficulty in making their plans without 'Grannie Times's' aid!!!
>
> I hope all goes well with you & that we shall have the pleasure of entertaining you in the Tower again before long.
>
> Yours sincerely
> Tom Butler.[1]

His letter was reinforced by one, also to Thomson, from Lady Balfour of Inchrye. Both were acknowledged in the proprietor's absence abroad by his personal assistant, I. Charles, who meanwhile evidently passed one of the letters to Rees-Mogg; because the following day the editor wrote to Miss Alexander: 'I have had a letter which suggests that there is some doubt that we will continue the list of forthcoming dances. I think they should be continued and perhaps we could discuss it'.[2] As a result it was arranged that lists should appear on the first Mondays in April and June, though a decision was soon taken to revert to an earlier month (March) to allow the hospitable matrons more time to make their plans. Yet the list of dances was a shadow of its former self, partly because the season was much less concentrated in London than it used to be before large private houses in the capital became a rarity, and partly because many of those giving dances in the country did not wish to advertise the fact for fear of attracting gate-crashers and/or burglars.

One item appearing on the page during the Thomson years epitom-

---

1 Colonel Sir Thomas Butler, Bart. to R.H.T., February 17 1967. (In writing as though it was only his wife who was bothered about such a trifling matter Sir Thomas was showing a male characteristic as old as Adam.)

2 Lady Balfour of Inchrye to R.H.T., undated. I. Charles to Butler and Lady Balfour, both February 22 1967. W.R.-M. to Margaret Alexander, February 23 1967. (On the last letter there is a note in pencil that the lists have been arranged for the first Mondays in April and June, and that Charles has been informed March 14.)

ised both the social changes of the period and the paper's relatively unchanging style. Under the heading 'Beatle Marriage' it read:

> Mr. George Harrison, the former member of The Beatles, was married in secret at Henley-on-Thames register office last weekend, to Olivia Arias, it was disclosed yesterday. They have a son aged five weeks.[1]

Readers of a staid disposition could at least feel confident that no such announcement was likely, as yet, to appear in the Court Circular.

On March 22 1972 the national executive committee of the Labour Party voted narrowly (13–11) in favour of a proposal by Tony Benn that the question of British membership of the European Communities should be put to a referendum. After the vote Benn went to the Connaught Hotel to have lunch with Rees-Mogg, whom he tried to convince that those who wanted a referendum were not necessarily opposed to British membership in principle. Rees-Mogg seems to have been chiefly concerned to press Roy Jenkins's claims to be leader of the Labour Party, telling Benn that Heath 'was very much afraid of Jenkins'. There was no meeting of minds between the two former presidents of the Oxford Union, whose public differences would, indeed, soon become more acute than ever. But Benn found the editor 'very friendly'.[2]

A week later Benn's referendum proposal was endorsed by the shadow cabinet, though again by a narrow majority (8–6). As a result Jenkins resigned as deputy leader of the party, while two senior colleagues, George Thomson and Harold Lever, also withdrew from the shadow cabinet, and three junior opposition spokesmen, Richard (Dick) Taverne, Dr. David Owen and Lord Chalfont, resigned their posts. It was clear from Jenkins's letter of resignation that his decision reflected his unhappiness about the trend of Labour policy in many fields, and his disapproval of Wilson's style of leadership. Yet the precipitating cause of the step he took was the referendum vote, and whether or not this was the best issue to choose will always be open to argument. Benn's proposal could be plausibly defended as a means of uniting the party without surrendering to pressure from the trade unions and constituency activists for a commitment to

1 September 9 1978.
2 Benn, op. cit., entry for March 22 1972, p.417.

withdraw from the Common Market. It was also a means of exploiting divisions on the Conservative side, where anti-Market sentiment was still strong and where many felt that Heath's pledge to take Britain into the EEC only with the country's 'full-hearted' consent had not been honoured. Moreover it was awkward for Heath, but convenient for Labour, that Pompidou had recently announced that he would be holding a referendum on British entry *in France*, and that the government itself had introduced a referendum, or 'border poll', for Northern Ireland. Jenkins regarded the referendum as a demagogic device, but his stand against it could too easily be represented as undemocratic.[1]

Rees-Mogg's leader on Jenkins's resignation described it as 'a political tragedy', and saw it as a portent of worse things to come as Labour's lurch to the left continued. 'The Conservative party does not have a monopoly of political wisdom, though it does have the great advantage that its extremists are less numerous and less dangerous than those of the Labour party'.[2] Early in September he was arguing that it might soon become impossible for anyone who believed in the European Community to play an active part in Labour politics. The Labour Party would then 'lose a small proportion of its Parliamentary Party but a high proportion of its most gifted leaders'. Shorn of these, 'and of many moderate supporters, [it] would be likely to be out of power for an indefinite time to come'.[3]

At the end of the month, and on the eve of the Labour party conference at Blackpool, *The Times* published a poll specially commissioned from Opinion Research & Communication (ORC) and based on questioning 2,206 citizens over the age of sixteen during the week ended September 25. The poll showed 53 per cent feeling, either strongly or fairly strongly, that the existing party system did not work properly. With the same varying degrees of intensity 40 per cent seemed to favour 'a right-of-centre party of Conservative moderates allied with the present Liberal party', while 35 per cent seemed willing to support 'a centre party which would be left of centre'. Most of those

---

1 Early in the century the idea of a referendum had been used as a tactical ploy by the Conservative Party. During the constitutional conflict of 1910–11, with which Jenkins was particularly familiar as an historian, the Tories had proposed that disputes between Lords and Commons on matters 'of great gravity which had not been adequately submitted to the judgment of the people' should be resolved by referendum. But the Liberals challenged them to apply this to tariff reform, and Balfour, the Tory leader, fell into the trap of agreeing. In the event, the referendum proposal came to nothing at that time.

2 'A political tragedy', April 11 1972.

3 'Labour Party and Europe', September 8 1972.

questioned, including a majority even of Labour supporters, appeared to feel that the trade unions had too much influence in the Labour party. Details of the poll were set out on the op. ed. page, and on the front page it was summarised under the truthful (so far as it went), though also slightly tendentious, headline 'Poll shows support for a Labour-Liberal centre party'.[1] Readers had to study the text of the report to discover that support for a Conservative-Liberal centre party was rather stronger.

In his accompanying leader Rees-Mogg did not ignore this aspect of the poll. The figures, he said, had a warning for the Conservative Party as well as for Labour.

> Twelve million potential Jenkinsites is a concept hardly likely to appeal to Mr. Scanlon [the left-wing leader of the AUEW] or indeed to Mr. Benn. Yet the other figures in the poll would suggest that this is not even the limit of a centre party's theoretical support. Oddly enough, if the Conservative Party split, a centre party including a group who could be called Lord Butler's grandchildren or the young Rabbites would get 40 per cent. of the vote; that is surely a very clear indication to the Conservative Party of the danger of moving in a Monday Club direction.

Most of his argument, however, dealt with the chances of a Labour split, which was naturally the outcome he would have preferred. (It was also the more likely, because parties are more fissiparous when in opposition than when in power.) He still thought it would not happen, but regarded it as 'not inconceivable' if the moderates of the left felt they had been 'forced to unite'.[2]

The *Times* poll was news, and it made further news. Indeed it led to a drama in which Benn and Rees-Mogg appeared as direct antagonists. On the last day of the Labour conference, over which Benn was presiding as that year's chairman of the party, Taverne held a press conference in London at which he announced that he would be resigning his seat at Lincoln and offering himself for re-election as a Democratic Labour candidate. Benn heard the news just before the afternoon session at which he was due to give the closing speech, and he decided without consulting anyone to attack the media, and more especially *The Times* and its editor, as the supposed cause of Taverne's

1 September 30 1972.
2 'Twelve million Jenkinsites', same date. The Monday Club was a right-wing pressure group within the Conservative Party.

defection. Next day's paper carried a front-page report of the speech from John Winder at Blackpool:

> In what many delegates must have interpreted as an encouragement to take industrial action to influence or restrict press and television reporting, Mr. Anthony Wedgwood Benn . . . told the party conference here today: 'The problems of Fleet Street may be difficult to handle when we are coping with their newspapers. I sometimes wish that trade unionists who work in the mass media – those who are writers, broadcasters, secretaries, printers and lift operators at Thomson House – would remember that they, too, are members of the working-class movement and have a responsibility to see (loud applause) that what is said about us is true. We have in our history taken on kings, landowners, factory owners. Now, in this impending by-election, make no mistake, we are taking on the mass media'.

Labour would be fighting 'a political party invented by the press'. The inventor was the editor of *The Times*, who had sent out his market research people to ask the electorate what kind of party they would like, 'as if he were designing some soap, detergent or beer'.[1]

According to Benn, he had been told three days before by Macbeath that the *Times* NUJ chapel had protested to the editor at the way he (Benn) had recently been treated in the paper.[2] Did this plant a seed in his mind? As he spoke, it was clear to him that his colleagues on the platform were 'absolutely livid'. Wilson 'had been smoking his pipe furiously'. The speech provoked a rumpus that lasted for days and cannot have done Labour much good. Even Benn's wife and close advisers felt that he had made a mistake.[3]

A few months later Taverne won an overwhelming victory in his by-election, and soon afterwards candidates of his description swept the poll in the local elections at Lincoln. But he was defeated in the second general election of 1974, and the great Labour schism which was largely to determine the course of politics in the 1980s was delayed for a number of years, mainly because Labour was back in office between 1974 and 1979. Rees-Mogg's judgement that the schism would

---

1 October 7 1972. On the same day there was a leader not surprisingly supporting Taverne. *The Times* refused to give Benn the style 'Tony Benn', though it had no compunction about calling Grimond 'Jo Grimond'.

2 Benn, op. cit., entry for October 3 1972.

3 Benn, op. cit., entry for October 6 1972. (Both this and the above entry were dictated at the end of October; not, as was usual with Benn, at the end of each day.)

Father and son: Roy and Kenneth Thomson, 1974

Editorial conference, summer 1967. Left to right: J. Caminada, James Bishop, Colin Webb (foreground), E. C. Hodgkin, John Hennessy, Susanne Puddefoot, C. Winchcombe, P. Davis, William Rees-Mogg, Ion Trewin, Michael Cudlipp, J. Petty, D. Holmes, Henry Stanhope (foreground), K. Smith, Peter Evans.

The board of Times Newspapers Limited, January 1967. Left to right: Kenneth Keith, James Coltart, Kenneth Thomson, Sir Eric Roll, George Pope, Lord Robens, G. C. Rowett, Sir Donald Anderson, W. Macleod (acting secretary), Sir William Haley, Denis Hamilton, Lord Shawcross, Gordon Brunton.

A trim, military figure: Denis Hamilton in 1973.

Media event in an Essex garden, 31 July 1967. Left to right: Mick Jagger, Rees-Mogg, Fr. Thomas Corbishley, Lord Stow Hill. (Dr. John Robinson is out of the picture).

Farewell to Susanne Puddefoot, 1969: between her and Rees-Mogg, Moira Keenan.

Meeting of night staff. Left to right, Michael Hardy, Michael Hamlyn, Ernest Russell, Rees-Mogg (coat over arm), John Bryan.

Innis Macbeath

Geoffrey Woolley

Michael Cudlipp on Ludgate Hill.

Mark Boxer

Farewell to Iverach McDonald, May 1973. Left to right: McDonald, Rees-Mogg, Haley.

Thomson party at the Great Wall of China, October 1972. Far left, Kenneth Thomson and Hamilton. Centre: Roy Thomson (with David Bonavia behind him), Louis Heren and Frank Giles (*Sunday Times*).

Charles Douglas-Home in his garden at Knight's Mill, Cirencester, summer 1977.

The editor's rocking chair carried out of Printing House Square, June 1974.

Its destination: the still unfinished new building at Gray's Inn Road.

probably not occur in 1972 turned out to be correct, but meanwhile the idea of a centre party was highlighted by *The Times* poll and its immediate consequences.

Harold Wilson's apparent fury at Benn's outburst against the press, and specifically against the editor of *The Times*, did not mean that his own relations in those quarters had become entirely cordial since he ceased to be prime minister. There were still numerous occasions when Wilson, now leader of the opposition, felt that he had cause to complain of ill-treatment in the paper. At the end of 1970 there was another row over David Wood, when Wilson took something that Wood had written as associating him with the *Morning Star* and militant shop stewards. There were hints of legal action, but Rees-Mogg cleared the air with a letter of apology which ended on a warmly personal note:

> I hear from our children that you have now moved into Lord North Street. I hope that in the New Year we shall have a chance to entertain you as neighbours, and that you are very comfortable in your new home.

Wilson replied that Wood had come to talk with Joe Haines and himself, and they had 'parted amicably'. He also reciprocated the neighbourly spirit:

> Yes, we have moved into Lord North Street, and we are very happy there. We shall be delighted to accept your invitation in the New Year; but for an accidental miscalculation we might have had to travel even further – from Cowley Street. Had we done so, at least we would have had less difficulty with the parking of our sons' cars.[1]

Yet there was more trouble the following year, when Haines complained to Douglas-Home that *The Times* had 'gone beyond straight reporting or fair comment to mount what many people, inside and outside the Labour Party, regard[ed] as a personal vendetta against Mr. Wilson'. In retaliation it would be 'impossible for Mr. Wilson to fulfil the promise . . . to review LBJ's [President Lyndon Johnson's]

1 W.R.-M. to Wilson, December 16 1970; Wilson to W.R.-M. December 18 1970. Lord North Street runs into Smith Square, where the Rees-Moggs lived. Cowley Street is slightly further away, and closer to the House of Commons.

memoirs', since to do so 'would appear to the general public to condone, forgive, or even justify the views that *The Times* ha[d] seen fit to print'. Douglas-Home replied that there was no vendetta, invoking the dubious argument that that was 'not the way any newspaper collectively behave[d]'. He regretted Wilson's decision, but insisted that the columns of the paper would always be open to him.[1]

Soon after the Labour conference in 1972, at which *The Times* and its editor became an issue, and when Wilson showed displeasure at Benn's attack, the former prime minister and Rees-Mogg appeared together on the Granada television programme *World in Action*. The interviewer, David Boulton, first asked if it was true that Rees-Mogg had 'set out to split the Labour Party and to get rid of Harold Wilson'. Rees-Mogg replied at some length, but definitely in the negative. Wilson, at even greater length, was more equivocal:

> I don't think that Mr. Rees-Mogg has got a vendetta against me. In fact he's told me he hasn't. He's said some pretty extraordinary things . . . and he ran quite a campaign to get rid of me when we were in government. I don't think really that this is a vendetta against the leader of the party. I think he wants to destroy the Labour Party and he knows as long as I'm the Labour leader there'll be a Labour Party. He would like to see something different.

There was then an argument about whether or not the majority of the press was anti-Labour, which Rees-Mogg could be said to have won on points. He also defended himself against the charge, put to him by the interviewer, of having plotted with 'some Labour leaders' to secure Wilson's replacement. Any editor, he said, who plotted with the colleagues of a man on either side to achieve a change of leadership 'would have to be out of his mind'. He did not deny having clearly and openly expressed the view that Wilson ought not to be prime minister again since he had changed his position on Europe for fear that the European issue would split his party. Wilson agreed that Rees-Mogg would never plot against him, but continued to complain of *The Times*'s way of reporting, and commenting on, Labour's objections to the government's terms of entry.[2]

---

1 Haines to C.D.-H., October 28 1971; C.D.-H. to Haines, November 1 1971.
2 *World in Action*, Granada TV, October 16 1972.

Two days after their television debate Wilson wrote Rees-Mogg a letter in which he described the paper's most recent parliamentary report as 'back to the Gamma minus and the Omega minus', since it showed 'the usual pro-Market obsession with Roy Jenkins'. Rees-Mogg in this instance offered no apology. Though he had not himself heard Jenkins the previous day, he saw no reason to doubt the judgement of the paper's sketch-writer, Noyes. Jenkins, who was 'at his best as a parliamentary speaker', in his experience 'easily commanded the House'.[1]

Wilson's righteous indignation against *The Times*, and his principled gesture in refusing to review a book, has to be judged in relation to the large-scale publishing contracts with Times Newspapers Limited into which he entered a month after leaving office. In November 1970 Heath told Cecil King that, on the plane returning from de Gaulle's memorial service in Paris, Wilson had been correcting proofs of a book for which 'he was getting £250,000 from *The Times*'. Heath was surprised that the paper should have paid so much for Wilson's memoirs, 'as the Macmillan memoirs that ha[d] been appearing in *The Times* just recently ha[d] been an expensive failure'.[2] The figure quoted was essentially correct, and it was also true that the Macmillan memoirs had been very expensive without noticeably affecting sales. The deal with Wilson, which was on the same lines as that with Macmillan, included an agreement for all publishing rights in an autobiography for which he would be paid £26,000 in four annual instalments of £6,500. But a far more important agreement was for the purchase from trustees appointed by Wilson of 'certain private papers, letters and photographs', with 'private notes and documents prepared both during the period prior to his becoming Prime Minister and also during his period in office'. For these assets he was to be paid £220,000 in four annual instalments of £55,000. There was something in it for Haines, too; under a separate agreement he was to be paid £4,000 for assisting Wilson with the book 'to the utmost of his ability and powers'.

In addition, there was an agreement with Wilson for writing twenty-five articles within a period of not more than five years, and for an exclusive relationship with Times Newspapers (absolute for one year, qualified for the remaining four years). He was to be paid at the

1 Wilson to W.R.-M., October 18 1972; W.R.-M. to Wilson, October 20 1972. Rees-Mogg ended by saying that he had 'enjoyed the television dialogue and hoped he would see Wilson again before long'.
2 *Cecil King Diary 1970–1974*, entry for November 14 1970 (p.60).

rate of £250 per article, and was also to have the services of a research assistant at £2,000 a year and a secretary at £1,000 a year.[1] If, as seems likely, the review of Lyndon Johnson's memoirs would have been a contribution within the terms of this agreement, then Wilson in refusing to do it was in the curious moral position of rejecting £250 for honour's sake while accepting a thousand times that amount without, apparently, feeling that his honour was compromised.

The deal with Wilson was initiated by Hamilton, though Rees-Mogg was a party to it. It did not work out well. The memoirs, serialised in the *Sunday Times*, made little impact, and the arrangement for articles in *The Times* was virtually a dead letter.[2] A far better arrangement was proposed by Rees-Mogg to his favourite Labour politician soon after the election, and formalised early the following year. Roy Jenkins was to write ten 'contemporary biographies' of 6,000 words each, and six 'current political pieces' of 1,500 words each, to appear at stated intervals over a three-year period. For these contributions he was to be paid, in instalments, a total of £16,250. The first of his biographical essays, on Robert Kennedy, was run in *The Times* on February 8, 9 and 10 1971. In the event there were eight, rather than nine, more: on Bevin, Keynes, Cripps, Léon Blum, Senator Joseph McCarthy, Halifax, Adlai Stevenson, and Jenkins's friend and mentor, Gaitskell. After first appearing in *The Times*, the essays were published in book form, in 1974, under the title *Nine Men of Power*.[3] The publisher was Hamish Hamilton, who paid Times Newspapers an advance

---

1 Four agreements all dated July 24 1970. Wilson's trustees, with whom the big contract was negotiated, were Lord Goodman and Lord Lloyd of Hampstead. In Macmillan's case the trustees of documents were Lord Poole, Sir Philip de Zulueta and Anthony Forbes Moir, to whom Times Newspapers paid £326,000. For the memoirs themselves (to be no fewer than three volumes) Macmillan was paid £34,000. Some of the money was recouped in a book-publishing contract under which Macmillans' paid Times Newspapers £40,000, and an agreement with Harper & Row for the American rights (up to $200,000). The book rights in Wilson's account of his 1964–70 government were bought jointly by Weidenfeld & Nicolson and Michael Joseph for £30,000 (agreement dated June 7 1971). Later, when there were negotiations (which came to nothing) for an account of Wilson's 1974–6 ministry, the figure involved was to be only £20,000 for the newspaper rights, and Hamilton minuted: 'I do *not* want the documents. I assume that as the gross amount is small compared to the first book he is *not* doing a tax arrangement or avoidance deal as he did with the first'. (MS note to Enid Knowles, dated March 29 1978.)

2 On March 30 1971 Enid Knowles wrote to A. Leighton Davis of the firm of Goodman, Derrick & Co., that 'as very little written by Mr. Wilson ha[d] emerged it would seem that this whole matter [was] one for discussion between him and Mr. Hamilton'. But Wilson continued to be paid for secretarial and research assistance.

3 At first the title was to have been *Great Contemporaries*, but no doubt it was thought best not to plagiarise Churchill.

of £3,000. Though not all of quite equal merit, the essays were eminently stylish and readable. The author's current affairs pieces were good copy for the paper, too; the first, on 'The European choice in the sweep of history', appearing on May 10 1971.

Another Labour front-bencher recruited as a contributor was Richard Crossman. In May 1972 Rees-Mogg asked him to write weekly pieces to appear on Wednesdays on the op. ed. page. For these he was offered £75 per article, but held out successfully for £100. The terms agreed were, therefore, that he would receive £4,600 for forty-six articles per year; if he wrote more or fewer, £100 for each would be added or subtracted. His pieces were called 'Personal View' and adorned with a mini-caricature by Marc, featuring the author's eyebrows and spectacles. The first, appearing on June 14, was on the subject of the controversial book, *Portnoy's Complaint*.

When, in August 1972, the extremely unbalanced president of Uganda, Idi Amin, decided to expel all Asians in his country lacking Ugandan citizenship, the British government promptly acted on its duty to admit those who were British citizens. The first plane-load arrived in mid-September and by the end of the year 25,000 had been settled temporarily in camps until work and proper accommodation could be found for them. This influx was extremely unpopular with the still massive section of the British public indiscriminately opposed to coloured immigration. Though the Ugandan Asians were to prove model immigrants – hard-working and, in many cases, people of substance who brought wealth as well as talent to the country – in the eyes of many members of the 'host community' (a sociological term full of unconscious irony) they were automatically undesirable on account of their race and colour. So intense was the feeling that the foreign secretary, Sir Alec Douglas-Home, who with the prime minister was most clearly responsible for the decision to give the Ugandan Asians the asylum in Britain to which they were entitled, and who in the ordinary way was quite a favourite with his compatriots, received at the time thousands of abusive letters.

The Times, however, gave wholehearted backing to what was indeed one of the most praiseworthy acts of the Heath government. In a leader at the beginning of September Rees-Mogg wrote:

> In this country the Government, despite great political difficulties, has responded with humanity and with a sense of responsibility to people to whom we gave passports and rights of entry. There

> are some moments when governments deserve to have firm and unequivocal support. This is such a moment.
>
> The problem of immigration to Britain is not going to be made radically worse by the Ugandan Asians whom we receive, though the emotional response has been made worse . . . [They] went to Uganda as indentured labour and in fifty years have made themselves a prosperous mercantile and industrious class. No doubt they, like many other Asians, will by hard work, family loyalty and thrift achieve the same results here.
>
> This does not mean that we do not have a coloured problem, or that we ought not to minimise it both by restriction on entry and by good neighbour policies. The long-term problem of the black community which, like the Irish, is developing as an under-privileged, badly housed proletarian group, is almost certainly more serious than the problem of the Asians.[1]

The same day a reader's eye travelling a few inches to the correspondence column could read a remarkable letter from six people in Maharashtra. It conveyed a tribute which Heath and Douglas-Home, at any rate, deserved:

> Some of us have been in your country and as young Indians we have come to love and respect Britain . . . We have been inspired by the British Government's readiness to accept the Ugandan Asians with British passports at a time when the country faces unemployment, crisis in industry and in Northern Ireland.[2]

But a few days later Crossman wrote with cynical worldly-wisdom, justifying Wilson's silence on the issue:

> The truth is that by accepting the Asians' right of entry the Prime Minister has already struck what may be a mortal blow against his chances of winning the next general election. Part of the undertow which carried him to power in 1970 was the working class dislike of coloured immigrants . . . Now that Mr. Heath has shown himself as soft on colour as Mr. Wilson, working class Toryism may well go into a decline from which (so long as Mr. Powell stands

1 'The suffering of exiles', September 1 1972. The distinction here drawn between Asian immigrants and those of Negro stock tended to be blurred by thoughtless use of the term 'blacks' by people on both sides of the argument.
2 From Ruby Kaur Chatwal and others, September 1 1972.

> aside) Labour will be the chief beneficiary – which is another reason for Mr. Wilson's silence.[1]

The mention of Enoch Powell was very much to the point, because by the latter part of 1972 he had become the most deadly leader of opposition to the government. Having, as he believed, contributed to the Tories' victory by his influence with voters, particularly in the West Midlands, he was all the more resentful of his exclusion from office. This personal grudge sharpened his disapproval of what the government was doing over the whole range of policy, domestic and foreign. He was appalled by what he regarded as betrayal of principle in the nationalisation of Rolls-Royce, surrender to the Clyde workers and the miners, and acceptance of the notion of a formal prices and incomes policy to combat inflation.[2] In his view the government itself was the prime cause of inflation through its failure to control the money supply. He was indignant, too, at the imposition of direct rule in Northern Ireland, without thorough integration of the province into the United Kingdom on a basis of equality. Above all he execrated British accession to the European Community, which he saw as abandonment of the sovereignty of Parliament and the most vital elements of British nationhood.

Yet it was not on any of these issues that he chose to challenge the government at the Conservative party conference in the second week of October, but rather on the issue which had transformed him from a scholarly eccentric, appreciated up to a point by his political peers though otherwise little known, into a populist hero and a household name. In an op. ed. piece a week before the conference Humphry Berkeley posed the question: had the Ugandan Asian issue revitalised Powellism? He then discussed the man himself, beginning with the contention that Powellism, seen as a body of doctrine consistently preached and practised by Powell, really did not exist:

> Enoch Powell is commonly regarded as a man of unswerving views, complete unwillingness to compromise and of Cromwellian integrity. In fact he has changed his mind as much as any contemporary politician, for which he should not be unduly criticized. Mental pliability is the only evidence of intellectual life.

---

1 'Understanding the profusion of shrinking violets', September 6 1972.

2 At the end of September Heath held tripartite talks at Chequers at which he put to the TUC and CBI proposals for limiting wages and prices. This initiative was welcomed by *The Times*, which argued that the government had resisted incomes policy for too long. Now it must try to achieve one that would be implemented voluntarily, to be 'followed quickly by a compulsory policy if the voluntary policy fails to be achieved'. (Leader, 'Inflation must be beaten', September 26 1972).

The implied moral was that he had no right to attack anyone else for performing U-turns.

Berkeley tried to dispose of Powell by treating him not, in the way most of his opponents did, as a man of dark passions and evil intent, but as a pathetically outdated figure who hardly understood the harm he was doing:

> I have known Mr. Powell for 25 years, and find in him much to admire. Yet . . . he is one of Yesterday's Men. The India which he loved has gone, as has the Germany upon which he continued to lavish his lonely affection until 1934. The EEC battle is all but over. The lame duck policy of which he was an enthusiastic supporter has been abandoned. All that remains is immigration and race, and I cannot predict whether he will do still further lasting damage in this sensitive field.[1]

Powell's challenge on the 'precipitate' admission of the Ugandan Asians was defeated by more than two to one at the conference, and *The Times* welcomed the vote, which however was probably not a true indication of the state of feeling in the party. The day it was reported an anonymous 'leading Conservative' wrote scathingly in the paper about the government's climb-down over miners' pay, and said that there was growing uneasiness about the concentration of power in the prime minister's hands. His standing in the polls was 'alarmingly low', and he 'would now have to go into a general election without a single lieutenant who would win him votes, while the only Conservative who ha[d] a worthwhile following would be in biting antagonism'.[2] So much for the idea that Powell was a man whose hour had passed. As a focus for multiple discontents he was still uniquely formidable.

In the autumn of 1972 Rees-Mogg made one of his best and most original appointments when he chose Clifford Longley for the new post of religious correspondent, responsible for covering all religious affairs – not only Christian – and for doing so from a newsy point of

1 'Mr. Powell: still Yesterday's Man', September 5 1972. Berkeley had been Conservative MP for Lancaster 1959–66. In 1970 he left the party to join Labour. Later he joined the SDP, then Labour again. He wrote a number of books, including *The Odyssey of Enoch: a political memoir* (1977). His career was no less wayward than Powell's.

2 Leader, 'Victory for moderation', and op. ed. article, 'Problems of one chief and too many Indians', October 13 1972.

view, without undue reverence. This was the first such appointment on any British newspaper, and it anticipated by five years the BBC's selection of Gerald Priestland for a similar role, in which he proved comparably successful.

Longley had joined *The Times* in 1967, as a general reporter, after learning the trade on local papers in Essex and Portsmouth. He was a Roman Catholic, though not from the cradle. His home background was atheistic, but he was converted to Catholicism at the age of twenty-one while reading engineering at Southampton university. The chaplain who converted him was very much in the Newman tradition, to which Longley attributed his freedom from the usual convert's tendency to be more Catholic than the Pope. His Catholicism survived a broken marriage and subsequent remarriage, but was, understandably, never of a kind to satisfy the strictly orthodox.

When he joined the paper there was a churches correspondent whose attention was confined to the Church of England and the Nonconformist churches. Longley, however, working on the newsdesk, felt that religion should be treated as an ordinary subject for news, and in that spirit began collecting stories from all the churches, including his own. In 1969 he was brought to Rees-Mogg's notice by a passage of arms with Cardinal John Heenan, archbishop of Westminster. This was not initiated by himself, though it reflected the annoyance already felt by members of the Roman Catholic hierarchy at his style of religious reporting. Towards the end of the previous year a letter appeared in the paper, signed by fifty-five Roman Catholic priests, protesting against the recent papal encyclical *Humanae Vitae* in which all artificial birth control was condemned. One of the signatories, Father Benedict Sketchley, was headmaster of a church school at Stevenage, and soon afterwards he was forced to resign by his ecclesiastical superiors. Early in the New Year Heenan addressed a parents' meeting at the school to explain why Sketchley had resigned. After claiming that the *Times* letter was not the precipitating cause, he went on to complain of the way the incident had been reported in the paper (not, as it happened, by Longley):

> In passing I would warn you to be very careful in reading *The Times* when things of Catholic interest are reported. There is a member of the staff of *The Times* who is a Catholic – I am not referring to Mr. Rees-Mogg . . . – who seeks every opportunity to produce slanted news which is not trustworthy. And this is a very good example.

After the meeting the Cardinal explained that the alleged culprit was 'a member of the Home News staff'.[1]

Before being sent to press the story was referred to McDonald, who was editing on the night in question. He took legal advice and then spoke to Longley, telling him that since he was clearly the target of the attack, though not explicitly named, the story was judged to be libellous. Longley nevertheless insisted that it be published, and his *nihil obstat* was richly rewarded. Heenan himself was soon under attack for what he had said, in, of all places, the *Catholic Herald*, and prominent Catholics, including Rees-Mogg and Norman St. John Stevas, made representations to him on Longley's behalf. As a result the cardinal asked Longley to tea and promised that in future he would give forewarning of any complaint he might have to make.[2] It was also arranged that he should write an article for the paper effectively retracting his remark, and that his fee of £100 should be paid to a charity of Longley's choice. The article duly appeared, containing the words:

> In the course of [my] speech I mistakenly attributed a biased report to one reporter. In fact this journalist was not responsible for the story. I have since privately expressed regret if I was unjust to *The Times* and to the journalist. It is well to confess publicly that it is sometimes the church and not the press which is at fault.[3]

The fee was paid, at Longley's request, to the Catholic Housing Aid Society.[4]

This was not, in fact, the end of his troubles with Heenan, and he never ceased to be regarded with disfavour by conservative members of his own church.[5] But he was equally suspect to some in other churches. At the time of his appointment as religious correspondent

---

1 'Cardinal Heenan tells why priest left school', report by Ronald Faux, January 27 1969.

2 Longley talking to author.

3 Turnover article, 'Problems of publicity for the church', February 19 1969.

4 Office memo dated February 21 1969.

5 When there was a controversy, reported by Longley, about Heenan's attitude to proposed lectures by the liberal Catholic scholar, Hans Kung, the cardinal sent Longley the advance text of an address he was to give on the subject at a private meeting. But in the actual speech he attacked Longley extemporaneously by name, not expecting, presumably, that his remarks would be leaked. (Longley to author.) In 1976 Rees-Mogg received a complaint from Father Michael Richards of Heythrop College, protesting strongly against Longley's handling of Catholic affairs, to which Rees-Mogg replied: 'His attitudes are indeed somewhat more radical than my own, but there has to be a range of opinion in *The Times* as indeed there is in the church'. (January 14 1974.)

the Revd Michael Saward, then the Church of England's radio and television officer, apparently sensing a popish plot, arranged for the matter to be considered at a meeting presided over by the archbishop of Canterbury, Michael Ramsey, who had the good sense to deprecate hasty judgements.[1] Yet in the next (84th) annual issue of *Crockford's Clerical Directory* the anonymous editor stated that the reporting of church affairs had 'suffered a sad decline'. Longley's supposed hostility to Anglicanism, and desire to undermine the Church of England, was a theme that persisted over the years in complaints to the editor, though always rebutted.[2] Rees-Mogg took pride in the work of his religious correspondent, and also gave him a column on the court (social) page after discontinuing the traditional practice of printing selected sermons there. There were, however, ups-and-downs in their personal relations, partly resulting from Longley's Labour sympathies and his very active role as a trade unionist on the paper.

---

1 Longley to author.

2 On June 11 1980, for instance, the Duchess of Buccleuch wrote to Rees-Mogg: 'As one who has been a dedicated supporter of the ecumenical movement for many years, may I say with what regret and disappointment I now read the reports by your Religious Affairs Correspondent, Mr. Clifford Longley? That one in his position should use his authority to disparage so constantly the Anglican Church, and should do so unchecked, is distressing . . .'. Rees-Mogg replied regretting that the duchess thought Longley had 'a bias against the Church of England', but assuring her that this was 'not the case'. (June 23 1980).

XIV

Hussey's damned inheritance • Expulsion from Moscow; excursion to Peking • New typeface • Significant departures • The Middle East to Yom Kippur • Office lunches • Home news team

WHILE THE HEATH government was trying to transform the nation's economy by means of a 'quiet revolution' (which turned out to be anything but quiet, and not much of a revolution), the new chief executive of Times Newspapers, M. J. Hussey, had a similar task within his own far more restricted sphere. He was expected above all to swing *The Times* from being a heavy loss-maker into earning a profit within a year or two at the most, since Roy Thomson had suddenly decided, despite all that he had said and implied at the time of the take-over, that he would no longer continue to subsidise the paper's development. Hussey's message to his colleagues as he assumed control was practical and down-to-earth. At the first meeting of his executive management committee, which he brought into being as a substitute for Hamilton's executive board, and from which Hamilton was excluded, he stressed the need to deal successfully with short-term problems, because unless evidence of success could be produced in that regard the company 'would not have a long-term problem to solve.'[1]

If managerial types can be divided broadly into 'people men' and 'figures men', Hussey was beyond question a 'people man'. He believed that the best way to get results was to have direct contact with his staff at all levels and to infuse them with a sense of common purpose. During his first year he met, 'very informally and very frankly, nearly all the chapels in Printing House Square', so giving *The Times* his prior attention.[2] Later he repeated the process with the the *Sunday Times* chapels at Thomson House in Gray's Inn Road. As for the chain of command, Hussey wanted no intermediate link

1 TEMC, February 18 1971.
2 M.J.H. interviewed by Macbeath, *Times News*, issue for January-March 1972.

between himself and his team of top managers. Whereas Hamilton had been, in effect, more of a chairman than a managing director, delegating much of his executive responsibility to the general manager, Geoffrey Rowett, Hussey made all heads of departments directly answerable to himself. Rowett's role thus became increasingly redundant until his departure in March 1972.

Yet there was no general purge. One most important member of the team, already there when Hussey came, was the finance director, Michael Brown. Brown was a Lancastrian, whose basic qualification was that of a chartered accountant but who had worked in the construction industry before being head-hunted by the Thomson Organisation. In joining it he accepted a cut in salary, but had no cause to regret his decision. In the new climate of austerity and realism his influence naturally grew, and when he left the board of Times Newspapers in mid-1972 – to be succeeded by his deputy, Ian Clubb – he soon became a key figure in the development of Thomson's North Sea oil interests. Later, his efficiency and tireless industry earned him the highest promotion, as president of the Thomson Corporation with his office in New York. But by then *The Times* was no longer a Thomson newspaper.

Hussey did bring in one colleague with whom he had worked closely at Associated Newspapers, to help him in a vital sector of *The Times*. This was Michael Mander, who became advertising director early in 1971. Mander was a public-school boy (Tonbridge) who had also attended a school in up-state New York (Hackley). After school he hitch-hiked round America, and in later life retained more friendships from Hackley than from Tonbridge. During his two years' National Service with the Green Howards he spent some time in Egypt and Cyprus. Then, to his parents' chagrin, he declined to take up a place at Oxford, since he was impatient to begin his active career. At Associated Newspapers he was at first largely concerned with circulation, though his scope broadened to include management and marketing.

When he joined *The Times* he felt he had a chance to tackle a defect shared, in his view, by the whole British newspaper industry: that circulation, marketing and advertising departments operated in virtual isolation from each other. He was determined to achieve more coordination. Another prime objective was to restore the paper's reputation with advertisers, which had suffered from the widespread belief that space was sold at cut prices or on the basis of contra arrangements. His target for the paper was A1 readers, since he was convinced that in this department an advantage could be gained over the *Financial Times*, much of whose readership consisted of clerks obliged to read the paper for the sake of their work. Mander was a lively and resourceful man, still in his thirties. He had the energy, but not the reckless euphoria, of youth. Soon after he arrived he told his colleagues that he was not optimistic about *The Times*'s short-term prospects, but that he was 'mildly optimistic' long-term.[1]

Before long there were encouraging results to show for the new regime, though in fairness it should be said that these resulted in part from decisions taken while Hamilton was still chief executive, such as the successive price rises and the staff cuts. The loss on the paper, which was over £1 million in 1971 and 1972, was cut to £187,000 in 1973. Moreover the paper would probably have been in profit that year but for nationwide industrial trouble during the final month. Much of the improvement was due to Mander's efforts. By the summer of 1971, though the performance in display advertising was still disappointing, *The Times*'s position within the total market was already significantly better. In the spring of the following year display was still a problem, but otherwise advertisements were doing well. By November 1972 there was objective evidence that, during the period January-June, the paper's 'AB profile' had risen, while the *FT*'s had not changed, and the *Guardian*'s and *Daily Telegraph*'s had fallen. At the end of the year *The Times*'s advertisement revenue was £165,000 better than budget.

In circulation, too, there were distinct signs of improvement. Until the autumn of 1971 *The Times*'s circulation was still in decline, though markedly less so than the previous year. In October 1971 a steady recovery was reported and it seemed that the figure might be firming up at about 340,000. There was, however, some countervailing bad news. At the end of the year the *Guardian* was only a thousand or two behind, and by the following summer it was ahead. Though *The Times* made gains over the same period, the *Guardian* gained more. To have been overtaken once again by a paper which had only been fully national since 1961 (when it started printing in London) was a considerable indignity.[2] Yet the number of copies sold mattered less than the unique prestige of *The Times* which, though never lost among readers, had suffered temporary damage among advertisers. In that crucial quarter it was now substantially restored.

All the good that was being done, however, could not prevent the dire consequences of a decision already taken before Hussey was appointed, and irreversible by the time he was in charge. One of the

1 TEMC, May 11 1971.

2 The *Guardian*'s circulation had passed *The Times*'s in 1962, but had fallen behind again during the early Thomson phase of expansion.

great benefits expected to flow from the Thomson take-over was the pooling of resources and functions as between the two newspapers; and in this process the most salutary effects were, it was thought, to be achieved by concentrating the production of both papers on a single site. In April 1969 Hamilton was authorised to sell Printing House Square, including the land, buildings, plant, fixtures and fittings, to the *Observer*. The price was to be £5½ million, and two months later the deal was through. At the same time negotiations were in progress, though far from complete, for the acquisition of premises adjacent to Thomson House in Gray's Inn Road. About an acre of land on the north side was to be bought, not by Times Newspapers or the Thomson Organisation but by a property company, Westmoreland Properties, which would then erect a building, to agreed specifications, that would be leased to *The Times* for fifty years. The initial rent would be £1,360,000 a year, though the figure would be subject to five-yearly reviews. Only the cost of building the basement would be borne by *The Times*, and for that it would consequently pay only a peppercorn rent. Planning difficulties delayed completion of this deal, and involved further substantial cost. But eventually it went through, and at least the danger that the paper might have nowhere to go at the time when it was obliged to leave Printing House Square, in 1974, was averted.

Nevertheless these transactions can only be regarded as disastrous. Quite apart from the false and flawed logic of the whole idea of producing both papers on the same site, which will be discussed later, the financial implications of the two deals were appalling. If Thomson had acquired the real estate of Printing House Square for a bargain price in 1966, he certainly let it go for a bargain price in 1969. The excuse was that he had promised the Monopolies Commission to do nothing to harm the *Observer*, and that if it were decided that *The Times* should vacate Printing House Square the property would be offered to the *Observer* on a sitting-tenant basis, that is for a price much lower than could be obtained by sale to a third party. Even so, £5½ million was a low figure for all the assets that were being transferred, and the *Observer* at the time could hardly believe its luck.[1]

Within a few years its luck was compounded, as was *The Times*'s discomfiture, by an explosion in property prices. By 1972 the market value of Printing House Square was at least double what the *Observer* had paid. Moreover, payment to *The Times* was to be in instalments over the five-year period of notice, which meant that the price was,

1 Lord Goodman talking to author. Goodman was chairman of the Observer Trust from 1967 to 1976.

in effect, heavily devalued. For the same reason, and in proportion, the cost of the new building in Gray's Inn Road increased, so that most of the money received from the *Observer* went into building and equipping the basement there. In any case the ineptitude of disposing of Printing House Square, at whatever price, before alternative premises for *The Times* could be counted on by the required date, is surely almost incredible. Thomson in his prime would never have committed such folly, or allowed it to be committed. The decision to leave Printing House Square and move to Gray's Inn Road was a *damnosa hereditas* for which Hussey was in no way responsible, but which was to poison and prejudice his stewardship in the years ahead.

In the spring of 1972 David Bonavia, who had been the paper's Moscow correspondent for the past three years, was summoned to the Soviet foreign ministry and asked to leave the country. The reason given to him was that he had engaged in 'systematic activities incompatible with the status of a foreign correspondent'. For a fortnight or so he had been under attack in the weekly newspaper of the Soviet Writers' Union, *Literaturnaya Gazeta*, which had asked how long he would be allowed to stay in the Soviet Union, accusing him of 'slanderous' writings 'misinforming' his readers. A retired worker from Vitebsk and other members of the proletariat were quoted as having expressed outrage at his disregard for truth and abuse of their country's hospitality.

In his last report from Moscow Bonavia described these quotations as 'distorted and even fabricated'. As to the true reasons for his expulsion, he could only speculate: 'The Soviet authorities may have objected to articles I wrote on political, economic and cultural matters, or they may have objected to the fact that I maintained good personal relations with Soviet citizens who were prepared to speak their mind about conditions in their country'.[1] A leader the same day began, most effectively, with a paragraph from one that had appeared in the paper on August 17 1937, when *The Times*'s Berlin correspondent was expelled by the Nazi regime. Only the names were changed: 'Bonavia' for 'Ebbutt', 'Moscow' for 'Berlin', and 'Russia' for 'Germany'. 'Any easy equation', the leader said, 'between the Nazi and Soviet systems and philosophies is misleading and dangerous, but their attitude towards free newspaper reporting shows uncomfortable similarities'. There could be no question of replacing Bonavia by someone more

1 Double-column front-page story, May 6 1972. The attacks in *Literaturnaya Gazeta* were reported on April 27.

likely to please the Soviet authorities. 'Once again the fundamental difference between a totalitarian and a liberal attitude towards information has been made absolutely clear'.[1]

The author of this leader was Hodgkin, whose private view of the matter it did not, however, reflect. In his diary at the time he wrote:

> Returning to the office after lunch found that R[ees] M[ogg] had gone and that David Bonavia had been served with an expulsion order from Moscow – not surprising as he made no effort to please his hosts and has had innumerable warnings. As Richard D[avy] said, if he had written an occasional piece saying how well something or other was done they might have forgiven the rest. But I had of course to write a leader saying that the Russian action was shocking, using quotes from the leader written when Ebbutt was expelled from Germany in 1937.[2]

Nevertheless he attended an office lunch the following month in honour of Bonavia and his wife, and was impressed by the 'great force and coherence' with which Bonavia spoke of the Soviet dissidents, 'the only people in Russia who speak the truth'.[3]

Bonavia did not have to wait long for another foreign posting. In October it was announced that *The Times* would be opening an office in Peking and that Bonavia would be the first resident correspondent there. The announcement coincided with the start of a visit to China by Thomson and a party in which Bonavia was included, and of which the other members were Kenneth Thomson, Hamilton, Heren, Frank Giles (foreign editor of the *Sunday Times*), Don McCullin (a famous war-photographer from the same paper) and George Rainbird (assistant managing director of Thomson Publications).[4] At Heathrow

---

1 Leader, 'Expulsion from Moscow', same date.

2 Hodgkin op. cit., entry for May 5 1972. Davy's remark is puzzling, because at precisely the same time he was at loggerheads with the Czech authorities about his unwillingness to write 'helpful' pieces about the Husak regime. (Davy to McDonald, May 9 1972.)

3 Ibid, entry for June 2 1972. The last words quoted were Bonavia's own describing the dissidents.

4 Richard Harris, *The Times*'s principal Far Eastern leader-writer and China hand, was at the last minute invited to join the party, but probably only because Hamilton heard he was offended by not being consulted about the trip while it was being planned. He was indeed rather hurt and, partly for that reason, partly because he knew he was not altogether *persona grata* in China at the time, he refused the invitation. Most of the planning of the trip was done by Heren, who had been in China during and immediately after the war, and who had also been the paper's correspondent in South-east Asia.

Thomson said that he was 'anxious to get to know China as it was one of the great nations of the world'; and he was photographed for *The Times* with Bonavia and the Chinese ambassador who saw the party off.[1]

Though he had never visited China, Thomson had scored quite a hit in the Soviet Union ten years before when he had taken a party of British businessmen to Moscow, to celebrate the first anniversary of the *Sunday Times* colour magazine, and had had a long talk with Khrushchev. Tycoons and dictators are naturally drawn to each other, whatever their ideologies, because they share the habit of command. In Peking Thomson was received by the Chinese premier, Chou En-lai, and Heren, who was also present, suffered acute initial embarrassment when Thomson delivered a long lecture on capitalism to his sophisticated host, 'as if he was addressing a Rotary lunch for small-town businessmen'. But Heren need not have worried:

> . . . Chou listened intently. I knew that the Chinese were always inscrutable, but I did not expect one of the greatest communist leaders in history to show such intense interest, especially in the suggestion that China should borrow from abroad instead of trying to pull itself up by its bootstraps. Thomson went on to explain the advantages of borrowing with considerable expertise . . . his knowledge of financial markets was a major reason for his success, but I marvelled at the two old men, so very different in every possible way, hobnobbing together. Then after offering to buy the *People's Daily*, which Chou politely declined, Thomson looked over to me with his cheeky grin, and said, 'It's all yours, Lou'.[2]

Between them Thomson and Heren spent three-and-a-half hours in conversation with Chou.

The Thomson party was allowed to visit provinces of China that for some years had been barred to Westerners, and there were 'long journeys by car and obsolescent aircraft'. Wherever he went, 'in chilly Peking or sweltering Canton', Thomson 'wore his homburg and dark, three-piece serge suit . . . with black shoes and discreet socks'. He enjoyed the respect accorded to him as proprietor of *The Times*, and was confirmed in his view that the paper was the world's greatest by

---

1 Reports and photograph in the paper, October 6 1972.

2 Heren, op. cit., pp.214–15. The meeting with Chou was front-page news in *The Times* on October 14 1972. During his talk with Khrushchev ten years previously Thomson had offered to buy *Pravda* and *Izvestia*.

a feat by Bonavia in Canton. When the party arrived there the manager of Chiang Kai-Shek's old residence, converted into a resthouse for VIPs, could speak only Cantonese, while the foreign ministry official accompanying the party was a Mandarin-speaker. As the official was beginning to lose his temper the situation was saved by Bonavia, who was fluent in both dialects.[1]

Throughout the period of the visit the paper carried more items on China than usual, all with an unmistakably favourable slant. There had, indeed, been much courting of China in advance of the visit, to which Hodgkin strongly objected despite his earlier disapproval of Bonavia's churlishness to the authorities in Moscow:

> Rather shocked at the attitude now shown by the Thomson organisation over China . . . there is much *empressement* to be nice to the Chinese . . . after R[ichard] H[arris] had written a centre-page article about the leadership in China, L[ouis] H[eren] said, 'I don't think there's anything in it that could offend them'. Good heavens! Afraid of offending Peking![2]

On October 3 1932 *The Times* underwent a typographical revolution when the ornamental gothic lettering which had been at the head of the paper for 140 years was replaced by capitals of classic design. Times New Roman type was, indeed, introduced for the whole paper and all its printed manifestations, including posters, notepaper and other stationery. Though planning the change took three years, it was put into effect over a single weekend. The moving spirit behind it was Stanley Morison.[3]

Forty years later almost to the day *The Times* had another change of typeface, referred to by some as its second October revolution. In fact, the change was less comprehensive than the first, since it applied to only three body sizes, 7, 8 and 9 point; but these comprised most of the editorial text. There were two main reasons for the change, both technical rather than aesthetic. Times New Roman had been designed for monotype machines, since abandoned in favour of linotype, to which it was less well suited. It was also apt to cause trouble

---

1 Ibid., same pages.
2 Hodgkin, op. cit., entry for August 17 1972.
3 But since he was also editor and (largely) author of the first four volumes of this History, including the one in which the change is recorded, modesty no doubt dictated the omission of any mention of his name. (*HTT*, vol.IV, pt.II, p.952.)

with the lighter newsprint to which the paper had recently been obliged to change for the sake of economy. A committee with Harold Evans, editor of the *Sunday Times*, as chairman, and Walter Tracy, an expert designer for linotype, as consultant, had been asked to propose a new typeface. The committee's choice was known as Times Europa – a name appropriate to the paper's current political stance – and it was described in the house magazine as 'a robust and well-rounded letter, wider than Times Roman, with good stroke-contrast and crispness of cut, giving it sufficient strength and colour to survive thin inking and fast running on lightweight newsprint'.[1]

Times Europa was introduced on Sunday October 8 1972, the following day's paper being the first to carry it. A lot of standing copy set in the old type, including scores of obituaries, had to be reset, and about 73,000 new matrices had to be installed. But the change was accomplished with remarkable smoothness and, it would seem, largely unnoticed by readers.

In April 1973 *The Times* lost two most important members of its editorial staff, one representing the old guard of the Astor period, the other a newcomer brought in when Thomson bought the paper. The former was Iverach McDonald, retiring after thirty-eight years' service. In presenting him with an inscribed silver tray, at a farewell ceremony in the board room, Rees-Mogg said that he had 'acted as a pilot' during the merger. Thanks to him a relationship of trust was established between old and new. 'When Northcliffe took over Printing House Square the "Black Friars" rejected him. In 1967 that disaster was avoided'. Rees-Mogg may have been slightly exaggerating the degree of trust, but certainly McDonald had done his best to foster it, despite his painful disappointment at the outset when denied the editorship.

In his reply he recalled his early years on the paper:

> Many people have described the atmosphere of the old *Times* – something I always used to think was between a regiment and a monastery. There were the coal fires regularly stoked up of an evening – cloistral calm – and the strict rules of style. We were not allowed to write 'scientist': that was a new-fangled Americanism, we had to say 'men of science'. And we could not write that, say, 'Atkinson, the murderer would be executed'. We had to say

1 Allen Hutt writing in *Times News*, November–December 1972.

> that 'the sentence of death would be executed on Atkinson'.
>
> I remember too towards the end of the Second World War the very scholarly assistant editor, Brodribb, a minor but quite considerable poet, objecting to the heading 'Germans Hurled Back Three Miles'. 'They were not hurled back', he cried, 'what happened was that our men opened fire, some Germans dropped down dead without further ado, the others did not like what they saw and ran away'. So the headline had to be altered . . .
>
> But I would not like you to think it was all discipline and dullness. In the foreign subs' room there was a pleasant collegiate atmosphere . . . in those months – before my wife and I were sent off to Berlin – I was going on with my Russian lessons in the morning and sometimes the afternoon . . . and in the early evenings I was often called in to do a leader; then back to subbing for the rest of the night. And I used to wonder uneasily whether I was really earning my £400 a year.[1]

The other major figure to leave in April was not only a 1967 interloper but the very embodiment of all that the old guard disliked and resented in the new, though some of the prejudice against him had lately been softening. Michael Cudlipp was still only thirty-eight; his entire life-span coincided exactly with the number of years McDonald had spent on *The Times*. He left ostensibly to become the first chief editor of London Broadcasting, and it was indeed to that job that he went. But did he really want to go? Beyond question he and Heren did not get on; indeed, they had been barely on speaking terms since Heren one day came into Cudlipp's office with a complaint only to be told: 'Run along and complain to the editor – I've got work to do'. Cudlipp had understood, when he and Heren were appointed deputy editors, that he would be designated senior deputy editor and would have the same authority as before.[2] But he was not formally given the title and in fact had to share his authority with Heren. He did not, therefore, feel that there was quite the same confidence between him and Rees-Mogg that had existed before 1970. Moreover, he could see no prospect of ever becoming editor of *The Times*. Among younger colleagues he could not fail to be aware of the growing influence of Douglas-Home, for one, and in any case Rees-Mogg was only a few years older than himself. Much as he enjoyed working for *The Times*, he was honourably ambitious and had to consider his future.

1 *Times News*, April–June 1973. See also I. McDonald, *A Man of the Times*, p.49.
2 Cudlipp talking to author.

Even so, there is evidence that he might have been persuaded to stay on. Less than two months before his resignation he wrote this 'private and confidential' letter to the editor:

> My dear William,
>
> I don't usually write to you about money, However, thanks to the freeze we are faced with a situation which I feel should be aired sooner rather than later.
>
> The facts are simple. Since you appointed me as senior Deputy Editor I have assumed more and more responsibility for the smooth running of the paper . . . In your absence, with the exception of the leaders and letters, I take sole charge of the paper and because Iverach has for a considerable period now leaned on my advice (which I obviously welcome) there is no question in the minds of the staff as to who is in charge when you are absent.
>
> When Iverach retires . . . my responsibilities will automatically grow. By this I do not mean I intend to usurp Owen Hickey's editorial page function; but by experience and training I will be filling a bureaucratic gap that Iverach's retirement will make apparent. All this I look forward to and but for the freeze have no doubt you could have recognised the situation financially. However, what can be done now?
>
> I know you know this note is in no way a threat. You know I hope my career lies within the Thomson Organisation and that *I have no intention of leaving*. But by present Fleet Street standards I am not extraordinarily well paid for a man at my level. Again, since joining *The Times* I have steadfastly set my face against freelance activities. My time and energy are devoted to the newspaper.
>
> Perhaps we could talk it over when you have a few moments.
>
> Yours
>
> Michael.[1]

When he said that the letter was not a threat Cudlipp was doubtless sincere. But surely it was a cry for reassurance. The total omission of Heren's name is telltale. Cudlipp knew that he was not in 'sole charge' of the paper when Rees-Mogg was absent; since 1970 he had had to share the responsibility with Heren. In the letter Cudlipp was asking, therefore, not merely for more money but above all for the position he thought he had been given in 1970. The role that he claimed to be

1 Cudlipp to W.R.-M., January 31 1973. Author's italics.

already apparent to the staff – but which was not, of course, apparent at all – he wanted Rees-Mogg to grant and formalise. Though we can never know for sure how he would have acted if Rees-Mogg had responded to his appeal, it seems probable that he would have stayed at *The Times*. But the gesture was not made. If Rees-Mogg replied, either in writing or viva voce, no record of a reply exists; and fifteen years later neither man could remember the letter at all.[1] No increase of salary was authorised, no memorandum establishing Cudlipp's status as chief deputy sent round. Clearly both his financial plea and the more urgent plea that underlay it were alike ignored.

In the absence of direct evidence we can only speculate about Rees-Mogg's motives. He genuinely liked Cudlipp and appreciated what he had done for the paper. Yet the editor may have been more shaken than he realised by the White Swan affair. While stoutly defending Cudlipp against his critics, he may have felt that a man who could be so tactless, and who could provoke so much animosity, needed to be balanced and controlled. Hence his creation of the Heren-Cudlipp dyarchy which, though patently not a success, may have seemed to him distinctly preferable to any return to the status quo ante. Yet such a return was precisely what Cudlipp had shown he wanted. Faced with such an implied request, the editor may have decided that Cudlipp was expendable if he would settle for no less. Whatever went on in the minds of the two men, the outcome is not in doubt; soon after writing his letter to Rees-Mogg Cudlipp had accepted the offer from London Broadcasting, and so was about to do what he had said he had no intention of doing. His departure from *The Times* was a serious misfortune for the paper and a tragedy for himself.[2]

There was a farewell ceremony for him, too, at which he was presented with the first four volumes of the paper's History (the fifth having yet to be written by McDonald), a cassette tape-recorder and a brass page-rule set in a glass case. In making the presentations Rees-Mogg said: 'Michael has seen us through a period which needed seeing through. I owe him an enormous debt of gratitude'. Without Cudlipp's

1 Conversations with Cudlipp and W.R.-M.

2 He resigned formally towards the end of March (Cudlipp to W.R.-M., March 22 1973). The job at London Broadcasting lasted less than a year. Then, after an interlude in the public service attached to the Northern Ireland Office with the rank of under-secretary, and three years as director of information at the National Enterprise Board, he returned to the Thomson Organisation as a senior executive. In this capacity he earned vastly more than the £10,000 a year he was receiving when he left *The Times*. But did he ever again achieve anything like the same job-satisfaction?

help, he added, it would not have been possible for him to be a writing editor.[1] The tribute was generous but also just.

After the Six-day War the Israelis hung on to their conquests, despite a UN resolution and attempts at mediation, while the Arab states seemed as divided and impotent as ever. At the end of 1971 Rees-Mogg decided to try his hand at mediating between Israel and Egypt. In this he had the benefit of Hamilton's friendship with the influential Egyptian journalist Mohamed Heikal. Through Heikal Hamilton had got to know Nasser and had formed the view that, had he 'been respected as the lynchpin in the Middle East (as we later came to treat the oil sheikhs), our whole standing in the area might have been significantly altered'.[2] Now, again through Heikal, Rees-Mogg was able to obtain an 'extended interview' with Nasser's successor, Anwar Sadat.

Impressions resulting from this and 'a series of other conversations' were reported in an article for the paper. Cairo he described as 'a city at war'. Yet he sensed that there was a chance of peace. Five issues had to be settled: the territorial question between Egypt and Israel; the security of both countries after the territorial question was settled; the future of the Palestinian refugees; territorial and security questions between Israel and Jordan; and the same between Israel and Syria. As to the first, Egypt was adamant that Sinai must be returned. Gaza, Rees-Mogg thought, might be regarded as negotiable, because it was originally part of Palestine, though Sadat insisted that it was equally non-negotiable. The president felt that the Americans had let him down, extracting concessions from him without applying any comparable pressure to Israel. 'Most Egyptian opinion', Rees-Mogg commented, 'exaggerates the ability of the United States to influence Israel'. He felt that Sadat would not go to war until he was finally convinced that 'the present diplomatic measures ha[d] failed'. Egypt had lost one battle in 1967 but, in the president's opinion, could 'afford to lose, two, three and four such battles rather than accept permanent loss of Sinai'. The mood of Egypt seemed to Rees-Mogg more that of

1 *Times News*, April-June 1973. A spoof issue of *The Times* itself was produced in Cudlipp's honour, with contributions from Hamilton, Rees-Mogg and other colleagues, and with a picture of him riding his bicycle down Ludgate Hill. It was dated April 30 1973, and he said he would treasure it all his life. (Cudlipp to W.R.-M., April 27 1973.)

2 Hamilton, op. cit., p.126. This was not, unfortunately, Hamilton's view at the time of the 1956 Suez crisis.

Egyptian than of Arab nationalism, and he saw Sadat as to some extent a Pompidou to Nasser's de Gaulle. His regime was 'prepared to make peace, and wanting to make peace', and the present opportunity was, therefore, 'as good as there is likely to be'.[1]

The article did not report one most significant impression conveyed by Sadat, that he would be willing to do a deal whereby Egypt would regain Sinai in return for giving Israel a free hand on the West Bank. When Rees-Mogg asked if he might put this to the Israeli premier, Golda Meir, Sadat agreed to his doing so while expressing doubt that she would react positively. The editor then asked if Sadat was planning to go to war should the overture be rejected, because he was hoping to take his family to Bethlehem for Christmas. In reply the president promised that he would anyway refrain from hostilities while the Rees-Moggs were in Israel. Golda Meir proved just as unresponsive as Sadat had anticipated. During a long talk with her Rees-Mogg got no change out of her at all.[2] In retrospect it is easy to see that the Israelis would make no territorial concession so long as they felt they had nothing to fear from Egypt. Rees-Mogg's mission was, therefore, inevitably a failure, though what he heard and deduced in Cairo provided an accurate pointer to the deal that would be struck at the end of the decade by the same Egyptian president and another Israeli premier, Menachem Begin.

Begin was *The Times*'s guest at an office lunch soon after Rees-Mogg returned from his trip. Others present at the lunch were Hodgkin, Heren, Cudlipp, Spanier and a bearded deputy from Begin's party. The Herut leader and former terrorist had been out of office since 1970, when he resigned from the government of national unity. Printing House Square was swarming with police before and during the lunch, because there had been threats to his life. He turned up three-quarters of an hour late and sat next to Hodgkin, whose understandable prejudice against him was amply confirmed:

> . . . he started by asking if I had ever been to 'his country'. I said I had been in Palestine while he was on the run and that his people had more than once tried to blow us up. 'I am sorry if I caused you any inconvenience', he said. He is an ugly, unimpressive man, presenting set answers which weren't necessarily relevant to the questions asked . . . he believes his own myths. Thus,

1 'Egypt and Israel: the bargain that could bring peace', signed op. ed. piece, December 7 1971.
2 Rees-Mogg talking to author.

> he solemnly said that Israel could easily absorb all the Jews from Russia because in the time of the Maccabees the land had contained 8 million people. 'Do you really believe that?' I asked, and he said he did. But what is perfectly clear is that he would hang on to all the conquered territory, including Sinai, though he would allow the Arabs on the West Bank full citizenship.[1]

The determination of Begin and others of his way of thinking to retain all conquered territory would probably never have been shaken but for unforeseen events towards the end of 1973. In March of that year Sadat assumed personal control of the Egyptian government, replacing his prime minister Sidky, and also appointed himself military governor-general. These changes were reported in *The Times*, though without any apparent sense of what they might portend. Indeed, as late as the beginning of October the paper was commenting in a leader that 'the Arab world as a whole seem[ed] to be turning away from violence and towards an attempt to solve its problems by political and diplomatic methods'.[2] Within a week the Egyptians and Syrians had launched a concerted onslaught on Israel and the so-called Yom Kippur war had begun.

Yom Kippur, the Jewish Day of Atonement, was a sabbath, so the Sunday newspapers on October 7 were the first to handle the story. On Monday *The Times*'s front page was largely devoted to the war, with Eric Marsden reporting from Jerusalem and Paul Martin from Beirut. The only report from Cairo, however, was on an inside page, and from a stringer. This set the pattern for reporting of the war. *The Times* throughout had no correspondent of its own in Egypt. Martin in Beirut had to provide most of the information from the Arab side, while there was abundant first-hand staff reporting from inside Israel, and from the Israeli front lines. Rees-Mogg's friendly exchanges with Sadat two years before had not led to strong permanent representation for the paper in the Egyptian capital, as might have been expected.[3]

The Times's opening leader on the war began with a fair statement of the basic position: 'This time the Arabs started it . . . It is clear that the Egyptians, who in 1967 felt the devastating effect of a surprise

---

1 Hodgkin, op. cit., entry for January 10 1972. The initiative for asking Begin came from Heren, who had known him since he emerged from the underground in 1948.
2 'Looking to Dr. Kissinger', October 1 1973.
3 Egyptian censorship was harsh, and it was difficult to get re-entry visas for Cairo. Hence the paper's decision to base its main Middle East correspondent in Beirut, which was then a far more open place.

attack, were determined that this time they would get in their blow first'. The paper's recent false optimism was admitted, though with the qualification that it was widely shared: 'We were wrong, but we were in good company'. And the leader concluded that there was no comfort for anyone in the affair:

> Not for Israel, which is faced not only with human losses but with the prospect of fighting a new war every few years and with the temptation to over-extend her resources by occupying yet more Arab territory. Not for the West, which will find it more difficult than ever to persuade Israel to pay any political price that the Arabs demand for their oil. Not for the Arab states, which face new physical devastation and quite possibly yet another moral humiliation, bringing yet more divisions and recriminations in its wake. And perhaps least of all for the Palestinians, the original victims of the whole conflict, whose liberation is no longer even an official Arab war aim and whose legitimate interests seem further than ever from fulfilment.[1]

This leader was written by Edward Mortimer. None of the paper's leaders on the war during the following days and weeks was written by the editor. Why? Perhaps he was torn between his moderate pro-Israeli sympathies and his awareness of the Arab case, enhanced by his personal regard for Sadat. Of all the statesmen he met while he was editor Sadat was one of the two he most admired. (The other was Helmut Schmidt, chancellor of West Germany from 1974 to 1982).[2] But the principal reason for his abstinence from writing on the Middle East crisis was that simultaneously a major industrial and political crisis was developing at home, and this pre-empted his attention.

There was, indeed, a most important link between the two crises – oil – and soon a leader written by Stephenson was calling for consideration of a drastic measure:

> It remains . . . in the clear interest of governments of industrial countries not directly involved in the dispute that they should reduce to the maximum degree possible the threat which a shortage of oil supplies could pose to their freedom of political action.

1 'The Fourth Arab-Israel War', October 8 1973. There was also an op. ed. feature, 'Israel and the Arabs: old wounds reopened', in which Heren assessed the military, and Nicholas Ashford the political, aspects of the war.
2 W.R.-M. talking to author.

> It would thus seem wise to consider whether it is necessary to introduce planned and mild rationing of the use of oil products at an early stage.[1]

A week later another leader proposed the appointment of a 'figure of standing', preferably with knowledge of the oil industry, to a place in the cabinet office with direct access to the prime minister, and that the government should adopt as rapidly as possible the policy of investing in 'proven methods of nuclear generation for electricity'.[2] In fact, Heath appointed a secretary of state for energy (Carrington) early in the New Year.

Militarily the war began with dramatic successes for the Syrians and Egyptians, and unprecedented losses of men and *matériel* by the Israelis. But after a few days the tide turned. The Israelis, with the benefit of massive American aid, launched an effective counter-attack on the Golan Heights, and in Sinai a tank battle, allegedly exceeding in scale even the battle of Kursk on the Russian front during the Second World War, was followed by a bold Israeli foray across the Suez Canal and the cutting-off of an Egyptian army. Jordan, having lost so much of its territory in 1967, prudently confined its participation in the war to sending a contingent to the Syrian front. By the end of the month it was clear that the attempt, if such it had been, to destroy Israel had failed, and ceasefire overtures were being made. There were still to be many hitches, however, and it took many months of shuttle diplomacy by the American secretary of state, Henry Kissinger, to establish even an uneasy armed truce in the region.

Shuttling was also done by the paper's defence correspondent, Henry Stanhope, as he covered operations alternately on the Syrian and Sinai fronts, always from the Israeli side. He identified the Egyptians' fatal mistake as their neglect of the west bank of the Suez Canal, which had allowed the Israelis to split their northern from their southern forces.[3] Apart from Martin's regular reporting from Beirut Michael Binyon sent some reports from Jordan, and Ashford a few from Syria. Ashford also described the false hopes of the West Bank Arabs:

> [They] listen to their radios and hope. 'For the first time we . . . sense victory', said [the] Mayor of El-Bireh, north of Jerusalem

1 'The Implications for oil', October 13 1973.
2 'An overlord for oil', October 20 1973. Thomson, of course, had substantial North Sea oil interests.
3 'A bitter lesson for the Arabs', op. ed., October 22 1973.

> . . . His words may prove to be premature, but for the moment the feeling persists that six years of occupation may soon be over.[1]

The mayor's words were premature indeed.

Comment on the implications of the war was on the whole shrewd and fair. When it was apparent that the Israelis had saved themselves, Heren warned against any return to the triumphalism of 1967. They could no longer assume that Arab troops were always inferior. The Arabs had proved that there were 'no secure borders for Israel', and the Egyptians in particular had demonstrated that the Suez Canal was 'not a secure frontier'.[2] Soon afterwards a leader drew conclusions for the country which had so narrowly survived:

> [Israel] would surely be mistaken to suppose that any real peace could be based on continued Israeli occupation of large areas of Arab territory, and indeed that would not be compatible with any interpretation of [UN] Resolution 242.
>
> If Israel has the political strength to realize this, she is probably better placed now than ever before to achieve a lasting peace with her neighbours.[3]

The conclusion actually reached by the Israelis may have been that they could never again afford a war on two main fronts, and that a deal would therefore have to be done with one of their enemies. At the same time the Egyptians began to consider that further hostilities against Israel would be useless and intolerably costly, and that their aim should be to regain Sinai at the price of a separate peace. Hence the Sadat-Begin deal a few years later. Meanwhile the Arabs' oil embargo, punishing the West for its support of Israel, had far-reaching and traumatic consequences, more especially for the Heath government.

Entertaining, such as the lunch for Begin, was a regular feature of life at Printing House Square, and later in Gray's Inn Road. There was a lunch in the Blue Room most days, though the hosts and guests varied. The editor would entertain there roughly once a week, and his guests were mainly political and journalistic, though he also asked a number

---

1 From the Allenby Bridge, West Bank, dateline October 14 1973 (op. ed. in the paper next day).
2 'Israel must think again now myth of might is shattered', op. ed., October 16 1973.
3 'Will peace follow ceasefire?' October 23 1973.

of people distinguished in other fields, notably the theatre. The various editorial heads of department would have their days for entertaining appropriate guests, and so would management chiefs such as Hussey and Mander. Apart from his own lunches, Rees-Mogg would occasionally attend one given by a colleague, in particular the editor of *TBN*.

Food was cooked on the premises and served (with some casual assistance) by two old butlers inherited from the Astor regime. Another part of the inheritance was a stock of good wine, but when this ran out it was replaced by more ordinary vintage. Thomson hospitality was adequate without being sybaritic. Brandy and cigars were exceptional.

Guests were encouraged to talk freely on their own subjects, but some were apt to overdo it. When the Chief Rabbi, Dr. Immanuel (later Lord) Jakobovits, came to lunch he:

> spoke most eloquently about the Sabbath – one day when man should think of himself as the created not the creator. It had been pointed out in advance that feeding the rabbi would be difficult, so we [staff members present] all had melon, followed by hot salmon, and for Dr. J. by salad. He hardly bothered to eat this, and we had all finished while he was still with a slice of tomato poised on his fork. Every now and then he would lift the fork from the plate towards his mouth, and the waiters, who had been growing impatient to bring on the next course (strawberries) would cluster round like slips round a last wicket batsman. Then the fork would be put down again, the waiters would withdraw, and a sigh would go up from the rest of us eyeing the strawberries.[1]

So long as Cudlipp was on the paper he dominated the news-gathering process, more especially at home. The News Team, earlier described, was the spearhead of a more urgent approach, which had its effect on the whole paper. For this reason, as well as economy, the team was phased out in the early 1970s, being to some extent the victim of its own success. In June 1968 its first leader, Peter Evans, became the second home news editor of the Thomson period, succeeding Frank Roberts, who had been in the job since 1965. But Evans held it for only eighteen months, after which he was appointed race relations correspondent, the first such appointment on a national newspaper.

---

1 Hodgkin, op. cit., entry for June 17 1971.

His successor was Colin Webb, who remained in the post for five years.

Webb came from an unprivileged background in Portsmouth, but a master at his grammar school, noting that he was good at English, advised him to go into journalism, with the result that he started work on a local paper at the age of sixteen. Four years later he was called up for national service, during which he was commissioned in the army and served for some time in Jamaica. After his discharge he worked for a year or so at the Press Association (to which, in 1986, he returned as editor-in-chief), and then for a similar period at the *Daily Telegraph*, before being recruited for *The Times* shortly before the Thomson take-over.

In London, Webb had twelve to fifteen reporters under him. In addition, there were resident correspondents in various parts of the country, whose activities were coordinated by the regional news editor, Cyril Bainbridge, a genial, efficient all-rounder from Bradford.[1] Scotland was covered first by Richard Sharpe, then by Ronald Faux, who had previously been the correspondent in Yorkshire, where he was succeeded by Ronald Kershaw. *The Times*'s man in Manchester was the Sussex-born John Chartres, and until 1972 his bailiwick included, as we have seen, Northern Ireland. The Midlands were covered by a correspondent based on Birmingham; until 1968 Brian Priestley, thereafter Arthur Osman. Wales was the territory of Trevor Fishlock, who was also responsible for the west and south-west of England, until Craig Seton was given the job of covering that large area from Exeter.

When Cudlipp left, one part of his empire was assigned to Douglas-Home, with the title of home editor. The following year Webb left to become editor of the *Cambridge Evening News*, and Rita Marshall became home news editor in his place. But this arrangement did not work well, and in 1976 Douglas-Home secured her removal. Brian MacArthur was then brought back to the paper from the *Times Higher Education Supplement* to succeed her as home news editor, to the accompaniment of an imbroglio which will be recorded in a later chapter. In 1978 Heren succeeded Douglas-Home as home editor, while remaining deputy editor, and Rodney Cowton filled the vacancy

1 Bainbridge's range of interests and all-round ability may be judged from the fact that he later proposed writing a series of articles on: the renaissance of brass bands, the tradition of choirs and operatic societies, the social side of religion, the growth of gardening as a leisure pursuit, ballroom dancing, the revival of crafts, and outdoor activities such as orienteering, shooting and cycling. (Memo from Bainbridge – by then managing news editor – to W.R.-M., February 28 1980.) Bainbridge had been with the paper since 1963.

caused by MacArthur's departure to be deputy editor of the *Evening Standard*.

Under pressure from Douglas-Home and MacArthur extra space was provided for home news. At this time labour reporting was a major strength of the paper, and obviously of special importance; Peter Hennessy acquired an outstanding reputation as Whitehall correspondent; and Pat Healy was a keen reporter on social services, though with a marked left-wing bias. In 1976 the paper's saleroom correspondent, Geraldine Norman, scored a great coup with her exposure of Tom Keating's art forgeries, for which she received the News Reporter of the Year award. In her book on the subject she acknowledges the editor's vital support:

> That my article ever saw the light of day was due to William Rees-Mogg . . . [According to legal advice] the amount of damages which we should envisage having to pay if a successful case were brought was of the order of £100,000' [and] *The Times*'s chances of winning such an action were roughly 60:40.
>
> Mr. Rees-Mogg decided in favour of publication. He took the view that a matter of principle was being established: the authenticity of works of art was . . . of public interest and therefore a subject on which newspapers should be free to comment.[1]

Despite a general belief that the *Daily Telegraph* carried more home news than *The Times*, the reality was rather different. In a typical eight-day period in early 1977 *The Times* carried more home news stories on seven of the eight days, and on five of the days many more. Yet even when the number of items was substantially larger, the *Telegraph* tended to give more space. For instance, on one day when *The Times* had seventy-nine stories to the *Telegraph*'s fifty-two, the number of columns in *The Times* was nineteen to twenty compared with twenty-six in the *Telegraph*. Moreover, the *Telegraph* had more regional reporters, and its coverage of a certain type of court case 'of interest' (as MacArthur put it) 'to the 8.17 from Surbiton' was never emulated by *The Times*.[2]

---

1 *The Fake's Progress*, pp.225–6. The article in question appeared on July 16 1976. (The book includes Keating's own account of his activities, told to Geraldine Norman's husband Frank.)

2 'Private and confidential' memo from MacArthur to W.R.-M. and C.D.-H., March 30 1977.

XV

The Times as good European • More Ulster experiments • The Times and Watergate • Government in crisis • Anatomy of a conversion

BRITAIN'S FIRST YEAR in the European Communities, after becoming formally a member on New Year's Day 1973, was by no means reassuring to those who had doubts about entry, and still less effective in converting outright opponents. The inflation of food and other prices was blamed indiscriminately on British membership, and in April opinion was inflamed by news that 200,000 tons from the EEC 'butter mountain' had been sold to the Soviet Union at 8p per pound, while the price of butter in Britain was 28p per pound. The argument that the Common Agricultural Policy would have had many fewer defects if Britain had been in 'Europe' from the beginning was perfectly valid, though of course little heeded. Euro-enthusiasts from Heath downwards were thrown on the defensive, with little to say about the economic benefits of membership other than that they would become apparent later on. The Labour Party stuck to its policy of holding a referendum after re-negotiating the terms of entry, and at its conference a motion calling for unconditional withdrawal was only narrowly defeated.

In these dispiriting circumstances Rees-Mogg soldiered on manfully, keeping *The Times* on its chosen track as the most European of British newspapers. To him, of course, the economic aspect was never paramount. Invited to make a personal statement for the German public at the time Britain was joining, he said (in part):

> When as a child I first read about the French Revolution, a historical event which always interested me because the fall of the Bastille had occurred on the same day of the year as my birthday, I remember being puzzled by the slogan Liberty, Equality and Fraternity. Liberty and equality were concepts which I could understand easily enough and I remember feeling that on the whole liberty was the more important of the two. Fraternity

> seemed to me to be incapable of a sufficiently precise definition. Yet in the making of Europe it seems to me that this is a truly revolutionary idea because it calls on all of us to change the way in which we regard our relationships and the relationships of our nations.[1]

He was prepared to interpret fraternity in a quite specific and concrete sense. His view of the European future was distinctly federalist, as he showed when discussing the role of the European parliament with Andrew Shonfield:

> I accept that there is a risk that if you have two elected parliaments they may quarrel with each other and dispute for jurisdiction. On the other hand, I believe that if we make the individual nation democratic and leave the Community non-democratic except through a system of indirect election we continue thereby to emphasise national identity and diminish Community identity.
>
> I am not sure that this is conventional wisdom. *The Times* is at present in a minority in taking the Dutch/Italian view of the future of the European parliament. Certainly Heath, Pompidou and Brandt are all inclined to move slowly and are reluctant to give up their own power.[2]

One instance among many of *The Times*'s enhanced coverage of Europe was to be the publication of reports of debates in the European parliament, in the same style, and on the same page, as the reports from Westminster. Another was to be the fuller publication of European law reports, which *The Times* had been the first British newspaper to give space to at all, and which were now, in a more extended form, to appear with the British law reports. European business and financial stories were to receive more attention in *TBN*; the arts page was to

1 Statement sent by W.R.-M. to Dieter Stadach, correspondent in London for a number of German papers, November 27 1972. It was, perhaps, hardly necessary to have been born on July 14 to find the French Revolution interesting.
2 W.R.-M. to Andrew Shonfield, January 16 1973. The correspondence arose from Shonfield's Reith lectures, *Europe: Journey to an Unknown Destination*. The European parliament, or assembly, was indirectly elected through national parliaments until 1979, when the first direct elections to it were held. Britain, though entitled to thirty-six members, was represented at the outset by only twenty-one, of whom eighteen were Conservatives, because Labour had decided to boycott the parliament. The leader of the Conservative group was Peter Kirk, a former junior minister, who explained in his maiden speech (reported in the paper on January 17 1973) that his group consisted of opponents and doubters as well as impassioned pro-Europeans like himself.

include more cultural events on the Continent, which the paper's London critics were to visit more; the women's page would 'study social trends in Europe, life styles and changing family structures'; sports reporting was to be similarly broadened; and there would be a resumption of vintage reports from the wine-growing countries of Europe. This comprehensive programme, foreshadowed at the Ston Easton weekend conference eighteen months before, was announced in a front-page story on entry day.[1]

The occasion was marked also by publication of two special reports. The first, running to twelve pages, had a coloured cover depicting the nine Community flags stitched together. Inside there were contributions from a wide variety of British notables, among them Heath, the Archbishop of Canterbury (Michael Ramsey), Lord Denning, Lord Zuckerman, Asa Briggs, Angus Wilson, Jonathan Miller, Roger Bannister, Richard Attenborough and Roy Strong. Each piece was illustrated by a small caricature of the author, in an attempt, no doubt, to give an air of liveliness to the feature. But the material to which the 'names' were attached was cumulatively of a kind to deter any normal reader. The second special report, entitled 'Forward into Europe', was similar in character: fourteen pages-worth of messages from Continental leaders, including Pompidou, Brandt, Andreotti and Dr. Sicco Mansholt, president of the European Commission, together with articles on different aspects of life and how they would be affected by the enlarged Community, and with a running cartoon by Gale across the top of each page, based on the Bayeux tapestry.[2] In general it must be said that there was considerable overkill in the paper's celebration of British entry.

At the same time it was decided, after months of preliminary discussion in the four countries concerned, to launch a monthly backset tabloid in conjunction with *Le Monde*, *Die Welt* and *La Stampa*. The initial cost would be about £50,000, including launching costs of £20,000, but it was hoped that the advantage of access to European as opposed to merely domestic advertising budgets would abundantly justify the expense.[3] There were also encouraging signs of support from the United States, where the reaction of senior agency personnel was found to be very positive.[4] Before the launch in the autumn large presentations, attended by Hussey and Mander, were held in Chicago

1 'The Times: meeting challenge of new frontier', January 1 1973. The story was written by Heren.
2 January 2 and 3 1973.
3 TEMC, January 11 1973.
4 TEMC, July 12 1973.

and New York, at which, it was said, much interest was shown in the pioneering venture of a European magazine appearing simultaneously in four languages, and in four newspapers of outstanding prestige in their respective countries.[1]

The first issue of the magazine, called *Europa* (but not to be confused with the typeface of that name), was published on October 2 1973. The lead feature was an interview with George Shultz, secretary of the US treasury, conducted by four journalists representing the constituent papers, but gaining nothing from the number of interviewers. There were eight pages in all, and features on the inside pages included an article on inflation by Raymond Barre (a former vice-president of the European Commission and future prime minister of France) and a boring profile of a French industrialist. On the back page there was an article on hotels in Europe, another work of collaboration – written by two journalists from *Die Welt*, but based on research by journalists from each of the other papers – which would almost certainly have been better as the work of a single hand.

On the score of readability this was not an auspicious beginning, and as time went on *Europa* acquired a reputation similar to that of the back-set *TBN*, as an offering of which thousands of copies were discarded unread. Mander's assistant, Garry Thorne, who had much to do with its inception, considered in retrospect that *Europa* failed because the contents were too dull and advertisers 'could not be convinced that anybody read it'. Another misfortune was that Lothar Rühl left *Die Welt* for government service soon after the launch. He was a man of bright ideas who believed that there should be plenty of opinion in the magazine, and in Thorne's view his departure removed the best chance of making it lively.[2] Mander's subsequent judgement was that it appeared ten years too soon. Though in America and Japan Europe was already regarded as one market, no European companies yet had European budgets. The magazine did quite well in syndication, though even there not well enough.[3]

Despite its disappointing performance *Europa* was not scrapped,

---

1 TEMC, October 11 1973.
2 Garry Thorne talking to author. Thorne was by birth an American, but having served during the Second World War with a Canadian regiment he had Canadian as well as US citizenship. Both his parents were actors and he was brought up in Hollywood, where his father helped Aubrey Smith to found the Hollywood Cricket Club. After training, himself, as an actor at the Bristol Old Vic, and spending ten years on the boards, Thorne became a journalist, with Fleetway and then IPC. He joined *The Times* in 1971 as advertising manager under Mander, working at first on special reports.
3 Mander talking to author.

and every year there were meetings of those involved, which rotated country by country. In 1977 it was Britain's turn and the Continentals were entertained at Woodstock, where they stayed at the Bear and a cricket match was staged for them in front of Blenheim Palace. On this occasion Rees-Mogg went to the length of putting on pads, but did not go in. Afterwards a representative of *La Stampa* wrote to thank him for a meeting held 'in the peaceful and friendly atmosphere of Old England'.[1]

Whatever the causes of direct rule in Northern Ireland, the consequences were predictably grave. The removal of Stormont had been a prime objective of the IRA, which naturally deduced that its campaign was succeeding; while the Unionist majority, equally naturally, felt betrayed. The newly-appointed secretary of state, William Whitelaw, had to operate at first in a state of complete political isolation, with only his officials and security chiefs to advise him. He began with a policy of cautious conciliation, directed mainly at the minority. Some detainees were released and the ban on marches and demonstrations was lifted. But this was not enough for the constitutional Nationalist party, the SDLP, which refused to cooperate until detention without trial was ended. The IRA intensified the violence and in Derry consolidated itself in 'no-go' areas where the government's writ did not run. The Unionists were at one in demanding that these enclaves should be eliminated, though in other respects they were divided. Some, such as Ian Paisley, favoured full integration within the United Kingdom; others, notably William Craig, were moving towards advocacy of a Protestant UDI; while Faulkner hoped to find some basis for collaboration with the government. Above all, the paramilitary organisations on the Unionist side were becoming much more powerful and active.

Soon after the imposition of direct rule *The Times* published an interesting article by Nigel Lawson, not yet a politician though soon to become one. Noting that direct rule was supposed to last for only one year, he argued that a decision what to do next could not long be avoided. He ruled out any return to the status quo ante, since responsibility for security could not be divided. So the choice lay between integration and independence, of which 'government thinking'

1 Arrigo Levi to W.R.-M., June 4 1977. Rees-Mogg regarded *Europa* as a success in the sense that it established *The Times* as *the* serious British newspaper on the Continent. But was it not that already?

seemed to incline towards the first. Yet Ulster Catholics would resent what they would regard as English rule, Dublin would reject it, and even Unionist support for the idea was suspect. As for Great Britain, 'the integration of Northern Ireland in the United Kingdom would mean integrating . . . the disaffection and violence'. He ended by stressing the need for the government to make up its mind one way or the other, and showed clearly, if not quite explicitly, which way he thought it should be. 'Direct rule became, temporarily, inescapable: integration is not'.[1] The only logical conclusion to be drawn from this article was that Britain should withdraw its troops and leave the Northern Irish to their own devices.

While the secretary of state was trying to learn about a province of which he previously knew next to nothing, *The Times*'s new resident correspondent, Robert Fisk, was doing the same. But he was learning more quickly, because his contacts were wider and closer to the ground – in the political parties, the police and the army, as well as in the IRA and the Protestant paramilitary organisations, the UDA and the UDF. At the end of April 1972 he interviewed Whitelaw in his office at Stormont Castle, from whose French window he could 'see the city of Belfast spread out below him, its scars and ruins usually hidden by a grey industrial haze'. The interview was unattributable, but direct quotation would hardly have conveyed Whitelaw's attitude and meaning more effectively. Fisk described his almost permanent 'hopeful smile', and said that he was playing a waiting game 'until the people of Northern Ireland ha[d] chosen their leaders'. So for the time being no invasion of the IRA areas of Londonderry was to be expected. If the SDLP failed, and the IRA was accepted as truly representing the people of the Bogside and Creggan, he might be 'faced with the prospect of talking to their front men'. The report ended: 'Mr. Whitelaw is fond of saying "If I show faith in people, I think they should be prepared to show some faith in me". If either community's patience snaps before the summer, however, faith will not be enough'.[2]

The truth of Fisk's final comment was soon demonstrated. When, as a misconceived gesture to the SDLP, Whitelaw accorded political status and special privileges to some detainees, the patience of Unionists nearly snapped and their paramilitaries mounted an alarming show of strength. Soon afterwards he made a worse error. When the

---

1 'Ulster: independence or integration?' Op. ed. piece, April 19 1972. Lawson was under contract to *The Times*. Two years later he was elected Conservative MP for Blaby.

2 'Mr. Whitelaw's patience and calculated faith': op. ed. piece, May 1 1972 (dateline Belfast the previous day).

Provisionals declared a ceasefire he fell into the trap of holding secret talks with their leaders in London, despite having stated categorically that he would not do so. The talks inevitably broke down, because the Provisionals had no interest at all in compromise. Having won a sort of recognition, they promptly ended the ceasefire and announced that the talks had taken place. This destroyed any remaining confidence the Unionists might have had in Whitelaw, and to prevent action by them which would probably have led to civil war he was forced to send the army into the 'no-go' areas at the end of July. In Crossman's view, he had 'pushed the conciliation of the Roman Catholic community far further, and accepted risks of a Protestant backlash far greater, than any Labour minister would have dared'. But his 'heroic enterprise' had manifestly failed, and a deadline would have to be set for the withdrawal of British troops.[1]

Whitelaw and the government did not, however, take the course which Crossman, and before him Lawson, recommended. Nor did they adopt the policy of integration. Gradually, over a period of months, an intermediate policy was evolved. In the autumn Whitelaw held a conference at Darlington, which only the Official Unionists, the non-sectarian Alliance Party and the Northern Ireland Labour Party attended. After this a Green Paper was issued which in most respects foreshadowed the policy put forward in a White Paper the following March, though the government was first compelled, by a Protestant agitation, to hold the border poll which had been promised when direct rule was brought in, to reaffirm the obvious fact that a majority of the population wanted to remain in the United Kingdom. The White Paper policy involved holding local elections and elections to a new assembly (not 'parliament'), on a new franchise and using the STV system of proportional representation. An executive was to be nominated on a non-sectarian and inter-communal basis, with powers that would be increased if it were successful, though responsibility for security was to remain with London.

The local elections were held in May and the assembly elections in June, with results that were disappointing to the government. Whitelaw had hoped that a fair voting system would allow moderation to prevail, but since the whole point of such a system is that it reflects the true state of opinion, and since opinion in Northern Ireland in mid-1973 was sharply polarised, the elections gave only a few assembly seats to the Alliance Party, and to Faulkner's Official Unionists only

1 'Personal View', July 12 1972 (the anniversary of the battle of the Boyne and the principal folk festival for Ulster Protestants).

twenty-two seats, compared with twenty-eight for other Unionists most of whom were implacably opposed to any form of power-sharing with the Nationalists. There was, indeed, potentially an overall majority to support a power-sharing executive if and when such a body could be brought into being, but the hostility of a large proportion of Unionists was ominous. Reporting the assembly elections, Fisk and Penny Symon wrote: 'The people of Northern Ireland have retreated into their tribal camps'.[1]

Not long after the elections Fisk had his first serious brush with the authorities. On August 14 a story from him appeared under the headline 'Army departure on Ulster arrests procedure'. It reported an 'extraordinary instruction to troops in Northern Ireland, telling them to hand arrested men over to the military police rather than to the Royal Ulster Constabulary'. This was to be circulated in a new and 'restricted Ministry of Defence document which would be issued to all 16,000 troops in the province during the following week'. The document was to take the form of a blue card 'remarkably similar to the yellow card carried by all soldiers containing instructions for opening fire'. The story was illustrated by a photograph of the blue card's heading.

Next day Fisk reported a denial by the army that the rules were new, together with a statement that the procedure had been in use for many months 'with the full knowledge and agreement of the RUC'. It was necessary, the army claimed, for record purposes, so that due help could be given to the RUC about the attendance of military witnesses at trials. Arrested persons were handed over to the RUC 'at the earliest opportunity'. A blue card had been in existence 'for well over a year', and if a new version of it was being produced it was merely to take account of the new emergency provisions legislation. Fisk, however, also reported the chairman of the police federation's reaction to the army's statement, which was that 'he had not yet met a policeman who knew of the existence of the blue card'. He further quoted an unnamed RUC man as saying that the army might have told the chief constable, 'but that doesn't mean it always gets down to us'.

This story caused quite a rumpus. A signal was sent out from army headquarters at Lisburn to the effect that Fisk should henceforth be

1 June 30 1973. There is some irony in the reflection that British politicians who applied PR in a community where there was no strong centre to benefit from it refused, for reasons of party interest, to apply it in Great Britain, where the true wishes of a majority of the people were repeatedly frustrated by the voting system.

regarded as a hostile reporter and given minimum cooperation. He was to receive no unattributable or off-the-record background briefings, and all requests from him should be referred to the press desk at headquarters. The army's recently appointed chief information officer in Northern Ireland, Peter Broderick, was particularly indignant because the army's denial and explanation did not appear with the original story, which as it stood was extremely damaging to army-police relations. In fact Fisk had filed the army's comments for later editions on August 14, but through no fault of his they were not included until the following day. He insisted that he had a good source for the story, and as the row developed this was more or less conceded by the army. In any case Douglas-Home gave him robust support and intervened on his behalf with the ministry of defence in London, with the result that the ban on him was soon rescinded.[1] (Douglas-Home's close relationship to the foreign secretary can hardly have been a handicap to him in his dealings with senior officials at this time.)

In November, after long negotiations which until the last moment seemed likely to fail, Whitelaw was able to announce the formation of a power-sharing executive, which was to consist of eleven members – six Unionist, four SDLP and one Alliance. Faulkner was to be chief executive, with Gerard Fitt, leader of the SDLP, as his deputy. *The Times*, which had backed the government's policy throughout, whatever its columnists might say, hailed the deal as 'a great achievement'.[2] So in many ways it was, but unfortunately there was a rider to it which ensured that the executive would not have time to settle down and prove itself in action without further agony and controversy. The rider was that agreement had to be reached between the executive and the British and Irish governments for establishing a Council of Ireland. This 'Irish dimension' was insisted on by the SDLP and by Dublin, where a new Fine Gael government under Liam Cosgrave had to show that it was no less devoted than its predecessor to the national and republican cause, despite memories of 1921–2. A tripartite conference was held at Sunningdale in early December, and after fifty hours' talk agreement was reached. *The Times* carried the news as its lead story,

1 Army signals dated August 17 1973 (leaked to Fisk and reported by him to C.D.-H.); Broderick to C.D.-H., August 14 1973; C.D.-H. to Colin Webb, news editor, August 21 1973; Broderick to C.D.-H., August 30 1973; C.D.-H. to Broderick, September 19 1973. Douglas-Home found that the army 'had developed a certain amount of paranoia about Fisk', to the extent of regarding him as 'a convinced republican sympathiser', which he certainly was not. Later, Douglas-Home discovered that Broderick had been called to London and given a 'roasting' by the permanent under-secretary at the MOD, Sir James Dunnett. (C.D.-H. to Fisk, February 27 1973.)
2 Leader, November 23 1973.

and alongside it a picture of Faulkner and Cosgrave shaking hands, with Heath, Fitt and the Alliance leader, Napier, looking on. On page 2 the text of the Sunningdale communiqué was printed, and there was a report from Fisk on the anger of loyalist politicians about the 'sell-out'. In its leader the paper said: 'They got there in the end . . . but will they be able to make it stick?'[1]

The agreement provided for a Council of Ireland through which, it was piously hoped, cooperation between North and South would grow, not least on police matters. To many Unionists this was anathema – a foot in the door for the Republic, and a first step towards their absorption into a united and Dublin-based Ireland. The reciprocal gestures by the Republic of acknowledging that the status of Northern Ireland could not be changed except by a vote of the majority there did not mollify them at all. By putting his name to the agreement Faulkner had not, like Michael Collins in 1921, signed his death warrant in the literal sense; but, as things turned out, he had signed his political death warrant.

American politics have always been corrupt, and in the modern age have become more rather than less so. Money is the fuel on which the system runs, and the competition for office at all levels is nearly always a dirty process. The vast expansion of government resulting from the growth of American power, and the enhanced role of the state even in a country dedicated to private enterprise, have together given politicians far greater patronage, which in turn has increased the attractions of a political career and intensified the activity of lobbies seeking the support or favour of public office-holders. At the same time the control of candidates' expenditure has remained utterly inadequate, and the voting system itself has never ceased to be open to grave abuse. The two parties enjoying a duopoly in American politics are not associations of principle, but rather coalitions of interest-groups varying from time to time and from region to region. Finally, American law is notoriously weak in the protection it offers against defamation.

The office of US president is peculiar in that the person who occupies it is both the head of state and the sole embodiment of federal executive power. In the first capacity he has to be respected, even revered, as a symbol of national unity; in the second, he is a controversial party politician who has hurt a lot of people on the way up and

1 December 10 1973.

is often execrated by his opponents. As a rule, the forces of opposition, more especially in the media, have tended to exercise just enough moderation in their attacks on a president to enable the dignity of his office to be maintained. But this tradition of limited restraint was abandoned in the case of Richard M. Nixon, who in his second term was hounded so relentlessly and effectively that in the end he was driven to resign.

The Watergate scandal which brought about his downfall was, of course, an extremely serious matter, but in other times, and with another man as president, its consequences might have been less drastic. The Democrats were in a state of exceptional disarray and bitterness, their regime having foundered in the morass of Vietnam; and their resentment was compounded by the spectacle of Nixon as the beneficiary of their self-inflicted woes. Nixon had long been a bogeyman to all liberal-minded Democrats, partly for valid reasons deriving from incidents in his early career, but partly for the bogus reason that he was invidiously contrasted with Kennedy. In fact, the Kennedy clan was second to none in political ruthlessness which, combined with enormous personal wealth, enabled John F. Kennedy to secure the Democratic nomination at the expense of Hubert Humphrey. Moreover, the 1960 election itself was won only by a hair's-breadth, a few thousand votes determining that the vital electoral college votes of Illinois and Texas went to Kennedy; and the genuineness of those votes is, to say the least, widely questioned. As for Lyndon B. Johnson, who inherited the presidency when Kennedy was assassinated, and then won it in his own right in 1964, it would be hard to think of an American politician less fastidious in the pursuit and exercise of power.

The media helped to bring Johnson down on the issue of Vietnam, but neither he nor Kennedy suffered on account of his way of working the system. Indeed, so far as Kennedy was concerned, the media created the 'Camelot' myth. Apart from sheer partisanship operating against the Republican successor to Kennedy and Johnson, Nixon had one other fatal disadvantage. He lacked the charm which, in politics at any rate, is often a useful working substitute for virtue. This quality was abundantly present in Kennedy, and by no means absent from Johnson. They were skilful communicators who could exploit the media for their own purposes, including the projection of a speciously attractive image. Nixon, on the other hand, was an awkward, secretive and introverted character, who never established an easy relationship with journalists or broadcasters. There was no fund of goodwill on which he could draw when an act of (literally) criminal folly was uncovered.

In June 1972 there was a burglary at the offices of the Democratic national committee in the Watergate building in Washington DC. Through the persistence of two journalists from the fiercely anti-Nixon *Washington Post* it was established that the burglars were CIA agents. During the year following Nixon's re-election further investigation revealed that close aides of his had authorised the burglary; and in the course of hearings before a federal judge it came out that throughout his presidency Nixon had tape-recorded all business discussions in the White House. The tapes naturally became an issue and, despite strenuous efforts to avoid releasing them, Nixon was eventually forced to give way. Transcripts of the tapes were then heard by a congressional committee and the effect produced by them was very damaging, though the tape of an interview in which, according to one aide, the burglary had been discussed with the president himself was said to have been accidentally erased by his secretary. This seemed too convenient to be even remotely plausible, and, at long last, under threat of impeachment, Nixon resigned the presidency in August 1974.

The incident which led to his ruin was foolish as well as criminal, because there was no need for him to resort to dirty tricks to defeat the Democrats in 1972. In the event he scored a landslide victory over Senator George McGovern. Moreover, while it was odd enough that he should ever have had the idea of bugging all conversations, including his own, it was surely much odder to have failed to have all the tapes destroyed at an early stage, before they could be used as incriminating evidence. In one respect, however, his troubles were unjustly compounded. Just when the Watergate affair was coming to the boil in 1973, his vice-president, Spiro Agnew, had to resign after accusations of corruption. The two cases were entirely unconnected. Nixon had chosen Agnew as running mate in 1968 for the adequate political reason that he had a 'liberal' image, having been Nelson Rockefeller's campaign manager in the primary fight for the Republican nomination. The choice was made for no other reason than to balance the ticket, and Nixon was no more involved in the activities that brought Agnew down than Agnew was in Watergate. Yet the coincidence of the two scandals suggested a general rottenness and further weakened Nixon's already crumbling position. (Agnew was replaced as vice-president by Congressman Gerald Ford, who the following year inherited the presidency when Nixon resigned.)

Watergate was for some time an issue on which Rees-Mogg and the paper's head of bureau in Washington, Fred Emery, disagreed. Emery felt that the press campaign against Nixon was justified, and in any case wanted the story to be covered uninhibitedly. Rees-Mogg was at first indignant at the way Nixon was being treated. In June 1973 he attacked the hue and cry against the president in a three-column leader:

> The President of the United States is in the unenviable position of being tried by his fellow countrymen in three different forms [a Congressional committee, a grand jury and the media], each of which has its own particular deficiencies . . . That is not to say that the President is innocent . . . It is perfectly possible for a wholly guilty man to be tried in a wholly unjust way. Indeed many of the men who have been lynched in the course of history were lynched for crimes they had actually committed. That does not alter the fact that what Mr. Nixon is now receiving is a Washington variant of lynch law.[1]

The leader did, however, praise the *Washington Post* for its investigative achievement.

About a week later that newspaper published the full text of Rees-Mogg's attack and replied to it in a leader of its own. What Rees-Mogg had said was being reprinted because it was 'eloquent', and because it 'faithfully reflect[ed] the thinking of Mr. Nixon's supporters' at home: 'so much so that White House propagandists [were] circulating it approvingly'. It was a sign of weakness in Nixon that he should have to fall back on ordinary civil rights when he had such privilege and could always state his case on three television networks. The American system was different. 'We are not Britain; we have a different set of checks and balances, which grant a President a fixed, firm term of office while holding him answerable, every day, to the judgment of the people he serves'. The *Washington Post* argued that Watergate was not just a question of 'specific isolated crimes', but of 'a whole style and manner and method of governing'.[2]

Rees-Mogg travelled to Washington to pursue the controversy on the spot. At a lunch meeting of the Press Club he again paid tribute to the *Washington Post*, and also to the *New York Times* – both 'fine newspapers' – but maintained that the First Amendment (concerning freedom of the press) 'could only work if the separate powers in the constitutional process respect each other'. It did not override the rest of the constitution, and should not prejudice the right to trial by an impartial jury decreed by the Sixth Amendment. He suggested that

---

1 'Due process of law', June 5 1973. Rees-Mogg's sympathy for Nixon may have gained just a little from the almost certain recollection of his praise of an editorial during the Six-Day War (see pp. 55–6 above).
2 June 13 1973.

Nixon had always been unfairly treated by the press, and in the case of Watergate the press was behaving like a 'hunting pack'.[1]

Emery was unhappy about the editor's line, though 'hunting pack' was perhaps a slight improvement on 'lynch law'. When they together visited the FBI, and a senior man there told them in so many words that he had enough evidence to proceed against the president, Rees-Mogg was outraged by what he saw as treason, whereas Emery would have liked to make use of what seemed to him a marvellous scoop. When they had a joint interview with Agnew it was apparent to Emery that the vice-president was savouring the prospect of taking over if and when Nixon had to go.[2] In fact Agnew had to go first, and by then *The Times*'s attitude to the Nixon regime was becoming more shaded, though the president was still given substantial credit:

> The historian will list the senior figures in Mr. Nixon's administration against whom criminal charges were brought, and those who had to resign their offices. The list is without parallel in any previous administration . . . On *The Times* we have always recognized that President Nixon, whatever the failings of his administration, has a general and admirable desire to achieve historic benefits for the United States . . . He is far from being the contemptible creature that his critics make him out to be, and until a few months ago his achievements greatly outweighed his failures in office.

It would, however, be disastrous for him to nominate in Agnew's place 'any politician who could possibly be accused of the practices of corrupt politics', though it would be difficult to avoid doing so granted that 'American politics have usually been a dirty business and some of the dirt sticks to only too many of those who fight their way to the top'.[3]

When Nixon resigned the following year the paper ran a four-page feature on 'The Unmaking of the President', edited by Emery, Brogan and Frank Vogl in Washington, and by Heren and Davy in London.[4]

---

1 June 15 1973. (Both the *Washington Post*'s leader, and Rees-Mogg's address, were reported in *The Times* on the following days.)
2 Emery talking to author.
3 'Who should succeed Mr. Agnew?', October 11 1973 (also written by Rees-Mogg).
4 August 9 1974. The feature included articles on various related themes, such as 'How could it have happened in the White House?', 'President who broke rigid mould of foreign policy imposed only sullen calm at home', 'America's hope for a second Truman', 'Ford – a hope not realised', and 'Unholy alliance that swung impeachment vote'. Key dates in the Watergate saga were listed, and there were pictures illustrating Nixon's career.

There was also a valedictory leader by the editor, which began by reasserting the view that Nixon had in many ways been a worthy occupant of the world's most powerful office, but immediately added that he had 'placed himself and his entourage above the law and sought to debauch the processes of law'. When threatened with exposure he had 'lied systematically to the Congress and the people'. The tapes 'had revealed not only the moral squalor of his inner councils, but the extraordinarily low level of debate, analysis and information at which he dealt with problems ranging from Watergate to the world monetary situation'. The Watergate inquiries had 'swept through the whole system exposing much that was endemic in American life, such as political corruption, tax evasion, invasion of privacy, and the abuse of power'. Yet the leader had an upbeat ending, referring to 'the extraordinary resilience of the United States', which would enable it to 'correct its errors' and to 'renew its faith and its values'.[1]

Rees-Mogg may have been too charitable to Nixon in 1973, but he was right about the prejudice and hypocrisy of many of Nixon's enemies, and justified in drawing attention to underlying flaws in the American political system. Unfortunately his eventual optimism that the flaws would be removed as a result of Watergate did not prove justified. A later Republican president, after two terms in office (and so with nothing to lose by candour), complained of the disastrous effects of gerrymandering and other forms of corruption in his country's politics.[2] Watergate got rid of a president and may, therefore, have served as a warning against the grossest imprudence; but it left the system essentially unchanged.

The expansionist policies of the Heath government reduced unemployment by a quarter of a million in 1973, but at the same time gave a powerful boost to inflation. The retail price index rose by eighteen points during the year, while average earnings rose in exact proportion. The money released by earlier tax cuts did not fructify to any adequate degree in savings and investment; much of it was lured into property speculation, for which Barber's budget in March provided no fiscal deterrent, despite a widespread expectation that it would do so. The

1 'End of a presidency'.

2 'Because of their opportunities for bestowing political favors, generating publicity, and raising enormous sums of money for re-election campaigns from special interest groups that want favors from them, it is almost impossible, short of a major scandal, for a member of Congress to lose his or her seat involuntarily'. (Ronald Reagan, *An American Life*, p.482.)

budget was 'neutral' so far as inflation was concerned, neither increasing nor significantly moderating the pressure of spending in the economy. For the fight against inflation the government depended upon its measures to control prices and incomes by statute.

In January 1973 a White Paper was issued on the next stage of the counter-inflationary policy, to follow the Phase One freeze which had been introduced the previous November. The White Paper announced that controls would be imposed for three years, with a Pay Board and a Price Commission as the controlling bodies. Under Phase Two, to start on April 1, increases in income would be limited to £1 a week plus 4 per cent. Price increases would be only those necessary to cover unavoidable rises in costs. Dividends would be held at 5 per cent. The Pay Board was to investigate special pay anomalies and to consider ways of helping the lowest paid, while the Price Commission was to assess claims for price rises, balancing the needs of producers and consumers. Phase Three in the autumn would, it was hoped, be an agreed package in which the just demands of all interest-groups would be accommodated, without detriment to the overall control of inflation.

There was, however, no agreement. Despite some apparent success for Phase Two during the spring and summer, neither employers nor trade unions could be happy with a system that substituted bureaucratic regulation for the disciplines and opportunities of the market. The CBI complained that dividend limitation and the lowering of profit margins were deterring investment, while the TUC, anyway at war with the government over the Industrial Relations Act, insisted on a return to free collective bargaining. The government nevertheless introduced its Phase Three scheme at the end of October, just when the economic assumptions on which it was based were being exploded by the Yom Kippur war: more especially by the cut in Arab oil supplies. This not only sent the price of oil rocketing, and with it many other costs, but also gave the National Union of Mineworkers what was, in effect, a blackmailing position. Phase Three was more flexible for trade unions than its predecessor,[1] but the government felt that it could not give way to the miners' demands without reopening arrangements already reached with other unions. On November 12 the miners started a ban on overtime, without holding a ballot, and the following

1 Pay rises were to be limited to 7 per cent, but with a 1 per cent margin for the removal of anomalies, and extra payments for 'unsocial hours' and proved efficiency schemes; also with an indexing mechanism in case inflation rose above 7 per cent. At the same time the Phase Two controls on prices, profits and dividends were rigidly maintained.

day the government declared a state of emergency to protect energy supplies. Powers were taken to restrict the use of energy for heating and lighting, and preparations were made for petrol rationing which was not, however, immediately introduced.

At the end of November matters were made worse by the threat of industrial action on the railways. On November 13 Heath announced a three-day working week for many areas of industry and commerce, to take effect from the end of the month, and soon afterwards Barber brought in a crisis budget which cut expenditure by £1,200 million and belatedly imposed an extra tax on property speculation, together with a surcharge on surtax, while also tightening the control of hire purchase and credit. But it did not increase income tax, VAT or duties on beer, tobacco and petrol. The year ended with the spectacle of a government defiant but scarcely, if at all, equal to the pressure of events.

The Times had been advocating an incomes policy for some time, with a preference for one that was voluntary, but with an evident readiness to accept the force of law as an alternative to no control at all. When the government decided that only a more permanent statutory policy would do the trick, the paper wholeheartedly endorsed the decision. The day after the Phase Two White Paper was published its proposals were set out in full in a double-page spread, while a leader written by Jay explained why compulsion had become necessary, and looked forward to its further development:

> The bargaining power of labour, even in a buyer's market, has not been reduced, nor has the gap between the desired annual increase in living standards and the actual rate of increase in national productivity been eliminated since 1969. Thus, the task facing incomes policy in Britain is different from and much greater than in the United States, where the need was only to overcome inflationary expectations left over from a past period of excess demand.
>
> For this reason Phase Three, *and indeed an indefinite succession of Phases to Phase N*, are of critical importance in the United Kingdom . . . It may well be true that unlimited [i.e. free] collective bargaining ended in Britain on November 6 last year [when Phase One began].
>
> There is really little need to weep copiously for it.[1]

This leader may be regarded as a classic statement of the *dirigiste*

1 'Fair, workable and necessary', January 18 1973. (Author's italics.)

approach. In Britain trade unions were so strong that control of inflation could be reconciled with a reasonable level of employment only by state management of pay and prices – that was the argument. But if unions were so strong, how in the last resort was the state to enforce its pay norms? Jay's argument, and the government's policy, surely assumed tacit labour assent to what the government laid down. In the absence of such assent the power of the unions was bound to tell – since the discipline of unemployment was still taboo.

When the miners' overtime ban was imminent, a leader in the paper denounced it as 'deplorable', while calling for tough measures to meet the threat:

> By taking industrial action when the country's need for domestically produced energy resources is at its most critical for many years, the miners stand to alienate the very public sympathy which supported their last fight with the government . . . The last dispute gave rise to unexpected and effective sanctions such as the picketing of power stations. This time the Government must be prepared to move more swiftly and with greater competence to counteract the impact of a determined body of men insistent upon imposing their will on the nation.[1]

The author of this leader was Paul Routledge, a young red-headed Yorkshireman who had recently taken over Macbeath's job. The son of a railway worker, Routledge was very different from the man he replaced. Whereas Macbeath was a leftishly-inclined but uncommitted member of the middle-class clerisy, Routledge was a working-class cradle Labourite with views well to the left, but robustly concerned with getting on. After grammar school and university (Nottingham), where he read philosophy and English, he became a Westminster Press trainee, having discarded his earlier ambition to be an academic. In 1969 he was writing on industry for the *Sheffield Telegraph* when he was recruited for *The Times*'s labour staff. He was only twenty-seven when he succeeded Macbeath, and his pride in doing such an important job for *The Times* took precedence over ideology.[2] His relations with Rees-Mogg were as good as Macbeath's had been bad, partly because he did not make the mistake of becoming so closely involved in trade union affairs within the office, but above all for reasons of temperament. Each man felt he knew where he was with the other. Routledge

1 'The miners' new threat', November 9 1973.
2 Ideology prevailed, however, during the Wapping dispute in the 1980s, when he was sacked for joining the strike.

had excellent trade union contacts, not least within the NUM, and one of his best sources was the union's communist vice-president, Mick McGahey. When McGahey threatened to withhold information if Routledge continued to write leaders critical of the union, Routledge obtained the editor's permission to stop actually writing them, but instead to advise on their contents: a jesuitical solution that would have shocked Macbeath.[1]

On November 14 the paper's lead story on the state of emergency just proclaimed had the headline 'Lights go out as emergency powers bite'. In the same issue a leader by Jay ended:

> The Government have made serious mistakes in the framing of their policy, but their mistakes have been made in the honest attempt to combine economic growth with a reduction of the rate of inflation. If their policies are now to fail, there is little prospect that an alternative government would be able to achieve growth or to contain inflation. They deserve therefore to be given support in what they are trying to do.[2]

About a fortnight later another leader, also written by Jay, gave firm backing to the government's stand against the miners:

> . . . the cost of buying the NUM off is to admit that democratic government in Britain cannot keep inflation down . . . that democratic government cannot govern. And if democracy cannot produce the essentials of government, democracy itself will not be able to survive.[3]

Mistakes in the government's policy were chiefly identified by the paper with the chancellor of the exchequer, Barber. Before his budget in March a leader had called in vain for 'a substantial general increase in personal taxation', suggesting that a neutral budget would be 'dangerously beguiling'.[4] The crisis budget in December was condemned in the strongest terms, and Barber's removal demanded. 'Of course there are great psychological difficulties in shifting a chancellor at a time like this. But they are not so great as the psychological opportunity which Mr. Barber missed yesterday'.[4] Did Rees-Mogg

1 Routledge talking to author. Other sources on the far left were cultivated through the *Morning Star*, with which he had close relations.
2 'We cannot afford the cost of surrender', November 27 1973.
3 'It should be a tough budget', February 28 1973.
4 'Not much of a budget', December 18 1973.

remember, as he attacked Barber for inflationary tax cuts the year before, which he now had an 'obsessive concern' to protect, that *The Times* had then questioned whether the 1972 budget had been reflationary enough? The government's supreme task was then, in *The Times*'s view, not the fight against inflation but the fight against unemployment.[1]

Between Jay's leader calling for a tough budget in March and Rees-Mogg's attack on Barber's December package the editor's position had decisively shifted. Jay had called for a cut in the budget deficit of at least £1,000 million and for reining back the prospective growth in home demand by the equivalent of about 1½ per cent of national output, from 5 per cent to 3½ per cent. Nevertheless, when Barber took the gamble of allowing the economy to continue to expand at 5 per cent a year or more, Rees-Mogg in his leader on the budget was by no means unqualified in his condemnation. While arguing that *The Times* would have preferred a more prudent budget, and while ending on a note of foreboding, he admitted the possibility that the chancellor's policy might succeed:

> There is room for widely different judgments. The Chancellor's plunge is neither necessarily nor obviously disastrous. But it is certainly incautious, and we fear that it is ill-judged.[2]

By the end of the year his conversion to fiscal stringency was complete.

In bringing it about Jay was undoubtedly the principal influence. As economics editor, and as a close friend, he more than anyone had the editor's ear on the subject. His own conversion to monetarism, though somewhat confused by earlier allegiances, had started soon after he joined *The Times*. He quite often had occasion to visit Washington for short periods, and in 1969 was sent there for the whole year (from January to December) to cover the beginning of the Nixon administration. In Washington he saw much of a Treasury friend, Geoffrey Bell, who was on secondment there at the embassy. Bell introduced him to American monetarists, and himself persuasively endorsed their arguments. Jay's mind was thus changed, and he in turn gradually changed Rees-Mogg's.[3]

---

1 See p. 223 above

2 Leader, 'Mr. Barber's big gamble', March 7 1973.

3 He did not at all share the editor's whimsical desire to return to the gold standard, but may have regarded it as a step in the right direction.

Jay remained, however, considerably attached – in the intellectual as well as the personal sense – to his old mentor, Nicholas Kaldor, who regarded monetarism as nonsense and was a strong believer in incomes policy, including taxation, as the appropriate cure for inflation. We thus find Jay simultaneously advocating tighter fiscal discipline and the statutory control of prices and incomes. We also find him, in his leader before the March 1973 budget, proposing higher taxes as the means of reducing home demand. He convinced himself that, while it was necessary to reduce government expenditure as the only effective way of fighting inflation, it was also necessary to control prices and incomes for the purpose of maintaining employment at the highest possible level. He and, through him, *The Times* were, therefore, far from advocating what was to become the 'Thatcherite' policy of free collective bargaining subject to monetary control, to the accompaniment of drastic cuts in personal taxation and steeply rising unemployment. But they were equally far from what had, until very recently, been the paper's clearly proclaimed policy.

XVI

The fall of Heath • May days in Ulster • The move to Gray's Inn Road

DURING THE FIRST two months of 1974 there was mounting industrial and political conflict culminating in a general election. In the New Year honours a peerage was awarded to Victor (Vic) Feather, who had recently retired as general secretary of the TUC. Though Heath's arch-opponent on trade union reform, Feather was congenial to the prime minister as a man of aesthetic sensibility. His successor, Lionel (Len) Murray, was markedly less so, inspiring at the time a distrust among leading Conservatives for which there was insufficient justification. In the same honours list there was only one knighthood for a Conservative MP, illustrating the fact that Heath had departed from Macmillan's practice of using to the full the prime minister's honours patronage as a means of keeping his backbenchers in line. This virtuous self-denial was to contribute to Heath's loss of the party leadership the following year.

Three op. ed. pieces in the first week of January focused attention on the miners' executive, with which the author, Routledge, had close contacts. The six Communists on the executive were, he said, dedicated to one objective in the union's rule book, that the NUM should 'join with other organisations for the purpose of, and with a view to, the complete abolition of capitalism'. The influence of the hard left had been growing in recent years. In addition to the outright Communists there were five left-wingers who normally sided with them. The leader of this group was the thirty-five-year-old Arthur Scargill, a Marxist who had left the Communist party in 1962 but who still found the Labour party 'far too liberal' for his liking. Even the sixteen moderates on the executive had become less moderate. 'In a world desperately short of energy the miner has recalculated his worth to society'.[1] A leader by Stephenson hinted that the government might

1 'Why miners look to the left wing for leadership', January 3 1974; 'Newcomers who hardened the miners' line', January 4 1974; 'Why the moderates of the NUM are behaving less moderately', January 7 1974 – all by Routledge.

have to reconsider its pay policy. Though hitherto it had had 'little option but to insist on the integrity of the Phase Three pay code', nevertheless 'since the recent dramatic change in the relative price of oil and coal, the industry as a whole could reasonably bear a higher wage bill, particularly if this was coupled with genuine productivity agreements'.[1]

This theme was developed by Rees-Mogg in a leader the following week, on the day Parliament was recalled to debate the crisis. Since neither of the big parties was free from blame for the miners' dispute, there should be 'a fair and constructive settlement' of it which both would back. The government could not be 'seen to be defeated' by the NUM; yet there should be 'a comprehensive revision of the expansion plans of the mining industry', designed to bring the level of miners' wages 'quickly' to the level at which all the new labour needed by the industry could be recruited. There should be some increase even within Phase Three for the year 1974–5, and 'substantial further increases in terms of real earnings for the years after that'.[2] But how could the miners be satisfied without any appearance of defeat for the government? And was the recruitment of more miners, in any case, the right way to expand the industry and make it more efficient?

Heath was under pressure from free marketeers in the Tory Party to scrap his prices and incomes policy altogether. In a speech early in the New Year the strongest advocate of this view, Enoch Powell, described the policy as 'bogus'. Did the government need 'to treat every wage bargain and every price change as if it were a cause and not a symptom of inflation'? And was it really necessary 'to pretend that a sophisticated interpretation of a price and pay code which would have baffled the theologians of the Middle Ages [was] a self-evident requirement of the national interest, which only a communist or a traitor could dispute'?[3] Most Tories, however, still accepted the case for wage and price restraint, and anyway wanted the government to stand up to the miners. The belief grew in the minds of leading figures, notably Carrington and Prior, that there would have to be an appeal to the country. George Clark was soon reporting on the front page: 'There is no doubt that Conservative Central Office has been alerted by the party managers to the possibility of a sudden dissolution of Parliament for a snap election if the Government finds the country is ungovernable'.[4]

1 Leader, 'A ruinous dispute', January 3 1974.
2 Leader, 'The duty of the House', January 9 1974.
3 Speech at Derby, reported in the paper (p.2) on January 9 1974.
4 January 10 1974.

Unlike most of his advisers Heath was extremely reluctant to have an election, and surely he was right. Very few elections are decided on a single issue, whatever the hopes and intentions of those who seek the people's verdict. The Heath government had a working majority and a mandate to govern which still had nearly eighteen months to run. By asking the question 'Who governs Britain?' the Tories would be inviting the voters to reply, in effect: 'You are meant to be governing, and if you find the country ungovernable there must be something wrong with you'. Given the chance to vote, the people would be likely to take all current grievances into account, refusing to be limited to the one issue which the government chose to emphasise. Heath's reluctance to hold a snap election on the constitutional issue was, therefore, justified. But the challenge from the miners still had to be faced, and Heath failed to see that there were only two practical responses to it: either to present a totally unyielding front whatever the consequences, or to settle at once whatever the cost. By dithering between these two courses he found himself after all fighting a snap election, but without the credibility needed to win it.

In the third week of January the TUC offered him a way out with some vestige of honour. He was told that an immediate and generous settlement with the miners would not be used by other unions as an excuse for higher wage claims, and it was obvious from lobby briefing at the time ('Prospects of snap election fade'[1]), that he was interested in the offer. But when it became apparent that other unions would not commit themselves to precise figures, he felt that Phase Three as a whole was threatened and the negotiation broke down. Probably Phase Three was doomed anyway and should have been reconsidered in the light of new world economic conditions. What is certain is that Heath's rejection of the TUC's face-saving formula deprived him of his best chance, at that stage, of avoiding catastrophe.

Crossman, identifying himself mischievously with the view of Tory hard-liners, wrote in his column: 'At the moment when the Prime Minister should have abruptly broken off relations and declared war, Ted was still hankering for one more talk with Len'. Why did he falter when it seemed he would go for a February 7 election? 'For this disastrous about turn for the Government, the main credit must go to the TUC'.[2] If Crossman was suggesting that the TUC deliberately trapped Heath into forfeiting a great political advantage, the suggestion seems doubly unfair. The TUC was, in fact, scarcely less

1 Front-page report by John Groser of the political staff, January 21 1974.
2 Personal View, January 23 1974.

apprehensive than Heath of the consequences of all-out industrial strife; and it cannot be assumed that a February 7 election would have gone any better for the Tories than the one actually held at the end of the month.

After the failure of the TUC's initiative the NUM at once announced that it would ballot its members on a national pit strike, and Heath further delayed his appeal to the country in the hope that the rank-and-file would prove less militant than their leaders. But militancy was in the air. The vote for strike action was overwhelming, and meanwhile the train drivers (ASLEF) also had decided on a series of one-day strikes. The prospect of another general strike began to loom, and Ronald Butt argued that Heath would be less well placed than Baldwin in 1926 to defeat a *levée en masse* by organised labour: 'the very fact that [the government] cannot, apparently, see a way forward to victory without recourse to an election is an indication that it is more vulnerable in its confrontation with the unions than the Baldwin Government was'. Butt concluded that there should be a new Conservative government, and a new policy, without an election.[1]

On February 6 the paper's lead story was that the NUM had called a pit strike from the following Sunday, and David Wood reported that Heath was at last preparing for an election, the necessity for which was accepted by Rees-Mogg in his leader the same day.[2] Two days later the paper announced that the election would be held on February 28, and the front page also carried the news that Powell would not be standing in what he called an 'essentially fraudulent' election.[3] The campaign that followed was the shortest for forty years. As in 1970, Rees-Mogg was stirred to a marathon effort: nineteen leaders between February 4 and March 5. In other respects, too, the paper's election coverage was much the same as on the previous occasion. There were regular opinion polls, provided this time by Opinion Research Centre (ORC), with commentary again by Richard Rose; area and constituency reports by members of the staff; and op. ed. pieces giving background and explaining the issues. Instead of the 'Minority View' pieces (ostensibly by people outside politics, but in fact largely by well-known establishment figures), there were articles under the heading 'Independent View', whose authors were even more narrowly selected and

1 'Why Mr. Heath may not be able to count on the spirit of '26', January 31 1974.
2 Leader, 'Only the nation can decide'. Rees-Mogg had supported Heath's delaying tactics. For instance, on January 29: 'For the next ten days the aim should be to see whether, after all, it is possible for Britain to be pulled back from the brink.' (Leader, 'The harshest of harsh choices'.)
3 February 8 1974.

hardly to be described as independent, since they were all politicians standing in the election.[1]

In his opening broadcast Heath took his stand on firm government, while at the same time saying that the pay board would undertake a study of pay relativities, with the miners at the top of the list, and that the resulting recommendations would be backdated. Wilson ridiculed this as 'the most remarkable election platform of all time', in which Heath was asking for a mandate to pay the miners after the election what he refused to pay them before it. 'For the first time in history' a general was leading his troops into battle 'with the deliberate aim of giving in' if he won.

Though Rees-Mogg gave the government solid support in his leaders, some articles on the op. ed. page were markedly less helpful. For instance, Routledge pointed out that during the three-and-a-half years of Tory rule 'a quite staggering total of 50,605,000 working days were lost through strikes, compared with 21,729,000 during the entire life of the last Labour Government'. The industrial relations act had had 'little discernible effect on the number of stoppages', though if anything the toll had been greater during the two years since it came into operation. The explosion of militancy could not be blamed simply on left-wing leadership in the unions, though that had contributed. With the benefit of hindsight the source of conflict could be traced to the breakdown of Labour's 'severe restraint' period following its statutory incomes policy. Routledge was, in effect, saying that the fundamental error was the attempt to control incomes: a critique which chimed with that of the radical right.[2]

In mid-campaign the Conservative and Labour programmes were coolly assessed by Jay in an op. ed. piece:

> So the choice comes to this. Mr. Barber depends on strict control of pay, plus the greater credit of his party in private financial circles abroad and with the Arabs, to avoid a sharp jump in taxes and to live with a balance of payments deficit of up to £5,000 million. Mr. Healey depends on a better balanced budget and a smaller balance of payments deficit with the implied threat of

---

1 The authors were: St John Stevas, Maudling and David Walder (Conservative); Shirley Williams, Raymond Fleet and Brian Walden (Labour); Grimond and David Steel (Liberal); and Dick Taverne (Democratic Labour). There was no representative of the Labour left.

2 'How unions found that confrontation pays', February 15 1974. It was ingenious to identify the policy of wage restraint as the prime culprit, to which left-wing trade union leaders and the Industrial Relations Act were alike only accessories.

> unemployment to help him hold the pound up while paying out more rope to those who earn. Neither promises big prizes until the crock of gold at the end of the North Sea rainbow is reached.[1]

Since Heath's open-ended commitment to the relativities review had thrown doubt on the government's 'strict control of pay', readers could hardly fail to take Jay's argument as favouring his father's and father-in-law's party, despite his apparent objectivity.

Whereas in 1970 economic statistics had been a plague to Labour, in 1974 they were a much worse plague to the Conservatives, chiefly because the statistics themselves were so much worse. The unemployment, inflation and balance of payments figures were harmful enough, but in addition there were disconcerting noises-off from unexpected quarters. In January, before the election was called, the governor of the Bank of England, Gordon Richardson, forecast 'years of economic austerity' until the huge trade deficit was corrected. During the campaign a press briefing on behalf of Sir Frank Figgures, chairman of the Pay Board, suggested that the statistics of miners' pay on which the government had based its negotiating position were significantly incorrect. The government denied this, but the 'Figgures figures' were obviously a gift to Labour. No less so was a statement shortly before polling day by the director-general of the CBI, Campbell Adamson, to the effect that the Industrial Relations Act had sullied relations between employers and the unions.

But probably the most damaging blow of all was struck by Powell. Not content with refusing to stand in the election, he intervened in the last week of the campaign in support of Labour, on the specific ground that Labour alone would give the country a chance to reconsider its membership of the European Communities. Rees-Mogg noted that he had thus made common cause with Benn. 'It is ironic, and has an agreeable flavour of the absurd, particularly when one remembers how *The Times* defended Mr. Powell in the 1970 election against Mr. Benn's Belsen speech'. Like Benn, Powell was both ultra-nationalist and an opponent of incomes policy. 'What the Labour Party has come to accept because of the influence of the trade unions, he believes as part of a rigid intellectual structure'.[2]

Despite all the adverse factors, opinion polls showed the Conservatives taking the lead early in the campaign and maintaining it, by varying margins, to the end. But they also showed growing support

1 'A choice between two risky cures for our economic ills', February 18 1974.
2 Leader, 'An endorsement to be feared', February 21 1974.

for the Liberals under their ebullient leader, Jeremy Thorpe. On February 25 (as ORC gave them 21 per cent to Labour's 35 and the Tories' 41) the main headline on the paper's front page was 'Liberals go for majority as party climbs in polls', accompanied by a picture of Thorpe vaulting a barrier in Barnstaple. The same day Rees-Mogg reacted to the Liberal revival with some ambivalence. 'In this crisis the Liberals are not a significant party. They are, in our hope and belief, a very significant party in the broader future of British politics'. Earlier in the campaign he had advised that Liberal candidates should be voted for wherever they already held seats, but that even sympathisers should refrain from voting for them elsewhere, in view of the 'need to face this direct challenge to our national life'.[1] His evident concern was to prevent them letting Labour in by splitting the vote in the current election, though he wanted them to be available to help de-socialise the left after another Tory victory.

Levin, too, hoped that a realignment of the left might follow from the election, and was therefore convinced of the necessity to vote Conservative. 'I want a Tory victory because it is only through a Labour defeat that the mass party structure of the left can be recaptured for the social-democracy in which I believe'.[2] On the morning of polling day it seemed that his hope might be realised. 'Four polls show Conservatives holding lead' was the paper's top headline on February 28, and its own ORC prediction was that the percentages for the three main parties would be Conservatives 38.7, Labour 34.9, Liberals 23. But the day before ORC had shown a narrower Conservative lead over Labour (36½ per cent to 35) and this proved the more reliable pointer. On March 1 the lead story was 'Mr. Heath's general election gamble fails', and the following day 'Political crisis as election leads to deadlock'.

No party had won outright, and for the second time since 1945 the party with the largest number of votes did not win the largest number of seats.[3] The Conservatives, with 37.9 per cent of the vote, had 297 seats in the new Parliament, whereas Labour with 37.1 per cent had 301. It was the Liberals, however, who suffered most severely from the injustice of the system, obtaining only fourteen seats in return for a 19.3 per cent share of the poll and over six million votes. By contrast, the Scottish Nationalists with only 2 per cent of the poll and barely a

---

1 Leader, 'Holding the Liberal beach head', February 13 1974.
2 'On voting Conservative for the first and I hope the last time', February 26 1974.
3 The previous occasion was 1951, when Labour received a larger aggregate vote than the Conservatives, but twenty-six fewer seats.

tenth the number of votes won seven seats. Rees-Mogg, an electoral reformer, was quick to emphasise the cost to the country of a system which so distorted the will of the people. 'A proportional system would in fact have produced a more stable parliament than the one we have elected in 1974 . . . It would have allowed a Liberal Conservative or a Liberal Labour grouping to form a coalition with the clear prospect of a full parliament ahead of it, and with a clear overall majority'.[1]

Even with the Liberals grossly under-represented the chance of a Liberal-Conservative coalition was explored. Heath did not at once resign, but entered into negotiations with Thorpe, to whom he offered a Cabinet post (with a few lesser posts for other Liberals) and a common agreed programme. But on electoral reform he proposed only a Speaker's conference, which was not enough for the Liberals.[2] The offer was rejected and on March 4 Heath resigned. Next day's lead story was 'Mr. Wilson is back in Downing Street', and Rees-Mogg's valedictory comment on the outgoing prime minister was succinct. 'Mr. Heath has gone. As a Prime Minister he was a man of serious purpose and absolute integrity of character. He lacks some of the qualities of a politician.'[3]

In Northern Ireland the evidence that trade union militancy had, at the very least, contributed to the downfall of a government was not lost on hard-line Unionists outraged by the power-sharing executive and, above all, by the 'Irish dimension' foreshadowed in the Sunningdale agreement. Early in the New Year Faulkner lost control of his Official Unionist Party whose new leader, Harry West, formed an alliance with Paisley's Democratic Unionists and William Craig's Vanguard Party to fight the February election. This alliance (the UUUC) won a sweeping victory in the election, taking eleven of the twelve Ulster seats at Westminster. The election thus had the most unfortunate effect of depriving the power-sharing executive of democratic

1 Leader, 'Facing the challenge of events', March 2 1974.

2 When the Liberals under Lloyd George held the balance in the 1929 Parliament, they enabled Labour to form a government in return for a Speaker's conference. But this became a cockpit of party rivalry and, with Labour implacably opposed to PR, the best that the Liberals could obtain from it was a reform bill incorporating the alternative vote (AV), which sank with the Labour government in 1931. At the beginning of 1917 a more united Speaker's conference had recommended PR for the big cities, but Lloyd George as Coalition premier then poured cold water on the idea and it was not implemented – with consequences disastrous to himself and his party, as well as (arguably) the nation.

3 Leader, 'The return of Mr. Wilson', March 5 1974.

legitimacy and moral authority before it had had time to demonstrate its value to the people at large. (It had been in office for only two months.)

Meanwhile the IRA, which for its own reasons was as hostile as the Unionists to Sunningdale, was intensifying its campaign. Soon after the election Belfast's main thoroughfare, Royal Avenue, was ravaged by a bomb left outside the former Grand Central Hotel, which had been turned into a military barracks. This and other manifestations of IRA violence greeted the new secretary of state, Merlyn Rees. Rees, who had been shadowing the post under the Heath government, was a well-meaning man with a good war record in the RAF. But he did not convey an impression of decisiveness and soon became suspect among Unionists when the IRA leaked an indiscreet letter he had written the previous year to a Dundalk housewife. This was reported in the same issue of the paper as a statement by Wilson in parliament to the effect that the IRA was planning a scorched earth policy in Belfast.[1]

Scarcely noticed in Britain on the day Wilson spoke, and the IRA leaked Rees's letter, was a warning from a new body, the Ulster Workers' Council, that there would be a general strike in the province if the assembly ratified the Sunningdale agreement. This warning was disregarded and the following day, May 14, the agreement was debated, receiving conditional endorsement by a majority of forty-four to twenty-eight.[2] The ensuing scene at Stormont was described and commented on by Fisk in a report appearing on page 2:

> A few minutes after the members had left the chamber, Mr. James Patterson, a member of the Ulster Workers' Council, arrived at Stormont and told journalists that electricity workers would, as a result, reduce the power supply in the city tonight to an extent where industry would be forced to shut down. Most of the workers

---

1 Lead story, May 14 1974. The story of the leaked letter also began on the front page but ran on to page 2, where the full text of the letter was printed together with a photograph of part of it. Dated March 19 1973, the letter was written by Rees to a Mrs. Catherine Adams in reply to one from her. The damaging words were these: 'We have not the faintest desire to stay in Ireland and the quicker we are out the better'. Though Rees went on to say that Cosgrave and Fitt had told him the position of the minority in Northern Ireland would be very difficult if the British withdrew, the passage about wanting to withdraw as soon as possible could all too easily be quoted out of context. Mrs. Adams had probably been put up to writing to Rees, since she now admitted that she was '100 per cent behind the IRA'.

2 The endorsement was conditional upon all the terms of the agreement being honoured by all the parties. If, for instance, the Republic failed to deliver its side of the bargain in the matter of extradition, the endorsement would no longer apply.

> at the Ballylumford power station near Belfast are Protestants and in the past they have caused industrial disruption.
>
> There seems little or no enthusiasm among loyalists for an all-out strike and the UWC's claim to a membership of 58,000 should be taken with a very large pinch of salt indeed.
>
> The Government remained apparently indifferent to the threat of a power strike last night and *it seems likely that Belfast will suffer no more than a slight loss of power during the daytime hours*.[1]

In making what he later called 'the devastating mistake' of underrating the seriousness of the UWC threat, Fisk was in good company. Not only the government but all the other British journalists in Northern Ireland made the same mistake. The only journalist to get it right was a member of the *Irish Times*'s Belfast staff, David McKittrick, but the gloom of his reports was not reflected in the editorials of his paper, which continued to give a bland view of the situation until a very late stage.[2] Fisk had excellent contacts in many key sectors of Ulster life, including the army, the RUC and the IRA. But he had neglected the Protestant working class, which was now to assert itself with formidable effect.[3]

An organisation of loyalist workers had existed for some time, but Sunningdale brought the UWC, as such, into being, and more importantly drove it into alliance with the Protestant paramilitaries. Among the outstanding figures in the workers' movement were Hugh Petrie, a precision engineer at Short Brothers', Billy Kelly, a convenor from the Belfast east power station, Tom Beattie from Ballylumford, and Harry Murray from the Harland and Wolff shipyard. But while the February election was in progress Glenn Barr, an Ulster Defence Association (UDA) officer who was also a Vanguard representative in the assembly, was elected chairman of the UWC. Loyalist politicians tended at first to be uneasy about a political strike and reluctant to commit themselves; but Vanguard had the closest links with the UWC and provided space in its offices for the strike headquarters.

On May 15 the strike duly began. Workers left the power stations, at once reducing their output to 60 per cent of normal. Gradually factories and shops closed down, as to the loss of power was added considerable intimidation of hesitant workers. Uniformed UDA men

---

1 May 15 1974. (Author's italics.)
2 Robert Fisk, *The Point of No Return*. This full account of the Ulster workers' strike was published by Times Books and André Deutsch in 1975.
3 Fisk talking to author.

appeared on the streets and erected road blocks, unhindered by the police. For the first two days of the strike Fisk's reports of it appeared on the front page, though not as the lead stories.[1] On the third day the paper led with the news of car bombs in Dublin which had killed twenty-eight people. Both the IRA and the UDA denied responsibility for this outrage, but it was generally thought to be the work of some Protestant group. By the end of the first week of the strike many parts of the province were experiencing daily power cuts of up to six hours, and food supplies as well as all other economic activity were suffering.

Rees refused to talk to the UWC, but failed to act resolutely to break its growing control of the province's life. Had the RUC been instructed at the outset to dismantle the barricades, with support from the army if necessary, the battle of wills would probably have been won by the government. But Rees seems to have hoped that the UWC would collapse on its own, without any physical intervention by the forces of law and order. At the end of the week he declared a state of emergency, while continuing to assure Faulkner that he would not allow the strike to succeed. But he still took no action to match his words, and a secret reconnaissance of Ballylumford by military technicians in disguise brought him the information that it would be impossible for the army to run the power stations without help from UWC workers. Nevertheless, at the beginning of the second week *The Times* argued in a leader that troops 'must be used to secure the sustenance and safety of the civil population'. In the same issue Fisk described, on the op. ed. page, 'how the militants took power away from the politicians.[2]

On the Tuesday the lead story was that 500 more troops were being sent to Ulster as the strike took a 'stranglehold'. But what was the point of reinforcing an army which was not to be used? Fisk in a separate story reported signs of division on the executive, where the SDLP members were understandably suspicious and restive.[3] The same day Len Murray came over from England to lead a 'back to work' march in Belfast, but only a handful joined him and, despite heavy protection, he was pelted and spat on. A front-page picture recorded his discomfiture more eloquently than any words.[4] The following day Fisk's lead story reported that the strike had won its first political victory:

1 May 16 and 17 1974.
2 May 20 1974. The leader, 'The Protestant offensive', was written by Hickey, as were all the leaders on Ulster during the crisis.
3 May 21 1974.
4 May 22 1974.

> After almost resigning *en bloc* during a long and heated discussion at Stormont yesterday Mr. Brian Faulkner's coalition Executive watered down the Sunningdale agreement, reducing greatly for three years and possibly forever the powers of the proposed . . . council of Ireland. But their gesture did nothing to appease the 'loyalists' whose general strike continued to keep Ulster's industrial and commercial life in a state of atrophy.

This story was illustrated by a picture of the commander of a UDA patrol on a Belfast barricade. In an op. ed. piece Fisk suggested that there might be a future for power-sharing, but only between the SDLP and hard-line Unionists after a new Assembly election in which the latter would unquestionably be swept to power. In the same issue a leader, quite out of touch with reality, commended the Wilson government for its 'firmness' in meeting the challenge of the strike.[1]

In fact, Wilson was as weak in action as his secretary of state, though for a time equally tough-talking. On the Thursday he had three members of the executive, Faulkner, Fitt and the Alliance leader, Napier, over for a meeting at Chequers, at which he assured them that troops would be used to maintain vital supplies. A broadcast by him was announced for Saturday, and it was expected by the executive and the UWC alike that he would impose martial law. But when he spoke he did nothing of the kind. The speech was worse than an anticlimax because, while taking no practical steps against the strikers, he united the whole Protestant community behind them and against himself by an ill-judged reference to 'people who spend their lives sponging on Westminster and British democracy'. Glenn Barr commented later that Wilson deserved to be made an honorary member of the UWC, because 'any hope he had of wrecking the strike went with that speech'.[2]

Three days later the executive resigned and Ulster's brief power-sharing experiment came to an end. In an op. ed. piece Fisk conducted a post-mortem. 'Power-sharing excluded the loyalists and . . . the coalition had a larger minority against it when it fell today than did the old Stormont government in the final days of its power two years ago'. The executive had shown a lack of sensitivity, which Wilson had compounded by his broadcast.[3] There was rejoicing in Protestant areas of Belfast as the assembly was prorogued and the council of Ireland aborted.

---

1 May 23 1974. Op. ed. piece, 'What future is there for power-sharing in Ulster?'. Leader, 'A move to moderation'.
2 Fisk, op. cit., pp.201–2.
3 May 29 1974. Op. ed. piece, 'What went wrong with Ulster's brave experiment?'.

The Times's move from its historic native site at Printing House Square to a site adjoining Thomson House in Gray's Inn Road, where the *Sunday Times* was produced, occurred over the weekend of June 22–23 1974. On the 21st (Friday) the paper did not appear, because of a strike by SOGAT workers which stopped three national dailies. But it did appear the following day, with a valedictory piece on the op. ed. page by Philip Howard:

> This is our last issue from our ancient home; Monday's paper will be published from New Printing House Square, a mile away up the Gray's Inn Road . . . It leaves behind . . . much history and a dear, dusty phantasmagoria of journalists of long ago.

But he suggested that in one sense the break was less painful than it might have been, because the original building, as distinct from the site, had already been abandoned. 'It is not easy to feel sentimental or nostalgic about our present building, a grey, functional block with intimations of a battery hen house, which was opened in 1962'. In any case, it would be unprofessional to indulge in too much introspection: 'what exercises *The Times* now is issue Number 59,122, Monday's paper'.[1]

That issue was produced from the new building, but it was a close run thing. Work on the building, two months delayed by the winter's various industrial troubles, was still far from complete when the move occurred. The industrial basement was just capable of functioning, though it was only on the Saturday that the last linotype machines were swung into place. The first floor (editorial) was usable, but only just; the floors were strewn with wires and there was a great shortage of telephones. The second floor (supplements, commercial departments and sundry tenants) was in an even more rudimentary state, and the third (advertising and marketing), though more advanced, was still awaiting the installation of the ACD system for telesales.[2] The fourth and fifth floors were largely for *Sunday Times* use. The sixth (directorate) and the seventh (board, hospitality and catering) were as behindhand as the second, and would not be in a proper condition for several months. The lifts were not yet working, and the bridge to connect the new building with Thomson House would not be ready until the end of the year.

Nevertheless issue Number 59,122 came out on June 24 (Monday)

1 'Times remembered from 189 years at Printing House Square', June 22 1974.
2 The third floor would also soon have to accommodate new machines prematurely acquired by Thomson for setting the papers by photocomposition, unusable in the absence of agreement with the print unions. (See Chap. XXIII.)

and the fact that the first edition was seventy-five minutes late off the stone was not directly attributable to the move. Ominously, it was due to a last-minute dispute with the printers. The front-page story reporting the move was extremely brief and gave no idea of the chaos in the building, though the accompanying picture showed a tell-tale crane on the roof. There was also a hint of reality in the diary, which began: 'If this Diary ever reaches your eyes, it will mean that our great move from Printing House Square to Gray's Inn Road will have been completed. To say that it has been completed successfully would be tempting fate'.[1]

On the Friday there had been a farewell party for the editorial staff at Printing House Square, held in the boardroom and organised by Heren. Despite an abundance of champagne (which the management would otherwise have left behind) the 'party became a wake', because 'nobody wanted to go'. Moreover, while the journalists were trying to drown their sorrows, 'the floors below the boardroom were being stripped of machinery, furniture, files and the library'.[2] On the Sunday Enid Knowles collected the remains of this cold supper and took them to Gray's Inn Road, where she served them across the half-built wall of the editor's outer office to journalists too busy to leave their desks.[3]

To most of the *Times* staff the move to Gray's Inn Road proved as unwelcome in fact as it had been in prospect. Some found the new building no worse than the 'old', but they were a minority. The relatively open-plan design of the editorial floor was not generally popular, and the architecture of the building – by Richard Seifert and Partners, the creators of Centre Point – had few admirers. Above all the area of Gray's Inn Road, and more especially the upper end of it towards King's Cross, was considered far less pleasant and convenient than the Blackfriars area. Those members of the staff – a fair number – who had chosen to live in south or south-east London to give themselves easy access to work were faced with a longer and more difficult journey. Gray's Inn Road was altogether less well served by public transport; in particular, it was less handy for Parliament and the City. It also had a bad reputation gastronomically. Four days before the move the management produced a booklet listing among other things, all the restaurants, coffee houses and hotels in the area; but no amount of propaganda could make it seem an attractive *quartier*.

1 Diary, 'A tender and moving experience', June 24 1974. An Olympian leader, 'A day in two centuries', looked back over the paper's past and discussed how its role, and that of the press in general, had changed.
2 Heren, op. cit. p.236.
3 Enid Knowles to author, April 9 1990.

Though the move had been undertaken for business reasons, it turned out to be an utter calamity from the business point of view. As has been indicated earlier,[1] the sale of Printing House Square to the *Observer* had been on terms astonishingly favourable to the buyer, and the disadvantage to the seller was compounded by the need to stay on the old site two months beyond the agreed date, because of the delay in work on the new. *The Times* had to pay the *Observer* rent of a quarter of a million pounds for use of the premises and plant at Printing House Square for the extra two months, while at the same time roughly the same amount was demanded to compensate the *Observer* for damages claimed from them by a prospective tenant (Lazard Brothers), whose occupancy was delayed by *The Times*'s inability to move out.

The magic word to justify the upheaval was integration. Ever since the Thomson take-over the prospect of achieving greater efficiency and massive economies by treating the two papers as a single enterprise had danced before the eyes of management like a will-o'-the-wisp. Despite the evident failure of early attempts to merge journalistic operations, more especially abroad, the principle of integration was never re-examined, and the decision to move *The Times* to Gray's Inn Road was the most baleful consequence of the integrationist fixation.

Once the decision was taken, with a definite (if over-optimistic) date for implementation, the management was open to trade union blackmail. This soon took the form of insistence by the staff of the *Sunday Times* that Thomson House should be refurbished to the level of amenity that would notionally be enjoyed in the new building; and the cost of refurbishment ran to nearly one and a quarter million pounds. As the date for moving approached there were threats of non-cooperation from sections of the *Times* staff. Union general secretaries were then told that no further on-cost could be accepted, and were given to understand that the management was prepared, if necessary, to close both papers down.[2] Nevertheless the cost of meeting the postponed deadline, in bribes to the unions, was far beyond anything anticipated.

The only benefit of integration was the reduction of the total labour force by 228 and a consequent net saving on the payroll of £486,000, though even this had to be set against the loss of charges to the *Observer* for shared labour, so the true figure of net saving was about £300,000.[3] In other respects integration was a profound disaster,

1 Chap. XIV above.
2 EMC, May 9 1974. The worst trouble was encountered among the clerical staff (NATSOPA).
3 TEMC, September 12 1974.

because it brought the labour force of *The Times*, with its tradition of relative industrial harmony, into close contact with that of the *Sunday Times*, whose tradition was quite the opposite. Whereas *Times* staff on the production side normally held their jobs on a settled basis, most of their opposite numbers on the *Sunday Times* were casual workers without much loyalty to the paper or *esprit de corps*. On the Gresham's Law principle it was the influence of the *Sunday Times* workers that prevailed, with devastating consequences over the next few years. In the worsening climate of British industrial relations *The Times* could not have remained permanently immune in any case, and there had already been signs of trouble even before the move. But beyond question the move accelerated and aggravated the process.

The change of site was not made the occasion for the sort of drastic technological change that was known to be overdue. When the decision to move was taken it was assumed, for no very obvious reason, that the *Guardian* would volunteer to be released early from the contract under which it was printed on the *Sunday Times* presses at Thomson House. This would have enabled *The Times* to be printed on those presses for the time being (the composing equipment at Printing House Square having been sold with the building) until more far-reaching arrangements could be put in hand. In fact, the *Guardian* decided to stay until its contract was up in September 1976, which meant that the industrial basement at Gray's Inn Road had to be equipped immediately for printing *The Times*. The original idea had been to leave it empty until it could be developed for both papers with new technology, including the capacity for a potential *Sunday Times* circulation of two million. But, faced with the need to provide equipment for *The Times* in 1974, the management decided it would not be feasible to install photo-composition simultaneously with the move. The choice, therefore, was between buying new or second-hand machines of the traditional hot-metal kind, and the decision was to buy second-hand, in view of the policy of introducing computerised photo-composition at the earliest opportunity.[1] The American Goss presses that were put in cost nearly half a million pounds – yet another addition to the budgeted cost of the move – and, since they were multi-section presses, not designed for *The Times*'s configuration, created many problems for the men operating them, particularly when the paper ran to more than thirty-two pages.[2]

As the move took effect various messages of goodwill were

---

1 General manager's report on the project, July 1974.
2 TEMC, July 11 1974.

received, and one reader even sent flowers. From his cuckoo-in-the-nest position at Thomson House, John Cole wrote to Rees-Mogg on behalf of the *Guardian*:

> Those of us who have survived since our own 1961 transfer from Fleet Street will think of you with compassion in the early difficult days. We hope that difficulties will pass quickly there, and that you will be happy in your new home.

Rees-Mogg thanked him in a tone of optimism that must have been rather forced:

> We had a good move on the whole though we had a disappointing night last night. It is true I think that the early days are bound to be difficult but we are all enjoying the new building more than most of us expected.[1]

He was similarly upbeat a month later, in reply to a message from his predecessor:

> We have had a bad start in the machine room but apart from that things are going well . . . The advantages of being able to operate the editorial side on a single floor are already becoming manifest.[2]

In the correspondence column there was a pithy letter from the Bishop of Norwich:

> Sir,
> Every good wish for the maintenance of your high standards in your new home. I notice that on the day of your move your Scripture text said 'Depart from evil, and do good'.
> Yours faithfully
> Maurice Norvic.[3]

---

1 John Cole to W.R.-M., undated, but presumably June 24 1974; W.R.-M. to Cole, June 25 1974. Cole was writing as deputy editor, in Alastair Hetherington's absence. In 1961 the *Guardian*, though not yet printing in London, had a London editorial office in Fleet Street.
2 W.R.-M. to Haley, July 23 1974.
3 June 27 1974. The daily text appeared on the back page, under the instructions to classified advertisers and before births. The text in question was from Psalm 34, verse 14.

XVII

Tory heart-searching • The second election of 1974 • Episcopal leg-pull • Conservatives look for a new leader • Mrs Thatcher triumphs • Foreign desk • Sport in the paper

THE SHOCK OF DEFEAT threw the Conservatives into a state of strenuous self-examination, whose eventual consequences were to be drastic. At the heart of the argument was the problem of inflation, now coming to be regarded as an even more deadly menace than unemployment. How was it to be tackled? Rees-Mogg had his own idiosyncratic answer: a return to the gold standard. On May 5 a 'discussion paper on inflation' by him appeared on the op. ed. page under the heading 'Crisis of paper currencies: Has the time come for Britain to return to the gold standard?' – with a picture of Montagu Norman and a box containing a selection of *Times* headlines during the 1931 sterling crisis. 'Is it possible', the editor asked, rhetorically, 'that just as the chronic deflationary disease of the early 1930s was relieved by abandoning the gold standard – a gold standard fixed at too high a rate for the pound – so the chronic inflationary disease of the mid-1970s could be relieved by returning to the gold standard – but to a gold standard fixed at a realistic and competitive rate for the pound?' This option was 'almost unmentioned among the world's leading academic economists, our leading central bankers, or our Treasury officials'.

Not many responded favourably to this article, but one who did was Lord Boothby. In a letter for publication he warmly congratulated Rees-Mogg on suggesting a remedy which he claimed to have advocated himself 'ever since the breakdown of the Bretton Woods agreement'.[1] Another strong, but private, supporter was a former governor of the Bank of England, Lord Cromer,[2] and Rees-Mogg also received a cordial letter from Jacques Rueff, the veteran French economist whose unfashionable views on gold had earlier influenced de Gaulle.

1 Lead letter, May 4 1974.
2 Cromer to W.R.-M., May 2 1974.

Replying, Rees-Mogg acknowledged his own debt: 'I remember with great pleasure our meeting two or three years ago when Charles Hargrove brought me to your house. I need scarcely say that I have been influenced by your work . . .'[1] Later in the year Rees-Mogg published a book expounding his counter-inflationary thesis, which Andrew Shonfield reviewed with considerable rigour on the op. ed. page, endorsing the author's wish to see more effective control of the money supply, while dissenting strongly from his chosen remedy.

A prominent member of what, in due course, would be known as the 'wet' element in the Conservative Party, Ian Gilmour, contributed a pair of articles on the Tory dilemma following the election. In the first he argued that the Heath government, 'like the other great reforming government of the post-war years, the Attlee administration of 1945–50', tried to do too much. Even if all its measures had been perfectly conceived, 'which in the nature of things they were not', the people's appetite for radical reform would have been severely tested. To make matters worse the Labour Party did not live up to its 'better traditions' and accept the 1970 election result. Instead it swung sharply to the left and, except on Northern Ireland, abandoned positions it had taken up in government. Even so, if the Conservatives had won the election, 'at least two of the key issues would have been settled'. By the next election the British would have become accustomed to being in Europe, and the trade unions, 'after substantial amendment of the Industrial Relations Act', would have become reconciled to the rule of law. Only the control of prices and incomes would have remained contentious, and even there the unions would have 'learned the risks of taking on the elected government'. In his second article Gilmour advocated a firm stand on Europe and maintenance of prices and incomes policy in a 'refined' and 'much more flexible' form. Trade union reform, however, should be 'largely omitted from the Conservative programme', since it was 'more of a Labour Party problem than a Conservative one'. The Tories must 'try to heal the country – not divide it'.[2]

Very different, but more indicative of the future course of Conservative policy, was a speech by Sir Keith Joseph at Preston on September 5, reported as next day's lead story by Jay. 'In an extraordinary political testament' Joseph had rejected the whole bipartisan basis of postwar employment policies. How far would Heath and his shadow chancellor, Robert Carr, be 'willing to follow him in giving absolute

1 Rueff to W.R.-M., May 10 1974; W.R.-M. to Rueff, May 21 1974.
2 May 2 and 3 1974.

priority to conquering inflation by controlling the budget deficit and the money supply at whatever temporary loss to employment, living standards, investment and political support'? The speech was bound to provoke a heated debate within the Conservative Party, since it could not be read 'except as a root and branch condemnation of the whole economic strategy followed by Mr. Heath and Mr. Barber from the summer of 1971 to the last election'.[1]

Joseph, a fellow of All Souls, was intellectually one of the most distinguished of the Tory leaders, who for that reason, and by virtue of cabinet seniority, might have expected to be appointed chancellor when Macleod died. But, as we have seen, Heath preferred a more committed European, with whom he could work more easily. Joseph remained at the department of health and social security, where he put through an elaborate reform of the health service's administrative structure, which the next Conservative government felt obliged to unscramble. Earlier, as housing minister under Macmillan, he had been a champion of high-rise residential blocks, which proved a social as well as an architectural disaster. His fine mind was prone to serious errors of judgement, while his temperament was nervy and his conscience apt to be tortured. Nevertheless, with his Preston speech he stepped into the position vacated by Powell, as chief exponent of an alternative Tory strategy. As such he was a challenger for the party leadership.

The speech upstaged one by Wilson to the TUC. This was, indeed, reported at length on pages 4 and 5, but Joseph's was the story of the day, while the full text of it was printed on the op. ed. page (continued on page 16). It was also the subject of a leader by Rees-Mogg, in which the analogy with Powell was noted:

> Sir Keith Joseph's speech . . . is certainly one of the most important political speeches of recent years . . . It will be compared with some of the speeches of Mr. Enoch Powell. Sir Keith is basically monetarist in his view of the problem of inflation, as is Mr. Powell. His speech has the same clarity and like Mr. Powell's best, and worst, speeches is the product of a fine academic mind. Yet Sir Keith Joseph's analysis seems preferable to Mr. Powell's because it shows a deeper understanding of the difficulties of the argument.

---

1 Lead story 'Sir Keith Joseph blames full employment policies for inflation', September 6 1974. Jay might have added that the same strategy had been followed by *The Times*.

The main lines of the speech were 'unquestionably right'. Though there were 'still points of difference' (unspecified) between Joseph's attitude and the paper's, what he had said was 'wise' and came 'with the sharp shock of truth'.[1]

Next day a letter from Lord O'Brien, a former governor of the Bank of England, wholeheartedly endorsing the speech, was used as the paper's lead story. Other letters that day included one from Maudling, in which he contested Joseph's view of the relationship between money supply, unemployment and inflation. This led to an exchange between them, Maudling writing one more letter, Joseph two. Among others who contributed to a week-long correspondence on the speech was Wynne Godley contesting Joseph's facts about the 1950s, and Lord Thorneycroft attacking Powell for not giving Joseph his support but instead giving comfort to Labour.[2]

The controversy over Joseph's Preston speech occurred as the parties were preparing for another election, and it ensured that the Conservatives would enter the contest with the disadvantage of manifest disunity. Not since 1910 had two elections been held within the same calendar year. On the earlier occasion Home Rule for Ireland was a dominating theme, because after the first election the Liberal government was dependent on the Irish National Party for a majority. Similarly, in 1974 Labour was promising parliaments for Scotland and Wales, since the Scottish National Party in particular had become a serious force. Labour's main policy, however, was the 'social contract' which it claimed to have achieved with the trade unions. This was momentarily threatened when, at the TUC conference, the engineers' leader, Hugh Scanlon, announced that his union's block vote would be cast against the policy; but after an appeal from Murray, the TUC's general secretary, he withdrew his motion, and the appearance of unity was maintained. At the same time division on the subject of Europe was avoided by a pledge to let the British people decide within twelve months of the election whether or not to stay in the Common Market.

The Times treated the 'social contract' as spurious. In a leader commenting on Labour's manifesto Rees-Mogg argued that the nation wanted 'a new reconciliation and a new hope'. Granted Labour's

---

1 Leader, 'The sharp shock of truth', September 6 1974.

2 O'Brien's letter, September 7 1974. Maudling's letters, September 7 and 10 1974. Joseph's letters, September 9 and 11 1974. Godley's letter, September 9 1974. Thorneycroft's letter, September 10 1974. Sir Oswald Mosley wrote (September 12 1974) demanding 'comprehensive' rather than 'partial' policies to meet the situation.

historical and organisational links with the trade unions, reconciliation could be provided by the party 'only if there were signs that the moderate men . . . were in control'. Despite Scanlon's volte-face there could be no confidence that they were.[1]

The Liberals fought the election on a policy of 'breaking the mould', and Thorpe talked of the possibility of joining an all-party coalition to implement an agreed economic package. Rees-Mogg, though always ready to sympathise with Liberal aspirations, had to dismiss the policy as, in the circumstances, unrealistic. Realignment would be fine, but:

> Unfortunately this is not the basis on which this election is going to be fought. The leader of the party of realignment would presumably be Mr. Jenkins, and Mr. Jenkins, for better or worse, is not only standing as the Labour candidate for Stechford but is a member of the present Labour Cabinet and seems likely to be a member of the next Labour government if one is formed.[2]

Yet it was only coalition involving Labour that he ruled out. As the campaign developed he argued that the best result would be 'a small overall Conservative majority governing with some Liberal support, or a combined majority for the Conservatives and Liberals'.[3] Levin, for his part, strongly favoured all-party coalition and deplored Thorpe's insistence that Heath must stand down if he and the Liberals were to join one.[4]

Coalition was, in fact, the principal theme of Heath's campaign, though many of his supporters disliked it. Tory policy in the election was largely on the lines recommended by Gilmour in his *Times* articles. Membership of the EEC was strongly reaffirmed, and the need for incomes policy, which might have to be statutory, re-stated. (The best, as well as briefest, judgement on incomes policy during the campaign was made by George Mikes in a letter to the paper. 'Sir, I am no economist but as a careful reader of comments and analyses I am driven to two inescapable conclusions. (1) A voluntary prices and incomes policy cannot work. (2) A compulsory prices and incomes policy cannot work either. Yours faithfully'.)[5] As for trade union

1 Leader, 'Worse than expected', September 17 1974.
2 Leader, 'Better in heart than head', September 18 1974.
3 Leader, 'The best result would be a Conservative-Liberal coalition', October 9 1974.
4 'Now is the time for all good parties to come to the aid of the people', September 18 1974.
5 September 25 1974.

reform, it was made clear that this policy would be treated as expendable for the sake of consensus.

Throughout the campaign *The Times*'s editorial attitude to Tory policy reflected the struggle within the party itself. While there was undiminished support for Heath as the arch-European, and to some extent support for the idea of coalition, there was also growing evidence of movement towards the radical right. Jay, despite his recent advocacy of incomes policy in the most drastic and enduring form, had clearly made up his mind once and for all that monetarism was the only remedy for inflation:

> Those of us whose ivory towers command a lofty view of the meandering progress of postwar policies towards the brink of hyper-inflation find it harder and harder to avoid the conclusion that gradual disinflation by fiscal and monetary means should be the over-riding priority.

Though he added 'ifs' and 'buts', the direction of his thinking was unmistakable.[1] Significant, too, was the exposure given to Joseph in the paper: an op. ed. piece early in the campaign, and no fewer than three letters, two of them long[2] – all additional to the space so recently lavished on his Preston speech and the ensuing controversy.

The election itself was a tired and lacklustre affair. One of the few incidents to mitigate the tedium was described by Philip Howard in his 'Election notebook'. Teresa Moore, standing at Streatham for less government, produced 'the most spectacular visual aid so far' by paying her deposit in real gold, to demonstrate her belief in 'real money' (a candidate, evidently, after the editor's heart).[3] Guest articles on the op. ed. page were, again, almost exclusively by politicians: Joseph, David Howell and Maudling for the Conservatives; Raymond Fletcher, Andrew Faulds and Bryan Magee for Labour; Grimond and Steel for the Liberals; and Powell for the United Ulster Unionists. (Powell said that he was lucky to have found a way of resuming public life without doing violence to his conscience.)[4] Lord Chalfont was given space to explain why, at the beginning of the campaign, he had

1 Op. ed. article, 'Time to break the familiar cycle we stagger round each year', with pictures of Joseph and Healey, October 7 1974.
2 Op. ed. article, 'Inflation: Government has to resist temptation just to print money', September 20 1974. Letters, September 23, October 1 and October 2 1974.
3 September 23 1974.
4 Howell, October 3 1974; Maudling twice, September 27 and October 10 (polling day) 1974. Fletcher, September 25; Faulds, October 2; Magee, October 9 1974. Grimond, September 30; Steel, October 9 1974. Powell October 4 1974.

announced his defection from the Labour Party, and Alec Home to write a valedictory piece on his departure from the House of Commons.[1] There were also pieces by two trade union leaders, David Basnett and Kenneth Gill,[2] and an article by the editor's favourite industrialist, Arnold Weinstock, calling for a more representative electoral system.[3]

As before there were extra news reports, features and analyses. All thirty-nine constituencies with majorities under 1,000 were specially described and assessed, and there were also reports from the regions. The main party leaders were covered by individual reporters: Noyes for Wilson, John Winder for Heath, and Christopher Walker for Thorpe. Three opinion polls by ORC were published during the campaign, which all showed Labour leading, the last two by 9 per cent. A late attempt to recapture votes for the Tories was a pledge, announced by the shadow environment minister, Margaret Thatcher, that mortgage rates would be cut from 11 to 9½ per cent by Christmas. A few days later she promised that the rates would be scrapped by 1979, and reasserted the party's intention to transfer education costs to the Exchequer.[4] She thus gained prominence from the issue of local government finance, which sixteen years later was to prove her undoing.

The actual poll on October 10 confirmed Labour in power, though by a less decisive margin than the straw polls had suggested. The turnout was down 6 per cent compared with February, reflecting the public's lack of interest in the campaign. Even the Labour vote was slightly down, while the Liberal vote dropped by 800,000 and the Conservative by nearly a million and a half. On the other hand the Scottish National Party increased its vote by over 200,000. In seats, Labour had an overall majority of only three, but its majority over the Conservatives increased to forty-two. Rees-Mogg took what comfort he could from the result. In a three-column leader he noted that two particularly bad results had been avoided: an overwhelming Labour majority which would have put the leadership under pressure

---

1 Septemuer 23 1974. Chalfont, as Alun Gwynne-Jones, had been *The Times*'s defence correspondent for three years when, in 1964, he accepted office and a peerage from Harold Wilson – who, asked to comment on the defection, said he was unaware Chalfont was a member of the Labour party. Home re-entered the House of Lords as a life peer.
2 October 8 1974.
3 September 26 1974.
4 September 28 and October 4 1974: both front-page stories, the first with a picture of Mrs. Thatcher.

'to make a further major movement towards socialism', and a situation in which no one had a clear responsibility to govern.[1]

In a heavy year for both the country and the staff of *The Times* there were moments of comic relief, and one such occurred during the second election campaign. On September 25, 26 and 27 the following entry was to be found among the paper's classified advertisements: 'Middle-aged bachelor bishop intending to travel round the world for a year seeks an interesting man to accompany him. Box No. 1509D. *The Times*'. On the last of the three dates this entry also appeared: 'Middle-aged spinster/actress intending to travel round the world for a year seeks interesting bishop to accompany her. Box 2463. *The Times*'.

Both insertions caught the eye of Dr. Mervyn Stockwood, bishop of Southwark, on his return from a visit to Romania, and he lost little time in writing a personal letter to Rees-Mogg, in which, after quoting the advertisements, he said:

> As I am the only bachelor diocesan bishop, and as it has been announced that I am to have Sabbatical leave next year for a world tour, it has been assumed by some people, among whom are some of my brother bishops, that I was responsible for the advertisement . . .
>
> I realise that there are unmarried suffragan bishops and there are also curious people who call themselves bishops but who are not in any recognisable episcopal orders. At the same time I am sure you understand that the advertisement has caused and is still causing me much embarrassment. Also I am involved in having to give explanations to people who are disturbed.
>
> I appreciate the fact that you cannot divulge to me the name of the person who sent in the advertisement, but it would be a help if you would let me know whether the advertisement was genuine or not, i.e. whether or not it was submitted by a man in episcopal orders.
>
> Yours sincerely
>
> + Mervyn Southwark.[2]

Rees-Mogg asked for an explanation, and received the following memo from Mander, the advertising director:

1 Leader, 'A famous victory – but whose?', October 12 1974.
2 Stockwood to W.R.-M., October 1 1974.

The Bishop of Southwark's Letter
The advertisement 'middle-aged bachelor bishop' was received in the office on 13 September. Correctly, it was not immediately put through, and references were sought. These were obtained through the advertiser's bankers (Coutts), who considered the advertiser to be 'respectable and trustworthy'. On receipt of this information, the advertisement was published . . . We believe the advertiser concerned to be a doctor of theology, although not a Bishop of the Church of England.

In view of our policy not to give names of Box Number advertisers, it is more difficult to explain to the Bishop of Southwark the subsequent advertisement, 'middle-aged spinster . . .'. This advertisement was in fact placed by Spike Milligan. As the pulling power of *The Times* is a phenomenon that I take for granted, I suppose I should not be surprised that he received 4 replies.

From the Bishop of Southwark's point-of-view, I assume that he would require a letter making it clear that he was not the advertiser but that the references of the actual advertiser were in fact carefully checked.*

M.M.

* Despite this, I still have my doubts as to whether the advertisement should have been accepted. This is a difficult matter of judgment which I am discussing with those concerned.[1]

Armed with this background information, Rees-Mogg replied to Stockwood:

Dear Bishop,

Thank you very much for your letter. I am sorry that you should have been troubled by any confusion about this. The first advertisement was a genuine one. I am told that the advertiser concerned is a doctor of theology but that he is not a Bishop of the Church of England. The second advertisement was a joke which was put in by one of our leading national comedians and received four replies. I do not know whether any of the replies came from genuine Bishops. It never entered anyone's head that the advertisements could be laid at your door.

Yours sincerely
William Rees-Mogg.[2]

---

1 Mander to W.R.-M., October 3 1974.
2 W.R.-M. to Stockwood, October 4 1974.

There the matter rested. The identity of the doctor of theology, who may or may not have been a bishop in some other episcopal church, has to remain a mystery.[1]

Immediately after the second 1974 election Rees-Mogg discussed the Tory leadership question (in a leader already briefly quoted). The party must, he argued, take its time over resolving the question. There was certainly a good case for asking Heath to stand down. 'He has lost three out of four elections; he lacks public popularity; he has been leader of the Conservative Party for nine years and his party's inadequacies both in people and policy are his responsibility.' Yet with all his faults he was the party's 'one big national and international figure', and it was hard to be convinced that 'any one of the alternative leaders would do better'. Heath was 'a serious and courageous man', who had told the British people 'more important truths than they wanted to listen to'. The natural successor to him would be Whitelaw. He was 'a man of character and public appeal', but it had to be doubted – he would doubt himself – 'whether he had the intellectual force' to preside over the 'searching process of policy making' that would be needed. Heath had the intellectual force, but did he have 'the intellectual receptivity'? The question was so difficult that it had to be 'thrashed out, not suddenly disposed of'.[2]

Clearly dismayed by the equivocal tone and content of this leader, Samuel Brittan, principal economic commentator of the *Financial Times*, and at the time a close adviser of Joseph, wrote to Rees-Mogg the following day urging him in the strongest terms to say nothing that could have the effect of delaying Heath's departure. Replying, Rees-Mogg insisted that the absence of any agreed alternative to Heath was a great difficulty. But he said he would like to discuss the matter further with Brittan.[3]

To the growing number of Tories who believed in a return to free

1 Sixteen years later Mander could not remember, even if he knew at the time.
When Hussey became chief executive he was concerned at the number of 'escort agencies' advertising in *The Times*, and decreed that this line of business must stop, though it was worth about a quarter of a million a year to the paper. Mander accepted the ban with regret, but Rees-Mogg protested on behalf of one agency which was taking space every day, and after some discussion an exception was made in its favour: a compromise between ethical and commercial imperatives. (Hussey talking to author.)

2 Leader, 'A famous victory – but whose?', October 12 1974.

3 Brittan to W.R.-M., October 13 1974; W.R.-M. to Brittan, October 15 1974. The two men had earlier been colleagues on the *Financial Times*.

market principles the natural successor to Heath was not Whitelaw, but Joseph, who had stepped into the intellectual void left by Powell and who, after the October election, was prepared to admit to being a candidate for the leadership. But Joseph soon disqualified himself by a speech in which he declared, in effect, that the working class was breeding to excess. The speech was delivered on October 19, a Saturday, and the lead story in Monday's paper was a confession by the speaker that his remarks had been naïve and ill-judged. The full text of the speech was printed on page 3, together with comments on it, from various sources, and there was also a leader criticising not only Joseph's 'excursions into eugenics' in terms redolent of social distinction, but also his tendency to link all the sins of permissiveness with socialism.[1] Conservatives who had begun to look to him as the most promising replacement for Heath were sharply disillusioned by the ineptitude of his remarks, and still more, perhaps, by the spectacle of a potential leader apologising and agonising in public.

If Joseph had been, in a sense, the Powell-surrogate as champion of the radical right, who was to be the surrogate for him now that his credibility was blown? Before the end of November he had withdrawn his candidature, and Margaret Thatcher then at once decided that she would stand against Heath in the New Year. Marc's cartoon had a tweedy character saying: 'If Mrs. Thatcher really has thrown her hat in the ring one can only say good riddance'.[2] (Since she had entered the public eye as a cabinet minister her style in hats had failed to win general approval. But her hats – like so much else – would change in the years ahead.) Shortly before she announced her decision the political editor, Wood, reported her progress:

> Mrs. Thatcher is recognized everywhere as a rising Conservative star . . . Since Parliament opened she has made a formidable name as a Commons debater, and it is not unusual to hear Conservative back-benchers saying: 'She is the best man among them'.

He added that she had 'already risen as high in politics as any woman except Mrs. Castle', and that the probability must be that she would 'prove to be the first woman Chancellor'. But he also felt it was 'early days for the party to plump for a woman leader'.[3]

Her advance had indeed been rapid, and largely due to Heath.

---

1 Leader, 'The public morality', October 21 1974.
2 November 26 1974.
3 November 25 1974. Wood's story was on p.2, but flagged by a short item on the front page.

During the October election he had given her the task of expounding the new policy of 9½ per cent mortgages and easier home ownership, which had been denounced as bribery by Labour but welcomed by many on her own side. After the election, in a very limited reshuffle of shadow posts, he had moved her from environment to treasury matters, as number two to Robert Carr. This had given her the chance, which she eagerly seized, to shine in debates on Denis Healey's autumn budget. Her speeches were well reported, and marked by knowledge, confidence, combativeness and, at times, wit. In one, addressing the millionaire Labour minister, Harold Lever, she said that 'there were four ways of acquiring money – earn it, make it, borrow it and marry it' – and that he appeared to have done all four'.[1] Suddenly her name was always in the news, if only for such things as being named 'Non-smoker of the Year' by the British Anti-Smoking Education Society.[2]

Heath's greatest service to her cause lay in not resigning after the election. Had he chosen to go at once of his own accord, realising that his position was hopeless, it is most unlikely that she would have become a candidate, and still less likely that she would have been elected. Most members of the party, in Parliament and in the country, probably did not want a lurch to the right and might have agreed with Rees-Mogg that Whitelaw would be the natural successor to Heath. But Whitelaw, like other senior colleagues, felt debarred from standing unless and until Heath resigned. They thus left the field open to anyone who did not recognise the same moral constraint, while their unwillingness to stand could too easily be represented as moral cowardice.

There could be little doubt of Heath's unpopularity. In mid-November an ORC poll showed that 57 per cent of all voters thought that he should be replaced either immediately or before the next election, while only 54 per cent of Conservative supporters thought that he should stay as party leader.[3] Even his narrow escape, just before Christmas, from a bomb attempt on his life did not noticeably swing opinion back in his favour.[4] A month later the paper reported that businessmen and party workers in the Black Country – a key area,

---

1 Parliamentary report, November 15 1974. Mrs. Thatcher herself had acquired money by, at least, the first and last of the four methods.

2 Report in the paper, November 13 1974. A former would-be Tory leader, Lord Hailsham of St. Marylebone, was third on the Society's list.

3 November 12 1974.

4 The bomb exploded on the balcony of his house in Wilton Street, Belgravia, ten minutes before he arrived back there from conducting his annual carol concert at Broadstairs. (Report, December 23 1974.)

electorally – were 'disenchanted'.[1] Meanwhile a committee under Sir Alec Douglas-Home had recommended that there should be sessional election of the leader, and it had been decided that Tory MPs should vote, under slightly altered rules, in early February.[2]

For the first round there were three candidates: Heath, Thatcher and – a relative outsider – Hugh Fraser. The question it was expected to settle was whether or not Heath should stay. Few as yet anticipated, apparently, Thatcher's emergence as the eventual winner. Wood suggested that she might 'succeed only in smoking out into the open a more successful male challenger to Mr. Heath',[3] and this was certainly the outcome for which the editor was hoping. She had, however, an eloquent, though discriminating, champion in Levin, who devoted two of his columns to arguing the case for her. In the first he wrote that, somewhat to his own surprise, he found his 'dreams being haunted more and more frequently by the graceful form of Peg o' my Heart'. What was the objection to her? Chiefly that she was a woman, but in his view no one would 'think it ridiculous or dangerous for a woman to be PM five minutes after it had happened'.[4] In the second piece he argued that her sex would be an advantage rather than the reverse. Though he would personally support Heath 'through as many ballots as he entered', he was sure she would be the best bet if Heath were defeated or withdrew. She was a fighter, and also an artful politician. 'Note . . . the skill with which she has avoided giving the impression of being an ideologue like Sir Keith, let alone Mr. Powell'.

> Mrs. T. is clever; she has stamina; she can mix it with the best, not to mention the worst. It is a pity that she apparently has no vices . . . and a greater pity that she has no interests either . . . Mr. Heath's combination of the Steinway and the surging deep did him a power of good. It is also a pity that she does undeniably radiate a distinct chill, and the Tories may feel . . . that that is what is chiefly wrong with their present leader. But Heaven forbid that she should try to be what she is not . . .[5]

Thatcher's campaign was ably managed by Airey Neave, who at the end of January said that she was 'in a strong position', though

1 'Message from Black Country Tories is "Heath must go",' January 20 1975.
2 To win on the first ballot a candidate would need to get a majority plus 15 per cent of those entitled to vote, rather than of those actually voting.
3 December 30 1974.
4 'The Tories' best hope of salvation', January 23 1975.
5 'Find the lady should be the cry if Tories want a change', January 28 1975.

without giving numbers.[1] On the day of the election there was a report, no doubt deliberately planted, that she would offer Heath a post in any cabinet she might form.[2]

The defending leader, by contrast, did little to campaign for himself, and those who campaigned on his behalf may have done his cause more harm than good. A few days before the vote this advertisement appeared in *The Times*, at the bottom of page 2:

> Ted Heath is *still* the Tories' best bet . . . if you agree, say so now, send a telegram to your MP, c/o House of Commons . . . Ask him to VOTE HEATH in next week's ballot.

The message was signed 'Friends of Ted Heath'. Its whole tone implied lack of confidence, and George Hutchinson later described it as 'certainly injudicious', if not 'improper'.[3]

By now Rees-Mogg had turned unequivocally against Heath, using particularly the argument that he was insensitive to criticism and would not acknowledge the faults of his administration. On February 1 the thumbs-down was given in a three-column editorial. Heath's merits were again dutifully rehearsed, but the leader ended:

> The formation of a policy to deal with inflation matters most. In this essential respect Mr. Heath is actually the least suitable of the three candidates on the first ballot; he alone remains committed to his own wrong policies. He was wrong and he will not admit he was wrong. Both Mrs. Thatcher and Mr. Fraser see what the problem is and are moving in the right direction . . . Mr. Heath has not freed himself from his own mistakes and does not seem capable of doing so. However much one may appreciate his high standing in the world, and his honourable character and strength of purpose, Mr. Heath, whether elected or no, cannot offer a

---

1 January 27 1975.

2 Story from John Groser, political staff, February 4 1975.

3 'How Mr. Heath's career was ruined by his friends', February 8 1975. Earlier, Lord Lambton had written (in an op. ed. piece on January 20 1975) that supporters of Heath had intrigued to bring about Home's resignation as leader ten years previously. This was denied by Peter Walker (letter, January 21 1975), but he in turn was contradicted by Humphry Berkeley (letter, January 23), who claimed to have been approached by Walker with the suggestion that Home should go. The controversy, together with the advertisement, can hardly have been helpful to Heath.

> future to the Conservative Party so long as he is the prisoner of his own past.[1]

To this criticism Heath replied at the last moment, using the paper's political editor as his spokesman. In a pre-election review of the three candidates, after noting that Thatcher and Fraser – following Joseph – had made 'full confession' of mistakes, Wood wrote of Heath:

> [He] would also admit mistakes, though not mistakes of Conservative principle . . . [but] he will not make the same mistakes again. There will be, if he is re-elected, a more open kind of Conservative Government, with a wider range of ability called into front bench service, and there will be, if the 1922 Committee allows, a freer play of opinion between the Treasury bench and the back-bench committees. He has mellowed if his party gives him a chance to prove it.[2]

But the party did not give him that chance. Though there was still considerable support for him among the Tory faithful, it was not enough to counteract his general unpopularity in the country, which made his colleagues at Westminster regard him as a loser. It was they who were to decide his fate, and their doubts about ever winning again under his leadership were combined, in many cases, with personal animus against him for neglecting them (not least in the matter of honours). Their motives may have been complex, but the result of the first ballot was, in the negative sense, clear-cut. On February 5 the front-page headline across six columns was 'Mr. Heath steps down after 11 vote defeat by Mrs. Thatcher'. He was beaten and had accepted defeat, but Thatcher's vote was not large enough to bring her victory and the positive question of the succession had yet to be settled.[3]

---

1 'The question is: Heath or no Heath?'. The leader repeated the view that Whitelaw would 'almost certainly be the first choice' for restoring unity and morale to the party, but also admitted that 'intellectual leadership' in developing anti-inflation policy belonged to Joseph, and even suggested that Powell, 'whose best contribution has been in economic policy, should be brought into discussions'. Powell, however, was no longer a member of the party and had said only the previous evening, at a dinner of the Selsdon Group, that it was useless to look for a leader among those who had sat in the Heath Cabinet 'without a single resignation or public dissent'. (Report, February 1 1975.)

2 February 3 1975. Voting was to be the following day.

3 The figures were: Thatcher, 130; Heath 119; Fraser, 16.

As soon as Heath had stood down Whitelaw announced that he would be a candidate on the next ballot, to be held a week later; and he was soon joined by three other former colleagues of the fallen leader, James Prior, John Peyton and Geoffrey Howe.[1] Whitelaw was evidently the strongest challenger, and Rees-Mogg lost no time in renewing support for him and explaining carefully why he was to be preferred:

> It has been observed that Mrs. Thatcher and Mr. Heath are in some ways very similar politicians . . . they both have that driving energy which is a great executive advantage. They both have cool rather than warm and broadly popular public temperaments, though both enjoy the genuine affection and admiration of their friends.
>
> Neither Mrs. Thatcher nor Mr. Heath could properly be regarded as extremists in terms of Conservative policy. Mrs. Thatcher is not so much to the right nor is Mr. Heath so far to the left as might for the moment have appeared. Yet both hold their views, though moderate, with considerable intensity, to a degree which makes it difficult for them to sympathize with people with quite different opinions. In politics this tight focus is helpful for specific achievement, but it is not the best way to bring together the differing judgments of men of differing temperaments and experience. In business terms Mrs. Thatcher and Mr. Heath are managing directors; Mr. Whitelaw's gifts are those of a chairman, and it is a chairman's gifts which are at present wanted.[2]

Levin had already drawn attention to Thatcher's skill in not appearing to be as much of an ideologue as Joseph, let alone Powell. Rees-Mogg now went further in suggesting that she was a crypto-moderate. She had indeed never shown as much interest as Joseph in, for example, the literature of the Institute of Economic Affairs, and when he founded the Centre for Policy Studies at the beginning of 1975 she became a vice-president but did not write for it. Adherents of the intellectual right recalled 'just how episodic, in earlier years, her own

1 In the Heath government Prior had been minister of agriculture and then leader of the House of Commons; Peyton minister of transport; and Howe solicitor-general before becoming minister for trade and consumer affairs.
2 Leader, 'The question of party unity', February 5 1975.

attachment to their thinking had been'.[1] Her performance at the ministry of education was, in most respects, hardly that of an anti-socialist crusader, and if Heath had won the 1974 elections she would probably have remained, in practice, a centrist, whatever her instinctive prejudices. As it was, she became, by default, the champion of free market doctrines and in due course an -ism was named after her. Yet she remained less of an ideologue than she was thought to be or, perhaps, thought herself to be. (The policy of mortgage-interest relief, which had appealed to many Tories in the October election, and was to become the basis of her own highly successful policy of home ownership, had been wished on her by Heath and was, in any case, hardly consistent with non-interventionist theory.)

Whitelaw suffered from having allowed her a head start, and for having given an impression of weakness by his refusal to stand against Heath. He seemed, moreover, to represent nothing new. As Butt remarked in his column, it was to her advantage that she had 'declared herself from the start', and that she stood for 'a new Tory policy critique' more clearly than her rivals.[2] The case for her was summed up by a reader in Glasgow:

> Mrs. Thatcher sensed that most members of her party in the Commons considered a change desirable; her main rivals did not. Surely in a democracy an ability to appreciate what a majority is thinking and to act accordingly is the first requirement of a leader of a party that hopes to win an election.[3]

Whitelaw was a squirearchical figure, for all his political ambition and professionalism, and many Tories must have feared that he would be the wrong sort of leader for the times, more especially against a Labour leader such as Wilson.

His chances cannot have been improved by a picture of him in shirtsleeves doing the washing-up, which suggested, rightly or wrongly, that he was pretending to be what he was not. Thatcher teased him about it when they appeared together at a Young Conservative conference at Eastbourne during the weekend between the two ballots. She said that if he could be found doing the washing-up she might be found on a golf course, and this remark was double-edged, since it implied both that he was not the man to do domestic chores and that she did not waste her time playing games. At the conference she had the good

1 Hugo Young, *One of Us*, chap. 7 (p.86 in paperback edition).
2 Op. ed. column, 'Will they become accustomed to her face?' February 5 1975.
3 Letter to the editor, published February 7 1975.

fortune to reply to a debate on the economy, which was her subject. She made an effective speech, and Wood reported on Monday that she was 'already the front runner', the weekend having been, by general agreement, hers.[1]

On the morning of the second ballot the lead story was that the chairman of the Tories' national union had reported to the 1922 committee a 'two to one' majority for Thatcher and against Whitelaw in constituency opinion.[2] On the op. ed. page Levin emphasised that the choice was between those two, since the other candidates could and should be disregarded. He had already stated his view that the Tories 'would do well to choose Mrs. Thatcher' and had nothing to add on that score, though he did criticise 'her prose style as shown in her speech at Eastbourne'.[3] (His backing was probably all the more useful to her for having been conditional, at the outset, upon Heath's defeat, and for being free from sycophancy.)

Among letters to the editor, which were entirely devoted to the leadership election, the first was from Edward Boyle endorsing the editor's support of Whitelaw and quoting a remark of Churchill's: 'Those who are prone by temperament and character to seek sharp and clear-cut solutions of difficult and obscure problems . . . have not always been right'. (Churchill was referring to Neville Chamberlain, between whom and Margaret Thatcher others later came to see analogies.) The second letter was from Norman Lamont, supporting Thatcher but denying that he and others who wanted her to win were drawn exclusively from the right. He described himself as 'a strong supporter of Mr. Heath's Government, a Bow grouper and someone on the liberal wing of the party'. The last letter was from Val Gielgud, commenting on another correspondent's claim that Whitelaw would prove as popular and beloved as Baldwin: 'If this doesn't put Mr. Whitelaw out of the running . . . nothing on God's earth can'.[4]

Rees-Mogg's final leader on the election ended with a compact re-statement of his preference and the reasons for it: 'The older, the wiser, the warmer politician has a freedom [to convert the public to social market policies] denied the younger, the narrower and more zealous'.[5] But Tory MPs thought otherwise and next day's banner

---

1 Front-page story, February 10 1975.
2 February 11 1975. Story from George Clark, in which he also reported that Conservative peers were two to one for Whitelaw.
3 Same date. 'Fish out the Tory minnows aspiring to be whales'.
4 Letters to the editor, February 11 1975.
5 'Mr. Whitelaw or Mrs. Thatcher?', same date.

headline proclaimed that Thatcher had won outright. The front-page story was illustrated by a picture of her being congratulated as she left the House of Commons, holding a bunch of flowers. Marc's cartoon showed the Thatchers together, with her saying 'From *now* on, Denis, you can do the shopping . . .' Rees-Mogg accepted the result with resignation: 'Those who wear the livery of Conservatism have a duty to support their new leader loyally'.[1]

In 1975 Jerome (Jerry) Caminada retired as foreign news editor. He had been with the paper for nearly thirty-eight years. Soon after he joined the war began, and in 1940 he was captured by the Germans. He then spent some time in prisoner-of-war camps in Germany, Hungary and Romania. After several unsuccessful attempts to escape he eventually got away, reaching the Middle East after about two years on the run. Returning to *The Times* in 1946, after a spell in naval intelligence, he was special correspondent in Palestine for seven years. Later he served in South-East Asia and, again, the Middle East, before becoming foreign news editor in 1965. Like Hodgkin, he was markedly Arabist in sympathy. South African by origin, he had a gruff manner which those who knew him more than superficially found to be misleading. He was a notable *Times* character.

By the time he retired Heren was foreign (as well as deputy) editor, having succeeded Hodgkin in 1973. By tradition the post of foreign news editor would have gone to an experienced foreign correspondent, but Heren decided to break with tradition. At his suggestion, Caminada was followed by a much younger man, Ivan Barnes, who had never served abroad and had joined the paper after the Thomson take-over. Barnes came, like Heren, from a working-class background, but in Brighton, not the East End of London. After national service he showed an instinctive interest in foreign countries by taking jobs abroad and hiking round Europe. Then, after working for a time in an obscure publishing house, he was encouraged by a friend to try his hand at journalism, and entered the London office of the *Glasgow Herald*. There he became acquainted with Patrick Brogan who, as an early recruit to the Thomson *Times* in 1967, arranged for Barnes to join soon afterwards as foreign news editor (night). Over the next

1 February 12 1975. The figures in the second ballot were: Thatcher, 146; Whitelaw, 79, Prior and Howe 19; Peyton, 11. Rees-Mogg's leader was entitled 'Truth is made true by events' (which seems uncomfortably close to *Die Weltgeschichte ist das Weltgericht*).

eight years he worked under Caminada and learnt much from him, particularly to view all reports with a degree of scepticism.[1]

When he took Caminada's place he got on well with Heren and, after him, the next foreign editor, Douglas-Home. Though he saw Rees-Mogg regularly at conferences, his personal contact with the editor was minimal. As foreign news editor he travelled as often as he could, and when he was abroad made a point of visiting the paper's correspondents and stringers. But inevitably most of his time was spent in the London office, where he worked as a rule from about 10 a.m. to 7 p.m.

He was well placed to observe, and indeed to participate in, the new approach to news that marked the early phase of the Thomson regime. Some well-established *Times* foreign correspondents had fallen into the habit of reporting only on high politics, and even so of sending their copy with no particular sense of urgency. Cudlipp took the lead in discouraging this habit. Correspondents would be telephoned in the small hours to ask what they were doing about covering a story.

The specialist in the foreign department was the diplomatic correspondent, who until 1974 was the long-serving A. M. Rendel. (He had been in the post since 1949.) His successor was David Spanier, whose name has already cropped up several times in this volume. He had been at Charterhouse where, as a Jew, he experienced some anti-semitism. When he arrived there Rees-Mogg was at the top of the school.[2] At Trinity College, Cambridge, Spanier read English literature and was much influenced by Leavis. After a brief spell on the *Yorkshire Post* he joined *The Times* as a home news reporter in 1955. In the early 1960s he was the first Common Market correspondent, and quite close at the time to the chief British negotiator, Edward Heath. At the time of the Thomson take-over he was economic correspondent on Europe generally, and then he was sent in the same capacity to Washington. From 1969 until his appointment to succeed

1 Caminada's independent, sceptical outlook, on domestic no less than foreign matters, was shown during the 1970 election campaign when, at a conference a few days before polling day, the editor said that Labour was clearly going to win, and asked his colleagues who they thought would be leading the Conservative party in a year's time. When it was his turn, Caminada replied that the leader would be Edward Heath, who would also be the prime minister. (Ivan Barnes talking to author).

2 In a test for new boys in his house one question asked was 'What is a moot point?' – to which one of his contemporaries boldly and pertly replied 'Rees-Mogg'. Luckily for him the senior boys conducting the inquisition were amused. Charterhouse was never discussed by Spanier and Rees-Mogg when they were colleagues on *The Times*. (David Spanier talking to author.)

Rendel he was a leader-writer in London; and when *Europa* was launched he was its London editor.

On becoming diplomatic correspondent he took at once an important and symbolic step. For as long as anyone could remember *The Times* had been accorded the privilege of separate briefing at the Foreign Office. This Spanier voluntarily surrendered, holding the view that it was out-of-date and that the paper had less to gain from its continuance than from his being able to talk freely to his opposite numbers from other papers. Ending the privilege was, unquestionably, a self-inflicted blow to *The Times*'s status as the establishment newspaper. But was that status, in any casc, desirable? The paper had risen to greatness by being anti-establishment.

Among his various qualifications Spanier had two that were, perhaps, specially relevant to the role of diplomatic correspondent. He was an excellent chess player and poker player.

Mention of games prompts some consideration of the paper's coverage of sport during the Thomson period. Though few were likely to read *The Times* primarily for its sports pages, certain sports had for years been covered in the paper with distinction, by correspondents who continued to write under the new regime.

Cricket was an outstanding case in point. The cricketing correspondent throughout the period was John Woodcock, who had held the post since 1954 and was to hold it until 1987. For six years (1980–6) he was also editor of *Wisden*. Son of a Church of England parson, and himself the patron of a benefice in Hampshire, he gave 'the impression that he would have preferred living in the 1870s'. He had high standards of criticism, and in his reports, which were written 'in a small, swift hand on a long pad', lyrical descriptions alternated with shrewd, even waspish, comments.[1] He favoured bright and positive cricket. When a long run of English success ended with a defeat by India at the Oval, he wrote:

> Both India and Pakistan have appeared to enjoy their cricket more than England. They have contributed more liberally to our summer's pleasures. In Illingworth's time as captain, England have now won eight Test matches, drawn 12 and lost only one. Before that, under Cowdrey, they played seven more without defeat. But an unbeaten record has its complications. Now that

1 From the chapter on cricket writers in *The Boundary Book*, ed. Leslie Frewin.

> England have lost they should think in terms of building a side which plays the game with more of a smile and less of a frown.[1]

When A. W. (Tony) Greig was deprived of the England captaincy for secretly negotiating with Kerry Packer, Woodcock had an explanation for his conduct:

> What has to be remembered, of course, is that he is an Englishman not by birth or upbringing, but only by adoption. It is not the same thing as being English through and through.[2]

Greig was, by origin, South African. It was not that Woodcock had any objection to white South Africans as such. Indeed, some of his colleagues felt that he was insufficiently outraged by the policy of apartheid, and therefore unwilling to take a strong line in the d'Oliveira case in 1968.[3] His task of reporting cricket matches was shared with the academic freelance, Alan Gibson, and also, for a short time, with John Arlott, who wrote for *The Times* under the pen-name 'Silchester' but soon left to write, under his own name, for the *Guardian*. Some others contributed on cricket from time to time, but Woodcock and, next to him, Gibson were pre-eminent.

Early in the period there was a first leader on cricket, written by A. P. Ryan, in which the game was said to be on trial in both its aspects, international and county. As to the first, the leader took the view that three days were ample for Test matches between the less strong sides. In county matches, success had crowned two experiments, Sunday and one-day knock-out games. Yet the health of cricket depended ultimately on the mood in which it was played. Some sides had responded wholeheartedly to appeals for a more sporting approach, but unfortunately 'an obstinate coterie of dour, unimaginative players' remained deaf, 'concentrating on individual averages and letting everything else, including the interest of spectators, go hang'. The leader avoided, however, interpreting the trouble in class terms. The example of captains was indeed all-important, but 'happily

1 August 25 1971.
2 May 14 1977.
3 At the end of August 1968 the MCC announced that the team to represent England in the forthcoming Test tour of South Africa would not include Basil d'Oliveira, an all-rounder manifestly qualified for selection but, it was generally assumed, passed over because he was a Cape Coloured, who had emigrated to Britain. The selectors seemed to be pandering to racialism. After weeks of controversy the MCC decided to include him after all, but the South African prime minister, Vorster, then demanded that the tour be cancelled, and cancelled it was.

some of the best captains [were] drawn from the professional ranks'.[1]

Another game in whose coverage *The Times* had a notable record was golf. Since 1953, when the long reign of Bernard Darwin came to an end, the paper's golf correspondent had been Peter Ryde, and he stayed in the job under the Thomson ownership. An excellent writer, with a more restrained palette than some of the others who wrote on sport, he adjusted with some difficulty to the growing necessity to personalise his reports and to establish personal contact with star players. But he did not shirk the task: his first favourite was Arnold Palmer, and later he could claim to be one of the first to have spotted the talent of Severiano Ballesteros.

In Haley's time he had paid a few visits to the United States, for instance to cover the Masters' tournament, but after Tony Jacklin's victory in the US Open in 1970 it became normal for him to cover that tournament as well. Palmer had done much to enhance American interest in the (British) Open, and in 1975 Ryde's description of Tom Watson's first victory in the event, at Carnoustie, is a good example of his style. Watson won in a play-off against the Australian Jack Newton. The play-off took place, then, on the Sunday, 'when the great men ha[d] departed and the crowd was a skeleton of its usual self'. Five players, including Jack Nicklaus, had come to the last hole on the Saturday with a chance of winning: a phenomenon not seen since 1958. A slight change in weather conditions affected the outcome:

> The wind, though never strong, made all the difference to the scoring. Although most of the finishing holes were downwind, such is their character that in the mounting pressure they came fully into their own. The sleeping giant had opened one eye and it was enough.

It was significant that Watson, 'whose presence in the play-off was the least expected of those in contention, was the only one apart from Nicklaus to play the course in par'. His eventual victory gave him, at twenty-three, his first big title. Moreover, by winning it at the first attempt he achieved a feat not seen since Gary Player's victory in 1959.[2]

Tennis was a sport of ever-growing appeal during the Thomson period, and the tennis correspondent, appointed in 1967, was Rex

---

1 Leader, 'Cricket on trial', August 28 1967.
2 July 14 1975.

Bellamy. Though he had been on the staff since 1956, he was new to a top position and proved highly successful in it, receiving five awards from the Association of Tennis Professionals. Despite strong international competition for these awards, he always won by a wide margin in the players' ballot.[1] His style was more florid than Ryde's. When, in the Queen's silver jubilee year, the ladies championship was won by a British player, Virginia Wade, defeating Betty Stove of the Netherlands, his description of the scene was characteristic:

> What a roar there was, what a raging sea of hands. A minute passed before the umpire, dutifully observing the last rites, could announce the score. Then the Queen came on court – the monarch of a realm greeting the monarch of a sport. Flags waved everywhere. There was a spontaneous chorus of 'For she's a jolly good fellow' . . . Hurrahs rang round the centre court. Miss Stove tried to move modestly into the background. But Prince Philip covered a few yards with elegant agility and brought her back to enjoy the fun.[2]

Another paragon among *Times* sports writers was Geoffrey Green, the football correspondent. He had joined the staff in 1946 and over the years had written about various sports, though principally about football. His convivial habits might occasionally cause a flutter of anxiety, but as a rule he could be relied on both to produce his copy and to maintain a high standard. Like Bellamy, he was a colourful writer. When England beat Scotland at Hampden Park in the centenary year of the Scottish Football Association, his English triumphalism was uncontrolled:

> It was the start of Scotland centenary celebrations at Hampden Park last night, but the nasty predatory Sassenachs turned up to spoil the birthday party and in the process made the Scots look 100 years old. With three goals in the opening quarter of an hour England quickly blew out the candles on the cake and reduced the rest of the bitter night to a frigid academic exercise.[3]

Green retired in 1976, to be succeeded by Norman Fox. In the New Year honours he received the OBE, in contravention of Rees-Mogg's edict (see p. 74). In a tribute to him the sports editor, John

1 *Times News*, December 1977.
2 July 2 1977.
3 February 15 1973. The piece was entitled 'England put down Scots pretenders'.

Hennessy, wrote of his 'towering stature in the world of sports journalism', and said that he had 'the pen as well as the appearance of a poet'.[1]

There was nothing flash about Hennessy. He had been the department's anchor man since 1954, and he did the job with quiet efficiency. He had joined the paper in 1948 as a sports sub, after service in the army as a corporal followed by work in a City office and (briefly) at the board of trade. He did some writing himself. During the winter he might report a football match every weekend, and he was also capable of covering tennis, hockey, boxing, skiing, skating and (occasionally) cricket. But his main function, of course, was to coordinate the work of his colleagues and see it through the press. In 1979 he retired and his place was taken by Nicholas Keith.

Apart from the leading correspondents already mentioned, Michael Phillips covered racing – with a northern correspondent, Jim Snow, to help him – and Peter West wrote about rugby. Most other sports were covered by freelances or part-timers, and the number of sports covered increased during the period. According to Hennessy, Rees-Mogg took little interest in the subject unless there was a financial angle; but Grant and Douglas-Home took an active interest.[2]

---

1 *Times News*, July/August 1976.
2 Talking to author.

XVIII

Referendum on Europe • Foot and press freedom • Sensitive matters • Obituaries: tradition and change • In place of contract

HEATH HAD TAKEN the country into the European Community through the instrumentality of Parliament, despite clear evidence that public opinion was hostile or lukewarm. His interpretation of a phrase he had rashly used, 'full-hearted consent', was strictly parliamentarian, not plebiscitarian. Wilson, on the other hand, had committed himself to consulting the British people 'through the ballot box' after re-negotiating the terms of entry. Though the wording of this pledge was ambiguous as between a referendum and yet another general election, in January 1975 the government decided in favour of the former and a referendum bill was introduced. The Conservatives opposed it in principle, but once it was passed most of them, including the leadership, concentrated with other pro-Europeans on securing a 'yes' vote. By the end of March the process of re-negotiation had been brought to a successful, if largely cosmetic, conclusion, and a White Paper was then published setting out the new terms and recommending their acceptance. But the cabinet split 16–7 on the issue, and Wilson resorted to the almost unprecedented expedient of an 'agreement to differ', with members of the cabinet free to campaign on opposite sides in the referendum, provided they confined themselves to government policy when speaking from the despatch box.[1]

The cabinet majority did not represent the parliamentary party, the trade unions, or Labour activists in the country. While the White Paper policy was endorsed in the Commons by an impressive margin of 226 – more than twice the majority for entry in October 1971 – only 138 Labour MPs voted in favour, with 145 against and 32 abstentions. Soon afterwards a special conference of the party voted two to

1 An approximate precedent was the agreement to differ on Protection, adopted for the benefit of Liberal members of the National government in 1932. But this, as a *Times* leader said, 'did not last long, did not license campaigning', and was 'hardly a happy political precedent'. (Leader, 'The cabinet recommends', March 19 1975).

one for withdrawal from the European Community. Even Callaghan who, as foreign secretary, had led the re-negotiation, was at pains to dispel any idea that he might be enthusiastic about the policy that he was formally commending to the people.[1]

Mrs. Thatcher, by contrast, went out of her way to demonstrate that her commitment to Europe was just as strong as her predecessor's. Her speech in the debate on the White Paper 'ended once and for all any suggestion that the change in the Tory leadership had brought with it a lukewarm approach to membership of the Community', and this was judged to be the occasion when she 'finally established herself in Parliament as the undisputed leader of her party'. Her speech, it was said, 'was skilfully blended to give maximum support to Europe and minimum assistance to Mr. Wilson'. It earned her 'one of the warmest ovations that a leader of any party ha[d] received in the Commons for some time'.[2]

An inter-party organisation 'Keep Britain in Europe' was launched, with Jenkins as leader, in the second week of May, and there was a front-page picture of him sharing the platform with Heath and Thorpe at the opening meeting.[3] On the other side a National Referendum Campaign came into being, with Benn, a comparatively recent convert to the anti-European cause, as its leading figure. Throughout the whole period from mid-March until polling on June 5 *The Times* naturally devoted much space to the referendum. Berthoud, as correspondent in Brussels, was kept particularly busy, contributing think-pieces to the op. ed. page as well as news stories. For instance, he interviewed the Belgian prime minister, Leo Tindemans, who was preparing a report on European union, and was (Berthoud said) 'not too concerned about the dangers of Britain, if confirmed as a member by the referendum, taking over the old French role as the slowest and surliest camel in the EEC caravan'. There would always be some '*trouble-fête* (spoilsport)' – France, Britain, Germany or some small country. It depended 'on majorities, and on political personalities'.[4] Berthoud was also among the team of specialists who together produced, on May 19, a four-page '*Times* guide to the EEC referendum', in which the cases for and against were stated and there were articles on such topics as the

1 Interviewed by David Spanier for *Europa*, April 7 1975.
2 Hugh Noyes, parliamentary correspondent, April 9 1975. His report appeared on the front page under the headline 'Mrs. Thatcher stills anti-Europe clamour'.
3 May 14 1975.
4 'Mr. Tindemans treads warily on the way to European unity', op. ed., April 15 1975.

legal limits of the Community, regional aid and the Commonwealth connection.[1]

The pro and con arguments were rehearsed, also, in a series of op. ed. articles by outsiders, starting with Andrew Shonfield and including, among a number of predictable names, Jenkins, Thorpe, Benn, Powell and Shirley Williams. The anti-EEC bias of the trade unions was all too apparent in the fact that the only trade unionist who could be found to write in its favour was a former secretary of the National Union of Dyers, Bleachers and Textile Workers, now a paid servant of the Community as director of industrial relations in its social affairs directorate.[2] The contrary view was put by the most powerful of contemporary British trade union leaders, Jack Jones, who described the Community as 'a Charlemagne dream or Hitlerish nightmare'.[3]

The paper's editorials during the referendum campaign were, on the whole, familiar in content, though Rees-Mogg was under the incongruous necessity to show some solidarity with Wilson. When the White Paper was published the editor reflected that the government could hardly be expected to survive if the vote in Parliament went against the Cabinet's recommendation, but added: 'Mr. Wilson has not been short of either skill or luck in his EEC manoeuvres up to now. He has at this stage a better chance of achieving his European objectives than most people would have supposed when he returned to office just over a year ago'.[4] And after the massive Commons vote endorsing the White Paper, in which, however, a majority of Labour MPs did not join, the prime minister was seen as committed to a 'fight for his political life on the European issue', against not only the Tribune group but formidable colleagues, and in that fight would 'deserve support'.[5]

Throughout the campaign letters poured in, and so many were published that, on most days, Europe and the politics of the referendum seemed to dominate the correspondence columns. A few of the letters provided welcome comic relief. When the cabinet split, J. P. Day wrote: 'As if it was not bad enough having one Labour Government, we now have two'.[6] After the White Paper vote, J. C. Morgan made this comment on Labour and its leader:

---

1 Other members of the team producing the guide were Heren, Wood, Lewis, Geoffrey Smith, George Clark, Henry Stanhope, Marcel Berlins, David Blake, Nicholas Ashford, Hugh Clayton and David Cross. The articles were, however, unsigned.
2 'Why trade unionists can expect a better deal inside Europe', May 28 1975.
3 'We must not lose sight of the fact that Europe is more than just the EEC', May 30 1975.
4 Leader, 'The Cabinet recommends', March 19 1975.
5 Leader, 'Labour divides on Europe', April 10 1975.
6 March 25 1975 (from Warden's House, Lindsay Hall, Keele University).

Now from the Common Market vote
All Bolshies in the land will note
That Harold, after all his tricks,
Only leads the Mensheviks.[1]

On the day of the poll Basil Boothroyd confessed himself still unpersuaded by the arguments on either side:

Since rival propagandists shout
With equal force and din,
One moment I'm for pulling OUT,
The next for staying IN.
Thus reason wavers on her throne,
Craving a straw to clutch,
While one thing's certain, one alone,
They both protest too much.
So much, in fact, that screams for YES
May win my vote of NO
(Or vice versa. It's a mess.
Damn it, I *still* Don't Know.)[2]

Most voters, however, did not share Boothroyd's indecision; the policy of remaining in the Community was backed by a majority of two to one in a 64.5 per cent poll. The only parts of the United Kingdom which did not record majorities for membership were the Western Isles and the Shetlands, and Jo Grimond was reported as saying of the Shetlanders: 'They are excellent and independent people who have elected me to Parliament for 25 years; I have always suspected that they did not know what I stood for'.[3]

To Rees-Mogg, the referendum majority had a significance transcending the immediate issue:

> We know that on the basic issue of national revival there is a massive popular majority on the side of reform, rejecting both the obsolete class selfishness of the far Right and the embittered class socialism of the far Left. There is no reason to think that this majority exists only or even chiefly for the purpose of Europe . . . The politician who now offers the British people not only continued membership of Europe but a complete and, if necessary,

---

April 12 1975 (from Ashurst, Kent).
June 5 1975.
Report, June 7 1975.

> ruthless programme of national reform, will find that the majority which was created yesterday still survives for tomorrow.[1]

It did indeed survive, but within the existing party and electoral systems there was no way it could prevail.

In 1974 the incoming Wilson government carried a measure which purported to repeal Heath's industrial relations act, and substantially did so, though in the bill itself the provisions on unfair dismissal were retained. Moreover, Labour's position in Parliament was so weak that the Tories were able to insert amendments which preserved some of the curbs on trade union power. But after the October election, when Labour had a narrow overall majority in the House of Commons, the employment secretary, Michael Foot, introduced a new bill designed to get rid of these amendments and so give fuller satisfaction to the trade union leaders. In particular, the bill sought to facilitate the establishment of closed shops in all industries, including the press.

At a time when the National Union of Journalists was increasingly under the influence of militants, Foot's bill was seen by many as a grave threat to press freedom. Though the general secretary of the union, Kenneth (Ken) Morgan, was a moderate, his executive was well to the left of him, as was the editor of the union's paper, the *Journalist*. In December 1974, while supporting a printers' strike in Glasgow against an anti-IRA cartoon by Cummings, and an electricians' strike in London against an anti-strike cartoon by Jak, the *Journalist* used these menacing words: 'We shall need more actions of that kind in the struggles ahead as the trade unions' struggle intensifies and we need to chip away at that version of the truth trumpeted by the press moguls from the comfort of their investment portfolios'.[2]

Press freedom seemed to be threatened in two principal ways. The right to comment, or even to print news, might be restricted by a single, politically motivated union, using its blackmailing power to stop production. There was also the danger that editors would lose their freedom to ask whomever they wished to contribute to their papers. Already, in 1965, Fleet Street managements had been forced to agree that new reporters could not be recruited direct from college, but would first have to work three years in the provinces. Now there was reason to fear that the NUJ would succeed in curtailing the use of

1 Leader, 'A great majority for Europe: a new majority for Britain', June 7 1975.
2 Quoted in Nora Beloff, *Freedom under Foot*, p.52.

non-union writers, including politicians and others outside journalism, without whose contributions newspapers would necessarily lose much of their interest and quality.

After the October election a lead was given by the provincial editors in resistance to Foot's bill. Through their joint body, the Guild of British Newspaper Editors, they arranged an informal meeting with Alastair Hetherington of the *Guardian* and Harold Evans of the *Sunday Times*, after which Hetherington wrote to all his opposite numbers in the national press proposing a common stand. The response was unanimous that such a stand should be made, though it soon turned out that there was no unanimity on the precise form it should take. The so-called Fleet Street editors, together with the editors-in-chief from the BBC and ITN, had two meetings with Foot, in November and December, but these only served to show him how divided his antagonists were on the key issue. Opposition to the closed shop in journalism was not solid. Hetherington himself was willing to accept it in return for an agreed, though unenforceable, charter – an idea also promoted by Ken Morgan, though later rejected by his own rank-and-file. While NUJ militants were against the charter idea because it might impose some limit, if only moral, on the exercise of union power, Rees-Mogg from his very different standpoint was against it, too, because he could not reconcile it with the ideal of perfect freedom cherished by him as editor of *The Times*.

Undeterred, Foot went ahead with his bill, suggesting that freedom of the press was far less at risk from NUJ closed shops than from the tyranny of newspaper proprietors and managements. In view of his close professional and personal association with the late Lord Beaverbrook, this was a matter on which he could be regarded as an authority, though without being able to boast any record of heroic defiance. His slur on the press lords was, in any case, condemned by another Beaverbrook Press man, John Junor, in an address to Scottish bankers. 'A man like Lord Hartwell' could, he said, 'find easier and less harrowing ways of making money than by running the *Daily Telegraph*'; and Lord Thomson could not have 'got much pleasure out of the money . . . paid from his own pocket to keep *The Times* alive'. The sense of social purpose that these men and others like them had shown would be lost to the nation if every newspaper were subjected to trade union censorship and veto.[1]

Most editors held to the view that the closed shop was, in principle,

1 Report in the paper, February 21 1975. Hartwell (Michael Berry) was editor-in-chief of the *Daily Telegraph* and second son of the 1st Lord Camrose.

unacceptable for newspapers, and Hetherington's coordinating role passed to Denis Hamilton who shared the majority view. But leadership of the anti-closed shop campaign was assumed by Lord Goodman, legendary fixer and friend of both Wilson and Heath. As chairman of the Observer Trust he was in close touch with David Astor, who persuaded him to lead the campaign. He was also chairman of the Newspaper Proprietors' Association, which naturally blasted his bona fides in the eyes of trade unionists. His motives were, however, impeccable, though the same could not always be said of his tactical sense. In a five-column letter in the *Times Literary Supplement* Foot denounced Goodman's attitude as anti-union, while at the same time attacking the attitude of NUJ militants.[1]

Foot's bill made slow progress and was still in the House of Commons when Parliament rose for the summer recess. In the Commons it faced not only Conservative obstruction but critical scrutiny by Labour MPs belonging to the right-wing Manifesto Group. From one of these a proposal emerged which seemed to offer an alternative to the straightforward legal guarantees that Goodman originally demanded. The ancient doctrine of 'public policy' was invoked as a means of limiting the harmful effects of a closed shop in journalism. If, it was argued, the proposed press charter were to be made citable in any legal proceedings, the courts would then be likely to treat it as a declaration of public policy and so refuse to sanction any action or agreement that might appear to conflict with it. At best this offered only a negative power of enforcement – a shield rather than a sword – but Goodman was tempted by it into prolonged and eventually fruitless negotiations with the government. They were bound to be fruitless, because Foot was never prepared to allow enforceability under any guise whatsoever. The negotiations only succeeded in causing further division and confusion among the various elements opposed to the bill.

Meanwhile it was rejected on its first appearance in the House of Lords, despite dire warnings that the House might be courting its own abolition. In the debate Lord (Hugh) Cudlipp 'visualized a monumental stonemason carving on Lord Goodman's tombstone the epitaph:

1 *TLS*, May 9 1975. Foot had also written a long letter to *The Times* on February 18, which ended: 'Of course I recognize that past or present misdemeanours by the proprietors cannot be invoked to excuse present or future misdemeanours by the journalists. But they might induce a touch of reticence in the spokesmen of the proprietors who have exercised, since the days of Caxton or thereabouts, all the powers of suppression, distortion, malign influence and the peremptory removal of editors to which the members of my union, the NUJ, are alleged all to aspire'.

"the man who failed to defend the press by statute but succeeded in abolishing the House of Lords"'.[1] On the constitutional issue *The Times* spoke with two voices. In a leader the editor argued against rejection:

> Lord Goodman's approach is unquestionably more apt, [but the] question which members of the House of Lords must now decide is whether the Goodman form of charter is so much more valuable, and the principle embodied in its method so necessary to vindicate, that a clash with the Commons is justified, even though its practical outcome will be no more than to delay enactment of the Bill for six months or so.

The leader's conclusion was against a clash.[2] But three days later, in an article appearing on the same page, under the leaders, Wood dissented from the view expressed. He urged the Lords to fight for the Goodman amendments because they were 'right and necessary', and because the issue was one 'where no compromise or temporising [might] be eventually safe'. He hoped that the Lords would 'do for the people what the crude party system no longer [could] be trusted to do'. If they retreated, 'as the leader in *The Times* of Friday beckoned', they would lose 'more than one constitutional cause'.[3]

At long last the bill was passed, under Parliament Act procedure, in March 1976, providing the occasion for George Brown (now Lord George-Brown) to sever his remaining links with the Labour party. His departure was given rather more importance than it deserved by being reported as the paper's lead story, and his comment at the time did not err on the side of understatement: 'I now join Bernard Levin and the army of Solzhenitsyn and Sakharov who stand for freedom'.[4] Goodman's own comment the following day was bitter and doom-laden. It was now established, he said, that there would be a press charter which would 'regulate the proceedings of what is proudly claimed as the freest press in the world, dictated and created if necessary by a minister of the Crown'.[5]

In fact his campaign, though a shambles on the legislative side, was by no means all wasted effort. The public may not have been able to follow all the intricacies of the parliamentary in-fighting – what Nora

1 Parliamentary report, October 21 1975.
2 Leader, 'We must guard our freedoms', October 17 1975.
3 'The Lords must stand and fight, October 20 1975.
4 'Lord George-Brown quits Labour on press freedom vote', March 3 1976.
5 Speech at Newspaper Society lunch, reported March 4 1976.

Beloff in her near-contemporary account describes as an 'interminable series of amendments to amendments to a Bill itself designed to repeal amendments to another Bill'[1] – but the potential reality of a threat to press freedom from a monopolistic and ideological journalists' union did nevertheless get through. Public opinion may not have been aroused to the extent that Goodman and others would have liked, but it was effectively alerted by the controversy. In Hetherington's subsequent view, 'a number of lessons' were learnt.[2] Editors and managements were encouraged to resist closed-shop demands, seeing that they clearly did not enjoy popular backing, and both the government and the trade unions could see that Foot's measure, which in any case was permissive, not mandatory, had little moral authority so far as the press was concerned. The next few years therefore witnessed no drastic consequences, and in due course the whole situation was transformed by the trade union legislation of the Thatcher government.

Adjudication on questions of taste and propriety was always among the editor's trickiest duties, and of course such questions were constantly arising. Ethnic sensitivities accounted for many of them, some occurring in unexpected contexts, as when a leader on the EEC referendum provoked a complaint at the use of the word 'Chinaman'. In Elizabeth Dun's view, 'the description of a Chinese as a Chinaman is no more acceptable than Franceman or Englandman or Americaman might be and . . . these groups do prefer to be referred to as Frenchmen, Englishmen and Americans'. Rees-Mogg was at first disposed to defend the traditional word:

> It seems to me that 'Chinaman' is perfectly ordinary English usage parallel to 'Frenchman' or 'Englishman'. It was obviously not intended to be offensive . . . A 'Chinese' sounds as unnatural to my ear as an 'English' or a 'French' would be, though I agree that we do speak of an 'Italian' or an 'American'.

But he undertook to ask what others felt about it and, since the result of his enquiries was that opinion split about fifty-fifty, he decided that 'Chinaman' should be banned in the paper, and he put out an instruction to that effect.[3]

---

1 Beloff, op. cit., p.123.
2 *Guardian Years*, p.352.
3 Elizabeth C. Dun to the editor, 'not for publication', June 5 1975; W.R.-M. to Elizabeth C. Dun, June 9 and June 24 1975.

Homosexual sensitivities were no less acute, and the recent (1967) legitimising of homosexual relations between consenting adult males had encouraged the assertion of contingent or consequential rights. In this process the fortnightly *Gay News* was to the fore, and in the autumn of 1975 there was trouble with its editor, R. D. Creed, over his application to place a classified advertisement in *The Times*. Mander turned the application down and Creed then wrote to Rees-Mogg, claiming that his journal was 'highly responsible, highly respectable and well established, that all its editorial staff belonged to the NUJ, that every issue was vetted by counsel' (in any case he was himself a solicitor), and that the paper was 'sold openly throughout the country', even W. H. Smith having taken it for some of their branches and found that there was 'a favourable response' to it.

After some delay Rees-Mogg replied briefly that, despite very careful consideration, the adverse decision had to stand. Unfortunately the arrival of his letter more or less coincided with an article by Levin on the theme of homosexual equality before the law, and Creed made much of the irony of Rees-Mogg's having published 'a fine article in the great liberal tradition' while refusing an advertisement for one of the 'channels of communication' by which the law might be further changed. He could not, he said, seriously believe that the motive for refusal was 'an irrational fear of homosexuals or homosexuality'; the decision not to print could only have been due to 'ignorance'.

Thus challenged, Rees-Mogg was obliged to be explicit:

> The reason I cannot advise the acceptance of your advertising is that the character of the Gay Guide which appears in the middle of your magazine and some of your classified advertisements makes your magazine unacceptable to us. This would also apply to heterosexual magazines of the same kind.

There the correspondence ended.[1]

At about the same time there was a letter of complaint, with a copy to Kenneth Thomson, regarding the contents and tone of the

---

1 R. D. Creed to W.R.-M., September 25 1975 (sent to Mander with ms. note 'Mike. Can we discuss, I have not seen the ad. William'); W.R.-M. to Creed, October 14 1975; Creed to W.R.-M., October 21 1975; W.R.-M. to Creed, October 22 1975.

Gay News was started in 1962 and within a year had acquired a large circulation. Its name embodied the American-led and apparently irreversible change of meaning of a lovely old English adjective, for which in its original sense there is no equivalent: a linguistic perversion incongruously perpetrated by male homosexuals just as they were being freed, themselves, from the stigma of moral perversion.

paper's obituary of Sir Denys Lowson, financier and former lord mayor of London. The obituary had nothing to say about his mayoralty, except that he was the youngest man to hold the office and that he had shown in it 'a flair for publicity' which he was always at pains to avoid in his personal affairs. Most of the piece was devoted to his financial irregularities, which had eventually been brought to light by DTI inspectors without, however, leading to any criminal proceedings. One passage reads very quaintly in the light of subsequent events in the City of London:

> Lowson began his career in the City before the war, when the standards of financial morality and duty to shareholders were less developed than they are today. He showed consistently that he was more concerned to turn situations to the advantage of himself . . . than with his fiduciary duty to the companies of which he was a director . . . his methods never represented the best City practice. In the quarter century since the war, however, the ethics of the City generally advanced in a way which placed Sir Denys increasingly out of tune with the City establishment.[1]

A few days later a supplementary tribute appeared from Lord Inman, in which he did not contest any factual statement in the obituary but suggested that it lacked balance. 'It is so easy to publicize recent happenings which clouded his latter years'. Lowson had done much good 'in a kindly and unobtrusive way'.[2]

The letter to the editor, from Michael Donovan, was less restrained. Without stating what connection, if any, had existed between him and Lowson, he described the piece as an offence against 'all good taste', unkind to Lowson's widow and family, and in general 'unwarranted'. For a paper of *The Times*'s standing 'such a biased one-sided account [was] unbecoming', as well as violating the 'principle of speaking well of the dead'. In reply, Rees-Mogg accepted none of the criticisms. He did not think the obituary was 'unfair or in bad taste'. Just as he would expect an obituary of himself to deal mainly with his career as a journalist, so it was reasonable that Lowson's should deal mainly with his career as a financier. 'Unfortunately his work as a financier was badly done'; and when this was true of

1 Obituary, September 11 1975.
2 Inman's tribute, September 18 1975. Inman was himself a notable philanthropist as well as a substantial man of business.

anybody's work, whatever it might be, a truthful obituary had to say so.[1]

The argument was largely, though not, in this instance, wholly sound. If only good could be written of the dead obituaries would not be worth writing, and the good itself would lack credibility. Obituaries should not gloss over unpleasant facts or characteristics. On the other hand, when a person dies it is right that his or her virtues and positive achievements should be stressed, along with any defects, and the balance of judgement should err, if at all, on the side of charity. A comparison of the *Times* obituary of Lowson with the entry on him in the *Dictionary of National Biography* (by John Roberts, in the 1971–80 volume) suggests that the former erred in the other direction, to that extent supporting Donovan's complaint and Inman's implied criticism.

This may be the moment to take a general look at obituaries during the Thomson period. Particular pieces have already been referred to in the course of the narrative, but since obituaries probably constituted, along with leaders, the crossword and letters to the editor, the most admired and distinctive feature of the paper, to which as yet there was no serious competition, they clearly deserve a section to themselves.

Ideally, they provided both a factual record of important careers and a penetrating assessment, personal as well as public, of the deceased. The anonymity of *Times* obituaries was essential to their character, since it gave them an appearance of objectivity which, as a rule, their contents did not belie. Though most of them were based on material commissioned in advance from people with special knowledge, with the result that some element of partiality, for or against, was likely to creep in, the editing of pieces before they went to press normally involved some addition to, and modification of, copy extracted from the file. The illusion that the post of obituaries' editor was held by the Recording Angel was, therefore, to a surprising degree maintained.

The actual editor of the feature throughout the period, and for ten years before it, was the Norfolk-born Colin Watson, who attended Gresham's School, Holt, as a day-boy but did not go to a university. Instead, he went straight from school into provincial journalism,

1 Michael Donovan to W.R.-M., September 12 1975; covering note from him to Kenneth Thomson, with copy of above letter, same date; W.R.-M. to Donovan, October 14 1975.

before joining *The Times* as a sub in 1949. When, to his astonishment, Haley asked him to take charge of obituaries, he at first had to do the job on his own. But before long he was given the assistance of another journalist: first Richard Wigg, then Pieter Zwart and finally, from 1975, Peter Davies. Davies was a most versatile deputy, equally at home in tackling literary figures or members of the armed forces. Quite early in Watson's time the department acquired, in Juliet Lygon, a secretary who established herself as anchor-woman and tutelary spirit. At Printing House Square the department was housed in a pleasant room overlooking the railway; at Gray's Inn Road its accommodation was more nondescript, like everything else there, but at least Watson was able to insist on a separate room, to protect the confidentiality of the files.

Haley took a positive interest in obituaries, always asking at his afternoon conference what each day's entries would be. Rees-Mogg's interest was more intermittent, and largely confined to political obituaries, about which he often made helpful suggestions. In one instance, however, he acted in a manner that was far from beneficial. When Iain Macleod died he asked to see the obituary on file and, finding it excessively critical, had another written which, as already mentioned, erred very markedly the other way. Bland and pious in tone, it was subtitled 'a statesman of spirit and conviction', which surely captures the essence of Macleod far less well than Roy Jenkins's description, 'a politician of insight and insolence'. The piece was also defective on the purely factual side. There was no reference to the life of Neville Chamberlain which, though in fact ghost-written (by Peter Goldman), appeared under Macleod's name while he was a cabinet minister. Worse still, there was nothing in the obituary about his book on bridge or about his prowess as a gambler at cards, which was by no means irrelevant to his character as a politician. Only readers of the *Times* diary were given any information on this aspect of his personality.[1]

In addition to the obituary and the diary titbit, Macleod's death was also the occasion for a leader and for tributes on the op. ed. page, including the text of a broadcast by Heath and a piece by Butt. This tendency to spread obituary material throughout the paper was a

1 Obituary of Macleod, July 22 1970 (referred to on p. 158). Jenkins's comment in his autobiography, *A Life at the Centre*, p.311. The first item in the diary on the day of the obituary began: 'How far, I wonder, could Iain Macleod's skill as an extempore public speaker and his supreme ability to produce an ace during any political debate be attributed to the photographic memory he developed as a bridge player?' Mention was also made of his service as bridge correspondent of the *Sunday Times* and of his book *Bridge is an Easy Game*.

significant threat to the standing and impact of the obituary itself. Another example of it, already noted, was the treatment of Robert Kennedy when he was assassinated.[1] But the worst case of obituary overkill during the Thomson period occurred when Hamilton's hero, Field Marshal Lord Montgomery, died. Monty was given a whole-page obituary (not on the usual page, but on page 9), another page of pictures, a leader 'The victor of Alamein', and an op. ed. piece by Michael Howard discussing how history would judge his generalship. By contrast, Lord Portal of Hungerford, whose contribution as a war leader was on the same scale as Montgomery's, for good or ill, received an obituary of only three columns, and running to only half the depth of the page.[2]

The relative size of obituary notices followed, indeed, no clearly discernible pattern; and the sound principle that pictures should be accorded sparingly was apt to be carried too far. It is odd, for instance, that two such distinguished novelists as Henry Green and Elizabeth Bowen should have been given only double-column, half-page-deep obituaries, without pictures.[3] And, among scientists, it is perhaps even odder that Sir Robert Watson-Watt, who might be on anybody's short list of national saviours, should have received an obituary of three columns but quarter-page depth, also without a picture.[4] Among composers, Dmitri Shostakovich would be generally rated at least on a par with Benjamin Britten. Yet Shostakovich got three columns without a picture, whereas Britten got five columns with one.[5] Few readers, however, can have bothered to make systematic comparisons, enabling them to become aware of such disparities. So long as the

---

1 See p. 78–9 above.
2 Montgomery obit and other pieces, March 25 1976; Portal obit April 24 1971. The obituary of Monty contained hardly any criticism, but Howard's piece was more balanced, bringing out Monty's supreme defect as a strategist, that he was too cautious and ponderous in pursuit. Howard's conclusion was that, although Monty was just as egotistical as Nelson, he 'lacked the final Nelson touch' in his conduct of operations. The Portal obit, as well as giving too brief an account of the subject's career, was totally lacking in critical appraisal. The fateful controversy between the bomber and fighter schools before the Second World War, and the attempt in that war to win it for the Allies by the terror bombing of civilians, of which attempt Portal was a key protagonist, were simply ignored in the piece.
3 Green obit, December 15 1973; Bowen obit, February 23 1973.
4 Watson-Watt obit, December 7 1973. The piece was also marred by its rather grudging tone, as in this passage: 'Although Watson-Watt became widely known as the "father of radar", *a title which he believed to be justified*, there was never an occasion when its origins were being discussed that he failed to give generous acknowledgment to the work of others in the field . . .' (Author's italics.)
5 Shostakovich obit, August 11 1975; Britten obit, December 6 1976. A picture of the former did accompany the front-page announcement of his death.

obituaries were of the usual high quality, whatever their length, complaint was unlikely.

The Britten and Shostakovich pieces were both excellent in themselves, and Britten's was also of interest as illustrating a distinctive problem of the period: how to deal with the phenomenon of homosexuality. The subject was still virtually unmentionable; despite the recent legalising of sexual relations between consenting adult males, the taboo died hard. In most obituaries of homosexuals there was either the time-honoured formula 'He was unmarried' (for example Terence Rattigan) or no reference at all to that side of life (for example Noel Coward).[1] But in some cases the truth was indicated in a circumlocutory way. W. H. Auden's obituary dealt with the matter thus: '*The Orators* (1932) . . . one of the few modern poems that can stand comparison with *The Waste Land*, is at once a fantasizing analysis of a sick society and an examination of the predicament of the homosexual, though Auden was rarely explicit on this theme' – any more, one might say, than his obituary. In the Britten piece the true nature of his relationship with Peter Pears was unmistakably conveyed though not quite stated, the avoidance of absolute precision being, in the circumstances, a considerable feat. The *Michelangelo Sonnets*, it was said, were 'written for Peter Pears, who had travelled with him to America, with whom he formed a nonpareil *recital* partnership, and for whom he composed a procession of superb vocal works and operatic roles – *artistically* they were the making of each other, just as *socially* they proved ideally attuned when they came to share their home at Aldeburgh, a favourite resort of their innumerable friends *of both sexes*'.[2] (The evasiveness of the Britten piece contrasts with the obituary of Tom Driberg earlier the same year, in which he was explicitly described as 'a homosexual' – the only such reference during the period).[3]

From the rich diversity of obituaries during the period two may be cited as showing particularly well how the excellence of the feature was maintained, and how it was evolving into new biographical fields. When Eamon de Valera died in 1975, at the age of ninety-two, he was rightly given an obituary occupying five columns to full-page depth, and with a picture. But it was the quality of the text that mattered; both as a record of fact and as an anticipation of the verdict

1 Rattigan obit, December 1 1977; Coward obit, March 27 1973.
2 Author's italics. In the front-page story on Britten's death it was reported that the Queen had sent a message of sympathy to Pears 'as a representative of all who had worked with Lord Britten'.
3 Driberg (Lord Bradwell) obit, August 13 1976.

of history the piece was outstanding. De Valera's merits were fully acknowledged, while the disastrous aspects of his character and mentality were subtly analysed. 'There was a bleak integrity and refusal to count the cost about many of his actions that was in apparent contradiction to the transparent opportunism of others'. The most fateful moment of his career, 'by which all that followed must be judged', was his conduct over the 1921 Anglo-Irish Treaty. 'There is no need to impugn his motives to conclude that he was wrong [in repudiating the Treaty]; for from that grave decision flowed an atrocious period of civil war, animosities that bedevilled Irish politics for four decades and retarded the development of the country, and the continuance of the Irish Republican Army as a threat to civil order'.[1]

De Valera was in the traditional mould as a subject for obituary treatment in *The Times*. But the same could hardly be said of John Lennon, who at the time of his assassination in 1980 received a three-column obituary, two-thirds of the page deep, also with a picture. The subtitle of the piece was 'Dominant role in a pop music revolution', and the suggestion throughout was that Lennon's importance, like that of the Beatles as a group, was more as a social and psychological, than as a musical, phenomenon. The Beatles 'somehow gave an impression of being more musically literate than any of their predecessors – though in fact none of the four could either read or write music'. The obituary referred contemptuously to those critics who uttered 'immoderate rhapsodies . . . on their musicianly attainments', such as the absurd statement that they were the 'greatest song-writers since Schubert'. Nevertheless, with the help of skilful promotion, they did pluck the lead in pop music 'from America's grasp'. Lennon himself was the odd man out, not conforming to the Beatles' 'clean' image. He had always been a difficult character. 'A rebel in the era before child rebellion was officially subsidized by adult indulgence, he took little interest in the formal side of his schooling'. The obituary did not take seriously his later status as a cult figure, with saintly attributes in the eyes of contemporary youth, devoting only two short paragraphs to his years of seclusion with Yoko Ono. The ending was ironically succinct: 'At the time of his death Lennon's fortune was estimated at £100 million'.[2]

The tradition that *Times* obituaries are anonymous is sound and should not be transgressed. The authorship of particular pieces, in whole or part, should not, therefore, be betrayed even long after the

1 De Valera obit., August 30 1975.
2 Lennon obit, December 10 1980.

event. All the same, the names of some people whose work for the feature was frequent and of exceptional value can reasonably be given, provided there is no specific attribution.

For literary figures, J. B. Priestley, C. Day-Lewis, Paul Scott, Raymond Mortimer, Walter Allen, Roy Fuller, Oliver Warner and Alan Pryce-Jones were among the most valuable sources; for general historians, Roger Fulford and A. J. P. Taylor; for service personnel and war historians, Basil Liddell Hart, Cyril Falls and Stephen Roskill; for artists and art historians, Anthony Blunt; for composers and musicians, William Mann, the paper's long-time music critic; for actors and dramatists, J. C. Trewin; for politicians and journalists, T. E. Utley, John Beavan and Margaret Cole; for scientists, Rudolf Peierls and William Penney; for churchmen Bishop William Wand (Anglicans) and Douglas Woodruff (Roman Catholics). As well as Mann, many regular members of the staff contributed, including Hickey, Michael Ratcliffe, Douglas-Home, and *TBS* specialists for businessmen. Rees-Mogg was helpful in suggesting contributors for political obituaries, and Haley continued to take an interest in the feature after his retirement.

Those who wrote *Times* obituaries, or produced material for them, worked with an indifference to financial reward matched only by contributors to the *Dictionary of National Biography*. The normal rate of pay was one guinea (one pound plus one shilling) per hundred words, for pieces which did not even have the advantage of a byline. Marghanita Laski, when told the rate by Watson, said that she could not write for less than two guineas per hundred words, and an exception was made in her favour. Some writers, on the other hand, refused to accept any payment at all for recording and appraising the lives of friends. From the paper's point of view, the obituaries' section was a bargain next only to the correspondence.[1]

Labour had returned to office in 1974 because of a fight between the Heath government and the trade unions which the latter had effectively won. In the second 1974 election Labour had improved its position because of a supposed contract with the unions under which wage claims were to be moderated in return for the re-instatement of union privileges and welfare benefits constituting what was described as the 'social wage'. This contract, like its predecessor the 'solemn and

1 Since 1986 rates of pay for obituaries have been relatively fair to those producing them.

binding' (nicknamed Solomon Binding) agreement that followed the collapse of Wilson's attempt to reform the trade unions, proved of no value whatsoever. In the words of Labour's chancellor of the exchequer, Denis Healey, 'the unions defaulted on their part of the contract'.[1] By early 1975 wage rises were exceeding the rate of inflation by 10 per cent, despite Foot's propitiatory legislation, redistributive tax changes, and a 'social wage' estimated at about £1,000 a year for every member of the working population.

Since inflation was already intolerably high (20 per cent), through circumstances over which the new government had no control – including the inflation of oil and other commodity prices, and 'threshold' agreements inherited from the Heath government – a drastic change of policy was inescapable, and Healey was just the man to carry it out. Of formidable intellect and robust temperament, he had evolved from a youthful spell in the Communist party to a habit of pragmatic Labour loyalism, which meant that when Labour was in office he would do all he could to keep it there, regardless of party orthodoxy, and when in opposition he would use all his forensic gifts to justify Labour policy, whether or not he agreed with it. The connecting links between his Communist past and his Labour present were blind loyalty to party and an overriding interest in power. Yet another product of Balliol, he was a fine classical scholar and humanist without any training in economics. But he did not regard this as a disadvantage, taking the view that 'a minister who has studied economics at university usually has at best only a general recollection of what he was taught at least twenty years earlier, by academics who had studied the economy at least twenty years earlier still'. In any case, economics was 'not a science', but 'a branch of social psychology'.[2]

His first budget, introduced within weeks of the change of government, was on quite the wrong lines for the country, though helpful in the short term to his party. The steps he took in it to implement Labour's pledge to effect an 'irreversible transfer of wealth and power to working people and their families' added to the already rampant inflation, while his increases in corporate taxation drove many firms to the brink of bankruptcy. Later he blamed the treasury for underestimating the public sector borrowing requirement (PSBR) and overestimating company liquidity;[3] but had he cut general public expenditure while giving fiscal encouragement to business Labour might well have lost the second 1974 election.

---

1 Healey, *The Time of my Life*, paperback edition, p.394.
2 Healey, op. cit., p.377.
3 Ibid., p.393.

The following year's budget had to be very different. 'The Chancellor made no bones about it', Wood reported. 'Because the so-called social contract is not working, in spite of some ministerial claims, direct and indirect taxation has had to be increased immediately and next financial year cuts of £900 m. are planned'. Unemployment could be 'touching one million by the end of the year', with the budget itself accounting for the probable loss of 20,000 jobs. The full text of the budget statement occupied two pages, and the parliamentary report continued on a further page, where Mrs. Thatcher was quoted as condemning 'a typical socialist budget – equal shares of misery for all'.[1]

The budget was not enough, however, and in July the government introduced, in agreement with the TUC general council, a limit of 6 per cent on wage increases, to operate for a year from August 1, and a complete freeze on salaries above £8,500 a year. This return to the direct control of incomes was announced in a Commons statement and further expounded at a press conference, while the details were set out in a White Paper. The new policy was welcomed in a leader which awarded personal good marks not only to Healey, but to Wilson as well. 'One has to recognize, and put in the Prime Minister's favour, that he is accepting these strains [on the trade unions and the Labour Party] in serving what both he and Mr. Healey know to be an essential national interest'. The parliamentary correspondent, Noyes, was even more fulsome about the prime minister:

> Mr. Wilson yesterday seemed to have pulled off a feat of reconciliation that will go down in the annals of political wizardry as one of his greatest achievements. Out of the Babel that preceded the publication of [the] White Paper . . . he emerged with a Commons statement that produced not a single threat of resignation or instant revolution.

In fact, one junior Scottish Office minister (Robert Hughes) did resign a few days later in protest against the return to statutory incomes policy, and there were even for a time rumours that Foot would not accept penal sanctions. But on the whole the management of the cabinet and parliamentary party was quite a feat.[2]

---

1 April 16 1975.
2 Leader, 'A plan to save the country' July 12 1975 and Noyes's front-page report the same day. The Conservatives' decision to abstain on the government's White Paper proposals, after moving a reasoned amendment, was deplored in a leader on July 18: 'The loss is not merely the Conservative Party's; it is the nation's. The two great parties now reciprocate in opposition the evasion of the policies they adopt in government'.

In early September the change of policy had to be endorsed by the TUC conference at Blackpool, and Routledge reported on the mood as the delegates assembled:

> A casual visitor to last year's [conference] at Brighton might have been forgiven for thinking that he was at the wrong jamboree. It was much more like a Labour Party conference, and the debates were clearly directed as much to the electorate as to the faithful membership . . .
>
> Certainly, Labour's election campaign got off the ground there, with the establishment of the social contract as the chief electoral advantage of a Government that knew how to get along with the unions. It worked [i.e. for electoral purposes], but it all seems such a long time ago now . . .
>
> The failure of the original version of the social contract . . . is frankly admitted.

Routledge assumed that the new policy would receive the delegates' backing, and it was indeed endorsed by a two to one majority. But he emphasised that, in return, the unions would want 'greater long-term influence in the social and industrial fabric of the country'.[1]

At the end of the month Foot demonstrated his solidarity with Healey and Wilson when he urged the Labour party conference, also at Blackpool, to accept the government's volte-face, calling upon the delegates to show the 'red flame of socialist courage'. His rhetoric helped to defeat the government's critics,[2] but his support for penal sanctions had been won by making them applicable exclusively against employers in the private sector, who were to be denied government orders and state aid if they paid in excess of the limit. In the public sector the government had to rely on its own control of cash, a subject on which, Stephenson noted, the White Paper had little to say.[3]

Though the 6 per cent limit was to be in force for only one year, Healey stated clearly that incomes would have to be controlled for a longer period. This admission was welcomed in a letter from J. K. Galbraith, who used the occasion to attack his fellow-economists for their failure to evolve beyond Keynes to the necessity for control.

Op. ed. piece, 'With the social contract buried, the TUC has more than money in mind', September 1 1975.

Lead story, 'Mr. Foot's passionate appeal defeats wages policy critics', September 0 1975.

'Chancellor's tactful omission', *TBN*, July 14 1975.

Even Healey, he said, had not yet moved far enough. The indication that wage control would have to last for several years

> . . . still suggests the lingering belief that somehow, some time, there can be a return to the wonderful world of macro-economics – no serious unemployment, no intolerable inflation, no controls; a world that is possible, in fact, only if there are no trade unions, no powerful corporations, no unsatisfied claims to income that are coupled with the power to satisfy them. No one avows such hopes – or such a world.[1]

The world would change in the next decade, and was already beginning to change. Before the end of the year unemployment had risen above a million for the first time since the war.

---

1 Letter to the editor, July 16 1975.

XIX

Fisk and Colin Wallace • More fringe problems • An extravagant tribute • Wilson resigns: Callaghan succeeds • Belabouring Healey • Editorial tensions

AFTER THE COLLAPSE of the power-sharing executive in Ulster things went from bad to worse in the province. Moderation and compromise were discredited, and so was direct rule as exercised by Wilson and Rees. Moreover, towards the end of 1974 IRA violence escalated alarmingly in Great Britain (too often referred to as 'mainland Britain', as though Ireland were a small offshore island like Man or Wight). The worst outrages at this time were the pub bombings at Guildford and Birmingham, whose notoriety was later compounded by the grave miscarriages of justice that resulted from them. In reaction to the Birmingham explosions on November 21, which killed 24 and injured nearly 200, the home secretary, Jenkins, introduced emergency legislation with all-party support. The Prevention of Terrorism (Temporary Provisions) Act had some practical utility, though its chief value was psychological. Despite its title it was still on the statute book nearly twenty years later.

Jenkins himself in retrospect considered it justified, while describing it as a 'rush of blood to the head'.[1] The description could better be applied to Rees-Mogg's initial reaction to the bombings, which was more impulsive and less discriminating. In a leader entitled 'This *is* an act of war' he called not only for banning the IRA and all demonstrations in favour of it (with which Jenkins concurred), but also for bringing back the death penalty for terrorists, dismissing the objection that this would lead to retaliatory killing and the taking of hostages. He also argued that if there were further such IRA atrocities in Great Britain the 'eventual' consequence would be the return of Northern Ireland to 'Protestant supremacy as the only

1 Jenkins, op. cit., p.393.

force capable of controlling the terrorists [based in] the Catholic community'.[1]

A few days later the paper's line was quietly modified to accord with that of Jenkins, who was determined to resist an attempt to add capital punishment to his programme of emergency measures. When his bill was introduced another leader, by a different hand (Hickey's), welcomed it as necessary not least as a means of averting the more extreme measures that some were proposing, such as the death penalty for terrorists. This leader also stressed the need to ensure that the new powers were not used clumsily, so making 'the problem of Irish republican violence more intractable than ever'.[2] When the death penalty proposal was debated in the House of Commons on December 11, it was defeated by a majority of 152 on a free vote. Next day's paper published the full division list, showing that Joseph, Maudling and Thatcher were among the numerous Conservatives who had voted for the proposal, while those who had voted against included Whitelaw and Heath.[3]

In January 1975 Fisk was named 'Reporter of the Year' by Granada TV's *What the Papers Say* programme. The citation referred to his 'courage, energy and cool, restrained style'; and the award was reported on *The Times*'s front page with a picture of him.[4] Towards the end of March he was withdrawn from Northern Ireland, his last weeks there having been marked by a bizarre incident. On February 6 he was in Dublin, at New Jury's Hotel, when he was visited late at night by an official from the British embassy, who told him that unless he handed over documents belonging to HMG he would be committing an offence. The reason for this threatening approach to a British subject on Irish soil (which Fisk regarded as a breach of diplomatic protocol), was that a few days before a secret document had been left at his cottage at Hillsborough, Co. Down, and that it had since fallen into the hands of the police. An army press officer with whom he was in frequent contact had brought the document, meaning to show it to

1 November 23 1974.
2 Leader, 'A necessary bill', November 27 1974.
3 December 12 1974. Curiously, Thatcher's name was omitted from the list of leading Conservatives voting for the proposal, which Wood gave in his front-page story. Whitelaw had interrupted Jenkins's speech to make his own, and Heath's, position clear, since protocol inhibited him from actually speaking in the debate (Joseph being the official opposition spokesman on home affairs). Jenkins praises this 'remarkable display of courage' by both men, at a time when Heath's leadership was 'coming under heavy challenge' and Whitelaw was 'a possible contender for the succession'. (Jenkins, op. cit., p.398.)
4 January 22 1975.

him, but finding that he was away had pushed the envelope through the letter-box. If this part of the story was true, the envelope cannot have been well sealed, because Fisk's cleaning lady later found 'a large number of foolscap sheets' that had burst out of it on the doormat. Noticing the word 'restricted' printed at the top she passed them on to the RUC. Fisk was then interviewed by the police, who asked if he had ever before seen classified documents. He replied that he had, and had written articles based on them. The police did not show him the document left at his cottage.[1]

The army press officer who had delivered it there was Colin Wallace, of whom Fisk had made much use as a covert source, but who had also, apparently, made some use of him. Wallace was a native Protestant Ulsterman, a former chemist, who had started working for the army in the Sixties, shortly before the troubles began, and whose local knowledge made him increasingly valuable. He became involved in black propaganda directed against the IRA ('Clockwork Orange'), an activity long denied, but eventually admitted, by the ministry of defence. He also later claimed that members of MI5 in Northern Ireland were engaged in a conspiracy to destabilise the Wilson government, and that he had objected to this on constitutional grounds. Whether or not his removal from Northern Ireland, his dismissal soon afterwards as a result of the Fisk incident, and his subsequent trial and conviction for manslaughter in England, were all engineered by MI5, as he alleged, may never be known for sure and anyway need not concern us here. There is little reason to doubt, however, that in leaking information or, quite often, disinformation to Fisk and other journalists, he was acting in general with the knowledge and approval of his military superiors.[2]

One way or the other, the February incident made Fisk's position in Northern Ireland more difficult, and his own departure was clearly to some extent connected with it. In writing to congratulate him on his record of service in the province, his friend and patron Douglas-Home told him: 'I have said privately that the important thing . . . is to get you out of Ulster alive and I hope I am not tempting fate now by expressing satisfaction that we have jointly achieved this'. In his reply, Fisk thanked Douglas-Home for backing him whenever he was in a tight spot, as when 'diplomats [came] whirling through the doors

---

1 Fisk's report in the paper, February 8 1975.

2 Paul Foot, *Who Framed Colin Wallace?* Foot shows that Wallace was about to leave Northern Ireland, having already been posted to another army job at Preston, when he took the envelope to Hillsborough. The official claim that that particular would-be leak was not authorised is, therefore, on the face of it plausible.

of New Jury's Hotel demanding non-existent documents'; also for letting him 'roar off to New York' after the 'escapade'.[1] On leaving Northern Ireland he joined the paper's foreign news staff and was soon making a fresh reputation for himself in the Middle East, where there was even more scope for his zest for dangerous living and his talent for vivid, controversial reporting. When Douglas-Home became foreign editor, they were able to work together again.

At about the time of Fisk's departure Wilson paid a six-hour visit to Ulster and announced that elections would soon be held for a convention to work out a new system of government for the province. The convention was duly elected, on May 1, but after lengthy sessions no agreement emerged from it. Meanwhile Rees continued to release suspects held in detention, and he also reduced the army's presence in South Armagh, to the indignation of loyalists and of the opposition at Westminster. In that dangerous area thirty murders occurred during the year, mostly the work of the IRA. On December 5 detention without trial was brought to an end with the release of the last forty-six suspects, who left with defiant threats to carry on the war. Early in the New Year the paper's lead story, from Christopher Walker, was of an ambush near the border in South Armagh, in which ten Protestant workers were turned out of a bus and machine-gunned. The following day Walker reported an ominous speech by Ian Paisley, threatening another Ulster workers' strike, and the paper argued in a big leader that a temporary coalition should be formed in Northern Ireland for the sole purpose of suppressing terrorism. Responsibility for the RUC should be transferred to this body and, as a gesture to the Protestants, the idea of a council of Ireland should be explicitly dropped.[2]

Wilson did not take up this suggestion, but reacted strongly to the Armagh atrocity by announcing that a unit of the Special Air Service (SAS) would be sent to the area. The announcement met with protest from every section of the nationalist minority, from Gerard Fitt no less than Seamus Mallon, and there was talk of the SAS as a bunch of assassins. The army command in Ulster gave an assurance that the

---

1 C.D.-H. to Fisk, March 25 1975; Fisk to C.D.-H., March 27 1975. (Fisk papers.) Douglas-Home's letter lays the compliments on so thick one is bound to suspect a desire to remove Fisk from Northern Ireland without hurting his pride. Another complication in the affair was that Michael Cudlipp (whose stay at London Broadcasting was short-lived) had recently become adviser on public relations to the Northern Ireland Office.

2 Lead story, '10 Ulster Protestants massacred in ambush near border', January 6 1976. Story of Paisley speech and leader 'The Armagh massacres', January 7 1976. The outgoing GOC Northern Ireland, Sir Frank King, had given a public warning in April that the continued release of detainees would lead to a new IRA offensive.

men would 'operate in uniform', and in parliament a few days later Wilson tried to pacify some of his backbenchers with a pledge that the unit would be used only 'for patrolling and surveillance' under strict control of the GOC.[1]

The reputation of the SAS was defended at the time in an anonymous op. ed. piece, which seems to have attracted less attention than at least one remark in it deserved:

> To anyone who knows them well, the IRA claim that [the SAS] have been used as undercover assassins in Northern Ireland is absurd. Furthermore, had the Northern Ireland Office wanted to assassinate civilians in Ulster, they would be unlikely to use a regular regiment of the British Army, *there being far better-equipped government departments for that purpose.*
>
> They face the best trained, best equipped IRA active service unit in Ulster, led by Paddy O'Kane, an ex-colour sergeant in the Parachute Regiment. The IRA also has the great advantage of being able to choose when to come across the border and where to attack.
>
> For SAS men, however, South Armagh gives them an opportunity to demonstrate their professionalism as soldiers in a spotlight, *improve relations with the Regular Army*, and get rid of the much hated assassin label.[2]

The unnamed author of this piece was described as 'a Special Correspondent who has recently served with the Army in Ulster'. The reference to improving relations with the regular army was an oblique admission that they had not been good. Above all, the statement that there were departments of the official machine that could be used to mount a campaign of assassination might have been expected to arouse serious alarm and feverish comment, though strangely it appears not to have done so. The publication of such a piece shows that, despite the departure of Fisk and Wallace, the army was still capable of planting material to suit itself in the paper.

---

1 Reports, January 8 and January 13 1976; the first from Walker and Michael Hatfield in Northern Ireland, the second from Hugh Noyes at Westminster.

2 'The SAS, fighting hard to lose the "assassin label"', January 16 1976. (Author's italics.) Whatever their methods, the presence of the SAS in South Armagh proved highly effective in the short term.

While in Ulster the British government was trying in vain to re-establish some form of devolution, the same constitutional device was in prospect for two other Celtic countries, Scotland and Wales. The strong showing of the Scottish National Party in the two 1974 elections, and the Liberals' commitment to devolution, had put Labour under pressure to respond, in some measure, to the demand for more Scottish autonomy. At the same time there was a feeling that Wales would have to be included in the process, though the issue was of far less concern to the Welsh. Indeed, towards the end of 1974 a young Welsh backbencher, with a future that few would then have predicted, wrote to the paper:

> As incredible as it may seem . . . the Welsh people do not seem to feel that it is necessary to have a Parliament in order to be a Nation any more than they feel it necessary to speak Welsh in order to be Welsh. This is not because the Welsh are congenitally subservient – no one could call us that – but because we do not feel the need for new constitutional clothing at this time in our history.[1]

Nevertheless, the White Paper that the government produced about a year later proposed that Wales as well as Scotland should have an elected assembly. The extent of devolution was, however, to be greater in Scotland than in Wales, since whereas the governmental functions to be transferred from the Welsh Office would be exercised by committees of the assembly, in Scotland there would be an executive to administer the transferred powers. This executive, under the leadership of an individual who would, in effect, be a Scottish prime minister, would be chosen by the elected assembly and responsible to it. The secretary of state for Scotland would remain, with reserved powers in economic and industrial matters, with oversight of the assembly, and with the right to suggest a veto on any act of the Scottish executive or legislature, even within the devolved sphere, subject only to the Westminster Parliament's (that is the British government's) assent. Finance would come mainly from a block treasury grant, though there would be a minor devolved power to raise revenue by a surcharge on the rates.

In January 1976 there was a four-day Commons debate on devolution, and the day before it began the paper carried a leader, written

1 Neil Kinnock, letter to the editor, November 1 1974. He was replying to one from Gwynfor Evans, president of Plaid Cymru and MP for Carmarthen.

by Geoffrey Smith, which addressed itself chiefly to the Scottish aspect of the question. The debate would be 'a test of the breadth of vision of the House of Commons'. Since the publication of the White Paper the trend of opinion among English MPs seemed to have become increasingly critical of the intention to set up Scottish and Welsh assemblies. In Scotland, on the other hand, there was 'considerable disappointment' that the White Paper did not go further, and there could be 'no guarantee that any form of devolution [would] be enough to satisfy Scotland in the mood developing there'. Yet the evidence still suggested that most Scots wanted no more than increased control over their own affairs within the United Kingdom, and the best hope of averting separatism lay 'in a measured advance on the White Paper's proposals'.

The leader mentioned three ways in which an improvement on them might be achieved. The scope of the secretary of state's veto was too wide as proposed, and should be reduced. The economic part of the scheme should be rethought; more responsibility in this field should be given to the assembly, and it should also have 'a somewhat greater power to levy taxes of its own'. Finally, the method of election should not necessarily be first-past-the-post, as the White Paper envisaged.[1]

Both the main parties were divided on the devolution issue. On the Labour side two MPs regarded the proposals as so inadequate that they formed a separate Scottish Labour Party which, however, the UK party was reluctant to excommunicate. Other Labour MPs were unhappy about the scheme for the opposite reason, and when Wilson sat down after opening the debate there was 'scarcely a murmur of approval' from his own side, even from his colleagues on the front bench.[2] Mrs. Thatcher denounced the proposals as cumbersome, costly and bound to lead to conflict, and in her party, which was after all Unionist as well as Conservative, there was more solid support for the leader's view. But there were dissidents in her ranks too, and when in due course the government introduced its bill the shadow Scottish secretary, Alick Buchanan-Smith, and his deputy, Malcolm Rifkind (a future secretary of state), both resigned in protest against the shadow cabinet's decision to oppose second reading. The former prime minister, Heath, also came out strongly in favour of full and effective

1 Leader, 'Can the Scots ever be satisfied?', January 12 1976. The following day there was a signed op. ed. piece by Smith on the financial difficulties of the scheme and how they might be surmounted.

2 Front-page report by Noyes, January 14 1976. The first SLP defector was James (Jim) Sillars, who some years later joined the SNP.

devolution. The official party line, slow to emerge, was that there should be an elected Scottish assembly to act as a third house of Parliament, but no Scottish executive.

At the end of the preliminary debate in January there was a government majority of 258, though a Conservative amendment was defeated by only 71. *The Times* warned against any illusion that the scheme would go through as it stood. 'Despite the token success of the voting figures . . . there could be little chance of a Bill faithfully reflecting the White Paper being piloted on to the statute book in this Parliament'. There would have to be changes.[1] When, however, the bill was at length introduced, on November 30 (St Andrew's Day), the only important modification was that instead of the secretary of state's veto on measures supposedly *ultra vires* there would be reference to the judicial committee of the Privy Council. This was welcomed by the paper, which also reasserted the necessity for devolution to keep Scotland within the United Kingdom. But failure to extend the assembly's taxation powers was attacked, and so was retention of the first-past-the-post method of election. There was already a precedent for PR in Northern Ireland, and soon (it was over-optimistically stated) there would be a further precedent in elections to the European parliament, as the British government would be obliged to bow to Community practice. The *Times*'s leader on the bill also argued that there should be referenda, confined to the Scottish and Welsh electorates, before the scheme for either country was put into effect.[2] On the last issue the government had to give way, since it became apparent that without a pledge to hold referenda there would be no majority for the principle of the bill. Even so, the majority was only 45.

There was still plenty of trouble ahead. The first bill did not after all make the grade and another had to be brought in towards the end of 1977. This passed, though with an amendment prescribing, for the

1 Leader, 'Honest doubts on Scotland', January 22 1976. The author was Smith.
2 Leader, 'Necessary but imperfect', December 1 1976; again written by Smith. *The Times* would have preferred separate bills for Scotland and Wales. It also raised a tricky point about the scale of their representation at Westminster, which was not to be reduced though the Kilbrandon Commission had recommended that it should be. The truth was that Labour depended upon a full complement of MPs from the Celtic fringe, because England tended to be predominantly Conservative. Yet it was obviously unfair that Scottish and Welsh MPs should be free to vote in undiminished strength not only on United Kingdom matters but also on purely English matters. By the same token it was unjust that Northern Ireland's Westminster representation had not been increased since direct rule was imposed, but left at the lower level fixed for the devolved Stormont system. This grievance was strongly pressed by Ulster's Westminster MPs, and in due course had to be met.

Scottish referendum, a percentage majority vote which was not, in the event, reached; while the Welsh scheme was decisively rejected by the voters of Wales. One way and another devolution contributed substantially to the undoing of the Labour government.

In March 1976 Rees-Mogg wrote perhaps his best-known, though certainly not his best, leader. Its theme was essentially the same as that of the very first he had written, in 1967: the superiority of George Brown to Harold Wilson. He had then mentioned Brown in the same breath, as it were, with the two Pitts, Palmerston, Lloyd George and Churchill, and the contrast with Wilson was implied rather than directly stated.[1] The later piece, though even more questionable on the score of balance, could hardly be criticised for any lack of directness.

The occasion for it was Brown's resignation from the Labour party, already recorded.[2] The emotion of leaving his old party had, apparently, been too much for him, and several newspapers carried a picture of him 'fallen in the gutter'. Among the papers which had so disgracefully (in Rees-Mogg's view) exploited the misfortune of 'a great man at an awkward moment', the *Guardian* kept company with the *Daily Mail*, the *Daily Express* and the *Daily Mirror*. *The Times*'s companions in virtuous self-denial were the *Daily Telegraph*, the *Financial Times*, the *Sun* and the *Morning Star*.

No other paper, however, felt moved to comment on the incident, or on Brown himself, as *The Times* did:

> Perhaps Lord George-Brown had been drinking . . . He is a man of strong mind and strong heart who cares for the defence of the freedoms of his country and for the well-being of ordinary British people.
>
> Of course he is impossible . . . If he had not been impossible he would be Prime Minister, and if he were Prime Minister then the country might be better off than it is. There is no cause to be critical of Mr. Wilson at this moment when he is battling for causes he earlier failed to support. But the truth is that when it comes to the heart of the matter, Lord George-Brown is a better man drunk than the Prime Minister sober.[3]

---

1 See p. 49 above.
2 See p. 343 above.
3 Leader, 'An honest man's warning', March 4 1976. The *Sun*, acquired by Rupert Murdoch some years earlier from IPC, may seem a rather surprising member of the self-denying group.

Not surprisingly, there was considerable reaction to this comment from readers, much of it sympathetic to George-Brown and the editor. But an interesting, if partly mischievous, protest came from a friend of Rees-Mogg's whose own failure to measure words had cost him his place as a columnist on the paper:

> Sir, Like many of your readers who can't possibly afford more than one newspaper in these difficult times, I might never have learnt about Lord George-Brown's mishap if it had not been for your high-minded leader criticizing other newspapers for describing it.
>
> Unlike you, I find the episode a fitting commentary on our times . . .
>
> Your decision to suppress those aspects of the news which displease you strikes me as differing only in effectiveness from the Russian model. If there is more behaviour of this sort on your part, I shall seriously consider switching my order to the *Daily Mail*.
>
> Yours faithfully
> Auberon Waugh.[1]

One private letter of support for Rees-Mogg came from a former deputy editor of the *Guardian*, John Pringle: 'I was sorry to see your savaging of the old paper in today's issue, but I am afraid it was deserved . . . What a shadow of a shade it has become from the paper I used to know . . . My good wishes to you in your increasingly lonely fight for everything that matters'. In his reply, Rees-Mogg lamented the recent departure of Hetherington as editor of the *Guardian*, 'because he acted as a control on the young men'.[2]

Heren later claimed to have acted as a control on Rees-Mogg in the gestation of this controversial leader:

> William was . . . capable of great dislikes. For instance, after he had left early one Friday evening for the country I read a proof of a leader he had written condemning Harold Wilson . . . He began splendidly, but then getting into his stride he had written four or five paragraphs which . . . [were] unnecessarily hurtful . . . There was no way of getting in touch with William before the paper went to press. I deleted four or five paragraphs but not

1 Letter to the editor, March 6 1976.
2 Pringle to W.R.-M., March 4 1976; W.R.-M. to Pringle, March 9 1976. The *Guardian* was certainly not the 'shadow of a shade' in the matter of circulation.

> the punch line which read: 'Better George Brown drunk than Harold Wilson sober' [*sic*]. It was too good a line, but I still felt I had done what I ought not to have done. I need not have worried. On Monday morning he arrived, his face enlivened by a boyish grin, and thanked me for saving him from himself again.[1]

Heren's memory of the incident was clearly at fault, because the article in question appeared on a Thursday, not a Saturday. We know, moreover, that Rees-Mogg was in the office as the leader was going to press, because Levin read it and sent him a memo urging him to change the punch-line to 'Lord George-Brown drunk is ten times a better man than the Prime Minister sober', while praising the leader as a whole as 'splendid fighting stuff'.[2]

Within a fortnight of the drunk/sober leader the prime minister took the country, and not least the media, utterly by surprise in announcing his resignation which, he said, had been long planned. In *The Times*'s lead story Wood wrote: 'The Queen had known of his intention since December. Mr. George Thomas, now the Speaker, had been warned of it. Lord Goodman, by all accounts, had told one or two Cabinet ministers before Christmas that Mr. Wilson would retire in March. But no member of the Cabinet had believed a word of it'. As a caption to the front-page picture of Wilson, characteristically smoking a pipe, his own words were quoted: 'I have a duty to the country and the party not to remain here so long that others are denied the chance to seek election'. On page 2 there was a feature on six prospective contenders for the succession: Callaghan, Healey, Foot, Crosland, Benn and Jenkins. On the op. ed. page there were pieces on Wilson by Butt and Geoffrey Smith, and a selection of pictures of him, including the familiar one as a child on the steps of 10 Downing Street.

In a three-column leader the editor noted, for a start, that the previous twelve years had been a period 'of palpable decline for the United Kingdom', and that 'for nine of them Wilson had been prime minister'. His failures and failings were listed, with special emphasis on his decision in 1964 to maintain at all costs the fixed parity of the pound. Yet his part in the recent recovery had been 'crucial', and he left his party in better shape than when he became its leader, at least

---

Heren, op. cit., pp.218–19.
Levin to W.R.-M., March 3 1976.

in the sense that there were candidates 'of long ministerial experience, political weight and shrewd judgment' to succeed him.[1]

During the run-up to the first ballot, on March 25, the paper indicated its preference for Jenkins: 'Roy Jenkins was the most successful Chancellor and as a matter of judgment he was the best. Mr. Healey is very good now, but was bad to begin with. Mr. Jenkins in Downing Street with Mr. Healey continuing his fight against inflation would be a convincing arrangement . . .'[2] Levin, too, gave Jenkins strong support.[3] But in news coverage of the contest the likelihood that Callaghan would emerge the winner was never concealed or played down. He had the rare distinction of having held the three principal offices of state apart from the premiership, though in none of them had his performance been particularly distinguished. Above all, he was a favourite of the trade unions, who was also acceptable to a majority of the parliamentary party as a moderate. On the first ballot he came narrowly second to Foot, but decisively ahead of the other left-wing candidate, Benn, and of his three moderate rivals, Jenkins, Healey and Crosland.[4] Jenkins immediately withdrew, and *The Times* made a virtue of necessity in switching to Callaghan: 'The sooner we have a new Prime Minister the better, and Mr. Callaghan could be a good one'.[5]

There were still two more ballots because, although Benn and Crosland also withdrew after the first, Healey stayed for the second, in which, however, he added only eight votes to his first-round score, while Callaghan moved ahead of Foot. In the third round, a straight contest between those two, Callaghan won by 176 votes to 137. His assumption of the premiership was followed by important changes in the government. Jenkins, denied the foreign office by which he would have been tempted to remain, left before the end of the year to become president of the European Commission. His place as home secretary was then taken by Merlyn Rees, whose post in Northern Ireland was

1 March 17 1976. Leader, 'End of the Wilson era'. Butt's piece, 'The Wilson years: one man's great political balancing act'. Smith's piece, 'Age is the problem, but Mr. Callaghan must be considered the front runner'.

2 Leader, 'The day of nominations', March 22 1976.

3 'Is Mr. Jenkins the man to sweep the board for Labour?' March 24 1976. Jenkins was one of those forewarned by Goodman. On Boxing Day 1975, lunching with Ann Fleming in the country, he had been taken aside by Goodman and told that Wilson was 'resolved to resign in March'. Goodman's declared motive for giving the information was that Jenkins was his preferred candidate for the succession. (Jenkins, op cit., p.430.)

4 The figures were: Foot, 90; Callaghan, 84; Jenkins 56; Benn, 37; Healey, 30; Crosland, 17.

5 Leader, 'It looks like Mr. Callaghan', March 26 1976.

filled by the more decisive Roy Mason. Crosland became foreign secretary, and Foot leader of the House of Commons, while Barbara Castle, one of the bravest and ablest of Wilson's ministers – whose plan for trade union reform had been sabotaged by Callaghan – was dropped from the government. Healey remained at the treasury.

The last act of Wilson's premiership occurred more than two months after he had retired, with the publication of his resignation honours list at the end of May. This had been preceded by 'weeks of speculation and rumour', much of which turned out to be accurate. Even so, when it eventually appeared it 'provoked angry outbursts from left-wing Labour and other MPs'.[1] Wilson himself had meanwhile been appointed a Knight of the Garter by the Queen.

His list was exceptionally large, consisting in all of forty-two names, including nine new life peers. It was also the most controversial since Lloyd George's Birthday list in 1922. Though some of those whom Wilson chose to reward were party stalwarts, more seemed to be people whose allegiance to the Labour party was at best doubtful; and at least one was dubious in another sense.[2] *The Times*'s leader on the list avoided stuffy censoriousness and dealt with it in sardonic vein, even with some hint of approval. It was, certainly, a 'bizarre' list for a socialist ex-prime minister. Most of the baronies and knighthoods went to people who were 'very clearly capitalists . . . of a tough, risk-taking type'; not by and large the sort of men who ran the great industrial companies, but the sort who had 'carved out their own fortunes with their own sharp swords'.

> Whether these untamed capitalists hold theoretically socialist views or not, it is they – the tigers and wild dogs free-ranging on the veldt – rather than the captive pseudo-capitalists on display in the safari park of the CBI, who are capable of destroying socialism . . . they probably serve a better social purpose than more gentle and acceptable men.

Men such as those honoured were the living contradiction of

---

1 Front-page report by Craig Seton, May 27 1976. The most sensational and circumstantial leaked story was in the *Sunday Times* on May 2. A retired Whitehall mandarin was given the task of investigating the leaks, but failed to trace their source.

2 Among the new life peers one, Joseph Kagan, later did time. Bernard Delfont and his brother, Lew Grade, were moguls of the entertainment industry. George Weidenfeld was Wilson's publisher. Professor John Vaizey, though still nominally Labour, was soon to become an impassioned Thatcherite (and, it must be said, a most lively member of the House of Lords). Among the new knights, James Goldsmith and James Hanson were already bywords for acquisitive capitalism.

everything the Labour party stood for. Were they friends for whom Wilson felt 'the warmth of personal gratitude'? If so:

> what secret hunger for the company of capitalists led him to form so many ultra-capitalist friendships? It is rather pleasant to see the wilder shores of capitalism once again hung with coronets, but . . . very odd that such a scene should be set by the ex-Prime Minister of a socialist party.[1]

Two days later, on the op. ed. page, George Hutchinson wrote of the list with none of the leader's lightness of touch. Wilson had 'embarrassed the Crown' and brought so much discredit on the honours system that it might not survive 'in its present form'. Lady Falkender (formerly Marcia Williams), Wilson's private and political secretary, had 'claimed too much influence and responsibility in the past to escape comment and attention now'. She should 'lie low for a while, perhaps a long while, avoiding the House of Lords'.[2] This piece, which appeared on a Saturday, was not one of Hutchinson's best, but had the valuable effect of stinging Lady Falkender into an instant riposte. Monday's paper carried a letter from her, running to two columns of more than half-page depth. She denied having any responsibility at all for the list, despite what was being widely alleged. 'The Resignation List was Sir Harold Wilson's list and his alone'. Had *The Times* criticised Heath when he gave a peerage to 'the socialist Lord Feather', or Wilson himself 'when he knighted Sir Denis Hamilton'? She suggested that some of the criticism was due to 'covert anti-semitism'. Wilson had done more than most prime ministers 'to uphold our institutions, to protect the Crown, to give devoted and loyal service to his party, and to uphold the office of Prime Minister through difficult times'.[3]

Correspondence on the affair flourished for some days. Geoffrey Treasure from Harrow-on-the-Hill thought that the list 'would have brought a blush to the cheeks of Sir Robert Walpole'. The author Chaim Bermant disputed what Lady Falkender had said about anti-semitism, from an original and amusing angle:

> The furore about the honours has arisen not because so many of

1 Leader (Rees-Mogg), 'Whom he delights to honour', May 27 1976. In real life, of course, tigers might be found in a safari park but not on the veldt.
2 'After the fiasco of Sir Harold's list, can the honours system now survive?', May 29 1976. In fact, Lady Falkender had never shown any interest in the House of Lords.
3 May 31 1976

> those honoured are Jewish, but because they are newcomers. To be Jewish or new is just about forgivable but to be both is a solecism which may only be atoned for by a century or two of decent obscurity.

W. S. Hayes of Merseyside objected to the *lèse-majesté* of Lady Falkender's suggestion that Hamilton had been knighted by Wilson rather than by the Queen.[1] Desmond Crawley of London SW15 asked:

> What, Sir, do you all want? Not, I hope, to abolish the list altogether? It is, after all, one of the few harmless pleasures left to us which does not apparently damage the pound.[2]

Ruth Morrah (widow of the scholar, genealogist and *Times* man, Dermot Morrah) said that the list did honour to those left out. And K. S. Meakin of Cambridgeshire offered a quotation from Bernard Shaw: 'Titles distinguish the mediocre, embarrass the superior and are disgraced by the inferior'.[3]

By mid-1976 the rate of inflation had been more than halved, from nearly 27 per cent to under 13 per cent, but it was obvious that this result would not have been achieved without the strict control of incomes to which the government had been forced to revert. Knowing that further progress in reducing inflation depended on an extension of wage control, Healey offered the unions, in his budget in April, income tax relief of special benefit to the lower-paid in return for an agreed limit of 3 per cent for wage rises in the coming financial year. The figure later had to be increased to 4½ per cent before a deal was struck. The procedure was unusual, to say the least, involving a material concession by the state to the unions without any guarantee that their reciprocal pledge would be honoured.

Despite Healey's relative success in fighting inflation, for which the paper gave him qualified praise, sterling continued to slide. At the start of the year the pound stood at \$2.024; by late May it had fallen to \$1.780. At this point the chancellor received an almighty drubbing from Levin, in a piece which had, in most marked degree, the columnist's argumentative traits of hyperbole and humour, together with his stylistic tricks of parentheses, dashes and subordinate clauses.

---

1 June 3 1976.
2 June 4 1976.
3 June 5 1976.

He began by saying that Nero had been unfairly criticised for fiddling while Rome burned. Though Nero's life, 'both in its private and its public aspects, left much to be desired, his conduct on the occasion that gave rise to the myth was exemplary'. In any case the fiddle, in the sense of the violin, had not yet been invented, and even if it had been Nero would not have been likely to play it, because his musical character was more that of singer than instrumentalist, though he did, perhaps, occasionally accompany himself on the lyre.

All of which brought Levin to the chancellor of the exchequer:

> Is there no way to penetrate that hide, no possibility of blowing away the stinking cloud of complacency in which he floats, no metaphorical boot that can be applied with such force to his metaphorical rear, that he will notice? Has this country really got to be destroyed economically (and perhaps politically) to the sound of this insufferable blow-hard blaming other people? [He had] announced certain specific measures well calculated to allay fear and to help bring about the very recovery in the value of sterling which he was forecasting. Most important and exciting of these was his revelation that he [was] to hold 'discussions with Government departments' which would 'steady people's nerves' – a proposal that must surely have awakened, in millions of households, memories of Henry the Fifth before Harfleur . . . – and he concluded his magnificent blend of exhortation and reassurance with a promise – itself enough to send a thrill through every patriotic breast – that he would take action (I suppose it's a mercy he didn't call it 'resolute action') as soon as he sees – no, *if* he sees – 'the lights flashing amber'.

But, Levin continued, evidently indifferent to any effect his words might have on foreign holders of sterling, the decline of the pound was inexorable:

> It is a measure of this Government's failure to understand what is happening that they are afraid to impose real cuts in the real level of public expenditure until they have got the agreement of the TUC to the proposed wage-freeze, whereas the truth is that when they have got the TUC's agreement and made the cuts, the pound will go on falling – now faster, now slower, now remaining stationary for several weeks, now rising a little before falling again, yet all the time going on down and down – because what is causing the pound to fall is now neither the failure to contro

> public expenditure nor the danger of failing to control wage-increases. It is the growing belief, based on the growing evidence, that Britain is simply not worth investing in, and that sterling is simply not worth holding, because the forces driving Britain towards an economic (and even political) condition of shabby and hopeless servitude are too strong to be resisted and will shortly triumph . . . Why should any foreigner – or any Briton, for that matter – have any confidence in a country run by people who think that the cure for 30 years of increasing restrictions, increasing taxation, increasing waste of thousands of millions of pounds of the people's money, increasing debasement of the currency, increasing state control of the economy, increasing state *ownership* of the economy, increasing inefficiency in both state control and state ownership, increasing opportunities for even more of the same inefficiency, is more of the same?

Apart from anything else the news that Healey was chancellor of the exchequer could not be kept from the outside world, and the outside world would draw its own conclusions. Indeed, it apparently *had* heard the news, and the conclusions were already being drawn.[1]

This onslaught may or may not have penetrated the chancellor's 'hide'. It certainly penetrated the walls of 11 Downing Street, because Healey's wife, Edna, lost little time in writing a personal 'Dear William' letter from there to the editor. She could not, she said, allow Levin's 'hysterical attack' to pass without comment:

> As far as I know he has not met his monster for some twenty years, nor does he appear to follow very closely the events about which he writes with such fluency.
>
> It may be that he would prefer to keep his hatred pure, in quarantine. But it occurs to me that it might be helpful to him if I arranged that he should actually meet the Chancellor.
>
> I will willingly provide beer, sandwiches & a long spoon . . .
>
> As I have said before to you, it is a positive pain to me that one who writes like an angel should continue to think like poor Poll.[2]

Rees-Mogg replied with sympathy so far as she was concerned –

1 'A sterling performance needs a kick up the metaphorical rear', June 4 1976.

2 Edna Healey to W.R.-M., June 6 1976. In fact, Healey prided himself on offering 'good food and drink' at 11 Downing Street, rather than 'the traditional beer and sandwiches' – for trade unionists, at any rate. (Healey, op. cit., p.396.)

because it was 'obviously painful to have members of one's family subject to what one is bound to feel are unfair attacks' – yet essentially supporting Levin. He was, indeed, a polemicist who used 'weapons of ridicule and exaggeration in order to make his case'. But then so was Healey himself.

It was surprising that there had been so little bitterness in the recent discussion of economic policy. Since Healey became Chancellor 'the majority of readers of *The Times* [had] lost anything between 20 to 40% of real income while the real incomes of the great majority of trade unionists [had] increased over the period'. This was what Labour had promised to do and Healey had talked about making the pips squeak. Granted the damage he had done to many people's interests, on the whole he had 'got off quite lightly'. This did not alter the fact that he (Rees-Mogg) had a higher opinion of Healey's policy and intentions than Levin had. But he did not regret the critical case being put by Levin 'with the same vigour' that Healey habitually used in his own defence.[1]

The day before replying to Mrs Healey, Rees-Mogg had written a leader which could be read as a polite paraphrase of Levin's piece. It began:

> Sterling had one of its best days for some time yesterday, which is a relief after all the reverses suffered recently. But it is important to distinguish between the temporary effects of a purely psychological boost and an improvement based on more substantial factors.

Healey had just arranged with the central banks a standby credit of more than five billion dollars. But:

> . . . taking a tonic of this nature does not in itself do anything to solve the underlying problems of the British economy; and it is noteworthy that the source of the loan avoided the requirement of a letter of intent to the IMF, in which the British Government would have had to pledge itself to certain internal policies, most probably including public expenditure cuts.

He ended by urging the government to abandon its bill for nationalising the aircraft and shipbuilding industries. It was 'wise for any government to seek good relations with the trade unions, but not at any price'.[2]

---

1 W.R.-M. to Edna Healey, June 9 1976.
2 'A tonic not a cure' June 8 1976.

The course of subsequent events largely justified the line taken, in their different styles, by Levin and Rees-Mogg. Sterling continued to go down, almost certainly for the reasons stated, until later in the year Healey had to apply policies and disciplines enforced by the IMF.

After Cudlipp's departure in 1973 the state of editorial command during Rees-Mogg's absences from the office became not less, but more, complicated. Since 1970, as we have seen, there had been a dyarchy between Cudlipp and Heren, but from 1973 to 1978 three men jostled for control. They were Heren, who remained as the sole deputy editor, Douglas-Home, who in 1973 became home editor, and Michael Hamlyn, who inherited a part, but only a part, of Cudlipp's authority through his appointment as executive editor (night).

Hamlyn was somewhat in the Cudlipp mould. Before coming to *The Times* both men had been news editors of the *Sunday Times* and the youngest news editors in Fleet Street. Educated at Kimbolton school and St. Peter's College, Oxford, where he read modern history, Hamlyn had joined the Kemsley Provincial Press after doing his national service. But he had soon graduated to the *Sunday Times* as a reporter, having been brought to Hamilton's attention as a promising young man. When, in 1965, he followed Cudlipp as news editor there he was still under thirty; and when Cudlipp transferred to *The Times* he moved as well. Over the next few years the two worked closely together.

In the new dispensation after 1973 Heren's seniority was not in doubt; but, since he was also foreign editor, he could hardly concentrate on running the paper as a whole when Rees-Mogg was not there. His relations with Hamlyn were better than with Cudlipp, though by no means free from difficulty. Between Hamlyn and Douglas-Home relations were consistently bad. They were in a position of direct rivalry and, as Hamlyn put it, 'had very different backgrounds'.[1] Though it may not have been Rees-Mogg's intention to create a system of 'divide and rule', such was unquestionably the effect of his appointments.

As home editor Douglas-Home had a good deal of power, but not as much as he would have liked. His restless spirit chafed. Always prone to make enemies as well as enthusiastic friends, in 1976 he gave the former an opportunity to strike at him. In that year he secured the removal of Rita Marshall as home news editor – in the process

1 Hamlyn talking to author.

antagonising members of her circle – and for the benefit of her successor, Brian MacArthur, sent him typewritten notes on the reporters and specialists within the home department. MacArthur, a Leeds English graduate, had in 1967 been persuaded by Grant to leave the *Guardian* to become *The Times*'s educational correspondent. In 1970–1 he had served under Douglas-Home as deputy features editor, but he had then gone off to be founding editor of the *Times Higher Educational Supplement*, and had therefore been away from the main paper for five years. In the circumstances he certainly needed briefing on the human material with which he would have to work, but it was unfortunate for Douglas-Home that he chose to do the briefing in the form of written notes rather than by word of mouth.

He kept copies of the notes in his desk. This was broken into, the notes were read, and their contents were bruited around. For the most part they referred only to the subjects' professional merits or defects, but in some cases there were allusions to personal factors that could reasonably be thought relevant. A few specimen extracts, without names, should convey the flavour. One reporter is said to have 'few outside interests', and to be 'a total innocent' living 'on the outskirts of a fantasy world'. One specialist 'makes v. few mistakes', but 'the drawback to not making *any* mistakes is that you seldom get anybody in the field under pressure'. Nevertheless he 'writes rather nicely and should be encouraged to diversify'. Another reporter is 'a fluent writer and a very hard worker', who is 'willing to follow up things one puts to him'. Another specialist has become too much the 'pet' of the industry he is covering, and apt to be 'stupidly stuffy' about any initiatives 'which he regards as likely to snarl up his contacts'. Yet another has 'become rather hopelessly bogged down in her subject', and another again 'very bored and stale'. A woman reporter 'seems to be a girl of almost granite though rather uncomfortable integrity'. She has 'little tact but speaks her mind and will not be pushed around by anybody'. Another reporter 'has an extraordinarily complicated and involved private life, which means that he is rather footloose and subject to frequent depressions which he attributes on the face of it to his working conditions but which [Douglas-Home suspects] are more often the product of his chaotic love life'. Another 'initiates nothing, and, if he has good contacts, never seems to exploit them'. Yet another has 'great political nous' and 'the best contacts at the right levels of Whitehall'. One reporter is said to be 'essentially limited', and without 'critical or analytical faculty', and therefore unsuitable for appointment as a specialist. Another has a 'volatile temperament and breaks out sweating or shouting at the slightest provocation'. Yet another is 'extremely nice, cooperative and keen', though his writing is 'a little rough at the edges'.[1]

As guidance for an incoming news editor there could surely be no reasonable objection to such notes, and they were, of course, intended to be strictly confidential. That they ceased to be so was no fault of Douglas-Home's, unless it be a fault to run the risk of theft by leaving confidential documents in the locked drawer of a desk. Such was the atmosphere of the time, however, that *he* was treated as the culprit rather than the person who had broken into his desk (whose identity was widely suspected if not, perhaps, known for sure). At a meeting of about sixty members of the home department Douglas-Home consented to be put, as it were, in the dock, though he could never have been forced to attend. For several hours he had to listen to denunciations of his supposedly monstrous behaviour, and to defend himself as best he could, while saying that his future was in his colleagues' hands. A vote was taken and he survived it, but the incident was seriously damaging to his position, and even his buoyant self-confidence was temporarily shaken. He must have been quite relieved to exchange the post of home editor for that of foreign editor two years later.

---

1 Copies in *The Times* archive. The notes are all typed on Gray's Inn Road memorandum sheets, with a few words filled in by hand.

XX

From Roy to Kenneth • Power struggle in China • Monetarist manifesto • Healey turned back at Heathrow • An outsider to the White House

ONE DAY ROY THOMSON, on his way to some other part of the *Times* building at Gray's Inn Road, dropped into the obituaries office and sat down there to recover his breath. After asking Watson where he was, and being told, he exclaimed 'Oh God!'. Before long the Almighty, and the obituaries department, had indeed claimed him. On August 4 1976 he died, aged eighty-two, at the Wellington Hospital in north-west London. He had been there for a month with a chest infection, and had also suffered a severe stroke.

The following day's paper gave saturation coverage to the late proprietor. His obituary occupied a full page, with picture, opposite the normal space, in which by contrast an outstanding soldier, Field Marshal Sir Francis Festing, received only two columns, half-page deep and without a picture. In the Thomson piece any hints of criticism were barely perceptible through the clouds of incense, as in this representative passage:

> He was . . . the most unaffected [man] and made no effort to polish his rough diamond side. If he felt like drinking his soup direct from the plate, that was the way it would be, and the presence of a Prime Minister or Archbishop of Canterbury at the table did not deter him. Unlike Lord Beaverbrook, he was never a sharpshooter at the Establishment – he wooed it, rather. At the same time he never wished to be of it or to dim his own personality by adopting drawing-room manners. In his everyday life, as in his business life, he was an original.

There was a suggestion that his wife had thought, when he already had more than enough money, that he should have given more time to family life. But adverse comment even of this indirect kind was rare.

The first leader was entitled 'A great man of business' and broken into sections with headings such as 'drive and energy', 'generous attitude' and 'true Canadian'. It concluded that his most memorable quality was 'his instinctive habit of telling the truth', and that he would be remembered 'with special gratitude by those who care[d] for *The Times*'. Page 2, also, was largely devoted to him, with tributes from Wilson, Heath, Pierre Trudeau, John Diefenbaker, Margaret Thatcher, Goodman, Haley, Gavin Astor and Henry Grunfeld (president of Warburg's, and Thomson's adviser in many business dealings, including his recent North Sea oil partnership with Occidental, Getty and Allied Chemical). Edward Pickering, then with the Mirror Group but formerly a Beaverbrook editor, in a tribute described as 'particularly generous', said of Thomson that 'dictatorial attitudes were not his way'.

On the same page Kenneth Thomson was reported as having told a Canadian magazine that the independence of *The Times* was 'a bigger thing than the fortunes of the Thomsons', and on another page there was more about the new proprietor. He had announced that he would be keeping his father's title, though he would not use it in North America and it would not affect his Canadian citizenship, which he would retain 'at all costs'. He was assuming the title only because he had promised his father to do so, though it gave him 'a somewhat uneasy feeling'. He would have to make some changes in the division of his time between Canada and Britain. On *The Times*'s future he said that 'given the right economic conditions' the paper should be viable 'by the end of the decade'. As soon as it could exist without subsidy from his family it would be handed over to the Thomson Organisation. The state of the British economy would always be a governing factor, he added, but financial independence would have to come to *The Times* 'basically through the introduction of new automated processes of newspaper production which now [were] available'. Its implementation would require the cooperation of the staff and employees, and he was confident this would be forthcoming. Asked if he would continue his father's 'breath-taking pace of newspaper buying', he replied that in Canada and the United States he might, but that in the rest of the world he would not be as 'explosive' as his father. Significantly, he was talking in Toronto and the report of his interview appeared on an overseas news page.[1]

A few years earlier Roy Thomson had said in a BBC interview:

> Listen, I can't get on much further in years than I am right now. I'm approaching my 79th birthday and that's getting on pretty well. But the encouraging fact is that my son, who will take over, of course, is even more enthusiastic about it than I am. If – I would say this, if I was to suggest to him that we should close *The Times* and save the drain on our resources, he'd – I think he'd shoot me.[2]

As old Gobbo said, it's a rare father that knows his son, and in that interview Roy showed that he had a very imperfect understanding of Kenneth. The idea that Kenneth was even more enthusiastic than he was about *The Times* was pure self-deception. In fact, Kenneth had little sentimental loyalty to the paper, or to the country in which it was published. His loyalty was to his father, but even that was qualified by practical considerations and by a natural desire to exist in his own right.

One of three children, but the only son, he had grown up under the shadow of a father who was, however, seldom at home. A late-developer, he did not shine at his school, Upper Canada College, or at the university of Toronto which he attended for a year during the Second World War. But after service in the Royal Canadian Air Force he went to Cambridge, where he obtained a first in law before returning to Canada to work in his father's organisation. Cambridge 'firsts' are not lightly awarded, and his academic success proved that his intellect was, in its way, at least as good as his father's, if not better. He was also slightly less of a philistine, though his taste for

1 Obituary, leader and news reports, August 5 1976. Festing, who was given so much less space than Thomson, had served with notable success in the Second World War, above all against the Japanese in Burma, and had held the post of chief of the general staff in peace-time. He was also a very colourful character. By any objective criterion he should have received at least two full columns, with a picture.

Though only UK subjects can receive peerages of first creation, and it was therefore necessary for Roy Thomson to become a UK subject to be eligible for one, no such restriction applies to the inheritance of peerages. A citizen of any country in the world is free to inherit a UK peerage, and indeed hereditary holders of such peerages who are citizens of other Commonwealth countries, or of the Republic of Ireland, are also free to sit in the House of Lords. Kenneth Thomson was, accordingly, in a position to have it both ways, carrying on the title without sacrificing his Canadian citizenship. But he never took his seat at Westminster.

2 Interview for BBC 'Today' programme, January 23 1973.

ivory miniatures and the work of the Dutch-Canadian artist Cornelius Krieghoff suggests that his aestheticism was not of the subtlest. Certainly, in following his father into the world of business, he was not mistaking his vocation. There was no alternative life's work of a more congenial sort that he had to forgo in order to devote himself to the Thomson empire. Though he did not inherit Roy's force of personality and extrovert character, he did inherit a talent for operating on a large scale which enabled him, in due course, not merely to consolidate the empire his father had created, but greatly to expand it.

When Roy acquired the *Scotsman* and moved to Britain in 1953, Kenneth was glad for his sake, knowing that he was at a loose end and that success in the old country would be the ultimate fulfilment for him. At the same time Kenneth was glad for his own sake, because he was put in charge of the North American and Caribbean satrapies and seemed to have the chance, at last, to act more or less independently. During the happy interlude before he was summoned to join his father in Britain he married a Canadian girl, started a family, and became more rooted than ever in Canada. Though Roy did not consult him about taking a peerage, he nevertheless promised to accept the title should it devolve upon him, to please the old man. Yet he did not comply with Roy's wish that he should send his elder son to Eton. He was determined that his children should be as Canadian as himself.

With the growth of Roy's newspaper interests in Britain, and more especially after his acquisition of *The Times*, Kenneth's spell of quasi-independence ended. He was needed at his father's side, if only as a symbol and surrogate. His wholehearted identification with what Roy did was taken for granted, and the Monopolies Commission was assured that his commitment to *The Times* was, like his father's, total. In fact he did go along with Roy's decisions, since he was in awe of his father's achievements and had boundless respect for his judgement. But he could not help being a different person, with appreciably different values. Roy was born in the Victorian age, when the British empire was the world's only super-power and Canada no more than a self-governing colony within it. He was brought up to regard Britain as the centre of the universe, and this conception essentially remained, despite his admiration for the United States, and despite all the changes that he had witnessed during his life. Kenneth, on the other hand, was born when Britain and the empire were already in decline, and when Canada was asserting its independence within the Commonwealth. He could not fully share his father's reverence for British institutions, such as *The Times*; indeed, he shared it only to a very limited degree.

Even in Roy, as we have seen, there was considerable tension between the instincts of a nineteenth-century British colonial and those of a twentieth-century North American entrepreneur, with the latter tending to prevail in the longer run. Despite his reckless promises to the Monopolies Commission, and his open-handedness in the first phase of his proprietorship, he abruptly imposed a regime of relative austerity when £5 million of his money had been spent without the looked-for results. How he would have handled the problems of the late 1970s can never be known, but there is no reason to assume that even he would have continued indefinitely to subsidise an unprofitable newspaper with a refractory workforce, however flattering to his self-esteem the fact of owning it might be.

To Kenneth, ownership of *The Times* had hardly any of the emotional or snobbish significance that it had for his father, and it was therefore to be expected that his tolerance of losses and uneconomic practices on the paper would be that much less. So it would prove, though for a time he was influenced the other way by piety towards the man who had built the empire that he now inherited. The words quoted above from his first interview after Roy's death should, if read carefully, have left nobody in any doubt of his underlying attitude. He emphasised his Canadian and North American orientation. Though he said that the independence of *The Times* was a bigger thing than the fortunes of the Thomsons, he did not say that those particular fortunes would be forever devoted to maintaining it. The remark left him free, if necessary, to dispose of the paper, granted suitable undertakings from the purchaser that its independence would be maintained. It was clear from the interview that his commitment to *The Times* depended upon the introduction of new technology by the end of the decade, and upon cooperation from the staff. Would those two vital requirements be met?

Since Roy Thomson, accompanied by Kenneth and others, had visited China in October 1972, Bonavia had been discharging to the best of his ability the duties of resident correspondent in Peking: a task which was almost hopeless, because freedom to report from there was even more restricted than from Moscow. Yet in 1976 there was no lack of news in the country, if only it could have been properly reported, because the year witnessed the deaths of the two leading figures of the Communist revolution, and a resulting struggle for power.

Chou En-lai was the first to go. He died on January 8, and the news was reported, with a picture, on the following day's front page.

In the report Bonavia quoted 'observers in Peking' as suggesting that his death 'would not make an immediate impact on the political scene, as he was already inactive and most of his functions had been taken over by Mr. Teng Hsiao-ping' [Deng Xiaoping], who now seemed likely to become prime minister. Nevertheless the 'most important long-term effect of Mr. Chou's death [was] likely to be the loss of his influence as a moderating factor'. In the obituary of Chou (four columns) the key question was asked: why did he remain loyal to Mao when his instincts must so often have pulled the other way?

> Was he the chief of staff, the supreme bureaucrat, conscious that his own territory, the administration, could only be defended while supporting all the many swings from turmoil to order and back again to which Mao was drawn all through his revolutionary career? . . . Through the back-breaking pressures of the Cultural Revolution Chou remained a pivotal figure, protecting his ministries, negotiating – often all through the night – with rival Red Guards, trying to keep railway lines open, bargaining with powerful regional warlords and coming out at the end of a gruelling three years to be the central figure in China's recovery internally and externally from 1970 onwards.[1]

This was probably as good an explanation as any. Chou had lived to see the regime he helped to establish recognised, through his patient efforts, by the United States, and also admitted to the United Nations, taking over China's permanent seat on the Security Council hitherto occupied by Taiwan.

The power struggle began with Chou's death because, though Mao was still alive, his health was known to be failing. But the outside world had to make what it could of the scraps of information that emerged. After a month Hua Kuo-feng, the security minister, rather than Deng, was appointed prime minister. Reporting this, Bonavia reminded readers that Deng had been much criticised during the Cultural Revolution as one who hankered after the capitalist road, and that his subsequent comeback had been due solely to Mao's 'personal esteem' for him. There was a picture of Hua, and a leader stressing the impossibility of knowing much about what was going on. 'Unlike Spain's last years under Franco, China's struggle for the succession goes on behind the Chinese safety curtain. Not a word can be heard

1 Report and obit, January 9 1976.

from the inner sanctum of power'.[1] A few days later the start of a wall poster campaign directed against Deng was reported.[2]

Early in April there were dramatic riots in a place that would later become a household name throughout the world. In a front-page story Bonavia told of angry mobs, tens of thousands strong, burning vehicles and trying to break into the Great Hall of the People 'on Peking's Tien An Men [*sic*] square'.

> Tonight they broke into a house at the south-east corner of the square with a makeshift battering ram, set the building on fire and threw furniture out of the upstairs windows. Its identity was not known but *some sources believed* it was a police station. The mobs were *apparently* protesting against the removal during the night of wreaths put up to commemorate the late Chou En-lai on the Monument to the Martyrs of the Revolution in the centre of the square.

Troops, it was added, did not intervene when rioters overturned a car.[3] The following day there was an op. ed. piece by Bonavia in which he further evoked the scene and sought to explain the true meaning of the riots:

> Can this really be Peking, the city thought to be one of the most orderly in the world? The smoke of burning cars drifts across the Historical Museum, people are publicly beaten in the main square, foreigners are hounded and slapped. It looks like the Cultural Revolution all over again, but it is not – rather the reverse, in fact.

There were pictures of Deng and of Mao's wife, Chiang Ching, the former captioned 'carrying the mantle of Chou En-lai', the latter 'leading the "radicals"'.[4] Next day's paper had a front-page report that Teng had been dismissed, on the grounds that the recent rioters had been openly supporting him; though '*foreigners who observed the rioting* could recall only the name of the late Chou En-lai being defended'.[5] This was followed by news of a mass demonstration in

1 Report and leader 'Uncertainties among China's leadership', February 9 1976.
2 Report from Peking, without Bonavia's byline, February 13 1976.
3 April 6 1976. (Author's italics, indicating the tentative tone of Bonavia's reports.)
4 'The real reason for Peking's violent outburst', April 7 1976.
5 April 8 1976. (Again author's italics.) According to the New China News Agency, more than 120 had been injured in the Peking riots.

Peking in favour of Hua,[1] and of posters in Shanghai calling for the death of Deng, of whose whereabouts there was 'no official indication'.[2]

The next stage in the struggle was precipitated by Mao's death on September 9, which was the paper's lead story the following day, together with a picture of Mao. The obituary, oddly placed on page 6, and illustrated with three further pictures, occupied six columns, while the remaining two on the page carried, no less oddly, the full text of the official announcement from Peking. The obituary itself was astonishingly friendly, assessing the dead tyrant in terms that an acolyte could hardly have wished to modify:

> His great service to China was to give his country what it longed for after a century of chaos and indecision – the revolutionary leadership, the strategy, and the doctrine that could inspire its regeneration. Mao could never have done this simply as an importer of Marxism . . . All that he did for China, he did as a nationalist.

In an op. ed. piece Harris said that, with Mao's death, China had the chance 'to take a new great leap forward'. On the same page there were potted biographies, with pictures, of four people thought to be the main contenders for power, including Hua and Chiang Ching. A leader mentioned the cost of Mao's rule, though surely without sufficient emphasis:

> To Mao revolutionary struggle saw man's potentialities raised to their greatest height . . . If that confidence and dedication explains the great things he did for China as well as the price paid for them, it points also to the dying down of the revolutionary winds that is likely to follow his death.[3]

On October 7 Hua moved against Chiang Ching and her partners in the so-called Gang of Four. But nearly a week passed before news of their arrest appeared in the paper. The story leaked out first as 'rumours', but when it was more or less definite a leader suggested that the Gang of Four should be 'so treated by the new leadership as

---

1 April 9 1976. The same day there was another leader, 'Confusion at the top in China', stating the obvious fact that China faced a 'fresh period of uncertainty'.
2 April 10 1976. Deng had 'not been seen since mid-January'.
3 Lead story 'Mao succession struggle' from Bonavia, op. ed. piece by Harris, and first leader 'A revolutionary first and last'; September 10 1976.

not to seem a repudiation of the departed leader' – a curious comment, though hardly surprising after the Mao obituary.[1] By way of corrective, Levin attacked Western apologists for the Chinese communist regime, wondering how they would react to the new situation. 'It is . . . going to be interesting to see how the tireless boomers and bellmen of Chinese Communism . . . go about explaining the actual occurrence in their earthly paradise of . . . a political purge'. Of Chiang Ching he wrote: 'One moment she was consort to the God-King, and sat enthroned beside the temporal and spiritual ruler of more people than any man in the whole of human history; the next she is under house arrest, and her ultimate fate can hardly be guessed at by any of those millions'.[2] Soon Bonavia was reporting, though at second hand, that in Shanghai thousands had paraded with effigies and posters denouncing Chiang Ching, some calling for her execution and 'claiming that she virtually nagged her husband to death in the last months of his life'.[3]

The frustrations of a foreign correspondent's work in Peking were explained from afar, and with perhaps a touch of *Schadenfreude*, by Harris. In China all important items of news, especially those thought to be controversial, were sent down through party channels 'some time before being published in the *People's Daily*'. The presence in Peking of 'a number of foreign correspondents' had complicated matters in recent years. When millions of Chinese had to be informed some leaks were 'inescapable'. The correspondents then demanded confirmation and were met with no comment or, after a time, the admission of something which might not yet have been published in any Chinese newspaper. Since the information itself was likely to consist of propaganda or plain lies, the value of such scoops was, he implied, severely limited.[4]

Hua had ousted the Gang of Four, but his own period of rule was to prove temporary. The future belonged to Deng.

Over a period of three years or so Rees-Mogg's stance on economic policy underwent two fundamental changes. First he became convinced that inflation, rather than unemployment, was the supreme

1 Story on p.6 (flagged on front page), 'Peking rumours about Mao widow's arrest', October 12 1976; front page report of Hua's coup and leader 'Power in Peking', October 13 1976.
2 'Are the faithful already waiting in the wings to bury the Little Red Book?' October 15 1976.
3 October 18 1976.
4 'How Peking manages the news', article by Harris on p.5, October 18 1976.

economic and social menace in Britain; and then he moved from a belief in control of incomes as the best medicine against inflation to a belief that control of the money supply was the only sure antidote. This nostrum, of which the American professor Milton Friedman was the leading advocate, had been taken up in British politics by, in the first place, Enoch Powell. He had been followed by Keith Joseph, and Rees-Mogg's reaction to the latter's Preston speech in September 1974 showed that he was more than half-way to conversion. His own plea in May of the same year for a return to the gold standard may be seen as the first step on this road to Damascus.

In July 1976 he produced what amounted to a full-blown monetarist manifesto. This appeared not in the form of a leader, but as a signed article on the op. ed. page, presumably because he had some qualms about taking the paper quite as far as he was prepared to go himself. In the piece he argued that, whereas many economic theories could be neither proved nor disproved, the theory of monetarism could be 'tested scientifically'. After a dutiful bow to Friedman's 'classic work' (*A Monetary History of the United States, 1867–1960*), he gave figures intended to show that Britain's inflation since 1967 corresponded with, and had therefore obviously been caused by, the 'excess money supply' that had entered the system during the same period. The figures had changed his attitude to incomes policy, since if excess money supply determined the rate of inflation 'equally closely in years subject to incomes policy and in years without', there was no apparent evidence left that incomes policy had 'any significant influence on inflation'.[1]

Even if the correlation between inflation and excess money supply was indeed as close as Rees-Mogg alleged, it could still be argued that the correlation was accidental rather than causal. But was the statistical premise correct? Opening the large correspondence which the article aroused, Maudling immediately challenged Rees-Mogg's interpretation. Was it really credible that 'if, by methods unstated, the growth of Excess Money Supply in this country had been kept to nil since 1965, we should still be enjoying 1965 prices'? But it was Wynne Godley, of the Cambridge department of applied economics, who counter-attacked most effectively:

> The scientific test you offer readers is a comparison of annual per cent. changes in retail prices from 1967 to 1975 with the 'excess

1 'How a 9.4% Excess Money Supply gave Britain 9.4% inflation' July 13 1976. Rees-Mogg's article recommending a return to the gold standard had also appeared under his own name on the op. ed. page.

> money supply' two years previously, with the claim that the two series closely resemble one another.
>
> Ignoring your underlying hypothesis – which I regard as completely untenable in terms of economic theory and behaviour – it should be pointed out that the relationship between the two series between 1967 and 1973 entirely fails to generate an accurate prediction for 1974 or 1975.
>
> Taking your first seven years the price change more often than not moved in the opposite direction to the corresponding change in the Excess Money Supply . . . The predictions for price changes in 1974 and 1975 conditional on the excess money supply in 1972 and 1973 which the relationship yields are only about . . . half of what happened.
>
> Any systematic relationship at all between the two series depends entirely on the inclusion of the observations for 1974 and 1975, when price changes were predominantly determined by the rise in world commodity prices generated via the 'threshold' system of awards.
>
> You do not, I take it, contend that monetary expansion in the United Kingdom in 1973 – which incidentally you strongly supported at the time – caused the rise in oil and other world commodity prices in 1974.[1]

Godley was no stranger to *The Times*. In the latter part of 1973 an article by him and a colleague arguing the case for substantial deflation had appeared in the paper on the same day that a leader took the opposite line. After Joseph's Preston speech a year later he had written a letter questioning its statistical basis. Early in 1975 the alternative economic strategy evolved by his department at Cambridge had received the qualified endorsement of Jay, with whom he shared a background of Modern Greats at Oxford and practical service in the treasury.[2] Godley, like Keynes, was an academic economist with wider dimensions. For a time he had been a professional oboist, and his father-in-law, Epstein, had used him as model for the figure of St. Michael commissioned for the new Coventry cathedral. His brother, Lord Kilbracken, was known for his capacity to dream in advance the names of winning horses, an aptitude with which, some might say, economics had more in common than with the natural sciences.

---

1 Maudling's and Godley's letters, July 14 1976.
2 Op. ed. piece by Jay, 'The Cambridge way out of Britain's economic maze', February 17 1975.

His letter replying to Rees-Mogg's monetarist article led to a private correspondence between them, in which *The Times*'s record in 1973–4 was discussed. Rees-Mogg maintained that he had been 'anti-inflationary rather than concerned with unemployment' from June 1972 onwards, though he admitted that his 'views were mistaken' in late 1973. He was 'very much influenced by the desire not to stop investment if that could be avoided'. Godley argued that after July 1973 it was more, rather than less, 'urgently necessary to reverse engines', which was why he had so strongly differed from the paper's line at the time. Nevertheless he now felt, on reflection, that 'the Heath expansion was [not] such an important cause' of the country's existing troubles. At least as important was 'the threshold system on which we got skewered and the fact that public expenditure got out of control in *1974*'.[1]

In the published correspondence the only serious attempt to answer Godley came from Oliver Smedley, who thought it wrong 'to confuse the rise in oil and other commodity prices with inflation in the United Kingdom'. If there had been no increase in the money supply, the rise in the oil price would have brought about 'either a reduction in the usage of oil or a compensatory fall in other prices, or both'.[2] He did not, however, weigh the industrial or the social consequences of such a policy. Another Cambridge don, Philip Allott, criticised Rees-Mogg's argument from an angle rather different from Godley's:

> It was good of you to present a money supply argument in so unvarnished a form. In so doing, you draw attention with unusual clarity to the other means of eliminating what you call the Excess Money Supply. The other means is to increase the Gross Domestic Product. This is the constructive and imaginative challenge which Britain faces and it is not compatible with the timid and destructive approach which you advocate.[3]

But there were many who supported Rees-Mogg.

Despite the standby credit negotiated by Healey in June, the slide of sterling was not arrested for long. The task of restoring confidence was not helped by unofficial strikes by Leyland car-workers, a threatened

1 Godley to W.R.-M., July 21 1976; W.R.-M., to Godley, July 22 1976 Godley to W.R.-M., July 25 1976; W.R.-M. to Godley, July 28 1976. They addressed each other then as 'Dear Rees-Mogg' and 'Dear Godley'.
2 July 16 1976. Smedley was director of studies at the Reliance School of Investment Ltd.
3 July 17 1976.

(though in the event averted) seamen's strike, and demands from Labour left-wingers for nationalisation of the main clearing banks and insurance companies. It was no coincidence that the next crisis occurred while the Labour Party conference was in session at Blackpool in late September.

A week before, when the pound was going down but a major sterling crisis did not yet seem imminent, *The Times* excelled itself, in scale at any rate, by producing an enormous leader of four columns and full-page depth, written by Jay, in which a 'programme for economic stability' was set forth. The main points of the programme were summarised in a box, and monetarism had pride of place. Money supply growth should be kept to 9 per cent in the current year, 6 per cent the following year, and 4 per cent thereafter. The budget deficit should be kept to £4,000 million the following year and £1,000 million in 1978–9, after which it should more or less disappear. Necessary tax increases should be concentrated on the indirect VAT. There should be a 'cleanly' floating pound. Free pay bargaining should resume from the following summer, and there should be an early end to price and dividend controls. Nationalised industries should be required to earn sufficient surpluses to finance most of their investment, with freedom to charge realistic prices. There should be tougher policy against monopolies. Finally, government-TUC-CBI energies should be devoted to the industry-by-industry campaign for higher productivity. Conspicuously absent from the programme was any mention of trade union reform.[1]

On the eve of the Labour conference Callaghan let it be known that nationalisation of banks and insurance companies would not be in the party's next election manifesto if he could help it, though the government would undertake a review of City institutions, including the Bank of England.[2] Three days later crisis struck. Sterling fell below $1.70 and continued to fall despite massive intervention by the Bank. Healey was now immersed in what he later called the worst four months of his life.[3] He was about to leave, with Gordon Richardson, governor of the Bank, for two conferences in the Far East, when such alarming news reached them at Heathrow that they had to abandon the flight and return to the treasury, where meetings were held until a late hour. On next day's front page there was a picture of Healey leaving the treasury after these meetings, and a report by Jay sug-

1 Leader, 'Programme for economic stability', September 20 1976.
2 Report from Michael Hatfield at Blackpool, September 25 1976. The review of City institutions was in due course entrusted to Sir Harold Wilson, with predictably bland results.
3 Healey, op. cit., p.428.

gesting that a 'huge long-term loan' was the chancellor's preferred cure. There was also a report that Callaghan's 'grim speech' at Blackpool had won him 'little conference applause'.[1]

The following day the pound was said to be rallying on the strength of indications from the treasury that the government was planning to apply, with American support, for a loan of up to $3,900 million dollars from the IMF. *The Times* stressed the need for corrective measures at home; a soothing letter to the IMF would not be enough. Action which should have been taken earlier must no longer be shirked.

> What those steps should be has been fully spelt out here recently, though some will quarrel with our numbers, and others . . . reject the whole approach. The Government may yet be tempted, despite the Chancellor's trenchant counter-arguments . . . to restrict imports just because many of its supporters, including trade union leaders, have erected this into a symbol of socialist virtue. This would only increase the price that had to be paid in other ways both to build confidence in sterling and to bring inflation under control.[2]

One trade union leader, David Basnett, had indeed recently been given space on the op. ed. page to argue in favour of protection, a remedy also demanded by the ideological left and, in a selective form, by Godley and his Cambridge colleagues. But *The Times* held out firmly against it.

Having taken preliminary measures to steady the pound, Healey travelled north to address the body to whose collective character much of his present travail was attributable. Since he had lost his seat on Labour's national executive he was entitled to only five minutes' speaking time at the conference, but he made typically pugnacious use of it. Next day, under the misleading headline 'Mr. Healey wins Labour backing for defence of sterling', *The Times* described the scene:

> Mr. Healey had a mixed reception from the delegates, with sporadic booing and hissing from some left-wingers, but most of his Cabinet colleagues thought he had been right to fly to Blackpool. An attempt by some delegates to give him a standing ovation failed and it was obvious that the conference, or most of the audience, did not relish the facts of life that he presented.

---

1 Reports, September 30 1976.
2 Lead story from Jay and leader 'Buying time', September 30 1976.

All the same, union block votes ensured a large majority for 'a statement by the party's national executive backing the measures [he had taken] but rejecting conditions that might be sought by the [IMF] if they clashed with party and TUC policies'.[1] The headline was misleading because it referred to the block-voted statement rather than to the effect of Healey's speech on delegates in the hall, and in any case the terms of the statement were hardly such as to inspire much confidence in the IMF or other hard-headed outside agencies upon which the fate of sterling depended.

A week later the paper's lead story was the rise in Bank lending rate to the record level of 15 per cent, though it was presumably not known, and certainly not reported, that Healey had had to threaten resignation to secure this. A leader accepted the necessity for the rise, but insisted that further action would be required to give the country a proper stabilisation programme.[2]

Since Nixon's enforced resignation in August 1974 the US presidency had been held by Gerald Ford, formerly a congressman from Michigan, who had been appointed to succeed Spiro Agnew as vice-president eight months earlier. Ford was a decent and modestly competent man who did the job tolerably well and certainly restored credit to the office. But his intellectual scope was limited and his style pedestrian. Worse still, he could not entirely shake off the burden of seeming to be Nixon's man, since he had been minority leader in the House of Representatives throughout the Nixon presidency and, on becoming president himself, had felt obliged to grant a pardon to his disgraced predecessor.

The situation offered, therefore, a marvellous opportunity to the Democrats. But who was to be their candidate? Hubert Humphrey, who had run in 1968, was getting on and anyway was still tainted by his association with Vietnam. Edward Kennedy was, in a different way, even worse tainted. George McGovern, the candidate in 1972, had been so overwhelmingly defeated that he had to be regarded as a no-hoper. In these circumstances there was, unusually, a chance for a complete outsider to win the nomination, and by mid-June 1976 it was clear that such a man would, in fact, win it. His name was James Earl (Jimmy) Carter.

Well before then, at the end of April, *Times* readers were given a brilliant account and appraisal of him by the paper's chief Washington correspondent, Emery. Carter was a 'meteor' who had 'burst forth

1 Report from Clark and Hatfield at Blackpool, October 1 1976.
2 Leader, 'Sterling's grave crisis', October 8 1976.

from the Democratic primaries'. He was nearly forty before he turned to politics. Son of a Baptist peanut merchant from the small town of Plains, Georgia, he spent his childhood in a clapboard house with no electricity but, quaintly, a tennis court. He graduated from his local high school where, he claimed, nearly all his playmates were black: an assertion which Emery found 'difficult to swallow'. After leaving school Carter went to the naval academy at Annapolis, where he came fifty-ninth in a class of 820. It was too late for him to be a combatant in the Second World War, but he tried to suggest that he might have experienced enemy action, if only in a small way, since during the last days of the war one of his training ship's propellers was 'either hit by a torpedo or struck a coral reef'. While on leave from his first naval posting he married 'a pretty local girl, Rosalynn Smith', by whom he had three sons and a daughter. Later he applied for the nuclear submarine project under Admiral Hyman Rickover, but rose only to the rank of lieutenant before retiring. Though he described himself as a nuclear physicist, in fact he merely got a standard engineering degree. In Emery's view, this tendency to inflate his record was slightly disturbing. In 1952, when his father died, he returned to the peanut business, which 'flourished enormously' under his direction.

Ten years later he entered politics, aged nearly forty, securing election as a Georgia state senator. But in 1966 he ran unsuccessfully for governor of the state, and 'in his uncertainty afterwards came to his religious inspiration'. In 1970 he ran again, and won. There was not a great deal to show for his gubernatorial term, though he made some administrative changes. He did not run for a second term, but decided instead to work for the Democratic presidential nomination in 1976, which had been his full-time occupation ever since.

As well as giving a clear, sharp account of his career, Emery assessed him as a man, vividly and unsparingly. 'His sandy-haired, boyish good looks' were 'jarred by his cold blue eyes', and his 'soft-spoken, almost glib manner' was 'one of utterly unabashed soulfulness, of hyper-sincerity'. He wore 'the piety of devout evangelical Baptism', in which he claimed to have been reborn, 'far more prominently on his sleeve than did Kennedy his Roman Catholicism or McGovern his prairie puritanism'. He was always promising that he would never lie to the people, yet 'managed to speak with such multiple ambiguities about policy' that his party rivals could only 'splutter in frustration' over where he stood. His 'one priceless achievement' was to have refused, in 1972, to second Governor George Wallace's presidential nomination, and in the current primaries to have defeated him. Many black politicians were rallying to him as 'the best white available'.

It was clear that he had 'profited singularly from the post-Watergate aching for a new, respectable, honest face, and one not at all associated with Washington'. A point in his favour was that he understood the vital importance of strengthening the alliance with Japan, and said so. But he could not pretend to be much of a dove, having supported the Vietnam war until 1971. If he had any spontaneous humour, he hid it well; but he had 'almost overbearing self-assurance'. The piece ended:

> Is the country ready for such a man? In a sense it has already had one quasi-Southern idealist in Woodrow Wilson. The primaries suggest some are certainly ready. But it still lies within the talents of the Democratic party factions to tear themselves apart simply to deny such a man. We shall soon know.[1]

It was nearly six weeks before Carter could be described as 'over the last hump',[2] and Emery's profile of him was a remarkable piece of anticipatory journalism, well-written and well-judged.

On the Republican side Ford had to face a strong challenge from Ronald Reagan, who fell only seventy short of the number of delegates' votes needed for nomination. Emery took Reagan more seriously than most European, and many American, commentators, though perhaps not seriously enough. The former governor of California had 'always tended to be underestimated'; yet he did not seem to be 'a viable national candidate', because 'sunbelt Republicans' were 'very much a minority within a minority'.[3] In view of what happened only four years later, this seems, to say the least, a doubtful judgement. Reagan, like Carter, had the advantage of being untarnished by the recent goings-on in Washington, and of seeming to stand for the simple primordial American virtues. It may well have been lucky for Carter that Reagan just missed the nomination in 1976, and that Ford was, after all, the candidate against whom he had to run.

The election campaign was a dull affair, apart from two extraordinary episodes. The first was Carter's interview with *Playboy* magazine, in which he was quoted as saying: 'I've looked on a lot of women with lust. I've committed adultery in my heart many times'. Though he had 'loved no other woman' than Rosalynn, he deprecated self-righteous fidelity: 'Christ says, don't consider yourself better than someone else because one guy screws a whole bunch of women while the other guy

1 'Times profile' of Carter, by Emery; 3 cols., full-page depth, with caricature, April 26 1976.
2 Op. ed. piece by Emery, June 10 1976.
3 Ibid.

is loyal to his wife'. Publication of this interview caused 'nervousness' in the Carter camp, and Emery reported that the couple, 'after campaigning separately for two days, kissed and hugged effusively and repeatedly in front of a cheering crowd' in Pittsburgh; also that Carter had told a man from the *Christian Science Monitor* that he could not remember using the word 'screws'.[1] Probably the interview did him no harm, on balance, and may even have done him a little good. No doubt some voters were shocked and offended, but on the other hand America's millions of adulterers may have been slightly reassured to know that what they had done he had done too, if only in his heart.

Ford anyway committed a more serious gaffe, which may conceivably have determined the result of what turned out to be a close election. Though the incumbent president, he started the campaign trailing in the polls and therefore decided that, being in that sense the underdog, it would be to his interest to enter into televised debates with his opponent. Three were held, and in the second Ford let fall the astonishing remark that there was 'no Soviet domination of Eastern Europe' and never would be under his administration. Carter made the most of his luck. The cameras cut to show him laughing at the president's remark, the laugh 'perhaps as potent as any words'; and he then said that he 'would like to see Mr. Ford convince the Polish-Americans and the Czech-Americans and the Hungarian-Americans' that those countries were not 'under the domination and supervision of the Soviet Union'.[2]

A *Times* reader in Texas sent a picture, which was reproduced in the paper, of a car sticker with the message 'Don't follow England down the drain! – vote Ford'.[3] But when America went to the polls at the beginning of November Ford narrowly lost. Shortly beforehand, in an op. ed. piece, Heren had written that the American electorate was dissatisfied with the political process,[4] and this seemed to be borne out by the fact that only 53 per cent bothered to vote in the election. Carter won with a margin of 2 per cent in the popular vote, and by 56 votes in the electoral college. In a leader *The Times* commented that he evidently had 'the potential to be a remarkable president'.[5] Remarkable or not, just as he had chosen to be a one-term governor of Georgia, so he was to prove, though not by his own choice, a one-term president of the United States.

---

1 Emery reporting, September 22 1976.
2 Emery reporting, October 8 1976.
3 October 27 1976.
4 'What the American voter wants is a party he can believe in', same date. Heren had re-visited America in July to write a diary of the Democratic convention.
5 Leader, 'Mr. Carter's qualities', November 4 1976.

XXI

Ominous setbacks for Hussey • Astor incident and Bullock report • India rejects dictatorship • Lib-Lab pact • A surprise appointment • New lobby chief

BEFORE THE CATACLYSMIC events that hit the whole of British industry at the end of 1973, *The Times*'s financial performance had been steadily improving under Hussey's direction. Indeed, but for those events the paper would probably have made a small profit, rather than a relatively small loss, in 1973. The following year, however, brought a sense of acute crisis to the management of Times Newspapers, as to most of the rest of the national press. During 1973–4 the price of newsprint doubled, while general inflation and increased trade union militancy further boosted costs. At the same time the depressed state of the economy halted the all-important growth of advertising revenue, and the necessity to charge more for newspapers, to readers who were themselves feeling the pinch, caused a drop in circulations. Not only the weak, but strong papers too, began to falter; in 1974 and 1975 even the *Sunday Times* made a loss.

Hussey was not alone in believing that the problems of the industry had reached a point where only drastic action could avert ruin, but he was foremost among those who felt that it should, if possible, be taken jointly. Newspaper managements had to work together, preferably in collaboration with trade union leaders, though if necessary without them, to make the industry viable. In particular, it was essential that the more efficient methods of production already widely used in North America should be introduced in Britain. On this issue he was no sudden convert; in August 1973 he had sent two teams from TNL, consisting of both managers and printers, to inspect new technology in the United States. They had visited a number of newspaper offices where the traditional linotype 'hot metal' process had given way to computerised photocomposition, with all the attendant economies in money and manpower. Their 'overall impression' was that the advances they had seen were worthwhile but costly, and that they could be matched in Britain 'only with cooperation'.[1]

The aim of reducing staff was, of course, closely allied with the need to simplify and rationalise the trade union structure in the industry, and to bring some discipline into its labour relations. The *Times* management had to deal with no fewer than seven trade unions (or eight, if one includes the small Institute of Journalists, not affiliated to the TUC). Four were print unions: the National Graphical Association (NGA), the National Society of Operative Printers, Graphical and Media Personnel (NATSOPA), the Society of Graphical and Allied Trades (SOGAT) and the Society of Lithographic Artists, Designers and Engravers (SLADE). The NUJ (and IoJ) represented the journalists, and there was also a substantial presence of the electricians' union (EEPTU) and the engineers' (AUEW). The unions were organised in chapels, some of which were subdivided. Thirteen of the chapels were capable of stopping the paper by official or unofficial action, and all the mechanical unions operated closed shops. The complexity of the system was akin to that of a ramshackle medieval town, with its narrow streets, buildings set at odd angles, jostling humanity, and unhealthy atmosphere. In some respects, indeed, the functions and ethos of the print unions might be seen as a direct legacy from the Middle Ages. The craft unions, NGA and SLADE, jealously guarded their mysteries and their differential rewards, while the others sought by every available means, fair and foul, to improve their position.

Such was the employers' dependence on the print chapels from day to day, even from hour to hour, that they were always at the mercy of people who exercised a virtual *imperium in imperio*, based on blackmail and a variety of time-honoured rackets. From 1974, however, there seemed a chance that desperation might prevail over short-term expediency. In the mood and circumstances of the time a would-be reformer like Hussey could hope for more solidarity from fellow employers than they were normally in the habit of showing; and he also began to look to a few newly-installed trade union leaders, who shared his belief that without fundamental change the whole industry was doomed.

Between 1974 and early 1977 his search for a magic formula involved him in two major initiatives. The first was an attempt to establish a printing consortium with the other quality dailies, the *Financial Times*, the *Daily Telegraph* and the *Guardian*. In this his most active partner was Alan Hare, managing director of the *FT*,

1 John Dixey, 'Shedding the Caxton image in USA', *Times News*, December 1973.

though from the outset there was a significant difference between them, in that Hare regarded the participation of others as essential, whereas Hussey merely regarded it as desirable.[1] The proposal was that there should be a jointly owned printing company, whose operations would be concentrated on a single site, probably Gray's Inn Road, with 'joint printing and servicing staff' responsible for printing all the papers in the consortium, 'the only staffs left with each parent company [to be] the top management, the journalists, and the sales and marketing staffs'. This would enable new technology to be introduced, far lower manning levels to be achieved, and trade union power to be much reduced by the resulting absence of alternative work within the same field. There would need to be 'a very imaginative compensation package for the many, many people' who would be made redundant, but the cost of this, as well as of the new equipment, should be covered 'within two years'.[2]

The *Guardian* and *Telegraph* took the idea seriously and for a time showed considerable interest. But by the spring of 1975 it was clear that the *Guardian*, at any rate, would not play, and that the *Telegraph* was unwilling to move without the *Mail*. Yet to have included the *Mail* would have been to abandon the idea of a group limited to the quality broadsheets, more especially as the *Mail* would have been unlikely, in turn, to move without the *Express*. The *FT* might conceivably have gone ahead without the *Guardian*, but would not do so without the *Telegraph*; so the project foundered.[3] An additional reason was that some of those who controlled the *FT* feared the proposed printing merger would lead, inevitably, to the sort of comprehensive one they had rejected nine years previously.[4]

Hussey's second initiative had the apparent advantage of being a management-union affair. Indeed, it was a joint initiative by himself and W. H. (Bill) Keys, who had recently become general secretary of SOGAT. Keys was Hussey's exact contemporary, and it was as obvious to him as to Hussey that things could not go on as they were in the industry. Sooner or later, the uneconomic and often corrupt practices which flourished in Fleet Street would have to end, and he could see

1 Hussey's 'strictly confidential' notes on a lunch with Hare, August 23 1974.
2 Draft summary of the project, December 9 1974.
3 David Kynaston, *The Financial Times: a Centenary History*, pp.407–8.
4 'They [the board of Pearson Longman] didn't wish . . . to get too involved with us because they thought that inevitably as the years roll by some form of merger will take place in which TNL would come out on top . . .' (From an undated, but clearly contemporary note in Hussey's personal papers, 'Reasons why FT and Telegraph not prepared to join TT in consortium'.)

that the sooner they ended the better his members' interests would, in the long run, be served. As a national leader, he had to contend with the traditional power of the print chapels, aggravated by the pusillanimity of managers and the failure of the employers to stand together as a body. During the war he had served in the army, attaining the rank of regimental sergeant major. It was said of him that he 'had the hide of an ox, obscuring the kindest of people'.[1] His attitude to change was broadly shared by two other men who emerged as leaders in the industry at about the same time: J. F. (Joe) Wade, who became general secretary of the NGA, and Owen O'Brien, who became general secretary of NATSOPA, succeeding Richard (Lord) Briginshaw, an outstanding symbol of the old order.

During 1975 a joint standing committee (JSC) was created by the TUC and the Newspaper Publishers' Association (NPA), to enable union and management representatives to work together on all the problems of the industry. The JSC's chairman was Keys, its vice-chairman Hussey (inverting their military ranks). Most other unions in the industry were, through their leaders, associated with the work of the committee, though SLADE stood aside. One sign of the new cooperative spirit among the industry's leaders was that the JSC submitted a joint statement to the royal commission on the press that was sitting at the time (the third since 1945).[2] But the committee's most remarkable product was a document entitled *Programme for Action*, in which an all-embracing scheme of reform was put forward.

This scheme, which was agreed in October 1976 after ten months of discussion, contained proposals for dealing with almost every important matter under review, including pensions, decasualisation, disputes procedure, redundancies and new technology. Since the authors of the scheme realised that its fate depended upon the establishment of effective joint institutions at house level, it was proposed that joint house committees should be set up, on each of which there would be up to seven management representatives and two from each union (apart from NATSOPA, which would have three, to take account of its clerical workers). The union leaders on the JSC commended *Programme for Action* to their members in a vigorously-worded preface:

> If . . . the provisional agreements are rejected, there will be no

1 Obit. in *Guardian*, May 21 1990.

2 Under the chairmanship of, first, Sir Morris Finer and, after his death, Professor Oliver (later Lord) McGregor. The commission reported in July 1977, and was as futile as its predecessor.

> agreed overall framework through which the problems facing the industry can be dealt with, and the consequences of this could well, in our view, be extremely grave and have a serious effect on the viability of some titles in the industry, the maintenance of employment, and the continuation of a strong and effective trade union organization.[1]

As usual with news of anything relating to labour relations in the industry, the agreed programme was given no prominence in *The Times*, but was reported down-column on an inside page. The most significant words were the last, that the recommendations would 'shortly be circulated by the unions for consideration at house and branch levels'.[2] Two days later a speech by Hussey was reported, in which he stressed the appalling financial state of the industry ('unprofitable and living on borrowed money'), but announced that Times Newspapers would nevertheless be investing £9 million in new machinery, an act of confidence to which, he trusted, the unions would respond.[3] In a leader in early December *Programme for Action* was not mentioned by name, but praised by implication as the best hope of regeneration by consent' that the industry had ever had.[4] This leader was soon followed, however, by a report from Routledge which suggested that the 'best hope' was likely to be disappointed:

> The joint union-employer Programme for Action designed to restore Fleet Street's fortunes through the introduction of new technology and manpower shrinkage is running into serious shop-floor opposition . . . Chapel officials of two key unions involved [NGA and NATSOPA] have overwhelmingly rejected the programme on the ground that it would cause too many redundancies. Meetings of these officials over the past few days have come out strongly against the proposals, and craft print-workers belonging to the NGA have suggested that Mr. Joe Wade, their secretary, should withdraw from talks . . . based on this document.[5]

1 Roderick Martin, *New Technology and Industrial Relations in Fleet Street*, p.198.
2 Report by Tim Jones on p.2, 'Fleet Street accord on new technology'.
3 October 15 1976. He was addressing the Bristol Junior Chamber of Commerce. On October 19, as if to emphasise the need for economy as well as investment, there was a front-page box announcement that *The Times* was, from that day, the first newspaper to be printed entirely on lightweight newsprint made from 'thermomechanical pulp'
4 Leader, 'Fleet Street's troubled labour relations', December 10 1976.
5 Report down-column on p.2 'Fleet street union officials reject redundancy plans' December 16 1976.

Balloting on the programme was carried out early in the New Year. In mid-January there was another gloomy report from Routledge. A leaflet, he said, was being privately circulated among NGA members, urging them to reject the plan and complaining that there had been 'virtually no consultation' before the plan was produced. The membership was 'expected to give blanket approval to a package detailed [*sic*] in extremely vague and ambitious terms', and apparently 'not subject to amendment or variation except at working party levels'.[1] On March 2 came the news that the NGA in London had rejected the plan by 'more than two to one', and that NATSOPA had also voted against it 'though by a considerably smaller margin'.[2] The *coup de grace* was rejection by SOGAT a fortnight or so later, by the crushing majority of 2,232 votes to 977.[3] *Programme for Action* was then effectively dead.

Hussey's failure to find a way of tackling his major problems all at once in partnership with either fellow employers or the unions was full of ill omen. His two setbacks might have suggested to him that he would never be able to count on the necessary cooperation from other employers, and that the agreement of national union leaders to a scheme would always be worthless, because their writ did not run in the chapels. In these circumstances he might well have concluded that any attempt to tackle the problems all at once was bound to fail, and that a more gradual and piecemeal approach was indicated. But he did not reach that conclusion, perhaps because he felt that the new proprietor would not be satisfied with such tactics. Instead, Hussey immediately decided that Times Newspapers would have to press on alone. Union leaders were informed that a new document, *Opportunity for Success*, would be put forward by the management, since 'the need for new technology and staff reductions' had not altered, but had become more acute than ever.[4]

While *Programme for Action* was under consideration by the unions' rank-and-file, an incident occurred which did nothing to improve the climate in which a hard choice had to be made, though there is no

1 Down-column p.4 report from 'our labour editor', 'New press technology plan seen as "mouldy old carrot"', January 18 1977. So far as *Programme for Action* was concerned, Routledge seems to have made a point of reporting only the bad news, leaving any encouraging items to be reported by juniors.
2 Front-page, but down-column, report from Routledge, 'Two Fleet Street unions reject technology deal'.
3 Short report down-column on p.2, 'Technology plan rejected again', March 19 1977.
4 Report from Tim Jones, down-column on p.2, 'Technology plans to go ahead at "The Times"', March 29 1977.

reason to suppose it decisively affected the outcome. Normally, as we have seen, the reporting of anything to do with trade unions in the newspaper industry was furtive and elliptical, since managements had learnt from experience that reticence was the only safe policy. They had come to know that loss of production, through sudden stoppages or mechanical 'accidents', was the likely penalty of any news item or comment displeasing to the print workers. All the same, in January 1977 Rees-Mogg decided, on an impulse, to break with the tradition of cowardly self-restraint, by offering on one occasion a direct challenge to the unions on the issue of editorial freedom. The decision was brave, whatever may be thought of the timing.

The affair began when David Astor, recently retired after his long and (particularly in the early phase) most fruitful editorship of the *Observer*, wrote an article on the way the print unions were restricting freedom of expression in newspapers. The article was written for the magazine *Index on Censorship*, which existed mainly to draw attention to the plight of writers and political dissidents living under foreign dictatorships. Rees-Mogg had a report of the article prepared for *The Times* of January 13, to appear not on an inside page but on the front page; and the task of preparing the report was entrusted to a home affairs reporter, Diana Geddes, rather than to the labour staff. When the NGA and NATSOPA machine-room members saw the copy they objected to it, and protracted discussion followed with the management. Eventually the NATSOPA men agreed to allow the report to appear, on the understanding that they would have the right to reply, but the NGA men, acting unofficially, made the further demand that a disclaimer by the management should be put at the foot of the report. This demand was refused, and consequently *The Times* did not appear on January 13.

The matter was raised that day in Parliament, where Callaghan, asked to comment, was evasive. He did not 'set himself up as a pundit' on such matters, but felt that freedom of the press 'depended on accurate reporting', which was too often absent. Nobody, so far as he knew, had heard the views of those who had stopped *The Times*, and without knowing their side of the case he would not pass judgement. He added that the *Guardian* seemed to have managed to print the story 'with general satisfaction'. (In fact, the *Guardian* had printed only a four-paragraph report, with a management disclaimer, and even so its London editions were delayed.) Mrs. Thatcher shouted across the Chamber that she 'little thought ever to hear a prime minister uphold the censorship of the press', and two Conservative backbenchers, Norman Tebbit and Nicholas Ridley, tried in vain to have the House adjourned for an emergency debate.

These Commons exchanges were front-page news in the paper on January 14, together with an account of the dispute; while the delayed report of Astor's article appeared at the top of page 2.[1] Next day the lead letter was from K. P. Smith, father of the chapel, writing 'for and on behalf of' *The Times's* NGA machine managers:

> Recently workers on national newspapers were presented with a booklet *Programme for Action*. It set out proposals for the introduction of new working arrangements and technology . . .
>
> On Wednesday night (January 12) a protest was made over an article which was to appear on page one of *The Times* subtitled 'Featherbed tactics in Fleet Street condemned'. The article was not complete but an edited version from a magazine *Index on Censorship*. It is strange that even in an edited version references to sabotage in machine rooms with all its undertones were left in. We do not wish to be associated with criminal actions.
>
> This is not the time for an obscure personality who has recently lost his editorship to blame everyone but himself.
>
> Whatever action we, the printers, took over the accuracy of the article or our request for a disclaimer over the charge of sabotage, the media would make us wrong; the article was written in this way. Every dispute has two points of view and it is significant that all reporting on Thursday, including radio and television, gave only one point of view and failed to find out the other side of the coin.
>
> Was someone trying to prove a point?[2]

Alongside this letter was a leader by Rees-Mogg, in which he first summarised what had happened; then, after a passing reference to Callaghan, asserted the importance of being on good terms with trade unions, as with proprietors, advertisers and governments. But it was more vital still to preserve 'the freedom of the editorial process'. In modern society the power of trade unions was very great, but if newspapers admitted their right to alter copy, 'either by addition or

1 'Mrs. Thatcher accuses the Prime Minister of supporting censorship', from Hugh Noyes, parliamentary correspondent; 'Union men's objection to story stops "Times"', from Christopher Thomas, labour staff; 'Mr. Astor condemns "featherbedding tactics in national newspapers"', from Diana Geddes, home affairs reporter.

2 January 15 1977. The apparently irrelevant mention of *Programme for Action* at the beginning of the letter will not have been overlooked.

subtraction', then the range of such interference, 'or the inhibitions which might arise from the possibility of such interference', would be very wide:

> Anybody, a citizen, a reader, a member of the printing staff, a trade union official, an ambassador, a private soldier, a public figure, can come to *The Times* and by way of letter or by word of mouth put his views or information to us, but he must not come on a claim of power. The editorial process entirely welcomes outside opinion and totally rejects outside pressure.[1]

Astor wrote to Rees-Mogg: 'I cannot begin to express my admiration of The Times' behaviour over my Index piece. Your paper has again made a piece of newspaper history and I am glad to have been an accessory'.[2]

Soon after this incident the Bullock committee on industrial democracy reported. The committee included, among others, representatives of both sides of industry. The trade unionists on it were the worthy, authoritative Jack Jones and the clever, but much less trusted, Clive Jenkins. The chairman, Alan (Lord) Bullock, was the eminent biographer of Bevin, as well as Hitler (and, later, Stalin). The committee was unable to reach a united conclusion, and therefore had to issue majority and minority reports. These, despite leaks in advance, received much space and attention when they appeared. In the majority report the most conspicuous proposal was that there should be worker-directors on boards, though since they were to be placed there under trade union auspices their democratic credentials would often be extremely doubtful. This proposal had few sincere friends outside the TUC. The Conservative and Liberal parties denounced it, the CBI would have nothing to do with it, and even within the Labour movement enthusiasm for it was limited. Left-wingers in parliament, in the constituency parties and on the shop floor were naturally opposed to any arrangement intended to mitigate the intensity of class warfare. The government, for its part, felt obliged to welcome a proposal that had the TUC's backing, though it did so with many unspoken reservations.

The Times gave blanket coverage to Bullock: two reports on the front page; pages 4 and 5 devoted to the majority and minority texts, together with comment from various sources; parliamentary

1 First leader, 'The conditions of freedom', same date.
2 Astor to W.R.-M., January 17 1977.

discussion of the proposals on page 9; finally in *TBN*, a critical piece by Edwin (Lord) Plowden and a column on the subject by Jay. The leader said that what was being advocated was not industrial democracy but, to coin a Greek word, 'syndicarchy'. True friends of the unions would oppose this, while those who wanted 'to gorge the trade unions with power, like a Strasbourg goose', were false friends.

Jay, too, evoked the brute creation, beginning his piece with a quotation:

> The 'orse 'e knows above a bit
> The bullock's but a fool,
> The elephant's a gentleman,
> The battery mule's a mule;
> But the commissariat cam-u-el,
> When all is said and done,
> E's a devil an' an ostrich an' a
> Orphan child in one.

'Available historical scholarship', Jay added, 'gives no warrant for the view that when Kipling wrote those lines he was musing on the introduction of industrial democracy into Britain, which only goes to show the limitations of historical scholarship . . . in the face of overwhelming internal evidence'.[1]

Readers had much to say about Bullock, but none was more succinct or to the point than Mrs. Sue Nightingale of Sheriff Hutton, near York, who asked: 'Sir, Am I to understand that managers are not workers?'[2]

Since 1975 the Indian prime minister, Indira Gandhi, had been ruling by decree, having declared a state of emergency not, as she claimed, to avert anarchy, but because she had lost the confidence of her party colleagues and was in danger of being ousted. She had acted to forestall a threat to her own power. Though in some quarters her pretexts were accepted, *The Times* did not accept them but condemned, editorially, her betrayal of India's democratic tradition, which her father had

1 January 27 1977. Lead story from Wood, 'TUC urges swift action on Bullock call for worker-directors', and Routledge front-page report 'CBI rejects idea of imposing directors on board by law'; leader, 'The British abhor a monopoly of power'; Plowden, Bullock – setback for worker participation'; Jay, 'The 'orse 'e knows above a bit'.
2 January 31 1977.

established and scrupulously upheld. An early casualty of her dictatorial regime was press freedom, and in July 1975 a *Times* correspondent, Peter Hazlehurst, was ordered out of the country.[1] (He was, at the time, the correspondent in Tokyo, but had been covering events in India since the promulgation of Mrs. Gandhi's emergency measures.) Since then the paper had been largely dependent on heavily censored news from India.

In early January 1977 Levin wrote a strong indictment of her regime, which provoked a passionate reply from Michael Foot, speaking at an India League reception in London. Of Levin's final comment that she wanted to be a dictator and was going to be, he had this to say: 'So little is that the truth that it adds up to a monstrous lie. Furthermore the peddling of such lies can do infinite damage to relations between our two countries'. After a few words of concern about certain aspects of the emergency, he ended strangely:

> Of course, one way was open to Mrs. Gandhi which would have spared her the strictures of Mr. Levin and everyone else. She could have had herself assassinated . . . My guess, and mine may be better than Mr. Levin's, is that the vast majority of Indian people are glad that Mrs. Gandhi chose a different course. Her departure from the Indian scene at this period . . . would have been a tragedy for the Indian people.[2]

Within days of the Levin-Foot exchange Mrs Gandhi surprised everybody by relaxing the emergency laws, releasing a number of political prisoners, and calling an election for March. Why did she perform this astonishing volte-face? There were probably three main reasons, all reflecting the complexity of her nature and the confusion of her motives. She was stung by the disillusionment and outrage of people in the outside world whose opinions she could not quite ignore; people like Levin (whether or not she read his article of January 6). She was embarrassed by the fact that the Pakistani leader, Zulfikar Ali Bhutto, would be holding elections in March; embarrassed, because it had always been a point of pride that India, unlike Pakistan, was a democratic state. Above all, wanting unfettered power but also wanting to feel that she had it by popular consent, she made the mistake of believing (with Foot) that the Indian people were in a mood to give

---

1 In 1971, as correspondent in India, he had received an award for his coverage of the crisis leading to the birth of Bangladesh.

2 Levin's piece, 'The simple truth about Mrs. Gandhi and her path to dictatorship', January 6 1977. Report of Foot's speech, January 7 1977.

it to her. As her father's daughter, uncomfortably aware of the odious comparisons that were being drawn, she sought the blessing of democracy for her authoritarian rule; but she would surely not have called an election when she did if she had thought there was any serious chance of losing it.

Her false optimism was not disputed by *The Times*, which said at the outset there could be 'little doubt' she would be returned.[1] But when the campaign started doubts soon arose. Kuldip Nayar, an experienced Indian journalist who was sending regular reports to the paper, described the scene at her launching rally in Delhi, when the crowd was smaller than in previous elections, and when she was met with jeers.[2] On the same day that this report appeared there was a picture of her aunt, Mrs. V. L. Pandit, speaking for the opposition parties at Delhi university.[3] A week or so later the paper published an article by Mrs. Pandit's daughter, Nayantara Sahgal, in which she said that her mother's re-entry into politics was symbolic 'of the widespread and passionate feeling that India must return to civilised values, to the standards represented by Jawaharlal Nehru', which Mrs. Gandhi's party no longer represented.[4]

Her younger son, Sanjay, was the principal bogey in the campaign, because his influence on her was thought (with reason) to have been nefarious, and above all because the methods by which his policy of 'voluntary' sterilisation had been carried out had aroused fierce resentment. About a week before the poll it was reported that he had escaped an assassination attempt, when gunmen fired shots at his jeep. On the same day there was an op. ed. piece by Richard Wigg, who had been sent out to cover the last stage of the campaign. He noted the significance of the defection to the opposition of the veteran Jagjivan Ram, leading representative of the Untouchables and a member of every Indian cabinet since independence. Wigg saw that Mrs. Gandhi had an uphill fight in north India, but suggested that a contrary trend in the southern states might 'save the balance'. The chief explanation of her difficulties was 'the impact caused by the Government's controversial sterilisation drive under the emergency [which had] emerged as the single most important popular issue of the campaign – for it took untrammelled executive action to the rural areas, above

1 Leader, 'India's elections are welcome', January 19 1977.
2 At one point Nayar was arrested and imprisoned, but Rees-Mogg secured his release.
3 March 2 1977.
4 'The romance and the reality of Mrs. Gandhi's rise to power'. March 11 1977.

all in northern India'. This assessment was largely correct, though it just came, tentatively, to the wrong conclusion.[1]

On March 21 the lead story in the paper was 'Mrs. Gandhi loses her seat in Congress disaster'. Wigg reported the big news; also that the coalition of opposition parties, Janata, had 'chosen Morarji Desai as its candidate for the premiership'. Desai was a puritanical octogenarian, with long experience of government, who had been detained by Mrs Gandhi under the emergency, but released when she announced the election. Janata had an absolute majority in the new parliament, but its gains were, as Wigg had more or less predicted, all in the north, while in the south Congress and its allies had held their own. Mrs Gandhi was gracious in defeat, resigning at once and offering 'constructive cooperation' to the new government, while Sanjay Gandhi announced that he was leaving active politics. *The Times* commented in a leader that his power had seemed to carry the threat of dynastic permanence, but that he had proved a liability and had been overwhelmingly defeated.[2]

The heading of the leader, 'Fall of the Nehru dynasty', turned out to be premature, however, because the Janata government squandered its opportunity, not least by its foolish and petty treatment of Mrs Gandhi. Instead of responding to her offer of goodwill, and letting bygones be bygones, it tried to bring her to book for her wrongdoing. The only effect of this was to make her seem a martyr and to restore her prestige. In due course she returned to power, with her elder son, Rajiv, as political heir apparent in place of Sanjay, who had been killed in an air crash. This dynastic revival was to have tragic consequences, personal and political.

By the early part of 1977 Labour's tenuous overall majority in the House of Commons had disappeared. By-election losses and the defection of two of its MPs to form the Scottish Labour Party had reduced its strength from 319 to 310, and it had begun to lose parliamentary votes, notably in its attempt to impose a guillotine on the devolution bill. Towards the end of March the opposition put down a no-confidence motion and it seemed likely that the government would be

1 Front page news report, 'Sanjay Gandhi shot at', and op. ed piece, 'Mrs. Gandhi has a fight on her hands, but she will win', March 15 1977. Wigg was an experienced foreign correspondent, who had served as correspondent in Latin America during the period of expansion following *The Times* take-over. Since 1972 he had been at rather a loose end.

2 News reports, March 21, 22, 23 and 24 1977, and leader, March 22 1977.

defeated, unless it could secure the support of the Liberals with their thirteen MPs.

Since the previous year the Liberals had a new leader. In May 1976 Thorpe had to resign, because of a bizarre, melodramatic scandal which damaged his credit beyond repair. Pending the election of a new leader in July Grimond was brought back as caretaker. The leadership was contested by two candidates, and for the first time all members of the party voted in the election. The two candidates, both MPs and each backed, as the new rules required, by at least one-fifth of their parliamentary colleagues, were John Pardoe and David Steel. The younger was Steel, and Levin, while favouring him for the longer term, argued that his election at that time would be 'premature' and that Grimond's return to the leadership should be prolonged. But the paper's support went to Steel, as 'the better qualified' to give the Liberals a sense of purpose and a reason why non-Liberals should turn to them.[1] After a campaign not free from acrimony Steel was elected, on July 7, by a large majority.

A son of the manse and a professional broadcaster, Steel was in some ways a representative figure of the Sixties, the decade during which he entered Parliament as the youngest MP. He soon made his name there with a private member's bill to reform the abortion law, which was passed, with government assistance, in 1967. This brought him into close contact with Roy Jenkins, then home secretary, anticipating their much closer cooperation, some years later, in a more ambitious enterprise. Steel had, indeed, more in common with the right wing of the Labour Party than with old-fashioned Liberals or even some who, without being old-fashioned, were more attached than he was to traditional Liberal policies. As an undergraduate at Edinburgh he had been greatly influenced by John Mackintosh, then a lecturer in modern British history, who had remained his 'mentor'; and in his last speech as president of the university Liberal club he had predicted the emergence of a 'social democratic party' uniting the Liberals and the Labour right.[2]

About a fortnight before the confidence debate in March 1977 Steel gave an interview to *The Times* in which he set out the terms on which his party 'would be prepared to enter into a working arrangement with

---

May 11 1976. Levin's piece, 'The one man, the one way, for the Liberals'; leader, 'Forced out'.

David Steel, *Against Goliath*, pp.21, 26 and 146. Mackintosh (who has already appeared in this volume as a *Times* columnist) had a varied academic career before being elected to parliament in 1966, a year after Steel. His early death from cancer in 1978 robbed British politics of one of its more brilliant personalities.

the Government to enable it to continue in office'. While denying that he had any thought of coalition, he said that he would like the government to adjust its programme to reach a 'wide area of agreement', failing which the Liberals would vote with other parties to bring it down. He listed four subjects on which agreement would have to be reached: the form of devolution, elections to the European parliament with PR, legislation on industrial partnership, and tax reform. Strangely absent from the list was any mention of PR for the Westminster parliament, the policy of most vital concern to the Liberals.[1]

Shortly before the debate *The Times* gave the incipient deal its backing. There was 'much to be said . . . for an arrangement that would permit the present Government to remain in office for a bit while ensuring that there would be no more extremist measures'. As for the Liberals, they stood to gain two advantages. Evidence that they had exercised a moderating influence on the government could strengthen their claim for more representation in the next parliament; and the deal might also 'possibly bring nearer that realignment in British politics' of which they had 'dreamt for so long'.[2] The readiness to keep Labour temporarily in office reflected no fundamental change of allegiance on the paper's part, but rather a feeling that it would be better for the IMF's stern discipline to be administered by a Labour government, which would then have to bear the inevitable popular odium. The suggested benefits to the Liberals of supporting the government in such circumstances ignored the probability that they would be made, thereby, to share the odium, with little or no compensating credit. So, indeed, it turned out.

Callaghan responded to Steel's offer, first through intermediaries and then by holding direct talks. Their first man-to-man meeting was on the Monday before the Thursday when the debate was to take place. On the Wednesday morning *The Times* reported in its lead story that no deal had yet been struck, but that it seemed increasingly likely Labour would survive the vote. Steel was demanding 'in effect a contractual undertaking' that the government would act in consultation with the Liberals. In a leader, the paper was at pains to correct any impression it might earlier have given of wanting the government to last beyond a limited period. Though the government had, for the immediate future, 'a useful purpose to serve', this did not mean that, if a general election were called, it would 'deserve to be returned to

1 Front-page story from George Clark, 'Mr. Steel states Liberal terms for keeping Labour in government', March 12 1977.
2 Leader, 'Liberals in the limelight', March 21 1977.

power for another five years'. In the paper's view, it would not.

A letter the same day from Neil Kinnock attacked *The Times*'s line on the proposed pact:

> You seek to disarm with the hope for something which 'would permit the present government to stay in office for a bit while ensuring that there would be no [more] extremist measures'. What 'extremist measures', pray? The most effective wage control policy in modern history? A £5 billion cutback in public spending programmes? A repeatedly demonstrated determination to save the pound and cut the PSBR regardless of electoral consequences? Obviously I have my own critical views of such policies and they are no secret. But only the most jaundiced Establishment eye could regard the Labour government as 'extremist' and only the blindest Liberal leader [could] think of full blooded socialism . . . [If Labour wins the vote] Extremism, mortal sin and unfulfillable deals will play no part. Practicality will.[1]

The author of this letter would later show an acute regard for electoral consequences, and a preference for practicality over ideology.

Labour did win the vote. The deal with the Liberals was clinched in time for Callaghan to announce it in his speech, and as a result the government had a majority of twenty-four at the end of the debate. *The Times* reported the news under a five-column headline on the front page, and in a leader commented that the Liberals had 'already made their mark', since direct elections to the European parliament would 'now definitely be presented to the House of Commons'. But the leader added that the history of Labour governments depending on Liberal support was not encouraging; the experience of 1924 and 1931 suggested that it could 'too easily end in confusion and recrimination'. All the same, it would be enough if the arrangement served its purpose for the next few months.[2]

Among Steel's colleagues, Grimond and the promising young MP for Truro, David Penhaligon, opposed the pact with Labour. Wood recalled the negotiation with Heath three years before, when the Liberals had been offered a formal coalition, with a Cabinet seat for Thorpe, lesser posts for other Liberals, and a Speaker's conference

---

1 Lead story from Wood, 'No inter-party deals signed that Labour can win', leader 'Verdict tonight', and lead letter from Kinnock, March 23 1977.

2 Lead story, 'Liberal support gives Government victory by 24 votes', and leader, 'Lib-Lab lifebelt', March 24 1977.

on electoral reform, including PR. 'All that the Liberals rejected'. Through the present consultative machinery they could hope 'only to influence here and there the drafting of the Finance Bill', but essentially the budget would be what Healey anyway intended. There would soon be 'a rude awakening' from 'another Liberal dream'.[1]

In February 1977 Crosland, whom Callaghan had appointed foreign secretary, died suddenly of a cerebral haemorrhage, and the shock of this event was compounded when the prime minister chose as his successor the minister of state at the foreign office, David Owen. Owen thus became the youngest occupant of the post since Eden in 1935 and, at thirty-eight, the same age that Eden had then been. He also resembled Eden in glamour and ambition, while differing from him in two important respects. Whereas Eden's ministerial experience had been entirely in foreign affairs, Owen was a doctor of medicine who had served as minister of health in the DHSS. The other difference was that, whereas Eden always had the deepest regard for the service over which he presided, Owen soon showed that he had little time for the traditional methods and standards of the foreign office and its missions abroad. It was therefore no wonder that, during only two years as foreign secretary, he made himself cordially disliked by his subordinates at all levels.

Soon after succeeding Crosland he turned his mind to a post within his new sphere of patronage, the requirements for which he could plausibly claim to understand better than most of his advisers. This was the Washington embassy. Since he was married to an American, he naturally felt he had a special rapport with Americans. He also had a less justifiable belief that there was a substantial affinity, almost an identity, of outlook between Carter Democrats and British Labour politicians like himself. For these reasons he decided to appoint as ambassador in Washington somebody whom he regarded as an outstanding representative, in his generation, of the moderate left, and who also shared his impatience with the airs and graces of the so-called establishment. His choice for the post was the economics editor of *The Times*, Peter Jay.

One day in April Jay returned to the office at three minutes to

1 Leader-page piece, 'Perchance to dream of Liberal glory', March 28 1977. It was true that the government's ostensible concessions to the Liberals were largely on matters where it either needed or wanted to act, or to refrain from acting, in the same way. For instance, it was convenient to it to have an excuse for shelving the Bullock proposals. In return, the Liberals did not even get PR for the European parliament.

4 p.m., after a long lunch at a restaurant in Regent's Park, to find two messages on his desk: one from the editor asking him to write a leader on unemployment, the other from the foreign secretary asking to see him at the House of Commons at 4.15. Since taxis were notoriously scarce in Gray's Inn Road, he at first abandoned any thought of making it to Wesminster in time and started to write the leader. But after a few minutes he decided, after all, to try his luck, and miraculously not only got a taxi at once but reached the House of Commons by 4.15. Owen took him out on to the terrace and said 'I want you to go to Washington'. Jay thought he was being offered the post of third secretary (economics), about which there had been some speculation in the press, so began to explain that he and his wife had discussed it and felt they could not interrupt their children's schooling. But when he grasped what was actually being proposed he took a different view. In the knowledge that his own employment was about to change dramatically, he went back to the office and wrote the leader on unemployment.[1]

Since the Jays were close friends of the Owens, and Margaret Jay was Callaghan's daughter, the appointment could hardly fail to come under strong attack, not only from the opposition but from Labour quarters as well. When it was announced, in the second week of May, Owen said that Jay was his personal choice and that his hardest task had been to persuade the prime minister to agree to it, because of 'the obvious risk of charges of nepotism'. But he had at length convinced Callaghan that it was right, on merit. Defending the appointment, he added that Jay would 'establish an easy and informal relationship with many of the people of his own generation who [had] prominent positions in the new American administration'. (He was forty at the time.) Reporting 'a move which took the diplomatic world by surprise', *The Times* said that for the foreign office, which was 'anxiously awaiting the report on its activities by the Think Tank', the news could not have been 'other than shattering'. On an inside page Berthoud contributed a profile of the new ambassador, which was on the whole very favourable, referring to Jay's 'intellectual brilliance, great charm', friendliness, 'profound grasp' of economics, 'wide range of human experience' and 'knowledge of how bureaucracies work'. But he did strike one cautionary note: 'If Peter Jay has a fault, it has been occasionally to carry self-confidence to the point of arrogance'.[2]

1 Jay talking to author.
2 Front-page report from diplomatic correspondent, and Berthoud profile on p.8, May 12 1977. Berthoud also praised Margaret Jay, who had 'remained her forceful and lovely self'.

Owen had paid an overt tribute to the existing ambassador, Sir Peter Ramsbotham, who was being replaced after two years and consoled with the governorship of Bermuda; while Brogan had reported from Washington that Ramsbotham had worked hard and achieved 'considerable success' in his dealings with the new administration. But 'inspired' press briefing from the prime minister's office led to reports in the evening papers that Ramsbotham was 'snobbish, old-fashioned in style, and rather a figure of fun'. These aspersions were hotly denied on both sides of the Atlantic, and official clarification made matters, if anything, worse. Suggestions that Owen disapproved of Ramsbotham's lifestyle were not roundly denied, but said to be 'more than slightly overdoing it'; and it was further explained that Owen, having decided on a change of style at the Washington embassy, had 'looked around for someone to embody it, and lighted on Mr. Jay'. Such a partial and half-hearted *démenti* was worse than none at all.

Meanwhile Callaghan was facing recriminations about the Jay appointment, not least from his own side. Dennis Skinner attacked it, with 'the backing of the ever-voluble Mr. Neil Kinnock . . . who spoke of the "enormous, stupendous, political insensitivity" of it'; and Willie Hamilton asked for a debate. In *The Times*'s correspondence columns one letter criticised the appointment from a different angle, John Scrope of Wood Street, London EC2, asking: '. . . is the United Kingdom entering an era of obscure diplomacy? If Mr. Jay should carry across the Atlantic his convoluted expression of . . . thought, this habit might cause confusion in the relationship between the two countries'. There was, however, unexpected support for Jay in a letter from Lord Aldington, Arnold Weinstock, Richard Powell, R. H. Grierson, William Waldegrave and Sara Morrison.[1]

The following day's lead letter was from Lord Caccia, provost of Eton and a former ambassador in Washington. Nepotism was, he said, a factor in the appointment, or anyway perceived to be. Besides Jay had never made any bones about being a socialist, which would create difficulties if there were a change of government. He added a postscript: 'Poor Ciano, for whom in the end his father-in-law would, and probably could, do nothing. *Absit omen*'. Another former ambassador, Lord Sherfield, deplored, as Caccia had done, the rubbishing of

1 Front-page report (from Noyes), and letters, May 13 1977. Lord Aldington, formerly Toby Low MP, was a businessman who had been a middle-ranking Conservative minister; Weinstock, Powell and Grierson were leading industrialists; Waldegrave, a future Conservative cabinet minister, had been a member of the Think Tank and then on Heath's staff at 10 Downing Street; Mrs. Morrison had recently been a vice-chairman of the Conservative party.

Ramsbotham, but on the whole supported Jay's appointment. George Mikes had his reason, flattering to the paper, for regretting it: 'From Economics Editor of *The Times* to Ambassador. What a comedown'.[1]

Rees-Mogg did not commit the paper to a view on the appointment, but instead warmly commended it himself in a signed article on the op. ed. page. If he had been asked to advise, he said, 'with no idea of Peter Jay's appointment in [his] mind, [he] would have suggested that the next ambassador should be someone very good on television, preferably young and of dynamic appearance, able to deal convincingly and *realistically* with the most tough-minded questions about the economic decline of Britain'. His piece ended: 'I am on the side of merit, even if the Provost of Eton is not'.[2] This was too much for Ian Gilmour, who wrote next day that he did not doubt Jay's abilities, but it was absurd to suppose he would have been thought of for the job if he had not been who he was. 'Patronage is patronage, and nepotism is nepotism; and nothing is gained by hailing them as triumphant meritocracy'. Besides, Jay's 'reported opposition to Concorde, his distaste for the EEC and his evident belief that the British political and economic systems [were] doomed, hardly [made] him an obvious choice as the protagonist in America of present day Britain'. The art-dealer Hugh Leggatt wrote from St. James's Street congratulating the people of Bermuda on their luck. 'I should know; I was once Sir Peter Ramsbotham's fag at Eton'.[3] One way and another, Eton kept being brought into the argument.

The same day a row in parliament was reported, over the Ramsbotham leak. A Conservative MP, Peter Blaker, had identified the source as the prime minister's press secretary, Tom McCaffery, and Callaghan, while denying that what had appeared in the press reflected his own or the government's judgement of Ramsbotham, at the same time impugned Blaker's honour. Asked to withdraw, he lamely said it was not Blaker himself, but his role in the affair, that was dishonourable.[4] The following day there was a leader in the paper on the lobby system, written by Smith, noting that the big disadvantage of it, to be set against certain advantages, was that it facilitated management of the news by ministers. The remedy was not to sweep the system away entirely, but to have fewer unattributable briefings. The balance should be changed.[5]

---

1 Letters, May 14 1977. Sherfield was the former Sir Roger Makins.
2 May 16 1977.
3 Letters, May 17 1977.
4 Front-page story and parliamentary report, May 17 1977.
5 Leader, 'The lobby should go public', May 18 1977.

Jay's term of office in Washington did not prove at all disastrous (except to his marriage), though a less obviously clever and more conventionally diplomatic man might have done the job even better. Moreover, Caccia's warning was borne out; after the fall of his father-in-law's government two years later, he was soon recalled.

In early 1977 Grant circulated a memo to all heads of department:

> After 20 years as Political Correspondent and Political Editor of *The Times*, David Wood feels that enough is enough and wishes now to concentrate on the development of the European Parliament. He has therefore been appointed European Political Editor.
>
> Fred Emery, Washington Correspondent, has been appointed to succeed David Wood as Political Editor.
>
> These appointments will come into effect immediately after the 1977 political party conferences.[1]

Under Emery, as under Wood, the second man in the team was George Clark, a most experienced and knowledgeable parliamentary reporter, with a command of shorthand that was already becoming rare. Michael Hatfield, a member of the parliamentary staff since 1972, continued to give the paper the benefit of his excellent contacts in the Labour party, while Hugh Noyes combined writing the parliamentary sketch with reporting important government statements. A further reporter might be assigned from time to time from the general pool.

From 1978 to 1980 Emery was also presenter of the BBC's leading current affairs programme *Panorama*.[2] There were some among his colleagues who slightly resented his dual role, but on balance his greater public exposure was probably an advantage to the paper, since it was made a condition of his work for the BBC that he should always be announced as 'Fred Emery of *The Times*'. When his first contract with *Panorama* ended, in the summer of 1980, the reason was an editorial change on the programme, not any pressure from the paper.

The choice of Emery for the key post of political editor could be interpreted as an admission by Rees-Mogg that he had been right about Watergate. Certainly his promotion was not due to any excess of deference on his part. He could react sharply when crossed, and

1 January 28 1977. Wood had been political correspondent from 1957 to 1969, and political editor since the latter date.
2 The period included nearly a year when the paper was closed down.

there was a further hiccup in the course of 1977, before he returned to take up his new duties, when a piece by him recording adverse comments by a senior American official on Ramsbotham's withdrawal, and Jay's appointment as ambassador, was spiked in the office.[1] But Rees-Mogg respected Emery's independence of mind, and Emery knew that there were few editors under whom he would be freer to exercise it.

1 Emery to W.R.-M., May 16 1977.

XXII

Silver jubilee • Good Bourbon wins through • Wrongful exposure • Grunwick • Double Dutch • Allen fights for her rights

QUEEN ELIZABETH II'S silver jubilee was celebrated in June rather than February, the month of her accession, in the hope (which turned out to be vain) of suitably benign weather. The celebrations were to be immediately followed by a Commonwealth conference, and two of the would-be participants were, in different ways, a source of difficulty. The president of Seychelles, Sir James Mancham, was overthrown by a coup at home after his arrival in London. He did not take part in the conference and, out of consideration for the Queen, decided to stay away from the jubilee service in St Paul's. The president of Uganda, Idi Amin, mass murderer and psychopath, was advised by the British government that his presence would not be welcome. All the same he threatened to attend, and the threat hung over the celebrations, though in the end he did not come.

The jubilee was a significant and popular event, which deserved to be well covered by the quality press as well as by the tabloids. Even so *The Times* may have gone a little too far in devoting three whole inside pages to it on successive days, in addition to front-page reports, op. ed pieces and a leader. On June 7 there was a report on the front page that the Queen had lit the first of a hundred bonfires to be kindled throughout the country. Pages 4, 5 and 6 were given over entirely to jubilee material, including accounts of George III's golden jubilee (which started the modern practice), Victoria's golden and diamond jubilees, and George V's silver jubilee. On the op. ed. page there was another, surely superfluous, piece on Victoria's golden jubilee. The leader, written by Hickey, observed that jubilees had been occasions 'for the expression of loyalty and affection towards the person of the Sovereign', and also 'for celebrating the deeds and worth of the nations over which the Sovereign reign[ed]', but that on the present occasion 'jubilation bubble[d] up more naturally in respect of the first of those blessings than of the second'. 'All the imperial and most of the

Commonwealth scent' had evaporated, while even 'the very integrity of the Kingdom' was under attack in Northern Ireland and 'called in question' in Scotland. Nevertheless:

> The Queen's faithful fulfilment of her representative role encourages her subjects to link her with whatever pleasure they take in the beauty, familiarity, antiquity and genius of their country. And her own qualities of dutifulness, grace, cultivation of family life, dignity, reliability and unimpressibility by publicized fashion . . . are readily perceived to be qualities of which the world stands much in need, especially in high places. We are grateful to her for possessing them.

When Masefield was poet laureate *The Times* used on such occasions to feature short poems by him, often of staggering vacuity, but set in large type. In June 1977 there was no such offering from the poet laureate, Sir John Betjeman, but instead a curious ode by an anonymous versifier who signed him- (or her-) self 'Pangloss'. Appearing not in the main body of the paper, but in the *Europa* section, this ode attempted to combine a tribute to the Queen with heavy reproach to her subjects in the United Kingdom for their lack of European enthusiasm. After an opening of routine homage, the note of complaint was soon introduced:

> Direct elections, once our dearest prize;
> Are fading fast before our very eyes;
> And while much European ardour cools,
> Perverse Britannia once more waives the rules.

The ending was as obtuse politically as it was poetically banal:

> Is all awry? Must Europe fade like this,
> Its love-match ended with a Judas-kiss?
> It cannot be! Great monarch raise thy voice!
> Against the barons back thy people's choice!
> Lest Europe to the East become a martyr –
> Or fall a prey instead to Magna Carter.
>
> Hail noble Queen! May God thy reign prolong
> Till Eurovision means far more than song;

Till Europe rules the unpolluted waves,
And Europeans never more be slaves.[1]

The day this ode appeared was the day the Queen drove in procession to St Paul's for the jubilee service of thanksgiving. The weather was cold and damp, though fortunately less so than for her coronation at the same time of year in 1953. Next morning the paper's front-page headline, across the full width of the paper, was 'One million people greet the Queen on her Silver Jubilee Day', on which the *Annual Register* later disobligingly commented that 'as this would have meant an average of 50 deep on both sides of a three-mile route it must be taken as a symbolic rather than an actual figure'. Whatever the true figure, the crowds were certainly very large.

The story under the headline, by Penny Symon, was resolutely glowing: 'It was one of those occasions that the British are still able to do so well. The pomp and pageantry were magnificent, everything ran like clockwork, and no one stumbled over his lines'. In the cathedral, the archbishop of Canterbury, Dr Donald Coggan, gave the congregation the news that many were 'seeing through the hollowness of a way of life which seeks to build on a basis of materialism'. The only embarrassment, according to Symon, was that Lord Snowdon, by now separated from Princess Margaret, was 'seated eight rows behind the Royal Family' and 'watched his wife enter the cathedral in a procession with Lord Linley and Lady Sarah Armstrong-Jones, his children'. But at the end of the service 'the children left the procession to greet their father affectionately in a side aisle'. Some readers must have wondered why such an awkwardly contrived encounter was necessary even in the side aisle of a packed cathedral, when presumably he and his children had plenty of opportunities to see each other in private.

As well as the main report, the front page carried a story from Berthoud about the patient vigil of crowds, and one from Heren about the attitude to the jubilee of his native East End of London. There was also a picture of the Queen talking informally to people in the crowd as she walked from St Paul's to Guildhall: an experiment new

1 Leader, 'Grateful for her possessing', and 'A jubilee ode' (in the Europa section), June 7 1977. The author of the ode (unless writing with tongue in cheek) seems to have thought that the Queen's ministers were anti-European while her ordinary subjects were pro-European: more nearly than not the opposite of the truth. Britain had, in the first place, become a member of the European Community through the action of enlightened 'barons'.

in Britain, and generally appreciated. Three inside pages were, again, wholly occupied with jubilee matter, one of them all pictures.[1]

Though Hickey's leader the previous day had ended with the words 'Long may she reign', Hutchinson had suggested in his column a few days before that she might not, after all, choose to reign all that much longer. Expressing himself with courtly floweriness, he said that, while we were in no danger of losing her 'just yet', it would be 'ungenerous to complain if she wished to retire within the next 10 years, bequeathing to Prince Charles the soundest throne in the world'. This suggestion did not appeal to the distinguished war historian, Dr. Noble Frankland, who wrote from Eynsham to describe it as 'misguided'. 'Abdication or exclusion, save in utterly exceptional circumstances, such as those concerning James II and Edward VIII, is a dangerous and basically republican instrument'. Better succession 'by the Grace of God', he said, than 'by decision of the Privy Council or advice in the newspapers'.[2] Fifteen years and more later it was clear that Elizabeth II's own view was closer to Frankland's than to Hutchinson's.

In July the Prince of Wales visited New Printing House Square, but only the editorial departments. There was a front-page picture of him leaving the building between two rows of smiling and applauding girls, with Hamilton behind him; and another on the court page of him talking to 'senior executives' including Heren and Douglas-Home, whose names, however, were not given in the caption.[3]

Another European monarch, with family links to our own, and with a more than symbolic role, was also making important news at this time. When Generalissimo Franco died in November 1975, nearly forty years of personal rule ended. But what was to be Spain's future? He had restored the monarchy as an institution though not, during his lifetime, the person of a monarch. Yet with undeniable wisdom he had arranged that on his death Juan Carlos, son of the pretender Don Juan, grandson of the last King of Spain, Alfonso XIII, and a great-great-grandson of Queen Victoria, should succeed him as head of state and king. Juan Carlos was a young man, still under forty, who had shown remarkable patience and good sense during his difficult

1 June 8 1977. Berthoud's story was headlined 'All-night wait brings its own reward'; Heren's, '"Liz rules OK" the Cockney way'.
2 Hutchinson's column, June 4 1977; Frankland's letter, June 9 1977.
3 July 13 1977.

years as successor-in-waiting to Franco, saying nothing to alarm the country's powerful conservative elements, cultivating the armed forces, yet at the same time 'hinting at some vague sympathy towards the spirit of the new generations'.[1] After Franco's death he soon revealed political qualities of the highest order, presiding over and largely effecting a peaceful transition from dictatorship to democracy which won universal admiration. Before him, the name of Bourbon had been commonly associated with political ineptitude or reaction. He redeemed it and gave it a quite different image.

During the early months of his reign he allowed the old system to discredit itself and prove its incapacity to handle the post-Franco situation. Franco's last prime minister, Arias Navarro, remained in office until July 1976, while the popular demand for true democracy grew. Arias tried to impose it from above, and in a limited form, but this approach was unacceptable to Spain's political parties, now once again free *de facto*, if not yet *de jure*; and it was also discreetly opposed by the king. When Arias resigned, Juan Carlos had to choose a successor from among three names submitted to him by the Council of the Realm, and he chose the candidate least favoured by the Council, Adolfo Suárez, a man of much the same age as himself, with impeccable credentials in the Franco regime but committed, he knew, to thoroughgoing reform.

At first the significance of the appointment was imperfectly understood. A stringer for *The Times* reported that the opposition had 'reacted with a mixture of bewilderment and outright criticism'.[2] A few days later a leader in the paper referred to the frustration that had set in since Arias was succeeded by Suárez. Leading liberals in the previous government had refused to serve under him, and his cabinet was composed mainly of 'personal friends' who, like himself, could be 'classified as reformers only within the context of the National Movement' (Franco's corporatist *Movimiento*). It might be paradoxical that people who had served under Arias should refuse to serve under Suárez, and their attitude was partly due to personal vanity. Nevertheless, the disappointment of liberals was 'not without political justification', and if the new government tried to 'stick to the political line of its predecessor', it would run into serious difficulties. 'Both the King and the new Prime Minister have made eloquent general statements about the need for democracy. It is increasingly necessary to make

1 Raymond Carr and Juan Pablo Fusi, *Spain: Dictatorship to Democracy*, p.208.
2 Report from Madrid, July 5 1976. The stringer was an American, Harry Debelius, who later sent bylined reports.

these statements more precise, and to translate them into action'.[1]

By the New Year there could no longer be any doubt about the government's intentions. A referendum in December had overwhelmingly endorsed a law under which the political system could, and would, be transformed. A new Cortes was to be elected by universal suffrage, and the way was open to the legalisation of democratic parties, trade unions and other organisms of a free country. The opposition, 'surprised and delighted', was now willing to help the government to overcome 'its genuine tactical problems'. The veteran Communist leader, Santiago Carrillo, living in Spain no longer clandestinely, but legally, gave an interview to *The Times* in early January, in which he helpfully disclaimed any immediate desire to form a popular front. 'This is not the time for unification of the left. It is the time for a wider collaboration of the democratic forces to establish freedom'. His only precondition for collaborating was that there should be a full amnesty.[2]

The elections were held in mid-June, and the result was a triumph for moderation. The far left was marginalised, and so were the spiritual heirs of Franco. Indeed, even the democratic right did badly. The big winners were the Democratic Centre Union (UCD), led by Suárez, and the Socialist Workers' Party (PSOE), led by the future prime minister, Felipe Gonsález, which had won, respectively, 165 and 118 seats in the new Cortes. After the poll, in which nearly 80 per cent voted, Suárez was confirmed in the premiership, but the country also had a strong opposition.

The Times commended the result in its best school-prizegiving style. In a leader written by Mortimer, and entitled 'Well done, Spain', it said that the Spanish people were to be congratulated on the tone of the election and on the sensible way they had voted. It also looked forward to Spanish membership of the European Community. Before this could come about there were, to be sure, problems to be faced, but the 'political will to find solutions must not be lacking'. Surprisingly, the leader did not mention the king, but amends for this were made in a piece on the op. ed. page, in which he was hailed as 'the real victor'. More than anyone else, he was responsible for the result. He had 'achieved the remarkable feat of being at the helm of a country which ha[d] moved from dictatorship to free elections in just 18 months without serious upheavals', so creating what must be regarded as 'some kind of historical precedent'. He and Suárez had executed 'a calculated

1 Leader, 'Spain's unknown cabinet', July 9 1976.
2 Leader, 'Progress of reform in Spain', and interview on p.4, January 7 1977.

manoeuvre' designed to avoid 'the dangerous polarization which occurred after the last general election in February, 1936'.[1] Evidently, they had succeeded.

At about the time the Spanish people went to the poll *The Times* committed a serious gaffe on a matter within the tricky area of espionage and security. This took the form of a front-page story with the headline 'Fourth man in inquiry on Philby, Burgess and Maclean', and with a picture of 'Donald Beves, a beloved Cambridge figure'. The story revealed that Beves, a man of wealth and a scholar of Renaissance French literature, who was a fellow of King's College, Cambridge from 1924 until his death in 1961, was suspected by security circles of having played a critical role 'in transforming Philby, Maclean and Burgess from undergraduate communists into Soviet agents'. His name had 'figured strongly in the intensive investigation of the Cambridge connection by MI5 in the early 1950s'. Though the story itself concluded that the evidence against him fell 'short of final proof' a piece the same day on the op. ed. page described him in terms that were distinctly tendentious. 'His position as a great cultivator of youth placed him admirably for the distasteful activities ascribed to him'. Though not much of an academic, he 'contrived to be an exemplary supervisor'. He was 'that rare individual, a man accepted easily by both the aesthetes and the hearties'. He 'never married' but 'lived the life of a bachelor don in King's'. The news of the doubts attached to his name would 'come as a severe shock to the Cambridge generations who knew him'. Most damaging of all was the sub-heading given to the op. ed. piece: 'His political extremism was mixed with a passion for acting' – which combined the *fact* that, as an undergraduate, he had made his mark in amateur theatricals, with the *unsupported suspicion* that he had held extreme left-wing views.[2]

The author of both the news story and the op. ed. piece was Peter Hennessy, a reporter of kindly and scholarly disposition, who was later to write impressive books on the civil service and postwar history. But the story did not come through him in the first place. Rees-Mogg was the channel through which it reached the paper, since he had heard about Beves from a source which, though not in the security services,

1 Leader and op. ed. piece, 'King Carlos [*sic*] is the real victor in Spain', June 17 1977. The author of the latter was William Chislett, a specialist not on the staff, who had also conducted the interview with Carrillo.
2 June 15 1977.

he nevertheless regarded as very strong.[1] Hennessy, acting on Rees-Mogg's lead, then consulted sources of his own inside the system and, having done so, felt justified in writing the story in the form he did.[2]

The lead letter in next morning's paper was from Noel Annan, a former provost of King's, whose protest against the story was all the more effective for being measured and controlled. He did not show any sign (as some later did) of standing on the divine right of King's, but appealed to reason and a sense of justice. The only evidence against Beves seemed to be that he was once under suspicion merely because he was a nodal figure in the university. But this was surely not good enough:

> Where spies are concerned, anything is possible . . . [But] the picture of Mr. Beves as a Soviet agent is so *prima facie* improbable that *The Times* must produce firmer evidence . . . It is a smear to say of a man that 'he would have been admirably placed' to recruit agents. That could be said of practically every hospitable don.

Why had *The Times* rung him (Annan) 'to ask among other things if Mr. Beves was a homosexual'? He was 'an old style bachelor don of great charm and goodness'. The letter ended with a shrewd question: Could it be that the paper's source was 'reporting one lead which petered out and not the considered and final opinion of MI5 on this matter'?[3]

Many more letters followed. Sir Michael Clapham, King's man and

---

1 The source was close to Conservative politicians, though not a politician himself. Despite his subsequent death Rees-Mogg felt inhibited from disclosing his name to the author.

2 Hennessy joined the paper in 1974 as a member of the news staff and occasional leader-writer. In 1967 he had a brief interlude as lobby correspondent on the *FT.*, but within months returned to *The Times* as Whitehall correspondent. He had been educated at Marling School, Stroud, St John's College, Cambridge, the LSE, and Harvard, where he was a Kennedy scholar. At the time of the Beves affair he was thirty years old.

3 June 16 1977. Noel (Lord) Annan was a fellow of King's from 1944 to 1956, and provost from 1956 to 1966. During the war he served at the war office, in the war cabinet offices and in military intelligence, so he was no stranger to the shadowy world of state security. In March 1977 the report of his committee on the future of broadcasting was published, and on the eve of its publication a 'man in the news' feature on him predicted that the report's 'prose style would reflect the gamy, erudite language of its chairman'. (March 24 1977.) The following day the text of the report was given on p.4, and a leader observed that it had 'some pertinent comments to make on the state of British broadcasting today', while doubting that its 'main proposals for change' would 'set the pattern for tomorrow'. (Leader, 'A fair audit but a weak blueprint', March 25 1977.)

businessman, wrote 'as one who knew Donald Beves well over 30 years', to say that he could 'recall no remotely political conversation with him'. If such a 'cultivated, infinitely kind, generous-hearted man' were to be turned into a 'communist spymaster', the grounds of suspicion should be published.[1] Five King's men wrote together: 'In the absence of real evidence, we prefer to retain untarnished our memories of an honourable English gentleman, and to regard the allegations in your report as unfounded'.[2] And the doyen of King's men, George Rylands, wrote two letters, the first of which ended: 'The hundreds and hundreds of those who knew him will not have given a moment's credence to what must be a grievous error or a cruel hoax or vindictive intent'.[3]

Geoffrey Grigson (without a Cambridge background) said: 'I did not know Donald Beves, but I thought I knew *The Times*. I never supposed that [it] . . . would indulge in posthumous assassination . . . Isn't this the kind of journalism that you would be the first to condemn in less exalted newspapers – rightly?'[4] From Christ's College, Cambridge, the senior tutor, G. S. Gorley Putt, addressed the editor still more *ad hominem*: 'It is true that if a Russian master spy wished to disguise himself, an affluent don might not be a bad shot. But I can think of an even more deceptive nodal figure – the Editor of *The Times*'.[5]

Eventually two members of the Beves family wrote to protest, but by then Rees-Mogg had decided to climb down, and the leader containing his recantation and apology appeared alongside their letters. The key passages in the leader read:

> Two weeks ago we published a story which reported that the security services had in the 1950s suspected a late Fellow of King's, Mr. Donald Beves . . . of being, in university terms, the senior member of the conspiracy. It is indeed true that Mr. Beves was suspected, but we now believe the suspicions were mistaken and regret having reported them.

Beves, though 'not a homosexual', fitted the 'pattern of association', but:

---

1 June 17 1977.
2 June 18 1977. The five were Peter Orr, David King, Bruce Nightingale, M. W. Turnbull and Ronald Watkins.
3 June 21 1977.
4 June 17 1977.
5 June 18 1977.

> Further inquiries, the letters of his friends, and private information not previously available to us lead us to reverse that judgment . . . We now apologize for our story because we think it was wrong; that is bad in two ways – it hurts the innocent; it tends to protect the guilty.[1]

The following day Hennessy took the 'unusual step' of associating himself with the apology in a letter to the paper:

> As the author of two articles printed in *The Times* of June 15 concerning the character and career of the late Donald Beves, I wish to retract in full the grievous allegations they contained about his involvement in the Philby/Burgess/Maclean affair.
>
> I would like to apologize unreservedly to the family, friends and former colleagues of Donald Beves for the harm and distress caused.[2]

Annan's hunch was correct. The sources consulted by Hennessy, after he was given the lead by Rees-Mogg, were out of date. Beves had indeed come under suspicion, but when his past was investigated no evidence against him had emerged. After the story appeared in *The Times* other, and more authoritative, sources in MI5 deprecated it; hence Rees-Mogg's reference to 'private information not previously available'. His own original informant had, presumably, been going on the suspicions entertained by MI5 a quarter of a century before.[3]

The incident was not quite closed. Though most people seem to have been satisfied with the expressions of penitence, a few were not. One was Rylands, who in a second letter dismissed the editor's apology as 'smug and shuffling', adding that even if *The Times* were to give £50,000 to King's College chapel or the Fitzwilliam Museum the 'evil smear [could] never be erased.'[4] Two Oxford academics, the historian Michael Howard and the economist Peter Oppenheimer, were equally dismissive of the apology and further demanded, in effect,

---

1 June 29 1977. Letters from Geoffrey Beves Crow, and from Paul Howard Beves and Brian Montague Beves (writing jointly); leader, 'The Cambridge conspiracy'. The second letter asked for a retraction on the front page, where the original story had appeared, but this request was not met.

2 June 30 1977.

3 Rees-Mogg and Hennessy talking to author. The suggestion sometimes heard that Beves was mistaken for Blunt, as a Cambridge bachelor intellectual with a five-letter name beginning with the letter B, appears to be a complete canard.

4 July 1 1977. Rylands also said in this letter: 'Beves was an addict of *The Times* crossword and the novels of Agatha Christie. Is this your evidence?'

that Hennessy and Rees-Mogg himself should resign.[1] This demand provoked a telling riposte from an unexpected quarter. Joe Haines, who as Harold Wilson's press officer had in the past often clashed with *The Times*, wrote to defend it, and more especially Hennessy, against the attack from Oxford:

> I did not know Donald Beves . . . Indeed, until I read the Howard-Oppenheimer letter I imagined I was the only reader of *The Times* not to have been tutored by him. But I do know Peter Hennessy, who is one of the best and most scrupulous reporters in Fleet Street. He made a mistake and has generously admitted it.
>
> Before Howard and Oppenheimer repeat their call for his resignation . . . they might wonder what the effect would be if that duty was imposed upon Mr. Oppenheimer's profession. If every economist who made a mistake was then to resign his post, none of them would be in work, though a great many more ordinary people might be.[2]

A sorry affair thus ended on a chivalrous and humorous note.

Despite the absence of formal control, wage increases were, on the whole, kept within reasonable bounds in 1977, and Britain's economic position improved, at any rate superficially. But industrial tension was growing and there were many strikes, of which one of the smallest, initially, developed during the year into a national *cause célèbre*, both legally and in a broader sense, as Grunwick, the name of an obscure photographic processing plant in north London, became a household name.

The dispute began in August 1976, when 137 Grunwick employees walked out in protest against their working conditions and approached the Association of Professional, Executive, Clerical and Computer Staffs (APEX or Apex). The management offered to take the strikers back if they would drop the idea of joining the union, but they refused and were then sacked. They represented a minority of the workforce, while the majority was content to be non-unionised and showed no disposition to strike. Most of the workers were women of Indian or

---

1 July 6 1977. The letter ended: 'We hardly think that we can be alone in wondering whether you, Sir, and the journalist principally responsible are considering . . . where your own duty lies'. Howard wrote from All Souls, Oppenheimer from Christ Church.
2 July 8 1977.

Pakistani origin. APEX demanded recognition at Grunwick and sought the support of the whole trade union movement for its demand. Its general secretary, Roy Grantham, was essentially moderate, but found himself swept along by more radical forces. During the winter there was unofficial action by postal workers to black the company's mail, and in the spring of 1977 mass picketing began, which in turn led to violence and conflict with the police.

Grunwick's boss, George Ward, was not a man to give way to intimidation. Ethnically Anglo-Indian, he differed from the average British employer at the time in being a full-blooded capitalist ideologue, who did not shrink from a showdown with militant trade unionism but, on the contrary, relished it. With backing from a radical right pressure-group, the National Association for Freedom (NAFF), he showed no interest in compromise. When the government tried to resolve the dispute through the conciliation service (ACAS) which it had recently established, he refused to cooperate; and when, nevertheless, ACAS unwisely recommended recognition of the union, he took ACAS to court, eventually winning his case in the House of Lords.

Meanwhile the picketing campaign had seized the attention of the media, whose coverage of it involved relatively little trouble or expense, since the scene of action, in the metropolitan area, was so easily accessible. While the numbers outside the factory were still fairly modest, and before there had been any violence, two cabinet ministers, Fred Mulley and Shirley Williams, and the minister of sport, Denis Howell, visited Grunwick and stood for a short time on the picket line. As members of APEX they went to show solidarity, and a smiling picture of them appeared on page 2 of *The Times*, though without an accompanying story.[1] Before long, however, they had less reason to smile, because they became associated in the public mind, however unfairly, with the ugly turn the picketing took, and the mere fact that they had been Grunwick pickets was damaging to the government as well as to themselves.

Within a month the paper was reporting that policemen had been pelted with flour, and their helmets knocked off, in scuffles outside the factory, and that eighty-four pickets had been arrested. In the same report, however, supporters of the strike were said to have complained to the Metropolitan Police about 'unnecessary brutality' and 'aggressive and provocative tactics'.[2] Soon afterwards a measured leader noted that intimidation by pickets was forbidden, and that case

1 May 20 1977.
2 Report from Clive Borrell and Tim Jones, June 14 1977.

law had 'sensibly established' that force of numbers was itself 'a kind of intimidation'. But in practice the police had 'considerable discretion' as to what they would allow, and this often led to 'ill-feeling and confusion'. After that week, the leader concluded, it was unlikely that the majority of Grunwick employees, who had stayed at work, could 'feel much warmth towards trade unionism or towards APEX'.[1]

Ward was soon featured as 'Man in the news', asserting that he would 'never give in to this sort of thing', and claiming that he was entitled to dismiss the people who had walked out. 'Mr. Ward sprinkles his arguments with Latin quotations, and religious, historical and even marital analogies. He says Apex is like the husband whose wife has been granted a divorce but who still demands to see her'.[2] But the following day Grantham was given the chance to state his case, and a few days later the home news editor, Brian MacArthur, admitted that there was a danger of over-simplification and distortion in media coverage of the dispute. 'Night after night on television, morning after morning in newspapers, millions of viewers and readers have been presented with film and pictures of violent clashes between the pickets and the police. How often, however, have there been explanations of the complexities of the dispute or of the case put by Apex and the strikers [as by Grantham in *The Times*]?'[3] In a subsequent account of Grunwick approved by the strike committee *The Times* was praised for its fair reporting, and for its attempt to give both sides of the case, which 'balanced its right-wing editorials'.[4]

The editorials did, indeed, become more right-wing as the affair progressed, and the appearance at Grunwick of Arthur Scargill and Mick McGahey, who had contributed so powerfully to the downfall of the last Conservative government, did nothing to counteract the spirit of political partisanship. In his first leader on the dispute Rees-Mogg wrote:

> At Grunwick the picketing is not a form of peaceful persuasion. It is a form of exercise of power. Neither the language nor the conduct of Mr. Scargill or Mr. McGahey is that of peaceful

1 Leader, 'Freedom for employees', June 18 1977.
2 Interviewed on p.2 by Robert Parker, June 22 1977. Ward's knowledge of Latin quotations may have derived from his education at Roman Catholic schools in India
3 Lead letter from Grantham, June 23 1977; op. ed. piece by MacArthur, 'Here is the news, but is there enough of it and is it biased?', June 29 1977.
4 Jack Dromey and Graham Taylor, *Grunwick: the workers' story*, p.128. Dromey as secretary of the TUC's south-east region and of the Brent trades council, was a major participant in the strike; Taylor was a left-wing lecturer, trade union activist and occasional contributor to the *Morning Star*.

> persuasion; they use the argument of superior force. Unless the trade unions can enforce limited and peaceful rules of picketing the Government will have to do so. The right to work has to be defended against the threat of mere numbers.

Scargill had been arrested at Grunwick the previous day, and Heren, visiting the scene, quoted an unnamed 'trade union leader' as having told him, at the back gate of the factory, that Scargill 'went out of his way to get arrested'. In a letter to the editor a former chief inspector of constabulary, Eric St Johnston, recalled Scargill's first triumphant use of flying pickets: 'We must not have another Saltley when mob rule overcame the forces of law and order'.[1]

In another leader Rees-Mogg depicted Scargill as the scourge of coloured immigrants, a white bully seeking to deny them the right to work:

> If the Grunwick picketing were taking place in South Africa or even in the United States everyone would have seen the colour contrast. In the street around the site the population is about evenly mixed . . . At the site a predominantly white crowd, with a small minority of coloured pickets, tries to stop a bus largely full of coloured people getting to their jobs. Mr. Arthur Scargill led a group of white miners from Yorkshire to overawe the Asian workers.

If Grunwick were closed down, would he and his followers be able to offer the 'Asian ladies' of Grunwick alternative employment? Among the numerous letters that appeared day after day there was one from a dentist, Dr. J. D. Harrison, saying that a patient of his was a policeman who was attacked by five Grunwick pickets and had a front tooth smashed. His assailants were caught and fined £10 each, and Harrison wondered if there was 'any other country in which people who attack[ed] the police [were] dealt with so ridiculously leniently'.[2]

The government was deeply embarrassed by the dispute, and at a loss how to reconcile its loyalty to trade unionism with a desire to act, and to be seen to be acting, responsibly in the national interest. At

---

Leader, 'The argument of numbers', June 25 1977. Op. ed. piece by Heren, 'Out with the pickets in Chapter Road', and letter from St Johnston, June 24 1977. The same day there was a front-page picture of a policeman lying on the ground 'after being struck by a bottle'.

Leader, 'Where else will they get jobs?', and Harrison letter (written from Forest Hill, London SE), June 30 1977.

the end of June, the home secretary, Rees, who could never give an appearance of decisiveness, visited Grunwick and was told by one of the picket organisers that there was 'a history of police antagonism', and that 'only once had pickets been allowed to speak to pickets on the buses'. Rees in reply said: 'We must not have this situation. The trade union I belong to, and my father, believed in doing this by peaceful means'. But there were 'people around who [did] not want to do that'. He made no attempt to see Ward, though urged to do so by a local Conservative MP much concerned in the dispute, John Gorst.[1] He thus made the worst of both worlds.

The mass picketing culminated in a 'day of action' on July 11, when 18,000 people converged on Grunwick and there were many clashes with the police. After this the government waited anxiously, but hopefully, for the report of a court of inquiry under Mr (soon to be Lord) Justice Scarman, whose other two members were a trade unionist and the chief industrial relations executive of British Leyland: hardly a team likely to seem balanced to a small independent businessman. Such courts of inquiry are a favourite device of governments, as well known for their short-term utility as for their probable eventual futility. Scarman was no exception to the general rule. When the report was published, in late August, it was seen to have described the history of the dispute and expounded the issues, but without offering any magic formula for a settlement. A whole page of *The Times* was devoted to the text of the report, and there was a profile of Scarman by Berlins. A leader made the point that our legal system depended ultimately on goodwill:

> The law that we have can work only if both sides are prepared to accept compromise and conciliation. Employers who exploit loopholes in the law to avoid those very things, and trade unionists who demonstrate, picket and 'black' up to the very limit the law permits . . . are acting fully within their rights. That is not to say that they are wise to do so, either in terms of public spirit, or of self-interest.[2]

Since goodwill was conspicuously lacking on both sides, there was

---

1 Report of Rees's visit to Grunwick (from Stewart Tendler and Craig Seton), June 28 1977. The picket organiser who spoke to him about the police was Dromey, joint author of the book quoted above.

2 Page 3 report of the text under headline 'Both sides blamed but company is advised to reemploy strikers'; profile of Scarman, 'Neither cloistered judge nor rebel' (p.2 leader, 'Where the law does not apply'. August 26 1977.

Marmaduke Hussey and Rees-Mogg leaving St Paul's after the memorial service for Roy Thomson, 26 October 1976.

Above: Peter Jay between his father-in-law, James Callaghan (left) and the German chancellor, Helmut Schmidt, 6 February 1975. Right: Bernard Levin receiving a columnist of the year award from Roy Jenkins, 23 April 1975.

Conference trio, Brighton 1980. Left to right: Heren, Margaret Allen, Fred Emery.

Paul Routledge (centre) and Douglas-Home (on his left) visiting Hickleton Main colliery, near Doncaster.

Brian MacArthur, home news editor (centre), with colleagues. Left to right: Cyril Bainbridge, Craig Seton, Robert Parker, Stewart Tendler, Dan van der Vat, Philip Howard.

Irving Wardle

Owen Hickey

John Higgins

John Grant

Hugh Stephenson

Clifford Longley

Announcing the shutdown. Left to right: Michael Mander, Hussey, Dugal Nisbet-Smith.

Union demo, November 1978. To left, hatless, behind girl with NATSOPA placard, Barry Fitzpatrick; to right, wearing coat, Russian-style hat and dark glasses, R. A. Brady.

Jake Ecclestone preaches the word.

Monday April 30 1979
No 60,471A
Price fifteen pence

THE TIMES

International
Weekly Edit

Threat to clear win in UK poll after 'scare campaign'

With the Conservatives' lead over Labour in the British election narrowing in the opinion polls, the possibility of an indecisive result for the third successive time could centre on whether the voters will heed Labour's warnings against a woman leader. Mrs Thatcher said on the issue: "I did not get here by being some strident female." Meanwhile a Tory spokesman has declared that a Liberal vote was a "dangerous" vote.

Callaghan challenge on new laws to curb union wreckers

By Fred Emery
Political Editor

Would the Conservatives manage to throw away an almost certain victory in next Thursday's British election? That question hangs over the final hectic days of the campaign. And it raises again the possibility of an indecisive result in the third successive election.

It raises also a faint hope for Labour, and the spectre for the Conservatives of having to rely on the Liberal Party for parliamentary support to form a government.

Towards the close, as the Conservatives' lead in the opinion polls began to falter, Mrs Margaret Thatcher and her colleagues sought to shake themselves out of the defensive posture they were continually being forced into by what they alleged was the Labour Government's scare campaigning.

Unexpected help came their way on the most unpredictable issue – whether British voters could, at the last, bring themselves to vote for their first woman leader. "It is just because she is a woman that my wife would vote for her," was the way the London *Daily Mail* quoted Sir Harold Wilson, the Labour Prime Minister who preceded Mr James Callaghan.

Sir Harold complained later that what he said had been "capable of misrepresentation", but the agreed that his wife Mary, was the sort of woman "more likely to vote for a party because the leader was a woman, Tory or Labour".

Sir Harold, although held in little regard these days by political sophisticates, still retains a popular following among traditional Labour voters.

Some Labour ministers admit that in their constituencies people frequently complain that he should never have resigned in 1976. One likely result of his latest intervention was to bring the "woman" issue to the fore again.

It has been in the back of most minds all through. And the month-long recriminatory campaign has been fought largely on it as an unspoken premise, with Labour trying to warn voters against taking a perilous leap in the dark with a government led by a woman, and such a right-wing Tory woman at that.

Mrs Thatcher, towards the close, has confronted the issue of her own stridency head on. Living dangerously with her words, she told questioners in Glasgow: "I did not get here by being some strident female... I do not like strident females".

And she added, in a seeming invitation to all women to take a chance with her, that were she defeated, the chance might not return for a generation. "I could do a lot for women at the top, and indeed for women on the way to the top."

Until the final days of the campaign the Conservatives have tried to ride the wave of popular discontent stirred up in last winter's strikes while avoiding two things: mistakes, and specific detail in their promises.

Serious discussion was only sporadic – as distinct from continual slanging – about what either party would do in government to revive Britain's industrial health.

The Prime Minister, who has enjoyed a successful personal campaign, took up Mrs Thatcher on her repeated castigation of some union members as "wreckers".

Mr Callaghan gave warning that using the law to "get at them", as Mrs Thatcher wanted, was a sure recipe for confrontation and chaos in industry, worse even than that seen at the end of Mr Heath's term of office in 1974.

The apprehensions were taken up by Mr Len Murray, the TUC general secretary. In a notable speech at Scarborough he said: "We need industrial confrontation like we need a hole in the head".

Accusing the Tories of being two faced, he said: "It has been left to Mr Prior to make soothing noises about wanting to cooperate with the trade unions while Mrs Thatcher has been launching against the unions a series of unfair, inaccurate and irrelevant attacks".

Mr Prior, whose position as secretary of State for Employment would be crucial to Conservative relations with the TUC, has repeatedly sought to blunt the offensive. Although originally he had no more favoured using the law for union reform than had Mr Callaghan, he insisted that strikers' abuses during the winter now made reform vital.

But equally he insisted that the legal reforms prosposed were "limited", as well as enjoying the support of most "reasonable" people.

Mr Prior was one of several leading Tories towards the close of the campaign who chose to accentuate their apprehension of the Liberal vote.

Mr Norman St John-Stevas, who expects to be in a Conservative Cabinet, perhaps as Leader of the House of Commons, notably declared: "Beware of the Liberals. A vote for a Liberal candidate is not a wasted vote, it is a dangerous vote. They supported socialism before, and given a chance they will do so again."

Mr Callaghan at his morning conference before going out to campaign.

The Mori poll in the *Daily Express* gives the Conservatives a 3 per cent lead over Labour: Conservatives 44 per cent; Labour 41 per cent; Liberal 12 per cent. Earlier in the week the same poll had shown a 6 per cent lead for the Tories.

Queen's visit to Africa complicates Tory policy

By Charles Douglas-Home

The Queen's visit to Africa in July and August has now become an important factor in future British policy towards Rhodesia, particularly if an incoming Tory Government responds favourably to the outcome of the Rhodesian election.

The Queen will visit Lusaka for the Commonwealth Prime Ministers Conference in August, but is due to pay state visits on the way, first in Tanzania and then in Malawi and Botswana. It is the Tanzanian visit which may present unexpected complexities for a Conservative Government, since President Nyerere has been one of the fiercest critics of the internal settlement in Rhodesia which has now, after the election, produced a government led by Bishop Muzorewa.

The Foreign Office hopes that a Conservative Government will postpone making any decision on Zimbabwe-Rhodesia as it will now be called by its first black-majority government, until Britain has met the full Commonwealth at Lusaka. Conservative leaders do not think that they can wait until then, but intend to start immediate consultations with Washington, the Commonwealth and the EEC in which they will register their belief and hope that the Muzorewa Government should now be recognized.

If this action causes the Tanzanians to have second thoughts about the Queen's state visit, a Conservative Government would regret the fact, but find it difficult to mortgage its whole Rhodesian policy to this one visit.

Some hope is expressed in Whitehall that the Tanzanians will be preoccupied with their conquest of Uganda. There is also the fact President Nyerere and the Queen have a warm friendship and the President is known to have been particularly keen for the Queen to return his own state visit to London of 1975.

The visits to Malawi and Botswana are not considered a difficulty in this context.

The Times weekly: voice that has earne a right to be heard

By Louis Heren

The international weekly edition of *The Times*, of which this is the first issue, is intended to maintain the title of the paper and serve our many overseas readers while daily publication of *The Times* remains suspended. It is written and prepared by our editorial staff in London and overseas, is printed by union labour in western Europe, and will not be sold in Britain.

We cannot, unfortunately, provide our usual service with a weekly edition, the size of which is also limited by available printing capacity. Obviously, we cannot pour a gallon into a half-pint pot, but careful distillation will, we hope, maintain standards and provide an informative and readable newspaper.

Special emphasis has been given to home, foreign, business, sports and social news, and to leading articles and letters to the editor. Some of our features, reviews of arts and books, law reports, obituaries and of course the crossword are included.

Thomas Jefferson once said that if he had to make a choice between newspapers and government he would choose newspapers. He changed his mind when elected President of the United States, but neither democratic governments nor the people they represent can flourish without the free exchange of news and opinion.

That is one reason why we are publishing a weekly edition, despite the opposition of unions in Britain. We also believe that newspapers can help to improve understanding between peoples, and if we cannot publish in Britain we can at least hope to serve our overseas readers, whose interest and support have made *The Times* a world newspaper.

We have long treasured this relationship with Commonwealth, European, American and third-world readers: not for financial gain, which is in fact slight, but because it has helped to give a global dimension to our contents.

The Times is also a voice of Britain, and we believe a voice that has earned the right to be heard. Many people overseas depend upon it for an understanding of British life, now all the more necessary because of the condition of the country.

Britain is in a state of disequilibrium. There can be no doubt about that; the suspended publication of *The Times* is but one example of the dissension that has plagued this once tolerant and pragmatic country for so many years.

A new internal balance will be achieved, if not by the new government then by the next. Until that happy day arrives, only impartial news reporting and fair and considered views and opinions can help readers towards an understanding.

We must also declare an intensely personal interest. *The Times* has been published since

1785, without interrupt
recent years, and is reg
home and abroad as a
institution.
We are grateful for suc
esteem, but we prefer t
ourselves as a newspa
independent newspaper
involved in the concern
present but conscious
lessons of the past and
our responsibility
future.
We also know that a ne
is more than the sum of it
rich man can buy a print
and recruit journali
production workers, bu
not necessarily cre
newspaper.
At least, not a newspa
as *The Times*. Tradition
the obvious reasons, but
others.
The Times has always
honest reporters and goo
and has generally moul
in its own image. And t
always been interaction
the journalists and the i
each gaining from the o
continuity has been vi
development and pro
both.
That continuity ca
broken for an indefini
without damage to the n
and the men and wor
write and edit it. We kno
readers and advertiser
loyal to the paper and w
when we publish agai
cannot put our journali
storage.
It is the nature of jou
respond to the events th
and comment upon. Fr
them the story the repo
realization of wha
happened, and the wri
important as the event.
We can no longer put
of *The Times*, wh
corporately represent, a
me, this is the decisive r
launching this inte
weekly edition. It will he
alive the spirit and tra
The Times.
The unions disagree,
seem determined to
considerable power to
publication although th
cannot possibly affect
prospects at Times N
Ltd.
Trade unions can
negotiate agreements w
believe, rightly or wrong
in the best interest
members. That is their
another right is at st
freedom of the pres
instance, the freedom
Times to print good n
without fear or fav
governments, p
advertisers and trade u
The Times has foug
right for nearly 200 yea
new international week
is but another skirmish
battle. Let us hope i
become a thriving sup
the paper when T
returns, restored
renewed robustness.

Brzezinski optimism on future of Europe

By Our Foreign Staff

The United States is prepared to pay the price of increased competition from Europe in the interests of a stable international system, Mr Zbigniew Brzezinski, the United States national security adviser, told correspondents of *Europa*, the economic monthly published by *The Times*, *Le Monde*, *Die Welt* and *La Stampa*.

Mr Brzezinski said that one of the inherent dilemmas of the American-European relationship was that Washington did not want a weak, pliant Europe and yet it recognized that as Europe became stronger and therefore more of a partner, Europe was also bound to contest the United States more.

"But that is a price we are prepared to pay because our historical perspective is one which involves a commitment to a world of diversity with a number of key players in it collectively contributing to world stability. For these players to be genuine players, they have to have the capacity and self-confidence from time to time to disagree with us.

"If the choice is between a passive and pliant Europe, or an allied, active but occasionally contesting Europe, it is the latter which is more in keeping with our image of a stable international system", Mr Brzezinski said.

Asked about European concerns that their security needs were not adequately met in Salt II, particularly on cruise missile technology transfer and theatre nuclear forces, Mr Brzezinski said that he felt there had been more frequent and more wide-ranging United States European consultations than on any other issue.

US swop spies for Mr Ginsberg

Five Soviet dissidents, including Mr Alexander Ginsberg, have been exchanged for two Russians jailed for spying in the United States.

The other four are Mark Dymshyts and Edward Kuznetsov jailed for an attempt to fly an aircraft to the West, Ukranian Velentyn Moroz, and the Baptist leader Georg Vins.

The two Russians arrived back in Moscow on Saturday. The exchange was the result of lengthy negotiations by Mr Brezezinski, the US national security adviser and the Soviet ambassador.

French steel troubles endanger Barre plan

The French steel industry exemplifies the cause and effect of the plan of M Raymond Barre, the Prime Minister, to restructure the French economy on a sound basis. The resulting unemployment and other troubles in the industry could also prove to be the undoing of the plan, Ian Murray writes from Paris. Page 6

Close study of manifestos

Party manifestos are not compulsive reading for most voters, but three important groups do study them closely. The Civil Service monitors them for possible changes in legislation; the House of Lords for important Labour policies that it judges it must not oppose; and party activists who use the documents as a moral yardstick to chastise a wayward leadership Page 2

M Chirac aims at presidential goal

M Jacques Chirac, the leader of France's Gaullist party, is set on a collision course with the Government over the European elections which he sees as a direct threat to national sovereignty. The motive behind his action is seen as a step towards his goal of the presidency. Page 6

Uganda's task

The civilian government in Uganda is faced with the daunting task of restoring the country's shattered economy after the damage done by the eight-year Amin regime. The problem of law and order also looms large as the retreating Ugandan army leaves a trail of chaos Page 7

Rich pickings in postal vote

The Conservative superiority in mobilizing the postal vote appears to be slowly eroding as the Labour Party becomes more aware of the rich electoral pickings to be gained. In past elections, the Conservative advantage, crucial in a close poll, has been estimated to be worth between five and 13 seats. Page 4

US budgets: California's Proposition 13 has started a bandwagon rolling in America for more prudent federal spending 15

Tennis: Leading women players returning in force to European circuit 12

Racing: Henry Cecil strongly represented in both Guineas races 13

International Edition

Pre-paid subscribers outside the United Kingdom and Eire receive this issue free of charge. A further announcement will be made in the next issue.
Overseas selling prices
[illegible]
Published weekly. 2nd class postage paid at New York, N.Y. [illegible]

Published by Michael Mander, and printed by Tercüman, Neu Isenburg/Zeppelinheim. Setting by Otto Gutfreund und Sohn, Darmstadt.
Responsible Editor: Michael Hamlyn, Darmstadt.

Mr Mulley angers specialists over successor to Polaris

By Peter Hennessy

Mr Frederick Mulley, Secretary of State for Defence, has provoked a private but outspoken dispute with an all-party select committee of the Commons by his refusal to permit serving officers, civil servants and government scientists to give evidence about the options for a third-generation British nuclear deterrent to replace the Royal Navy's Polaris submarine squadron.

Feelings between the Ministry of Defence and the defence and external affairs sub-committee of the Select Committee on Expenditure have become progressively strained over recent months, with MPs and their advisers taking the view that the ministry has been niggardly in the provision of documents and witnesses across a range of inquiries.

Differences deepened into strongly worded exchanges about the constitutional rights of backbench committees when Mr Mulley made it clear that the only witness from the ministry on the deterrent issue would be himself.

The argument continued until Parliament was dissolved, with Mr Mulley determined to avoid widening, through public or private debate, the pronounced rift of opinion within the Labour Party about the desirability of a successor system to Polaris and the committee increasingly jealous of its rights.

A meeting was arranged for March 27 between the committee's chairman, Sir Harwood Harrison, then Conservative MP for Eye, its clerk, Mr Matthew Cooper, Mr Mulley and Sir Frank Cooper, permanent secretary to the ministry, to air the committee's accumulated grievances.

The meeting was postponed, however, because of the confidence debate in the Commons the next day. Mr Mulley replied to the committee's criticisms by letter instead. Sir Harwood's last letter to Mr Mulley, drafted by Mr Cooper in blunt terms, caused offence inside the ministry, which feels the committee has exhibited faults of its own 'in its approach to the deterrent inquiry.

Mr Mulley's reply reaffirmed his view that the Secretary of State must decide who appears before the committee on behalf of the ministry.

Among the officers and officials debarred by Mr Mulley from attending the committee's private hearings were Marshal of the Royal Air Force Sir Neil Cameron, Chief of the Defence Staff, Rear-Admiral Sir David Scott, Chief of the Polaris Executive, Rear-Admiral Ronald Squires, Flag Officer Submarines, Admiral Sir Henry Leach, Commander-in-Chief Fleet, and Mr David Cardwell, Director of the Atomic Weapons Research Establishment.

Continued on page 16, col 3

Trade hopes in Giscard Moscow trip

From Michael Binyon
Moscow

The Russians have always had a soft spot for France, and President Giscard d'Estaing's state visit comes at a time when Moscow appears eager to revive a special relationship that in recent years has been in danger of losing some of its warmth.

The meeting was not expected to lead to any important new political initiatives. But the Russians are anxious for reassurance that France retains some vestige of de Gaulle's vision of Europe from "the Atlantic to the Urals", and that President Giscard is not about to draw any closer to the Americans and Nato.

The French in turn hope the visit will reinforce their privileged trading position with the Russians.

Such an exchange of good political relations for increased trade has led to resentment from other West European countries.

The meeting in many ways was a test for President Brezhnev, whose uncertain health has been a topic of considerable speculation in the West. At the summit in Bonn last May there were reports that he was not able to depart easily from his negotiating brief or keep up intensive discussion for long.

UN force facing long stay in Lebanon

From Robert Fisk
Tibnin southern Lebanon

You only have to sit on the hills above the village of Houle just east of here to understand why last week's truce in southern Lebanon is likely to go the way of all ceasefires in this country.

Every few hours, a cloud of grey smoke will rise from the wadi to the north and then – far along the horizon near Metullah – artillery explosions will obscure the local Israeli observation post on the border.

The curiously innocent "popping" sound that the exchange of fire makes at this distance has a special meaning for the United Nations peacekeeping troops down here. It is not just one more truce violation – another unexplained artillery duel which will provoke their two-way radios to crackle with questions – but also a reminder that the United Nations Interim Force in Lebanon (Unifil) is no longer "interim" at all.

For what was intended to be a small-scale peacekeeping role is fast becoming a permanent and large-scale military operation that could conceivably go on for years.

The events of the last week in southern Lebanon only confirm the suspicion of United Nations officers here that the Security Council's desire to see Lebanese sovereignty extended over the entire country is a pipe-dream. They do not say so in those words, but there is no mistaking the new and graver tones in which they talk of their duties in the wild and mountainous countryside around Tibnin.

Colonel Vincent Savino, commander of the United Nations Irish 44 Infantry Battalion and a veteran of the Congo campaign, says that the shelling which his men underwent last week was "a very traumatic experience" and he is clearly under no illusions about the new truce.

"For me personally, the Congo was a very cut and dried operation," he says, with a soldier's interest in tactics rather than history. "I knew what was doing there. I knew what the mission was and I knew the mission could be fulfilled. Here in Lebanon, the mission cannot be fulfilled at the present moment...

In the Congo, although we lost a lot of men, we had a good idea of what was happening. Here we are in a vacuum in which various factions mill around, and from time to time we are completely lost."

It is not difficult to see why. The Irish – like their Norwegian, Dutch, Nigerian and other colleagues in Unifil – find it difficult to understand why the Israelis also want to shell them.

Officially, they say they do not know who fires the shells which land around their posts, bu

Continued on Page 16, col 3

Front page of the the solitary international edition, printed at Frankfurt, 30 April 1979.

Unwarranted celebration: the first edition piped off the stone, 13 November 1979.

Anthony Blunt interviewed at Gray's Inn Road, 20 November 1979.

Gordon Brunton announces the choice of Rupert Murdoch as buyer of Times Newspapers: Portman Hotel, London, 22 January 1981.

Old technology: the composing room at Printing House Square, 1973.

New technology: what the Thomson management fought for in vain.

The new proprietor meets the press, 22 January 1981. Left to right: Harold Evans, Murdoch, Rees-Mogg.

never much chance of a compromise solution; and in any case the 'compromise' proposed by Scarman was bound to be taken by Ward as a demand for surrender on his part. Though the report was critical of the trade unions as well as of him, he was asked to reinstate the strikers or, failing that, to compensate them financially. Moreover, though the question of union recognition was still *sub judice* as between him and ACAS, he was in effect asked to allow his workers to be represented by a union. Predictably he rejected Scarman, and *The Times* was generous in the space it gave him to justify his stand.[1] Soon afterwards Routledge reported that the TUC was mobilising its forces for further action against Grunwick,[2] and in mid-September Rees-Mogg argued in a leader that the underlying problem revealed by the dispute, the need for trade union reform, would have to be tackled:

> Like most such issues, it has not gone away; it has become more serious. It has not become easier to resolve, but more difficult, yet [it is] clearly inevitable. It is like looking forward to the assertion of parliamentary authority in the 1630s, or to Parliamentary Reform in the 1820s; you cannot tell when it will happen, in what precise form, or after what bitter conflict, but you can tell that trade union reform will come, and the longer delayed, the more root-and-branch it will be.[3]

Though it was certainly true that the issue of trade union power and privilege would not go away, the Grunwick dispute itself did gradually die, despite the unions' efforts to keep it alive. Without conceding union recognition, Ward judiciously improved the conditions of work for his employees, so weakening the case against him. In that sense the strike was effective, but at what a cost in reputation to the trade union movement and its Siamese twin, the Labour party. The extent to which the unions were losing the battle for hearts and minds was evident in a piece by Grimond towards the end of the year, reviewing two instant books on Grunwick. The dispute had shown, he said, that unions had become a threat to workers as well as the general public; that the behaviour of Labour ministers (and he specially mentioned Shirley Williams) had not been impartial; and that ACAS was,

---

1 Front-page story, 'Grunwick rebuff of Scarman report angers union chiefs', from Robert Parker; text of Ward's reply to Scarman (occupying half p.4); op. ed. piece by Ward, 'Why I believe the Scarman inquiry was a political "con-trick"'. September 1 1977.
2 September 3 1977.
3 Leader, 'It won't go away' (3 cols. with crossheads), September 14 1977.

in effect, 'an arm of government designed to further the interests of the trade unions'.[1] That such conclusions could be drawn by an outstanding Liberal was both a sign of the times and a portent for the not distant future.

With unabated Friedmanite zeal Rees-Mogg pursued his crusade against inflation. In July he advocated 'an independent central bank operating a policy of gradual monetary growth';[2] and in September, evidently concerned that semantic rigour on the subject should be practised throughout the paper, he circulated a 'style note' to all departments, not even excluding the social and sports editors:

> The words relating to inflation need to be treated with the greatest care. They all refer primarily to the rate of increase or decrease in the supply of money and by extension to the effect of changes in the supply of money on prices.
> *Inflation* means that the supply of money is being increased and prices are rising, as is happening at present.
> *Hyper-inflation* means that the money supply is being increased very rapidly and should not be used unless the supply of money or prices is increasing at an annual rate of twenty per cent or higher.
> *Disinflation* means that the supply of money is still being increased but at a lower rate.
> *Deflation* means that the supply of money is being reduced or that prices are falling.
> *Reflation* means that the supply of money is being restored to a higher level after deflation has occurred.
>
> In present circumstances deflation is extremely unlikely and until deflation has occurred reflation is logically impossible. The phrase 'a reflation of the economy' or references to reflation should therefore be avoided. The Government is under pressure from some quarters to increase the rate of inflation of the money supply. This should be referred to as such, as increased inflation or higher inflation, and should not be referred to as reflation.[3]

---

1 Op. ed. review article, 'In the aftermath of Grunwick, the three vital issues that must be faced', December 8 1977. The books Grimond was reviewing were *Grunwick* by Joe Rogaly and *Fort Grunwick* by Ward himself.
2 Leader, 'Money and wages', July 14 1977.
3 September 5 1977.

Though there may have been few opportunities for giving effect to this edict on the court page or in football reports, the editor's thoroughness on a matter close to his heart is impressive.

At the end of September he wrote the first of two big signed articles on productivity, which attracted wide notice and copious correspondence. In the first he began with a clear statement of his theme: 'The British disease is low manpower productivity; too many man hours per unit of output. It is an underlying cause of *all* the other weaknesses in our economy'. Though 'the ordinary housewife' was free to decide 'whether to employ one Boy Scout or two to clean her car' (perhaps not yet quite a decision facing the *ordinary* housewife), the chairman of British Steel could not decide 'whether to employ 50 or 200 to make a bar of steel'. In a table accompanying the article the comparative figures were given for six European countries during the period 1955–74. The countries were the Netherlands, Belgium, France, West Germany, Italy and the United Kingdom, and they came out in that order, the percentage rise for the Netherlands being 228 against the UK's 92. In another table productivity in steel for the year 1976–7 was compared as between the United States, Japan, West Germany, Italy and the United Kingdom, showing the USA top and the UK, again, bottom.

Because British productivity was below the international competitive level, Britain's standard of living had fallen below that of other advanced industrial countries. Moreover, investment was 'artificially depressed', because manufacturers would not invest in new equipment which, they knew, would not be operated efficiently, and because, granted that they already had overmanned equipment, they often believed less would be saved by investing in new machinery than by improved manning agreements for the use of their existing machinery. Rees-Mogg therefore concluded:

> If the world is now destined to move into a recession next year, then the British economy will face the pressure of more efficient competitors at a time when every nation is struggling to retain its share of world trade. In times of prosperity low productivity is extremely damaging . . . In times of slump [it] is not only damaging, it is very dangerous. If our response to a slump should be a further retreat into job saving and deliberate overmanning then that danger will certainly prove a disaster. On the other hand if we started to raise our productivity to international levels we could have a unique period of growing prosperity. All we have

> to do to double our standard of living is to become as efficient as the Dutch.[1]

Among the many letters that followed publication of this piece, one of the first was from Robert Heller, editor of *Management Today*, who said that the trade unions had to be held responsible for the state of affairs correctly analysed by Rees-Mogg. 'Nobody wants to be identified with "bashing the unions": But on this crucial economic issue, who else is there to bash?' J. R. Holden, of Croydon, thought that management was at least partly to blame, and that until the managers came down from 'their self-appointed positions of high command' they would 'remain unable to motivate their fellow workers'. William Shepherd, of George Street, Portman Square, suggested that Rees-Mogg's comparison of the British and Continental standards of living was misleading, because the internal purchasing power of the pound was 'something like 30 per cent. higher than its international exchange rate'. But the best letter after the first article, a classic of the genre, was from D. G. Pumfrett, of Twyford, Hants.:

> Your headline . . . in fact shows considerable improvement on our performance 300 years ago.
>
> Samuel Pepys on February 13, 1665, wrote 'But to see how despicably they (the Dutch) speak of us for our using so many hands more to do anything than they do, they closing a cable with 20 that we use 60 men upon'.
>
> There's no telling what we may be doing by AD 2277![2]

The second article did not add very much to the first, but gave more instances of Britain's poor relative performance. A Japanese steelworker produced five-and-a-half tons for every ton produced by a British steelworker, an employee of Pan Am handled three times the traffic of a BA employee, Britain's share of world tonnage in shipbuilding had fallen from 38 per cent in 1950 to 4 per cent in 1976, and so on. No one could pretend that restrictive labour practices were not imposed by labour on management. 'Managements do not choose to waste labour; they lack the power to organize labour to the highest production result.' Higher real wages could only be paid out of higher

1 Op. ed. article, 'One Dutch man hour = two British man hours', September 28 1977.

2 Heller's letter, September 29 1977; Holden's letter, September 30 1977; Shepherd's and Pumfrett's letters, October 1 1977.

productivity, and higher employment could only be assured if industry was competitive.[1]

More letters flowed in. One, from Ben Vincent of Radlett, Herts., protested against Rees-Mogg's argument from the standpoint of a pure old-fashioned socialist: 'Security of employment and labour-intensive industry are a blight on capitalism but a blessing of socialism'. Graham Cleverley, of Southampton, claimed to have detected a 'fundamental technical flaw' in the argument, which was that Rees-Mogg confused 'actual productivity – output per capita – with potential productivity – output per worker'. The former, Cleverley said, might actually be increasing, through the effects of North Sea oil. Evidently the unions were not making the same mistake. 'They are perfectly conscious of the fact that if a hundred men are being paid, say, eight thousand pounds to produce the same ten thousand units of something, and subsequently fifty men are paid, say, eight thousand pounds to produce the same ten thousand, then the working force as a whole is *worse* off (even without progressive taxation). So they won't let it happen, no matter how much *The Times* thunders at them'.

Throughout the entire correspondence on both articles, however, it was significant that there was no letter from any leading trade unionist. The nearest approach to one was G. H. B. Cattell, director-general of the National Farmers' Union (a union of employers, not affiliated to the TUC), who agreed that greater productivity was needed, but held that the prime responsibility for obtaining it lay with management. 'I do not believe that trade union officials can or should be expected to exercise discipline over their members . . . people do not work for trade unions. They subscribe to them for protection, for advice . . . but they work for employers and they take their instructions from managers'.[2] Many on the management side, reading those words, must have assumed that the author intended irony, since he could hardly be suspected of innocence.

At about this time Rees-Mogg wrote to Andrew Shonfield: 'I now believe in three propositions: that Europe is the essential context for Britain's future, that control of inflation depends on control of the

1 Op. ed. article, 'The machinery for wasting manpower', October 5 1977. As he was writing Rees-Mogg obviously had the newspaper industry very much in mind, and early in the first article he said that Fleet Street was a striking example of the evil to which he was drawing attention, though he would not be 'concerned primarily with Fleet Street'. In fact he never mentioned it again (no doubt for the prudential reasons earlier explained).

2 Ben Vincent's letter, October 7 1977; Cleverley's and Cattell's letters, October 11 1977.

money supply and that low productivity caused by trade union restrictions is Britain's chief economic problem. These clear and simple beliefs, two of which I think you share, greatly simplify my life'.[1] With his mind so settled, he was about to enter a most difficult and testing period.

Since 1975 Margaret Allen had been editing features with Shona Crawford Poole as her deputy.[2] Their characters – Allen dynamic and radical, Crawford Poole calm and conservative – went well together. Crawford Poole's father was a corporate businessman, very different from Allen's tool-maker father. Not surprisingly, the political leanings of the two women were dissimilar, though they shared a strong belief in sexual equality. Above all, they were both dedicated professionals.

Crawford Poole had wanted to be a journalist since the age of twelve, and she entered journalism straight from the last of the many schools which (mainly because of her father's peripatetic life) she had attended. After serving a three-year apprenticeship on the *Croydon Times*, and then working for three more years as a feature writer on the *Daily Express*, she joined *The Times* in 1970.[3] Her assignment to special reports brought her into contact with Allen, with the result that she was in due course chosen by Allen to help her on features. As the only woman who was the head of a department, Allen was therefore the only woman to attend editorial conferences. When she was away Crawford Poole would attend on her behalf, and was exceptionally proud to do so, being as a rule the youngest person, as well as the only woman, present. She much appreciated the spirit in which Rees-Mogg conducted these meetings.[4]

Towards the end of 1977, before leaving for a climbing trip in the Himalayas, Allen sent the editor some thoughts on the future development of features, to be discussed on her return. She suggested that the paper's columnists were preponderantly right-wing, and that the left should be given more of a say. But her most disturbing statement was this: 'I am very unhappy with our fashion coverage and have

---

1 W.R.-M. to Shonfield, October 3 1977. By his own acknowledgement he was indebted to Shonfield for some of the ideas in his second productivity article.

2 Her first deputy (1973–5) was Sheridan Morley. During this time Crawford Poole was assistant features editor (women's pages), the post of women's page editor having lapsed.

3 Newspaper apprenticeships were three years for non-graduates, two years for graduates.

4 Crawford Poole talking to author.

a plan which might help . . . it will mean being very tough with Prudence and I will need your backing'.[1]

'Prudence' was Prudence Glynn, who had been fashion editor since 1966, becoming at her prime so influential in her field that she was almost the dictator of style. She was an intelligent and witty woman, whose interest in fashion extended beyond the design of clothes to underlying social trends, and whose criticism of both commanded wide attention. But her temperament was uneven, creating difficulties for those who worked with and for her. After 1975 she was past her best, and Allen came to regard her as an impossible colleague. Perhaps they were fated to clash in any case, but matters were made worse by the deterioration in Glynn's performance. Her copy was increasingly repetitive, and sometimes defective in other ways; yet she was unamenable to criticism. She was the *grande dame* of fashion, and her attitude was 'take it or leave it'. Allen was determined that she should be replaced as fashion editor, while remaining an occasional or even a regular columnist. This was the plan that she wished to discuss with Rees-Mogg on her return from the Himalayas.

The conflict between Allen and Glynn was embarrassing to the editor for more than one reason. In addition to any doubts he may have had about the wisdom of replacing one of the paper's stars, there was also a personal consideration: Glynn was married to the Conservative politician, Lord Windlesham, who was a friend of his. The device by which he sought to resolve the dilemma facing him might have had the effect of enabling Glynn to keep her job, but was wholly unacceptable to Allen. His idea was that she should lose her quasi-autonomous position as features editor, and become instead deputy to Douglas-Home as home editor, with responsibility, under him, for features. This proposal was not only a response to the conflict between her and Glynn, but also brought to the fore a power struggle between her and Douglas-Home.

Both were ambitious, and both saw themselves as potential successors to Rees-Mogg. To Douglas-Home, Allen was his former subordinate who had been gaining ground at his expense. While she was controlling the empire that had once been his, one of the most important on the paper, he was occupying the slightly nebulous new post of home editor, in which his freedom of action was limited. (One of the arguments used by Rees-Mogg in his attempt to commend his scheme to Allen was that Douglas-Home was underemployed and needed to be given more to do.) To Allen, Douglas-Home had been conspiring

1 Allen to W.R.-M., October 14 1977.

with the editor, behind her back, to diminish and demote her. She reacted furiously, both face to face and on paper:

> . . . you must realise [she wrote to Rees-Mogg] that I have found the events of the past few days very distressing. You have always made it clear to me . . . that you have found my work in all respects to be of the highest order. Imagine, therefore, my feelings this week when you suggest that you wish me in future not to report to the Editor, but to another executive. As you will understand, this can only be regarded in the same light as a demotion to a Deputy Features Editor . . . You appear, in effect, to be telling me that you no longer have confidence in my ability to take decisions and that you yourself no longer wish to deal with me . . .
>
> I must . . . ask you, having put me into this position within the last few days, that you now give me assurances which will restore my confidence. It may be that . . . you are searching for checks and balances to satisfy problems with other executives. I wish you to understand that I have no desire to be a check or a balance to enable a situation to be resolved elsewhere.[1]

From this trial of strength Allen emerged the winner. She remained features editor, and after some delay (partly due to the 1978–9 shut-down of the paper) she secured the removal of Glynn, who was given a consolatory column to appear on Thursdays. Allen acknowledged that she would need a desk in the office, but was not sure that there would be space for one in the features department.[2] Her successor, chosen by Allen, was Suzy Menkes, who had been on the paper from 1966 to 1969, before going to the *Evening Standard* as fashion editor. Later she had been women's editor of the *Daily Express*. At Cambridge, before her first stint on *The Times*, she had read English and edited *Varsity*, and she was one of the last to be taken on, at the age of twenty-two, without having to go through the probationary period in the provinces laid down by the NUJ. After her appointment in 1980 she was soon to acquire a prestige in the world of fashion entirely comparable with Glynn's.[3]

1 Allen to W.R.-M., 'Private and confidential', January 17 1978.
2 Ditto to ditto, copies to Grant and Crawford Poole, May 27 1980.
3 In 1969 Suzy Menkes married David Spanier – an office romance.

XXIII

Sadat's separate peace • Relations with Mrs Thatcher • Crisis in Italy • Management decides to risk all-out war • Preparing after deciding

AT THE END OF 1977 there was a major new development in the Middle East. Fisk at the time was on sabbatical leave (writing a book about Ireland), and his place had temporarily been taken by Mortimer. Since Cairo was still considered an unsuitable base for a Middle East correspondent, Fisk had established himself in Beirut, and in his absence Mortimer, too, was reporting from there. But in early December he decided to spend a few days in Cairo, and so happened to be present at the opening of the Egyptian national assembly when Sadat made an historic statement.

This occurred towards the end of a two-and-a-half hours' speech, and the substance of it was conveyed in Mortimer's words: 'President Sadat said today he was so anxious to open peace negotiations with Israel that he would even go to the Knesset'. The tone of the statement was 'emotional', but Mortimer had no doubt that it was serious and meant to be taken seriously. Unfortunately it was not so taken at Gray's Inn Road, and before the report appeared phrases were added to it which suggested that Sadat's words might be no more than empty rhetoric. Moreover, the report was buried in a small down-column space on page 7.[1] But a few days later the true importance of Sadat's overture was brought home to *Times* readers by a report from Moshe Brilliant in Tel Aviv, which was placed on the front page: 'The Cabinet in Jerusalem agreed today to invite President Sadat of Egypt to speak from the rostrum in the Knesset and to exchange views with all factions in the 120-member parliament'.[2] Soon afterwards, in a leader written by Mortimer, the paper praised Sadat for his 'spectacular gesture'.

1 November 10 1977.
2 November 14 1977. The regular correspondent in Israel was also absent at the time, in his case through illness. Brilliant was an able stringer, but subject to the disadvantage that his religious scruples forbade him even to speak on the telephone between sundown on Friday and sundown on Saturday.

While there was certainly a risk that he might seem weak and so be 'giving the wrong signal to the Israelis', it was nevertheless 'good that at least one Arab ha[d] the courage to take that risk', because the only alternative was the continuance of the existing 'deadlock'.[1]

Before going to Jerusalem Sadat visited Damascus in an attempt to square the Syrian president, Assad. But the attempt failed, and his unilateral move was denounced not only by Syria, but by Iraq, Libya and the Palestinians, while his own foreign minister and deputy foreign minister resigned in protest. But he was not deflected from his chosen course, and on November 20 he duly arrived in Jerusalem and addressed the Knesset. Mortimer was there, having also covered the Damascus visit, and his account appeared the following day as the lead story under a five-column headline, with a picture of Sadat mopping his brow during the speech, and of 'Mr. Isaak Shamir', then speaker of the Knesset, sitting beside him. Of Begin's immediate response to the speech Mortimer wrote that it 'surprised many of his hearers by not even alluding to the Palestinian problem, either directly or indirectly'. Though he had spoken 'respectfully' of Islam and the 'great Arab nation', his speech 'did not contain any new element remotely comparable to the enormous gesture Mr. Sadat had made in coming in person to Israel'. Leader comment was suitably cautious, noting that Carter and the US Congress were scarcely less important as an audience, and that 'the same shake-up' was needed in that quarter. Sadat remained 'a singular spokesman', who had failed to disarm his Arab opposition and who might not draw any concessions from the Israelis. 'Like a rocket this flamboyant journey has sent gasps round the world but the black night could as quickly envelop it once again'.[2]

The second day of the visit was again the paper's lead story, this time with a picture of Golda Meir handing Sadat a present 'from a grandmother to a grandfather'. At a joint press conference Begin 'was at pains to set the record straight about his speech in the Knesset'. He would 'invite genuine spokesmen of the Arabs of the land of Israel' to hold talks about 'our common future'. But neither leader was prepared to say who would represent the Palestinians, and both 'conspicuously avoided' any reference to the PLO.[3] Sadat did not, however, at

---

1 Leader, 'President Sadat's initiative', November 16 1977.

2 November 21 1977. As well as the main news story and the leader (by Harris), there was a report of 'PLO fury', and partial texts of the two speeches, on p.6; a report (from Brilliant) of the 'ecstatic welcome' for Sadat, together with another picture, on p.7; and on the op. ed. page pieces by Mortimer and Eric Moonman (who was also in Jerusalem).

3 November 22 1977. Lead story from Mortimer, 'Mr. Sadat returns home with no concessions from Israel'.

this stage invite Begin to pay a return visit to Egypt, and for a few days it seemed that he might hold out for the involvement of the PLO, Syria and others in any further negotiations. But before the end of the month Mortimer was reporting from Cairo that Sadat was 'ready to continue talks with Israel alone', and that Begin had been 'quick to accept his invitation'.[1]

The return meeting took place at Ismailia, on Christmas Day, and was covered for the paper by its diplomatic correspondent, Spanier. Because of the holiday his report appeared three days later. There was, he said, 'widespread disappointment' that the talks had 'failed to produce full agreement', but negotiations for 'an overall peace settlement' were to continue in the new year. The principal difference concerned the future of the Palestinians, since Sadat was insisting 'that a Palestinian state should be established on the West Bank and the Gaza Strip', while Begin was merely proposing 'self-rule for the people of Samaria and Judea for a period of 20 years', and 'utterly rejecting the idea of a separate state'. From Tel Aviv Brilliant reported a general view in Israel that Sadat had 'got the best out of the Ismailia summit', since Begin had 'met almost fully the Egyptian demands for the return of the Sinai peninsula and made a substantial concession regarding the Palestinian Arabs by offering administrative autonomy' in the West Bank and Gaza. Sadat, on the other hand, had 'not yielded an inch on his initial demand for a total evacuation on all fronts and self-determination for the Palestinians'. A leader the same day suggested that it might be possible for Israel to go further to meet Sadat without jeopardising the country's security.[2]

In fact, Sadat was determined to regain Sinai and to have peace

---

1 November 28 1977.
2 December 28 1977. The leader, 'After Ismailia', was written by Davy. Rees-Mogg seems to have been reluctant at this period to write about the Middle East, though a leader by him on the subject, 'The cockpit of the world', did appear on Christmas Eve.

The previous year he had revisited Cairo and had another meeting with Sadat. At their meeting in 1971, it will be recalled, Sadat had more or less foreshadowed his recent initiative, when speaking off the record; and had authorised Rees-Mogg to convey the gist of his proposal to Golda Meir. Mrs Meir, however, as Sadat expected, had been quite unresponsive. In 1976 Rees-Mogg went from Cairo not to Israel but to Jordan, where a meeting with King Hussein had, as he thought, been arranged. But on arrival he was disconcerted to find that the King and all his ministers were in Damascus, leaving no word of explanation or apology. On his return to London after this wasted trip he wrote a letter of dignified protest to the King, from whom there was no reply. Instead, he received an effusively apologetic letter from the prime minister. (W.R.-M. to King Hussein, May 17 1976; Zaid Al-Rifal to W.R.-M., May 30 1976.)

with Israel, even if it had to be a separate peace. His strong line on the Palestinians' behalf was dependent on American support, which, it was soon made clear, would not be forthcoming. On the day Spanier was reporting on Ismailia, Carter made a statement to the effect that 'he preferred limited autonomy for the West Bank along the lines suggested by the Israelis rather than the creation of a separate Palestinian state'. Sadat was said to be 'disappointed' by the statement, but did not announce that his quest for peace would be abandoned unless and until he could get a better deal for the Palestinians.[1]

In the long and complicated sequel there were times when it seemed that he might, after all, be ready to sacrifice Egypt's national self-interest to the Palestinian cause; but such quixotism was hardly to be expected, and the eventual outcome was a separate Israeli-Egyptian peace and no overall settlement. At Camp David in September 1978 two papers were signed by Sadat and Begin, under Carter's auspices. One, providing for Israeli withdrawal from Sinai, was in the event implemented, though not without many further doubts and difficulties. The other, offering a 'framework of peace', with phased and partial evacuation of occupied Palestine by Israeli forces, became a dead letter. Indeed, the deal with Egypt facilitated Israel's toughness on other fronts, with the encouragement of Jewish settlement in the West Bank and the invasion of south Lebanon.

The Camp David accords were reported in a lead story from the Washington correspondent, Brogan, illustrated by a picture of Sadat and Begin embracing while Carter stood by 'applauding enthusiastically'. Below the Brogan story was one from Fisk, now returned to duty, and a report from Cairo that another Egyptian foreign minister had resigned. In an op. ed. piece the same day Fisk discussed the unanswered questions left by Camp David. For instance, since it was evident that the PLO was 'no longer considered a viable negotiating partner by the United States', who was to take its place, and how? Fisk did not hold much of a brief for the PLO. To judge from its conduct in west Beirut, a Palestinian state under its control would 'probably be as violent, greedy and undemocratic as many of its neighbours'. But 'it would at least have come into existence for all of its people'. In a leader written by Mortimer the paper gave this assessment: 'The Camp David agreements have so far been received by and large with acclaim in Israel, with mixed feelings in Egypt, with wailing and gnashing of teeth in Syria and among the Palestinians, and so far

1 Front-page report, December 30 1977.

with studied silence in Jordan. In the West, they are bound to be warmly welcomed'.[1]

Soon after Camp David the Nobel peace prize was jointly awarded to the two Middle Eastern principals. In Mortimer's view, Sadat deserved it for his 'courageous and imaginative' gesture, but Begin had no such claim. His 'most spectacular initiative' during the past year had been to invade Lebanon, and in his approach to Camp David he was 'only pursuing a line of diplomacy well marked out by previous Israeli governments: that of prising Egypt away from the Arab coalition facing Israel'. In making Sadat share the award with him the Nobel committee had 'detracted a great deal from its value'.[2]

As a Conservative editing a newspaper that was broadly, if independently, Conservative, Rees-Mogg wished to be on adequate working terms with Mrs. Thatcher. But she was not the sort of politician, or indeed the sort of person, with whom he had many obvious affinities. With Heath he shared a background of Balliol and the Oxford Union, and a passionate belief in Britain's European destiny. Even so they had never been really close, and in any case it was not Rees-Mogg's policy to be too close to any party leader. Mrs. Thatcher had been at Oxford, too, but as a woman and a scientist her milieu there was very different from his, and the values that might be summed up as Oxbridge elitism were as repugnant to her as they were, on the whole, attractive to him. He had opposed her candidature for the leadership, preferring as we have seen the more unifying personality of Whitelaw, and since her election he had more than once criticised her excessive partisanship and her failure to be consistent, in opposition, with views to which the Conservatives were committed when they were in power. Such conduct reminded him of the behaviour that he had found so deplorable in Wilson. For instance, he condemned her decision to abstain on Healey's anti-inflation package in August 1975.[3]

Nevertheless, Rees-Mogg felt there was some common ground

1 September 19 1978. Lead story, 'Mr. Sadat believes treaty will lead to complete Israeli withdrawal'; Fisk story, 'Divided Arabs react with fury and contempt'; news story from Cairo stringer; texts of agreements, p.6; op. ed. piece, 'The questions Camp David has left unanswered'; leader, 'A big step towards peace'. Jordan soon felt obliged to distance itself from Egypt, whose only overt supporters were Sudan and Morocco.

2 Leader, 'Sadat, yes, but why Begin?' October 28 1978.

3 'The loss is not merely the Conservative Party's; it is the nation's. The two great parties now reciprocate in opposition the evasion of the policies they adopt in government'. (Leader, 'The decision not to decide', August 18 1975.)

between them. Though he had not wanted her to be leader, he had at least turned against Heath's leadership and to that extent had been of assistance to her. Moreover, he convinced himself that she shared his interest in political ideas and economic theories. This was almost certainly self-delusion. Those whose talent is overwhelmingly for the exercise of power are seldom very interested in ideas. They may pretend to be, for the purpose of flattering and seducing intellectuals; they may even fancy that they possess such interests, but the fancy is usually little more than a psychological mechanism for dignifying their prejudices. In reality there is nearly always a deep gulf between those who seek power in the world of practical affairs and those who strive after objective truth.

Of course there may be bridges over the gulf, and some genuine contact between the two sides, because human beings are never absolutely one thing or the other. As a politician *manqué* Rees-Mogg retained a lively interest in the practical side of politics, and as an editor who was also a director of his newspaper he was no stranger to problems of management, including man-management. But he did not live for power, as Mrs Thatcher did; their casts of mind were, in the end, profoundly different. If, therefore, they were tending by 1975 to talk the same economic language, it was largely for quite different reasons; Rees-Mogg because he had been converted to monetarism by reading and discussion, Mrs Thatcher because she needed an ideological justification for the bold and ruthless stroke by which she had obtained the party leadership.

Her attitude to the media was as anti-elitist as her attitude to other established institutions. She set less store than most party leaders by the quality press, regarding the *Daily Mail*, the *Daily Express* and the *Sun* as more important, politically, than the *Daily Telegraph*, the *Guardian* or *The Times*. Nevertheless she did not cold-shoulder the Conservative 'heavies', whose personal goodwill was worth having, and not entirely to be counted on without a little effort on her part. In July 1975 following her election she lunched at *The Times* and wrote afterwards to say that she always welcomed the opportunity of 'meeting and talking with' the paper's leader-writers. She was still, then, addressing the editor as 'Dear Mr. Rees-Mogg', but by 1976 they were on Christian name terms.[1]

On February 13 1978 Rees-Mogg arranged an office lunch for her to meet a few trade union leaders and industrialists, as well as members of the editorial staff. The trade unionists were David Lea (TUC),

1 M. Thatcher to W.R.-M., July 22 1975. W.R.-M. to M. Thatcher, October 19 1976.

Gavin Laird (AUEW), Leif Mills (National Union of Bank Employees) and Jim Slater (National Union of Seamen); the industrialists, Sir Hector Laing (United Biscuits), W. B. Duncan (ICI) and Sir Kenneth Bond (GEC). Apart from the editor, the paper's representatives were Clark, Emery, Grant, Michael Hatfield, George Hill, Stephenson, Routledge, Donald Macintyre and Christopher Thomas. The lunch went well, and her letter of thanks was cordial:

> Dear William,
>
> Thank you so much for arranging lunch today and particularly for making it possible for me to meet a number of Trade Unionists. It was most valuable having their views although there is obviously a diversity of view amongst themselves as well as in some cases between myself and them.
>
> In any case it was a wonderful discussion and I am most grateful.
>
> Yours sincerely
> Margaret Thatcher.[1]

Rees-Mogg's memory of the occasion was that the 'discussion' was somewhat one-sided, because for most of the time she was lecturing the trade unionists.[2] Even so, at least one of them went away with a much improved opinion of her:

> It was my first, but not my last, meeting with Margaret Thatcher. She struck me as very attractive . . . very confident amongst a horde of men, well able to ask perceptive questions and respond quickly and with conviction to the few questions put to her. In short, I was impressed.[3]

Not long afterwards Hamilton had an encounter with her which showed her abrasive side, and her lack of reverence for the quality press. As he reported at the time in a private memo to Harold Evans and Rees-Mogg:

> I spoke to Mrs. Thatcher at the United Newspapers lunch yesterday.
>
> 'Good morning', I said, 'How are you? We haven't spoken

1 February 13 1978.
2 W.R.-M. to author.
3 Gavin Laird to author.

for a while'. (She rather brusquely refused my IPS dinner invitation earlier this spring).

'That's your fault', she replied smartly. No comment from me!

'And now you are here, why no coverage in *The Times* and the British Press this morning on the nine countries forming a Conservative Union?

'You only want sensations. You people don't recognise the importance of liberty'. Her voice had, by now, risen many decibels. She repeated 'Liberty, liberty, liberty. That's what I want'.

I fled.[1]

During the late 1960s and the 1970s the Italian state came under serious challenge, when it had to face mass revolutionary action by students and workers, followed by the terrorism of the Red Brigades. But the political establishment, which included the Communist party, held firm. The turning-point in the fight against the Red Brigades was the reaction of the regime to the kidnapping of the leading Christian Democrat, Aldo Moro, in March 1978. The news of this was reported by the Rome correspondent, Peter Nichols: 'Left-wing terrorists today carried out a bloody ambush on a Rome street, which saw Signor Aldo Moro carried off a prisoner and the bodyguard of five men left dying. The most incredible of all the many Italian kidnappings took place about an hour before a crucial sitting was about to open in Parliament'. Moro had been kidnapped 'after his daily visit to a small church near his home'. From there 'he was about to attend a parliamentary debate due to seal his latest and most remarkable political victory', since he had persuaded his party colleagues 'to approve the type of government he favoured: a minority Christian Democratic administration supported by, among others, the Communists'. If the terrorists 'wanted to strike at the political system and astonish the public, Signor Moro was their man'.

On the op. ed. page Caroline Moorehead described 'Italy's new breed of bodysnatchers', and reached a chillingly tough conclusion about how the menace should be met. 'Kidnapping is growing. And it will go on doing so . . . until the life of the victim is made secondary to stopping the kidnappers'. This view was also expressed in a leader.[2] The Italian authorities were of the same mind. Despite letters from

1 April 26 1978.
2 March 17 1978. Lead story from Nichols, with picture. Profile of Moro, with picture, p.7. Op. ed. piece by Caroline Moorehead. Leader, 'The challenge of terror'.

Moro, written either in desperation or under duress, in which he pleaded for clemency for jailed terrorists as the price of his life, and even threatened to reveal compromising secrets of his colleagues if they did not take action to save him, the regime did not crack. The Christian Democrats and the Communists maintained a united front against the blackmail, even though the Socialists weakened.

In early May the agonising ordeal reached its climax. A message was received from Moro's captors that the death sentence passed on him by a 'people's court' would be carried out. But still the authorities refused to bargain. According to Nichols, the Communists were describing political kidnapping as 'a conspiracy against the republic', while one leading Christian Democrat had 'remarked ruefully that the system for delivering Signor Moro's letters was much more effective than the state's postal service'.[1] Four days later a four-column lead story from Nichols gave the news that Moro was dead. 'The full ugliness of the truth came home to an angry Italy today with the discovery of the body of Signor Aldo Moro, five times Prime Minister, lying behind the back seat of a shabby parked Renault with 11 bullets fired into the chest. The discovery was made in the early afternoon in the centre of Rome, after police had been told by an anonymous telephone call that a car in the area had a bomb in it'. There was a further story from Nichols on an inside page, and a picture of the street where the body was found, with an arrow indicating the car. In addition, there was a chronological record of the crisis from the day Moro was kidnapped, and reports of tributes and shocked comments from world leaders, including the Queen, Callaghan, Carter, Schmidt and Giscard.

In a leader the paper commended the government and political parties in Italy, whose conduct had 'undoubtedly' been right. 'Numerous examples from the past few years have shown that human lives saved in this way are saved only at the expense of other lives. Only a state strong enough to resist this kind of pressure has any chance of defeating terrorism'. Nevertheless, 'Italy and Europe ha[d] lost a man of moderation and wisdom'. With admirable objectivity, the obituary of Moro was candid about his defects as a statesman. 'He maintained his coalitions in a state of suspended animation: he saw that they did not fall but left the animating to others. Some of the blame was certainly due to him that the great reforming decade promised when he put together the first of his five governments in December, 1963, never came about'.[2]

---

1 May 6 1978. Front page and p.4 stories from Nichols.
2 May 10 1978. Lead story and p.6 story from Nichols. Chronology and world tributes. Leader, 'A life cruelly taken'. Obit.

The comment was just. By a cruel irony, Moro's martyrdom was his greatest service to his country. Thereafter the Red Brigades began to lose momentum and cohesion, and before very long they had ceased to be a threat.

The year 1978 began, as it was to end, badly for Hussey. On the first day of the year he lost a particularly valued colleague, with the sudden death of the general manager of Times Newspapers, Harvey Thompson. Thompson was a grammar-school boy from Cumbria, of country stock, who had done national service and read geography at Manchester University before entering newspapers on the management side. After experience with the Mirror Group he had joined the *Guardian*, and it was from there that Hussey recruited him in 1972, giving him responsibility for production, administration, new projects and labour relations. Round-faced, tubby, physically slow-moving, humorous and friendly, he appeared relaxed but was, in fact, quite a worrier. He also drank and smoked more than was good for him. It was, therefore, not altogether surprising that, as labour problems at Gray's Inn Road were going from bad to worse, he succumbed to a heart attack at the age of forty-seven.

His obituary in the paper was followed by signed tributes from Rees-Mogg and Hussey. The editor praised him for not making agreements that were 'easy but ambiguous', and Hussey paid him a seemingly double-edged compliment: 'The new building in Gray's Inn Road . . . will be a lasting memorial to him, because he, more than any other single individual, was responsible for its construction'. The intention was not, of course, to associate him with the architecture of the place, and still less with the idea of leaving Printing House Square (adopted before he or, indeed, Hussey joined the company), but rather to acknowledge his paramount part in getting the building work completed and the move effected.[1] Hussey was not alone in regarding his death at a time of mounting crisis on the labour front as a singularly malign stroke of fate, whose implications for the subsequent course of events were incalculable.

When the board of Times Newspapers Limited met at the end of January the directors were told the name of Thompson's successor.[2] He was to be Dugal Nisbet-Smith, a New Zealander who had come to England, as a journalist, in 1956, at the age of twenty-one, to work

1 Obit. and tributes, January 3 1978.
2 TNL board meeting, January 30 1978.

for Express Newspapers. After four years he had gone to edit a paper in Barbados, and while there had come to the notice of a senior executive of the Mirror Group, who decided he had management potential. As a result, he was made deputy general manager of the Group's paper in Trinidad. Returning to Britain in 1966, he was soon sent by the chairman of Daily Mirror Newspapers, Edward Pickering, to install the first colour web-offset in the group's Scottish papers, the *Daily Record* and *Sunday Mail*. This mission was carried through to success despite intense local resistance to the new technology, and only after the whole Scottish board, including the chairman, had been eased out. With such a battle honour he seemed the right man to tackle the problems of Times Newspapers, and on Thompson's death was head-hunted for the job, though not previously acquainted with Hussey. He was formally due to begin in April, but lost no time in getting to grips with his new task.

There was, indeed, every need for urgency. Throughout 1977 the papers had been suffering the effects of unofficial industrial action on an unprecedented scale. The group as a whole had lost 7,337,000 copies, £1,136,000 in profit, and £911,000 in advertisement revenue during the year. For *The Times* alone the figures were 3,533,000, £340,000 and £228,000, respectively. On two days in January and six days in March no copies of the paper had appeared, while on many other days issues had been partly lost. The entire press was facing similar trouble, because trade union militancy and anarchy were growing while newspapers were no longer able to plead, as they could two years previously, that their financial circumstances were grave or, in some cases, desperate. General economic conditions had changed; recession had given way to growth. Whereas in 1974 *The Times* made a loss of well over £1 million, and in 1975 lost nearly £1½ million, in 1976 the loss was down to under £900,000 and in 1977 the paper nearly broke even (making a loss of only £60,000). But for unofficial stoppages, it should have made at least a modest profit. The problem was that labour relations in the industry were deteriorating steeply, while the general state of the economy was improving.

On *The Times* the problem was aggravated by two special factors. One, mentioned earlier, was the harmful effect of close contact with the *Sunday Times* workforce, resulting from the move to Gray's Inn Road. The other, which applied to both papers and the supplements, was that the Thomson management, unlike any other in the industry, chose to pay strict regard to the government's guidelines on pay. The motive for this was not exceptional civic virtue, but fear that the group's other interests might suffer if it failed to give the government total support in its anti-inflation policy. The Thomson Organisation had a contract to fly British troops to and from Germany; it also published the Yellow Pages directories for the Post Office. Above all, its stake in North Sea oil was subject to government regulation. While other managements were finding ways of breaking the government's rules and paying the traditional print unions' blackmail, Times Newspapers Ltd was being forced, for reasons extraneous to the newspaper industry, to allow its employees' earnings to drop to the bottom of the league table. The only means acceptable to the government of reversing this trend was to achieve significant improvements in productivity, which in turn could only be achieved if working practices on the papers were transformed.

Even for the existing machinery and methods of production Gray's Inn Road was grossly overmanned. As in other London newspaper plants, the union chapels controlled recruitment and did so in such a way as to ensure that as many names as possible were on the payroll. Moreover, since not all the names necessarily corresponded to real people, there was all the more money to be shared between those who were genuine employees. The function of management had been largely abdicated to the chapels, whose threats of instant disruption – at a potential cost of thousands in lost copies and millions in lost advertisement revenue – were usually enough to produce instant *ad hoc* pay concessions. (Times Newspapers' recently increased resistance to such threats, in order to comply with government policy, was indeed causing the added disruption and loss already described.) The ascendancy of union power on the shop floor was enhanced by the fact that so-called managers at the lower levels were themselves obliged to be union members. The system that had evolved over the years left management facing a monopoly on the production side that was, within itself, fragmented and anarchic: an extraordinary combination of evils.

So far as productivity was concerned, substantial improvements could be achieved without new technology only if numbers could be reduced and a normal degree of discipline established between management and employees. The Thomson leadership was determined to secure these improvements, but it also wanted to achieve the greater boost to efficiency that would result from using the technique of photocomposition ('cold type') instead of setting by linotype ('hot metal'). At Roy Thomson's instigation, a system known as SDC (from the initials of the Californian corporation that produced it) had been acquired and installed at Gray's Inn Road, where it had been lying unused on the third floor for over a year. Failure to persuade the relevant union (the NGA) to operate it had added massively to the unforeseen costs of the move, and represented a continuing frustration to the management. Photocomposition was no longer new technology in North America, where many newspapers were already using it, but where, one should observe, it had been introduced gradually. Roy Thomson was known to regard it as top priority at the time of his death, and his son had promptly expressed the same view in the clearest terms.

For the NGA the introduction of SDC, even with inputting still entirely reserved for members of the union, would mean a cut of about 50 per cent in the labour employed, because photocomposition was so much quicker than hot metal setting. The company might guarantee that there would be no compulsory redundancies, and that the financial economies obtained would be used, as to two-thirds of the total, to improve pay and conditions for those remaining employed; but this could not alter the fact that the union would in due course suffer a heavy loss of membership. The NGA knew, moreover, that there was an ulterior threat to its very existence as a craft union with exclusive privileges. Much larger economies were available, and maximum efficiency could be achieved, only if journalists and tele-ad girls could have direct access to computer terminals for setting their copy. Without such direct inputting the full benefits of the new technology could never be gained. But to the NGA it seemed, naturally enough, a matter of institutional life-or-death that the process of setting by 'single keystroke', which computer terminals made possible, should forever be controlled by members of the union. A drastic reduction in the size of the workforce might, over time, be conceded, in return for much higher rewards; but on the single keystroke issue there could be no compromise.

Since the collapse of *Programme for Action* Hussey and his colleagues had made no progress in their attempts to rationalise methods of production and working practices at Gray's Inn Road. On the contrary, as we have seen, matters had been going from bad to worse. Now there was strong pressure from the new chief proprietor and the Thomson Organisation that urgent and decisive action should be taken. In the middle of March Hussey's executive committee, noting that industrial relations problems on the papers had become 'intolerable', braced itself for a fundamental showdown:

> The going will be tough. T[he] T[homson] O[rganisation], the TUC and the relevant Government department are fully aware of what we plan to do. *It is more than likely that we will be faced with confrontation. Negotiations must therefore be done in the right*

> *way and we must be seen as taking a reasonable attitude against an unreasonable response.*[1]

The desire to act 'in the right way' led Hussey to arrange a meeting with the print union general secretaries at a time when the latter were together for a conference at Birmingham. He travelled there on April 13 with a full complement of senior colleagues, including the two editors, Rees-Mogg and Evans, and the meeting took place in the Metropole Hotel. The management's case was stated firmly and comprehensively, and no doubt the general secretaries made some encouraging noises, varying from person to person. A further meeting was held in London, at the Waldorf Hotel, on April 24. No written agreement emerged from either of these encounters, nor would any such agreement have been of the slightest value, since the *Programme for Action* experience had demonstrated that power in the unions belonged not to the general secretaries, but to the chapels.

Hussey seemed, by implication, to acknowledge as much in a message that he addressed to all members of the staff of Times Newspapers shortly before the Birmingham meeting. This began with a stark account of the papers' recent industrial relations record, and its cost. Every dispute causing loss of production during the current year had, he stressed, been unofficial. 'If the disputes procedures, agreed and signed at house and national level, had been followed, there would have been no loss of copies and no loss of revenue'. Then he said:

> A series of meetings are taking place, involving the Executive Board and the Thomson Organisation, and of course meetings with officials of the unions specifically involved in our recent problems. In addition, a meeting [at Birmingham] has been arranged with all General Secretaries.

Precedence was clearly given to the in-house negotiations, and the meeting with the general secretaries was mentioned, seemingly, almost as an afterthought. Hussey promised to write again to give details of the company's 'plans and aspirations', and to describe the measures that would be taken to secure 'uninterrupted production'.[2]

After the Waldorf Hotel meeting Hussey wrote to each of the general secretaries summarising the company's grievances and putting forward a set of proposals for urgent discussion:

---

1 Minutes of TEMC meeting, March 16 1978. (Author's italics.)
2 April 10.

1. The common purpose will be the absolute continuity of production. All arbitrary restrictions will be lifted. No unofficial action will be taken. Dispute procedures and current agreements will be honoured. Overtime will be worked as necessary . . .
2. We negotiate a fast-acting and effective disputes procedure.
3. We negotiate, in consultation with Union representatives, a general wage restructuring. This will be based on new technology systems, and on efficient manning levels in all departments. A considerable improvement in earnings and conditions could accrue . . .
4. We have already stated, and confirm now, that no compulsory redundancy will arise from the introduction of the new technology systems.
5. All these negotiations shall be concluded by November 30th, 1978.

The sting of the letter was in the tail:

> Finally . . . I have to tell you that it is the firm decision of the Board of Times Newspapers that, if it is not possible to negotiate a joint approach to resolve these problems and if disruption continues, publication of all our newspapers will be suspended. Suspension will last until we are wholly satisfied that publication can be re-started on a basis of reasonable staffing, efficient working and uninterrupted production.
>
> We earnestly hope that you can join with us in a final endeavour to avoid this inevitably painful measure.[1]

This letter did not precisely state that, in the absence of agreement, suspension would occur on November 30, but insistence that negotiations must be concluded by then, followed by the threat of suspension, could hardly be interpreted otherwise. In early May the letter was leaked to the *Guardian*, and the *Times* staffs thus received further information, and learnt of the imminent crisis, from another newspaper rather than from Hussey himself.

---

1 April 26 1978.

Whatever doubts and disagreements may have arisen during the months ahead, the Thomson management was of one mind as the decision was taken to tackle head-on the interrelated problems of labour and technological change. Those who later came to be regarded by their colleagues as 'doves' were as hawkish as any at the outset. Harold Evans was all for the new technology, as was Hamilton, to whom Roy Thomson had expressed his urgent wish that it be brought into service, just before suffering the stroke from which he never recovered. Gordon Brunton, chief executive of the Thomson organisation, was for his part eager to give effect to the new proprietor's stated desire, which was, indeed, the implied condition of his willingness to maintain his father's commitment to *The Times*.

The group seemed, at last, to be well placed for a trial of strength. Whereas at the beginning of the decade it was seriously overstretched, by 1978 its general position could hardly have been more favourable. Its North Sea oil (from the Claymore and Piper fields) was on stream, its travel business was prospering, and altogether its financial resources could be regarded as more than adequate for what might be a prolonged struggle. During the year financial responsibility for Times Newspapers reverted from Thomson British Holdings to the main Thomson organisation, with which the family's oil interests were merged to form a new Canadian holding company for the entire group, to be known as International Thomson Organisation Ltd (ITO). The purpose of this was to escape the effects of British monopolies legislation, exchange control and dividend limitation. A statement was made on behalf of International Thomson that the future of *The Times* was secure provided 'the necessary cooperation, effort and goodwill' were forthcoming.[1]

The decision to fight on a broad front was, therefore, firm and unanimous. But it was preceded by very little detailed thought for the practical implications. The original idea was that all staff should receive about ninety days' notice before suspension of the papers, but this had to be abandoned when lawyers pointed out that it would give rise to actions for unfair dismissal under the 1975 employment protection act. So, after much discussion and considerable delay, it was decided that the department of employment and others concerned should be notified in mid-September that publication of the papers would cease

1 Press announcement, July 26 1978. Responsibility for Times Newspapers had been transferred from Thomson Scottish Associates to Thomson British Holdings in September 1975. Under the 1978 arrangements shareholders in the Thomson Organisation (TTO) became, in exchange, shareholders in the new holding company (ITO).

after November 30, and that negotiations would be held with the unions about redundancies that would then arise. No notices would be served before November 30 unless continued publication proved impossible in the interval.

Hussey's meetings with, and letter to, the general secretaries certainly produced no sign of greater cooperation on the part of the chapels, while the leak of the letter resulted in a spate of rumour and speculation throughout the staff. To counteract this Hussey wrote a second, and longer, letter towards the end of July, which was sent to all employees at their private addresses. In it he said that, since he had written to the general secretaries, a further 1¼ million copies of the papers had been lost through unofficial action, making a total of nearly 9 million, so far, during the year. He summarised the proposals he had put to the unions thus:

> Guarantees on the continuity of production; an effective and fast-acting disputes procedure; the lifting of all arbitrary work restrictions; efficient manning levels and operating arrangements for the future; general wage restructuring reflecting all the above.

If these could not be negotiated, and the disruption continued, then the papers would have to be suspended, but the requirements of the law concerning notice to employees would, of course, be observed.[1]

The response of those general secretaries who bothered to reply at all to Hussey's April letter was thoroughly unhelpful and negative. However encouraging they may have been in private at Birmingham – and on the management side it was believed that the suggestion of a time-limit had come from them – their attitude for the record, when writing on behalf of their executives, was very different. Owen O'Brien, for instance, the general secretary of NATSOPA, who at least sent Hussey a formal reply, and within a month, said that his executive was as concerned as management about the loss of production, but felt that 'they were being asked to negotiate under duress'.[2] The NGA took nearly three months to reply, and then adopted an even more obdurate stance. In his letter the NGA general secretary, Joe Wade, wrote:

> My Council have . . . directed me to inform you that until such time as you are prepared to withdraw the threats to suspend

1 July 22 1978.
2 O'Brien to M.J.H., May 15 1978. (Hussey papers.)

> publication . . . and remove the deadlines for completion of negotiations, we shall not agree to negotiations taking place between the NGA and the company at any level, either about the problems referred to in your letter or about the introduction of new technology.[1]

Soon afterwards Hussey heard from a group of those who, on the union side, wielded the real power. They were eleven NATSOPA fathers of chapel (FoCs), including two men, B. A. Fitzpatrick of the *Sunday Times* clerical chapel and R. A. Brady of the *Sunday Times* machine chapel, who were to prove the sharpest thorns in management's flesh. Their letter, ostensibly a reply to Hussey's second message to all employees, read:

> Following your letter . . . we the undersigned . . . have unanimously decided to inform you as follows:
>
> 1. We will not accept negotiations under the duress created by your letter . . .
> 2. We will not accept any new Agreements unless negotiated and agreed by individual Chapels.
> 3. We oppose the setting up of a working party of National Officials and Management as suggested by Mr. Keys [of SOGAT] . . . and as contained in Programme for Action.
>
> As these points are the basis of a firm and binding commitment between us, we would suggest that you arrange a meeting with all of us in order to discuss this very serious situation.[2]

This was a naked assertion of chapel power not only against management but, quite as much, against the national leadership of their union.

Hussey's reply to the FoCs restated the company's position, and then tackled two of the specific issues raised:

> . . . We have not said that these negotiations will not include Chapel Officers. What we have done is approach the General Secretaries first as is the custom in this industry when the future of publications is at risk.

1 Wade to M.J.H., July 19 1978. (Hussey papers.)

2 July 26 1978. Apart from Fitzpatrick and Brady, the other signatories were: J. A. Britton, *Sunday Times* RIRMA chapel; K. Braidwood, *The Times* day machine chapel; J. Freedman, *The Times* machine chapel; D. Edwards, *The Times* clerical chapel; P. Frizzel, *The Times* darkrooms chapel; J. Payne, *The Times* lino assistants chapel; somebody per pro R. Dolling, *The Times* day readers chapel; and P. Donovan, *Sunday Times* RIRMA readers chapel. (Hussey papers.)

> We do not accept that giving the General Secretaries and unions six months' opportunity to negotiate . . . can possibly be described as duress. This is particularly the case when there are many instances . . . when action contrary to agreements puts the Company under such duress that weekly and daily publication suffers.

Having got this justifiably tart comment off his chest, he concluded that, in view of current discussions with the general secretaries, a meeting at house level would not be 'appropriate'.[1]

Throughout the late summer a team of managers, supported by a firm of consultants, drafted fifty-four detailed proposals (NAPs) suitable for each negotiating unit, with some clauses common to all staff. This was a lengthy and complicated business, which might with advantage have been undertaken at an earlier stage. The NAPs were to be presented to the chapels from October onwards. Meanwhile, on September 15, Hussey wrote to the employment secretary, Albert Booth, enclosing a draft of the notice of suspension which he proposed to send to the general secretaries three days later. The notice was duly sent, and on the same day Hussey wrote his third message to all staff, reporting the action the company had taken.

He stressed that notice of suspension of the papers on November 30 was 'not in itself notice of termination of any contract'. No such notices would be issued before the date of suspension, because the company wanted 'to give everyone the maximum opportunity to reach agreement'. Even then notices would not be issued, 'subject to unforeseen circumstances', to managers or senior executives or members of any union which agreed meanwhile to the company's proposals. If agreement was reached with all unions, there would be no notices and no stoppage. He ended by quoting the prime minister in support of his view that without high productivity there could not be high real wages.[2] But for Callaghan, as for him, a winter of discontent lay ahead.

1 M.J.H. to the above-mentioned. (Hussey papers.)
2 September 18 1978.

XXIV

Three Popes • Labour and 5 per cent • Ferment in Iran • Towards the deadline • Commons debate – then silence

A **MAJOR REFORMING** pope who was nevertheless, on one issue, widely seen as a major reactionary, died on August 6. Paul VI carried forward the conciliar movement initiated by his predecessor, John XXIII, and fulfilled the promise of his chosen name by travelling more extensively than any former pope. But he lacked the warmth and geniality of Pope John, and his encyclical *Humanae Vitae*, in which he took an uncompromising stand against artificial birth control, was defied by millions within his own church, while it was also a blow to the better relations that he genuinely sought with other churches. In a leader assessing his pontificate the irony was noted that 'he who was so anxious to sustain papal authority should have left it noticeably weakened'. *Humanae Vitae*, which was 'composed to vindicate the supreme teaching authority of the papal office', in fact 'conspicuously undermined it' by becoming 'an object of contradiction, reservation and, more deadly to its authority, of undeclared reinterpretation'. It was 'a broken instrument', and in the matter of birth control 'the right of private conscience' was cultivated.[1]

Attention quickly turned to the choice of a successor, and Longley observed that one of Paul VI's main contributions to the reform of his church lived on after him, 'in the form of the most international College of Cardinals in history'. Whereas Italians used to dominate the Sacred College, now only 28 of the 118 cardinals were Italian, while 46 were from the Third World. It was therefore distinctly possible that a non-Italian pope, the first since the Renaissance, would be elected, and the most likely areas for such a pope to come from were Europe and Latin America. Various names were mentioned by Longley, including England's Basil Hume, but not including any Polish name.

1 Leader, 'The post-conciliar Pope', written by Hickey, August 8 1978. (*The Times* had criticised *Humanae Vitae* when it was issued, in July 1968.)

Nichols thought that Italian cardinals were still the front-runners, but his list of names did not include the winner.[1].

In the event 111 cardinals assembled for the conclave, and Nichols described the 'Spartan ritual' awaiting them. There was a picture of them, white-mitred, attending the pre-conclave mass in St Peter's. Then they took the oath of secrecy and, after being searched, were sealed into the Sistine Chapel.[2] Their work was soon done. On the fourth ballot a new pope was chosen, and the choice confounded all predictions. After 'one of the shortest and most astonishing elections in papal history', a man 'almost unknown outside Italy, and even within it, was given the greatest religious office in the world'.[3] He was the Patriarch of Venice, Albino Luciani, who combined the names of his two predecessors to become Pope John Paul I.

The new pope's modesty matched the relative obscurity from which he had emerged. Longley speculated that the cardinals had deliberately cut the papacy down to size by electing someone who would be '*primus inter pares* in the community of bishops'.[4] He decided to forgo the traditional coronation in St. Peter's, and instead to be installed at a simple liturgical ceremony out in the square. Nichols was captivated by him: 'He laughs easily. When he puts aside a prepared text to make some observation which has come into his mind, a kind of irrepressible amusement lightens his face as he goes on to explain his ignorance about the workings of the Curia or what sort of a journalist St Paul would have made'. Paul VI had been quite different. 'There can hardly have been many more solemn Popes.' The new man's papacy 'could be as surprising as his election'.[5]

So indeed it was, though not, unfortunately, in the sense Nichols intended. Sudden death was its principal feature. On September 5 the visiting metropolitan of Leningrad fell dead at the pope's feet, at an audience in his private library for delegations from Orthodox churches. By the end of the month he was dead himself. During the night of September 28 he died, officially of a heart attack, after a reign of only thirty-three days, the shortest since 1605. *The Times* reported the fact that a post-mortem had been called for but 'bad-temperedly rejected'.[6]

1 Front-page piece, under news report, 'Non-Italian successor possible', August 7 1978. Op. ed. piece by Nichols, August 8 1978.
2 Reports from Nichols, August 25 and 26 1978.
3 Nichols report, August 28 1978.
4 Op. ed. piece, 'Why the cardinals are taking a gamble', same date.
5 Op. ed. piece by Nichols, 'The lighter side of Pope John Paul', September 2. Incidentally, the new Pope was the first since 914 'to add a one after his name'.
6 Nichols reports, September 2 and 6 1978.

Apart from that, there was no hint of the controversy later aroused by the circumstances of his death.

Nichols paid him a touching farewell, describing the scene of his lying-in-state in the Clementine Hall. 'John Paul lay on his catafalque this morning, suddenly serious in death, with his red shoes scarcely showing any signs of wear.' The cardinals now had to decide 'who, from among themselves, should follow this brief apparition of old-fashioned good nature which momentarily made itself felt within the sacred hall'.[1] A fortnight later Nichols discussed the field, concentrating again on the Italians, while admitting that there might, this time, be a better chance for a non-Italian. At the previous conclave the leading conservative, Cardinal Siri of Genoa, was 'said to have been runner-up', and although he was still unlikely to win the interest that he represented would be 'a real force'.[2] Longley had meanwhile put forward much the same list of potential non-Italian winners as before, with the same key omission.[3]

On October 16, on the eighth ballot, the cardinals elected the first non-Italian since Adrian VI in 1522, and his identity and nationality were alike sensational. Karol Wojtila, archbishop of Cracow, was a complete outsider, though the strength of the conservative element in the Sacred College (perceived by Nichols), combined with a growing sense that the time had come for a non-Italian, might have given shrewd punters a hint of his chances. Among the non-Italians he was indeed, as time was to demonstrate, just about the most conservative available. Nichols's report began: 'The smoke blew strong and unmistakably white tonight from the improvised chimney above the Sistine Chapel, sweeping away centuries of tradition in this amazing election'. On the balcony of the Vatican the new Pope, who had chosen the name John Paul II, appeared with Cardinal Siri and Cardinal Wyszynski, primate of Poland, until that day his senior colleague. Nichols commented that Siri 'might find something to approve of in the generally conservative views of His Holiness'.[4] In all probability his approval existed before the election, and helped to bring it about.

Rees-Mogg felt moved to write a leader on Wojtila's election, and

1 Ditto, September 30 1978.
2 Ditto, October 14 1978.
3 Longley column on court page, October 2 1978.
4 Lead story from Nichols, with headline across five columns 'Polish Cardinal becomes Pope John Paul II', October 17 1978. There had been talk, which came to nothing, of giving the first news of a successful ballot by telephone rather than by the traditional smoke signal. This was because at the conclave in August the chimney had belched smoke of an uncertain colour.

appealed urgently for background information to Berthoud, whose father had been ambassador to Poland. The leader that emerged was interesting on the historic role of the church in Poland, though misleading in the statement that it had not been reactionary. The Polish church might, indeed, have 'led the Poles to regard Russia with prudence and Germany with reconciliation', but in other respects it was, surely, among the most illiberal and obscurantist in the world. In Rees-Mogg's opinion, not only would oppressed Christians in Russia and throughout eastern Europe be encouraged, but others too had reason to feel confidence:

> . . . what is known of Pope John Paul II suggests that his views are moderate and open to reform. He was ordained a priest after the war when he was 26, and as a young man must have had more experience, and more tragic experience, of life than any but a very few of modern Popes. He is an athlete and, for a Pope, he is young [58].[1]

A better idea of what was in store might have been gained from a headline the following day: 'New Pontiff places much weight on discipline'. According to Nichols, he would 'evidently be a demanding Pope on matters which he regard[ed] as of fundamental importance'.[2] He would, in fact, combine the charisma of the young Pio Nono with the inflexibility and bigotry of the old.

While *The Times* was moving towards its moment of truth with the unions at Gray's Inn Road, the Callaghan government was doing the same on a much larger scale. Considerable success had been achieved in the fight against inflation, which had fallen to 7.4 per cent by the middle of the year. Incomes policy, based on a norm of 10 per cent in 1977–8, had kept the actual rise in earnings to 14 per cent. For 1978–9, therefore, the government decided to push its luck with a much more stringent norm, and in July a White Paper laid down the figure of 5 per cent. This had no advance backing from trade union leaders, and in retrospect Healey described it as an act of 'hubris' which in due course 'met its nemesis, as inevitably as in a Greek tragedy'.[3]

---

1 Leader, 'A Polish Pope', October 17 1978.
2 Nichols report, October 18 1978.
3 Healey, op. cit., p.462. Since the Thomson Organisation was, as explained, abiding strictly by the government's pay norms, the new figure could only aggravate its difficulties.

The TUC's conference at Brighton in September was the first act in the drama. As the delegates assembled Routledge assessed the likely political impact of the dispute between government and unions:

> The 'election Congress' of the TUC gets underway today with the unions loyally attempting to prove that it is feasible and indeed laudable to believe in two contradictory notions: unswerving support for the Government and fundamental opposition to a key plank of its economic policy . . . Complete fracture, no. But the trump electoral card of a working relationship with the unions to which no other party may aspire looks on closer inspection to be a misdeal. The risk of the public at large finding that out may push Mr. Callaghan into asking for his mandate sooner rather than later.[1]

There was, indeed, a general expectation that the prime minister would go to the country in the autumn, which his whimsical speech to the TUC failed to dispel. As Emery reported:

> He departed from his prepared text to sing, somewhat tunelessly, the whole verse of 'There was I, waiting at the church . . .', and added: 'I have promised nobody that I shall be at the altar in October'. However, all that was taken as an elaborate tease . . .[2]

The headline of the paper's lead story as the TUC conference ended summed up the prevalent view: 'TUC rejects 5% pay limit as general election fever rises'.[3] That very evening, however, Callaghan announced on radio and television that he would not be calling an early election. The announcement 'astounded virtually the entire political establishment, including his own party, union leaders, many ministers (although not the most senior ones), not to say his opponents and many of the general public'.[4] A *Times* leader judged the decision unwise:

> The economic indicators are at least as favourable now as they are likely to be [in six months' time]. Inflation is expected to rise in the coming months and there will be all the uncertainties of

1 Op. ed. piece, 'Another round of collective bargaining', September 4 1978.
2 September 6 1978.
3 September 7 1978.
4 Lead story, 'Prime Minister's decision against election angers opponents', September 8 1978.

> another round of wage bargaining. If that gets seriously out of hand Labour will have lost their most persuasive argument: that they are better able to control inflation because they know how to get on with the unions.[1]

Evidence in support of this comment was soon to hand, as 57,000 Ford workers went on strike in defiance of the pay norm. *The Times*, no longer the advocate it had once been of incomes policy, gave them its backing:

> [Ford] should be allowed to negotiate a reasonable commercial settlement with its employees. It is only by breaking out in this way that there is any hope of restoring the minimum necessary degree of flexibility to an excessively rigid policy.[2]

Butt explained the differences between the dispute with the Ford workers and Heath's with the miners, 'despite superficial similarity'. Heath's policy was statutory. The Callaghan government, in threatening sanctions in the form of withdrawal of grants, was acting with doubtful legality. And the showdown with Ford was with a multinational in the private sector, whereas Heath had been dealing with a nationalised industry. The differences were all to the Callaghan government's disadvantage.[3] A clergyman commented on the Ford dispute from another angle:

> Is there not a certain irony in the fact that, in the same week, the Church of England asks its committed members to give 5 per cent. of their income to keep it solvent and the clergy paid, and the Ford trade unions reject a 5 per cent. wage rise as 'derisory'.[4]

When the government's policy was heavily defeated at the Labour Party conference at Blackpool, there were rumours that the pay norm would be relaxed. 'The Whitehall view is that Mr. Callaghan and his senior Cabinet colleagues will listen to any ideas that the TUC is prepared to put up as an alternative to the White Paper on countering inflation'.[5] But no compromise emerged and the 5 per cent norm stood.

1 Leader, 'Three faults for refusing', September 8 1978.
2 Leader, 'The impossibility of 5 per cent', September 26 1978.
3 Op. ed. piece, 'Playing the Government game of 5 per cent. bluff', September 28 1978.
4 Letter to the Editor from the Revd R. J. Macklin, from Stanwell Vicarage, near Staines, September 30 1978.
5 Lead story from Routledge, October 5 1978.

Even a vaguely worded proposal that the TUC should give guidance to unions, to keep inflationary consequences in mind when pressing wage claims, was not carried by the general council.[1]

The threat of unrestrained trade unionism was increasingly apparent, and a solemn warning was given in the paper by F. A. Hayek, an oracle of the radical right:

> I am not qualified to judge what is today politically possible. That depends on prevalent opinion. All that I can say with conviction is that so long as general opinion makes it politically impossible to deprive the trade unions of their coercive powers, an economic recovery of Great Britain is also impossible.[2]

Paul Johnson, a convert from the left, expressed the same view:

> In Britain it is *demonstrably* true that the legal privileges of the trade unions, which virtually exempt them from any kind of action for damages (including, now, libel) led directly to restrictive practices, over-manning, low productivity, low investment, low wages and low profits.[3]

At the Conservative conference held, like the TUC's, at Brighton, Margaret Thatcher promised to restore free wage bargaining, while Heath reasserted the need for incomes policy. Towards the end of October, on a visit to Germany, Callaghan told a press conference that 'the Government believed it could win the battle against inflation . . . even if this meant standing up to industrial disputes'.[4] In mid-November, Len Murray foresaw 'more aggravation on the industrial scene this winter'.[5]

Mohammed Reza Pahlavi had been Shah of Iran since 1941. His father, a soldier who had seized the throne in 1925, was suspected of pro-German sympathies in the Second World War and therefore deposed by the British and Russians, who installed the son, then a very young

1 There was a tied vote, and the chairman was obliged, by rule, to use his casting vote against the proposal.
2 Op. ed. piece, 'The powerful reasons for curbing union powers', October 10 1978.
3 Op. ed. piece, the second of two on the dangers facing Western capitalism, October 12 1978.
4 Report from David Blake in Bonn, October 20 1978.
5 November 15 1978. The comment, reported by Routledge, was made after the general council's vote mentioned above. It proved, of course, an understatement.

man, as a puppet. Throughout his reign he was largely dependent on outside support, and in 1953 had to be reinstated, after fleeing the country, by a coup engineered by the British and American secret services. The two governments concerned felt that the nationalist regime of Dr. Mohammed Mossadek was a menace, and so helped to overthrow it: a step that appears, in retrospect, to have been a disastrous error. For a time the Shah was able to cut quite a grand figure in his part of the world, exploiting the mineral wealth of his country and the opportunities provided by the Cold War, introducing some measures of internal reform in a Westernising spirit, and making Iran an industrial and military power of some importance. But in the process he incurred the hostility of many elements, including the traditionalist Islamic clergy; his attempt to Westernise the country was only superficially effective; corruption flourished; and his regime rested ultimately on the army and brutal police repression.

By the latter part of 1978 there were mounting signs of revolutionary ferment in Iran. The Shah's policies had created a high rate of inflation which, in the mid-Seventies, he recklessly compounded by nearly doubling wages. All the various and disparate forces opposed to him began to coalesce, willy-nilly, and there were demonstrations which it was increasingly hard to control. In the heated atmosphere people began to turn to the Shah's most implacable enemy, Ayatollah Ruholla Khomeini, who had been an exile since 1964, first in Turkey, then for thirteen years in Iraq, and recently in France. Khomeini's revivalist and anti-Western message was finding an audience, ominously, in the army as well as among the civilian masses.

Events in Iran became big news in early November, when a lead story from Tony Allaway reported that anti-Shah rioters were going on the rampage in Teheran.[1] The following day he gave the news that the Shah had appointed a military government to halt the riots, and the same day there was a front-page picture of Khomeini 'leading prayers . . . near his suburban Paris villa'. He was quoted as saying: 'Only the departure of the Shah and the cleansing of the regime can provide a way out of the present situation. As soon as the Shah goes, we want an Islamic republic to be set up on the basis of a popular vote'.[2]

The Shah's backers in the West began to sound the alarm. In the United States ex-President Nixon, in one of his 'rare forays into the spotlight since resigning', told an enthusiastic crowd at Biloxi,

---

1 November 6 1978.
2 November 7 1978.

Mississipi, that America should support the embattled Shah.[1] The British foreign secretary, Owen, took the same line. But *The Times's* first leader on the crisis was, on balance, hostile to the Shah:

> The question is whether the corruption, inadequacy, even beastliness . . . of the regime can be admitted, as they now have been, and the man who *is* the system yet emerge as a credible guarantor of reform and democratization.[2]

Soon the foreign editor, Douglas-Home, decided to go to Teheran to report and assess the situation himself. After an interview with the Shah he wrote a lead story in which he showed that he was far from sure the regime would survive:

> Fortified by the conviction that there is nothing between his own rule and chaos, [he] still appears to be baffled about what to do next to cool Iran's temper . . . Although some of [his] recent visitors have reported signs that he is beginning to recover his confidence and resilience, those signs were not evident . . .[3]

In an op. ed. piece a few days later Douglas-Home concluded:

> The strikers have to make it clear to him that only a real, visible and irreversible change in his position will take the pressure off. This time the token concessions of previous crises, which he has always managed subsequently to exploit to regain his position, will not be enough.[4]

And in a leader the following day the foreign editor argued that, although sudden abdication by the Shah would plunge the country into chaos, he should declare that his retention of the throne was 'only temporary' and devote himself to arranging an orderly transition to constitutional monarchy under his son.[5]

It was not to be. In January 1979 the Shah was forced to leave the country for good, and Khomeini returned in triumph to establish his Islamic republic. But *The Times* was unable to report these developments.

1 November 13 1978.
2 Same date.
3 November 23 1978.
4 'Will the Shah be toppled from his shaky throne?' November 28 1978.
5 Leader, 'The monarchy in Iran', November 29 1978.

Soon after three months' notice of the papers' suspension had been given in mid-September, the board of Times Newspapers reviewed the course of the crisis to date and considered the outlook. Hussey reminded his colleagues that, in April, the union general secretaries had privately supported the company's proposed strategy. But he acknowledged the irrelevance of their support, by implication, when he stressed the fact that the company had to deal with fifty-six bargaining units, and drew the conclusion that a stoppage in December was that much more likely. After discussion, the board agreed that '*the credibility of management must be maintained*', and that '*the real issue [was] to re-establish authority*'.[1]

This was, indeed, the nub of the matter. The dispute was essentially about power. The company's proposals threatened the interests of many individual members of print unions, who did well out of the existing corrupt system, and who might not be employed at all if it were replaced. But above all it was a threat to the entrenched power of the chapel bosses, whose little empires would disappear if the newspapers were produced efficiently, rationally and honestly. Some of these men exercised their power as genuine class warriors, seeing the trade unions as the means whereby capitalism could be overthrown and workers' control established. Others were at heart neither socialists nor syndicalists but crypto-capitalists. Others again were confused in their motivation, working the system by instinct and living in a fog of ideological cliché. But all knew that they had positions of more or less independent authority to defend.

If the management ever hoped that the mere threat of closure would have a sobering effect on the chapels, the hope proved vain. Unofficial action continued to plague the papers in 1978. By the end of October *The Times* had lost 3.9 million copies, the *Sunday Times* 6.3 million and the Supplements 600,000. Before the closure the management had two further meetings with the union leaders, both in London: on September 18 at the Russell Hotel, and on November 10 at Gray's Inn Road. Neither made any significant progress towards breaking the deadlock. At a lower level the NAP negotiations proceeded with very patchy and limited success. There was never any chance of general agreement before the deadline, or indeed at all, because general agreement would have involved effective capitulation by all the chapel bosses.

Nevertheless it was the attitude of the NGA on the issue of single

---

1 Minutes of TNL board meeting, September 25 1978. (Author's italics.)

keystroking that attracted most attention, creating the false impression that it was that issue, rather than the underlying one of authority and discipline on the shopfloor, that was truly vital in the dispute. On single keystroking the management made an enormous concession to the NGA, stating that freedom of inputting by journalists and tele-ad girls would not be a prior condition of agreement on other matters, and assuring the union that 'until further notice' there would be no inputting from other sources without its agreement. But this was not enough for the NGA, which refused to commit itself even to discuss 'the principle and the practice of single keystroking' at a later date. Moreover, it was adamant in insisting that even on other matters it would agree to nothing unless the threat of closures were first withdrawn.[1]

Despite their resentment of the NGA's privileged status, the other unions found its obduracy on the new technology a useful distraction, and its absolute refusal to negotiate against the company's deadline equally convenient. All complained that they had too little time for negotiation on the proposals put to them, and NATSOPA in particular published in November its correspondence with the company, purporting to show that the company was entirely to blame for delay. It was, of course, true that the NAPs had not been produced until October, but if all the chapels had then settled down to negotiating with reasonable goodwill and a due sense of urgency there should have been time to reach agreement by November 30. Goodwill and a sense of urgency were, however, not much in evidence on the union side, and least of all in the NATSOPA chapels run by Brady and Fitzpatrick. Out of ninety meetings held with NATSOPA chapels after the end of September, the *Sunday Times* clerical chapel (Fitzpatrick) attended only four and the *Sunday Times* machine chapel (Brady) only three. Shortage of time was essentially a canard, but in the propaganda war it served the unions well.

On November 10 Hussey wrote again to all members of the staff. The company's proposals had, he said, been made known to them through chapel representatives 'wherever possible', or through chapel managers. He summarised the benefits available to those who reached agreement before the deadline. Millions of pounds would go into a new wages structure which would 'fully recognise people's skills and their working hours'. This would mean better pay for 'the vast majority'. Everyone would have six weeks' holiday in addition to Bank

1 Nisbet-Smith to L. S. Dixon, president of the NGA, November 10 1978; J. Wade, general secretary of the NGA, to Hussey, November 16 1978. (Hussey papers.)

Holiday entitlements. Sick pay would be granted on 'the most up-to-date terms in industry'. Pensions would be higher because an extra £5½ million would go into the pension funds, and the higher pensions would be payable to those who might volunteer for redundancy, though he emphasised that redundancy would indeed be voluntary. The benefits together would take up about two-thirds of what the company planned to save by more economical and efficient working. The balance would be invested in further expansion of the papers. In return the company was asking for guarantees of continuous production, a new disputes procedure which would be strictly honoured, new working methods including new technology, and 'appropriate' levels of manning.

The full text of the letter was published in the paper, and Hussey was reported as hoping that it would 'cut through the rumour, speculation and half-truths that ha[d] been circulating within the company and outside',[1] A week later NATSOPA's dossier of correspondence was also reported.[2] On November 24 there was a big leader by Rees-Mogg on the issues in the dispute. Since the early 1960s unofficial strikes had become increasingly common, he said, and had 'received the full support of union solidarity which was naturally given to official strikes'. Union leaders realised that this was dangerous. 'They were asked by Times Newspapers Ltd for a new disputes procedure to help to bring this continuous disruption to an end, and *subject to procedures* they have now agreed to that', though 'unfortunately' the NGA was not party to the agreement. The second 'historic theme' was new technology. Times Newspapers had always recognised that 'time, patience and consultation' would be needed. But the NGA could not be allowed 'perhaps to delay for ever'. The third theme was productivity, which in Britain was very low by international standards. Without strong management unions were 'helpless in trying to raise real wages'. He ended: '*The Times* now stands on the brink of suspension, but the future of *The Times* would be in greater jeopardy if the crisis had not been faced'.[3]

Four days later there was a front-page report that hopes of avoiding the shutdown were fading, and on the same day the company took space in other papers to answer the question: 'What forces us to consider suspending publication of some of the best newspapers in the

1 November 10 1978.
2 November 18 1978.
3 Leader, 'The issues at *The Times*'. (Author's italics.) The words 'subject to procedures' were a somewhat euphemistic way of saying that agreement could, in effect, be vetoed by the chapels.

world?'[1] On November 29 it was reported that the NUJ had reached agreement on the company's proposals, and that NATSOPA was recommending a new disputes procedure if the threat of suspension were lifted, or at least postponed. The same day there was a signed op. ed. piece by Rees-Mogg, in which he asked: 'If *The Times* is serious about truth, how can [it] not face the truth about itself?'[2]

The last issue before suspension contained a number of letters on the dispute, of which the first was from Major Hugh Walter, a descendant of the founder. He quoted from the leading article of November 29 1814, which was about the difficulties of installing the Koenig and Bauer steam-driven press, and his letter ended: 'Introducing new technology does not seem to me, a great-great-great-grandson of John Walter I, to have been much easier than it is today, 164 years of publication later'.[3] Routledge's front-page story had the headline 'Management and unions dig in', and the lead story, from Emery, referred to a 'last-ditch' move in Parliament to avert the stoppage; there was to be an emergency debate that evening in the House of Commons.

Shortly after 4 p.m. on November 30 Patrick Cormack, the Conservative MP for Staffordshire, South-West, moved the adjournment of the House on 'the crisis at *The Times* newspaper and its serious consequences'. His tone was studiously impartial. This was no time, he said, 'for bashing management or unions'. The dispute should be treated as industrial, not political. Most national union leaders were moderate, sensible and honourable, whatever might be thought of some lower down who did not 'behave as the shepherds would wish'. Management, though he had some 'reservations' about its handling of the dispute, was definitely not hostile to unions as such, only to 'reckless, militant, unofficial union action'. He appealed to management and, specifically, the NGA to settle their differences within fourteen days, that being the shortest period of notice any employee of the company would be receiving after the suspension. (Evidently he shared the common assumption that, if agreement could be reached with the NGA, other unions would fall into line.) In one form or another, the idea of a

1 November 28 1978. The advertisement was carried by the *Financial Times*, *Daily Telegraph*, *Guardian*, *Daily Mail*, *Daily Express*, *Daily Mirror*, *Sun*, *Evening News* and *Evening Standard*, but rejected by the Communist *Morning Star*.
2 Op. ed. piece, 'A decisive test for *The Times*', November 29 1978.
3 November 30 1978. Major Walter wrote from Blaxhall Heath, Woodbridge, Suffolk. His letter was immediately followed by one from J. Freedman, a NATSOPA FoC.

fourteen-day moratorium was to be echoed by other speakers in the debate.

Cormack was followed by the employment secretary, Albert Booth, whose remarks were equally measured. He ended by saying that his good offices were available at any time. Not all speakers, however, followed the example of the openers in avoiding acerbity. Julian Critchley had sharp things to say about the Fleet Street print unions, as did Jonathan Aitken, who described them as 'the most overpaid and underworked group of workers in Britain'. On the other hand, Max Madden, Austin Mitchell and Robin Corbett were bitter in their condemnation of management.

Eric Moonman, while declaring himself a member of the NGA, refused to say that one side was right, the other wrong. But he argued that the introduction of new technology should be gradual. A similar line was taken by another Labour MP, Phillip Whitehead, who maintained that the Times management had fallen into the trap of attempting to tackle three problems at once, 'in the wrong way and on the wrong timetable'. The problems were overmanning, new technology and 'loss of production through disputes which [could] not be controlled by unions or management'. He criticised the deadline and hoped that the next fourteen days would be used constructively.

Ronald Bell did not at all agree that technological change should be more gradual. In his view, it should be faster, and he thought the Times management's approach 'absolutely right'. So did another Conservative MP, Michael Brotherton, who advised the company to 'stand firm and not to give way'. (He had once been employed by it 'in a commercial capacity'.)

The last Conservative speaker was the shadow employment secretary, James Prior, who was as even-handed as Cormack. Though he could see that management 'had to take a firm line', and dismissed the arguments that had been used against setting a time-limit, he felt nevertheless that management was 'vulnerable to criticism about not getting on with the negotiation sooner'. At the same time he was 'shocked by the labyrinth of different agreements' that had to be obtained. Now there had to be a break, but the shorter the better. He appealed to management to make 'some positive gesture to create a better climate', and to unions 'to accept that gesture and to make one themselves by all agreeing to get on with the negotiations'.

Harold Walker, minister of state at the department of employment, quoted Margaret Thatcher as having said: 'I wish Lord Thomson well. I wish him victory'. He (Walker) congratulated Prior on not having spoken in such a vein. Without wishing to set any target date, he agreed 'that there should be constructive talk as soon as possible'. So the debate ended. It had lasted just under three hours.[1]

There were still about five hours to go until the midnight deadline, and during that time Hussey and his colleagues decided that it would be expedient to make some response to the appeals for a gesture. Their solution was to adhere to immediate suspension of the papers, but to postpone for a fortnight the issuing of notices to members of unions which had not settled.

On December 1, therefore, *The Times* did not appear. In a leader the day before Rees-Mogg had apologised to readers for having to deprive them of the paper 'for some time'. It would be 'a sad period' for all concerned, but it had 'become necessary to get to the other bank and not to flounder like a drowning kitten in the middle of the stream'. He mentioned the 'very heartening number of letters of sympathy and support' received by the paper. One printed in the correspondence column that day may be taken as representative. It was from Mr. and Mrs. Nicoll of Chiswick, and it read:

> Sir, Just to say that whoever we read while you're away, when you come back, so shall we – so don't worry.[2]

The period of suspension turned out to be far longer than Rees-Mogg or, no doubt, the Nicolls expected. But, amid all the frustration and disillusionment of the months ahead, the fidelity of readers proved equal to the test.

---

1 Hansard, fifth series, Vol. 959, cols. 715–7.
2 Leader, 'There will be an interval'. Letter from Anthony and Inga Nicoll, 9 Netheravon Road, Chiswick, W4. November 30 1978.

XXV

Futile initiatives • Foreign adventure • Journalists unhappy and divided • Management in retreat • Peace without security

THE MANAGEMENT'S GESTURE in delaying notices to staff by two weeks proved worse than useless. At a meeting at the department of employment shortly before the time expired Hussey's old partner in *Programme for Action*, Bill Keys of SOGAT, said that the disputants had 'gone into a backward situation since the closure'.[1] Instead of using the extra time to intensify efforts to reach a settlement, most of the union negotiators spent the fortnight demanding more time and protesting further about the very existence of a time-limit. Hussey's gesture was interpreted by union hard-liners as a sign of weakness to add to those already shown, more especially the concessions vainly offered to the NGA on the subject of key-stroking.

Hussey himself was at heart less confidently pugnacious than he felt obliged to appear. He was acting under pressure from the Thomson organisation, and a few days after the suspension Kenneth Thomson, on what he called, with some exaggeration, one of his 'frequent visits to London', reaffirmed his endorsement of the tough policy which had been implicit in his first statement as proprietor:

> Unofficial disruption cannot be allowed to continue. It cannot be denied that some departments have too many staff. Nor can I accept that new and more efficient equipment should stand idle when it has been in use throughout the world for many years, nor that we should be prevented from replacing ordinary machinery which is worn out.

He politely but firmly rebuffed a request from Wade for a meeting between them.[2]

---

1. Record kept by Mander of meeting at department of employment between four representatives of Times management and the union general secretaries, with the employment secretary, Booth, in the chair: December 13 1978. (Mander papers.)
2. Statement by Lord Thomson of Fleet, December 4 1978.

As well as being conscious of what Thomson expected of him, Hussey was also kept up to the mark by his colleague, Nisbet-Smith, whose success in overcoming union resistance to technological change in Scotland, where chapel power was altogether less formidable than in London, made him excessively optimistic about the current dispute, into which he had been precipitated after the sudden death of Harvey Thompson. The relative militancy of Hussey and Nisbet-Smith is manifest in the draft of a letter that the former proposed to send to Wade during the fortnight following the suspension of the papers. Beginning 'Dear Joe', the letter is a heartfelt plea for cooperation, as this typical passage shows:

> Please believe me, Joe, that my one single objective is to ensure the future of our newspapers and I have nothing but goodwill towards you, your Union, and your members, and I sincerely believe that their future lies, as ours does, in a civilised acceptance of change in a changing world.

In red ink, Nisbet-Smith has ringed 'Dear Joe' and written beside it 'No'. He has also put a red line through the entire draft and appended this comment:

> *MJH*: I don't agree with the content of this letter, or its tone. It is too supplicating & exudes a false bonhomie. If a letter is needed at all, it should be direct, courteous – and should *say* something. Gordon [Brunton]'s secretary will telex any revised draft to Toronto for Ken [Thomson] to send. D.[1]

In fact, the letter was not sent at all.

On December 15 notices of dismissal were sent to about 3,000 Times Newspapers' employees. They were the members of those unions which had not reached agreement when the extended time-limit passed: the NGA, NATSOPA, the EEPTU, SLADE and the London central branch of SOGAT. No notices were sent to about 1,200 employees whose unions or branches had settled: the AUEW, UCATT (construction workers and technicians), the printing machine branch and circulation representatives branch of SOGAT, and – though not without a strong element of dissent – the NUJ.

The period of notice was to begin three days later, on the 18th,

1 Draft in M.J.H.'s papers, dated December 8 1978.

and the hope was expressed that agreement would be reached before anyone's notice expired. In that event arrangements would be made for those under notice to return, should they so wish. Meanwhile they would not be entitled to any redundancy payments. No further settlements were negotiated and the first notices ran out on January 2 1979. But the company had to continue paying most of the dismissed staff until well into the New Year, having already incurred considerable extra cost by extending the time-limit. In addition, of course, it had the burden of paying those who were not dismissed through the whole period of the stoppage, though the full financial significance of this was beyond anyone's imagination at the outset.

Before long it became evident that the unions were less at a disadvantage in the trial of strength than optimists on the management side had supposed. One reason was that there was less solidarity among employers than even pessimists had reason to expect. Hussey made no approach to the NPA before embarking on the dispute, and he did not count on any positive action by other newspaper managements. He was even prepared for them to offer work to printers from Times Newspapers on a casual basis. But he was not prepared for them to offer full-time work, or to go out of their way to exploit for their own gain a struggle in which, as he saw it, his company was fighting for the common good.

In this he underrated the opportunism and short-term cupidity of Fleet Street employers. The *Guardian*, the *Financial Times* and the *Observer* – the last, particularly – were the worst offenders. They printed extra pages or even, in some cases, extra sections, and brought more machines into operation, recruiting Times Newspapers printers to man them. Lord Hartwell was the last to succumb, and did so with reluctance, but after a time the *Daily Telegraph* and the *Sunday Telegraph* followed the others. As Eric Jacobs puts it, in his admirable account of the dispute: 'Almost magically, an industry that was already notoriously overmanned absorbed the staff of the *Times* and the *Sunday Times* as it came off the company's payroll'.[1]

For the most part, the unions did not need to finance their members. The NGA and SLADE paid theirs at the full rate they had been receiving, and they could well afford to do so, since they had comparatively strong resources and anyway their London chapels represented less than one per cent of their membership. But hardly any financial demands were made on the poorer unions; their members were looked after by Times Newspapers' competitors. To quote Jacobs

Eric Jacobs, *Stop Press*, p.72.

again: 'Within a very few weeks the balance of forces looked very different from how it had seemed in November. The company was no longer self-evidently stronger than the unions. Its financial power had been misleading; the unions had discovered means of resistance, and the two sides were now more evenly matched than anybody had thought possible.[1]

In these unpromising circumstances two attempts at a settlement were made in the early months of 1979, the first on the initiative of the TUC, the second on that of the employment secretary. Both involved, again, only the national union leaders and were based on the fantasy that they had the power to deliver. Meanwhile those who did have the power formed themselves into a negotiating body in waiting, as the Times chapel fathers established a liaison committee with Fitzpatrick as its chairman. The TUC initiative came to an abrupt end in early February when a (more or less) agreed programme for negotiations was leaked and immediately rejected out of hand by the liaison committee. Soon afterwards Callaghan, in the throes of his own losing battle with the unions, talked to Hamilton and Hussey, congratulating the latter on 'handling the matter extremely well'. At about the same time he told Rees-Mogg that he wanted the company to 'stand firm', and assured Brunton that he was 'ready to intervene' at the right moment, whenever that might be.[2]

His colleague Albert Booth, the employment secretary, did intervene at the beginning of March. His initiative culminated in a marathon session at the department on March 8, at the end of which an agreement was signed in the small hours of the following day. The agreement aimed to secure resumption of publication by April 17, with reinstatement then of all dismissed staff, and their re-engagement meanwhile. All the seriously contentious matters were not agreed but set out as being 'for negotiation'. They included the question of a disputes procedure and the means of maintaining continuous production; efficient working arrangements with a productivity deal and wage restructuring; application of new technology with a timetable; and implementation of new staffing levels, also subject to a time-limit, though preserving the principle of voluntary redundancy. It was agreed that negotiation on these matters should proceed 'without precon-

---

1 Op. cit., same page.

2 Record by M.J.H. of his meeting with Callaghan, February 19 1979, with Hamilton also present. In the same note he refers to what Callaghan had recently said to Rees Mogg and Brunton. (Hussey papers.)

ditions imposed by either side', and the intention was also stated that 'chapel officials should be fully involved' in the further talks.[1]

News of this 'breakthrough' quickly got around and George Clark found 'a mood of joy in the office', where 'celebrations started: somewhat prematurely perhaps'. He did not fail to observe important signs of retreat by the management. 'They have virtually withdrawn the notices of dismissal [and have] agreed to debate and possibly amend the time-table for the introduction of the new technology'.[2] This was indeed true, and it was also true that celebrations were premature. The so-called agreement was, in reality, no more than an invitation to further deadlock. When the issues of substance were tackled they proved as intractable as ever. There was no breakthrough on keystroking with the NGA, despite fugitive hopes at one stage, and in any case Brady's NATSOPA chapel rejected the company's proposals outright. Booth's initiative duly went the way of the TUC's, and the prospect that the papers might reappear on April 17 turned out to be another mirage.

Evidence abounded that *The Times*'s natural constituency, which covered all parties, was increasingly feeling its absence. Eric Heffer, a left-wing Labour MP who often wrote for the paper, begged Clark 'with tears in his eyes' to do something to get it back into print. 'You look at all the other bloody papers', he said, 'and there's not one which allows the same freedom to all points of view to reach the public. You may think that it is only the Tories who miss it. It is missed just as much by Labour MPs'.[3] This sense of deprivation extended far beyond the world of professional politics. At about the same time Hamilton received from a friend at W. H. Smith's the findings of an ORC survey of *Times* readers, which showed that nearly all were now, perforce, reading another paper, but that 89 per cent thought it not as good as *The Times*, 96 per cent would be likely to take *The Times* again regularly, and 77 per cent were missing it either as much as, or more than, they did at first.[4]

---

1 The agreement was signed by Owen O'Brien for NATSOPA, Wade for the NGA, Ken Ashton for the NUJ, J. A. Jackson for SLADE, Keys for SOGAT and Hussey for TNL. Though dated March 8 1979, it was actually signed at 3.30 a.m. on the 9th. The distinction between re-engagement and reinstatement was crucial, because if and when people were reinstated they would need to be given another full term of notice if there were any further trouble.

2 George Clark's diary, entry for March 9 1979.

3 Ibid., entry for February 6 1979.

4 Peter Bennett to C.D.H., February 16 1979, enclosing letter to him from J. T. Hanvey, managing director of ORC, dated February 13 1979.

As it became obvious that the negotiations entered into under Booth's auspices were doomed to fail, the thoughts of *Times* and Thomson directors turned to a project which, though risky, seemed to offer them some hope of regaining the initiative. This was the idea of producing a weekly edition of *The Times*, to be printed abroad. The arguments for doing so were, in theory, cogent. It would provide occupation and a sense of purpose for journalists, managers and marketing staff. It would enable the paper to tap some of the 36 per cent of advertisement revenue that normally came from overseas. It would help to hold the paper's overseas readership, considered to be more vulnerable than its readership at home. It would demonstrate the efficiency of modern methods of production. Finally, it would emphasise the company's determination to soldier on, so (it was hoped) bringing further pressure to bear on the unions. An additional spur towards resuming publication somehow, somewhere, was that on April 7 Parliament was dissolved, and it was against Rees-Mogg's instincts for a British general election to take place without his being in a position to comment on it.

The prime mover in the search for suitable foreign printing facilities was Mander, and it certainly involved him in a lot of movement, to the accompaniment of elaborate subterfuges, even at times physical disguises, in what eventually proved a vain attempt to maintain secrecy. After many peregrinations his choice fell on a plant in suburban Frankfurt, where the German edition of an Istanbul daily, *Tercuman*, was printed for the benefit of Turkish 'guest workers' in Germany. This was a very modest plant by Fleet Street standards, and the Turkish paper was not set there; negatives were flown from Istanbul. It was necessary, therefore, for Mander to find a typesetter in the neighbourhood, and he discovered a very small firm down the road in Darmstadt, Otto Gutfreund and Son, who would set *The Times* by photocomposition. Arrangements were made to have the first weekly edition produced by the combined efforts of Gutfreund and Tercuman on Monday April 30.

The indispensable cooperation of *Times* journalists was secured by a narrow vote of the NUJ chapel a week before the deadline, though some were already cooperating covertly. Hamlyn was put in charge on the editorial side, and he established a residential qualification in Darmstadt. As the day of the launch approached there were ominous developments. The print unions vowed to mobilise international union action against the project, even though copies of the paper were not to be sold in Britain. By April 26 the location of the printing was no longer a secret, and that day a member of *The Times*'s marketing staff,

Karin Dahmen, arriving at Frankfurt, was struck and seriously injured by two men on an escalator.[1] The men were never caught, but since there was no robbery or sexual assault the motive of intimidation was plausibly suspected.

Already pickets were beginning to gather outside the Tercuman plant, which was inconveniently situated in a cul-de-sac. By Saturday, when printing was due to begin, the street was filled with a menacing crowd that included, as well as genuine German trade unionists, many agitators of the extreme left and men who, according to the police, had records of political violence. Nevertheless Hamlyn, with Patricia Clough, drove with the plates from Darmstadt. When he arrived his hands were sweating so much that he could hardly hold the steering wheel, but fortunately the pickets did not grasp the significance of the package under his arm and he was able to enter the building unmolested.[2]

Shortly before 9 p.m., however, when printing was due to begin, newspapers and rags impregnated with petrol were found in a chamber containing the compressor, the machine that was to drive the presses. The chamber was under the street, ventilated by a grille through which the objects must have been inserted. If they had been lit when printing began, as was doubtless intended, the resulting fire would have sabotaged the process. There might also have been casualties, possibly some fatal, because lighting the inflammable material in the enclosed space might have caused an explosion. That night and the following day there was intense discussion with the federal and *Land* police, involving not only Mander and the Turkish director of the plant, Serhat Ilicak, but also Rees-Mogg, Heren and Douglas-Home who had flown out for the launch. A complication was that the weekend would run into the May Day holiday, an ideal time for left-wing militancy. Since the police could not guarantee the safety of the plant or those who worked in it, the decision had to be taken not to go ahead with printing the projected 80,000 copies. When the pickets were told the news, they dispersed.

In fact, after their dispersal, Ilicak ran off 10,000 copies which were thinly distributed around the world, soon becoming collectors' items.[3] But no second issue of the international edition was produced.

---

1 A German whose task was to act as an interpreter said she 'had two wounds, one on her head behind her right ear and the other on the ear itself, the latter a cut so severe that her ear-lobe was almost detached'. (Jacobs, op. cit., p.86.)
2 Hamlyn to author. Mander had taken the precaution of ordering a second set of negatives from Gutfreund, which were delivered to his hotel.
3 Within a few months they were selling for £100. (Jacobs, op. cit., p.102.)

Even before the violence in Frankfurt there were signs of divided counsels among the management on the advisability of the project. In view of what happened, opinions against it hardened. Certainly it would have been dangerous to try to continue printing at the Tercuman plant. Ten days later a plastic bag was found outside it, containing explosive and flint stones, and not long afterwards Ilicak escaped death when his car was machine-gunned by an unidentified assailant.[1]

The solitary edition of the international *Times* was praised as 'recognisably its old self' by one columnist, who also noted that Levin's sentences had 'not diminished in size through disuse'.[2] The lead story was about the general election then in progress, and there was a front-page picture of Callaghan. The first leader gave predictably solid backing to the Conservatives, while preserving a certain equity as between Callaghan and Thatcher:

> So far as the main personalities are concerned we are fortunate with both party leaders; we cannot expect a leader who combines the fire of Mrs. Thatcher with the phlegm of Mr. Callaghan, but we have had many worse leaders than either. Yet it is not on personalities that the issue should depend, but on the central historic issue. The Conservatives are the party who offer to reverse Britain's decline, but if they fail, the decline may accelerate. Is that a risk that Britain ought to take? Our own sympathies are on the side of change.

The second leader, on the dispute at *The Times*, focused on the issue of power. With the NGA the matter might be one of principle, but it was 'very much one of power with the militant fathers of Natsopa chapels'. Did readers want the management to admit that trade union power was too strong for them, and that, having 'made a perhaps honourable mistake', they should settle as best they could in order to get the papers going again? To do so 'might not be a complete surrender, but it would be a big climb down', with potentially 'dangerous consequences'. Thus, in hypothetical terms, the actual course of events was anticipated.[3]

On the op. ed. page, as well as Levin, there were pieces by Emery and Anthony Howard, and a Leapman diary from America. The

1 Jacobs, op. cit., p.103. Racial feeling against Turks may well have been a further exacerbating factor in the demonstrations against Tercuman.

2 Iain Murray in *Marketing Week*, May 18 1979.

3 First leader, 'The choice for the country'; second leader, 'The choice for *The Times*', April 30 1979.

sixteen-page paper also had reports from most of its leading correspondents at home and abroad, and all its familiar features were in place. Among letters to the editor, there was the traditional one about the choice of Christian names during the previous year, showing that James and Elizabeth were the two most favoured by those announcing the birth of their offspring in *The Times*. Another letter of the vintage sort read:

> On the afternoon of April 2 I walked up on to the moor where snow was still lying from the storm in the morning. I saw a lizard in the snow and a few minutes later, low to the ground, like a shadow, a swallow.
>
> I thought the annual swallow followers might like to know of this when you are back in print.[1]

Most of the objectives which the Frankfurt adventure had been designed to attain were, manifestly, not attained, or attained only to a very limited degree. But there was one notable exception; in demonstrating the efficiency of modern technology the experiment could hardly have been more successful. Whereas linotype setting at Gray's Inn Road was at the rate of 3,000 characters per hour, Gutfreund's two computer terminals at Darmstadt, worked by German operators who did not understand English, had set the paper at the rate of 12,500 characters per hour. Had they been setting in their own language, the rate would have been more than 17,000 per hour. As for wage costs, it was estimated that for every £1,000 paid by Gutfreund and Tercuman, Times Newspapers were paying £2,868 at Gray's Inn Road. Nor was this due to the employment of cheap labour by the former; the German and Turkish workers involved were all members of unions and paid above union rates.

After the Frankfurt fiasco, many offers were received from other overseas firms to print *The Times*. Wherever accompanied by detailed estimates, these showed a productivity improvement of between 80 per cent and 350 per cent. Compared with these the improvement sought by the management in London, without any compulsory redundancy, was extremely modest. Yet even a productivity improvement of 50 per cent would have been enough to bring about an amazing

1 Emery's piece was entitled 'How the bitterness came through in this back to front campaign'; Howard's, 'My mind is made up, but it's been a struggle'. The letter about Christian names was from Mrs Margaret and Mr Thomas Brown, of Badger Hill, York; the swallow letter was from Susan Wigan, of Combe Martin, North Devon. The leading obituary was of Sir Leon Bagrit, the pioneer of automation.

transformation in costs and, therefore, in the quality of service to readers and advertisers.

Denied the stimulus of urgent work to do and deadlines to meet, *Times* journalists gradually settled into a routine of boredom tinged with resentment. They were expected to put in an appearance at Gray's Inn Road on one or two days a week. Courses were arranged for the improvement of shorthand and sub-editing, and there were lessons in French and Arabic, paid for by the company. Specialists were encouraged to keep their knowledge up-to-date, and reporters were put to work on research projects. Obituaries were regularly prepared, and so was a file of events to enable *The Times* to maintain its index, vital for its reputation as a journal of record. Freelance work was allowed, within reason, and some journalists wrote books. But none of this was any substitute for the excitement of producing a paper to appear the following morning.

Few of the journalists had much sympathy with the print unions, but few had much confidence in the management, either. The attitude of most of the editorial staff was, as Heren records, 'at best ambivalent'.[1] Their mood is well reflected in the diary that George Clark kept at the time, as for instance in these extracts:

> *10 January 1979.* Fixed up to write for the Country Landowner, 1,000 words for £80 . . . Fred Emery says that the Editor was despondent at the weekly meeting. Gloom, gloom everywhere. He seems to believe in divine intervention.
>
> *11 January 1979.* Black ice on the roads. Black gloom at the office . . . Went to the chapel meeting. Well attended. But 55 minutes was spent discussing whether we should go to collect our mail from the mail room. The NATSOPA chapel had asked that we should not do any job done by their members, but they were prepared to let us collect personal mail. A letter addressed 'G. Clark, The Times' would be personal, one addressed 'G. Clark, Political Correspondent, The Times' could not be taken . . . Then, from one triviality to another, we had a rigmarole about confidential memoranda passing between the *Sunday Times* NUJ chapel and their Editor, and references to the treachery of Rees-Mogg and such-like . . .
>
> *28 February 1979.* Three months of the shutdown now complete

1 Heren, op, cit., p.242.

and I was overcome by a feeling of *black despair* when the mandatory chapel meeting began with a long wrangle about the management's refusal to agree with the chapel's claim for 'parity' with the salaries of the *Sunday Times* journalists. The two chapels are now at daggers drawn. Brothers all!

1 March 1979. Editorial staff meeting, addressed by Louis Heren, produced the same gloom that was all-pervading at the union meeting. He saw little hope of the paper starting up again before June . . . the last notices would expire on March 9 and we could expect pickets around the building from then on . . . Pay clerks and pensions staff will continue at work. Expenses will continue to be paid . . . 'I seem to be spending all my time signing away money for you lot', said Louis . . . There will be a restricted service in the canteen. For emergency duty, one engineer and one electrician will be allowed in. Only the telephone supervisor will be on the switchboard.[1]

The chapel to which Clark and most other *Times* journalists belonged was that of the NUJ, though there was no closed shop and about forty, including the editor, belonged to the IoJ, while a few did not belong to either union. The NUJ chapel was divided, with the father of the chapel both reflecting and accentuating the division. Jacob (Jake) Ecclestone had been elected to the post in 1976. He was the son of a Church of England clergyman who joined the Communist party, and of the somewhat rebellious daughter of an Anglican suffragan bishop. Ecclestone was brought up and educated in Sheffield, where his father was a parish priest. He did not go to a university, though later in life (before the stoppage) he acquired credits in a number of Open University courses, including politics and economics. He went straight from school into journalism, moving from a weekly at Mexborough to the Doncaster office of the *Yorkshire Evening News*. In 1962 he was recruited to *The Times*, starting work there as a sports reporter.

Three years later he left the paper to teach in China, but his teaching career there was cut short by the almost immediate onset of the Cultural Revolution. Returning to England he was taken back on to the sports desk as a sub-editor, and then worked for a time on the 'back bench' at night before becoming a home news reporter. By 1976

1 Clark was chairman of the parliamentary lobby journalists from May 1978 to May 1979. This meant that he remained in frequent contact with leading politicians even though he was not writing about them.

he had come to feel rather aggrieved that he had not progressed further on the paper.[1] Yet with him personal dissatisfaction was a less important motive than devotion to the cause of socialism, which had survived even his unpleasant experience in China. His view of politics and industrial relations was essentially Marxist, though on his father's advice he did not join the Communist party of Great Britain, regarding it as hopelessly ineffective. To his way of thinking socialism was good, and all the better when it was international. By the same token, capitalist enterprises were inherently bad, and all the worse when they were multinationals, like the Thomson Organisation. He believed in class struggle, and had no doubt that all trade unionists, whatever their apparent differences, had an overriding common interest as 'workers' and employees.

His election as father of the chapel was a sign of the changing climate, both nationally and in the little world of *Times* journalists. Before him the post had been held by people of relative seniority, in status if not in age or length of service. After Innis Macbeath's stint the job had been done for two years by Longley, and after him by Rodney Cowton. In 1976 Longley was prepared to serve again, but a substantial number of his colleagues felt that he had not, earlier, been a tough enough negotiator on their behalf. The desire for greater toughness was reinforced by invidious comparisons with the pay of *Sunday Times* journalists, resulting from the move to Gray's Inn Road. Ecclestone had played no very conspicuous part at chapel meetings, and his highest ambition at the time was to stand for the committee. But those who wanted a stronger FoC knew just enough about him to be satisfied that he would fill the bill. When the idea was put to him he agreed to stand and was elected.[2] Thus he leapt from obscurity to a position of power and influence on the paper, and before long his gaunt, bearded figure was becoming familiar to the general public.

His attitude to the 1978 dispute was consistent with his philosophic stance, though not necessarily with the interests of NUJ members. In theory, he was not opposed to new technology or more efficient working procedures, but he was implacably opposed to what he saw as the ruthless treatment of trade unionists for the benefit of a distant plutocrat, and this meant that, in practice, he largely supported the print chapels' resistance to the management's proposals. To him the dispute

1 In 1971 he had applied for the post of deputy features editor (Ecclestone to W.R.-M., May 5 1971), but it had gone to Margaret Allen.

2 He was approached in the first instance by Leapman, but on the day was formally proposed by Ross Davies, the business diary editor, because Leapman was unable to attend the meeting.

was a classic case of bosses versus workers, and nobody could have convinced him that the real interests of the NUJ were incompatible with those of the print unions, more especially the NGA.

A few *Times* journalists in some degree shared his ideological commitment, though most did not. But a large number – often a majority – were behind him when he seemed to be putting up a good fight on matters of concern to them. They, too, were victims of the management's policy of rigid adherence to the government's pay guidelines, and this alone was enough to ensure frequent support for his militancy. He carried the chapel with him in refusing to accept the management's proposals before the original November 30 deadline, and when agreement was eventually reached before December 15 it was on terms thought more favourable by the NUJ journalists.[1] During this fraught period Longley told Rees-Mogg that any attempt to undermine Ecclestone's leadership would only strengthen it, and that the chapel would not get rid of him so long as it needed 'a crusading militant to stand up to a bloody-minded management'.[2]

Left-wingers produced a broadsheet called *The Times Challenger*. With the famous clock's hands at five-past twelve, and with the motto 'Unity is Strength', the masthead displayed the NUJ's name along with

---

1 Requirements for extra productivity were dropped. The package as a whole had been accepted before November 30 by the *Sunday Times* chapel and by *Times* journalists who were not NUJ members.

2 Longley had written a letter to the *Guardian*, published on December 4 1978, calling on Rees-Mogg to resign for allowing his staff, 'with no just cause, to be exposed to the intolerable threat of dismissal'. The same day Rees-Mogg wrote Longley this characteristic note:

> Dear Cliff,
>
> I saw your letter in The Guardian and I have a feeling that you may at some future time feel embarrassed by it.
>
> I thought therefore that I would send you a note to say that I did not in the least resent it and that when the present difficult situation has been resolved I, for my part, shall very much look forward to your resuming your coverage as our Religious Affairs Correspondent.
>
> Yours ever
> William

Evidently touched, Longley replied with a letter 'basically' of apology (December 6 1978), and also wrote again to the *Guardian* saying that his earlier letter no longer applied, but praising Ecclestone as well as Rees-Mogg for the 'wisdom and courage' that had enabled agreement to be reached (December 19 1978). The incident served to establish good relations between Longley and the man who had defeated him.

Another *Times* journalist who wrote to the *Guardian* that month was Routledge (December 29 1978). He welcomed as a basis for discussion a proposal by Tony Benn that *The Times* should be taken over by the BBC, and criticised the management's use of 'imported American labour relations tactics'.

the names of the unions which had not settled and whose members were under notice. The paper was edited by John Jennings, a journalist working for SOGAT. A front-page leader set the tone:

> The suppression of Times Newspapers by a Canadian based multinational corporation has now continued for eight weeks . . . The journalists have been gagged: several thousand print workers and office staff have been dismissed: the public's freedom of choice is diminished.

There was a cartoon of Hussey and Nisbet-Smith, and a piece by David Basnett, general secretary of the municipal workers (GMWU). A few *Times* journalists contributed, including Ecclestone, who wrote on 'Why the "loyal moderates" no longer trust management'.[1]

Moderates were, however, equally mistrustful of his own activities as a member of the chapels' liaison committee, and were particularly indignant when he voted with the print FoCs to reject the TUC initiative.[2] When *Times* journalists were asked to contribute to the Frankfurt edition, moderates in the chapel just managed to swing the vote in favour of leaving themselves free to do so, despite an instruction from the NUJ executive that no work should be done for any publication which other unions opposed. But after the failure of the Frankfurt adventure the vote was soon reversed, and members of the chapel were prohibited from working on any further foreign editions.

Dissatisfaction with their NUJ chapel was one reason, though only one, why a number of *Times* journalists took the initiative of setting up a body known as Journalists of The Times (JOTT). The main reason was that they feared Thomson would sell the paper over their heads, despite repeated assurances from the management that he had no intention of doing so. In any case the journalists, looking to the example of *Le Monde* in France, were attracted by the idea of greater participation by themselves in the running of their paper.

The prime movers in the creation of JOTT were Stephenson, Mortimer and Geraldine Norman. In June they circulated a proposal to their colleagues on the main paper and the supplements, inviting them to join an association whose precise character was as yet undefined, and to attend an inaugural meeting the following month. The

---

1 January 1979. *The Times Challenger* carried many advertisements from union chapels, and one from the Lewisham Communist Party wishing 'success to *Times* workers in their struggle'. Jennings was editor of SOGAT's journal.

2 Clark diary, entry for February 9 1979. In fact, Ecclestone proposed the rejection, with Brady seconding the motion.

strategy of the association would be to work on 'detailed contingency plans for any of the possible eventualities in the present dispute': republication at some point under the existing ownership, long-term or permanent closure of all titles, and sale of the titles to another owner, either together or separately. *Sunday Times* journalists were it was said, 'considering a similar initiative', and it was hoped to keep in close touch with them.[1] (Predictably, this did not occur.)

At the same time Stephenson wrote personally to Rees-Mogg, inviting him to join and listing merits of the scheme that might be expected to appeal to him:

> 1) It provides a forum for *all* journalists, that is not the NUJ. 2) At a time when journalists feel totally helpless & inconsequential in the present dispute it gives them something to think about & do. 3) If it got anywhere . . . it would provide a way in which journalists could talk to each other outside the NUJ.

Rees-Mogg replied that his attitude to JOTT had to be one of 'sympathetic neutrality'. While agreeing with what Stephenson had said in its favour he felt he could not join, because the association, might need to talk to him and he could not be 'usefully engaged' in talking to himself.[2]

On July 23 about sixty journalists turned up for the first meeting of JOTT, at the Conway Hall, at which there was a preliminary discussion of the association's nature and purpose. Lord Young of Dartington (Michael Young) attended to 'put forward his ideas on reader participation in a rescue plan'. Stephenson summed up the consensus of the meeting as favouring 'a loose structure for the time being'. A steering committee was elected to 'look at the practical details of forming a company'.[3] The next meeting was held in the same place, on September 20, by which time the steering committee had dismissed as 'unrealistic' the idea of a journalists' cooperative, deciding instead to recommend a limited liability company to be 'owned and run democratically by journalists'. A trust was to be established 'in close parallel to the company', for the technical purpose of being legally competent to buy shares from departing members and sell them to new ones, and

---

1 Proposal for an association of journalists, June 22 1979.

2 Stephenson to W.R.-M., June 25 1979; W.R.-M. to Stephenson, July 5 1979.

3 Minutes of the meeting kept by Geraldine Norman. As well as Young, there were other well-wishers hovering in the wings in the early days of JOTT, including Grimond and Robert Oakeshott, idealist and expert on cooperatives.

of being able to lend money for the purchase of shares.[1] These proposals were endorsed at the meeting, and by the time JOTT held its first annual general meeting, on January 17 1980, it had recruited 221 shareholders from approximately 290 journalists on *The Times* and supplements. Each journalist had one £4 share and one vote.

Before the shutdown of the papers and the issuing of notices to staff, there were already signs of doubt and potential dissension within the circle of management. Hamilton and Evans were showing the preliminary symptoms of what was soon to become a profound disenchantment with the whole policy. Brunton was asking questions which suggested that he had reservations about some aspects of it. Even Hussey, as we have seen, was less confident in December than he, like all the others, had been earlier in the year.

In February the *Observer* and the *Daily Express* did deals with the NGA for the installation of new technology on the union's terms. This increased the management's sense of isolation, and played into the hands of those who mistakenly believed that all would have been well if conflict with the NGA on the issue of keystroking had been avoided. In fact, the dispute was about power in the workplace, and settlement with the NGA on keystroking would not have resolved that issue. Besides, it was principally because of Roy Thomson's investment in new technology, and his son's determination that it should be brought into use, that the management of Times Newspapers had been told it must take the unions on. It was wrong to suggest, as some did, that keystroking was an issue gratuitously introduced by Hussey.

Faced with union resistance of unforeseen stubbornness and effectiveness, and faced also with a lack of solidarity on the part of other Fleet Street managements that surpassed expectation, the Thomson high command was fatally confused in motive and structure. In London, the board of Times Newspapers was entirely absorbed in the task of trying to rationalise production of the newspapers, and in the resulting struggle with the unions. In Toronto, this was only one of Kenneth Thomson's many preoccupations, among which the most recent was his bid for control of the Hudson's Bay Company. Between London and Toronto the link man was Brunton, and his position was increasingly awkward. As president and chief executive of International Thomson (ITO) his responsibilities extended far beyond the Gray's Inn Road dispute. Yet he was, obviously, much closer to it

1 Circular letter from Stephenson, September 12 1979. (Stephenson papers.)

than the proprietor, since he was an Englishman with his office in London (in Stratford Place, off Oxford Street), and since he had been among those most intimately involved in the decision to confront the unions. By the spring of 1979 it was scarcely possible for him to reconcile his conflicting loyalties. Should he continue to back his embattled colleagues, whatever the cost, or should he, in the interests of ITO and the proprietor, find some way out of what seemed an unwinnable struggle? In any form of warfare victory is likely to go to the side which is the more single-minded and the better organised. Despite its vast financial resources, the Thomson set-up lacked the necessary cohesion and fixity of purpose.

Frankfurt decided the issue. After the failure there Brunton's mind was swiftly made up. He could see no future in pursuing the dispute with all the objectives previously agreed; indeed, he was convinced that it had to be ended. This opened a breach between him and Hussey, and their relations were further impaired by a misunderstanding over Frankfurt itself, Brunton maintaining that the plan to print there had not been properly explained to him in advance, while Hussey contended that he had been fully party to it. Such misunderstandings often occur when things go wrong, and it was the fact that Frankfurt had gone wrong that was significant. Hussey thought it would be disastrous to abandon foreign printing altogether, under duress; he wanted to try again in some other place, and there was no shortage of offers. Rees-Mogg favoured printing in America, or even on some 'green field' site in Britain, though the latter option was hardly realistic, since other unions would have prevented distribution of the paper. In any case Brunton and, behind him, Thomson were in no mood for further risky experiments. They were already of a mind to retreat, and Frankfurt was just the last straw. At a meeting of the main board of TNL on April 30, immediately after the critical weekend at Frankfurt, Hussey received the 'clear message' that Thomson's were 'not prepared to foot the bill any longer'.

The words quoted were those of one of the national directors, Robens, speaking on the telephone to Hussey the same night, and confirming their shared recollection of the meeting. Hussey in turn reported them in a letter to John Tory, Thomson's most trusted Canadian adviser. The letter was, in fact, never sent, but it conveys Hussey's state of mind at the time, and his sense of being badly let down:

> Whatever may be our current negotiating position . . . I feel I must write to tell you how very disturbed I am about the drift in our position and attitude to this stoppage. Since before it started,

> even going back to December 1977, on the subject of technology and our industrial aims we have been told . . . that [Thomson's] would forgive us mistakes, would forgive us misjudgment, but . . . would never forgive us breaches of principle. We have been consistently told that we would forfeit . . . confidence and financial support . . . if we abandoned the objectives which we have so often outlined.
>
> This is an issue on which I feel extremely strongly because TNL were urged and directed first to make *The Times* profitable, the *Sunday Times* more profitable, and then to abide by the government's wage policy, and finally to force the issue with the trade unions. Much of the current confrontation stems from the first and second of these directives . . . I myself believe it was the right policy . . . but I have always warned that I could not guarantee success, most certainly if we had a suspension. I readily admit that I thought we could resolve it more quickly than we have so far been able to do. Nevertheless I still believe that we would be better advised to continue our present policy rather than publicly submit to these pressures. There is no doubt that we have almost the unanimous support of everybody in industry, in the Government, in the opposition, the advertising and distribution trades, our readers and the general public.
>
> The European issue which we have been ordered to abandon . . . has to my mind already yielded results . . . I think we would be making a terrible tactical error if we abandoned all thoughts of republishing a European edition.
>
> I cannot understand the sudden shift in policy nor can many of my colleagues . . .[1]

The day after this letter was drafted an event occurred whose impact on the power of trade unions would, over the next few years, be drastic. On May 3 Britain went to the polls and, as a result, the Callaghan government was replaced by the Conservatives under Margaret Thatcher. When, at Transport House the following day, Clark told Callaghan that *The Times*'s future was 'in the hands of the unions', he 'murmured his sympathy and said he had also been sunk by the unions'.[2]

The incoming Tory government was pledged to reform trade union

1 Draft of unsent letter from M.J.H. to John Tory, May 2 1979. (Hussey papers).
2 Clark diary, entry for May 4 1979. As the man who had sabotaged *In Place of Strife*, Callaghan perhaps deserved this particular fate.

law but, mindful of the fate of Heath's industrial relations act, intended to go about the job in its own time and its own way. It could, therefore, offer no immediate assistance to Times Newspapers. The new employment secretary, Prior, favoured the softly-softly approach, and his speech in the Commons debate before the *Times* stoppage had, it will be recalled, included some criticism of the management's tactics. Soon after his appointment he told Hamilton: 'I can't see what we can do. Fundamentally we want to keep out of it, we don't want to be a fire brigade rushing round every trade union dispute'.[1]

The policy of appeasement at Gray's Inn Road brought Hamilton once again to the fore. Though he had spoken strongly, early the previous year, for giving effect to Roy Thomson's dream of modern and economic methods of production, his instincts were above all those of a newspaperman, and the reality of the stoppage altered his scale of priorities. The same was true of Evans. Both now felt that the resumption of publication was worth almost any price. On June 12 Hamilton attended a meeting of the chapel's liaison committee and listened to complaints. The mere fact of the meeting was a notable climbdown, since management had hitherto refused to recognise the committee. At the same time Evans was leaving his numerous contacts in the chapels in no doubt of his dissent from the policy represented by Hussey and Nisbet-Smith.

Three days after Hamilton met the FoCs Hussey talked to Rupert Murdoch, at Brunton's request, and his record of the conversation is of special interest, in view of the future:

> He said he didn't think we would get the technology. 'But you must get everything else . . .' He said 'It is perfectly obvious what is happening to you. GCB [Brunton] has sent Denis [Hamilton] in to wave the white flag, and he is waving it in all directions. This could be very damaging for your company. If this attitude goes on, the management will lose all credibility. Your chances of getting . . . a commercially viable newspaper company are negligible. There are only two people who have the authority to make a surrender or compromise proposal, and they are Ken Thomson and GCB. If GCB is sending Denis in to do it for him, he is making your position absolutely impossible. He started you off on this road in the first place . . . and now if Denis waves the white flag, he is absolutely slaughtering you . . . You have sacrificed your working credibility and your neck, and he should give

1 Hamilton, op. cit., p.168.

> you £200,000 and tell you to run an oil well. On the other hand, if you can salvage a good compromise on the technology, it is absolutely vital that you get the manning and the continuous production'. He knew that Gordon Brunton was waving the white flag as soon as he [Murdoch] sat down at lunch yesterday and said 'I hope you are not going to pay these bastards any back money'. GCB replied 'Well of course we might have to have a special £1 million for hardship'. 'I knew then that the balloon was going to go up and that everything was lost . . . . You shouldn't have agreed to the Booth formula and to pay them the back money . . . That was a mistake. I don't think you will have any trouble at all getting the market back. Your problem has been that the rest of Fleet Street have behaved like a pack of real bastards, particularly Jocelyn Stevens [the *Daily Express*] and the *Observer*. . . You are not being helped either by Harry Evans . . . Gordon and Denis must be stopped from giving this surrender atmosphere to everyone'.[1]

The surrender atmosphere was getting through to the journalists. Rees-Mogg told Clark that Hamilton was 'flapping about like an old washerwoman', and that Evans had 'lost his nerve', wanting to 'capitulate'. 'Oh dear', Clark commented, 'when the big shots get like this, what *can* we expect?'[2] From New York Leapman contributed a 'Lock-out Diary' to the *New Statesman*, in which he summarised the balance of forces within the management on the basis of 'the observations of transients from *The Times* and the *Sunday Times* who pass through New York trying to sell their books to American publishers':

> The hawks are led by Duke Hussey, flanked by his spiritual adviser Rees-Mogg. The moderate camp seems now to be headed by Gordon Brunton . . . backed by Denis Hamilton . . . who has kept his profile low throughout. The irony is that Brunton provoked the showdown when he summoned Hussey last April and said something must be done to end production losses. Hussey, with Brunton's approval, chose strong-arm tactics, believing that they would achieve his object by April of this year. Now that the deadline has slipped, Brunton is said to be getting impatient with the increasingly despairing Hussey. So is Harold Evans . . .[3]

1 June 15 1979. (Contemporary record in Hussey papers.)
2 Clark diary, entry for June 18 1979.
3 June 8 1979. This diary was not well received by Douglas-Home, the foreign editor, or by some others at Gray's Inn Road.

Rees-Mogg remained a hawk to the end, so distancing himself not only from Evans, but from most of his own editorial colleagues. The politician in him took precedence over the journalist.

In the last week of June Thomson was in London for the annual general meeting of ITO. On the 25th his confidant, Tory, had a discussion with Brunton and Hussey (whose drafted but unsent *cri de coeur* to him in early May has been quoted). According to Hussey's record, Tory confirmed that every part of the policy which Hussey had been carrying out was indeed, in the first instance, agreed by all:

> We all agreed what TNL set out to do. I thought the objectives were right at the time and I think so still. We probably all thought in our hearts they [we?] were trying to do too much but we all thought it was worth it to try and get as much as we could. All right it has not worked out for a variety of reasons mainly, in my view, because other newspapers have ratted on us . . . On the question of technology we all knew that it was not in the original list of objectives and it was put in, as Duke said, because he did not want to land us in two strikes and we all agreed that was the right thing to do then. All right, so if we have to make a compromise now on technology we have to . . . and I think we all accept that . . . but nevertheless I agree with the way Duke has put it. It must be done in such a way that the staff don't see it as a surrender and so we don't lose their confidence . . . because we have to come out of this with a manageable and viable company.

He asked Hussey if he and his board agreed to act on the lines indicated, and Hussey replied:

> Yes, I agree with the way you have put it. I think they agree we have to compromise but equally that we must end with a manageable and viable company . . . We have to have something better than the *Observer* in order to make certain of our other agreements and preserve the confidence of the management.

At this point Brunton intervened to say that Hussey was the chief executive and that in the end the decision was his, which his colleagues 'had to accept'.[1]

1 Contemporary record in Hussey papers.

In fact, the ultimate decisions were never exclusively his, but were dictated by general Thomson policy. On the other hand it is also clearly true that he accepted the necessity to compromise on technology, though 'compromise' was, in the circumstances, a euphemism for surrender. On the substance of the dispute he had anyway offered compromise to the NGA before the shutdown, but to no avail. The union had refused to budge on keystroking, or to negotiate at all unless the threat of closure was first withdrawn. As a result of this obduracy the papers had been out of circulation for six months and the company was suffering enormous financial loss. Now the union was saying that its 600 members formerly employed by Times Newspapers would be instructed to look for jobs elsewhere, and that the papers had no chance of surviving.[1] Against such a background to have any truck at all with the NGA was, as Murdoch put it, to show the white flag.

As Thomson arrived for the ITO annual general meeting at the Portman Hotel on June 27 he was greeted by pickets, including some from the NUJ. In his speech to shareholders he said that ITO's 'businesses and developments internationally, especially in the US', were up to expectation, and that, in the UK, the travel, book, regional newspapers and oil concerns were all doing well. But the dispute at Times Newspapers had already cost £20 million, and the estimated ongoing cost of it was £1.7 million per month, representing mainly the salaries of the 1,300 staff retained. He ended with an appeal to the unions:

> We realise that there is a strong need for better communication between management and work force . . . There has already been one recent meeting between our chapels and the chairman of Times Newspapers [Hamilton] and his two senior management colleagues . . . There is a need for both sides to come together to create a new atmosphere, to heal wounds. This time we must get it right.
>
> We are resolute people; we are fair people; we seek confrontation with nobody. I will simply express the hope . . . that what I have said will evoke a response in the hearts and minds of those with whom we are negotiating, which will secure the very earliest resumption of publication of these irreplaceable titles.

---

1 Statement by Wade, reported June 23 1979. The NGA had been paying its ex-Times Newspapers members strike pay, having the resources to do so. An attempt by members of the NUJ to find common ground with the NGA on keystroking had predictably come to nothing. (Jacobs, op. cit., pp.117–120.)

From the body of the hall Lewis Chester, a shareholder who was also a *Sunday Times* journalist, denounced the management as 'arrogant' and addressed himself directly to Thomson:

> You do not have the loyalty of the journalists. In fact you do not have the loyalty of any of the employees. The only way to resolve this matter is for you personally to involve yourself in these negotiations.

Thomson replied:

> Maybe we did not give enough time to negotiations. Maybe we did make a few mistakes. If it would be helpful I would be prepared to take part in talks between unions and management. I would discuss with my colleagues the advisability of doing that.

A motion of no confidence in the management was easily defeated.[1]

Strangely, the immediate reaction to Thomson's performance was that he had stood firm and given nothing away. But in fact he had shown weakness by admitting error and conceding the possibility of a meeting between himself and union leaders, which he had refused to countenance earlier in the dispute. Two days later he did indeed meet Dixon and Wade at Stratford Place, to discuss a formula which Evans had already agreed with them at the union's Bedford headquarters. Afterwards a short bulletin was issued. News of this encounter swiftly reached *Times* journalists, and Clark drew the right conclusion:

> Well, you could have knocked me over with a feather . . . It is a complete surrender to the print unions, and I am amazed that there have been no resignations from the board. Duke Hussey's policy, and the editor's arguments, have been rejected, and rejected by no less a person than Lord Thomson, the man who puts up the money.[2]

The only mistake was to suggest that the policy now abandoned had been exclusively Hussey's; it had been Thomson's own, which Hussey and others had been trying to carry out.

However lamentable the circumstances, the road to republication was now open; yet nearly five more months were to pass before the

1 *Daily Mail*, June 28 1979.
2 Clark diary, entry for July 29, 1979.

papers actually reappeared. Though Hamilton met the chapels' liaison committee again on July 4, the management soon reverted to the provenly sterile procedure of trying to negotiate a deal with the unions' national leaders. At the end of the month such a deal was, in fact, negotiated, but the chapels then insisted that the company must negotiate with them individually, and that there would be no return to work unless and until they had all agreed. This inevitably involved long delay and further large concessions by management, as well as much jockeying for advantage and differential gain between the trade unionists. Until September the company at least stuck to the line that it would not reinstate any of those who had been dismissed, before there was agreement with all concerned. But when the NGA renewed its threat to instruct its members to find jobs elsewhere, they were reinstated even though there was still no general settlement.

Finally, on November 11 – a suitably symbolic date – a return to work was agreed between all the parties. The dismissed employees were to come back on terms that represented an increase in wage costs to the company of 55 per cent. Apart from much higher wages, each employee was to receive a bonus (though it was not called that) of £500. On the union side there were undertakings about overtime, manning levels, greater efficiency and more reliable print runs. But these were not legally enforceable and were, in the event, largely dishonoured. The company's concessions were solid and immediate; the unions' were mere words dependent upon future good faith and goodwill.

The fate of one union concession was a bad augury for all the others. Wade and Dixon gave, at the last moment, a written promise (they had wanted it to be only verbal) that there would be no victimisation of members of their union who, as supervisors, had continued to work during the stoppage. But the promise was soon broken, when the NGA punished some with expulsion and others with a fine of £1,000. Under threat of legal action by the company the penalty was reduced to a fine of £70; but it was still a penalty and the pledge of no victimisation was not redeemed.

For Times Newspapers the stoppage has to be regarded as an almost unqualified disaster. There was not even a Pyrrhic victory to show for the £46 million that it eventually cost the Thomson regime. Any apparent gains lacked the means to make them secure and lasting. The real victor, in Jacobs's judgement:

> . . . was not the company, the unions or the staff, but the fact of chapel power. That power had been partially hidden throughout

> the first half of the dispute by the issue of the new technology . . . Once that issue had been cleared out of the way, the chapels stood revealed as the dominating force. It was the chapels . . . that dictated the pace of the protracted negotiations which led to the newspapers' return. Chapel power had not been overridden, either by the company or by the unions . . . And when the newspapers were back in print, the chapels continued to bestride the company's operations and to be the arbiters of production.[1]

The management had set out, above all, to assert its right and freedom to manage. In that endeavour it had comprehensively failed.

If blame for the failure were to be apportioned, it would have to be apportioned very widely. But it is profitless to attempt a precise allocation of responsibility for all that was wrong and all that went wrong. The story should speak for itself, in all its sadness, silliness and complexity.

---

1 Jacobs, op. cit., p.151. Chapel power was humiliatingly evident in the fact that, during the last phase of the dispute, Nisbet-Smith had to travel to Blackpool to see Brady, and soon afterwards another TNL director, Donald Cruickshank, had to go to Brighton to see Fitzpatrick. (The two FoCs were attending, respectively, the TUC and Labour conferences.)

Though roughly equivalent in power and obstructive effect, Brady and Fitzpatrick were very different characters. Brady was a natural boss who had applied, unsuccessfully, for a job with the NPA and was later to accept a managerial post under Murdoch. Fitzpatrick, though not averse to the exercise of power, was a committed ideologue and trade unionist, with views similar to Ecclestone's.

XXVI

Back in business • Timely scoop • Sermon for the new decade • The centre beckons again • From Rhodesia to Zimbabwe • Carter agonistes

SINCE AGREEMENT TO republish was reached in the late afternoon of November 11, which was a Sunday, there was no time to produce a paper for Monday morning and *The Times* made its reappearance on Tuesday 13th. The event itself was recorded down-column on the front page, with thanks to 'readers, advertisers and newsagents for their patience and loyalty'. The lead story was, rightly, less parochial: a report from Brogan about the cutting-off of Iranian oil imports by Carter. But there was plenty more about the paper's return on inside pages.

At the Lord Mayor's banquet the previous evening Mrs Thatcher welcomed the news, saying that *The Times*'s absence had been 'tragic and overlong'. This was reported on page 6. On the op. ed. page there were articles representing both sides in the dispute. From the management side Rees-Mogg himself wrote a signed piece in which he criticised governments, Conservative as well as Labour, for their failure to reform trade union law. He also expressed some bitterness about the 'negative attitude' of other Fleet Street managements, pointedly thanking the *Daily Telegraph* for printing an article of his during the stoppage, which '*The Observer* commissioned, never even saw, but were too cowardly to print'. He ended on a note of doubtful bravado: 'I am glad that we have achieved higher productivity, even at this cost, and believe that it can lead to better rather than worse relations with our staff, on whose quality everything depends'.

The article from the trade union side was interesting above all for the identity of the author, since it was written not by Keys or Wade or any of the national leaders, but by Fitzpatrick. That he rather than any of them was asked to write it shows with eloquent symbolism how Rees-Mogg, like his colleagues, had been brought to recognise the realities of power. He began by complaining that it was normally hard for unions to get a fair hearing in the media, and that only 'the more sensational aspects' of the dispute had been properly covered, while the real issues had been largely ignored. The management's proposals had been resisted for three reasons: that they were hurriedly conceived and presented as an ultimatum, that they offered no concessions 'other than redundancy payments in return for enormous job and skill losses', and that the strategy 'relied on abusing the readers . . . by suspending publication'. The vast amount of money spent on the dispute did not 'represent a penny invested in either plant or employees'; it was simply 'money squandered'. 'A fraction of it well-spent could have secured the new technology and many of the benefits and social improvements that we all want to see'. With laughable understatement he admitted that there might be some wrong on the union side: 'Of course unions and their members from time to time bear some responsibility for interrupting newspaper production. In my experience, however, it is rare for this responsibility to be found solely on one side or the other'. He appealed to the management not to 'manage remotely', but to listen to employees and to acknowledge that the real owner of a newspaper is the readers'. In his last paragraph, however, he said that a newspaper belonged 'to the nation', and that new technology should be used 'to bring a greater diversity to the press'.

Not content with his signed op. ed. piece, Rees-Mogg also wrote a thumping three-column leader, in which he reasserted the familiar argument that low productivity was killing Britain, and claimed that 'without a willingness to press the question home, it would not have been possible to negotiate the new agreements'. Among letters to the editor, the first was from Goodman, welcoming the paper back and (somewhat ironically, from a director of the *Observer*) praising it for its stand. The last letter, from D. J. Connolly of Berkhamsted, parodied the genre to good topical effect:

> Last Monday I believe I heard the sound of the first phoenix of the year. Who said it was extinct? Welcome back.[1]

Over the next fortnight or so *The Times* tried to compensate for its year-long dereliction of duty as a journal of record by publishing a series of supplements, which appeared in the middle of the paper between the op. ed. and leader pages. The first provided a summary of world events during the period of the stoppage, with contributions

1 November 13 1979. Op. ed. pieces: 'The terrible price we have paid' by W.R.-M., and 'Why both sides must change their attitudes' by Barry Fitzpatrick. Leader, 'The sparks are falling on the gunpowder'. (Donald Trelford, editor of the *Observer*, defended himself in a letter, November 16.)

from specialists in various departments ranging from foreign affairs to sport. This was followed by four supplements of obituaries and one in which the paper's leading reviewers presented a selection of the books they had most enjoyed during the year. On December 31 there was a diary of the year giving a review of events of all kinds, month by month.[1]

The loyalty of the readership, of which there was already encouraging evidence from tests conducted during the stoppage, was amply demonstrated in the event. Whereas the last six-monthly average of circulation before the stoppage was 297,738, the seven-week period from the paper's return to the end of 1979 showed an average figure of 360,257. This was certainly boosted by freak sales during the early days of republication; by the end of January 1980 the figure had dropped to 335,000, and the figure for the whole of 1980 was roughly the same as before the stoppage. But clearly the paper's core readership had, to a marvellous degree, remained faithful to it. The sense of quiet but joyous relief at *The Times*'s return was comically but touchingly conveyed by one reader: 'Today, for the first time since November 30, my husband smiled at breakfast. Undoubtedly a sign of *The Times*'.[2]

Though the paper's addicted readers needed no special inducement to return, it was felt, nevertheless, that a good scoop would be helpful in the early days after republication; and the opportunity to obtain one soon presented itself in a surprising and controversial form. On November 15 the prime minister announced in the House of Commons that Sir Anthony Blunt, the eminent art historian who for twenty-seven years (until 1972) had been surveyor of the royal picture collection, had been a Soviet agent before and during the Second World War. In 1964, after the American FBI had found a witness prepared to testify that Blunt had tried to recruit him in the 1930s, Blunt had made a confession to the British security services in return for a promise of immunity from prosecution. The Queen had agreed to collaborate in

---

1 The supplement on world events consisted of eight pages and appeared on November 14. Three of the obituaries' supplements also ran to eight pages each and appeared on November 16, 19 and 23; the last, consisting of two pages, appeared on December 17. The books' supplement, of four pages, appeared on November 24; it included, on the back page, a short selection of children's books. The diary of the year on December 31 occupied the same position in the paper, and ran to three pages.

2 Letter to the editor from Mrs Iris Schoenewald, of Greenford, Middlesex; published November 15 1979.

this deal to the extent of retaining Blunt as a member of her household, while knowing that he had been a traitor. But Lord Home, who had been prime minister at the time of the confession, had not, Mrs. Thatcher said, been informed of it. She also stated that the evidence against Blunt had been insufficient as a basis for criminal charges.

No doubt the matter would have remained a secret, and Blunt a publicly respected and honoured figure, but for explicit allegations in *Private Eye*, followed by hints in a book by Andrew Boyle, *The Climate of Treason*, which received much attention in the press. As it was, Blunt was stripped of his knighthood and soon afterwards forced to resign his fellowships of Trinity College, Cambridge, and the British Academy. *The Times*'s first comment on the affair, in a leader written by Rees-Mogg, noted that Blunt was 'a more substantial figure' than the other Cambridge traitors, and criticised the decision to leave him in his Buckingham Palace post after he had confessed:

> That was an extraordinary decision. It ought to be a cardinal principle to protect the Queen . . . In such matters the Queen acts under advice. The responsibility for that advice is that of the Government, not of the Queen's Private Secretary, let alone of the Queen herself. The Government of the day, though Lord Home . . . appears to have had no knowledge of the transaction . . . must have decided that the supposed advantages to the Service justified leaving a traitor on the Queen's staff . . . It is a bit late to strip a man of his honours when he has been knowingly permitted to hold royal posts as a retired traitor for 15 years.[1]

Next day there was a letter in the paper from Brian Sewell, antique dealer and close friend of Blunt, complaining that Labour was 'baying for vengeance with cries of *Privilege* and *Establishment*', while the government had reneged on an undertaking by which it should have

---

1 Leader, 'A most distinguished traitor', November 16 1979. The same day Blunt's exposure was reported on the front page, while the parliamentary report included the full text of Mrs. Thatcher's statement.

Was Rees-Mogg right to argue that the Queen had no responsibility for the objectionable decision? Though on political issues the sovereign must, of course, speak and act on ministerial advice, the composition of her own official family is not a political issue in the accepted sense, but definitely a matter for her. She would have been entirely within her rights, and surely justified, in refusing to do what she was asked to do. In any case the request did not come from the prime minister, who should have been her confidant on such an important matter. Willie Hamilton raised the interesting question: did she 'advise or warn her Prime Minister', which was 'the constitutional role of the Monarch according to Bagehot'? (House of Commons, reported in the paper November 22 1979.)

felt bound: '. . . a bargain is a bargain, and they had not kept their side, for immunity of [*sic*] prosecution is meaningless if there is no immunity from publicity'. The withdrawal of Blunt's knighthood was 'a petty response'.

Told of Sewell's letter as soon as it arrived in the office, Stewart Tendler, the paper's crime correspondent, who was covering the Blunt story, immediately contacted Sewell and also spoke to Blunt's lawyer, Michael Rubinstein. As a result he discovered Blunt's whereabouts and the paper was able to lead with the news 'Professor Blunt still in Britain', when it was widely believed that he had gone abroad.[1] Better still, from the paper's point of view, the contact with Sewell and Rubinstein led to a negotiation whose outcome was a full-length interview with Blunt, conducted at Gray's Inn Road on November 20. The scoop was not quite exclusive, because at the request of Blunt and his advisers the interview was given simultaneously to the *Guardian*. But in the words of Heren, who took the principal part in the negotiation and in the interview itself, 'half a scoop was better than none'.[2]

On November 21 the interview was summarised on the front page under the five-column headline 'Professor Blunt describes double life as MI5 man and Soviet agent', with a picture of him taken the previous day. The full text appeared on pages 4 and 5. Throughout the interview 'he was remarkably composed and clearly believed that his confession to MI5 in 1964 and the immunity granted to him was an absolution', putting him, 'in Roman Catholic terms, in a state of grace'. He said that he had stopped giving information to the Russians after the war, when he became 'disenchanted with communism and the Soviet Union', and 'convinced that the British way of life and constitution was the best'. It was not he who had alerted Maclean and Burgess; that was Philby. But when asked 'Did you not feel obliged to warn the security services?' he replied 'No, because they [the two defectors] were my friends'. He refused to discuss what information he had given the security services in return for immunity.[3]

News of the interview and its venue got around in advance, and when Blunt arrived at Gray's Inn Road the place was besieged by

---

1 Letter and report, November 17 1979. Tendler, who was assisted on the story by Ian Bradley, had been recruited for the paper by Cudlipp and Heren. Like Heren he was an East End boy, though unlike Heren he had been to university (Cambridge), where he had read history. Before joining *The Times* he had worked on an evening paper in Reading and on the *Daily Telegraph*.

2 Op. ed. piece, 'That Blunt interview: a scoop is a scoop', November 27 1979.

3 For *The Times* the interview was conducted by Heren and Tendler; for the *Guardian* by David Leigh, until recently a *Times* reporter, who cannot have expected to have occasion to return so soon to Gray's Inn Road.

reporters from other papers, some of whom managed to break into the building. A further difficulty was that Edward Heath was also there, as Rees-Mogg's guest at an editorial lunch. Though the interview with Blunt took place in an adjoining room, and though he partook of at least some of the fare that was offered to Heath, the embarrassment of a direct encounter between the two men was avoided. Blunt's discrimination in favour of *The Times* and the *Guardian* was not obtained by any financial inducement, but probably reflected his preference, as a natural elitist, for the two papers that he must have regarded as the prime organs of respectable educated opinion, right and left. Nevertheless, their rivals were understandably vexed, and some expressed moral outrage that a traitor should have been not only interviewed but entertained to lunch.[1]

Correspondence on the Blunt affair and its security aspects lasted for many days. One of the best letters consisted of a single sentence: 'Why not institute a new order of knighthood, the KGB?'[2] In a second leader on the subject Rees-Mogg linked the case of Blunt with that of Derek Robinson ('Red Robbo'), a well-known trade union militant who had caused much disruption at Longbridge and had just been dismissed by British Leyland amid cries of indignation from the left. Robinson, the leader argued, was currently far more important than Blunt, because he was 'part of a Communist led infiltration of the trade unions'. He and his friends were 'not traitors'; their activities were not furtive or underhand. They were 'open advocates of an extreme socialist solution, but as such they had 'done far more to destroy the prospect of our maintaining a free and prosperous society than all the Cambridge traitors put together'.[3]

The end of the 1970s put Rees-Mogg into a more than usually sermonising mood. And as the new decade opened he unburdened himself, in a signed article, of his thoughts on Britain's contemporary state of mind. There were, he said, as many different ways of thinking of a nation as of the coach in Bishop Berkeley's *Essay towards a New Theory of Vision*. He had his own way. The British 'no longer, as a nation, set themselves to achieve high economic objectives'. Many of

1 According to Heren (article already quoted), some who claimed to be morally outraged had offered Blunt large sums for an interview. As for the lunch, he (Heren) had 'expected sandwiches', but the steward had taken pity on him and produced some smoked trout from the Blue Room.
2 From Frank Hodgson, Plymouth, published November 20 1979.
3 Leader, 'Mr. Robinson and Mr. Blunt', November 22 1979.

them had an economic ambition, but it was 'to be comfortable, not to be rich'. This was understandable, granted the national character. 'It is not surprising that the nation whose poet is Shakespeare should at heart be indifferent both to the doctrines of Adam Smith and of Karl Marx'. But the British now seemed to respond neither to metaphysical nor moral challenge.

St Paul's cathedral was, he suggested, not only a great Christian building but, within the baroque style, distinctively British. The baroque was a style of movement, but 'St Peter's movement is a general outward explosion of the circumference, like plum pudding aflame with brandy; St Paul's drives forward, a stern vehicle of grace determined to arrive at its destination'. Yet the British no longer crowded into St Paul's, Sunday after Sunday. If asked by a public opinion poll, most of them said they believed in God, but for most it was 'a cool and indifferent belief'. The British were perhaps to be seen at their best in morality. 'They are peaceable. Their moderation makes them good neighbours; they are often good citizens; they support charity'. But that was not enough: 'the morality which requires hard thought and difficult action, in particular the morality which cuts against the grain of sentiment, finds out their weakness'. They were good about dogs, starving children and cancer, but not so good about single parents and no good at all about prisoners.

How would such a nation fare in the 1980s? The economic problems that the country faced would not be solved unless the spiritual need was met. 'Britain will not be saved by silicon chips, though Britain might well be undone by failing to use them. The sickness of the nation is that it lacks a guiding purpose, a central idea'. A nation seldom found inspiration in 'abstract ideals, like justice or compassion', but far more often in religion. He could not perceive the real state of the British nation. He could 'hear the coach, the clatter of hooves and wheels and harness, [and] see the colours, a pattern of paint and light. But the coach itself [was] an idea [that could only be known] through separate and imperfect perception'. Perhaps the country was 'already pregnant' with the idea that would save Britain.[1]

This rumination was in some respects muddled and contradictory. If the British were incapable of responding to a moral challenge, then why was morality (of however soft and sentimental a kind) said to be the department in which they might be seen at their best? And were there not important differences between the nations constituting the United Kingdom, glossed over in, for instance, the author's reference

1 January 2 1980. Op. ed. piece, 'Bishop Berkeley's coach'.

to the spirit of Shakespeare? All the same, it was a piece entirely characteristic of Rees-Mogg, and the theme was worthy of the somewhat artificial occasion of a new decade. Readers could be reassured by it that their paper and its editor were, indeed, like no other.

If she read the piece, Margaret Thatcher may have wondered why Rees-Mogg merely said that Britain might be 'pregnant' with a new and saving idea, which he could not yet perceive. Had such an idea not already been born with her advent to the premiership? Rees-Mogg was, after all, a Friedmanite convert. Did it not follow that he should be an enthusiastic Thatcherite?

Certainly he was a supporter of her government, and hoped that it would succeed. But he had reservations, as we have seen, about her personality and style, and for that reason alone was bound to have difficulty in regarding her as the ideal national saviour. In any case, he had doubts about her chances of success and was therefore concerned that there should be a tolerable alternative to her. So his thoughts turned again, as in 1972, to the idea of a centre party which would have the effect of separating moderate Labourites from the socialist left. As a contribution to this process he commissioned again an opinion poll from ORC, and as on the previous occasion the key figure in the hoped-for development was to be Roy Jenkins. Indeed it was an intervention by Jenkins that acted as a spur to Rees-Mogg to commission the new poll.

On November 22 1979 Jenkins, still president of the European Commission, delivered in London his famous Dimbleby Lecture, in which he argued that the British political system was out of date. Calling for a proportional method of voting to replace the traditional method of first-past-the-post, he rebutted the charge that this would involve exchanging strong, clear-cut and homogeneous governments for coalitions that would lack internal cohesion and would therefore be weak as well as unprincipled. Existing governments were, he maintained, coalitions in all but name, often between the most disparate elements. Under a reformed system coalitions would be overt, whereas at present they were covert; and it was easy to imagine a coalition that would be more united on major issues of policy than either of the big parties currently alternating in government.

Emery was among the lecture's immediate audience at the Royal Society of Arts, and at the party afterwards gave Jenkins the impression of being, like other journalists, sceptical of his argument.[1] But it

1 Jenkins, *European Diary 1977–1981*, entry for November 22 1979, p.524.

was sure of a good reception from Rees-Mogg. In next day's paper the lecture was fully reported on page 5, with a picture, and it was also the subject of a first leader by the editor. It was, he said, too early to say if Mrs Thatcher's policies would or would not succeed. If they did, then national politics would 'follow a mainly Conservative course in the 1980s'. But meanwhile it was 'sensible to look at the alternative'.

> This in essence is what Mr. Roy Jenkins did in his Dimbleby Lecture. There is a real risk that the failure of Mrs. Thatcher's government would be followed by the election of a Labour government commanding no real public confidence, but committed to an extremist manifesto . . . The obvious way to remove this danger is to change to a system of proportional representation.

Mrs Thatcher's opposition to PR was 'the worst defect in her position', since it amounted to saying that it was 'so important to have a Conservative government that Britain must take the risk of having a Marxist government emerge'.

> A coalition of the centre could well win an election outright . . . the creation of an alternative government which would not be a disaster for Britain is now both feasible and necessary. It would give a new form to Mr. David Steel's Lib-Lab pact. It would make the institutional changes which would allow Britain a greater stability of government than we have had since 1964.[1]

There was further evidence of Rees-Mogg's doubts about the viability of the Thatcher experiment in a leader that he wrote at the end of the year. The medicines she was prescribing, strict monetary control, reduced government spending and the restoration of enterprise – of which, of course, in theory he thoroughly approved – ran the risk of killing the patient before they had 'a proper chance to cure him'.[2]

The poll inspired by the Dimbleby Lecture was carried out between January 4 and 6, using a sample of more than 1,000 voters in 100 constituencies, excluding Northern Ireland; and the results were published in the paper on January 17. They showed that 54 per cent of British voters would like to see some sort of centre party formed, but that there would not be strong enough support for it to win a general

1 Leader, 'An alternative government', November 23 1979.
2 Leader, 'Still on the downswing', December 31 1979.

election outright. The likeliest outcome would be three parties of similar size, but with Labour and the Conservatives just ahead of the centre party. Paradoxically, 59 per cent thought that it would be a bad thing for the Labour Party to split. As for potential leaders of a centre party, the top choice was Steel, followed by Heath, Shirley Williams and Jenkins, in that order. Compared with the 1972 poll, the desire for a centre party had definitely increased, or at any rate opposition to it had declined from 40 to 32 per cent.

Though Conservatives still appeared to believe, by a small majority, that the existing political system was working properly, Labour as well as Liberal supporters seemed to believe the contrary by majorities of two to one. Overall, almost three to one thought that Labour was moving too far to the left, and almost half of Labour supporters held this view. A small overall majority thought that the Conservatives were moving too far to the right, but only 21 per cent of Conservatives seemed to agree; 75 per cent overall regarded the trade unions as having too much power over Labour; 72 per cent wanted reform of the voting system on proportional lines. There was, indeed, a substantial majority in all three parties for electoral reform.

Commenting on the results in a leader, Rees-Mogg said that they 'conclusively' vindicated Jenkins's basic argument. Yet it was also clear that no split would occur on the left unless the extremists tried to assert a 'hegemony' over the moderates. The possibility, even the desirability, of a centre party involving Labour defectors turned on 'future developments in the two major parties'. If Labour moved back towards the centre the threat of a split would be eliminated. For the Conservatives there was no substitute for success in government. If they proved to be 'even reasonably successful in reducing inflation and in their general handling of the economy,' Mrs. Thatcher would win and would deserve to win. 'From the national point of view' that was 'highly desirable'. But if Labour went further left, and Conservative economic policy failed, 'a centre alternative' would become possible. He ended by stressing that electoral reform and trade union reform were vital, and also interdependent, since effective trade union reform needed 'a permanent majority' to support it, such as only electoral reform could provide.[1]

Two days later there was an op. ed. piece by the social democratic

1 January 17 1980. Front-page story (Emery) '54% would welcome centre party but it would fail in election'. Details of poll on p.3, with picture of Steel. Leader, 'The idea of a centre party'. A further ORC poll was published on January 21, showing that 86 per cent disapproved of flying pickets, while a similar majority favoured strike ballots.

pioneer, Dick Taverne, in which he argued that, 'whatever its merits or demerits', the Thatcher government would probably be even more unpopular in 1984 than the Heath government was in 1974. At the same time the Labour Party would apparently be fighting the next election on a manifesto 'even more left wing and ill designed for our predicament' than ten years previously. It was therefore 'not unreasonable to suppose that an alliance of Liberals and social democrats fighting side by side could make an impact in 1984 far greater than the Liberals alone made in 1974, and the electoral obstacles could be swept aside'.[1] At the end of the month David Owen, who had reacted unfavourably to Jenkins's Dimbleby Lecture, stated his position on general policy in terms that scarcely anticipated his grounds for leaving the Labour Party a year later.[2]

With the break-up of the Central African Federation, Nyasaland and Northern Rhodesia became independent black African states, by agreement, as Malawi and Zambia. But soon afterwards, at the end of 1965, the white minority in Southern Rhodesia elected a government which, under the leadership of Ian Smith, unilaterally declared the country independent as Rhodesia. The Smith regime was almost universally ostracised and soon subjected to mandatory UN sanctions, which, however, proved ineffective for a time because the regime could count on help from South Africa and from the Portuguese in Angola and Mozambique. In 1974 the balance of forces changed when Portugal's long period of dictatorship was brought to an end and the policy of trying to maintain Portuguese colonial rule was abandoned. Two new 'front-line' black African states thus came into being, whose support strengthened the internal black resistance to Smith. At the same time the South African government began to regard the Smith regime as more of a liability than an asset, more especially since the Russians, through their Cuban surrogate, had become involved in Angola. Under growing pressure Smith introduced a constitution which, in effect, entrenched white supremacy behind a facade of black

1 Op. ed. piece, '1984: the year Labour break-away could work', January 19 1980. Taverne had been Democratic Labour MP for Lincoln from March 1973 (when he won a sensational by-election there under his new colours) till September 1974.

2 Op. ed. piece, 'This serious challenge Labour must fight', January 30 1980. Owen said that the case was 'for matching the right with their cry of financial incentive, reduced tax . . . private control and wider shareholding . . . by reawakening interest in decentralized socialism . . . the social wage and cooperative ownership'. No word of electoral reform.

majority rule. The constitution was endorsed in a referendum by the Rhodesian whites, but Britain and the United States made their acceptance of it conditional upon inclusion of the black resistance forces, the Patriotic Front, whose exclusion it had been carefully designed by Smith to ensure. An election was nevertheless held, as a result of which a government nominally led by the African Bishop Muzorewa was returned at the beginning of June. But the Patriotic Front and most of the world treated this government of 'Zimbabwe-Rhodesia' as a puppet regime.

One who was tempted not to do so was the newly elected British prime minister, Margaret Thatcher, whose first inclination was to recognise Muzorewa and lift sanctions. But after one or two indiscreet remarks at the outset she was dissuaded from this course. At the Lusaka conference of Commonwealth leaders in early August she made an excellent impression and accepted responsibility for promoting a viable settlement. Representatives of the Patriotic Front were then invited, together with Muzorewa, Smith and other representatives of the existing regime, to a conference in London, at Lancaster House. By the end of the year a new constitution, drafted by the British government, had been accepted, however grudgingly, by Muzorewa and the Patriotic Front (with Smith dissenting); arrangements for the transition to legal independence put in place; and terms for a ceasefire agreed.

When *The Times* resumed publication, the transitional arrangements were about to be agreed, though the prospects of a ceasefire were still doubtful. There was also much ignorance and misunderstanding of black politics in Zimbabwe-Rhodesia, which the paper's chief correspondent there, Ashford, did his best to remove. Ideological differences should not be taken too seriously, he suggested, since 'the tribal factor [would], regrettably, be of far greater importance to the final outcome'.[1] Within the foreign office there was, throughout the conference, a marked tendency to work for a solution which would legitimise Muzorewa while dividing and marginalising the Patriotic Front. Among the relatively few who could see that Muzorewa was a bad bet, and that the future was bound to lie with the Patriotic Front, Joshua Nkomo was seen as the most likely, as well as the preferable, figure to emerge as winner within the Front. He was the Ndebele (Matabele) leader, who for the purpose of defeating white supremacy had made common cause with Robert Mugabe, the dominant figure in the rival Shona (Mashona) tribe. Mugabe was suspect to the

1 Op. ed. piece, 'The crucial choice before Zimbabwe-Rhodesia', November 23 1979.

government as a Marxist but, unlike Nkomo, had never had any dealings with Smith; and his tribe was the more powerful. Ashford, though less concerned than British officialdom about Mugabe's Marxism, nevertheless underrated him at this stage through failure to perceive his pre-eminence within the Shona tribe.[1]

In the last stages of the negotiation the British government took considerable risks, more especially in deciding to lift sanctions before white power was dismantled. This it did as a gesture, probably unnecessary, to the Conservative right. But success justifies all, and on December 17 the Patriotic Front agreed to the terms of a ceasefire. Its leaders had been under pressure to settle, not least from the frontline states, just as the whites and Muzorewa had been under pressure from South Africa, as well as from the rest of the world. Meanwhile legality was restored through the appointment of a governor. On December 7 Lord Soames accepted this difficult job, and he left for the colony without waiting for the ceasefire to be agreed. Ashford's report of his arrival was the paper's lead story on December 13, with a picture of him inspecting a guard of honour.[2] A few days later another lead story announced the ceasefire agreement.[3]

Zimbabwe-Rhodesia remained in the forefront of the news for the next two or three months, as effect was given to the ceasefire and an election held to determine who would rule the country after independence. The parties composing the Patriotic Front were legitimised and its guerrilla fighters returned from the bush to a tumultuous welcome in Salisbury, soon to be Harare.[4] Soames was an experienced politician, who left a senior post in the cabinet to supervise the transfer of power in Zimbabwe-Rhodesia, and who afterwards returned to the cabinet (though not for long). His prestige was enhanced by his wife, Churchill's daughter Mary, who accompanied him on his mission.[5] Though he shared the government's hostility to Mugabe, and its preference for Muzorewa or, if the Patriotic Front had to win, for Nkomo, he maintained the necessary appearance of impartiality, for which *The Times* praised him: 'British sovereignty is accepted by the rival forces because it is convenient to them both. For this reason Britain could

1 He suggested that even within Mugabe's section of the Shona, the 'most martial' Karangas, there were many cross-currents. (Ibid.)

2 'Arrival of Lord Soames marks end of Rhodesia's rebellion', December 13 1979.

3 'Patriotic Front leaders agree to Rhodesia ceasefire', December 13 1979.

4 The ceasefire agreement was actually signed on December 21, and with its signature the ban on parties was removed (lead story, December 22). The return of the guerrillas was reported in a front-page story from Frederick Cleary, December 27.

5 When they left for Salisbury there was a front-page picture of the foreign secretary, Carrington, embracing Mary Soames at Heathrow.

not, if it wanted, deliberately favour one party, such as the Bishop's, more than another, for then the ceasefire would collapse with dire effects'.[1]

The ceasefire was anyway often near to collapse, and there was much talk of intimidation, particularly by the ZANU (Mugabe) camp. But Soames managed to keep up an outward show of confidence. On February 9 there was a front-page picture of him walking along a colonnade at Government House, Salisbury, smiling and with a jaunty air, though the caption mentioned that he had just been presented with 'a gloomy view of political coercion' by his election supervisors.[2]

Shortly beforehand Smith had further damaged Nkomo's chances by declaring in favour of him, which showed his contempt for his now useless puppet, Muzorewa. The day this lethal endorsement was reported *The Times* commented:

> Mr. Smith has long shown that he thinks Mr. Nkomo would make the best black leader for Zimbabwe . . . [He] negotiated for months to bring Mr. Nkomo in . . . but he could not carry his party with him on any offer to Mr. Nkomo that Mr. Nkomo could have sold to his wing of the Patriotic Front . . . in the end the internal settlement was reached – and a much more far-reaching one under the stress of events.[3]

Yet in New Printing House Square, as in Whitehall, the illusion that Nkomo might win died hard, and the virtual inevitability of Mugabe was not grasped.

In the middle of the month the paper ran an eight-page Special Report on the country, as the moment of decision approached. Between the numerous advertisements there were articles by almost every relevant specialist, including two by Ashford which could not be criticised for blandness. They were entitled 'Partnership dream unlikely to come true' and 'Shona differ crucially from Ndebele'.[4] Voting had already taken place for the twenty seats on the roll reserved for whites, and these had all been won by Smith's Rhodesia Front. But the poll that mattered, for the eighty common-roll seats, was held over two days at the end of the month. The process was supervised by a team of British officials and policed by five hundred British

1 Leader, 'Lord Soames on his high wire', January 15 1980.
2 February 9 1980.
3 Lead story 'Mr. Smith tells whites to campaign for Mr. Nkomo', and leader 'Rhodesia's hazardous election', February 1 1980.
4 February 19 1980.

constables flown in for the occasion. The main contenders were Mugabe's ZANU, Nkomo's ZAPU (Patriotic Front partners campaigning separately), and Muzorewa's UANC. In a poll of nearly 95 per cent ZANU won fifty-seven seats, ZAPU twenty and UANC three. Mugabe was, therefore, the overwhelming winner.

Though Muzorewa denounced the election as 'totally and absolutely unfree and unfair', the official observers gave it a clean bill of health, while Nkomo said that the result must be accepted, and even Smith adjusted his position to the extent of saying that he regarded Mugabe as 'a pragmatist' despite his Marxist 'past'. Mugabe himself insisted, pre-emptively, that the governor had no choice but to send for him, and was indeed asked to form a government which, he promised, would be one of 'national unity'. In a three-column leader the paper gave him a guarded welcome to the ranks of established power, noting his 'considerable if perhaps calculated generosity' on the subject of cooperation with whites.[1] The following day there was another leader on his ideological stance, arguing that his victory was unlikely to turn out to be a victory for Moscow. Smith's assessment of him was endorsed, and it was also pointed out that the Russians had chiefly supported Nkomo. Whites should now act in such a way as to make sure that he did not need the Russians. In the same issue the Liberal leader, Steel, reminded readers that a year before he had predicted that 'true African opinion was 85 per cent. behind Mr. Mugabe and Mr. Nkomo, with Mr. Mugabe clearly the favourite'.[2]

Election year in the United States found President Carter grappling with two major crises in foreign affairs, without receiving as much support from his allies as he felt he had a right to expect. They, on their side, regarded his response to events as often ill-judged, and his tendency to act on his own without consulting them as unacceptable. The two critical areas were Iran and Afghanistan. In the former country the Shah's regime, tottering when *The Times* ceased publication, had duly fallen soon afterwards, to be replaced in February 1979 by an Islamic republic in which Ayatollah Khomeini was all-

1 Lead story from Dan van der Vat 'Mr. Mugabe insists he must be given first chance to govern', March 3 1980. Lead story from Ashford, with five-column headline, and leader 'Mr. Mugabe's Zimbabwe', March 5 1980. The leader ended with an accolade for Carrington and Soames. There was a front-page picture of Mugabe, smiling and with clenched fist.

2 Leader 'Mr. Mugabe's Marxism', and op. ed. piece by Steel 'I told you so from the start', March 6 1980.

powerful. Rabid anti-Americanism was, from the first, a feature of the regime, and this came to a head shortly before *The Times*'s return, when a mob of students stormed the US embassy in Teheran and took sixty-three Americans hostage, demanding the handing-over of the Shah as the price of their release.[1] Thirteen were soon let go, but the remaining fifty were held in captivity with the Ayatollah's full approval. The effect on American public opinion was understandably traumatic, though Carter made the issue of their liberation so much of a crusade that his personal and political credibility came to depend on its fairly early success. He thus became a hostage of a sort himself.

At the end of the year the second crisis arose when the Soviet Union invaded Afghanistan in strength. The motives for this drastic step were doubtless mixed, but it was certainly an act of aggression and was seen by the Americans as a most threatening move by the rival superpower, placing its air forces within an hour's flying time of the Persian Gulf. On the other hand it had the advantage, from the West's point of view, of uniting Muslim opinion against the Russians. Carter condemned the aggression, as did *The Times*:

> What matters is the realization that if the Soviet Union continues to get away with direct and indirect interventions as it has in Africa, Cambodia and Afghanistan, the world will become a more dangerous place and Western influence will inexorably diminish.[2]

Only a clairvoyant could then have foreseen that the move into Afghanistan would, in fact, lead inexorably to the collapse of Soviet communism and the break-up of the Russian empire.

Carter was no clairvoyant, and in any case his preoccupations were more immediate. He tried to mobilise international action against Iran and the Soviet Union, but his efforts were largely fruitless. The UN Security Council was inhibited, on both issues, by use of the Soviet veto, and massive votes in the General Assembly had no practical effect. Even America's friends were, in varying degrees, reluctant to commit themselves to economic sanctions which, they thought, would be damaging to themselves without achieving the desired result. As another form of pressure on the Soviet Union Carter called for a boycott of the Olympic Games, due to be held in Russia in July; but the response was patchy. Canada fell into line with the United States, as did a few other countries which, like Japan, were unlikely to do

---

1 The embassy was stormed on November 4 1979, when the ex-Shah was in New York for medical treatment.

2 Leader, 'Annexation of Afghanistan', January 2 1980.

well in the Games, or which, like Kenya, were dependent on America economically and had authoritarian governments that could give orders to their athletes. In Britain the government wanted to cooperate and, on a free vote, Parliament voted by a large majority in favour of a boycott. But the sporting organisations were free to take their own decisions, and only a few decided to boycott the Games. The issue was much discussed by readers in the columns of *The Times*, and Arthur Koestler was one who challenged the comfortable view that politics could be kept out of sport:

> May I suggest that the BBC shows one of the excellent filmed reports of the 1936 Nazi Olympiad in Berlin for the benefit of those innocents who still maintain that sporting events have no political propaganda value.[1]

The government, however, did not seek to move beyond persuasion in the matter.

The Times took the same view, favouring boycott but insisting that it had to be voluntary. In a leader following a decision by the rugby unions that a British Lions' tour of South Africa should go ahead despite representations from a British government that 'could hardly be labelled left-wing or soft', the paper maintained that in all analogous circumstances the liberty of individuals and bodies should be upheld. If it was 'right that the government, now that persuasion ha[d] failed, should play no active part in stopping the Lions' tour', it was equally right for it 'not to seek to impose a decision on participation in the Olympic Games in Moscow'.[2]

Meanwhile events on the ground were being well covered in the paper. Fisk's reports from Iran during six weeks at the end of 1979 earned him the title International Reporter of the Year, and the citation referred to his 'ability to convey the flavour of life in the country he [was] covering, allied with a deep insight into the political and economic problems'.[3] In the New Year he was transferred to Afghanistan, where these qualities were no less in evidence. As usual, he liked to be part of any action, and when a thousand Afghan men and women invaded a prison in Kabul and released the inmates under

---

1 Lead letter, published March 18 1980.

2 Leader, 'Sport on the altar of politics', January 8 1980. One reader wrote to ask 'Would Mr. Peter Hain [leader of the campaign to boycott South African sport] let us have his views on the Moscow Olympics?' (Letter from Geoffrey H. Jacobs of Portobello Road, London, published January 25 1980.)

3 Reported on front page of the paper, with a picture of Fisk, February 22 1980.

the noses of the Russian guards, he was swept into the prison along with the crowd:

> The most notable phenomenon about this amazing prison break-in . . . were the Islamic chants from the crowd. Several men shouted for an Islamic revolution – something the Russians have long feared in Afghanistan and in their own Muslim republics. Only in the early afternoon did Russian soldiers form a line inside the main gate with rifles lowered . . . When I walked up to the line of troops with a colleague, I said *dosvidanya* (goodbye) and two Soviet soldiers stepped smartly to one side. We walked out of the jail.[1]

He took the risk of riding for hundreds of miles in the company of Russian troops, receiving looks of hatred from the inhabitants of villages which had remained 'virtually unchanged since Genghis Khan'.[2] He was surprised by the freedom he enjoyed 'to roam around a Russian operational area and talk to ordinary Soviet troops'.

> For the West, the door is closing on Afghanistan and the Afghans, whose individual courage and overwhelming hatred of the Russians are two of the most immediately impressive and consistent features of the country.

The BBC was, he reported, far more impartial in its news service than the Voice of America, though Pushtu speakers (the majority) complained that its broadcasts were all in Farsi.[3] He lasted longer in the country than most Western correspondents, but was eventually expelled at the end of February.

There could be no question of using force against the Russians, but Carter had never ruled out the use of it against Iran, and as his hopes of concerted alternative action faded the danger that he would resort to it increased. In early April he broke off diplomatic relations with Iran, and *The Times* warned him not to go further:

> He has two main interests to pursue. One is to get the hostages out; the other is to restore normal relations with Iran. Neither would be served by a naval blockade or other deployment of

1 Front-page story, January 12 1980.
2 Reports, January 18 and 21 1980.
3 Op. ed. piece, 'What is going on in Afghanistan? The real difficulty is getting at the truth', February 11 1980.

force. Military action would more probably endanger the hostages, rally Iranian opinion against the United States, and give the Soviet Union an excuse to come to the aid of the Iranian revolution.[1]

A day or two later the EEC postponed a decision on economic sanctions against Iran, and Emery reported a mood of 'angry frustration in Washington'.[2] The paper noted that Carter was saying that his policy would have to become tougher if his allies would not show more solidarity, and concluded that the alliance would 'have to go some way with him if only to hang onto his coat tails'.[3]

Such action was then taken, or at least promised, as the EEC agreed a plan to stop oil purchases from Iran. But it was too late. On April 24 Carter launched an operation with transport aircraft, helicopters and commando troops, which ended in tragic and ignominious failure. Eight American lives were lost, a helicopter and a transport were destroyed, and the raiders got nowhere near the hostages. The front-page headline two days later, across five columns, was 'President Carter takes full blame for failure of Iran rescue'. The Ayatollah was reported as describing it as 'a stupid act', but apparently would not be retaliating against the hostages.[4] While the operation was in progress, though still not known to the world, the paper reported that opinion in the White House was 'deeply divided' over the use of force.[5] This was shown to be correct when, as a consequence of the raid, the US Secretary of State, Cyrus Vance, resigned. Carter was lucky not to have the hostages' blood on his hands, but the necessity to him of securing their release was greater than ever. So was the difficulty.

---

1 Report, April 8 1980; leader, 'Running out of patience', April 9 1980.
2 Report, April 11 1980; op. ed. piece, April 12 1980.
3 Leader, 'Helping President Carter', April 14 1980.
4 April 26 1980. On the op. ed. page there were pieces by Stanhope ('The insuperable hurdles that doomed the raid'), Emery, and Michael Binyon in Moscow. There was also a three-column leader, 'Lawful but not wise'.
5 Report from David Cross in Washington, April 25 1980.

XXVII

Thatcherism on the home front • 'My money' • Labour rifts grow • Reagan nominated • Golden oldies • Journalists' strike

LIKE W. E. GLADSTONE, Margaret Thatcher came to the premiership with a sense of mission. Hers was not to pacify Ireland (though she tried her hand at that later, without much success), but to save the country from a relentless drift to socialism, which she more or less equated with communism. Egalitarian taxation, public ownership, ubiquitous state control and unfettered trade union power were, she believed, strangling enterprise and depriving individuals of both their liberty and the habit of fending for themselves. She was determined to reverse the trend and to give the country a new direction. At the same time she was committed to conquering inflation exclusively by monetarist methods, and to making drastic cuts in government expenditure. Yet she was enough of a realist to know that she could seldom afford to push her policies to their logical conclusion. Some socialistic institutions, above all the national heath service, were so popular that she was obliged to promise to maintain them. Private arrangements for health and pensions, as for education, might be actively encouraged, but the central bastions of the welfare state could not be touched. What came to be known as Thatcherism was, therefore, a mixture of principle, prejudice and pragmatism, whose consequences were similarly mixed.

When *The Times* returned, her special brand of counter-revolution was already taking shape. Pay, price, dividend and exchange controls had been scrapped. The standard rate of income tax had been cut from 33p to 20p in the pound, and the top rate of taxation from 83p to 60p. To a marked degree the tax burden had been shifted from direct to indirect, in that VAT rates were sharply increased – on some items almost doubled – while the tax on petrol also went up. These taxes on consumption added to the inflationary pressure which was already being boosted by pay awards in the public sector set in train by the Clegg commission, a legacy from the previous government. Against inflation the weapons deployed were the attempted (but ineffective) control of the money supply, the fixing of cash limits, and the raising of interest rates from 12 per cent to 14 per cent. On the eve of *The Times*'s return, November 12 1979, they were raised again to the record level of 17 per cent. Not surprisingly, output was sluggish. The conditions had been created for the disastrous slump in manufacturing industry, and the steep rise in unemployment, that were soon to follow.

At first the Thatcher government's moves to denationalise (the term 'privatise' had not yet come into fashion) were on a fairly modest scale, with only British Aerospace totally, and British Petroleum partially, affected. But the bill to give council tenants the right to buy the freeholds or long leases of their houses or flats, below market value and with the help of 100 per cent local authority mortgages, was certainly of far-reaching significance. The environment secretary who introduced it, Michael Heseltine, was justified in describing it as 'the foundation for one of the most important social revolutions of our time'. The other outstanding achievement of the Thatcher regime, the reform of trade union law and the taming of the unions, was undertaken more cautiously and gradually. James Prior, who had been shadow employment secretary before the election, was appointed to the substantive post, though many of the prime minister's supporters on the radical right would have liked it to go to somebody less 'wet' (in the jargon of the day). At heart she sympathised with them, but her resolve to 'get it right' this time and not to suffer the fate of Heath prevailed over her aggressive instincts. Prior had experience of industry and genuinely disliked industrial conflict. As we have seen, he had thought the shock tactics employed by Times Newspapers were mistaken, and he made sure that his own approach was different.

Before preparing a bill he submitted a consultative document to the TUC and the CBI, which gave the former the opportunity to put itself in the wrong by rejecting out of hand proposals that seemed moderate and reasonable to most people, including most rank-and-file trade unionists. His bill, introduced nine months after the formation of the government, provided for strict limits on secondary picketing, for modifying without abolishing the closed shop, and for the promotion of secret ballots before strikes and in the election of officers. These ballots were to be assisted by state aid. While trade union leaders condemned the bill as a violation of sacred union rights, it was attacked from the opposite quarter as being too weak.

Rees-Mogg joined in the attack with a three-column leader, which began: 'The trouble with Mr. Prior – or is it, perhaps, his strength? – is that he does not have a conceptual mind'. (The parenthetical question was very much to the point, since conceptual minds are more often than not a liability in politics.) The leader drew extensively on *The Times*'s recent troubles, and called for amendments to the bill to deal 'effectively with at least some aspects of the problems of excessive trade union power'. Then in the next session the unions should be forced to be more democratic. A piece by Emery on the op. ed. page had a different tone, referring to 'the spasm of impotent rage that ha[d] convulsed Conservatives in and out of politics . . . over the Government's inability instantly and drastically to change trade union law'.[1] But opinion polls showed strong public support for Prior's approach, and later in the year he scored a hit even at the party conference when he emphasised the need to achieve 'a harmony of wills' with trade union members.

He was, of course, assisted in his task by the effects of a world recession which began in the spring of 1980: effects that were aggravated by government policy. Mass unemployment naturally weakens trade unions, and in 1980 the figure of unemployed climbed to levels that would have been unacceptable to Rees-Mogg and other oracles of *bien pensant* opinion ten years before, or less. By the end of April it had reached nearly 1,400,000; by the end of the year it was well over 2 million. A significant part of the unemployment had, no doubt, previously been 'concealed' in overmanned industries, and represented a healthy process of 'shake-out'. But much of it was due to an adverse economic climate gratuitously made more adverse by the doctrinaire application of monetarism, which ruined many firms that were neither overmanned nor inefficient. The measures were held to be justified as the only way of fighting inflation (itself to some extent government-induced), which was indeed rising to alarming levels; 18.4 per cent in March, 19.8 per cent in April, and 21.9 per cent – the peak figure – in May. With perverse symmetry the Thatcher government followed the Heath government's error of inflating during a boom by deflating during a slump.

Rees-Mogg threw *The Times* solidly behind the doctrine that there was no alternative (TINA). When the chancellor of the exchequer, Sir Geoffrey Howe, introduced his second budget in March 1980, the editor's only criticism was that his policy to date might not have been quite tough enough. The day after the budget speech the op. ed. page carried an extract from a speech to the Monday Club by Hayek, one of the leading prophets of Thatcherism, in which he took an 'even

1 Leader 'We have bad laws and we must put them right' and op. ed. piece 'Can Mr. Prior win a third union war?' February 9 1980.

more radical position' than Friedman on inflation. In his leader on the budget Rees-Mogg wrote:

> The Chancellor has committed himself to a long and painful reduction of inflation which will unfortunately be accompanied by a period of recession and high unemployment. There were three policy options: to go on spending, to go on borrowing, and to go on inflating; to follow the line the Chancellor has taken of a gradual and painful approach to price stability; or to follow the course Professor Hayek advocated . . . and take the strain of a violent attack on inflation – going for a knock-out. In retrospect, a more Hayekian approach last year might have been preferable, but this year's middle course Budget does seem both to recognize the reality of the political situation and to offer a coherent but gradualist policy. Perhaps a rather tougher Budget would have been rather quicker. The Conservative Party will need both skill and resolution to maintain the support of this moderately painful policy for a more than moderately long time.[1]

At the beginning of 1980 a dispute over pay in the largely nationalised steel industry enabled the government to demonstrate its non-interventionist attitude in such matters. The cost was heavy to an industry anyway doomed to contract by inexorable market forces, and the general economy suffered, too. But the government felt that it had won a moral victory by standing aside for three months, and by not settling the dispute, even at the end of that time, over 'beer and sandwiches' at 10 Downing Street. A contingent victory of greater significance was an overwhelming vote by the South Wales miners to reject a call from their union's executive to strike in support of the steelworkers.

A portent for the future was the announcement, soon after the steel strike, that the outgoing chairman of the British Steel Corporation, Sir Charles Villiers, would be succeeded by Ian MacGregor. The choice was intensely controversial, not only because some chauvinists held it against MacGregor that, although born a Scotsman, he had spent most of his working life in America and was a naturalised American; but above all because of the financial terms of his appointment. His

1 Op. ed. piece 'How to deal with inflation', and leader '5 per cent inflation by 1985', March 27 1980. Two days later there was a letter from Hayek complaining about the editor's use of the term deflation when what was meant was the reduction of inflation (March 29): ironically, since Rees-Mogg had earlier gone to the trouble of circularising the entire editorial staff on this very point (see p.434 above).

existing employers, Lazard Frères, were to be paid a large sum as compensation for the loss of his services, and the sum would be spread over three years, varying upwards according to the performance of BSC under his direction. There was a big row in Parliament, and Emery reported 'strong indications' that the terms of the deal had not been put to the full cabinet, some of whose members 'were worried at the public reaction to the news'. *The Times*, while welcoming the appointment itself, condemned the terms as 'a major error of judgment'. The analogy with a footballer's transfer fee, which the industry secretary, Joseph, had drawn in the House of Commons, was 'distasteful'. The sum to be paid to Lazard Frères was 'uncomfortably high', and in any case it should not increase on the basis of MacGregor's performance at BSC. MacGregor had been given 'the worst possible start'.[1]

The same issue of the paper reported sweeping Labour gains in the district council elections. But the government still had plenty of time in hand, and as Mrs Thatcher passed the first anniversary of her premiership there was no serious threat to her authority. The occasion was marked by a 'profile' of her in the paper; really an interview in which she did most of the talking. Her final remark was revealing in more ways than one:

> My pleasure reading ordinarily is the John le Carré kind of thing, which I love. Of course I do read biography and some philosophy and anything in connexion with the home. I love going through the *House & Garden* magazines, seeing what other people are doing who have the time and money [*sic*] to do it.[2]

Soon afterwards the weakness of trade union opposition to her was made pathetically obvious when a 'day of action' organised by the TUC turned out to be largely a flop.[3] She was in no imminent danger of having the leisure to cultivate her garden.

---

1 Lead story 'Government "buys" a new chief for BSC from America', and leader 'What's good for Lazard Frères', May 2 1980. The leader was written by Stephenson.
2 'The Times profile', by Brian Connell, May 5 1980.
3 Front-page story from Craig Seton 'Patchy response by workers to TUC call for day of action', May 15 1980. In anticipation, Routledge had said that it could not be both a flop and a threat to society, but did not commit himself as to which it would be (op. ed. piece, May 13).

On the international stage the impact of Mrs. Thatcher's personality was most acutely felt in the long wrangle over Britain's net contribution to the EEC budget. No reasonable person could deny that the system was working unfairly from Britain's point of view. Because the United Kingdom imported more than other member-states from outside the Community, the amount levied on customs duties for EEC purposes, in addition to the fixed percentage of VAT receipts also earmarked for Europe, was relatively higher for Britain, while the relatively small size of its agriculture meant that it received only a modest proportion of the 70 per cent of EEC resources devoted to agricultural support. Unless the system was changed the absurd position would soon be reached that Britain, though one of the least affluent members of the Community, would be paying more than West Germany, the richest. Any government, any prime minister, would have been bound to fight for a change; Mrs Thatcher did so in her own disconcerting style, and with peculiar relish. Though committed to British membership of the Community, her instincts were Anglo-Saxon and Atlanticist rather than Continental. Moreover, it suited her politically to have an issue on which she could play to the anti-European gallery in her own party and in the country.

At her first European Council meeting, at Strasbourg in June 1979, she forced her fellow leaders to admit that Britain might have genuine cause for complaint, and the matter was adjourned for further consideration at the next meeting in November, in the light of a report that the commission was instructed to prepare meanwhile. Roy Jenkins, still president of the commission, was convinced that change was necessary, for the Community's sake no less than for his own country's. Some of his colleagues, and their governments, however, suspected him of partiality, and his efforts to promote a reasonable settlement involved him in difficulties with them as well as with Mrs. Thatcher. His chief problem in dealing with her was that, despite the 'nerve and determination' of her advocacy, she 'did not begin to understand the case against her', or 'to appreciate the importance of not boring the judge and jury'.[1] She had already succeeded in annoying the German chancellor, Schmidt, whose cooperation was essential if she was to overcome the principal opposition Britain faced, which was from the French.

Shortly before the November Council meeting she was in Paris for two days of talks with the French president, Giscard d'Estaing. Hargrove reported that, when the talks ended, the Elysée spokesman

1 Jenkins, op. cit., p.498.

said they had been 'frank and cordial', but he said it with 'a broad smile' and his words 'were greeted with equally broad smiles by French journalists'.[1] The Council meeting was held in Dublin, the six-monthly presidency having passed from France to Ireland. On the eve of the meeting *The Times* urged her to press Britain's case with patience and circumspection:

> The proper course is to try reasoned arguments coupled with proposals for constructive reform, and then, if this fails, to move cautiously towards a gradual and flexible building up of pressures.[2]

But Mrs Thatcher was in no mood for such old-world diplomacy. At the Dublin summit she subjected her Continental partners to a relentless barrage, culminating at a dinner when she kept them 'sitting over the table for more than four hours, for the greater part of which she talked without pause, but not without repetition'.[3] Her insistent refrain was that she must have 'her money' back, and she defined the required sum as £1,000 million a year. Since the others were not willing to concede more than £350 million, the matter had to be adjourned again. While agreeing, reluctantly, to discuss it on the next occasion in a spirit of compromise, for the benefit of her home audience she said publicly that she was giving the Community one more chance. She was not afraid, she said, to 'precipitate a crisis', though she 'ruled out withdrawal from the EEC'. *The Times* basically supported her at this point, while reminding her that she needed allies, and while criticising her for not backing the European Parliament in its attempt to cut farm spending.[4]

Whether or not the memory of her performance in Dublin acted as a deterrent to her partners, influencing them to do whatever might be necessary to avoid another such experience, the terms offered to her in Luxembourg five months later were certainly a great improvement. In the view of Jenkins and most of her other advisers they were the best she could hope to obtain. Hornsby reported that the dispute was 'near solution', and Wood wrote that compromise was 'in the air at Luxembourg'.[5] But they were wrong; Mrs Thatcher turned the new terms down. The other leaders were 'stunned', and Hargrove quoted

---

1 Front-page report, 'M. Giscard is shown the Thatcher steel', November 20 1979.
2 Leader, 'The battle of Dublin', November 28 1979.
3 Jenkins, op. cit., p.498. Schmidt pretended to go to sleep during the tirade.
4 Lead story from Michael Hornsby and Peter Newman, 'Mrs. Thatcher ready for crisis action after rebuff by EEC'. Leader, 'Everyone lost at Dublin'. December 1 1979.
5 April 28 1980.

a French official comment that Britain was 'now isolated from the Continent'. *The Times* regarded her behaviour as indefensible, more especially when the Western alliance was in such trouble elsewhere (with the Russians in Afghanistan and Carter's disastrous raid on Iran having just occurred):

> Despite the little England attitudes struck in the House of Commons – which make Britain seem so ludicrously insular and chauvinist – it is Mrs. Thatcher who has made the mistake of rejecting large concessions and sending Chancellor Schmidt and President Giscard home angry and alienated. To do this with the world in its present state shows lack of judgment, a failure to put first things first. Sometimes it is wise to be tough – but it is never wise to quarrel with your friends in the crisis hour which calls for unity.[1]

After desperate efforts by the EEC foreign ministers and Jenkins a revised package was negotiated over the next four weeks and, at the end of May, agreed. Reporting it, Hornsby noted that in 1980 alone Britain would now do less well than under the previous offer, but would be £60 million better off in 1980 and 1981 taken together. The paper's comment was, in the circumstances, surprisingly charitable. The new agreement was 'clearly better for Britain than the Luxembourg package . . . [but] not necessarily so much better that it wholly vindicate[d] what she did'. She had scored 'a great success', though it fell 'far short of meeting her original demand'.[2] Jenkins regarded her obduracy in Luxembourg as entirely without justification:

> Nothing worthwhile was gained, but the eight lost their faith in Tory Europeanism, and Mrs. Thatcher became an instinctive Euro-basher . . . It was an appalling price to pay for the narrow difference, almost undiscoverable by the naked eye, between the settlement which was rejected at the end of April and that which Carrington skilfully but nervously accepted at the end of May.[3]

1 Reports from Hornsby and Hargrove, and leader 'Disunity in crisis', April 30 1980.
2 Lead story 'Britain's EEC budget payments agreed by foreign ministers', and leader 'The Community's victory', May 31 1980. In an op. ed. piece earlier in May Hornsby argued that Mrs Thatcher was on balance 'right to hold out for better terms in Luxembourg. Since she would be obliged to concede a 5 per cent increase in EEC farm prices,' she ought at least to get a better deal on budget payments'. ('EEC budget: Mrs Thatcher was right to hold out', May 8). She did indeed give way on farm prices (report, May 30), but the question remains: was the eventual gain on budget payments remotely large enough to justify the waste of time and loss of goodwill?
3 Jenkins, op. cit., p.508.

Mrs Thatcher, however, was thoroughly pleased with herself after Luxembourg. 'Exulting in the claim that her EEC tactics made her partners say that "I'm a she-de-Gaulle", [she] boasted . . . that one main achievement of her first year in government was that "Britain really does count on the world scene"'.[1] Nearly a decade was to pass before her personal style of diplomacy, or non-diplomacy, in Europe was to contribute to her downfall.

At the end of May the Labour Party held a special one-day conference at Wembley, to consider a policy statement, *Peace, Jobs and Freedom*, on which it was hoped the party could unite. But it was a fudge which, in fact, satisfied nobody. On the eve of the conference one right-wing Labour MP, Tom Ellis, told *The Times* that the document was 'a load of rubbish', if only because the objectives set out in it were incompatible with Britain's long-term membership of the European Community.[2] At the conference itself Callaghan introduced the document in a speech which combined an attack on the Thatcher government with reassertion of the need for an incomes policy. Benn, however, in his winding-up speech at the end of the day, 'virtually repudiated' everything that Callaghan had said in the morning. He stirred the delegates to great enthusiasm by calling for renationalisation without compensation, expansion of the public sector, and abolition of the House of Lords. But the conference was imperfectly representative even of active members of the party, because many moderates stayed away. According to *The Times*, the conference increased the likelihood that the party would be 'saddled with unrealistic or irresponsible policies', and was particularly disturbing in the field of foreign affairs and defence, since it seemed to indicate that unilateralism would 'once again take a central place in Labour's internal debate'.[3]

The question of the party leadership now came to the fore. A few days after Wembley Benn further dramatised his challenge to Callaghan by saying that the unions must not be 'shackled again' by an incomes policy. There was much talk at this time of Callaghan being a lame-duck leader, and since it seemed unlikely that he would lead the party into the next election, *The Times* took the view that he

---

1 Interview on the Jimmy Young Show, BBC Radio 2, reported by Emery, May 1 1980.

2 Front-page story, 'Disaffected right will stay away from Labour conference', May 31 1980.

3 Front-page story (Emery) 'Mr. Benn steps up the pressure on Labour's moderates'; full report of conference, p.5; leader, 'Labour refights the past'. June 2 1980.

should go before the end of the year. Delay only increased the uncertainty about his successor, and his early retirement would give 'the most appropriate candidate', Healey, the best chance of succeeding him. To blight Healey's chances would be 'unforgivable'. The only circumstance in which Callaghan would be right to stay on would be 'if the party conference in October were to vote in favour of changing the system of electing the leader'. But if the conference confirmed the existing system, election by Labour MPs, 'it would be best for Mr. Callaghan to go in November'.[1]

Healey himself was so confident of being chosen as the next leader that he conveyed to Jenkins (via Shirley Williams) an invitation to return to British politics as foreign secretary in his government. But Jenkins, whose term as president of the European commission was due to expire in the New Year, had other ideas. He certainly intended to return to British politics, but the thought of serving as foreign secretary under Healey did not appeal to him. In any case, he had despaired of the Labour Party, and was increasingly attracted by the idea of a new political force uniting Labour moderates, the Liberal Party, and many who were at present alienated from politics. On June 9 he made another speech in London, developing the argument of his Dimbleby lecture in November. This time he spoke at a lunch of the parliamentary press gallery, attended mainly by lobby journalists but also by a few politicians, including Neil Kinnock. The most striking feature of the speech was a word-picture of the kind that Jenkins often produced, showing how truly he belonged to the tradition of Welsh oratory, despite his Balliol overlay. He likened the new party that he was prefiguring to an experimental plane which might 'finish up a few fields from the end of the runway' or 'soar into the sky'. If the latter, it might go 'further and more quickly' than many then imagined, 'for it would carry with it great and now untapped reserves of political energy and commitment'.

The speech had a mixed reception, even the *Guardian* commenting on it in discouraging terms, though the *Financial Times* was favourable. *The Times* led with the speech next day, Hatfield saying that it 'left little room for doubt' that Jenkins would 'lead a campaign for a realignment in British politics' when his time in Brussels was up. Healey's and Shirley Williams's reactions to the speech were reported, and a partial text of it appeared, with a picture of Jenkins, on page 2. A leader on it was friendly, as was to be expected, but also circumspect:

1 Lead story (Emery) 'Struggle for Labour leadership erupts', reporting speech by Benn at Eastbourne. Leader, 'When should Mr. Callaghan go?' June 4 1980.

'So Mr. Jenkins is poised on the brink of an initiative of great boldness, but which depends for its success on conditions which still remain improbable'.[1]

Though there was still a more or less moderate majority among Labour MPs, the National Executive (NEC) was dominated by the left. In July this body published its own statement of party policy, which included such items as reform of the Common Agricultural Policy as the price of Britain's remaining a member of the European Community, the removal of Polaris bases and refusal to produce a new generation of British nuclear weapons, abolition of the House of Lords, repeal of the Prior Act 'in its entirety', public ownership extended to banking, insurance and road haulage, renationalisation without compensation of 'the assets and activities of our public sector industries sold off by the Tories', and an annual progressive personal wealth tax for those with more than £125,000, rising to a top rate of 5 per cent: all to be achieved within the lifetime of a parliament. Reporting this manifesto on the front page, Clark said that while the party leaders agreed with 'parts of it', and also had to acknowledge that 'most of the proposals ha[d] at some time been approved by Labour Party conferences', they nevertheless believed that in its present form it could only be 'an electoral handicap'.[2] They could not prevent its publication, but Callaghan and, significantly, Foot managed to stop Benn and the NEC majority holding a press conference to launch it.

A striking example of anticipatory journalism appeared in the paper at the end of July. This was a substantial profile of Kinnock by Caroline Moorehead. At the time Kinnock was the chief opposition spokesman on education, and he had earlier served briefly as PPS to Foot. He was a unilateralist and a director of Tribune, and had been a member of the NEC since 1978. According to Moorehead, there were few MPs on either side who did not 'at least speculate about his role as a possible future leader of the Labour Party', though they asked themselves, 'somewhat perplexed, just why . . . a thirty-seven-year-old Welshman with great charm, but almost nothing in the way of a past, ha[d] suddenly come to look so promising'. In education debates he had 'not proved a master of detail', and there was 'a certain lack of substance in his speeches'. Yet he was 'canny', having refused to say

1 Lead story 'Labour rift too deep to be bridged, says Mr. Jenkins', and leader 'Home thoughts from Brussels', June 10 1980. Shirley Williams, out of Parliament since the previous election, had condemned the idea of a centre party in a broadcast shortly before Jenkins's speech.

2 Front-page story, 'Manifesto of the Left disowned by leaders', June 11 1980.

that all Tory cuts would be restored, or that parents should be forbidden to contribute. Even those who doubted his ability 'to engage in the drudgery of routine politics', felt 'real affection for him'.

The profile referred to his informality, and his 'unmalicious mimicry'; also to the qualities of his 'widely admired' wife, Glenys, and the priority he gave to family life. He was generous, and did not go in for gossip. Politically, there was just one respect in which he had not run true to form. The passion with which he had opposed Welsh devolution had surprised people. 'Neither the emotion he showed, nor the stand he took, was entirely in keeping with the package of views he share[d] with fellow members of the Tribune group'. He had incurred unpopularity for this, but the result had been 'something of a personal triumph'.

When asked about his future, he said: 'I want to retire at fifty. I want to play cricket in summer, geriatric football in winter, and [to] sing in the choir'. He had an idea of writing novels, 'the most direct and painless way of telling the truth for politicians'.[1] Few could then have imagined that he would indeed retire from the predicted office at the age of fifty, having led the party to defeat in two elections.

In November 1979 Ronald Reagan, who had come close to being the Republican candidate for president in 1976, announced that he was in the running for nomination in 1980. At a dinner in New York observers noted 'less stridency' in his political tone than during earlier campaigns, which seemed 'to reflect a conscious effort by his staff to give him a more moderate image and attract more of the Republican middle ground'. He said that his aim was 'not to run against any of his Republican colleagues, but to be selected for his principles'. This comment, together with his 'advanced age' (sixty-eight), suggested to *The Times*'s correspondent that he 'might not have the stamina for a protracted Presidential campaign'.[2]

Rees-Mogg had no prejudice in favour of Reagan. In his letter to his son, published in 1966, he had said that Europe was going the way of America, that America was going the way of California, and that California was going 'to the devil and Mr. Reagan'.[3] (Reagan was elected governor of California soon after Rees-Mogg became editor, and served two terms.) A few months later, when Reagan was doing

1 The Times profile, 'Golden boy with a silver tongue', July 28 1980.
2 Report from David Cross in Washington, November 15 1979.
3 See p.17 above.

well in the primaries, the editor reflected on presidential prospects from the vantage-point of Berkeley. He had not 'heard a single enthusiastic endorsement' of Carter, though he had 'many reluctant supporters'. The difficulty was 'to find a Republican of quality'. Some had retired from the race; others had left it too late. That left Reagan and George Bush. The Californian 'intellectual community' did not 'particularly dislike' Reagan. Rees-Mogg had even met a Democrat who said he would rather vote for Reagan than for Carter. Yet Reagan was 'regarded as unqualified and inadequate for the Presidency'. Bush was 'in some ways the most plausible candidate in intellectual terms', though the intellectual community was 'not easy about him', either. His 'energetic manner' seemed to be 'artificially imposed on a dry personality, an introvert pretending to be an extrovert', who looked 'more like somebody else's Secretary of State than his own President'. The academics with whom Rees-Mogg was consorting were 'ready to back' any first-rate man who might show up, though none was yet in sight.[1]

Before leaving the United States he had become reconciled to the idea of a Reagan presidency. From Chicago he wrote: 'I am not afraid of Mr. Reagan. He seems a perfectly normal kind of conservative to me'. The election would probably turn on whether people were 'more angry at the Carter record or afraid of the Reagan image'.[2] In May, when it was virtually certain that Reagan would win the nomination, Brogan gave readers of *The Times* an assessment of him less full and penetrating than Emery's of Carter four years previously, but nevertheless interesting. Reagan was 'wedded to the idea that the panacea for inflation, the federal deficit and declining productivity is a huge tax cut'. In California he was 'remembered with some affection and approval, even by people who opposed him. He chose competent people, usually businessmen, to run the departments . . . and left them alone. He uttered terrible threats against the universities, but in fact quickly came to an understanding with them.' He believed that the 1980s could be a 'replay of the 1920s or, better still, of the Truman years when America was overwhelmingly rich and universally respected'. That was his appeal, and his success would be 'a measure of American nostalgia'.[3]

In Truman's day, and indeed more recently, Reagan had been a Democrat. According to his own testimony he did not formally leave

1 Signed op. ed. piece from W.R.-M., March 8 1980.
2 Ditto, March 18 1980.
3 Foreign report from Brogan, p.10, May 23 1980

the Democratic Party until 1962, though he voted for Eisenhower in 1952 and 1956.[1] Heren found him rather reminiscent of Eisenhower:

> Even his closest associates privately admit that he is an unusual candidate. They say that he does not have fire in his belly, but only wants to do right. That was an apt description of President Eisenhower, upon whom Mr. Reagan is said to model himself . . . one should not dismiss him because he was an actor. There are many intelligent actors, and many more unintelligent politicians who are ham actors. President Eisenhower also delegated authority in order to play golf, if not nap, but he was also the Supreme Allied Commander.[2]

More to the point, he was a successful president.

In mid-July Reagan was nominated, announcing that his running-mate would be Bush. *The Times* showed at once that it preferred him to Carter:

> One of Mr. Carter's greatest weaknesses has been his inability to put together and run an efficient collective operation. There are good reasons for hoping that Mr. Reagan would do much better.

He was unlikely to be either 'the great President that his more ardent supporters believe[d]' or 'the extremist in the White House that both his opponents and much overseas comment portray[ed]'.[3] Evidently America would not be going to the devil with him as the editor had once thought California would.

In July the paper's front page carried a large picture of two very healthy-looking veterans. The caption read:

> A couple with 80 years married life behind them, Mr. John Orton, aged 104, and his wife Harriet, aged 102, celebrate their anniversary today. They are devout Methodists and credit their happiness to 'hard work, give and take, and a little help from the Lord', and Mrs. Orton added: 'We do not drink, smoke or swear'. The couple, who live in Great Gidding, Cambridgeshire, were married in Great Casterton, Rutland. Mr. Orton, who worked a 16-hour

1 Ronald Reagan, op. cit., pp.133–4.
2 Op. ed. piece, 'Do the Americans see Mr. Reagan as another Ike?' July 5 1980.
3 Leader, 'A moderate extremist' (Geoffrey Smith), July 17 1980.

> day as a farmer, added: 'We did not have time to quarrel. It was all work in those days'.[1]

Shortly after the Ortons were married in 1900 a girl was born whose eightieth birthday naturally commanded more space in the paper. Queen Elizabeth the Queen Mother's actual birthday was August 4, but for many days preceding it there were celebratory events to be reported, among which a service at St Paul's on July 15 was outstanding. The lead story describing it the following day was written with warmth, but also with wit, by Berthoud. He was far less definite about the number of people witnessing the procession to St Paul's than *The Times* had been on the occasion of the Queen's silver jubilee, leaving himself an exceptionally wide margin of error. 'Between a quarter of a million and two million people . . . turned up to provide a human corridor of affection as . . . [the Queen Mother] drove in a 1902 state landau from Buckingham Palace to St. Paul's Cathedral'. Along the Mall the crowds stood ten deep. Inside the cathedral about 2,700 invited guests, who had to be seated an hour before the Queen Mother arrived, talked in a 'relaxed atmosphere . . . reminiscent perhaps of a cross between the royal enclosure at Ascot and a seated, tea-less garden party'.[2]

On the birthday itself the paper reported that the Queen Mother would be spending the whole day at Clarence House until the evening, when the Royal Ballet would be giving her 'a special treat' in the form of the world première of Sir Frederick Ashton's ballet *Rhapsody*, created for, and danced by, the Russian Mikhail Baryshnikov. Meanwhile bonfires and beacons would blaze along the south coast in honour of her in her capacity as lord warden of the Cinque Ports. In his leader to mark the occasion Rees-Mogg observed that royal personages, to do their job successfully, normally needed to be trained for it from birth. Yet it was the virtue of the Queen Mother that she 'came from outside', the first queen consort since Catherine Parr not to have been of royal provenance. The way she had brought up her children was praised, but above all the singular charm of her personality was emphasised.

> Making royalty human is what [she] has achieved . . . who else

1 July 9 1980.
2 Lead story, 'London's day of affection for Queen Mother', July 16 1980. There was also a front-page picture of the Queen Mother with her two daughters on the balcony of Buckingham Palace, and the whole of p.9 was devoted to the occasion, with more pictures.

> could plant the third or fourth thousandth tree of a lifetime of planting trees, and still leave on the Lady Mayoress the impression of really being pleased to meet her? What is more, of whom else would that impression be true?

This was indeed 'one of the memorable birthdays of the British nation'.[1]

If there were any on the management side of Times Newspapers, or on the editorial side, for that matter, who thought that the agreement to resume publication in November 1979 would usher in a period of harmony and prosperity, they were soon undeceived. The old troubles persisted, particularly on the *Sunday Times*. Week after week the paper failed to achieve its full run or to be distributed on time. At the April 1980 board meeting the directors noted that 'the one single and acute problem [was] the continuing failure to complete the *Sunday Times* print run'. The previous weekend alone 420,000 copies had been lost. The cause was 'not really sabotage, but a general malaise and a lack of cooperation'. Production of *The Times* was not as good as could be wished, though there at least full runs were being achieved; and *The Times*'s sale figure was better than expected, 326,000 in March (compared with an average of under 296,000 during the eleven months before the stoppage).[2] The price had, however, been held at an unrealistic level until late March, when it was raised from 15p to 20p. After the price increase the sale figure began to decline; two months later it was down to 312,000, and the eventual average for 1980 was only a little higher than for 1978.

In any case the economics of the company depended above all on the *Sunday Times*, whose poor showing counteracted any pleasure that might have been derived from the relatively satisfactory performance of *The Times* during the early part of the year. Advertisers and

---

1 Front-page story and leader 'A grandmother's 80th birthday', August 4 1980. The Queen Mother was said to 'get up at 7.30 a.m. and read all the papers thoroughly'. The same was not, apparently, true of all members of her family. When Clark met the Duke of Edinburgh at a Buckingham Palace garden party during the stoppage, and ventured to say that he assumed the Duke was missing *The Times*, the Duke replied that he certainly was not missing it because he never read it.

2 TNL board minutes, April 28 1980. Writing later, Hamilton did accuse the unions of sabotage. 'One by one, every agreement made in getting a resumption of work was broken or repudiated; production sabotage resumed with the same irresponsibility, even anarchic fervour, as before. At one point the head printer had to write to the combined chapels demanding an apology for deliberate defiance of his authority, as well as intoxication and abuse to his staff'. (Hamilton, op. cit., pp.175–6).

wholesalers were becoming 'restive and disenchanted' because of the bad record of production and distribution on the *Sunday Times*.[1] There was no question of the company's being profitable; on top of the enormous cost of the stoppage, a further heavy loss was to be expected during the current year.

The management team which had led the company into and through the stoppage – at the prompting, certainly, of higher authority – was still in place, and hoping against all the evidence to make a success of the deal, or deals, supposedly struck the previous November. Every effort was made to foster a spirit of cooperation and togetherness. In May a conference was held at Gatwick Park, at which FoCs, managers and editorial staff discussed the future in a convivial atmosphere, under the chairmanship of Lord McCarthy, who had begun his career as an industrial relations 'expert' with a trade union scholarship to Ruskin College, Oxford. The conference, at which in any case not all chapels were represented, achieved little beyond conviviality. It was divided into syndicates; Heren recalled that his 'produced very little', and he 'only acquired a hangover'.[2] According to Hamilton: 'Impassioned speeches were made about a better, even a glorious future. But the fine words belied an ever-deteriorating situation at Gray's Inn Road'.[3]

At the end of June the structure of business control was drastically changed. A new holding company, Times Newspapers Holdings Limited (TNHL), was formed, of which Hamilton was to be chairman while retaining the (largely honorific) post of editor-in-chief, and Hussey was to be vice-chairman. At the same time it was announced that 'the management of the business' would be 'placed in the hands of a new board of Times Newspapers composed of full-time executives', with two executive committees, one for the *Sunday Times*, the other for *The Times* and supplements. The new chairman of TNL was to be James Evans, who would keep his existing post of joint managing director of Thomson British Holdings. Nisbet-Smith was promoted from general manager to managing director of TNL.[4]

Evans was a barrister turned solicitor, who was legal adviser to the *Sunday Times* in Kemsley's time, and then acted in the same capacity for both papers under Roy Thomson. For several years he was diverted to dealing with the Thomson oil concession, but was brought on to

1 Same TNL board meeting as above.
2 Heren, op. cit., p.251.
3 Hamilton, op. cit., p.176.
4 Report in the paper, June 25 1980.

the boards of British Thomson Holdings and Times Newspapers just before the stoppage. Obviously his advancement, and the rustication of Hamilton and Hussey, meant that in future there would be less journalistic sentiment in the conduct of the company's business. Evans did not come in with an express remit to get rid of the papers, but he was the sort of cool, detached professional under whom such a step could more easily be taken, if necessary. Meanwhile the combination of him as chairman and Nisbet-Smith as managing director signalled an end to Gatwick Park-style make-believe.

Before long trouble occurred on *The Times*, and in a surprising quarter. At the board meeting in July consideration was given to a wage claim from the paper's journalists. Before the stoppage their pay had fallen behind that of other Fleet Street journalists, but at the time of republication they had been given increases of between 30 and 40 per cent. They were now as well paid as their equivalents on the *Daily Telegraph* and better paid than those on the *Guardian*. Nevertheless the NUJ chapel put in a claim which, Rees-Mogg said, would 'effectively add 32 per cent. to the wage bill'.[1] Management said that 18 per cent was as much as it could afford to pay, and probably most members of the chapel would, in a secret ballot, have accepted this. But a minority of militants, led by Ecclestone, succeeded in mounting a challenge whose consequences were incalculable.

In April there was an exchange between Ecclestone and Rees-Mogg which showed, on both sides, a touchingly eirenic spirit. Ecclestone thanked the editor and TNL for the time off allowed him during the past year to attend to NUJ business. He asked if he could take up a Churchill Trust fellowship for a month in the autumn to study the effects of new technology in America. Rees-Mogg replied:

> Dear Jacob,
>
> Thank you very much for your letter. *I think you had an excellent year of office and have been very impressed by the way you carried it through.* Not an easy year.
>
> Naturally I should be delighted for you to take up the Churchill Trust Fellowship . . .
>
> With all best wishes,
>
> Yours ever
>
> William Rees-Mogg.[2]

---

1 TNL board minutes, July 17 1980. At the same meeting it was noted that *The Times*'s sales trend had turned adverse, the current estimated figure being 298,000.
2 Ecclestone to W.R.-M., April 29 1980; W.R.-M. to Ecclestone, April 30 1980. (Author's italics.)

Despite the 'Jacob' rather than 'Jake', this was surely a remarkable letter for the editor to have written in view of Ecclestone's activities during the previous year, and more especially his attitude to the Frankfurt experiment. But any hope that it might have helped to create a new mood of mellowness was soon dashed.

Ecclestone's deputy as FoC was Geraldine Norman, whose political philosophy was very different from his. During his absence on holiday she succeeded in having the pay claim referred to arbitration, with Professor J. R. Crossley of Leeds University as the arbitrator. She hoped, perhaps rather naïvely, that the management's arguments would thus receive independent support, or that some fudge would be produced that would end the dispute. On August 13 Crossley's verdict was delivered. Working on the principle that the journalists should be paid the rate for the job, as he saw it, rather than what the company's financial state might justify, he recommended an increase of 21 per cent. The company was not obliged to accept this recommendation. Mandatory arbitration had earlier been ruled out, on Ecclestone's initiative. Nevertheless Ecclestone, now returned, insisted that the company was morally obliged to pay 21 per cent, while the management stuck firm on 18 per cent.

Though Ecclestone was back, many of the journalists were on holiday, quite apart from all the foreign and regional correspondents who were unable to attend a meeting in London. Thus it came about that the chapel voted for a strike by a majority of 83 to 37, out of a total membership of about 280. Rees-Mogg was in America. Hamilton was in Italy, but rushed back in the hope of being able to convince the journalists that 'this was not the moment to press the company till the pips squeaked, given that it had kept them on full pay throughout the shutdown and had already given enormous salary increases'.[1] But he arrived too late. After useless talks at ACAS, the strike began at noon on August 22, and the paper was out of circulation for a week. During this period James Evans informed the board that the strike would have 'very serious financial repercussions', since it would add substantially to an estimated trading loss for the year of up to £12 million. He could say that both Thomson and Brunton were 'staggered' by the damaging action taken by the *Times* journalists, who were 'fully aware' of the company's financial position.[2]

On August 30 the paper reappeared with a front-page story headed 'Pay formula ends NUJ strike at "Times"'. The formula was for 18

1 Hamilton, op. cit., p.176.
2 TNL board minutes, August 24 1980.

per cent over the next year, but increased payments from the summer of 1981 which would amount to 27 per cent over an eighteen months' period. This delayed benefit was to prove academic. Rees-Mogg was reported as saying that the strike had not been one 'of necessity' but 'thoroughly avoidable', and that it would 'do great and permanent harm to the reputation of the paper in the eyes of the Thomson family'. Ecclestone's curious comment was that 'the real winner was *The Times* newspaper'. In a three-column leader the editor described Ecclestone as 'gifted but difficult'. He questioned the need for 'a professional earning an income broadly level with that of other professionals on other newspapers to strike' on a paper which was 'losing so much money'. The strike had been 'severely criticized' by readers – and there were indeed three columns of indignant letters from readers on the same page. He ended:

> The strike is over; the strikers have come back; they are welcome as colleagues and friends, but it must be obvious that what they chose to do has equally threatened their own jobs and the future of *The Times*.[1]

For the Thomson ownership of *The Times* the future would, in fact, now be brief.

Was the journalists' strike quite as significant an event as is often alleged? For Hamilton it was 'the last straw', and he lost no time in ringing Kenneth Thomson in Toronto to say that the papers should immediately be sold for the best price obtainable.[2] But how much longer, in any case, would Thomson have continued to sustain a company that had cost him, and was still costing him, so much money? The management changes in June suggest that his attitude towards Times Newspapers had already taken a markedly tougher turn. His patience was wearing very thin, and the state of affairs at the *Sunday Times* was just about intolerable. So could anything that happened at *The Times* have made all that much difference?

The answer, probably, is that it much accelerated a process that was anyway well in train. Even if *The Times*'s NUJ chapel had not gratuitously eased his conscience, it is unlikely that he would have been prepared to carry the incubus of Times Newspapers indefinitely or, indeed, for very much longer. But the journalists' strike gave him

1 Leader, 'How to kill a newspaper', August 30 1980. The front-page report was continued on an inside page, and the views of both Rees-Mogg and Ecclestone were quoted at length.
2 Hamilton, op. cit., p.177.

a handy pretext to act promptly as economic logic dictated. Insofar as he was inhibited by filial piety, it was towards *The Times* rather than the *Sunday Times* that he felt some moral obligation. So long as *The Times*, as it were, kept faith with him, it was bound to be rather awkward and uncomfortable for him to get rid of Times Newspapers, though circumstances would almost certainly have forced him to do it sooner or later. After the journalists had struck, he felt free to do it sooner, and without too much compunction. They were the key people on *The Times*, the people who gave it its character. He had paid them throughout the stoppage, but now they had let him down. That was his view of the matter, and it may well have served to precipitate an inexorable decision.

XXVIII

Polish miracle • New Labour leader • Reagan elected • Long shadow of Thatcherism • Decision to sell: Brunton's hour • Picking the winner

IN POLAND DURING the latter part of 1980 acute economic difficulties combined with passionate popular hostility to the communist regime to produce a dramatic crisis. In August there were strikes along the north coast and in the Silesian coalfield, while in Gdansk a committee representing trade unions throughout the country was formed. It became known as Solidarity, and the leading figure in it was an electrician with a long record of resistance, Lech Walesa. Soon both his name and his committee's were household words throughout the world.

The shadow of Czechoslovakia in 1968 lay over the course of events, inducing a measure of caution both in leaders on the spot and in commentators abroad. Thus towards the end of August Dessa Trevisan was reporting from Warsaw: 'The hard core, mainly young workers . . . , still insist on all demands being met and say that only far-reaching concessions can satisfy them. But others, like Mr. Lech Walesa, the strike leader – say that the men are ready to modify their demands'. At the same time the paper was saying in a three-column leader that the Polish government 'clearly' could not allow 'wholly free trade unions' or free expression, since the Russians would not agree to such developments. But this did not 'rule out' all change.[1]

The leader was unduly pessimistic. By the end of the month Solidarity was recognised as an independent body and as a partner in the shaping of economic policy. Describing the occasion, Trevisan wrote:

> Mr. Lech Walesa, the 37-year-old electrician, was unemployed three weeks ago. He was out of a job for four years as reprisal for his attempts to organize free unions in the shipyards. He

1 Lead story 'Warsaw rules out use of force to break Baltic strikes'; leader, 'The Polish nation in crisis'. August 20 1980.

> became the indispensable man of the strike, exhibiting his great talent for compromising on minor issues but standing firm on the crucial one of obtaining the right to set up independent trade unions. This is how the compromise was struck, and on [*sic*] the signing ceremony Mr. Walesa had a rosary with a picture of Poland round his neck and he signed the agreement with a huge pencil which bore the picture of Pope John Paul II.[1]

A few days later Edward Giereck, who had ruled Poland for ten years was removed from power, to be succeeded for a time by Stanislav Kania.[2]

One reason why the Poles could not be crushed as the Czechs had been was that the Church was so powerful internally and, since the election of a Polish pope, internationally. In late October the primate of Poland, Cardinal Wyszynski, visited Rome for two weeks, and Nichols commented:

> There is a feeling of conviction in Rome that the Polish workers' confidence in insisting on their rights to a free trade union movement, and the use of the strike weapon to obtain it, came about because of the wide support they felt was theirs as a result of the strong international position of the papacy under its first Polish Pope.[3]

All the same, would the Russians continue to hold off? Could they allow such developments to occur in a satellite state? On the last day of September it was reported that the Polish leaders had been 'summoned to Moscow', and that a tough line was expected from the Kremlin.[4] But still Solidarity survived, and *The Times* commented that things were looking better in Poland than for some time, with realism being shown 'by all concerned'. Kania was 'emerging as a very steady and skilful politician'. He had returned from Moscow with promises of economic help, and the Russians still apparently willing to allow him to carry on negotiations with Solidarity. Compromise was essential, but the country was 'fortunate to have found the political talent

---

1 Op. ed. piece, 'A revolution in the uniquely Polish style', September 3 1980.
2 Lead story (no byline), 'Mr. Giereck removed from party leadership in Poland', September 6 1980.
3 Nichols reporting from Rome, October 24 1980.
4 Lead story (Trevisan) 'Polish leaders summoned to Moscow for urgent talks', and another front-page story (Binyon) 'Tough line expected from Kremlin': October 30 1980.

available to handle a novel situation of such explosive delicacy'.[1]

Before long a leading Roman Catholic layman, Jerzy Ozdowski, was appointed deputy prime minister. This most significant appointment was 'believed to be the result of talks between . . . Kania and Cardinal Wyszynski'.[2] Soon afterwards Walesa was reported as appealing to his fellow workers 'not to provoke military intervention',[3] and a few days later there were warnings to the Poles in Moscow newspapers not to go the way of Czechoslovakia.[4] Faced with these warnings, *The Times* discussed how the West should handle the situation. It would be wrong to tell the Russians precisely how the West would respond, or that it would not respond. They should be left in a state of uncertainty, and encouraged to reflect upon the probable price of intervention. 'The result would be like having another Afghanistan on their hands.'[5]

Whatever the considerations that weighed with them, the Russians did not, in fact, try to crush the Poles as they had crushed the Czechs. Within a few days the paper had a lead story across five columns 'East block renounces use of force in pledge of support to Poland'.[6] This was soon followed by a ceremony at Gdansk when a memorial was unveiled to those killed in the food riots ten years previously. People came from all over Poland for the ceremony, at which Walesa made 'a forceful plea for reconciliation'.[7]

In mid-January 1981 he led a Solidarity delegation to Rome, which was welcomed on arrival by an official from the Vatican secretariat of state and by representatives of three Italian trade union confederations, including communists (who in Italy had strongly supported the growth of Solidarity). The Polish party was also mobbed by crowds.[8] Two days later the delegation was received by the Pope, who warned Walesa that 'Poland's independent trade unions must remain non-political': by which presumably he meant that they must be careful not to go too far or too fast in their defiance of communism. A leader commented:

---

1 Leader 'Compromise in Poland', November 1 1980.

2 Front-page story (Sue Masterman) 'Top Cabinet job for Catholic Pole', November 22 1980.

3 Report, November 28 1980. He was addressing workers at the Huta steel mill in Warsaw.

4 Front-page story, dateline Moscow, 'Remember the Czechs' warning to Poland', December 1 1980.

5 Leader 'What if they do go in?' December 2 1980.

6 December 6 1980.

7 Front-page story (Trevisan), with picture, 'Unity pleas in Gdansk at memorial ceremony', December 17 1980.

8 Report on p.8 (Trevisan), with picture, January 14 1981.

> It is a fitting coincidence that the commander in chief of the Warsaw Pact, Marshal Viktor Kulikov, should be visiting Warsaw just as Mr. Lech Walesa is in Rome. 'How many divisions has the Pope?' Stalin is said to have once asked rhetorically. If Marshal Kulikov were to ask the same question during his talks in Poland, he might well receive the answer, 'a good many more than the Warsaw Pact can count on'.

Nevertheless cooperation with the Polish government was still necessary if the perilous experiment were to succeed. The presence of a high government official in the Solidarity delegation suggested that, 'despite its dislike of alternative centres of power in Poland', the government understood this too.[1]

Poland was a controversial issue at the TUC's annual conference, held at Brighton in early September. The general council was due to pay an official visit to the country, which it showed no inclination to cancel even though the Polish government was at the time at the height of its conflict with the Polish workers on the issue of free trade unions. Frank Chapple, leader of the electricians' union, delivered an 'onslaught' on the attitude of his colleagues. The British trade union movement had, he said, 'a vast record of support for human liberty, dignity and freedom', which the general council's failure to support the Polish workers' movement was dishonouring. That failure was further denounced by Mrs. Kate Losinska, president of the Civil and Public Services Association, and the wife of a Pole, who said that 'the silence over supporting the Polish workers had been deafening'. Nevertheless the decision to go ahead with the visit was endorsed by the conference. In a leader *The Times* remarked that the test would be whether or not the TUC delegates insisted on meeting the would-be free trade unionists.[2] But the test did not have to be met, because the following day the Polish government itself called the visit off, on the grounds that it would be untimely.

At the same conference there was an overwhelming vote against pay restraint, and the Labour leadership came under intense, if confused, pressure at the end of the month, when the party met at Blackpool. The conference there voted for choice of the leader by a wider

1 Reports on front page and on p.8. Picture of the Pope embracing a kneeling Walesa. Leader, 'Poles and their Pope'. January 16 1981.
2 Conference report by David Felton, and leader 'The test of the TUC's Polish visit': September 4 1980.

electoral college, though the task of deciding on a precise method was referred to another special conference, to be held in January. In the debate on Europe Shirley Williams and another right-winger, or moderate, Thomas (Tom) Bradley, refused to speak from the platform 'because they could not accept the view of the executive'. In his speech to the conference Callaghan appealed for party unity and, according to Emery, left his colleagues in no doubt that he would soon quit.[1] Their judgement was correct. Despite a public appeal to him from Foot to stay on, he announced his retirement from the leadership a fortnight later.[2] A strong motive behind his decision was assumed to be the desire to have his successor elected under the existing system, by Labour MPs, rather than by a new electoral college which would almost certainly favour the left. For the same reason, left-wingers tried in vain to postpone the election until the new system was established.

The candidate of the right was Healey, who not surprisingly was also *The Times*'s preferred choice.[3] At first there were two candidates vying for left-wing support, Peter Shore and John Silkin, since Benn refused to stand under a system which he dismissed as 'not a real election'. Shore seemed to have the better chance against Healey, because he was a moderate on most issues while appealing to the left on account of his strongly anti-EEC views. He also had the advantage, as he thought, of Foot's backing. But left-wing MPs were not confident that he could beat Healey, and in any case there was much lobbying by trade union leaders, reported by Routledge, that their favourite politician, Foot, should be drafted and persuaded to stand. Before long he yielded to this pressure, reinforced by that of his wife, Jill Craigie ('If I refused my wife might divorce me'), and by entering the contest he scuppered Shore's chances.[4] On the first ballot, held on November 4, Healey led with 112 votes, but Foot was second with 83, while Silkin and Shore had, respectively, only 38 and 32. In the resulting straight fight a week later between Foot and Healey, Foot won with a margin of 10 votes.

To *The Times* his election as leader seemed 'a terrible mistake for the Labour Party'. In the paper's view, he was a unifier 'only in the

---

1 Conference report by Hatfield, September 29 1980; lead story from Emery, October 1 1980. During the conference Rees-Mogg went to Blackpool to address the party's newspaper group on press freedom.

2 Report by Hatfield, October 15 1980; lead story from the same reporter, October 16 1980.

3 Leader, 'Mr. Callaghan goes', October 16 1980, which said that Callaghan had taken the right decision and that 'the wisest course' would be to elect Healey.

4 Routledge reports, October 16 and 17 1980. On October 31 *The Times* published a poll showing that Foot was also the favourite of local Labour parties.

most superficial sense'; in reality, he was not 'well placed to restore harmony and coherence to Labour', but on the contrary made 'a breakaway much more probable'. Though he had been loyal to a right-wing leader, he remained at heart 'a man of the left, personally attached to policies . . . not favoured by a majority either of the general public or of Labour voters'. Moreover, he was remembered 'for the uncomplaining ease with which he succumbed to union pressure'. 'Mr. Jack Jones's poodle' was hardly likely 'to turn into the parliamentary party's watchdog'. He did not have a strong grasp of policy, and was 'more of a rhetorician than a leader'. Labour had done itself lasting damage by 'going for the easy option'.[1]

Evidence that his election would, indeed make a breakaway more probable was not slow in coming. Though Healey agreed to serve as deputy leader, Rodgers and Owen were soon attacking Foot for, as they saw it, conniving at an unruly Labour demonstration in the House of Commons on the subject of council rents. This was noted in the paper as the 'first sign of a split in the Shadow Cabinet'.[2] William Rodgers, excluded as spokesman for defence, refused the alternative posts that Foot offered him and before long ceased to be a member.[3] Shirley Williams declined to be a Labour candidate at the next election, since she could no longer 'honestly defend' party policies. Even before Foot's election she had written in *The Times* that the divide in the Labour party between reformers and revolutionaries was 'becoming explicitly – as implicitly it always ha[d] been – unbridgeable'.[4] Schism was clearly imminent.

Contemplating, in August, the early stages of the American presidential election, Heren described it as 'surely the longest and most expensive in the Western world'. Nor did he any longer seem disposed to take a favourable view of either candidate, though only the previous month he had compared Reagan with Eisenhower. The process had, he said, 'again produced two indifferent presidential candidates'.[5]

1 Leader, 'An unmitigated folly', written by Smith, November 11 1980. The idea that Foot was 'a romantic who might unify the party' had been mentioned, not least, in a profile of him by Hatfield (November 3).
2 Lead story, November 15 1980.
3 Front-page story, December 8 1980
4 Lead story, November 29 1980; op. ed. piece, 'Why the left's plan will not work', October 30 1980.
5 Op. ed. piece, 'America, still searching for the lost leader', dateline Washington DC, August 11 1980.

The paper, however, continued to support Reagan, while drawing attention to weaknesses in his programme:

> [Was it] practical to combine tax cuts on the scale outlined with sustained military spending and a balanced budget? It seems probable that in office [he] would have to trim some, if not all, of his policies to expediency. Still, the strategy he outlined shows a clearer appreciation of the needs of America and the world than the desperate succession of emergency packages which have characterized the Carter years.[1]

On the other hand Jay, who returned to the paper at the beginning of October, stated the case for Carter on the op. ed. page.[2]

Carter lacked the appearance of serene self-confidence that a candidate needs to show, and that Reagan excelled at showing. He did himself no good by what many regarded as ill-natured personal attacks on his opponent, and even less good, no doubt, by then apologising for them.[3] When they met for their one televised debate, at the end of October, he needed the sort of gaffe from Reagan that Ford had committed in the previous campaign. But Reagan did not oblige. Brogan reported 'no disasters, no triumphs'; but in reality the absence of disaster was the equivalent of triumph for Reagan.[4] When the American electorate (little more than half of those eligible) went to the polls a few days later, Reagan had a convincing majority of the popular vote and an overwhelming majority in the electoral college. Moreover, the Republicans gained control of the Senate and improved their position in, without controlling, the House of Representatives. Bush, who had been chosen, after some confusion, as Reagan's running mate, was to be the new vice-president.

News of the vote occupied much space in the paper on November 5, and the following day Brogan surmised that Reagan might succeed where his predecessors had failed. 'He has the wind behind him, unlike them. Congress will do his bidding, to begin with, anyway, and the

---

1 Leader, 'Mr. Reagan spells it out', September 11 1980.
2 'Why President Carter has clearly proved his right to a second term', October 2[illegible] 1980. Jay's second term on the paper was announced with a picture, on October 3 He would be contributing a weekly article 'covering public affairs in their widest sense'.
3 Front-page story (David Cross), 'Contrite Mr. Carter drops personal attacks on opponent', October 10 1980.
4 Front-page story, October 30 1980.

country is clearly responsive to his ideas'.[1] A big leader on the result ended:

> Mr. Reagan has shown that he can delegate, and there are able and experienced people around him from whom he can choose an impressive team. [He] could become the eloquent spokesman of a sound Republican government over which he presides with a shrewd common-sense.

The leader also said that he would have less difficulty than his predecessors in securing ratification for treaties limiting the scale of armaments.[2] The full extent of what would be achieved in this line during his presidency could not, of course, be foreseen.

The following month the president-elect began to announce seriatim the names of those who were to form his administration. The first batch, which included Caspar Weinberger as secretary of defense, was made public on December 11, and soon afterwards General Alexander Haig was named as the prospective secretary of state.[3] Only a few of those appointed were to prove as impressive as *The Times* had predicted the whole team would be, and by no means all were to last the course. Reagan's inauguration, on January 20 1981, coincided with the release of the American hostages in Iran. His inaugural address, much of which he was said to have written himself 'after studying those of his predecessors', contained near-paraphrases of Kennedy and even of Carter. He also echoed Churchill in proclaiming that he had not taken his oath of office 'with the intention of presiding over the dissolution of the world's strongest economy'.[4]

The divisions in the Labour party were obviously a godsend to the Thatcher government, whose difficulties, partly at least self-created, would have made it highly vulnerable to a united and intelligent opposition. In the summer of 1980 Emery could recall that only a short time previously 'even the purest monetarists in the Cabinet . . . feared that any turnaround would come too late'. But Mrs Thatcher was 'adamant that she would rather be right and lose the next election', and this might well have meant that she would, indeed, lose it. Now,

1 Op. ed. piece, 'A better chance for those fine promises', November 6 1980.
2 Leader, 'A Republican president' (Smith), November 6 1980.
3 News stories, December 12 and 17 1980. Leader, 'Good choice for secretary of state', December 18 1980.
4 Reports, January 21 1981.

however, there was a prospect that, when the election came, she would face 'at least four parties (Labour, Libs, Jenkins and Shirleyites)', and in that case the odds were that 'it would be a Tory decade'.[1]

In late November the government made some concessions to its critics. Though *The Times* expected severe cuts in social benefits, and a resulting 'storm',[2] in fact the chancellor's proposals were rather less controversial than those of his budget in March (and much less so than his 1981 budget was to be). The sum of £250 million was assigned to job preservation and training, and the rate of interest was lowered from 16 to 14 per cent. The NHS escaped 'lightly', while defence expenditure was cut by £200 million. On the other hand, there was a row about the addition of 1 per cent to employees' national insurance contributions, and local authority expenditure, with its heavy social content, was bound to suffer most from a further cut of over £1,000 million in public spending.

A leader commenting on this package wondered if the interest rate cut would prove sustainable, and also expressed more general doubt about the government's policy:

> It is the continuation of the task that remains worrying. Pay settlements are falling because unemployment is rising. What we do not yet have is firm ground for believing that inflation will stay low when output begins to pick up. That is the shadow which still hangs over the Government's strategy.[3]

The following day the paper's lead story reported unemployment at the postwar record figure of 2,162,874.[4]

Meanwhile, 7,000 miles away in the South Atlantic, a middle-ranking minister was grappling with an issue which before very long was to bulk large in the history and legend of Thatcherism. The day the paper led with the unemployment figure, the second story gave this news:

> Britain is suggesting that the sovereignty of the Falkland Islands be transferred to Argentina . . . This is said to be one of a number of options which are being put to the islanders by Mr. Nicholas

---

1 Op. ed. piece, 'Why Labour's troubles could make it a Tory decade', August 2 1980.
2 Front-page story (Hatfield), November 24 1980.
3 Leader, 'The counter-inflation strategy', November 25 1980.
4 Lead story (Blake), November 26 1980.

> Ridley . . . who is now in the Falklands. [The Foreign and Commonwealth Office] can neither confirm nor deny.[1]

Ridley, a strong exponent of monetarism and, as the decade unfolded, an increasingly prominent member of Mrs. Thatcher's praetorian guard, was at the time a minister of state at the foreign office. In a radio interview next day the foreign secretary, Carrington, said that Britain would respect the islanders' wishes, but was nevertheless keen to reach an amicable arrangement with Argentina.[2] He did not specify the idea of a transfer of sovereignty, combined with a lease-back, which were among the options put by Ridley to the Falklanders, but that was clearly what he had in mind.

In a third leader *The Times* gave qualified support to the idea. Since the future of the Falklands had come to the fore again, it was healthy that it should be discussed. The starting point, the leader agreed, was that nothing should be done against the islanders' wishes. On the other hand the status quo in which the Falklands were 'in a kind of limbo', was also unsatisfactory. 'The advantage of the lease-back option outlined by Mr. Ridley – similar to that of Hongkong's new territories – is that it nominally meets the Argentine requirement on sovereignty, while leaving the islanders to maintain their own pattern of life'. It would also provide a basis for agreements on oil exploration, fisheries and the development of tourism.[3]

Unfortunately the islanders had not been persuaded by Ridley's logic, and when he was about to leave for home they shouted abuse at him to the accompaniment of 'Rule Britannia'. He was no better treated in the House of Commons when, soon after his return, he was allowed by his superiors to make a premature statement. 'Seldom', Noyes reported, 'can a minister have had such a drubbing from all sides of the House . . . [He] was left stammering and confused'. Among speakers in the debate quoted in the report were the Conservatives Julian Amery and Lord Cranborne, the Labour Peter Shore, and the Liberal Russell Johnston who said that 'shameful schemes' for getting rid of the Falklands had for some time been 'festering' in the Foreign Office. Noyes concluded: 'The one certainty of yesterday's exchanges . . . was that even if the "festering plots" of the Foreign

1 Front-page report from Michael Frenchman, same date.
2 Spanier story on p.7, November 27 1980.
3 Leader, 'An option for the Falklands' (written by Peter Strafford), November 29 1980.

Office should reach the floor of the House of Commons, they will be given very short shrift'.[1]

So vanished a chance to resolve intelligently a dispute that was soon to lead to war and, thereafter, to an indefinite and disproportionately costly commitment of British resources. *The Times*'s reference to Hongkong was very much to the point. Later in the decade the Thatcher government was to agree to cede to the totalitarian communist government of China not only the leased-back New Territories there, but Hongkong island itself, which was sovereign British territory. This agreement was signed without regard to the actual wishes, as distinct from the notional interests, of the 6 million people of Hongkong. The population of the Falklands was by contrast minuscule, under two thousand, and far outnumbered by the British or British-descended population of Argentina. To have given such a tiny and remote community an absolute veto over political change, which was later denied to the people of Hongkong, cannot be justified by any objective standards. If the government had put its weight behind the Ridley lease-back scheme, as Heath had put his behind carrying the European legislation, it would surely have gone through. In that case Mrs Thatcher would have forfeited the prestige of war leadership that was soon to be hers, and might possibly (though this is more doubtful) have failed to win the next election. But the balance-sheet for the nation would have been wholly favourable.

Early in the New Year there was a government reshuffle whose most important feature was the dropping of Norman St. John Stevas, a colourful figure who had been leader of the House of Commons and minister for the arts since Mrs. Thatcher came to power, having previously been her under-secretary at the ministry of education. As leader of the House he had gone some way towards correcting the imbalance between parliament and the executive by developing the system of select committees: a most notable contribution. His offence was that he was regarded as 'wet' (in the jargon of the time) on economic and social issues, and that he was in the habit of making jokes about his colleagues, including the prime minister herself. She had to apologise, however, for suggesting on television that he had leaked cabinet secrets.[2] His dismissal marked a significant stage

---

1 News report, 'Falklanders give Mr. Ridley abusive send-off', December 1 1980; parliamentary report, December 3 1980.

2 Lead story (Clark) 'Mrs. Thatcher clears former minister of leaking Cabinet talks', January 8 1981. The apology resulted from an interview on Thames TV two days before, which *The Times* in a leader said was 'asking for trouble' ('The fall-out not as intended', also January 8).

in the assertion of her personal authority. Other dismissals were to follow in due course as her style of government became ever more monarchical.[1]

On October 23 the paper's lead story appeared under the headline 'Lord Thomson to sever connexion with The Times', while page 2 carried the full text of a statement by Thomson British Holdings (TBH) issued the day before. In this the company announced its intention of 'withdrawing from the publication' of *The Times*, the *Sunday Times* and the Supplements, the board having decided 'with the utmost reluctance' that 'despite strenuous efforts of management at all levels, and the expenditure of massive sums of money, the existence and development of the titles [would] have the opportunity of a more secure future in other ownership'. The major reason behind the decision was 'the continuing troubled history of industrial relations' going back over many years. The story was recalled in detail, and the financial consequences spelt out. Since the formation of Times Newspapers in 1967 'more than £70 million ha[d] been advanced from Thomson sources'. In the current year TNL was 'expected to incur a pre-tax loss of some £15m and to borrow from TBH £22m'. The board would ask the national directors, the editor-in-chief and the editors of the two main papers to 'advise' on the conditions of any sale, which would anyway include 'the interests of employees, readers and advertisers, [and] the national interest as well as commercial and financial criteria'. If it were to prove impossible to achieve continuation of any or all of the titles under new ownership by March 1981, the TBH board had concluded that it could no longer justify sustaining the financial losses and publication would then cease. If it seemed unlikely that a sale could be achieved by that date, it might be necessary to issue dismissal notices to all TNL employees 'in the near future', though the board undertook to fund the papers until the deadline date so long as their production and distribution were not disrupted. Meanwhile the department of

1 Soames, Gilmour and Pym were other leading 'wets' to be sacked between 1981 and 1983. During the same period Prior was moved, against his will, from the department of employment to the Northern Ireland office, having lost all credibility by first saying that he would resign rather than move. The cause of the 'wets' was, in fact, doomed from the moment they acquiesced in the exclusion of Heath from the government when it was formed, despite his declared willingness to serve under Mrs Thatcher. The only senior 'wet' she was careful not to lose throughout her regime was Peter Walker, whom she must have judged to have some following among the party rank-and-file. The same was true of Heseltine, whom she did lose in 1986, with consequences ultimately fatal to herself.

trade and industry had been informed, and consultation with trade unions and staff had begun.

The statement left open the question whether the papers would be 'kept together as an entity' or sold separately, though the former solution might be 'preferable'. Within the statement there was a personal one by Thomson, in which he said that the decision had been reached with great regret but with his full support. He ended: 'I believe that a change of ownership could provide Times Newspapers with the opportunity to create a new and constructive relationship with its staff. With their cooperation and goodwill Times Newspapers with its superb titles could be a viable and profitable business with excellent prospects for the future'. On the same page he was reported as having said, in an interview the previous evening on ITN's *News at Ten*, that 'he did not feel he was betraying his father's memory'. He was glad, however, that his father had not had to make the decision. 'It would have broken his heart to make it but make it he certainly would'. It was now Kenneth Thomson's turn to be taking his father's attitude for granted. The clear implication, anyway, was that the decision was not breaking his own heart.

Alongside a picture of him there was one, the same size, of Gordon Brunton, who was, indeed, to play the key part in the ensuing negotiations.[1] As managing director and chief executive of TBH, it was he who issued the statement announcing the intention to sell, and the responsibility for conducting the sale was largely entrusted to him. His presence has been felt at earlier stages of this narrative, but now it becomes preponderant. Instead of occupying an ambiguous and ill-defined position between the distant Kenneth Thomson and the TNL management in Gray's Inn Road, he now assumed virtually unfettered power to settle the fate of the papers.

Like Heren, Brunton was born in London's East End, but the circumstances of his childhood were different, as was the direction that his career took. His parents were divorced when he was five – a most unusual occurrence in an English working-class family in the 1920s – and his mother then married a Belgian of bourgeois provenance, who set up a trust fund of £1,000 for his education. On the strength of this he was sent first to a preparatory school at Broadstairs and then to Cranleigh. Later, and more profitably, he attended a private school in North London. In 1939 he went to the London School

1 Lead story (Heren), p.2 reports and pictures, October 23 1980. Also on p.2, Routledge reported 'Union leaders stunned', and there was a report from the political staff 'Dismay and disbelief among the politicians'.

of Economics, where he obtained an intermediate B.Sc. (econ) before joining the Royal Artillery, in which he was soon commissioned. After active service in Assam and Burma, he returned for a year to military government in Germany while awaiting demobilisation.

Back in civilian life, he took a job selling advertisement space in trade magazines, attending evening classes at the LSE to complete his degree. Soon he became a manager, and before long a director, of an Odhams subsidiary, but there was a hiccup in his progress when, in his mid-thirties, he abandoned this secure employment for a speculative venture running a group of companies making toys and children's games. It failed, but he was then recalled to Odhams by its then chairman, Sir Christopher Chancellor, who in 1960–1 attempted a merger with Roy Thomson. The attempt came to nothing, and Odhams was soon afterwards taken over by Cecil King. But Chancellor then recommended Brunton to Thomson, and Brunton's career was made as he became one of the latter's principal lieutenants.

He was a man well-equipped for high-level business management, with the gambling streak that goes with enterprise and which, in his case, found another outlet in racehorse owning. He was also an educated man with a taste for reading and a deep respect for cultural institutions such as *The Times*. Even more, perhaps, than Kenneth Thomson he had a conscience about the paper and was determined to do the best he could for it. To him, it seemed more important to secure *The Times*'s future than to sell Times Newspapers to the highest bidder.

This view was emphatically shared by the editor. Rees-Mogg had just enough warning of the decision to sell to be able to prepare an instant reaction to it, with the result that on the day the announcement was reported a signed piece by him appeared on the op. ed. page, in which he declared: 'I am determined to save *The Times* whatever has to be done'. After tributes to the paper and his colleagues, and after describing the connection with the *Sunday Times* as 'an unsatisfactory marriage', he gave some indication of the kind of solution he had in mind. 'Without specifying any particular scheme, it is the unanimous view of *The Times* journalists, and probably of managers as well, that they like those of *Le Monde* should have a share in the ownership of their newspaper', though at present this might have to be only a minority share. 'Next week', he said, 'I am going to the United States and Canada . . . from now on the main thrust of my work will be to try with like-minded colleagues to develop a partnership – commercial not charitable – which can keep *The Times* in being. I have no doubt it will be difficult. I have no doubt it can be done.[1]

Despite his reference in the article to 'like-minded colleagues', and to 'the unanimous view of *The Times* journalists', Rees-Mogg surprisingly made no specific mention of JOTT, with whose aims, however, his own were now clearly identical. Nevertheless he at once received the full support of JOTT for his efforts, however irritated most of its members may have been by his pre-emptive move, and on his return from the New World they joined with him in an attempt to acquire *The Times* and run it independently. The trip itself was a complete failure. He carried it out with deliberate theatricality, travelling with a BBC camera crew, since he believed that only by creating a big effect could he hope to obtain the necessary financial backing from American or Canadian sources.[2] But the trick did not work; nobody on the other side of the Atlantic was prepared to risk good money in an enterprise that appeared at best speculative, at worst suicidal. So he had no choice but to return and try, with others, to achieve the paper's salvation through a 'commercial not charitable' partnership at home.

In the consortium formed for this purpose he was vice-chairman under Sir Michael Swann (provost of Oriel College, Oxford and a former chairman of the BBC). Other members of the steering committee were Sir John Sainsbury, Hugh Stephenson and Lord Weinstock (with whom Rees-Mogg had long been particularly friendly, and whom he was soon to join on the board of GEC).[3] Barings agreed to act as merchant bankers to the project. An arrangement for printing *The Times* outside London was sought, and at the end of November a quotation was received from the provincial chain, United Newspapers, for printing the paper on its web-offset plant at Northampton.[4] Rees-Mogg told his colleagues that the paper would, in any case, have to close for at least six weeks before restarting on the new basis. Moreover, everything would depend on relations with the trade unions.

---

1 'Now the Times is going to fight for herself', October 23 1980. This title suggested to one veteran reader that the editor regarded the paper as feminine, and he was prompted to comment: 'as a consistent reader for nearly seventy years, I have never detected any feminine bias in your columns'. (Letter from John Gloag, East Sheen, October 25 1980.)
2 Rees-Mogg talking to author.
3 In December 1980 he accepted a non-executive directorship of GEC, the appointment to become effective after March 14 1981.
4 The figures quoted were £6,700,000 annually for 300,000 copies of a 20-page paper; £7,300,000 for a 24-page paper. (D. B. Anderson to W.R.-M., November 27 1980).

> A potential buyer would obviously make his bid conditional on getting union agreement to his proposals. It might be that the unions would recognize the true position and give the agreements that the Thomson Organisation had failed to get, but *the consortium was likely to come into things only after union negotiations with a potential buyer had broken down*. . . The chapels at present seemed to be demanding no de-manning except by agreement after the event, which was a quite impossible demand.[1]

On December 31, the required date for preliminary offers, the consortium made a token bid of £1 for the title and goodwill of *The Times*.

Meanwhile Harold Evans had been busy putting together a consortium with a view to running the *Sunday Times* either independently or in partnership with the *Guardian*, and his group also put in a bid. Despite its appalling record of industrial trouble, and the loss of profitability recently resulting from it, the *Sunday Times* was, of course, a far more attractive proposition, commercially, than *The Times*. Brunton, however, did not much fancy consortia as such or anyway the kind that Rees-Mogg and Evans were leading, since he regarded them as incapable of effective newspaper management in current circumstances. Above all, he soon became convinced that the two papers would have to be sold together if *The Times*'s future was to be assured, while the two editors' plans were based on the necessity for separation. It was also no less clear to Brunton than to Rees-Mogg that selling *The Times* to the latter's consortium would inevitably involve a breach in publication, which would raise the problem of

---

1 Minutes of the third *Times* journalists' representative committee meeting on December 16 1980, signed by Grant. (Author's italics.) The tensions between Rees-Mogg and his colleagues are evident in a letter written to him soon afterwards by Stephenson, in which the latter, seeking to 'clear the air', sets out two points in relation to JOTT and the editor:

> The first is that my JOTT colleagues have an understandable degree of suspicion about the fact that you have so quickly and openly embraced JOTT, when you and the company as a whole for a year failed to take up its implied offer to provide an alternative means of communication with journalists. The second is the way in which you used your leader column to attack your staff after the journalists' strike.

Stephenson believed, rightly or wrongly, that 'a viable business plan based on near continuous production would have been at an advanced stage before Christmas, if JOTT had got on with it alone'. Members had 'pulled £2,500 out of their pockets to finance the study'. (Stephenson to W.R.-M., December 26 1980.) Rees-Mogg thought in retrospect that the sudden death of the head of United Newspapers, Lord Barnetson, at the end of the year blighted an otherwise promising negotiation. (Rees-Mogg talking to author.) Perhaps both he and Stephenson, from their different standpoints, were equally over-sanguine about the consortium's potential.

redundancy payments. By the end of the year it was, therefore, certain that Times Newspapers (the two main papers and Supplements) would be sold as one package to a single owner, or to a group under strong personal control.

There was no lack of applications. By December 31 Warburgs, the merchant bankers acting for TBH, had received about fifty, including a bid for £1 million from Rupert Murdoch. Though a million times larger than the Rees-Mogg consortium's bid, this too was only a token offer. Things were, however, soon going Murdoch's way; indeed, he was Brunton's favourite from the moment that he showed interest, for reasons that will become apparent. Scarcely more than a week into the New Year the list of serious applicants had been reduced to seven, and Hamilton, after discussing them with the national directors – in the light of the criteria they had themselves laid down, in collusion with the editors – wrote to Brunton giving 'their views and rough order of merit'. Murdoch was already top of the list.

> 1. *News International* [Murdoch]
> *In favour*: Commercially viable, proved track record of successful newspaper management, ability in Australia to create a quality newspaper [the *Australian*], readiness to accept criteria that the newspapers will be developed as independent newspapers of high quality. Readiness to retain present editors. British based and Rupert Murdoch of Commonwealth origin and British education.
> *Reservations*: Mr. Murdoch's arrival in England has had some deteriorating effect on the standards of the daily tabloid Press and he undoubtedly has been deeply and often involved in the editorial function. Possible problems with Monopolies Commission.
> *Recommendation*: No objection, but promises of editorial independence and maintenance of quality should be made the subject of institutionalised guarantee. This would be especially important for Monopolies Commission.
> 2. *Associated Newspapers* [Rothermere group]
> *In favour*: Reasons very similar to News International. British Company and much experience. Considerable resources.
> *Reservations*: Some evidence that property potential is greater motivation than the development of these papers.
> No real evidence could cope [with] demanding problems of *The Times*. Strong and consistent bias towards Conservative Party which is incompatible with independent role of *The Times*.
> *Recommendation*: No objection but guarantees of editorial

independence offered would have to be translated into acceptable form.
3. *Atlantic Richfield* [which had controlled the *Observer* since 1976].
In favour: Limitless resources, some recent experience [of] Fleet Street through *Observer*. Non-interference with editorial, and preservation of quality guaranteed.
Reservations: All National Directors dislike prospect of a British institution such as *The Times* being owned by [an] American oil company headed by someone aged 70 and whose responsible attitude to the serious media may not be continued by successors. Ownership of *Observer* may raise problems with Monopolies Commission, who may ask for guarantees that merger of *Observer* with the *Sunday Times* is not the reason for purchase.
Recommendation: Heavily qualified go ahead but guarantees of non-intervention editorially from USA must be sought, especially in case of *The Times*.
4. *Newhouse*
Little known of competence to handle international type newspapers such as *The Times*. Too American.
5. *Sir James Goldsmith*
Not thought suitable.
6. *Lonrho* ['Tiny' Rowland's corporation, to which Atlantic Richfield was soon to sell control of the *Observer*]
Out of the question. Would provoke outrage in eyes of British society. Middle East money and African political involvement too evident and outweighs any packing of [the] Board by well known British politicians or any promises about the independence of editors.
7. *Maxwell*
Totally out of the question. Unacceptable to unions and journalists.[1]

Hamilton shared Brunton's conviction that it would be wrong to separate the two papers, and he also shared Brunton's preference for Murdoch over all other potential owners in sight. Brunton had observed Murdoch on the NPA and had formed the view that he was both tough and straight; that when he gave an undertaking, he could

1 C.D.H. to Brunton, marked 'strictly private', January 9 1981. (Brunton papers). In February Atlantic Richfield sold the *Observer* to Lonrho, to David Astor's extreme chagrin, and to *The Times*'s disapproval expressed in one of the last leaders of the Thomson regime (February 27 1981).

be relied on to honour it. Hamilton regarded him as 'a professional newspaperman, prepared – perhaps too prepared – to take off his jacket and go in and sub a story or do the negotiating with a union himself'.[1] Both men were suspicious of Associated Newspapers, which soon emerged as the only alternative to Murdoch worth considering. Financially, Associated was prepared to offer more; £20 million for the package, £15 million for the *Sunday Times* alone. But Brunton had no confidence that Rothermere and his organisation really cared about *The Times*, whereas he was sure that in committing himself to support and develop *The Times* Murdoch would be as good as his word. Hamilton agreed. In his opinion, Rothermere was interested in the *Sunday Times* and its printing plant, 'leaving him to sell his Bouverie Street site', but 'he didn't entertain much hope for *The Times*'.[2] In this matter Brunton's and Hamilton's judgement was correct.[3]

January 21 was the decisive day, when Murdoch spent hours at Gray's Inn Road haggling over money with Brunton and appearing before the vetting committee, on which he made a good impression. He agreed that the number of national directors should be increased from four to six, that Times Newspapers should not be absorbed into News International but should retain its distinct existence, and that editorial authority and freedom to set policy should be respected, with the national directors available to act, if necessary, as a court of appeal. The financial argument lasted until after midnight, but eventually a deal was struck under which Times Newspapers would be sold to Murdoch for £12 million, which – according to his calculations – was less than half the book value of the company's tangible assets, and which was, of course, substantially less than Associated Newspapers' offer. The preferential price reflected Brunton's belief that Murdoch, and Murdoch alone, would honour a pledge to keep *The Times* going. That pledge indeed he gave, though never in writing. Even so it was confidently accepted: an example of Brunton's readiness to gamble for high stakes.

The following day he and Hamilton announced the proposed sale, and on January 23 the paper's lead story was headed 'Mr. Murdoch has three weeks to seal purchase of *The Times*'. There was a front-page picture of him holding a copy of *The Times*, flanked by Rees-Mogg and Evans. All was not yet over, because the question had to be

---

1 Hamilton, op. cit., p.179. Soon after the announcement that Thomsons had decided to sell, Hamilton discussed the state of the papers with Murdoch on a flight to Bahrein, for a Reuters board meeting that they were both attending.
2 Ibid., same page.
3 Author's view, based on conversation with Lord Rothermere.

decided whether or not the deal would be referred to the Monopolies Commission. Murdoch had made it a condition, on his side, that he would be free to pull out if there were a referral, and there were ominous noises from the politicians. Another condition on which he insisted was that he should have an understanding with the trade unions. As to this, preliminary signs were promising, because unions were reported to have reacted to the news 'with optimism', and Wade in particular was said to be 'delighted'.

In a leader Rees-Mogg explained and commented on the sale. Murdoch had been selected by the proprietors, and had given assurances that had satisfied the independent directors and the editors of the two papers. A number of tests had been applied to the various bids and proposals, and he was 'in effect the only bidder who passed all of them'. If he could make *The Times* commercially viable, he would have done 'the greatest possible service'.[1] The next few weeks would show if he would be allowed the chance.

1 Lead story, reports on inside pages, and leader 'The future of *The Times*'. Rees-Mogg made a gesture to his consortium by suggesting that it might still be needed 'to save the paper after a closure'; i.e. if the Murdoch bid were disallowed and Thomsons then gave effect to the threat to close the papers.

XXIX

Opposition formally fragmented • Longley v. Opus Dei • Royal election and royal engagement • Special relationship • The new owner • The deal clinched • Rees-Mogg signs off

NEW YEAR 1981 saw the realignment of British politics, so long anticipated, at last in the process of occurring, if only to a limited degree. Jenkins's return from Brussels, his term as president of the EEC commission completed, liberated him for full and open involvement in the process. *The Times* judged his return to be of great importance for two reasons. First, it might affect the timing of any breakaway from Labour. Though he might 'no longer be seen as the natural leader of the defectors', they would be 'reluctant to see him set up a new party of his own' before they had acted themselves. Secondly, without necessarily being the leader of a new party, 'whether of social democrats or the centre', he still had much to contribute to any party or group of which he was a member. As 'the best Chancellor of the Exchequer of the past twenty-five years', he would particularly compensate for any weakness on the economic side.[1]

In the middle of January there were reports of meetings between Jenkins and the 'gang of three' (Williams, Rodgers and Owen) with a view to making it a gang of four. Owen had said in a TV interview that he intended to sound out the possibility of a social democratic party, and poll findings broadcast to coincide with the interview 'suggested that a social democratic-Liberal alliance led by Mrs. Shirley Williams would', if a general election were then held, 'come out ahead of Labour'.[2] Soon afterwards the special Labour conference at Wembley voted for future election of the party leader by an electoral college comprising trade unions (as the dominant element) and party activists, as well as MPs. This conference was the final watershed. On the eve

1 Leader, 'The return of Roy Jenkins' (written by Smith), January 6 1981.
2 Lead story (Emery), 'Mr. Jenkins moves to cement alliance with "gang of three"', January 19 1981.

of it the paper's op. ed. page was given over to statements by six prominent Labourites, ranging from Scargill to Shirley Williams.[1] On the day after it the lead story reported that Labour moderates were preparing to form a new party, and that the gang of four had become a reality. As yet, the rebels had stopped 'just short of a breakaway' by creating a 'Council for Social Democracy' rather than a party. But a leader saw this as 'a signal that the social democrats [were] preparing to break'. To all intents and purposes they had cut their links, but:

> If they are to have any further impact on British politics they will have to go forward, not back. There will never be a perfect moment for doing so, and there can be no assurance that they will be successful. But the more they are themselves decisive the better chance they will have of persuading others to decide in their favour.[2]

Routledge devoted a piece to praising the speech delivered at the special conference by Chapple, the electricians' leader, which was, he said, 'one of the few articulate and intellectually honest speeches of the day'. In it, Chapple attacked the proposed electoral college on the grounds that, through the trade union element, the choice of future Labour leaders would be influenced by 'Communists, Fascists and Conservatives'.[3] In a think-piece about the new party that seemed to be emerging, Butt said that it would have parliamentary standing, but would need also to develop an organisation in the country, for which purpose the Social Democratic Alliance that had already existed for six years should be helpful.[4] At the end of the month Owen announced that he would not be seeking re-selection by Labour in his Plymouth, Devonport, constituency.[5]

Within a week the gang of four issued what came to be known as their 'Limehouse declaration', the name deriving from Owen's house in that part of London, where it was drawn up, but also carrying an

---

1 January 24 1981. The statements had the general heading 'How I see the crisis in the Labour Party'. Scargill's was entitled 'The only fair way' (that the cabinet and shadow cabinet should be elected by an electoral college); Williams's, 'A time to fight'. The other contributors were Frank Longford ('Why I stay'), Mike Thomas ('The fatal college'), the Young Socialist NEC representative, Tony Saunois ('Back to socialism'), and David Marquand ('Hoping for a split').

2 Lead story (Emery) and leader 'The fall-out from Wembley' (Smith), January 25 1981. On the same day there was a front-page picture of the gang of four.

3 Op. ed. piece, 'The man who really scored at Wembley', January 28 1981.

4 Op. ed. piece, 'Finding the roots of a new party', January 29 1981.

5 Lead story (John Witherow, Plymouth), January 31 1981.

echo of Lloyd George's famous speech there in 1909. They also released the names of a hundred prominent Labourites who had already joined the Council for Social Democracy, including four former Cabinet ministers, George Brown, Edmund Dell, John (Jack) Diamond and Kenneth Robinson. As for the general public, it was reported that 8,000 people had expressed support for the Council during the eight days since its formation was proclaimed.[1]

Soon afterwards the paper carried an ORAC poll which showed that a social democratic and Liberal alliance would attract 39 per cent support, compared with 27 per cent for Labour and 21 per cent for the Conservatives. Among potential leaders Steel was the favourite with 29 per cent, followed by Williams (24 per cent), Owen (15 per cent) and Jenkins (11 per cent). The poll also revealed that 36 per cent said they would prefer a merged single party to two separate parties in alliance.[2]

The day after this poll appeared Shirley Williams's resignation from Labour's national executive was reported. Her move prompted one of Rees-Mogg's most striking leaders, which was also his last but one. In December he had written to her: 'I hope you are going to lead a new party; it will have my thoughts and prayers, and possibly even my financial support, but probably not my vote'.[3] Now, at any rate, it received his strong editorial backing. He had always thought very highly of Mrs. Williams, and he had a soft spot for the Liberal party as well. By contrast, he did not warm to the personality of Mrs Thatcher, despite the economic ideology that they had both come to share. The result was a leader which, in effect, advocated a Williams-led centre government instead of the existing Tory one led by Mrs Thatcher:

> Mrs Shirley Williams would make a good Prime Minister . . . she has a personal character that very large numbers of British people can relate to, can give their confidence to . . . Beyond the quality of the leaders and the form of the electoral system, there is the question of national unity. Mr. Foot divides the nation; *so does Mrs. Thatcher*. Mrs. Thatcher may well leave great achievements, as did Mr. Heath, but *she has the character of a partisan and not a peacemaker*. . . the nation believes in its unity, and may take

1 Reports, February 5 1981.
2 Front-page story (Emery), February 9 1981. Details of the survey were given on p.4. ORAC was ORC under a slightly new name.
3 W.R.-M. to Shirley Williams, December 11 1980.

> a terrible revenge at the next election on those who represent Britain.[1]

At the end of February Foot made a last appeal to the rebels, but there was no way they could be diverted from their course. Owen, assuming that a new party would soon exist, declared that it would challenge dogmatic extremism by introducing PR. Steel said on television that he would 'happily serve under any of the social democrat gang of four if they came to power', adding that he hoped they would take the same view of him, though 'he had never been motivated to become prime minister'.[2] At the beginning of March, twelve Labour MPs resigned the Labour whip to form a social democratic group in the House of Commons and, despite reservations on both sides, a joint consultative committee of Liberal and social democratic MPs was almost immediately formed.[3] At length, on March 26, the new party was launched nationally – but by then *The Times* had changed hands.

A feature in the paper that aroused considerable anger, as well as interest, in January was a long profile of Opus Dei, the Roman Catholic lay order founded in 1928 by a Spanish priest, José-Maria Escrivá de Balaguer. During the last phase of the Franco regime members of the order had been highly placed in the economic and political life of Spain, though its influence had, of course, spread to many other countries. The profile was written by Longley and Dan van der Vat, and owed much to revelations from Dr John Roche of Linacre College, Oxford. Opus Dei was described in the piece as a 'secretive and controversial Roman Catholic organisation . . . seeking to increase its power and prestige . . . by profiting from the new mood since the election of Pope John Paul II.'

The piece was illustrated with pictures of 'instruments of mortification' allegedly much in use in the order; a whip 'with five or six thongs' and the *cilus*, 'a strip of metal rather like chain mail with the points of the links bent inwards', which was meant to be worn for two hours a day 'usually around the top of one thigh'. There was also a

1 Lead story (Emery) and leader, 'The sooner the better', February 10 1981. (Author's italics.)
2 Lead story (Clark), '"Twelfth hour" appeal by Mr. Foot to Labour dissidents', February 28 1981.
3 Lead story (Emery), 'Labour rebels quit to form new party by Easter', March 3 1981. Lead story, 'Steel-Owen alliance moves closer in Commons', March 4 1981.

picture of Escrivá, whose canonisation the Pope was said to favour.[1]

Two days after the piece appeared Longley reported on the front page a statement from Opus Dei strongly denying that it was a secret society or that it had, as an order, any political role. The statement was also printed in full on an inside page.[2] The first two letters to the editor set the pattern of what was, on the whole, a hostile reaction from readers. In the first a Jesuit remarked, with irony, that the profile was 'pleasantly reminiscent of some of the sixteenth and seventeenth-century charges levelled against the Jesuits', and the second said that it did not accord with the writer's personal experience of Opus Dei.[3] In the next batch of letters a correspondent noted that the Franciscans were regarded as very dangerous when they started. Another, who said that her late husband had been 'one of the first married Englishmen to join Opus Dei after its arrival in this country', asserted 'confidently' that Longley's and van der Vat's 'lack of sympathy' had led them into error. Yet another described herself as a convert and 'now an ordinary, but happy, wife, mother and recently qualified doctor', and said that she still looked to Opus Dei for 'encouragement' in her Catholicism. On the other hand, one writer regarded the work of the movement as 'insidious' among 'always impressionable' young boys, while another said that her daughter, who was not a Catholic before she joined Opus Dei, was now 'completely indoctrinated' and had undergone a change of personality.[4]

The profile led to a quarrel between Longley and Rees-Mogg, whose Catholicism was no less free from bigotry than that of his religious correspondent, and who anyway never knowingly allowed it to influence his conduct of the paper, but who nevertheless felt that the Opus Dei piece was unfair. In his view, too much of it was based on the testimony of someone who had left the order and wished to denounce it, and he also felt that Opus Dei should have been given the chance to reply in the text. Longley, for his part, believed in his source and had given a lot of time to the piece. The reply of Opus Dei was, he thought, implicit.[5] The editor had his way to the extent

1 January 12 1981.
2 January 14 1981.
3 Letters from Hugh Thwaite SJ, from the Catholic International Student Chaplaincy, Upper Tooting Park; and from Dr. Anthony D. Clift, Middleton, Manchester – both published January 16 1981.
4 January 17 1981. The three 'pro' letters quoted were from Mrs. Hilda Marlin of Berkhamsted, Mrs Anne Scott of Oxford, and Dr Wendy I. Adams of Streatham; the two 'antis' from J. D. Barber of London E1, and Mrs B. Strange of Tavistock.
5 Longley talking to author.

of making sure that a thoroughly favourable account of the order appeared in the paper within a week or so.[1]

Members of the royal family seldom, if ever, expose themselves to the hazard of an electoral contest, but an exception in early 1981 was Princess Anne. When her grandmother, Queen Elizabeth the Queen Mother, retired as chancellor of London University, after long and popular service in the post, she suggested that Princess Anne might succeed her and the idea was adopted with enthusiasm by the university's establishment. Precisely for that reason, however, it acted as a goad to non-establishment elements in the graduate body, and the names of Jack Jones and Nelson Mandela were, consequently, put forward as alternative candidates. Jones was the former general secretary of the T&GWU, who was still prominent as a Labour worthy and champion of old age pensioners. Mandela, though a prisoner on Robben Island, was a cult figure in the eyes of all opponents of South Africa's white oligarchy, and of racialism generally.

Neither could be regarded as a negligible candidate (though Mandela, if elected, would obviously have to serve for the time being *in absentia*), and it would have been easy enough for Princess Anne to withdraw, pleading unwillingness to bring the monarchy into controversy. She was not yet, herself, anything like as respected as she was soon to become, her image being still more that of an abrasive horsewoman than of an intelligent and dedicated do-gooder on the world stage. There was a real chance that she might be beaten, but she was prepared to face possible humiliation and, showing that she had moral as well as physical courage, did not withdraw.

Levin sprang to her support in characteristic style. Wisely, he did not attack Mandela personally (being anyway a genuine admirer of his), but said that he had 'trodden every step of his stony and cheerless road . . . only to be used by a gaggle of modish London lightweights who want[ed] to demonstrate their lack of admiration for the Royal Family'. Jones, however, he described as a 'knackered old wheelhorse', which provoked letters of indignant protest.[2] How much, if at all, his intervention helped Princess Anne cannot be known, but at the very least it cannot be said to have cost her the chancellorship, because when the voting took place she won overwhelmingly, with

1 Op. ed. piece, 'Opus Dei: the ideals and the unseen influence', by John Horrigan, secretary of Netherhall House, January 23 1981.
2 Op. ed. piece, 'Why Princess Anne deserves to romp home', January 8 1981.

more votes than her opponents' put together. In the paper's report, she was seen to have secured 23,951 votes to 10,507 for Jones and 7,199 for Mandela, in a 'remarkably high total' of more than half the university's 83,000 graduates. There had never before been a contest for the office.[1]

At the end of February, after much anticipatory speculation, the engagement of the Prince of Wales to Lady Diana Spencer was announced. The paper led with the story under the five-column headline '"Blissfully happy" Lady Diana to marry Prince of Wales', with a picture of them both at Buckingham Palace. Her father, Lord Spencer, was quoted as saying that her life might now be easier, because she would have more protection from the attentions of the media. He also revealed that the Prince had telephoned the previous week to ask him for his permission, adding: 'I wonder what he would have said if I had said no'. Consulted about the genealogical background of the future Princess, the managing editor of *Debrett*, Harold Brooks-Baker, remarked that she would 'bring back Stuart blood to the family', since she descended 'five times from Charles II; four times on the wrong side of the blanket, and one on the right side'. In general, the announcement was reportedly 'greeted with enthusiasm and delight throughout the country'.[2]

The following day a Calman cartoon appeared with the caption 'Another royal romance?'. It showed two little men walking past a hoarding inscribed 'Maggie flies to Reagan'. Mrs Thatcher was, indeed, in Washington for her first meeting with the new president since he took office, and her visit was billed in the American press as 'one of the great love feasts in the long history of the so-called Anglo-American "special relationship"'. According to the *Washington Post*, 'it was hard to remember when a President of the United States and a British Prime Minister ha[d] been so remarkably of one mind, not just on their economic theories but on their fundamental world view'.[3]

On the third day of her visit Mrs Thatcher gave a long address at Georgetown university, in which she propounded her economic nostrums. In the American administration there were some reservations about these, as Cross reported:

---

1 Front-page report with picture, detailed report on p.4, February 18 1981.
2 Lead story (John Witherow) February 25 1981.
3 Calman cartoon and report from Cross in Washington, February 26 1981.

> Despite the similarity of views on how to tackle economic problems, the Administration here has been eager to avoid drawing too close parallels between Britain's economic experience under Mrs Thatcher and what Mr Reagan's virtually identical programme has in store for the United States.

During a press conference and in TV interviews Mrs Thatcher had conceded that Reagan's policies 'stood a better chance of success, not least because the world recession which had been plaguing both countries seemed to be nearing its end'. In fact, Reagan's and Thatcher's economic policies were not identical, the former's being concerned to bring unemployment as well as inflation down. Reagan's priority was tax-cutting; he did not allow himself to be inveigled into monetarist orthodoxy. In addition to economics, the prime minister also 'voiced firmly her views on such critical foreign policy issues as East-West relations, the Middle East and El Salvador'.

At the White House banquet in her honour Reagan was asked by a reporter if he would like to go to the Wales wedding in the summer, and replied: 'I'd like to go very much. It would be lovely'. But 'checking later with the First Lady, he discovered that he had not yet been invited'. For the paper to have described this, as it did, as a 'diplomatic gaffe', even though 'minor', seems rather pompous. (In the event Reagan did not attend the wedding, though his wife did.)

The report of the banquet included this item: 'Also there . . . was Mr Rupert Murdoch, new owner of *The Times*. He appeared on the guest list as publisher of the *New York Post*'.[1]

Murdoch was indeed the new owner, though not yet unconditionally. He had stipulated that the deal would be off, so far as he was concerned, if the government decided to refer it to the Monopolies Commission, or if he failed to obtain a satisfactory working agreement with the unions. The last stages of the transaction will be recorded in the next section; but meanwhile, what sort of man was Murdoch? Detailed description and appraisal of him will belong properly in the next volume of this History. Here only a brief, provisional sketch will be attempted.

Like Roy Thomson, he came from a white Commonwealth country – Australia in his case – and his paternal ancestry was also Scottish. But in one vital respect his background was quite different. Whereas

---

1 Front-page story (Cross) and reports on p.5, February 28 1981.

Thomson made his way in the world from obscure beginnings, Murdoch was a child of privilege. His father, Sir Keith, was a towering figure in Australian life; probably the greatest editor and newspaper entrepreneur in the country's history. His mother, Dame Elizabeth, much younger than her husband, was from a well-established Melbourne family. Among the four children of the marriage, Rupert was the only son.

He was sent to the exclusive and prestigious Geelong Grammar School, and then to Worcester College, Oxford. A close friend at school and university, and thereafter, was Richard Searby, classical scholar and sophisticate, who had a distinguished career at the Australian bar before becoming increasingly involved in his friend's business affairs. In his view, Murdoch had 'great intellectual ability but no intellectual ideas', and this was the key to his effectiveness.[1] When he was nineteen he accompanied his father to a meeting of the (then) Imperial Press Conference in Canada, and anyone who met him at that time cannot have failed to be struck by his raw vitality, and by his almost obsessive interest in the mechanics of newspaper ownership, more especially the struggle between rival proprietors in his own country.[2]

All too soon he was to be part of that struggle, because only two years later his father died, leaving a difficult and challenging inheritance. Though he had created a newspaper empire, Sir Keith owned, at his death, only a small part of it himself: the *News* and *Sunday Mail* in Adelaide, and a share of the *Courier-Mail* in Brisbane (which the executors of his estate immediately decided to sell). Unlike his son, Sir Keith was more journalist than tycoon; his entrepreneurship was undertaken for the sake of journalism, rather than for its own sake. Rupert had, of course, been brought up in an intensely journalistic atmosphere, and he had gained proficiency in the trade partly on brief attachment to the London *Daily Express*, where his mentor was Edward Pickering. The production of newspapers excited him, and he could, at a pinch, turn his hand to editing. Yet his predominant interest and supreme talent lay in building a great commercial empire, though his empire differed from the Thomsons' in consisting almost exclusively of newspapers and other communications media.

Young as he was, he had to prove that he was more than a match for his elders. Above all, he had to demonstrate that he was no pampered amateur, but at least as tough as any self-made competitor. Before

1 Richard Searby talking to author.
2 Personal knowledge.

long his toughness was abundantly, even painfully, apparent. Within a few years he had acquired newspapers in other states, and had also gained control of several television channels, showing the flair that served Thomson so well at the same period in Britain. Though he operated mainly in the popular market, he took the brave and technically daunting initiative of launching a quality paper for the whole country, the *Australian*.

In 1969 he entered the British popular market with his acquisition of the *News of the World* after a battle with Robert Maxwell. He did nothing to modify the paper's traditional stock-in-trade of prurient sleaziness, but if anything enhanced it. The same year he bought, as a daily partner for the *News of the World*, the ailing *Sun* newspaper, for which he paid IPC less than £1 million. His success with the *Sun* was phenomenal; within a year the paper had doubled its sale, and in 1976 it overtook the *Daily Mirror*, for long Britain's largest-circulating daily. The Murdoch *Sun*'s appeal cannot be ascribed solely to its exploitation of female nudity, though doubtless that played a part. More fundamentally, it was due to a recognition that the British working class liked to be entertained, in however crude a manner, rather than educated or improved. Working-class readers also liked to have their prejudices confirmed and played to, rather than contested, in the paper of their choice, and the *Sun* was only too pleased to oblige.

Murdoch's philosophy of newspaper proprietorship was strictly realistic. He did not feel that it was incumbent on him to cultivate, at the expense of himself and his shareholders, better taste or a higher moral tone than the law required. It was not, as he saw it, his business to supplement the efforts of legislators and bishops; his business was – business. He took human nature as he found it and provided what the public wanted, subject only to legal restraints. He therefore earned from *Private Eye* (hardly itself a model of decency and decorum) the nickname 'Dirty Digger'.

Though this was at least partly misleading, he certainly did not come to Britain with any of Thomson's hunger for old-world respectability. As a colonial aristocrat he was somewhat resentful of the British establishment and contemptuous of the flummery surrounding it. Yet he was discriminating in his attitude to British institutions, regarding some with favour. For instance, he was a major benefactor of his old college at Oxford, of which he became an honorary fellow. Towards *The Times* his feelings were mixed. His motive for acquiring it was in one sense quite different from Thomson's, since he had no desire to become a British 'top person' by virtue of owning *The Times*. On the other hand, he was not immune to the attraction of owning the most famous and historic newspaper in the world. He was rather like a tennis star from Down Under who might have no time for the Pommy ambience of Wimbledon, but would nevertheless covet, and be glad to win, the trophy.

In his last leader for the paper Rees-Mogg described Murdoch as 'somewhere between Northcliffe and Thomson in newspaper ownership'. The resemblance with Northcliffe was, supposedly, that he had 'always involved himself in the editorial character as well as the commercial efficiency of his papers'. To some readers this must have seemed a disturbing analogy; but how apt was it? Northcliffe had been Sir Keith Murdoch's hero, and he, like Northcliffe had been first and foremost a journalist. The same, as already observed, could not be said of Rupert; nor could it be said that he had much of Northcliffe's, or Sir Keith's, general interest in the world and its affairs. His political concern was more or less limited to ensuring that the environment in which he operated was as favourable as possible to his business activities. Rees-Mogg also described him as 'a newspaper romantic', and there was considerable evidence of this in his launching of the *Australian*; some too, perhaps, in the sense suggested, in his purchase of *The Times*. But on the whole realism, rather than romanticism, was his hallmark.

He was, unquestionably, as the leader also said, 'very much an international business man'.[1] Whereas his father and Northcliffe had been simple patriots, Rupert was a citizen of the world, or at any rate of the capitalist world whose heartland was the United States. Though he never quite cut himself off from his roots in Australia, he became increasingly American. In 1973 he started to live in New York, partly because his wife, Anna, had a revulsion against Britain after the wife of a Murdoch executive was kidnapped and horribly murdered, and it came out at the trial that she (Anna) had been the intended victim. But in any case the atmosphere of America suited Murdoch. At the beginning of 1977 he acquired, in the *New York Post*, his first major stake in the country. Later, technically in order to qualify to buy American television stations, he took American citizenship – rather as Roy Thomson had become a British subject to qualify for a peerage – and in due course Los Angeles became his home. But when he bought *The Times* he was still an Australian citizen, living principally in New York.

Apart from Rees-Mogg's remarks about him in the leader just quoted, readers of *The Times* had the benefit of a profile by Leapman,

1 Leader, 'The fifth proprietorship', Feburary 13 1981.

which appeared the day the sale was announced. The profile, though brief, could not be faulted for sycophancy. Most of Murdoch's Australian papers relied, it said, on 'a combination of sex and sensationalism', which also characterised his British publications. The *Australian* was 'a middle-brow paper, in British terms a cross between the *Daily Telegraph* and the *Daily Mail*'. The *New York Post*, which used to be 'New York's most liberal paper', had in the previous year's election supported Reagan.[1] The profile only omitted to mention that in the 1979 election Murdoch's British papers had given equally fervent support to Margaret Thatcher.

When he decided to buy *The Times* Murdoch turned for help to his old friend, Searby, who had been a director of News Corporation since 1977, though his chief occupation was still the law. Murdoch telephoned him in Sydney, where he was about to go on holiday with his wife, and asked him to come at once to London. Searby answered the summons and, as a result, not only became closely involved in the negotiations, but also soon afterwards gave up his legal career to concentrate on the affairs of News Corporation, of which he became chairman.

The first obstacle to be surmounted was the threat of referral to the Monopolies Commission. When Murdoch and Searby had their first meeting at the department of trade and industry, with the secretary of state, John Biffen, and his minister of state (for consumer affairs), Sally Oppenheim, they had a clear impression that the deal would be referred; the two ministers seemed unlikely to budge on the issue. Nor was this surprising, because the 1973 Fair Trading Act provided that all newspaper take-overs should, in principle, be referred, and the provision had very recently been applied to Lonrho's takeover of the *Observer*, which manifestly involved a less serious concentration of ownership than the proposed Murdoch deal. There was, however, a loophole in the Act. Under section 58(3) the secretary of state was empowered to sanction a transfer of ownership without referral to the commission, if he was satisfied that the paper concerned was unprofitable, or that its survival was a matter of such urgency that the time required for consideration by the commission would make the difference between life and death. On the strength of this sub-section, Biffen announced in Parliament on January 27 that he had decided to consent to the transfer, on certain conditions.

1 January 23 1981. Two years later Leapman published a biography of Murdoch, entitled *Barefaced Cheek*.

The announcement was made in an adjournment debate opened by a Labour front-bencher, John Smith. Biffen justified his decision on the grounds that even the *Sunday Times* had made a loss during 1980, that the chairman of the Monopolies Commission had advised that the absolute minimum of time needed for dealing with a referral was eight weeks, and that Thomsons had stated categorically they would not extend their deadline. The first of these statements came under strong challenge in the debate, and subsequently. The figures for the *Sunday Times* had been supplied to the DTI's accountants by Warburgs who, it was suggested, had given more encouraging figures in the prospectus earlier made available by them to would-be purchasers. Biffen's explanation that the difference related to the allocation of overheads between the two papers, and to taking into account interest on capital, failed to dispose of the matter. He was also attacked for allowing himself to be 'blackmailed' by Thomsons into a rushed decision. Patrick Cormack, the Conservative who had opened the Commons debate before the shutdown at the end of 1978, interrupted him to ask: 'Is he not profoundly unhappy about the pistol . . . put to his head?'. Biffen could only reply, rather lamely, that he would have been 'much happier' to work under a 'more generous' time limit than Thomsons permitted.

The conditions attached to his consent were, in effect, Murdoch's undertakings to the vetting committee, now to be incorporated in the articles of association of Times Newspapers and so given the force of law. And in his winding-up speech Biffen was able to quote what Harold Evans had said that very afternoon: 'No editor or journalist could ask for wider guarantees of editorial independence on news and policy than those Mr. Murdoch has accepted and which are now entrenched by the secretary of state'. Nevertheless, doubts were expressed during the debate about the practical value of such guarantees, and some who spoke had hard things to say about Murdoch's record as a newspaper proprietor. Jonathan Aitken recalled that the journalists of the *Australian* had come out on strike in protest against proprietorial interference during the 1975 Australian election, and Phillip Whitehead asserted that Murdoch's 'multi-media concerns' had 'caused legal challenges'. Significantly, however, two Labour MPs reflecting trade union opinion backed the sale to Murdoch as the best solution available in the circumstances. Ron Leighton, sponsored by NATSOPA, said: 'The printing trade unions and, I understand, a very large number of journalists take the view that the best chance of keeping the publications in existence is Rupert Murdoch . . . it is our view that the most viable offer is the one from Murdoch'. And the same point was made by a prominent left-winger, Norman Atkinson: 'The trade unions . . . are concerned about the situation in March. Above all else, they want continuity of production . . . They must therefore ask themselves what is the alternative to Rupert Murdoch's proposal. The conclusion must be that there is no viable alternative at the moment'.

Though a Conservative, Peter Bottomley, thought it wrong that the whips should be on for the division at the end of the debate, and himself voted with the opposition, as Aitken also did, the government did not risk a free vote. The House divided essentially on party lines and the government had a comfortable majority. So the Monopolies Commission threat was removed. Whatever the arguments put forward, the presumption has to be that the decision not to refer was, in reality, political. Though Biffen was the minister immediately responsible, it was clearly not taken by him alone. The matter was discussed by the cabinet, and the cabinet in Mrs Thatcher's day was not a notably collegiate body; what it decided tended to be whatever she wanted it to decide. If Murdoch had shown himself hostile to the prime minister and her party, who can doubt that his purchase of Times Newspapers would have been referred? In fact, he had shown himself anything but hostile; Hamilton's view that he was 'neither greatly to the Left nor greatly to the Right in politics' was wide of the mark.[1] He was as strong a supporter of Thatcher in Britain as of Reagan in America, and she was known to feel that her victory in 1979 owed more than a little to the robust partisanship of the *Sun*, whose editor, Larry Lamb, she had recommended for a knighthood the following year.[2] It was wholly in character for her to reward the *Sun*'s proprietor, if she could do so with even a semblance of plausibility. His own view, in retrospect, was that Biffen was 'probably told what to do by Margaret', though he (Murdoch) hardly knew her at the time.[3]

What would have happened if the government had taken the opposite decision? All the evidence suggests that Thomsons were not bluffing – that they would have held to the March deadline – and it is equally probable that Murdoch would have stuck to his declared intention to withdraw, if there had been a referral. Kenneth Thomson might then have concluded that he had done his best for *The Times* and so have abandoned the idea of selling the papers as a package. As a result *The Times* would almost certainly have ceased publication in

1 Handwritten memo. to Brunton, marked 'strictly confidential', January 16 1981.
2 A letter from Lamb appeared in *The Times* on January 29 denying that the *Sun*'s 'wholehearted support for the Tories' in the election had been dictated by Murdoch. It was, he said, decided by a 'consortium' of senior journalists.
3 Murdoch talking to author.

March, for an indefinite period, while a better price would have been obtained for the *Sunday Times* on its own, which would have gone some way towards compensating Thomsons for their redundancy payments to *Times* employees. (The Supplements might have stayed with *The Times*, or have been sold separately.) In due course *The Times* might have been revived by the Rees-Mogg/JOTT consortium, or by some other agency. But its revival would have been more doubtful, and anyway harder, after a second hiatus and in a time of recession. Beyond question, therefore, referral of the Murdoch deal would have involved a serious risk to the life of *The Times*, and anxiety about this was so widespread that the arguments for non-referral seemed to many plausible, whatever its true, or prevalent, motivation.

Before the referral issue was resolved, Murdoch lost no time in making sure that he would have the support of most, at any rate, of the journalists on Times Newspapers. In 1976 he had suffered the annoyance of being rejected by the journalists of the *Observer*, and did not fancy any repetition of such a setback. So far as *The Times* was concerned, he had reason to be optimistic. Early in the New Year an associate of his, Bruce Rothwell, telephoned Heren from New York to ask if 'the senior editorial men would object to Murdoch buying the paper', and Heren assured him that 'there would be no trouble'.[1] This assurance was largely borne out. When, on January 26, Murdoch addressed a crowded meeting of *Times* editorial staff in the news room at Gray's Inn Road, he made on the whole a good impression, and some of them afterwards issued a statement to the Press Association that they now approved of him as the new proprietor. He admitted, by implication, that they might have some cause for misgiving, but emphasised the restraints under which he would be acting. When Longley asked him about editorial independence, he replied: 'I can sell myself to you as the least of the alternative evils . . . What if I found a way of tearing up all those guarantees and firing an editor? The answer is, there would be a terrible stink and it would destroy the paper'. His only reason for being against referral to the Monopolies Commission was 'the length of time it took'.[2] Though some of the

---

1 Heren, op. cit., p.260.

2 News story from van der Vat, 'Mr. Murdoch outlines his plans for *The Times*', with picture, p.2, January 27 1981. Also Leapman, op. cit., p.196, where Murdoch is quoted as saying in reply to Berlins that he was wrong to have described *The Times* as 'a dead duck'; he should have called it 'a sick duck'.

The suggestion that firing an editor would cause enough of a row to destroy the paper was probably correct, but only on the assumption that the editor in question appealed to the national directors and was supported by them; also that he had the more or less full support of his fellow-journalists. None of these conditions applied when Harold Evans was dismissed the following year.

journalists still hankered after the consortium project, most realised that the position of *The Times* was desperately weak and that there would have to be substantial job losses among journalists if it was to have any hope of existing on its own. In the circumstances, Murdoch seemed the best bet.[1]

With the *Sunday Times* journalists his task was much more difficult, because they knew that the underlying position of their paper was strong, and were indignant to find it described as unprofitable solely, as they believed, for the purpose of bolstering the case for non-referral. Moreover, Murdoch made a tactical error when he visited the paper on the Saturday after the sale to him was announced. Looking at page proofs of a leader by the editor, he instinctively made a correction in his own hand, which was duly incorporated in later editions. The correction was trivial, accurate and entirely in line with the leader (which was a strong statement of the case against referral), but it could easily be represented as an ominous sign of Murdoch's tendency to interfere in the editorial process.[2] The incident served to reinforce the opposition to him, and the *Sunday Times* NUJ chapel voted to fight the government's non-referral decision in the courts. Harold Evans's attitude was by now equivocal. While still giving a measure of moral support to his colleagues, he had approved the Murdoch deal as a member of the vetting committee, and had argued in print that it should not be referred to the Monopolies Commission. His outlook can hardly have failed to be influenced by the fact that Murdoch had offered him the editorship of *The Times*. But the journalists' legal battle would surely have been abandoned in any case, as the financial implications became apparent to them. (They were advised that the first round would cost them up to £85,000.)

Murdoch, however, did not at all relish the prospect of litigation, and thought it prudent to make at least token concessions to the *Sunday Times* journalists. On February 6 he met a committee of them and proposed that the status of the national directors should be protected by a special voting share, and that there should, in addition, be two seats for journalists on the board. The following day the chapel agreed to stop the legal proceedings, with only fourteen voting against. Shortly afterwards he reached an understanding with the print unions. While letting the NGA have its own way on keystroking, he secured

---

1 An exception, among the senior staff, was Brogan, who wrote to Rees-Mogg strongly opposing the sale to Murdoch, and who in due course resigned.

2 The proof-correcting incident was played up in the first of a pair of vigorously anti-Murdoch articles written for the *New Statesman* by Bruce Page ('Into the arms of Count Dracula', January 30 1981).

agreement, on paper, to the gradual introduction of new technology, and to a cut of 40 per cent in the 4,000 payroll. According to Dixon, the same terms had been offered to Thomsons, but 'Murdoch had the common sense to accept'. The unions' complacency was singularly ill-founded. He gave some indication of what was in store for them when, asked about the risk of renewed industrial action, he replied that, if that happened, he would 'close the place down'.[1] At about the same time, in a private conversation with him, Len Murray said he had always felt the Fleet Street proprietors had got the trade unions they deserved. 'Well, now perhaps the unions have got the proprietor they deserve' was Murdoch's reply.[2]

The day the deal with the print unions was reported, it was also made known that a new board had been set up, with Murdoch himself as chairman. He would not, like Roy Thomson, be confined to presiding behind the scenes, or through surrogates. Hamilton and Sir Edward Pickering were soon added to the existing national directors, to bring the number up to six, and the two journalists appointed to the board, as promised to the *Sunday Times* journalists, were Peter Roberts from their paper and Heren from *The Times*. Other new directors were Gavin Astor, Lord Drogheda, Lord Catto (of Morgan Grenfell), and Searby, replacing four who had resigned. A new managing director, Gerald Long, was brought in from Reuters to take the place of Nisbet-Smith.[3]

Hamilton resigned the post of editor-in-chief, which then ceased to exist – having anyway been largely nugatory, so far as *The Times* was concerned. On February 19 readers were told that Harold Evans would be succeeding Rees-Mogg as editor the following month. Rees-Mogg had, it was reported, given the news to editorial staff the previous day, with the benison: 'Harold Evans is a great journalist and I am sure he will do an excellent job'.[4] Evans was not, in fact, his

---

1 Lead story (Routledge and Macintyre), 'Pact with unions clears the way for completion of "Times" purchase', February 1981.

2 Murray talking to author.

3 Reports, February 13 and 18 1981. The outgoing directors were Lord Keith of Castleacre, James Evans (the previous chairman), T. D. P. Emblem and Hussey, though Hussey, it was stated, would remain in the company's service 'as a special consultant'. Morgan Grenfell were Murdoch's London merchant bankers, and Catto had played a quite important part in the negotiations with Thomsons. Gavin Astor had been Lord Astor of Hever since succeeding his father in 1971.

4 Front-page, down-column story (van der Vat), February 19 1981, in which it was also announced that Evans would be succeeded as editor of the *Sunday Times*, by the deputy editor and former foreign editor, Frank Giles.

preferred candidate for the post. He thought Douglas-Home would have been the right man to appoint, as did several others, including Hickey, Levin and, most significantly, Hamilton, whose lieutenant and protégé Evans had been on the *Sunday Times*, and who was therefore exceptionally well placed to judge his suitability for *The Times*. Among existing *Times* men, none could quite match Douglas-Home's qualifications. Though still comparatively young (forty-three), he had covered a wide gamut of responsibility, as defence correspondent, features editor, home editor and foreign editor. Heren, who was a strong aspirant for the job, and obviously a most eminent *Times* man, had an experience that was less varied as between home and abroad, and also had the disadvantage of being nine years older than Rees-Mogg. Another candidate, Stephenson, was the right age, but his experience was too limited and his political views were unlikely to commend him to the new proprietor.

Murdoch's precise reasons for appointing Evans will be examined, no doubt, in the next volume of this History. He said at the time that Evans was 'one of the world's great editors', and later that he 'wanted to get the energy of *The Sunday Times* into *The Times*'.[1] These statements seem, between them, to provide the likeliest explanation of his choice, and the fact that, in the process, the *Sunday Times* consortium was decapitated need be regarded as no more than an incidental bonus.[2] When the appointment was discussed by the national directors Hamilton spoke against it, but the only one to vote against it was Lord Dacre of Glanton (Hugh Trevor-Roper). Admiration of Evans's talents as a journalist was almost universal, and justified, though his merits as an editor had not, perhaps, been fully tested. At the *Sunday Times* Hamilton as editor-in-chief still had considerable power to influence and guide him (though none whatever with Rees-Mogg at *The Times*). Moreover, the general difference between Sunday and daily journalism, and the specific differences between the two papers in question, were perhaps insufficiently weighed.

When he wrote to Shirley Williams the previous December Rees-Mogg was still thinking that he might stay on 'for an interim period', though not on 'any permanent basis', under a new owner.[3] But when it became clear that the new owner would be Murdoch he realised that a clean break would be necessary. In January he let it be known

---

1 William Shawcross,

2 The offer of the job was made in mid-January, though formalised only on February 17.

3 Letter already quoted, December 11 1980.

that he would definitely not be going on, so leaving Murdoch free to make his own appointment in advance of the transfer of ownership, without any unpleasantness.

Suitably, for the most personalised editorship in the history of the paper, Rees-Mogg's ended not with a farewell leader but with a signed piece on the op. ed. page. The job had been fascinating but very difficult, he said, and recently complicated by industrial and commercial problems which he left without regret, and which reminded him of Pope's allusion:

> To where Fleet Ditch, with disemboguing streams,
> Rolls the large tribute of dead dogs to Thames.

He welcomed his return to 'a second adolescency, full of freedom, impertinence and hope'. For fourteen years he had had to think as though he were an institution, and he admitted to having been 'chafed by the restraints of impartiality' (not always, perhaps, very obvious to his readers). He had been 'sensible for too long', and now needed 'not to be sensible again, at least for the time being'.

He ended by emphasising *The Times's* 'principle of openness':

> *The Times* is clearly not the newspaper of a party, but it is not even the newspaper of a single opinion. The uniqueness of *The Times* is that it feels an obligation to all opinions, to all perceptions of truth . . . Yet to be open to all views does not mean to be indifferent to all actions. To the destroyers of the open society, and in my 14 years most particularly to the Russian destroyers of the Czech movement to liberty, *The Times* has been and is most absolutely opposed.[1]

The paper under his editorship had, indeed, stood firmly for liberty, in the world, in the country and in the office. He had attracted much new talent to the paper, to reinforce all that he inherited, and he had been a thoroughly loyal, supportive and permissive editor. People might criticise him for being too 'hands-off', and for leaving too much to his subordinates, but not for being excessively domineering or censorious. He had championed many important causes, including above all that of British membership of the European Community. His natural bias towards the Conservative party had for most of the time been manifest, though he had often had hard things to say about individual

1 Op. ed. piece, 'My resumption of liberty', March 7 1981.

Conservative politicians or policies, and at the end had come out in favour of a government of the centre. His economic opinions, and therefore the paper's, had undergone a fundamental change in 1973–4, and on some other issues the volatility or eccentricity of his judgement had been apparent. But whatever he wrote tended to be read, and often remembered. Moreover he had always done his best to ensure that differing opinions were freely expressed in the paper, and there was abundant evidence that this aspect of *The Times* in his day was widely appreciated.

His farewell article appeared on a Saturday, and the following Monday's paper was edited by Evans. So ended the relatively brief, but eventful, Thomson period in the paper's history. In economic terms, it was undeniably a failure. The attempt to escape from the legacy of folly that enabled the *Daily Telegraph* to establish such a commanding lead in the general quality market, the *Financial Times* to become the paramount organ of City news and opinion, and the *Guardian* to become a dangerous competitor for the allegiance of intelligent younger readers, had not been carried through to success. After giving the impression, at the outset, that almost unlimited resources would be devoted to *The Times*, Roy Thomson had abruptly stepped on the brakes in 1970. His son had sought to transform the paper's fortunes by a showdown with the print unions, but this had cost more than would have been needed to stick with the original strategy, and all to no avail.

Yet in other ways the period was far from barren. The unique character of the paper was well maintained, and on the whole its reputation flourished. The idea that its standards were being betrayed was never remotely true, nor seriously entertained outside a limited circle. Of course there were changes, but most were for the better and accepted as such. Throughout the period the paper held the loyalty of its core readership, despite an unprecedented test, and its influence extended far beyond those who actually bought it. While it probably continued to be read, and written to, by more 'top people' than any other paper, it also appealed, as always, to many cultivated and idiosyncratic, but obscure, people; and the two categories together made it the organ of an elite that was all its own. A great tradition lived on.

APPENDIX A

Comparative circulations and prices of broadsheet dailies 1967–1981

	The Times *6d*	D. Telegraph *4d*	Guardian *5d*	Financial Times *6d*	*Comments*
1967	349,168	1,392,328	284,860	149,312 *8d*	
1968	408,301	1,393,094 *5d*	274,638 *6d*	159,536	
1969	431,721 *8d*	1,380,435	291,310	171,790 *9d*	
1970	388,406 *9d* *1s*	1,409,009 *6d*	303,717 *8d* *9d*	169,901 *1s*	
1971	339,948	1,445,705 *7d* *3p* *4p*	331,723 *4p* *5p*	170,466 *6p*	
1972	340,288	1,433,558	339,078	188,485	
1973	344,840 *6p*	1,419,487	345,766	194,290	*D. Telegraph: closed Nov. due to strike*
1974	345,400 *8p*	1,406,134 *5p* *6p*	359,169 *6p* *8p*	194,592 *7p* *8p*	*D. Telegraph: closed Jan. due to strike*
1975	318,565 *10p*	1,330,788 *7p*	319,417 *10p*	180,507 *10p*	
1976	309,560 *12p*	1,308,020 *8p*	305,289 *12p*	175,156	
1977	298,443 *15p*	1,318,124 *9p*	279,513 *15p*	177,546 *12p*	*FT: closed Aug. due to strike* *D. Telegraph: closed Jan. and Apr. due to strike* *Times: closed Jan. and Mar. due to strike*
1978	295,864	1,358,875	283,494	181,678 *15p*	*D. Telegraph: closed Mar., Apr. and Oct. due to strike* *Times: closed by management*

1979	360,257	1,493,827 *10p*	388,304 *est*	204,609 *20p* *est*	*D. Telegraph: closed Apr. and June due to strike Times: closed Jan. to Nov. 6*
1980	297,392 *20p*	1,439,455 *12p* *15p*	377,016 *18p*	197,097 *25p*	*D. Telegraph: closed May due to strike*
1981	289,987	1,371,471 *18p*	395,719 *20p*	198,488 *30p*	

APPENDIX B

Editorial and senior management personnel on The Times *during the Thomson period*

General Editorial

Rees-Mogg, William	Editor of *The Times*, 1967–81
Hamilton, C. D. (from 1976 Sir Denis)	Editor-in-chief of Times Newspapers, 1967–81
McDonald, Iverach	Deputy editor and associate editor, 1967–70; associate editor, 1970–3
Hickey, Owen	Leader writer, to 1969; chief leader writer, 1969–; associate editor, 1972–
Cudlipp, Michael	Asst. editor (night), 1967–9; joint managing editor, 1969–70; deputy editor (home), 1970–3
Heren, Louis	Deputy editor (foreign), 1970–
Hodgkin, E. C.	Deputy editor, 1967–9; associate editor (foreign) 1970–2
Grant, John	Joint managing editor, 1969–70; managing editor, 1970–

Boxer, Mark ('Marc')	Cartoonist, 1969–
Brogan, Patrick	Diplomatic leader writer, 1967–70
Butt, Ronald	Columnist, 1969–
Calman, Mel	Cartoonist, 1979–
Collins, Jeanette	Design editor, 1970–9
Davies, Peter	Deputy obituaries editor, 1975–
Davy, Richard	Special writer on foreign affairs, to 1968; asst. editor (night), 1969–70; special writer on East European affairs, 1970–9; chief foreign leader writer 1979–
Douglas-Home, Charles	Defence correspondent, to 1970
Eldridge-Doyle, H. E.	Asst. obituaries editor, 1973–4
Grenyer, Norman	Deputy letters editor, 1968–78
Hardy, Michael	Night editor, 1970–9
Harris, Richard	Leader-writer, to 1979

Hennessy, Peter	Special writer, 1976–
Holmes, Donald	Coordinating editor, 1967–71
Levin, Bernard	Columnist, 1971–
Lewis, Roy	Special writer, to 1971; leader-writer, 1971–81
Mortimer, Edward	Leader-writer, 1973–
Owen, Richard	Leader-writer, 1980–
Pilpel, Leon	Letters editor, 1980–
Russell, Ernest	Night production editor, 1967–9; executive production editor, 1969–81
Smith, Geoffrey	Home leader-writer, 1967–
Spanier, David	Special leader-writer, 1969–73
Stanhope, Henry	Defence correspondent, 1970–
Trott, Edward	Asst. design editor, 1976–81
Watson, Colin	Obituaries editor
Woods, Oliver	Chief asst. to editor-in-chief, 1967–70
Woolley, Geoffrey	Letters editor, to 1980
Zwart, Pieter	Asst. obituaries editor, to 1972

Home News

Aiton, Douglas	Reporter, 1970–1
Aldous, Tony	Architectural and environment reporter, 1971–3
Alexander, Margaret	Social editor, 1967–
Amey, Leonard	Agriculture correspondent, to 1974
Austin, Tim	Chief sub-editor, 1980–
Baily, Michael	Transport correspondent
Bainbridge, Cyril	Deputy home news editor, 1967–9; regional news editor, 1969–77; managing news editor, 1977–
Berlins, Marcel	Legal correspondent, 1971–; (also leader writer)
Borrell, Clive	Asst. news editor, 1977–8; deputy home news editor, 1978–
Carter, John	Travel correspondent, 1967–72
Cashinella, Brian	Reporter, 1968–74
Chartres, John	Northern correspondent, to 1972; chief northern correspondent, 1972–
Clare, John	Deputy home news editor, 1970; home news reporter, 1971–2
Colinvaux, Raoul	Editor of law reports, to 1969
Cochrane, Hugh	Scottish correspondent, to 1968
Courtauld, Simon	Legal correspondent, 1968–9
Cowton, Rodney	Home news editor, 1978–
Devlin, Tim	Education correspondent, 1973–7
Douglas-Home, Charles	Home editor, 1973–8
Dunkley, Christopher	Reporter, 1968–72
Ecclestone, Jacob	Asst. news editor, 1974–7; reporter, 1977–81
Elliott, Keith	Chief sub-editor, 1978–81
Ely, Gerald	Property correspondent, to 1981
Evans, Jack	Editor to Law Reports, 1969–81
Evans, Peter	Head of news team, 1967–8; home news editor, 1968–9; race relations correspondent 1969–
Faux, Ronald	Reporter, to 1970; Yorkshire correspondent, 1970–
Ferriman, Annabel	Reporter, 1977–80; health services correspondent, 1980–
Fishlock, Trevor	South Wales correspondent, 1968–78

Fisk, Robert	Belfast correspondent, 1972–5; Irish correspondent, 1974–6
Forbes, Brian	Joint deputy night news editor, 1971–
Ford, Richard	Reporter, 1980–1
Forse, Christopher	Joint deputy night news editor, 1972–4
Fowler, Norman	Home affairs correspondent, 1966–70
Geddes, Diana	Education correspondent, 1977–
Gingell, Basil	Religious affairs correspondent, 1970–2
Godfrey, Peter	Reporter, 1976–7
Golombek, Harry	Chess correspondent,
Gosling, Kenneth	Deputy night news editor, 1970–1; asst. news editor, 1971–4
Grant, John	Home news editor, 1966–9
Groser, John	Reporter, 1978; asst. home news editor, 1978–81
Hamilton, Alan	Labour reporter, 1969–75 and 1977–
Hammond, Norman	Archaeological correspondent, 1967–
Hatfield, Michael	Labour reporter, 1967–9; deputy home news editor, 1969–70; special news and features writer, 1970–7; political reporter, 1977–81
Healy, Pat	Reporter, 1966–70; social services correspondent, 1970–
Hendry, Alex	Labour reporter, 1968–9
Hodgkinson, Neville	Social policy correspondent, 1977–
Holohan, Renagh	Dublin correspondent, 1978–
Hopkirk, Peter	Reporter, to 1969
Horsnell, Michael	Reporter, 1973–8
Howard, Philip	Reporter, to 1979
Huckerby, Martin	Reporter, 1972–7; deputy news editor, 1977–81
Hunter-Symon, Penny	Reporter, 1971–81
Jessel, Stephen	Education reporter,
Jones, Tim	South Wales correspondent, 1977–
Knipe, Michael	Reporter, 1967–9
Leigh, David	Reporter, 1973–7
Lloyd, Garry	Reporter, 1968–71
Longley, Clifford	Reporter, 1967–72; religious affairs correspondent, 1972–
MacArthur, Brian	Education correspondent, 1967–70; home news editor, 1976–8
Macbeath, Innis	Labour editor, 1969–73
McKean, Charles	Architectural reporter, 1978–
Marshall, Rita	Deputy home news editor, 1971–4; home news editor, 1974–6
Mounter, Julian	Reporter, 1966–9; motoring correspondent, 1970–2
Mulvey, Gerry	Dublin correspondent, 1970–8
Murray, Ian	Deputy Labour correspondent, 1971–7
Norbury, Tony	Production night editor, 1971–81
Norman, Geraldine	Saleroom correspondent, 1969–
Osman, Arthur	Midlands correspondent, 1968–; regional crime correspondent, 1978–
Packham, Brian	Night news editor, to 1970
Parker, Robert	Reporter, 1974–9
Pilpel, Leon	Chief sub-editor, 1967–80
Priestley, Brian	Midlands correspondent, to 1968
Reed, Arthur	Deputy news editor, to 1967; air correspondent, 1967–81
Richards, J. M.	Architectural correspondent, to 1971
Roberts, Frank	Home news editor, to 1968

Robertshaw, Denis	Chief sub-editor (home), 1967–9
Rogers, Byron	Reporter, 1967–9
Roper, John	Reporter, to 1970; medical reporter, 1970–7; health services correspondent, 1977–80; reporter, 1980–1
Routledge, Paul	Labour correspondent, 1971–3; Labour editor, 1973–
Seton, Craig	Reporter, 1975–81
Sharpe, Richard	Scottish correspondent, 1968–70
Smith, Anthony	Medical correspondent, 1971–
Smith, J.	Deputy night news editor, 1967–9
Sweeney, Christopher	Reporter, 1971–4
Taylor, Denis	Irish correspondent, 1971–4
Tendler, Stewart	Reporter, 1972–8; crime reporter, 1978–
Thomas, Christopher	Irish correspondent, 1979–81
Thomas, Michael	Labour correspondent, 1969–71
Thomson, William	Medical correspondent, to 1971
Van der Vat, Dan	Deputy home news editor, 1977–8; special correspondent, 1978–81
Walker, Christopher	Irish correspondent, to 1971
Wansell, Geoffrey	Reporter, 1970–3
Warman, Christopher	Local government correspondent, 1973–81
Webb, Colin	Home news editor, 1969–74
Wigham, Eric	Labour correspondent, to 1969
Wilson, Colin	Reporter, to 1970; night news editor, 1970–
Wilsworth, David	Reporter, 1967–70
Young, Robin	Consumer affairs correspondent, 1977–

Foreign News

Aiton, Douglas	Asst. to foreign news editor, 1971–2; correspondent, Australia 1976–
Ashford, Nicholas	Correspondent, South Africa, 1975–81
Barnes, Ivan	Asst. foreign news editor, 1967–75; foreign news editor, 1975–
Best, John	Correspondent, Ottawa, 1974–
Berthoud, Roger	Correspondent, Bonn, 1969–72; Brussels, 1972–5
Binyon, Michael	Correspondent, Moscow, 1978–
Blandy, John	Asst. to foreign news editor, 1967–9
Bonavia, David	Correspondent, Saigon (stringer), 1967–9; Moscow, 1969–72; Peking, 1972–6
Brigstocke, Hilary	Correspondent, Ottawa, to 1971
Brittain, Victoria	Correspondent, Vietnam, 1973–4; Algeria, 1975
Britter, Eric	Correspondent, New York and U.N., to 1968
Brogan, Patrick	Asst. correspondent, Paris, 1970–3; asst. correspondent, Washington, 1973–7; chief correspondent, Washington, 1977–81
Brookes, Kenneth	Chief foreign sub-editor, 1967–9
Caminada, Jerome	Foreign news editor, to 1975
Clough, Patricia	Correspondent, Bonn, 1977–
Cross, David	Asst. correspondent, Washington, 1977–
Davis, Patrick	Deputy foreign news editor, 1967–
Douglas-Home, Charles	Foreign editor, 1978–81
Emery, Fred	Correspondent, South-East Asia (covering Vietnam), 1967–70; chief correspondent, Washington, 1970–77

Fisk, Robert	Correspondent, Middle East, 1976–
Guy, W. H.	Correspondent, Australia, 1970–6
Hargrove, Charles	Correspondent, Paris, 1966–
Harris, Richard	Deputy foreign editor, 1967–79
Harris, Stewart	Correspondent, Australia, to 1973
Hazelhurst, Peter	Correspondent, South Asia (for India and Pakistan), 1967–72; Tokyo, 1972–
Herbert, Nicholas	Correspondent, Middle East, to 1968
Heren, Louis	American editor, Washington, to 1969; deputy editor (foreign), 1970–3; foreign editor, 1973–8
Hodgkin, E. C.	Foreign editor, to 1972
Hornsby, Michael	Correspondent, Bonn, 1967–9; Tokyo, 1969–72; New Delhi, 1972–4; Brussels, 1975–81
Hogue, D. T. F.	Asst. to foreign news editor, 1976–9
Hotham, David	Correspondent, Bonn, 1966–9
Knipe, Michael	Correspondent, New York, 1969–71; South Africa, 1971–7 (Rhodesia, 1975–7); Israel, 1977–9
Leapman, Michael	Correspondent, New York, 1969–72 and 1977–81
Lewis, Roy	Asst. foreign editor, 1967–71
Macbeath, Innis	Correspondent, New York, 1968–9
Mackenzie, Kenneth	Chief foreign sub-editor, 1969–77
Martin, Paul	Correspondent, Middle East, 1968–76; Paris, 1976–7
Modiano, Mario	Correspondent, Athens
Mortimer, Edward	Asst. correspondent, Paris, 1967–70
Murray, Ian	Asst. correspondent, Paris, 1977–81
Nayar, Kuldip	Correspondent, New Delhi, 1966–
Nichols, Peter	Correspondent, Rome, to 1980
Nicholson, John	Correspondent, Rhodesia, 1966–9
Noori, S. Ibrahim	Correspondent, Aden, 1966–8
Norris, William	Correspondent, Africa, 1967–8
Rendel, A. M. (Sandy)	Diplomatic correspondent, to 1974
Singer, Peter	Asst. to foreign news editor 1969–70
Spanier, David	Correspondent, EEC, 1964–8; economic correspondent, Washington, 1968–74; diplomatic correspondent, 1974–
Stairs, Edward	Chief foreign sub-editor, 1978–81
Stokes, Scott	Correspondent, Tokyo, 1967–9
Strafford, Peter	Correspondent, Paris, to 1967; Brussels, 1967–71; New York, 1971–7
Tidmarsh, Kyril	Correspondent, Moscow
Trevisan, Dessa	Correspondent, Vienna, to 1971; Yugoslavia, 1971–
Van der Vat, Dan	Correspondent, South Africa, 1969–72; Bonn, 1972–7
Watts, David	Asst. to foreign news editor, 1975–
Wigg, Richard	Correspondent, Latin America, 1967–72; Paris (asst.), 1972–6; Iberian peninsula, 1976; New Delhi, 1977–80; Spain, 1980–
Wolfers, Michael	Correspondent, Africa, to 1972

Politics and parliamentary

Bonner, Sara	Parliamentary reporter, 1973–
Browning, G. K.	Parliamentary reporter, 1973–
Cheyne, Ernest	Parliamentary reporter, to 1974

Church, Ian	Parliamentary reporter, 1967–72
Clark, George	Political correspondent, 1973–7; associate political editor, 1977–81
Daglish, James	Parliamentary reporter, 1967–8; political reporter, 1968–9
Deans, John	Parliamentary reporter, 1968–71
De Wet, Hugh	Parliamentary reporter, 1968–70
Emery, Fred	Political editor, 1977–
Evans, Richard	Parliamentary reporter, 1979–
Forse, Christopher	Parliamentary reporter, to 1968
Goodwin, Stephen	Parliamentary reporter, 1975–81
Ivermee, Colin	Parliamentary reporter, 1975–9
Johnson, Stephen	Parliamentary reporter, 1972–3
Jones, George	Parliamentary reporter, 1969–72
Jones, Nicholas	Parliamentary reporter, 1968–71
Mercer, Iain	Parliamentary reporter, 1969–70
Moore, Brian	Parliamentary reporter, 1975–9
Morgan, Robert	Parliamentary reporter
Noyes, Hugh	Parliamentary correspondent, 1967–
Robinson, Stanley	Head of gallery staff, to 1968
Snoddy, Raymond	Parliamentary correspondent, 1972–3
Thomas, Craig	Parliamentry reporter, 1968–
Underwood, Howard	Parliamentary reporter, 1975–81
Webster, Philip	Parliamentary reporter, 1973–81
Wellman, Gordon	Parliamentary reporter
Winder, John	Parliamentary reporter, 1968–
Withers, Bernard	Parliamentary reporter, 1966–
Wood, Alan	Head of gallery staff, 1968–
Wood, David	Political correspondent, to 1969; political editor, 1969–77; European political editor, 1977–
Wyndham, Rupert	Parliamentary reporter, 1968–9

Features and women's pages

Akenhead, Edmund	Crossword editor
Allen, Margaret	Deputy features editor, 1971–3; features editor, 1973–81
Bishop, James	Features editor, to 1970
Black, Sheila	Features writer, 1973–9
Collins, Jeanette	Women's page art editor, 1966–70
Crawford Poole, Shona	Asst. features editor, 1973–4; deputy features editor, 1975–81
Crook, Anthony	Deputy features editor, 1967–8
Douglas-Home, Charles	Features editor, 1970–3
Edison, Alastair	Chief features sub-editor, 1970–1
Ellison, Peter	Chief features sub-editor, 1971–4
Gelson, Hilary	Women's page home editor, 1966–70
Glynn, Prudence	Fashion editor, 1966–80
Hatfield, Michael	Special features writer, 1970–7
Herbert, Nicholas	Deputy features editor, 1968–70
Hunter-Symon, Penny	Women's page reporter, 1968–71
John, Donald	Chief features sub-editor, 1975–9
Keenan, Moira	Women's page deputy editor, 1969–70; women's page editor 1970–2

King-Deacon, Anthony	Men's fashion correspondent, 1967–70
MacArthur, Brian	Deputy features editor, 1970
Mayer, Edward	Bridge correspondent, to 1980
Mead, Robert	Chief features sub-editor, 1970
Menkes, Suzy	Fashion editor, 1980–
Moorehead, Caroline	Special writer, 1977–
Morley, Sheridan	Deputy features editor, 1973–5
Puddefoot, Susanne	Women's page editor, 1966–9
Radford, Penny	Women's page reporter, 1970–1; women's page home editor, 1971–3
Raven, Susan	Women's page deputy editor, 1968–9

Arts and books

Brett, Guy	Art critic, to 1974
Higgins, John	Arts editor, 1970–
Howard, Philip	Literary editor, 1979–
Lawrence, John	Arts editor, to 1969
Mann, W. S.	Music critic
Overy, Paul	Art critic, 1974–5
Percival, John	Ballet critic
Pym, John	Deputy design editor, 1976–
Ratcliffe, Michael	Literary editor and deputy editor, arts page, 1970–72
Robinson, David	Film critic, 1973–
Ryan, A. P.	Literary editor, to 1967
Sargent, Valerie	Editor, special numbers (arts), 1967–76
Stephens, Jan	Arts page sub-editor
Taylor, Russell	Film critic, to 1972
Trewin, Ion	Literary editor, 1972–9
Twomey, Philippa	Asst. to literary editor, 1970–6; deputy literary editor 1976–
Wardle, Irving	Drama critic

Diary

Aldous, John	Reporter, 1967–9
Ashford, Nicholas	Reporter, 1969–72
Berthoud, Roger	Diary editor, 1967–9
Davalle, Peter	Diary editor, 1977–
Grigs, Derick	Reporter, 1969–71
Groser, John	Reporter, 1977–78
Hamilton, Alan	Reporter, 1975–7
Horsnell, Michael	Reporter, 1978–9
Leapman, Michael	Diary editor, 1972–7
Martin, Paul	Reporter, 1967–8
Pearson, Jennifer	Reporter, 1966–7
Reid, Stuart	Reporter, 1973–5
Trewin, Ion	Diary editor, 1969–72
Weir, Stuart	Reporter, 1967–72
Young, Robin	Reporter, 1968–77

Sport

Allen, Neil	Athletics, boxing and swimming correspondent, to 1976
Bellamy, Rex	Tennis and squash correspondent; general sports reporter, 1967–
Calder, Douglas	Rowing correspondent, 1967–9
Charles, Geoffrey	Motoring correspondent, to 1970
Ecclestone, Jacob	Chief sports sub-editor, 1967–9
Faux, Ronald	Yachting correspondent, 1968–70
Fox, Norman	Football correspondent, 1976–
Freeman, Tom	Chief sports sub-editor, 1969–71; deputy sports editor, 1971–80
Green, Geoffrey	Football correspondent, and special cricket correspondent, to 1976
Hennessy, John	Sports editor, to 1979
Horsbrugh-Porter, Andrew	Polo correspondent, to 1976
Keith, Nicholas	Chief sports sub-editor, 1976–9; sports editor, 1979–
Nicholls, J.	Yachting correspondent, 1970
Phillips, Michael	Racing correspondent
Railton, J.	Rowing correspondent, 1970–
Reading, Andrew	Deputy sports editor, to 1971
Ryde, Peter	Golf correspondent, to 1979
Seeley, Michael	Racing correspondent, 1975–
Snow, Jim	Northern racing correspondent, to 1976
Streeton, Richard	Sports writer, 1977–
Titley, Uel	Rugby football correspondent, to 1971
West, Peter	Rugby football correspondent, 1971–81
White, Clive	Chief sports sub-editor, 1979–81
Woodcock, John	Cricket correspondent
Young, John	Yachting correspondent, to 1968

Business news

Allen, Margaret	Asst. City editor, 1967–8
Allen, Richard	Financial writer, 1978; insurance correspondent, 1978–81
Appleyard, Bryan	Financial writer, 1977–9; asst. financial editor, 1979–81
Atkinson, Caroline	Economics writer and statistician, 1977–
Basham, Brian	Diary reporter, 1969–71
Blake, David	Diary editor, 1973–4; economics correspondent, and foreign editor, 1975–9; economics editor, TT, 1979–81
Brennan, John	Financial writer, 1976–7; insurance correspondent, 1977
Brophy, Warwick	Industrial writer, 1967; asst. news editor, 1967–70
Brown, Malcolm	Industrial writer, 1969–78; features editor, 1978–
Byland, Terence	Financial writer, 1971–
Cairncross, Frances	Economics and financial writer, 1967–9
Congdon, Tim	Economics writer, 1973–6
Corina, Maurice	Industrial writer, 1967–9; industrial editor, 1969–79
Cawton, Rodney	Night editor, 1972–8

Davies, Ross	Asst. news editor, 1970–2; industrial writer, 1972–4; diary editor, 1974–
Davies, Sara	Chief features sub-editor, 1971–2
Douglas-Hamilton, Andrew	Production editor, 1971
Doxon, Alan	Picture news editor, 1970; deputy news editor, 1970–4
Druker, Ashley	Deputy financial services editor, 1977–9
Drummond, Maggie	Financial writer, 1972–6
Dwyer, Dennis	Industrial reporter, 1969–71; deputy industrial editor, 1971–74; news editor, 1974–81
Egerton, Ansell	Asst. editor, 1967–8
Eisenstein, Roman	Banking correspondent, 1980–1
Emler, Ronald	Financial writer, 1967–74; deputy news editor 1974–6; industrial reporter, 1976–7
Felton, David	Asst. news editor, 1976–8; industrial reporter, 1978–
Ferrie, James	Deputy news editor, 1969–70
Frenchman, Michael	Night editor, 1969–71
Gleeson, Adrienne	Financial writer, 1974–7; banking correspondent, 1977–8; financial writer, 1978–80
Goodrick-Clarke, Andrew	Deputy finanical editor, 1970–3; financial editor, 1973–81; deputy editor, 1974–
Gunn, Catherine	Financial writer, 1980–1
Harris, Derek	Asst. editor, 1969–
Hewson, David	Asst. news editor, 1978–
Hill, Peter	Industrial writer, 1969–74; deputy industrial editor, 1974–79; industrial editor, 1979–
Hirst, Geoffrey	Financial writer, 1977–8; energy correspondent, 1978–
Huxley, John	Industrial and diary writer, 1977–81
Jackson, Wallace	Chief sub-editor, 1970–5; commodities editor, 1975–80
Jacobson, Philip	Investment writer, 1967–8; US financial correspondent, 1968–70
Jay, Peter	Economics editor TT, 1967–77; associate editor TBN, 1969–77
Jones, David	Industrial writer, 1967–70; features editor, 1970–3
Jones, Robert	Editor, special projects, 1967–8; features editor, 1968–70
Klinger, Larry	Night news editor, 1972–4
Lumsden, Andrew	Industrial writer, 1969–71; diary editor, 1971–2
Marley, Christopher	Investment writer, 1967–9; financial editor, 1969–81
Marriott, Oliver	Financial editor, 1968–69
Maugham, Raymond	Financial writer, 1977–9
Millham, David	Financial reporter, 1968–71
Mitchell, Alison	Company news writer, 1977–8; financial reporter, 1978–80
Morison, Ian	Banking correspondent, 1969–73; deputy financial editor, 1973–4
Norman, Peter	European business correspondent, 1975–
O'Connor, Gillian	Insurance correspondent, 1969–71
Owen, Kenneth	Industrial writer, 1967–8; technology correspondent, 1968–79; deputy industrial and technical editor, 1979–81
Pagano, Margaretta	Financial writer, 1980–
Payne, Keith	Banking correspondent, 1967–8
Petty, John	News editor, 1968–70

Phillips, Joseph	Asst. editor, 1980–
Pickering, Robert	Night production editor, 1971–2; chief features sub-editor, 1972–4; production editor, 1974–9
Prest, Michael	Financial writer, 1977–
Pulay, George	City editor and deputy business editor, 1967–8
Pullen, Ronald	Financial writer, 1975–7; banking correspondent, 1977–9; deputy financial editor, 1979–81
Quigley, Desmond	Financial reporter, 1975–8; company news editor, 1978–9
Ritchie Barry	Mining editor, 1967–71
Robertson, William	Chief sub-editor, 1973–5; night editor, 1975–81
Robinson, Philip	Financial writer, 1980–
Roeber, Joe	Industrial editor, 1967–9; retainer, 1970–1
Rowley, Anthony	Industrial writer, 1968–70; European industrial correspondent, 1970–5; Insurance correspondent, 1975–6
Senior, Robert	Deputy features editor, 1978–81
Shakespeare, R. (Bill)	Northern industrial correspondent (Manchester)
Smith, Giles	Industrial writer, 1968–71
Spiegelberg, Richard	Industrial writer, 1967–8; diary editor, 1968–70; managing editor, 1970–74; features editor, 1974–
Stephenson, Hugh	Economics correspondent and foreign editor, 1968–70; joint deputy and executive editor, 1970–1; editor TBN, 1972–81
Stone, Margaret	Personal finance editor, 1969–73; assistant editor, 1973–
Thomas, Anthony	Banking correspondent, 1968–9; US economics correspondent, 1969–74
Tisdall, Patricia	Industrial reporter and writer, 1969–76; diary writer, 1976–8; management correspondent, 1978–
Topping, Dennis	Deputy editor, 1969–71; managing editor, 1971–81
Townsend, Edward	Industrial writer, 1973–
Unsworth, Rosemary	Company news reporter, 1978–81
Tice, Anthony	Editor TBN, 1967–71
Vielvoye, Roger	Industrial reporter, 1970–4; energy correspondent, 1974–8
Vogl, Frank	Frankfurt correspondent, 1970–4; Washington correspondent, 1974–81
Wainwright, Peter	Financial writer, 1974–5; financial services editor, 1975–8; company news writer, 1978–
Webb, Clifford	Midlands industrial correspondent
Westlake, Melvyn	Financial reporter
White, Sally	Industrial writer, 1967–72
Whitmore, John	Financial writer, 1971–4; deputy financial editor, 1974–7; chief financial writer, 1977–
Wilkins, Christopher	Financial writer, 1972–4; banking correspondent, 1974–7; deputy financial editor, 1977–9
Williams, Frances	Economics writer, 1980–
Wilson, Charles	Mining correspondent, 1973–5
Wood, Roger	Production editor, 1980–
Wormleighton, Austin	Financial services editor, 1973–5; chief sub-editor, 1975–81
Young, David	Industrial writer, 1974–6; deputy news editor, 1975–81

Special reports

Allen, Margaret	Planning editor, 1969–71
Crawford Poole, Shona	Home planner, 1971–2
Frenchman, Michael	Asst. editor (planning), 1972–
Greig, John	Editor, 1967–
Hopkirk, Peter	Foreign planner and writer, 1975–
Jones, A. R. C.	Home planner, 1975–
Jones, David	Business editor, 1972–3
Kiley, Dennis	Foreign planner, 1969–71
Knight, J. S.	Senior sub-editor, 1967–9; asst. editor, 1969
Marshall, Rita	Asst. editor, 1977–
Miller, Donald	Chief sub-editor, 1969–76; asst. editor, 1977–
O'Leary, Patrick	Home planner and writer, 1969–
Robertshaw, Denis	Sub-editor, 1967–9; production editor, 1969–
Sachs, Richard	Home planner, 1969–
Sargent, Valerie	Art editor, 1967–76
Scott-Plummer, Simon	Foreign planner, 1970–
Taylor, Denis	Foreign planner, 1975–
Weston, Geoffrey	Home planner, 1970–
Young, John	Home planner, 1969–73
Zwart, Pieter	Home planner, 1973–81

Pictures

Barker, Jack	Photographer, to 1973
Bradshaw, Ian	Photographer, 1966–70
Bridgett, Geoff	Photographer, 1967–9
Forbes, Brian	Assistant picture editor (night) 1967–70
Hall, Norman	Pictures editor, to 1975
Harris, Brian	Photographer, 1977–
Harrison, Warren	Photographer, 1966–77
Jones, David	Photographer, 1977–81
Kerr, Harry	Photographer
Manning, John	Photographer
O'Gorman, Cathal	Photographer, to 1968
Risley, Derek	Photographer
Shepherd, Fred	Photographer
Smith, Keith	Assistant picture editor (day), 1967–75; picture editor, 1975–
Warhurst, G. H. (Bill)	Photographer

Management

Anderson, Sir Donald	Director, 1967–73
Argyle, Derek	Night production manager, 1978–81
Banyard, George	Production manager, 1980
Barrett, Donald	Advertisement director, 1977–81
Barron, Philip	Finance director, 1975–7
Brown, W.	Finance director, 1969–72
Brunton, Gordon	Director, 1967–81; managing director, and chief executive TT0, 1968–
Bryers, Jack	Personnel director, 1980

Carr, John	Project manager, 1970–5; senior projects coordinator, 1975–80
Clubb, Ian	Chief accountant, 1969–72; finance director, 1972–5
Collins, J.	Day production manager, to 1975
Coltart, James	Director, 1967–
Conaty, Seamus	Production manager, 1971–3
Cox, J. A.	Asst. general manager, 1974–7
Crowe, Paul	Production director, 1978–81
Cruickshank, Donald	Commerical director, 1978–
Dixey, John	Asst. general manager (personnel), 1967–9; production services director 1969–73; deputy general manager, 1973–4
Emblem, Thomas	Director, 1976–80; TNHL, 1980–
Evans, James	Legal adviser, 1967–73; director executive board, 1973–8; director, 1977–81; chairman, 1980–1
Ferrier, Allan	Chief accountant, 1972–
Floyd, Hugh (Pat)	Publisher, to 1976
Greene, Sidney (from 1970 Sir, from 1974 Lord Greene of Harrow Weald)	Director, 1974–80; TNHL, 1980–
Haley, Sir William	Chairman, 1967–8
Hamilton, C. D. (from 1976 Sir Denis)	Chief executive 1967–71; chairman, 1971–80; chairman TNHL, 1980–1
Henry, Harry	Alternate director, 1967–70
Heritage, Denis	Finance director, 1977–9
Hinton, R.	Publisher, 1977–
Hopkins, Tudor	Industrial relations adviser 1975–7; asst. general manager, 1977–80; asst. personnel director, 1980–
Hudd, Glyn	Deputy production manager, 1980–
Hussey, Marmaduke	Managing director and chief executive, 1971–80; vice-chairman, TNHL, 1980–
Jewell, Derek	Publishing director, 1968–
Jordan, Arthur	Personnel director, 1969–71
Kavanagh, J. B.	Production manager, 1974–7; technical director, 1977–
Keith, Kenneth (from 1969 Sir)	Director, 1967–81
Kenneth, C. G.	Deputy day printer, 1978–
Knowles, Enid	Executive assistant to C. D. Hamilton, 1969–81; external relations executive, 1977–81
Lawson, David	Chief accountant, 1973–6; financial controller, 1976–9; financial director, 1979–81
Macfarlane, James	Advertisement director, 1969–70
MacLeod, William	Company secretary, 1967–81
Mander, Michael	Advertisement and marketing director, 1971–7; deputy chief executive and marketing director, 1977–80
Mitchell, Peter	Administration manager, 1974–80; asst. general manager (admin) 1980–1
Nisbet-Smith, Dugal	General manager, 1978–80; managing director, 1980–1
Owen, Fred	Circulation manager, 1970–8; personnel and training manager, 1978–1
Pope, Sir George	General manager, 1967–8; director, 1968–76
Rees-Mogg, William	Director, 1967–81

Robens of Woldingham, Lord	Director, 1967–80; director TNHL, 1980–
Roll, Sir Eric (from 1977 Lord Roll of Ipsden)	Director, 1967–80; director TNHL, 1980–
Rowett, Geoffrey	Director and general manager, 1967–72
Selmon, Richard	Financial advertisement director, 1972–7; project manager, 1977–80
Shawcross, Lord	Director, 1967–74
Sims, J.	Day printer, 1975–
Stovold, Allen	Circulation manager, to 1970
Taverner, Philip	Marketing director, 1968–
Thomson, Kenneth (from 1976 Lord Thomson of Fleet)	Deputy chairman, 1967–8; chairman, 1968–70
Thompson, Harvey	General manager, 1972–7
Thorne, Garry	Advertisement director, 1974–7; advertisement and marketing director, 1980–
Todd, Bryan	Advertisement and marketing director, 1977–81
Tory, John	Director, 1973–80; TNHL, 1980–
Trevor-Roper, Hugh (from 1979 Lord Dacre of Glanton)	Director, 1974–
Tydeman, Paul	Asst. production manager, 1975–7; production manager, 1977–81
Vowles, George	Head printer, 1967–
Webb, John	Technical director, 1968–71
Weston, Michael	Display advertisement director, 1970–4
Woods, Oliver	Deputy to C. D. Hamilton, 1967–70

NOTE ON APPENDIX B

THE ABOVE LIST was originally compiled by a member of the *Times* archive staff, Caroline O'Sullivan, under the supervision of Melanie Aspey, and with her very active cooperation; also with that of their colleague, Eamon Dyas. It has, moreover, been vetted, in whole or part, by the following who were staff members during the Thomson period: Margaret Allen, Cyril Bainbridge, Ivan Barnes, George Clark, Dennis Dwyer, John Grant, John Hennessy, John Higgins, Tudor Hopkins, Michael Leapman, Brian MacArthur, Michael Mander, Michael Roffey, Richard Sachs and Professor Hugh Stephenson. To all of them I am exceedingly grateful.

Sadly, I could not make the list anything like comprehensive, giving the names of all who worked for *The Times* under the Thomson ownership. For obvious reasons of space, the production, printing, marketing and advertisement staffs are hardly represented, and I have also felt it necessary to exclude all secretaries, all but the leading sub-editors, and (in the foreign news list) all stringers. These omissions are much regretted, but the list had to be kept within manageable bounds.

Joining or leaving dates are, in principle, given only when they fall within the period. Where a person worked on *The Times* throughout the period, no dates are given. Since the list is broken down by departments, the names of those who switched departments during the period (e.g. Charles Douglas-Home) appear more than once.

Not all of those listed were strictly staff members; some were freelances in a special contractual relationship with *The Times* (e.g. Mark Boxer), whose inclusion is justified by their importance to the paper through all, or most, of the time covered by the book.

Titles are mentioned when conferred or inherited before or (with relevant dates) during the Thomson years. Those who received titles subsequently (e.g. Lord Rees-Mogg and Sir Gordon Brunton) are listed in the unadorned style that applied at the time.

J.G.

APPENDIX C

Awards to The Times *and contributors*

1968
'What The Papers Say', Granada TV:
Newspaper of the Year: *The Times*

IPC Awards:

Special award to Susanne Puddefoot for 'success in producing fresh lively pages'

1969
'What The Papers Say', Granada TV:

Reporter of the Year: Brian Priestley

Ilford's Print Competition:

Ian Bradshaw (photographer) and Reg Miller

1970
'What The Papers Say', Granada TV:
Reporter of the Year: Michael Hornsby. 'For consistently knowledgeable dispatches from Czechoslovakia

1971
IPC Awards:

Sports Writer of the Year (runner-up): Neil Allen

Womens' Pages (runner-up): Moira Keenan

1972
'What The Papers Say', Granada TV:

Columnist of the Year: Bernard Levin

IPC Awards:

International Reporter of the Year (shared): Peter Hazelhurst

News Reporter of the Year: John Clare

Special award to William Rees-Mogg for exposure by Garry Lloyd and Julian Mounter of corruption by two police officers

1973

'What The Papers Say', Granada TV:

Cartoonist of the Year: Mark Boxer

Glenfiddich Award for Wine and Food Writers:

Pamela Vandyke Price*

City of Rome Prize for Journalism:

Peter Nichols

Newspaper Design Awards:

Silver Award for Most Outstanding Editorial Design of a Newspaper Feature: Jeanette Collins

Silver Award for Most Outstanding Piece of Artwork for a Newspaper Feature: Franklin Wilson*

The Calabrian Prize for International Journalism:

Peter Nichols

1974

Wincott Award for Outstanding Achievement in Financial Journalism:

Financial Journalist of the Year: Peter Jay

IPC Awards:

Columnist of the Year (shared): Bernard Levin

1975

'What The Papers Say', Granada TV:

Reporter of the Year: Robert Fisk

Association of Tennis Professionals:

Tennis Writer of the Year: Rex Bellamy

1976

Midland Bank Press Pictures of the Year:

Third Prize, News Section: David Jones

Publishers Publicity Circle:

Ronald Politzer Award: *The Times*

Association of Tennis Professionals:

Tennis Writer of the Year: Rex Bellamy

1977

IPC Awards:

News Reporter of the Year: Geraldine Norman

News Reporter of the Year (commended): Neville Hodgkinson

Association of Tennis Professionals:

Tennis Writer of the Year: Rex Bellamy

Martini Royal Photographic Awards:

Best black-and-white photograph: David Jones

Sporting Life:

Silver Trophy for Outstanding Race Tipster of the Season: Jim Snow

Advertising Creative Circle:

Commendation for advertisements promoting *The Times* in trade press
Commendation for *The Times* classified Christmas gift guide

British Press Advertising Awards:

Special Award to *The Times* for its circulation campaign

1978

Management Journalist of the Year: Rodney Cowton

1980

IPC Awards:

International Reporter of the Year: Robert Fisk

Association of Polish Film Makers:

Special award for David Robinson as 'the international critic who during the year has done most to promote understanding of Polish cinematography'

1981

IPC Awards:

International Reporter of the Year: Robert Fisk

The David Holden Award: Michael Binyon

Columnist of the Year (commended): Peter Evans

Photographer of the Year (commended): Harry Kerr

The Glen Grant Cartoonist of the Year Awards:

Cartoonist of the Year: Mark Boxer

Baron de Lancey Trust Awards:

Prize awarded to Dr Rachel Davies, law reporter*

Pamela Vandyke Price, Franklin Wilson and Dr Rachel Davies were freelance contributors to *The Times* and their names do not therefore appear in Appendix B.

CHRONOLOGY

OUTSIDE EVENTS
1966

November–December Talks between Harold Wilson and Rhodesian leader, Ian Smith, on *HMS Tiger*, end in failure.

EVENTS ON *THE TIMES*
1966

December 21 Douglas Jay, President of the Board of Trade, tells House of Commons that Monopolies Commission has decided Thomson purchase of TNL not against public interest.
December 22 Announcement that Sir William Haley will be relinquishing editorship of *The Times* at the end of the year, to become chairman of TNL. Iverach McDonald then to be in charge of paper till new editor appointed.

1967

February *Torrey Canyon* wrecked.

June Six-Day War.

November 18 Devaluation of the £. Roy Jenkins succeeds James Callaghan as chancellor of the exchequer.

1967

January 12 William Rees-Mogg appointed editor of *The Times*.
January 23 Personal by-lines introduced.

April 11 TBN launched.

July 1 Leader on Rolling Stones case.

November Row between the paper and Downing Street over article by Peter Jay.

OUTSIDE EVENTS 1968	EVENTS ON *THE TIMES* 1968
February Tet offensive in Vietnam.	
April Lyndon B. Johnson announces he will not be candidate for re-election as president. Martin Luther King assassinated.	**April 22** Leader attacking Enoch Powell's Birmingham speech on immigration.
May Student riots lead to crisis of regime in France.	
August 20 Russians suppress 'Prague spring'.	
November De Gaulle vetoes British entry to EEC for second time.	
	December Haley stands down as chairman: succeeded by Kenneth Thomson. **December 9** Leader proposing coalition.
1969	**1969**
	February–March Strong editorial support for Biafra.
	March Peak sale of over 450,000 reached.
April De Gaulle resigns. Succeeded by Georges Pompidou.	
July Moon landing.	
August British troops sent to Northern Ireland.	

OUTSIDE EVENTS	EVENTS ON *THE TIMES*
	October Corruption in Metropolitan Police exposed.
	December 12 Letter from Denis Hamilton to staff, stressing need for economy.
1970	**1970**
June 18 Conservatives win general election; Edward Heath prime minister.	
	July 7 White Swan letter.
September Death of President Nasser of Egypt.	
	December 23 End of backset TBN.
1971	**1971**
	January 1 Hamilton replaced as chief executive of TNL by M. J. Hussey.
February 15 Decimalisation of the currency.	
	July 28 'Dermatitis' strike – the first time in its history the paper stopped on its own.
August 6 Industrial Relations bill becomes law.	
	September Re-styling of paper. Last turnover article.
October 29 House of Commons votes for joining EEC.	
1972	**1972**
January 22 Treaty of accession to EEC signed.	
January 30 'Bloody Sunday' in Londonderry.	

OUTSIDE EVENTS

February 18 Wilberforce report on coal dispute.

March 24 Direct rule in Northern Ireland.

August Ugandan Asian refugees from Idi Amin persecution admitted to Britain.

EVENTS ON *THE TIMES*

March 17 Nude advertisement in *The Times*.

May David Bonavia expelled from USSR.

October 8 Typeface changed to Times Europa.
October Thomson visit to People's Republic of China. Bonavia appointed correspondent there.

1973

January White Paper announcing statutory incomes policy.

October 6–24 Yom Kippur war.

November 13 Government takes emergency powers to deal with industrial crisis.

December 9 Sunningdale agreement.

1973

March 22 Michael Cudlipp leaves.

June 5 Leader defending Nixon.

October 2 First issue of *Europa* magazine.

OUTSIDE EVENTS	**EVENTS ON *THE TIMES***
1974	**1974**
February 28–March 4 General election results in fall of Heath government and return of Labour under Wilson.	
May 15–28 Ulster workers' strike brings down power-sharing executive.	
	June 24 Move to Gray's Inn Road.
August 9 Nixon resigns: succeeded by Gerald Ford.	
September 5 Sir Keith Joseph's speech at Preston presages shift in Conservative policy.	**September 6** Leader substantially supports Joseph, confirming shift of policy by the paper.
October 10 Second general election improves Labour's position.	
1975	**1975**
February Heath loses Tory leadership; Margaret Thatcher elected as leader.	**February–March** Imbroglio involving Colin Wallace; Robert Fisk leaves Northern Ireland.
June Referendum on EEC.	
October/November Controversy over Michael Foot's Employment Protection bill.	
1976	**1976**
March–April Wilson resigns as prime minister; James Callaghan elected to succeed him.	
	August 4 Roy Thomson dies.

OUTSIDE EVENTS

September 9 Mao Tse-tung dies.

September 28 Sterling crisis: Denis Healey turned back at Heathrow.

November 3 Jimmy Carter elected US president.

EVENTS ON *THE TIMES*

October *Programme for Action* agreed with union leaders.

1977

January–March Indira Gandhi ends period of dictatorship in India; holds election, in which she is heavily defeated.

March Lib–Lab pact.

June Queen's silver jubilee. Free elections in Spain. Grunwick strike.

November President Sadat visits Israel.

1977

March *Programme for Action* rejected in union ballots.

May Peter Jay appointed ambassador to the USA.

1978

March–May Moro crisis in Italy.

1978

January Harvey Thompson dies; succeeded by Dugal Nisbet-Smith.

April 13 Hussey and colleagues meet union general secretaries at Bedford.

OUTSIDE EVENTS | **EVENTS ON *THE TIMES***

April 26 Hussey writes threatening, in effect, suspension of papers on November 30, failing agreement meanwhile.

July 26 Letter to Hussey from 11 FoCs.

September Camp David accords. Callaghan decides against early election, while insisting on 5 per cent pay norm.

October 16 Election of Pope John Paul II.

November 30 House of Commons debate on TNL dispute.

December 1 Publication suspended.

1979

January Shah of Iran forced out; Ayotollah Khomeini establishes Islamic republic.

February TUC attempt at settlement ends abruptly when programme for negotiations leaked.

March–April Government initiative also comes to nothing.

April 30 Frankfurt printing forcibly stopped after one edition.

May 3 Conservatives win election; Thatcher government takes office.

OUTSIDE EVENTS	EVENTS ON *THE TIMES*
	June Management in retreat. JOTT established.
	November 13 End of stoppage; *The Times* reappears.
November 22 Roy Jenkins's Dimbleby Lecture presages Labour split.	**November 21** Anthony Blunt interviewed at Gray's Inn Road.
December 25 Soviet invasion of Afghanistan.	
1980	**1980**
February Robert Mugabe comes to power in Zimbabwe.	
April 24 Botched attempt to rescue American hostages in Teheran.	
May Eventual agreement for EEC rebate for Britain.	**May** Gatwick Park conference.
	June James Evans becomes chairman of TNL, and Nisbet-Smith managing director. Hussey sidelined.
	August 22–30 *Times* journalists' strike.
September Solidarity officially recognised in Poland.	
October–November Callaghan resigns labour leadership; Michael Foot elected leader.	**October 22** Thomsons announce decision to sell TNL, setting a time-limit.
November Ronald Reagan elected US president.	

OUTSIDE EVENTS
1981

January–February Labour schism begins; Limehouse Declaration, and Council for Social Democracy set up.

February Reagan–Thatcher meeting.

EVENTS ON *THE TIMES*
1981

January 22 Sale to Rupert Murdoch agreed, subject to non-referral to Monopolies Commission and satisfactory agreements with unions.
January 27 John Biffen announces in Parliament that Murdoch deal will not be referred to Monopolies Commission.

February Murdoch reaches agreement with unions.

March 7 Rees-Mogg's farewell article.

NOTE ON SOURCES

THE BEST SOURCE for any historian of *The Times* is the paper itself. The most important aspect of a newspaper's life is what it offers to the public; its reporting and interpretation of news, and its role as a reflector as well as a moulder of opinion. My time spent reading back-numbers of the paper through the Thomson period, in the *Times* room at the London Library, has been the most rewarding part of my research.

Needless to say, the archive of *The Times* has also been a vital source. The correspondence and memoranda of the editor, and of other leading members of the staff, have thrown much light on developments in the office and on the evolution of the paper's attitude to public affairs. Very useful, too, have been the minutes of TNL board meetings, of the successive executive board and management committee meetings, and of meetings of the *Times* management committee (1967–9). The book showing the authorship of leaders has been convenient, and the file of the paper's house journal, *Times News*, has yielded much information.

I have also drawn freely on two important diaries, which their authors most kindly allowed me to use: that of E. C. Hodgkin, covering (during my period) the years 1966–72; and that of George Clark covering the period of the shutdown, 1978–9. (The latter is deposited at Wapping.)

In addition to the archive of the paper, I have had the good fortune to be allowed access to certain collections of papers in private hands, above all those belonging to Sir Gordon Brunton, Mr Robert Fisk, the late Sir Denis Hamilton, Mr M. J. Hussey, Mr Michael Mander and Professor Hugh Stephenson.

The public records for the period are, of course, still closed, but on the other hand the fact that the period is comparatively recent has given me an abundance, even a superabundance, of living witnesses to consult. The perils of oral evidence some time after the event are well known, and I hope I have treated it here with due caution, nearly always preferring, where possible, a contemporary written record. Nevertheless, I am much obliged to those who have talked to me, above all for helping me to understand certain personal relationships, and for enabling me to sense the atmosphere of *The Times* during the Thomson years.

Among published works bearing on the period, or on key personalities in it, the following deserve special mention:

Beloff, Nora	*Freedom Under Foot*
Benn, Tony	*Out of the Wilderness* (Diaries 1963–67). *Office without Power* (Diaries 1968–72). *Against the Tide* (Diaries 1973–76). *Conflicts of Interest* (Diaries, 1977–80)
Braddon, Russell	*Roy Thomson of Fleet Street*
Callaghan, James	*Time and Chance.*
Carrington, Lord	*Reflect on Things Past*
Castle, Barbara	*The Castle Diaries* (1974–6 and Vol. II 1964–70)
Crossman, Richard	*The Diaries of a Cabinet Minister, ed. Janet Morgan* (Vol Two, 1966–8; Vol Three, 1968–70)
Evans, Harold	*Good Times, Bad Times*

NOTE ON SOURCES

Fisk, Robert	*The Point of No Return: The Strike which Broke the British in Ulster*
Foot, Paul	*Who Framed Colin Wallace?*
Goldenberg, Susan	*The Thomson Empire*
Grimond, Jo	*Memoirs*
Hamilton, Denis	*Editor-in-Chief*
Hart-Davis, Duff	*The House the Berrys Built*
Healey, Denis	*The Time of My Life*
Heren, Louis	*Memories of Times Past*
Hetherington, Alastair	*Guardian Years*
Jacobs, Eric	*Stop Press*
Jenkins, Roy	*A Life at the Centre.* *European Diary, 1977–81*
Jenkins, Simon	*Newspapers: the Power and the Money* *The Market for Glory*
King, Cecil H.	*Diary, 1965–1970. Diary, 1970–1974*
Koss, Stephen	*The Rise and Fall of the Political Press in Britain: Vol Two, The Twentieth Century*
Kynaston, David	*The Financial Times: a Centenary History*
Leapman, Michael	*Barefaced Cheek*
McDonald, Iverach	*A Man of The Times*
Martin, Roderick	*New Technology and Industrial Relations in Fleet Street*
Rees-Mogg, William	*The Reigning Error: The Crisis of World Inflation.* *An Humbler Heaven*
*Shawcross, William	*Murdoch*
Steel, David	*Against Goliath*
Thomson, Roy	*After I was Sixty*
Whitelaw, William	*The Whitelaw Memoirs*
Wilson, Harold	*The Labour Government: 1964–1970.* *Final Term: The Labour Government, 1974–6*
Woods, Oliver, and Bishop, James	*The Story of The Times*
Young, Hugo	*One of Us*

* Though this book was published after the present volume was written, William Shawcross kindly allowed the author to read the typescript of his chapter on the Murdoch take-over of *The Times*.

INDEX

Ranks and titles are those applicable in the period covered by this volume. The letter 'n' after a page number indicates a footnote.